D1517182

HMRL 1010
Human Relations Skills

Custom Edition for Metropolitan Community College

Taken from:
Human Relations: Interpersonal Job-Oriented Skills, Eleventh Edition
by Andrew J. DuBrin

*Human Relations for Career and Personal Success:
Concepts, Applications, and Skills,* Ninth Edition
by Andrew J. DuBrin

Professionalism: Skills for Workplace Success, Third Edition
by Lydia E. Anderson and Sandra B. Bolt

The Community College Experience, Third Edition
by Amy Baldwin

Resource Management for Individuals and Families, Fourth Edition
by Elizabeth B. Goldsmith

*Understanding Human Differences: Multicultural Education
for a Diverse America,* Third Edition
by Kent Koppelman and R. Lee Goodhart

Power Up: A Practical Student's Guide to Online Learning, Second Edition
by Stacey Barrett, Catrina Poe and Carrie Spagnola-Doyle

Cover Art: Courtesy of Digital Vision/Getty Images.

Taken from:

Human Relations: Interpersonal Job-Oriented Skills, Eleventh Edition
by Andrew J. DuBrin
Copyright © 2012, 2009, 2007, 2004, 2000 by Pearson Education, Inc.
Published by Prentice Hall
Upper Saddle River, New Jersey 07458

Human Relations for Career and Personal Success: Concepts, Applications, and Skills, Ninth Edition
by Andrew J. DuBrin
Copyright © 2011, 2008 by Pearson Education, Inc.
Published by Prentice Hall

Professionalism: Skills for Workplace Success, Third Edition
by Lydia E. Anderson and Sandra B. Bolt
Copyright © 2013, 2011, 2008 by Pearson Education, Inc.
Published by Prentice Hall

The Community College Experience, Third Edition
by Amy Baldwin
Copyright © 2013 by Pearson Education, Inc.
Published by Pearson
Boston, Massachusetts 02116

Resource Management for Individuals and Families, Fourth Edition
by Elizabeth B. Goldsmith
Copyright © 2010 by Pearson Education, Inc.
Published by Prentice Hall

Understanding Human Differences: Multicultural Education for a Diverse America, Third Edition
by Kent Koppelman and R. Lee Goodhart
Copyright © 2011, 2008, 2005 by Pearson Education, Inc.
Published by Allyn & Bacon
Boston, Massachusetts 02116

Power Up: A Practical Student's Guide to Online Learning, Second Edition
by Stacey Barrett, Catrina Poe and Carrie Spagnola-Doyle
Copyright © 2012, 2009 by Pearson Education, Inc.
Published by Pearson
Boston, Massachusetts 02116

This special edition published in cooperation with Pearson Learning Solutions.

All trademarks, service marks, registered trademarks, and registered service marks are the property of their respective owners and are used herein for identification purposes only.

Pearson Learning Solutions, 501 Boylston Street, Suite 900, Boston, MA 02116
A Pearson Education Company
www.pearsoned.com

Printed in the United States of America

20   16

000200010271699737

CT

ISBN 10: 1-256-86240-1
ISBN 13: 978-1-256-86240-6

BRIEF CONTENTS

Chapter 1   Intro to Human Relations 2

Chapter 2   Team Building 36

Chapter 3   Professional Presence and Interviewing 60

Chapter 4   Resumes and Cover Letters 102

Chapter 5   Communication 152

Chapter 6   Self-Esteem and Attitude 186

Chapter 7   Goal Setting and Motivation 232

Chapter 8   Ethics and Values 254

Chapter 9   Stress 280

Chapter 10 Anger and Conflict 312

Chapter 11 Diversity 340

Chapter 12 Life Plan 370

CONTENTS

The following content was taken from:
Human Relations For Career and Personal Success: Concepts, Applications, and Skills,
Ninth Edition by Andrew J. DuBrin

Chapter 1   Intro to Human Relations 2

What Is the Nature and Importance of Human Relations? 3

How Can Studying Human Relations Help You? 4

How Do Work and Personal Life Influence Each Other? 8

In What Way Does Human Relations Begin with
  Self-Understanding? 9

  General Information about Human Behavior 10

  Informal Feedback from People 10

  Feedback from Superiors 11

  Feedback from Coworkers 11

  Feedback from Self-Assessment Quizzes 11

  Looking at the Self through the Johari Window 12

  Two Self-Evaluation Traps 13

How Did the Human Relations Movement Develop? 14

  Scientific Management 14

  The Hawthorne Studies 15

  The Threat of Unionization 16

  The Philosophy of Industrial Humanism 16

  Theory X and Theory Y of Douglas McGregor 16

  Relevance of the History of Human Relations to Today's
    Workplace 17

How Does Human Relations Knowledge and Skill Help You Deal
  with Major Challenges in the Workplace? 17

  Emphasis on Teamwork and Collaboration 17

  High Expectations for Personal Productivity 18

  Dealing with Workplace Diversity and Globalization 19

  Emphasis on Employee Creativity and Innovativeness 20

  Being Part of the Virtual Workplace and Telecommuting 20

  Increased Emphasis on Skill Acquisition and Less on Upward
    Mobility 21

What Major Factors Influence Job Performance and Behavior? 21

The following content was taken from:
The Community College Experience, Third Edition by Amy Baldwin

Chapter 1 Special Topic 23

  Different Theories Provide Unique Insights 23

Learning Styles Relate to Career Choices 24

Concept Review and Reinforcement 29
Key Terms 29
Summary 29
Questions for Discussion and Review 30
The Web Corner 30

Developing Your Human Relations Skills 31
Human Relations Application Exercises 31
Human Relations Case Study 1-1 31
Human Relations Case Study 1-2 32
Human Relations Role-Playing Exercise 33
Class Activity: The Unique People 34

References 35

The following content was taken from:
Human Relations: Interpersonal Job-Oriented Skills, Eleventh Edition
by Andrew J. DuBrin

Chapter 2   Team Building 36

Face-to-Face Versus Virtual Teams 37
Face-to-Face (Traditional) Teams 37
Virtual Teams 38

The Advantages and Disadvantages of Teams and Teamwork 40
Advantages of Group Work and Teamwork 40
Disadvantages of Group Work and Teamwork 41

Team Member Roles 42

Guidelines for the Interpersonal Aspects of Team Play 47
Trust Team Members 48
Display a High Level of Cooperation and Collaboration 49
Recognize the Interests and Achievements of Others 50
Give and Receive Helpful Criticism 50
Share the Glory 50
Take Care Not to Rain on Another Person's Parade 50

Guidelines for the Task Aspects of Team Play 51
Provide Technical Expertise (Or Knowledge of the Task) 51
Assume Responsibility for Problems 51
See the Big Picture 52
Believe in Consensus 52
Focus on Deadlines 52
Help Team Members Do Their Jobs Better 52
Be a Good Organizational Citizen 53

Concept Review and Reinforcement 55
Key Terms 55
Summary 55
Questions for Discussion and Review 55
The Web Corner 56

Developing Your Human Relations Skills 57
Interpersonal Relations Case 2-1 57
Interpersonal Relations Case 2-2 58

References 59

The following content was taken from:
Human Relations: Interpersonal Job-Oriented Skills, Eleventh Edition
by Andrew J. DuBrin

Chapter 3   Professional Presence and Interviewing 60

Conducting a Job Search 60
Job-Hunting Tactics 61

The following content was taken from:
Professionalism: Skills for Workplace Success, Third Edition by Lydia E. Anderson and Sandra B. Bolt

The Interview 67
The Invitation to Interview 67
Company-Specific Research 68
The Personal Commercial 68
The Interview Portfolio 69
Practice Interview Questions 70
Pre-Interview Practice 70
The Day of the Interview 72
The Interview 73
Phone- and other Technology-Based Interviews 73
Interview Methods and Types of Interview Questions 74
Discrimination and Employee Rights 75
Tough Questions 76
Closing the Interview 77
After the Interview 78
Salary Negotiation 78
Pre-Employment Tests, Screenings and Medical Exams 79
When You Are Not Offered the Job 79
Workplace Dos and Don'ts 80
Executive Presence 81
Influences of Dress in a Professional Environment 82
Casual Workdays and Special Events 83
Tips from Head to Toe 84
Jewelry, Body Piercing, and Tattoos 84
Business Etiquette 85
Handshakes 85
Introductions and Business Networking 86
Appointments 87
Dining 87
Other Etiquette Basics 89
Workplace Dos and Don'ts 90
Concept Review and Reinforcement 91
Key Terms 91
Summary 91
Questions for Discussion and Review 92
The Web Corner 92
If You Were the Boss 93

Developing Your Human Relations Skills 94
   Interpersonal Relations Case 3-1 94
   Interpersonal Relations Case 3-2 94
Activities 96
   Activity 3-1 96
   Activity 3-2 97
   Activity 3-3 97
   Activity 3-4 98
   Activity 3-5 98
   Activity 3-6 99
   Activity 3-7 99
Sample Exam Questions 100
References 101

The following content was taken from:
Professionalism: Skills for Workplace Success, Third Edition by Lydia E. Anderson and Sandra B. Bolt

Chapter 4   Resumes and Cover Letters 102

The Job Search 103
Choosing the Right Career 103
Career Objective and Personal Profile 105
Industry Research 106
The Targeted Job Search 106
Preparation 107
Job Search Portfolio 107
Employment Applications 109
Personal References and Recommendations 109
Sources of Job Leads 110
Networking 111
Protecting Your Privacy 113
Keeping the Right Attitude 114
Workplace Dos and Don'ts 115
Building Your Résumé Package 115
Step One: Career Objective/Personal Profile 116
Step Two: Gathering Information 117
Step Three: Proper Layout 118
Step Four: Skills, Accomplishments, and Experience 119
Step Five: Complete the Résumé 121
Sharing Your Résumé 122
Cover Letters 124
Tailoring Your Résumé and Cover Letter 125
Tips for Ex-Offenders 125
Workplace Dos and Don'ts 126
Concept Review and Application 143
   Key Terms 143
   Summary 143
   If You Were the Boss 143
   The Web Corner 144

Activities 145

Activity 4-1 145

Activity 4-2 146

Activity 4-3 146

Activity 4-4 147

Activity 4-5 147

Activity 4-6 147

Activity 4-7 148

Activity 4-8 148

Activity 4-9 149

Activity 4-10 149

Sample Exam Questions 150

References 151

The following content was taken from:
Human Relations For Career and Personal Success: Concepts, Applications, and Skills,
Ninth Edition by Andrew J. DuBrin

Chapter 5   Communication 152

How Does Communication Take Place? 153

How Does Interpersonal Communication Relate to Relationship
Building? 155

What Is Nonverbal Communication (Sending and Receiving Silent
Messages)? 156

Environment or Setting 157

Distance from the Other Person 157

Posture 157

Hand Gestures 158

Facial Expressions and Eye Contact 159

Voice Quality 159

Personal Appearance 159

Nonverbal Communication and Airport Security 160

What Are Some Frequent Roadblocks to Communication? 161

Limited Understanding of People 161

One-Way Communication 162

Different Interpretation of Words (Semantics) 162

Credibility of the Sender and Mixed Signals 162

Distortion of Information 163

Different Perspectives and Experiences 163

Emotions and Attitudes 163

Communication Overload 163

Improper Timing 164

Poor Communication Skills 164

Cultural and Language Barriers 164

What Are Some Ways to Build Bridges to Communication? 165

Appeal to Human Needs, and Time Your Messages 165

Repeat Your Message, Using More than One Channel 165

Have an Empowered Attitude, and Be Persuasive 166

Discuss Differences in Frames of Reference 166

Check for Comprehension and Feelings through Feedback 166
Minimize Defensive Communication 167
Combat Communication Overload 168
Use Mirroring to Establish Rapport 168
Engage in Small Talk and Constructive Gossip 168
How Do You Overcome Gender Barriers to Communication? 169
How Can You Enhance Your Listening Skills? 170
Active Listening 171
Personal Communication Style 173
What Are the Formal Channels of Communication Within Organizations? 174
Company Blogs as Formal Channels 174
Social Networking Web Sites, Intranets, and Webinars 175
Concept Review and Reinforcement 178
Key Terms 178
Summary 178
Questions for Discussion and Review 179
The Web Corner 179
Developing Your Human Relations Skills 180
Human Relations Application Exercises 180
Human Relations Class Activity 181
Human Relations Case Study 5-1 181
Human Relations Case Study 5-2 183
Human Relations Role-Playing Exercise 184
References 185

The following content was taken from:
Human Relations: Interpersonal Job-Oriented Skills, Eleventh Edition
by Andrew J. DuBrin

Chapter 6 Self-Esteem and Attitude 186

The Meaning of Self-Esteem, Its Development and Consequences 188
How Self-Esteem Develops 189
The Consequences of High Self-Esteem 190
Enhancing Self-Esteem 192
Attain Legitimate Accomplishments 193
Be Aware of Personal Strengths 193
Rebut the Inner Critic 194
Practice Self-Nurturing 194
Minimize Settings and Interactions That Detract from Your Feelings of Competence 195
Get Help from Others 195
Model the Behavior of People with High Self-Esteem 196
Create a High Self-Esteem Living Space 196
How a Manager Helps Build the Self-Esteem of Group Members 196
The Importance of Self-Confidence and Self-Efficacy 197

Techniques for Developing and Enhancing Your
  Self-Confidence 197
    Develop a Solid Knowledge Base 198
    Use Positive Self-Talk 199
    Avoid Negative Self-Talk 200
    Use Positive Visual Imagery 200
    Set High Expectations for Yourself (the Galatea Effect) 200
    Develop the Explanatory Style of Optimists 201
    Strive for Peak Performance 201
    Bounce Back from Setbacks and Embarrassments 202

The following content was taken from:
Human Relations For Career and Personal Success: Concepts, Applications, and Skills,
Ninth Edition by Andrew J. DuBrin

What Is Emotional Intelligence? 203
    Key Components of Emotional Intelligence 203
    Consequences of High and Low Emotional Intelligence 204
    Acquiring and Developing Emotional Intelligence 206
    Concerns and Cross-Cultural Considerations 206
**What Are the Components of Attitudes, and How Are They
  Acquired and Changed? 207**
    Components of Attitudes 207
    How Attitudes Are Formed 208
    The Importance of Positive Attitudes 209
    How Attitudes Are Changed 209
    How Companies Encourage Positive Attitudes and Job
      Satisfaction 210
    Organizational Citizenship Behavior 211
**What Is Happiness, and How Can It Be Acquired and
  Enhanced? 213**
    The Spheres of Life and Happiness 213
    The Keys to Happiness 214
    The Five Principles of Psychological Functioning 218
Concept Review and Reinforcement 219
    Key Terms 219
    Summary 219
    Questions for Discussion and Review 221
    The Web Corner 222
Developing Your Human Relations Skills 223
    Interpersonal Relations Case 6-1 223
    Interpersonal Relations Case 6-2 224
    Applying Human Relations Exercise 6-1 225
    Applying Human Relations Exercise 6-2 226
    Human Relations Class Activity 226
    Human Relations Case Study 6-1 227
    Human Relations Role-Playing Exercise 228
    Human Relations Case Study 6-2 228
References 230

The following content was taken from:
Professionalism: Skills for Workplace Success, Third Edition by Lydia E. Anderson and Sandra B. Bolt

Chapter 7 Goal Setting and Motivation 232

The Importance of Personal Goal Setting 232
Influences of Goals 232
How to Set Goals 232

The following content was taken from:
Resource Management for Individuals and Families, Fourth Edition by Elizabeth B. Goldsmith

Goals and Motivation 234
Goals Versus Habits 235
Goal Attributes 235
Types of Goals 235
Setting Goals 237

The following content was taken from:
Power Up: A Practical Student's Guide to Online Learning, Second Edition by Stacey Barrett, Catrina Poe and Carrie Spagnola-Doyle

Reaching Goals Means Setting Goals 237
Steps in Goal Setting 238
College Students' Values, Goals, and Life Outcomes 242
Motivation 244
Concept Review and Reinforcement 247
E-Resources 247
Key Terms 247
Summary 247
Questions for Discussion and Review 248
Sample Exam Questions 249
Career Goal Setting 251
References 252

The following content was taken from:
Human Relations: Interpersonal Job-Oriented Skills, Eleventh Edition by Andrew J. DuBrin

Chapter 8 Ethics and Values 254

Why Be Concerned About Business Ethics? 256
Why We Have so Many Ethical Problems 257
Why Being Ethical Isn't Easy 258
A Survey of the Extent of Ethical Problems 258
Frequent Ethical Dilemmas 258
Choosing between Two Rights: Dealing with Defining
  Moments 262

Guidelines for Behaving Ethically 264
    Developing Virtuousness 264
    Following a Guide to Ethical Decision Making 265
    Developing Strong Relationships with Work Associates 268
    Using Corporate Ethics Programs 268
    Being Environmentally Conscious 271
    Following an Applicable Professional Code of Conduct 272
    Be Ready to Exert Upward Ethical Leadership 272
Concept Review and Reinforcement 274
    Key Terms 274
    Summary 274
    Questions for Discussion and Review 275
    The Web Corner 275
Developing Your Human Relations Skills 276
    Interpersonal Relations Case 8-1 276
    Interpersonal Relations Case 8-2 277
    Interpersonal Skills Role-Play 278
References 279

The following content was taken from:
Human Relations: Interpersonal Job-Oriented Skills, Eleventh Edition
by Andrew J. DuBrin

Chapter 9   Stress 280

Understanding and Managing Stress 281
    Symptoms and Consequences of Stress 281
    Personality and Job Factors Contributing to Stress 284
    Methods and Techniques for Stress Management 288
Improving Personal Productivity 293
    Dealing with Procrastination 293
    Enhancing Personal Productivity through Attitudes and
        Values 295
    Enhancing Personal Productivity through Work Habits and
        Skills 298
    Overcoming Time Wasters 301

The following content was taken from:
Human Relations For Career and Personal Success: Concepts, Applications, and Skills,
Ninth Edition by Andrew J. DuBrin

Concept Review and Reinforcement 305
    Key Terms 305
    Summary 305
    Questions for Discussion and Review 306
    The Web Corner 306
Developing Your Human Relations Skills 308
    Interpersonal Relations Case 9-1 308
    Interpersonal Relations Case 9-2 309
References 310

The following content was taken from:
Human Relations For Career and Personal Success: Concepts, Applications, and Skills,
Ninth Edition by Andrew J. DuBrin

Chapter 10 Anger and Conflict 312

  Why Does So Much Conflict Exist? 313
    Competition for Limited Resources 313
    Differences of Opinion on Work-Related Issues and Rights 314
    Personality Clashes 314
    Aggressive Personalities, Including Bullies 314
    Culturally Diverse Teams and Factional Groups 315
    Competing Work and Family Demands 315
    Micro-Inequities as a Source of Conflict 317
    Cross-Generational Conflict 317
    Sexual Harassment: A Special Type of Conflict 317
  The Good and Bad Sides of Conflict 320
  What Are Some Techniques for Resolving Conflicts? 322
    Being Assertive 322
    Confrontation and Problem Solving Leading to Win–Win 324
    Disarm the Opposition 325
    Reframing (Including Cognitive Restructuring and Asking
        Questions) 326
    Appeal to a Third Party 326
    The Grievance Procedure 327
    Negotiation and Bargaining Tactics 328
  What Are Some Suggestions for Managing Anger? 330
    Managing Your Own Anger 331
    Managing Anger in Other People 331
    Choosing a Tactic for Resolving a Conflict or Managing
        Anger 331
  Concept Review and Reinforcement 333
    Key Terms 333
    Summary 333
    Questions for Discussion and Review 334
    The Web Corner 334
  Developing Your Human Relations Skills 335
    Human Relations Application Exercises 335
    Human Relations Class Activity 335
    Human Relations Case Study 10-1 336
    Human Relations Role-Playing Exercise 337
    Human Relations Case Study 10-2 337
    Human Relations Role-Playing Exercise 338
  References 339

The following content was taken from:
Human Relations: Interpersonal Job-Oriented Skills, Eleventh Edition
by Andrew J. DuBrin

Chapter 11 Diversity 340

  The Diversity Umbrella 341

Understanding Cultural Differences 344
     Cultural Sensitivity and Political Correctness 344
     Cultural Intelligence 345
     Respect for All Workers and Cultures 346
     Cultural Fluency 347
     Dimensions of Differences in Cultural Values 347
     Cultural Bloopers 350
Overcoming Cross-Cultural Communication Barriers 350

The following content was taken from:
Understanding Human Differences: Multicultural Education for a Diverse America,
Third Edition by Kent Koppelman and R. Lee Goodhart

     How Do Negative Attitudes Develop? 353
     What Do Stereotypes Have to Do with Uncertainty and How Do
          They Cause Prejudice? 354
Diversity In The United States 356
     How Have Members of the Majority Responded to Diverse
          Groups? 357
Attitudes About Diversity 358
     What Does It Mean to Have an Anglo Conformity
          Perspective? 358
Institutional Sexism 359
     Why Are Men Earning More Than Women in The Workforce? 359
     What Are Economic Consequences of Institutional Sexism for
          Women? 362
     How Is Sexual Harassment a Significant Problem for Women in
          the Workforce? 363
     What Are the Most Common Behaviors That Women Regard as
          Sexual Harassment? 363
Concept Review and Reinforcement 365
     Key Terms 365
     Summary 365
     Questions for Discussion and Review 366
     The Web Corner 366
Developing Your Human Relations Skills 367
     Interpersonal Relations Case 8.1 367
     Interpersonal Relations Case 8.2 367
     Interpersonal Skills Role-Play 368
References 369

The following content was taken from:
The Community College Experience, Third Edition by Amy Baldwin

Chapter 12   Life Plan 370
     Time Management Resources: Calendars, Lists, and Work
          Space 370
     Time Management Routines: Daily Reviews and Back
          Planning 372

Manage Your Energy 376

    Avoid the "Black Holes" of Television, Video Games, and Social
        Media 379

    Multi-Tasking Should Be Used in Moderation 379

Money Matters 380

    Estimate Your College Costs 380

    Create a Budget 380

    Set Goals 382

    Don't Take Credit 382

    Practice Good Financial Habits 383

    Protect Yourself 384

    Learn More 384

Your Physical Health Matters a Lot in College 385

    Nutrition Gives You Fuel 385

    Exercise Gives You Energy and Relieves Stress 387

    Sleep Recharges Your Batteries 388

    Drugs and Alcohol Can Quickly Derail Your Health and Life 389

    Yes, We Do Need to Talk about Sex 390

    Depression and Suicide Are Sad but Real Occurrences in
        College 392

Healthy Living Is a Choice You Make for Life 392

    A Balanced Life Is a Healthy Life 392

    Relationships Impact Your Health 393

    Getting Help When You Need It 393

Concept Review and Reinforcement 395

    Questions for Discussion and Review 395

Apply & Analyze 396

    Critical Thinking 396

Evaluate 397

    Case Scenarios 397

Create 399

    Research It Further 399

Take This With You 400

References 401

Index 402

Intro to Human Relations

Sandy Bellows was being honored as the local Woman of the Year by a public relations trade association. Bellows was the executive vice president of a private organization that promoted tourism and convention business in her geographic area. During the awards ceremony, several people who either report directly to Bellows or work closely with her were asked to comment on what makes Sandy Bellows so special.

LEARNING
Objectives

After studying the information and doing the exercises in this chapter, you should be able to

1. Describe the nature and importance of human relations.
2. Understand how studying human relations will help you.
3. Pinpoint how work and personal life influence each other.
4. Understand how effective human relations begins with self-understanding.
5. Understand the timeline and development of the human relations movement.
6. Indicate how a knowledge of human relations will help you deal with major challenges in the workplace.
7. Understand the major factors influencing job performance and behavior.

Jack, the director of tourism publicity, spoke first. Among his comments were, "Sandy knows no limits to the kindness and respect she shows to others on her team. When a suggestion of mine might be way off base, Sandy will listen carefully and then compliment me for the good in my idea. But then she will ask me a few sharp questions that point me in the direction of coming up with a better solution to the problem I am facing."

Penny, the convention and banquet manager at a large hotel in the area, opened her comments about Bellows in these terms: "Sandy really knows what it means to *partner* with somebody in the community. She works with me and my staff in a fully cooperative way. She keeps emphasizing how the community can prosper only if we truly collaborate in finding ways to bring convention business to our city. Working with Sandy has helped we hotel managers realize that we are not competing against each other but against other areas of the country."

Megan, who has worked five years as the administrative assistant to Bellows, included this point in her comments: "Sandy makes me feel like the most important person in her workday. She asks my opinion about so many things. She frequently asks me what *she* can do to make my job run more smoothly. The impression I get is that Sandy makes a lot of other people feel important too."

The comments by this public-sector executive focus on the importance of effective human relations. Treating people with kindness helps Sandy Bellows deal effectively with the businesspeople her organization serves, as well as her employees. This book presents a wide variety of suggestions and guidelines for improving your personal relationships both on and off the job. Most of them are based on systematic knowledge about human behavior.

LEARNING OBJECTIVE 1

WHAT IS THE NATURE AND IMPORTANCE OF HUMAN RELATIONS?

In the context used here, **human relations** is the art of using systematic knowledge about human behavior to improve personal, job, and career effectiveness. Human relations is far more than "being nice to people," because it applies systematic

human relations

The art of using systematic knowledge about human behavior to improve personal, job, and career effectiveness.

knowledge to treating people in such a way that they feel better and are more productive—such as providing a more relaxed work atmosphere to enhance worker creativity.

Similar to the field known as *organizational behavior*, human relations studies individuals and groups in organizations. Human relations, however, is essentially a less technical and more applied version of organizational behavior. In this text we make some references to research and theory, but the emphasis is on a more personal and applied approach to the subject matter.

From the standpoint of management, human relations is quite important because it contributes to **organizational effectiveness**—the extent to which an organization is productive and satisfies the demands of interested parties, such as employees, customers, and investors. Steve Kent, an equities analyst (not a human relations specialist) at Goldman Sachs & Co., made extensive observations about the importance of treating employees well (using principles of human relations). He found that treating employees with respect and paying them fairly contributes to developing an efficient and creative organization. Business firms that go the extra mile to treat employees well often derive tangible benefits, such as a high quality of customer service.[1]

Why does paying more attention to the human element improve business performance? Organizational behavior professor Jeffery Pfeffer at Stanford University notes that people work harder when they have greater control over their work environment and when they are encouraged by peer pressure from teammates. Even more advantage comes from people working smarter. People-oriented management practices enable workers to use their wisdom and receive the training they need to perform better. Another contribution to improved performance stems from eliminating positions that focus primarily on watching and controlling people.[2] The accompanying Human Relations in Practice box insert provides additional information about the payoff from company management practicing good human relations.

HOW CAN STUDYING HUMAN RELATIONS HELP YOU?

LEARNING OBJECTIVE 2

Human relations knowledge and skills are also potentially beneficial for the individual as well as the organization. The following case history illustrates how a career-minded person made effective use of human relations principles to resolve a difficult situation that seemed to be blocking her career. You might be able to use the same approach if you face a similar problem.

Ashley worked as a business analyst at a large hospital. Her responsibilities included searching for ways to improve work processes at the hospital, such as developing better forms for collecting information about patients and reducing the time outpatients spent in the waiting room. Ashley enjoyed her work and believed that she was gaining valuable experience toward her goal of becoming a hospital administrator.

Another contributor to Ashley's job satisfaction was her relationship with Paul, her boss. Ashley perceived her work relationship with him to be ideal. Paul kept feeding Ashley interesting assignments, gave her useful suggestions from time to time, and frequently praised her work. On her most recent performance evaluation, Ashley was described as "an ideal hospital business analyst with great potential."

Ashley's smooth working relationship with her manager quickly changed one January. Paul informed the group that the hospital had offered him a promotion to a much bigger role at the hospital and that although he enjoyed his present position, he felt obliged to accept the promotion. In Paul's place, the hospital appointed Jody, an experienced supervisor in another department within the hospital.

Growing an Innovation Consulting Firm by Focusing on Positive Interpersonal Relationships

When the four founders of Jump Associates LLC were building the company, they wanted to avoid the ultracompetitive, sometimes backstabbing atmosphere found at other high-energy consulting agencies. So early on they began adopting a series of practices that promote considerate collaboration.

Every morning, all employees meet for a "scrum"—a short get-together where they're briefed on company news, do yoga-like exercises, and then play a quick brain-rousing game that forces them to think on their feet. Jump employees are also subject to a "no zinger" policy that bans them from saying anything demeaning or hurtful about another employee. What's more, employees are asked to occasionally do so-called affinity exercises where employees ask others to declare one thing they like about them and ask other icebreaker-type questions. The person who responded then poses those questions to the person who originally asked them. And a coach stops in the office a few days a month to help employees with any issue, such as improving their communications or resolving conflicts with a colleague.

"There are companies that try to systematize the nastier instincts in people," says cofounder and chief executive Dev Patnaik. At Jump, "we try to put in systems that make people better than they otherwise would be."

The layout and interior design of the office are also meant to spark team building. All employees, including all senior management, sit out in the open in "neighborhoods" of five or six workers.

Senior management also believes in relying on the latest team-building research and methods to improve effectiveness and camaraderie. New employees all take tests that measure learning knowledge and skills learning. Everyone's strengths are listed on a poster in the office in hopes that these skills will be used and discussed on a regular basis to improve team performance.

The test told Colleen Murray, a 35-year-old project leader, that among her top strengths are being disciplined, responsible, and deliberative. Her disciplined nature, she says, makes her a natural at spearheading projects and setting goals and deadlines. Managers say they took those qualities into account when moving her into leadership roles.

Question

Why would an emphasis on collaboration help a company that helps other companies be more innovative?

Source: Abridged from Kelly K. Spors, "Top Small Workplaces 2008: Jump Associates LLC," *The Wall Street Journal,* October 13, 2008, p. R5.

Within the first three weeks, Jody began criticizing Ashley's work. She told her that her approach to improving business processes was not up-to-date, and that it lacked the kind of depth the hospital needed. Ashley then worked diligently on her next project to make the kind of improvements Jody suggested. Jody then found something else to criticize, this time telling Ashley that her PowerPoint presentations supporting her report were too complex, making them difficult for hospital administrators to follow.

Soon Jody found ways to criticize Ashley personally, in addition to the work she was performing. She suggested that Ashley should be careful to never wear heels higher than one and one half inches to the office and that the tattoo on her neck was unprofessional. Jody also suggested to Ashley twice that she should make sure to use the Internet only for job-related purposes during working hours.

After five months of regular criticism from her boss, Ashley decided to talk over the strained relationship with David, a close friend. Ashley explained to David that the negative chemistry between her and her boss was giving her chest pains and interrupted sleep. Ashley also emphasized that she was worried about receiving such a poor evaluation that it would damage her career.

David advised Ashley to "do what she had to do," by confronting her boss about the unjustified criticisms. If that didn't work, Ashley should communicate directly with Jody's manager to get the problem resolved. David explained that "In the modern organization, you are expected to bring problems right out on the table."

Ashley thanked David for his advice and then did some careful reflection. On the surface, David's advice made sense, but with her career potentially at stake, Ashley did not want to operate on common sense alone. She remembered studying about attitude change somewhere in human relations or social psychology. A point that stuck in her mind was that favorable interactions lead to attitude change.

Ashley developed a game plan to look for ways to have positive interactions with Jody whenever possible. One day she thanked Jody for the suggestions she made about preparing less complicated PowerPoint slides. She also incorporated ideas from a recent article about business process reengineering into her next suggestion for improving the workflow in the hospital laundry. Another day Ashley complimented Jody about a business suit she was wearing. At a luncheon meeting with Jody and several other department members, Ashley wore a blouse that covered the tattoo on her neck.

Ashley's game plan of applying a little-known principle of human relations to improving her relationship with her boss soon started to pay off. Jody actually complimented Ashley's report and stated that she was a strong contributor to the hospital. The most concrete evidence of an improved relationship was that Jody rated Ashley as "exceeding expectations" the first time she formally evaluated her performance.

As the case history just presented indicated, another way of understanding the importance of human relations is to examine its personal benefits. A person who carefully studies human relations and incorporates its suggestions into his or her work and personal life should derive the five benefits discussed next. Knowledge itself, however, is no guarantee of success. Because people differ greatly in learning ability, personality, and life circumstances, some will get more out of studying human relations than will others. You may, for example, be getting along well with coworkers or customers, so studying this topic might seem unnecessary from your viewpoint. Or you may be so shy at this stage of your life that you are unable to capitalize on some of the suggestions for being assertive with people. You might have to work doubly hard to benefit from studying that topic. The major benefits from studying human relations are the following:

1. **Acquiring valid information about human behavior.** To feel comfortable with people and to make a favorable impression both on and off the job, you need to understand how people think and act. Studying human relations will provide you with some basic knowledge about interpersonal relationships, such as the meaning of self-esteem, why goals work, and win–win conflict resolution. You will even learn such things as effective methods of dealing with difficult people.

2. **Developing skills in dealing with people.** People who aspire to high-level positions or enriched social lives need to be able to communicate with others, work well on a team, manage stress, and behave confidently. Relating well to diverse cultural groups is also an asset. Studying information about such topics, coupled with practicing what you learn, should help you develop such interpersonal skills.

3. **Coping with job problems.** Almost everyone who holds a job inevitably runs into human relations problems. Reading about these problems and suggestions for coping with them could save you considerable inner turmoil. Among the job survival skills that you will learn about in the study of human relations are how to deal with difficult people and how to overcome what seems to be an overwhelming workload.

4. **Coping with personal problems.** We all have problems. An important difference between the effective and the ineffective person is that the effective person knows how to manage them. Among the problems studying human relations will help you cope with are self-defeating behavior, dealing with a difficult coworker, overcoming low self-confidence, and working your way out of heavy job stress.

5. **Capitalizing on opportunities.** Many readers of this book will someday spend part of their working time taking advantage of opportunities rather than solving

daily problems. Every career-minded person needs a few breakthrough experiences to make life more rewarding. Toward this end, studying human relations gives you ideas for developing your career, becoming a leader, and becoming more creative.

You are invited to take the accompanying Self-Assessment Quiz 1-1 to think through your current level of human relations effectiveness.

SELF-ASSESSMENT QUIZ 1-1

Human Relations Skills

For each of the following statements about human relations skills, indicate how strong you think you are right now. Attempt to be as objective as possible, even though most of us tend to exaggerate our skills in dealing with people. To help obtain a more objective evaluation of your capabilities, ask someone who knows you well (family member, friend, or work associate) to also rate you on these factors. Use the following scale: (1) very weak, (2) weak, (3) average, (4) strong, (5) very strong.

	Self-Rating	Rating by Other Person
1. Listen carefully when in conversation with another person		
2. Smile frequently		
3. Am tactful when criticizing others		
4. Am comfortable in dealing with people from a different generation than myself		
5. Am comfortable in dealing with a person from a different ethnic group than myself		
6. Am comfortable in dealing with a person from a different race than myself		
7. Let my feelings be known when I disagree with another person		
8. Let my feelings be known when I am joyful about something		
9. Have a neat, well-groomed appearance		
10. Congratulate the winner when I lose an athletic or any other type of contest		
11. Concentrate on another person when in conversation instead of accepting a call on my cell phone, making use of call waiting, or responding to e-mail		
12. Compliment others when a compliment is merited		
13. Have a good sense of humor		
14. Am patient with people who do not understand what I am saying		
15. Cooperate with others in a team effort		
16. Have a controllable temper		
17. Am respected for being honest and dependable		
18. Hug people when the situation is appropriate		
19. Am trusted by other people		
20. Motivate others to do something they hadn't thought of doing		
Total Score		
Combined Score (self plus other)		

(Continued)

Interpretation

1. **Self-ratings:** If your self-rating is 85 or more, and your scoring is accurate, you have exceptional human relations skills. Scores between 60 and 84 suggest moderate, or average, human relations skills. Scores of 59 and below suggest below-average human relations skills in the areas covered in this quiz.
2. **Rating by other person:** Because people tend to judge us a little more critically than we judge ourselves in human relations skills, use the following scale: 80 or more suggests exceptional human relations skills; 55 to 79 suggests moderate, or average, human relations skills; 54 and below suggests below-average human relations skills.
3. **Combined ratings:** 165 or more suggests exceptional human relations skills; 115 to 163 suggests moderate, or average, human relations skills; 114 or below suggests below-average human relations skills.

Action plan: Whether you scored high, low, or medium on this quiz, there is always room for improvement, just as athletes, actors, and musicians are always looking to improve their art. Scores in the bottom category suggest a more urgent need for improvement in human relations skill.

HOW DO WORK AND PERSONAL LIFE INFLUENCE EACH OTHER?

LEARNING OBJECTIVE 3

Most people reading this book will be doing so to improve their job effectiveness and careers. Therefore, the book centers on relationships with people in a job setting. Keep in mind that human relationships in work and personal life have much in common. Several studies have supported the close relationship between job satisfaction and life satisfaction. One such study conducted by Timothy A. Judge, psychology professor at the University of Florida, and Remus Ilies, psychology professor at Michigan State University, involved seventy-four university employees with administrative support positions, such as secretaries or office managers. The researchers collected reports of mood and job satisfaction at work, mood away from work, and job satisfaction. Data were collected using questionnaires posted on a Web site.

The major findings of the study were that mood influences job satisfaction, with a positive mood increasing satisfaction. The effect decreases rapidly because moods pass quickly. The researchers also found that employee's satisfaction with their jobs, measured at work, influences the mood at home. Workers who are more emotional by nature are more likely to experience these connections, such as joy or anger, on the job spilling over to home life. A related finding was that a mood developed on the job spilled over to the home later in the day.[3] In short, this study confirmed the old cartoons about a worker who is chewed out by the boss coming home and swearing at his or her dog or kicking the furniture!

Work and personal life influence each other in a number of specific ways, as outlined in Figure 1-1. First, the satisfaction you achieve on the job contributes to your general life satisfaction. Conversely, if you suffer from chronic job dissatisfaction, your life satisfaction will begin to decline. Career disappointments have been shown to cause marital relationships to suffer. Frustrated on the job, many people start feuding with their partners and other family members.

FIGURE 1-1 How Work and Personal Life Influence Each Other

1. Job satisfaction enhances life satisfaction.
2. An unsatisfying job can damage physical health.
3. Relationships with people on and off the job influence each other.
4. Certain skills contribute to success in both work and personal life.
5. How we behave at work is closely related to how we behave at home.

Second, an unsatisfying job can affect physical health, primarily by creating stress and burnout. Intense job dissatisfaction may even lead to heart disease, ulcers, intestinal disorders, and skin problems. People who have high job satisfaction even tend to live longer than those who suffer from prolonged job dissatisfaction. These benefits may be attributed to better physical health and passion for life. Finding the right type of job may thus add years to a person's life.

Third, the quality of your relationships with people at work and in personal life influence each other. If you experience intense conflict in your family, you might be so upset that you will be unable to form good relationships with coworkers. Conversely, if you have a healthy, rewarding personal life, it will be easier for you to form good relationships on the job. People you meet on the job will find it pleasant to relate to a seemingly positive and untroubled person.

Another way of explaining the third point is that how we behave at work is closely related to how we behave at home. Psychologist John M. Gottman, executive director of the Relationship Research Institute, has been studying married couples for over thirty-five years. He and his colleagues have used devices such as camcorders, heart monitors, and other biofeedback equipment to measure what takes place when couples experience moments of conflict or closeness. The research results indicate that successful couples look for ways to emphasize the positive and attempt to say yes as often as possible. Successful couples use conflict as a way of working through personality differences rather than to attack each other.

A useful inference from research at the Relationship Research Institute is that the way people manage their relationships in the workplace is closely linked to the way they manage their personal ones. People who frequently use the word *yes* in communications at home are likely to do the same on the job. Also, people who are abusive on the job are likely to be abusive at home.[4]

Personal relationships on the job also influence personal relationships off the job. Interacting harmoniously with coworkers can put one in a better mood for dealing with family and friends after hours. Crossing swords with employees and customers during working hours can make it difficult for you to feel comfortable and relaxed with people off the job.

Fourth, certain skills contribute to success in both work and personal life. For example, people who know how to deal effectively with others and get things accomplished on the job can use the same skills to enhance their personal lives. Similarly, people who are effective in dealing with friends and family members and who can organize things are likely to be effective supervisors.

Can you think of other ways in which success in work and success in personal life are related to each other?

IN WHAT WAY DOES HUMAN RELATIONS BEGIN WITH SELF-UNDERSTANDING?

Before you can understand other people very well, and therefore practice effective human relations, you must understand yourself. You already know something about yourself. An important starting point in learning more about yourself is self-examination. Suppose that instead of being about human relations, this book were about dancing. The reader would obviously need to know what other dancers do right and wrong. But the basic principles of dancing cannot be fully grasped unless they are seen in relation to your own style of dancing. Watching a video of your dancing, for example, would be helpful. You might also ask other people for comments and suggestions about your dance movements.

Similarly, to achieve **self-understanding**, you must gather valid information about yourself. (Self-understanding refers to knowledge about you, particularly with respect to mental and emotional aspects.) Every time you read a self-help book, take a personality quiz, or receive an evaluation of your work from a manager or instructor, you are gaining some self-knowledge.

In achieving self-understanding, it is helpful to recognize that the **self** is a complex idea. It generally refers to a person's total being or individuality. To help clarify the meaning of

LEARNING OBJECTIVE 4

self-understanding

Gathering valid information about oneself; self-understanding refers to knowledge about oneself, particularly with respect to mental and emotional aspects.

self

A complex idea generally referring to a person's total being or individuality.

public self

What a person communicates about himself or herself and what others actually perceive about the person.

private self

The actual person an individual may be.

the self, a distinction is sometimes made between the self a person projects to the outside world and the inner self. The **public self** is what the person is communicating about himself or herself and what others actually perceive about the person. The **private self** is the actual person you may be.[5] A similar distinction is made between the real self and the ideal self. Many people think of themselves in terms of an ideal version of what they are really like. To avoid making continuous distinctions between the various selves throughout this text, we will use the term *self* to refer to an accurate representation of the individual.

Some scientific evidence suggests that the self is based on structures within the brain. According to the research of Joseph LeDoux at New York University, the self is the sum of the brain's individual components, or subsystems. Each subsystem has its own form of memory, along with its interactions with other subsystems.[6] Two examples of subsystems in the brain are the center for speech and the center for hearing. The implication to recognize here is that the self could be an entity that is both psychological and biological.

Most of this text is geared toward using human relations knowledge for self-development and self-improvement. Throughout the text you will find questionnaires designed to improve insight. The self-knowledge emphasized here deals with psychological (such as personality traits and thinking style) rather than physical characteristics (such as height and blood pressure). As outlined in Figure 1-2, here we discuss six types of information that contribute to self-understanding, along with potential problems in self-evaluation.

General Information about Human Behavior

As you learn about people in general, you should also be gaining knowledge about yourself. Therefore, most of the information in this text is presented in a form that should be useful to you personally. Whenever general information is presented, it is your responsibility to relate such information to your particular situation, such as in studying sources of conflict. One such general cause is limited resources—that is, not everyone can have what he or she wants. See how this general principle applies to you. Here is an example involving others: "That's why I've been so angry with Melissa lately. She was the one given the promotion, whereas I'm stuck in the same old job."

In relating facts and observations about people in general to yourself, be careful not to misapply the information. Feedback from other people will help you avoid the pitfalls of introspection (looking into yourself).

Informal Feedback from People

feedback

Information that tells one how well he or she has performed.

As just implied, **feedback** is information that tells you how well you have performed. You can sometimes obtain feedback from the spontaneous comments of others or by asking them for feedback. An order-fulfillment materials-handling specialist grew one notch in self-confidence when coworkers began to call him "Net Speed." He was given this name because of the rapidity with which he processed orders. His experience illustrates that a valuable source of information for self- understanding is what the significant people in your life think of you. Although feedback of this type might make you feel uncomfortable, when it is consistent, it accurately reflects how others perceive you.

FIGURE 1-2   Six Sources of Information That Contribute to Self-Understanding

1. General information about human behavior
2. Informal feedback from people
3. Feedback from superiors
4. Feedback from coworkers
5. Feedback from self-assessment quizzes
6. The Johari Window

With some ingenuity you can create informal feedback. (In this sense, the term *informal* refers to not being part of a company-sponsored program.) For example, you might send an e-mail to ten people in your social network asking them for a candid evaluation of your strengths and weaknesses. Make the promise that you will not retaliate if you don't like what you hear.

A few skeptics will argue that friends never give you a true picture of yourself but, rather, say flattering things about you because they value your friendship. Experience has shown, however, that if you emphasize the importance of their opinions, most people will give you a few constructive suggestions. You also have to appear sincere. Because not everyone's comments will be helpful, you may have to sample many people.

Feedback from Superiors

Virtually all employers provide employees with formal or informal feedback on their performances. A formal method of feedback is called a *performance evaluation*. During a performance evaluation (or appraisal) your superior will convey to you what he or she thinks you are doing well and not so well. These observations become a permanent part of your human resources record. Informal feedback occurs when a superior discusses your job performance with you but does not record these observations.

The feedback obtained from superiors in this way can help you learn about yourself. For instance, if two different bosses say that you are a creative problem solver, you might conclude that you are creative. If several bosses tell you that you are too impatient with other people, you might conclude that you are impatient.

Feedback from Coworkers

A sometimes-used practice in organizations is **peer evaluations**, a system in which teammates contribute to an evaluation of a person's job performance. Although coworkers under this system do not have total responsibility for evaluating each other, their input is taken seriously. The amount of a worker's salary increase could thus be affected by peer judgments about his or her performance. The results of peer evaluations can also be used as feedback for learning about yourself. Assume that coworkers agree on several of your strengths and needs for improvement. You can conclude that others who work closely with you generally perceive you that way.

Teammates might rate each other on performance dimensions such as cooperation with other members of the team, customer service attitude, productivity, and contributions to meetings. If several teammates rated you low in one of these dimensions, it could indicate a **developmental opportunity**, an area for growth, or weakness.

peer evaluations
System in which teammates contribute to an evaluation of a person's job performance.

developmental opportunity
Area for growth or weakness.

Feedback from Self-Assessment Quizzes

Many self-help books, including this one, contain questionnaires that you fill out by yourself, for yourself. The information that you pick up from these questionnaires often provides valuable clues to your preferences, values, and personal traits. Such self-examination questionnaires should not be confused with the scientifically researched test you might take in a counseling center or guidance department or when applying for a job. Another source of useful self-assessment quizzes is www.queendom.com, which offers a variety of tests that contribute to self- understanding, including the classical intelligence quotient (IQ), mental toughness, risk-taking, and self-esteem tests, among many others.

The amount of useful information gained from self-examination questionnaires depends on your candor. Because no outside judge is involved in these self-help quizzes, candor usually is not a problem. An exception is that we all have certain blind spots. Most people, for example, believe that they have considerably above-average skills in dealing with people.

As a starting point in conducting self-examination exercises, you already completed Self-Assessment Quiz 1-1. Quiz 1-2 gives you an opportunity to write some things down about yourself.

The Written Self-Portrait

A good starting point in acquiring serious self-knowledge is to prepare a written self-portrait in the major life spheres (or aspects). In each of the following spheres, describe yourself in about twenty-five to fifty words. For example, under the social and interpersonal sphere, a person might write, "I'm a little timid on the surface. But those people who get to know me well understand that I'm filled with enthusiasm and joy. My relationships with people last a long time. I'm on excellent terms with all members of my family. And my significant other and I have been together for five years. We are very close emotionally and should be together for a lifetime."

A. Occupational and school: _____

_____

_____

_____

B. Social and interpersonal: _____

_____

_____

_____

C. Beliefs, values, and attitudes: _____

_____

_____

_____

D. Physical description (body type, appearance, grooming): _____

_____

_____

_____

Looking at the Self through the Johari Window

Johari Window

A grid showing how much information you know about yourself as well as how much other people know about you.

A systematic approach to looking at yourself is through a model of communication called the Johari Window, which focuses on self-disclosure. The **Johari Window** is a grid showing how much information you know about yourself as well as how much other people know about you. (The term *Johari* came about because the method was created by Joseph Loft and Harry Ingram.)

The basics of the model are outlined in Figure 1-3. One axis of the grid is the degree to which information about you is known to or understood by you. The other axis is the degree to which information about you is known to others. The horizontal dimension involves soliciting, or obtaining, feedback from others about you; the vertical dimension involves feedback about you to others, or self-disclosure.[7]

The basic premise of the model, as well as the lesson it teaches, is that we can improve our personal and professional relationships through understanding ourselves in depth. But you also have to take the next step of selecting those aspects of the self that are appropriate to share with others. A packaging specialist might want to reveal to coworkers that he does his best creative thinking when jogging alone. However, he might not want to reveal that he finds coworkers to be an annoying distraction while he is attempting to think creatively.

FIGURE 1-3 The Johari Window

Solicit Feedback →

	Known to Self	Unknown to Self
Known to Others	**Open Area:** known to self and others	**Blind Area:** blind to self, seen by others
Unknown to Others	**Hidden Area:** open to self, hidden from others	**Unknown Area:** unknown to self and others

Give Feedback ↓

Another premise of the model is that the more we share of ourselves with others, the higher the probability of developing high-quality relationships. To develop these positive relationships, we need to be aware of the four areas (or four panes of the window) indicating what is known about us and what is hidden. Observe that the four areas, or panes, of the window are the basics of the communication model.

- The **open area** consists of information that is known to us and others. Among these readily observable aspects would be hair color, skin color, physical appearance, and spoken communication skills. As a relationship builds we enlarge the open area by revealing more about ourselves. As the open area expands, relationships with others improve—unless you annoy others with too many details about your work and personal life.

- The **hidden area** contains information known to us about ourselves but is hidden from others. Frequent hidden areas are ambitions and dislikes of specific individuals. Over the long term, fewer hidden areas lead to more openness and closeness in relationships with others. Yet it is prudent to keep some areas hidden, such as describing a strong physical attraction toward your coworker's or manager's spouse.

- The **blind area** contains information that others are aware of but we cannot see in ourselves in reference to both positive and negative qualities. Many people suffer from thinking that they are not physically attractive, yet others in general have an opposite perception. In the opposite direction, many people perceive themselves to be highly skilled in getting along with other people, yet most people might have an opposite point of view. Feedback from others, if not blocked by defensiveness, will help reduce the blind area. As your blind area decreases, you are likely to enlarge your open area because you will have more accurate data to work with.

- The **unknown area** contains information that you and others do not know about you. It sometimes takes an unusual situation to bring out this unknown information, such as emerging as a leader when a crisis, such as a hurricane, hits your unit of the company.

The Johari Window is useful in reminding you of the importance of self-disclosure, such as in enlarging your open area. As you disclose more about yourself, others will reciprocate and disclose more about themselves. The mutual disclosures lead to enhanced positive feelings among people in both work and personal life.

Two Self-Evaluation Traps

The theme of this section of the chapter is that self-awareness is a positive force in our lives. Yet self-awareness also has two negative extremes or traps. One of these extremes is that focusing on the self can highlight shortcomings the way staring into a mirror can dramatize every blemish and wrinkle on a face. Certain situations predictably force us to engage in self-reflection and become the object of our own attention. When we talk about

open area
Pane of Johari Window consisting of information that is known to us and others.

hidden area
Pane of Johari Window that contains information known to us about ourselves but is hidden from others.

blind area
Pane of Johari Window that contains information that others are aware of but we cannot see in ourselves in reference to both positive and negative qualities.

unknown area
Pane of Johari Window that contains information that you and others do not know about you.

ourselves, answer self-quizzes, stand before an audience or camera, or watch ourselves on a video, we become more self-aware and make comparisons to some arbitrary standard of behavior. The comparison often results in negative self-evaluation in comparison to the standard and a decrease in self-esteem as we discover that we fall short of standards.[8] Keeping the self-awareness trap in mind will help you minimize needless underevaluation, thereby benefiting from gathering feedback about yourself.

In contrast to underevaluation, it is also true that many people tend to overestimate their competence, such as thinking they deserve a bigger raise or an A in every course. A particular area in which people overestimate their competence is in the moral domain. Many people suffer from a "holier than thou" syndrome. A study with college students, for example, found that they consistently overrated the likelihood that they would act in generous or selfless ways. Eighty-four percent of the students initially predicted that they would cooperate with their partner, but in reality only 61 percent did.[9]

Cultural differences help explain at least some of the differences in underevaluation versus overevaluation. Several studies have shown, for example, that East Asians tend to underestimate their abilities, with an aim toward improving the self and getting along with others. North Americans are more likely to overestimate their abilities and not be so prone to look for areas of self-improvement.[10] Cultural differences reflect stereotypes that apply to the average individual from a culture.

The antidote to the twin self-evaluation traps is to search for honest and objective feedback from others to help you supplement your self-evaluation. Competing against peers, such as in school, sports, and contests on the job (for example, a sales contest or creative suggestion contest), can help you evaluate yourself more realistically. Next, we look more at human relations from the standpoint of the workplace rather than the individual.

HOW DID THE HUMAN RELATIONS MOVEMENT DEVELOP?

human relations movement

Movement that began as a concentrated effort by some managers and their advisers to become more sensitive to the needs of employees or to treat them in a more humanistic manner.

The **human relations movement** began as a concentrated effort by some managers and their advisers to become more sensitive to the needs of employees or to treat them in a more humanistic manner. In other words, employees were to be treated as human beings rather than as parts of the productive process. The human relations movement was supported directly by three different historic influences: the Hawthorne studies, the threat of unionization, and industrial humanism (see Figure 1-4).[11] Scientific management, which predated the growth of human relations in industry, contributed indirectly to the movement.

Scientific Management

The study of management became more systematized and formal as a byproduct of the Industrial Revolution, which took place from the 1700s through the 1900s. Approaches to managing work and people needed to be developed to manage all the new factories

FIGURE 1-4 Influences Supporting the Human Relations Movement

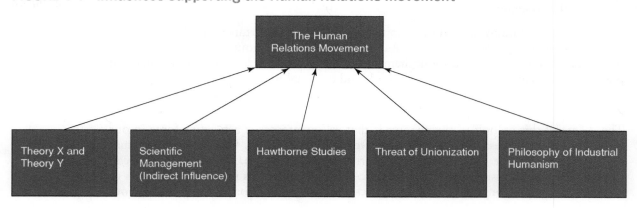

that were a central part of the Industrial Revolution. The focus of **scientific management** was on the application of scientific methods to increase individual workers' productivity. Frederick W. Taylor, considered the father of scientific management, was an engineer by background. He used scientific analysis and experiments to increase worker output. Taylor's goal was to remove human variability so each worker could become essentially an interchangeable part. His model for human behavior was a machine, with inexpensive parts, each of which has a specific function. Using the principles of scientific management, a worker might assemble a washing machine with the least number of wasted motions and steps. United Parcel Service (UPS) relies heavily on the principles of scientific management to get the most productivity from carriers and shipping personnel, including tightly timing their deliveries.

With scientific management sounding so dehumanizing, how could the movement have contributed to good human relations? Taylor also studied problems such as fatigue and safety. He urged management to study the relationship between work breaks and the length of the workday and productivity. He convinced some managers that work breaks and shorter workdays could increase productivity. Furthermore, scientific management proposed that workers who produced more be paid more.

Scientific management also contributed to the human relations movement by creating a backlash against what many people thought was mistreatment of workers. The industrial engineer with his or her stopwatch and clipboard, hovering over a worker measuring each tiny part of the job and the worker's movements, became a hated figure. [12] The objection to this approach called for a better way to treat people, which came to be known as the human relations movement.

The Hawthorne Studies

The human relations school of management is generally said to have begun in 1927 with a group of studies conducted at the Chicago-area Hawthorne plant of an AT&T subsidiary. These studies were prompted by an experiment carried out by the company's engineers between 1924 and 1927. Following the tradition of scientific management, these engineers were applying research methods to investigate problems of employee productivity.

Two groups were studied to determine the effects of different levels of light on worker performance. As prescribed by the scientific method, one group received increased illumination, whereas the other did not. A preliminary finding was that when illumination was increased, the level of performance also increased. Surprisingly to the engineers, productivity also increased when the level of light was decreased almost to moonlight levels. One interpretation of these findings was that the workers involved in the experiment enjoyed being the center of attention. In other words, they reacted positively because management cared about them. Such a phenomenon taking place in any work or research setting is now called the **Hawthorne Effect**.[13]

As a result of these preliminary investigations, a team of researchers headed by Harvard professors Elton Mayo and Fritz J. Roethlisberger conducted a series of experiments extending over a six-year period. The conclusions they reached served as the foundations for later developments in the human relations approach to management. It was found that economic incentives are less important than generally believed in influencing workers to achieve high levels of output. Also, leadership practices and work group pressures profoundly influence employee satisfaction and performance. An example of an effective leadership practice would be coaching and encouraging workers to higher performance. The researchers noted that any factor influencing employee behavior is embedded in a social system. For instance, to understand the impact of pay on performance, you have to understand the atmosphere that exists in the work group and how the leader approaches his or her job.

A major implication of the Hawthorne studies was that the old concept of an economic person motivated primarily by money had to be replaced by a more valid idea. The replacement concept was a social person, motivated by social needs, desiring rewarding on-the-job relationships and more responsive to pressures from coworkers than to control by the boss.[14] Do you believe that workers are more concerned with social relationships than with money?

scientific management

Theory that focuses on the application of scientific methods to increase individual workers' productivity.

Hawthorne Effect

Applying research methods to investigate problems of employee productivity using the scientific method; in the study, employees reacted positively because management cared about them.

The Threat of Unionization

Labor union officials and their advocates contend that the benefits of unionization extend to many workers who themselves do not belong to unions. Management in nonunion firms will often pay employees union wages to offset the potential advantages of unionization. A similar set of circumstances contributed to the growth of the human relations movement. Labor unions began to grow rapidly in the United States during the late 1930s. Many employers feared that the presence of a labor union would have negative consequences for their companies. Consequently, management looked aggressively for ways to stem the tide of unionization, such as using human relations techniques to satisfy workers.[15] Their reasoning is still valid today: dissatisfied workers are much more likely to join a labor union, in hope of improving their working conditions.[16]

Today the threat of unionization is primarily in the public sector. Although unionization has declined considerably in manufacturing, about 36 percent of government workers, including those in education, are union members, compared with about 8 percent of workers in private-sector industries. In 1945, about 36 percent of the U.S. workforce was unionized, versus about 12 percent today.[17] The decline of manufacturing jobs has contributed to the decline of union membership.

The Philosophy of Industrial Humanism

Partly as a byproduct of the Hawthorne studies, a new philosophy of human relations arose in the workplace. Elton Mayo was one of the two key figures in developing this philosophy of industrial humanism. He cautioned managers that emotional factors (such as a desire for recognition) were a more important contributor to productivity than physical and logical factors. Mayo argued vigorously that work should lead to personal satisfaction for employees.

Mary Parker Follett was another key figure in advancing the cause of industrial humanism. Her experience as a management consultant led her to believe that the key to increased productivity was to motivate employees, rather than simply ordering better job performance. The keys to both productivity and democracy, according to Follett, were cooperation, a spirit of unity, and a coordination of effort.[18]

Theory X and Theory Y of Douglas McGregor

The importance of managing people through more effective methods of human relations was advanced by the writings of social psychologist Douglas McGregor. His famous position was that managers should challenge their assumptions about the nature of people. McGregor believed that too many managers assumed that people were lazy and indifferent toward work. He urged managers to be open to the possibility that under the right circumstances people are eager to perform well. If a supervisor accepts one of these extreme sets of beliefs about people, the supervisor will act differently toward them than if he or she believes the opposite. These famous assumptions that propelled the human relations movement are summarized as follows:

Theory X Assumptions
1. The average person dislikes work and therefore will avoid it if he or she can.
2. Because of this dislike of work, most people must be coerced, controlled, directed, or threatened with punishment to get them to put forth enough effort to achieve organizational goals.
3. The average employee prefers to be directed, wishes to shirk responsibility, has relatively little ambition, and highly values job security.

Theory Y Assumptions
1. The expenditure of physical and mental effort in work is as natural as play or rest.
2. External control and the threat of punishment are not the only means for bringing about effort toward reaching company objectives. Employees will exercise self-direction and self-control in the service of objectives to which they attach high valence.

3. Commitment to objectives is related to the rewards associated with their achievement.

4. The average person learns, under proper conditions, not only to accept but also to seek responsibility.

5. Many employees have the capacity to exercise a high degree of imagination, ingenuity, and creativity in the solution of organizational problems.

6. Under the present conditions of industrial life, the intellectual potentialities of the average person are only partially utilized.[19]

The distinction between Theory X and Theory Y has often been misinterpreted. McGregor was humanistic, but he did not mean to imply that being directive and demanding with workers is always the wrong tactic. Some people are undermotivated and dislike work. In these situations, the manager has to behave sternly toward group members to motivate them. If you are a Theory Y manager, you size up your group members to understand their attitudes toward work.

Relevance of the History of Human Relations to Today's Workplace

Many of the pioneering ideas described in the history of human relations are still relevant, partly because human nature has not undergone major changes. Most of the core ideas in the history of the human relations movement are still part of the human relations and organizational behavior curriculum today, even though they have more research substantiation and new labels. A good example is the push toward creativity and innovation based on the involvement of many different workers, not only specialists from one department. The link to history is that Theory Y encourages empowering employees to use their ingenuity and creativity to solve organizational problems. Next is a bulleted summary of ideas from the human relations movement that still influence the practice of human relations today.

- Many principles of scientific management are useful in making workers more productive so business firms can compete better in a global economy.
- Ideas from the Hawthorne studies have helped managers focus on the importance of providing both congenial work surroundings and adequate compensation to motivate and retain workers.
- Industrial humanism is widely practiced today in the form of looking for ways to keep workers satisfied through such methods as flexible work arrangements, family leave, and dependent care benefits.
- Theory Y has prompted managers to think through which style of leadership works best with which employees. Specifically, a modern manager is likely to grant more freedom to employees who are well motivated and talented. Spurred partially by Theory X, few managers today believe that being the "bull of the woods" is the best way to supervise all workers.

HOW DOES HUMAN RELATIONS KNOWLEDGE AND SKILL HELP YOU DEAL WITH MAJOR CHALLENGES IN THE WORKPLACE?

Another major way in which human relations skills and knowledge can help you is in dealing effectively with major challenges in the modern workplace. Although it would be difficult to reach consensus on which are the major challenges in the workplace, our list at least touches the major themes. All of these themes, outlined in Figure 1-5, will be discussed in more depth at various places in the book.

LEARNING OBJECTIVE 6

Emphasis on Teamwork and Collaboration

The modern workplace emphasizes teamwork and collaboration. Similarly, many of the courses you have taken emphasize collaborative projects inside and outside of the classroom.

FIGURE 1-5   Major Workplace Challenges of Today

Human relations skills are helpful in dealing with the major challenges in the modern workplace.

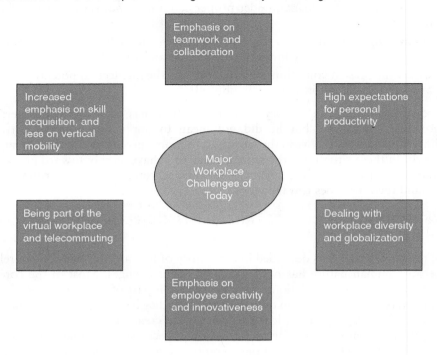

The story about the consulting firm presented earlier in the chapter indicates that company management invests time and money to enhance collaboration among coworkers. A current thrust in office design is to move people away from private offices and cubicles to encourage collaboration.[20] The reasoning being that you are more likely to confer with coworkers who are in open view than with those hidden in their own work area. Another approach to enhancing teamwork and collaboration is to send employees to offsite or outdoor training to participate in exercises that require collaboration, such as refurbishing an old house.

A subtle aspect of collaboration is that the modern employee is supposed to think of the demands of people working in different functions of the organization, not just in terms of his or her own function (or department). The buzzword for people who think only in terms of their own function or discipline (such as marketing or accounting) is having a *silo mentality*.[21] A silo, as you probably already know, is high and narrow, thereby blocking out other points of view.

The human relations lesson for you with respect to teamwork and collaboration is that you need to acquire skills that facilitate working smoothly in joint effort with others. Among these dozens of skills would be learning to accept criticism from coworkers and also being willing to offer them constructive criticism.

High Expectations for Personal Productivity

For many years business organizations as well as governmental and educational institutions have been focusing on getting more work accomplished with fewer people. Many large firms have shrunk their workforce almost in half without experiencing a substantial decrease in sales volume. Much of this increased productivity stems from advances in technology, yet some of the productivity gains stem from employees working harder, smarter, and longer. This translates into you having to produce more than your counterparts of yesteryear. Higher productivity is expected of workers at all levels, including managers, corporate professionals, and entry-level workers. Here is an example of productivity measurement applied to a store cashier:

> A clock starts ticking the moment a cashier at Meijer Inc. scans a customer's first item, and it doesn't shut off until his register spits out a receipt. To assess his

efficiency, the store's computer takes into account everything from the kinds of merchandise he is bagging to how his customers are paying. Each week, he gets scored. If he falls below 95% of the baseline score too many times, the 185-store megastore chain is likely to bounce him to a lower-paying job or fire him.[22]

With so many retail stores under the gun to cut costs and improve profit margins, "labor-waste elimination" systems such as the one mentioned above have come into widespread use. Employees working in manufacturing, whatever their job title, are typically expected to be highly efficient. An extreme example is that several automobile manufacturers worldwide, including Tata Motors of India, are attempting to produce automobiles that can be sold profitably for around $5,000. Initially, the hope was to sell a Tata auto for $3,500 which proved to be unrealistic.[23] In addition to using the latest labor-saving technology, these companies expect managers and professionals to work at a fast pace, relying on less staff assistance.

To deal successfully with the push for increased productivity, you have to acquire excellent work habits and time-management skills. Such skills are related to human relations because being in control of your work makes it easier to relate effectively to others, partially because you will be less stressed. Human relations skills at a high level are also called for in helping management determine which approaches to enhanced productivity are sensible, and therefore not counterproductive. A cashier who is working like a robot might lower customer service by failing to establish rapport with customers. The cashier might also neglect to smile, violating an important part of relationship building with customers.

Dealing with Workplace Diversity and Globalization

The domestic workforce has become more culturally diverse, and more people in high-level positions are from culturally diverse groups. You deal well with diversity when you relate comfortably to people from a range of cultural and demographic groups. (A cultural group refers mostly to values and customs, whereas a demographic group refers to a statistical category, such as being a Filipino or under age twenty-five.) *Diversity* includes all categories of people. A strong example of this inclusion is the global constituency teams formed by Merck & Co., the pharmaceutical giant. The teams represent the following diverse groups: Asians, blacks, Latinos, indigenous peoples, generational differences, interfaith, differently abled, and lesbian, gay, bisexual, and transgendered. (Age groups are not considered separately.) The leader of all these teams is chief diversity officer Deborah Dagit, who is four feet tall and who made the following comment:

> As a person with a visible disability, I have a special gift and a unique challenge. Because of my packaging, and because there are not many people with disabilities who do the work that I do, I have been given opportunities I might otherwise not have had. Having a disability is a tool in my toolbox.[24]

The globalization of the workforce requires many workers to work comfortably with people from different countries and time zones. Visiting another country might require a quick adaptation to another culture, such as being offered food during a business dinner that you consider to be a household pet or repulsive in some other way.

A specific career challenge created by globalization is that you have to develop skills so valuable that your job is not in danger of being sent offshore. We all know that countless thousands of manufacturing and call-center jobs have been sent overseas. Less well publicized is that many higher-level positions such as those related to research and development, product design, and medical diagnostics have also been sent to other countries. Many American patients now have surgery performed in India and China to lower costs, assuming the health of the patient allows for such rigorous travel. Your job is less likely to be outsourced if you have established valuable personal relationships, such as an industrial sales representative who knows his or her customers well.

The general challenge created by the diverse domestic and international workforce is that you need to develop cross-cultural skills, including being able to work comfortably with generational differences. So many workers today have been relating to diverse groups for so much of their lives that cross-cultural skills are more widespread than they were years ago. Participating in sports during youth, for example, has helped many people develop cross-cultural skills.

Emphasis on Employee Creativity and Innovativeness

Workplaces today frequently demand creativity and innovativeness from all types of workers, not just those involved in such functions as research and development, advertising, engineering, and product development. Creativity in the present context refers to having imaginative, useful suggestions. Many people have imaginative ideas that are not useful, such as suggesting that the company become more environmentally friendly by having employees commute to work via jet packs rather than private vehicles. (Maybe jetpacks will be useful by the next edition of this book.)

The creativity demanded by organizations from employees outside of traditionally creative roles, such as those in advertising, often focuses on searching for new ways to solve basic problems, including how to decrease costs and improve profits. A representative example is Costco, a discount warehouse chain that relies heavily on membership fees. The company fears that raising prices on merchandise might drive away dues-paying customers. As a result, employees search continuously for ways to reduce the cost of merchandise so the store price is lower. A few years ago, Procter & Gamble announced a 6 percent price increase on Bounty paper towels. Costco management responded imaginatively by purchasing hundreds of truckloads of Bounty paper at the old price and storing the towels. As a result, customers saved psychologically important pennies. At the time the company was also exploring the possibilities of growing its own pumpkins to help maintain a low price tag on its store-baked pies. Costco CEO James Sinegal says, "If that stuff doesn't turn you on then you're in the wrong business."[25]

Although being a creative problem solver is not directly an interpersonal skill, being creative will help you develop a better reputation within your company and perhaps help you hold on to an important job. The current emphasis on creative problem solving in the workplace suggests that you will have to emphasize the creativity that you probably already have—even if you don't yet use it extensively.

Being Part of the Virtual Workplace and Telecommuting

Workplace trends such as more emphasis on diversity and creativity are intangible, or difficult to measure. A tangible, or measurable, workplace trend is the movement toward many workers being given the opportunity, or forced to, work outside of the traditional office. Forcing refers to demand that employees work from home to reduce real estate costs for the company.

virtual office

One in which employees work together as if they were part of a single office despite being physically separated.

A **virtual office** is one in which employees work together as if they were part of a single office despite being physically separated. Highly coordinated virtual office members form a virtual team. For example, you might be on the same team with five other workers who are physically located in different parts of country or even another country. Or a few of your team members might be at different places of a large office building or factory. Communication among team members is mostly online, with telephone calls supplementing the online messages. Members of the virtual team might hold a physical meeting on occasion. Companies who make extensive use of virtual offices rely heavily on Web-based technology. Among the specific tools are an Intranet (company Internet), a method of scheduling meetings, document management, and news updates.[26]

Being a successful member of a virtual office and a virtual team requires that you have particularly good skills in relating to people you do not see frequently. Among these skills are knowing how to give sincere compliments with instant messaging, keeping your manager updated on your contribution, and making the most out of the occasional face-to-face meeting.

Telecommuting, or working from a remote location, makes a virtual office possible. Yet many workers telecommute as independent workers rather than as part of a team. About 26 million corporate workers in the United States now telecommute at least one day a week. The special human relations demands that telecommuting places on the worker include being sufficiently self-disciplined to work without a supervisor present and making a good face-to-face impression during the time one spends in the physical office. You also have to be able to size up the company atmosphere to understand whether telecommuting places you in a favorable or an unfavorable light with management.[27]

Increased Emphasis on Skill Acquisition and Less on Upward Mobility

A subtle trend in the workplace is for employers to encourage employees to continuously acquire new skills and knowledge, while at the same time offering fewer opportunities for promotion than in the past. A positive force behind this development is that technology and workplace procedures change so rapidly that continuous learning by workers is necessary for organizations of all types to stay competitive. A not-so-positive reason for the emphasis on growth by acquiring new skills is that organizations offer fewer opportunities for vertical mobility (essentially promotions). Most organizations today have substantially decreased their number of layers as well as the number of managers. Some of the best-known business firms, such as General Motors and Hewlett Packard, have eliminated over 30,000 positions.

An example of today's emphasis on continuous learning is the lifelong learning account (LiLA) offered by some employers. LiLA offers an investment program for adult education to which employees and employers contribute, with the employee owning the plan and keeping it even if he or she leaves the organization. An employee could use the money in the plan to invest in learning at the present employer or use the same funds to invest in education at a future employer. One of the goals of the plan is to assist working adults to remain competitive in the workforce.[28]

The new emphasis on learning in organizations requires that to succeed, you need to actively participate in learning through such means as self-study, taking courses, and participating in training and seminars. If you are concerned about the challenge of fewer opportunities for promotion, you need to place extra effort into tactics for career advancement, such as building your personal brand (your unique basket of strengths).

WHAT MAJOR FACTORS INFLUENCE JOB PERFORMANCE AND BEHAVIOR?

Part of understanding human relations is recognizing the factors or forces that influence job performance and behavior. In overview, the performance and behavior of workers is influenced by factors related to the employee, manager, job, and organization as discussed next and outlined in Figure 1-6. Here we present a sampling of these many factors, because a comprehensive understanding of them would encompass the study of human relations, organizational behavior, and management.

LEARNING OBJECTIVE 7

1. **Factors related to the employee.** The major influence on how a worker performs and behaves, or acts, on the job stems from his or her personal attributes. The worker's mental ability influences how quickly and accurately he or she can solve problems. Physical ability would influence some types of performance, such as the ability to stand up for long periods of time as a store manager or lift boxes as a warehouse attendant. Job knowledge is obviously important, such as a financial consultant being knowledgeable about a variety of investments. Employees who are well motivated and interested in the work are likely to perform better and behave in a more professional manner. Workers who receive encouragement from friends and family are likely to perform better. Being distracted, such as Internet surfing during the workday or experiencing heavy personal problems, can influence performance negatively. Having the right amount of stress can boost performance, whereas being overstressed can lower performance and lead to distracting behavior, such as being confused.

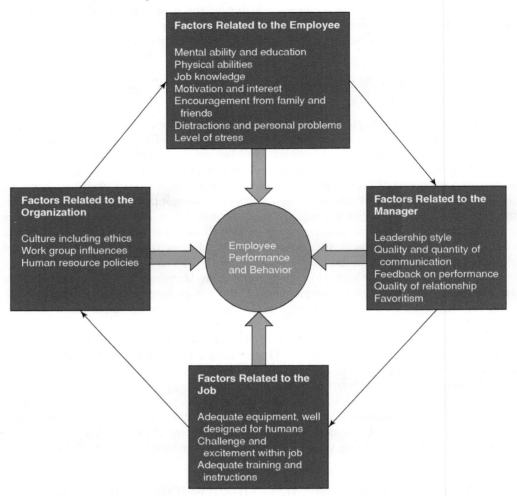

Factors Related to the Employee

Mental ability and education
Physical abilities
Job knowledge
Motivation and interest
Encouragement from family and
friends
Distractions and personal problems
Level of stress

**Factors Related to the
Organization**

Culture including ethics
Work group influences
Human resource policies

Employee
Performance
and Behavior

**Factors Related to the
Manager**

Leadership style
Quality and quantity of
communication
Feedback on performance
Quality of relationship
Favoritism

**Factors Related to the
Job**

Adequate equipment, well
designed for humans
Challenge and
excitement within job
Adequate training and
instructions

2. **Factors related to the manager.** The manager, or supervisor, is another major influence on work behavior. A manager whose style, or approach, is warm and supportive is likely to bring out the best in many employees. But some workers require a more directive and demanding supervisor to perform at their best. Ample communication among the manager and group members is likely to enhance performance and guide employees toward doing what is expected of them. Most workers need considerable feedback from their supervisor to stay on track and be highly motivated. A high-quality relationship between the manager and group members leads to high performance, more loyalty, and lower absenteeism. Favoritism is another key factor related to the manager. A manager who plays favorites is less likely to gain the cooperation of the entire group.

3. **Factors related to the job.** The job itself influences how well the worker might perform and behave. Given the right equipment, designed well for human use, a worker is likely to perform better, such as being less likely to have aches, pains, and wrist injuries as a result of many hours of keyboarding. A proven strategy for improving worker motivation is to give the employee an exciting, challenging job, such as the opportunity to make presentations to management about a project. Adequate training and instructions can also be a big boost to job performance.

4. **Factors related to the organization.** The organization as a whole can have a profound influence on the individual worker's performance and behavior. The

culture, or atmosphere and values of a company, establishes an unwritten standard for how employees perform and behave. At Google, for example, employees are placed in an atmosphere where being creative and making suggestions is expected. And all Southwest Airlines employees know that having fun is supposed to be part of the job. The culture of the organization also influences the ethical behavior of employees, with some companies expecting honest treatment of workers and employees. Other companies are much less ethical and encourage tactics such as deceiving customers. The work group, as part of the organization, can influence the employee by encouraging teamwork and high productivity, among other methods. Human resource policies are another notable influence on the individual. If your company offers you generous medical and dental benefits and allows time off for family emergencies, it becomes easier to concentrate on the job.

The four factors just listed often have a combined influence on the worker. Let us take an extreme example: Jack, a well-motivated and talented assistant hotel manager, reports to a manager with whom he has a great relationship, which includes giving Jack ample feedback on his performance. Jack finds his job challenging, and his hotel has the advanced equipment necessary for success. The hotel has a friendly climate, along with generous benefits. As a result of this combination of factors, Jack is an outstanding performer who approaches his job with a high degree of professionalism.

CHAPTER 1 SPECIAL TOPIC

Different Theories Provide Unique Insights

There are numerous ways to see yourself and understand your behavior in certain situations, and many education specialists and psychologists have provided theories on how we take in and process information. They have developed different inventories and personality profiles to enhance your understanding of yourself. As you will discover, the learning process is somewhat complex; it involves more than just our preferences in how we create knowledge, because there are many factors that affect our ability to take in and process information.

Theories about the two hemispheres of our brain, known as the left brain and the right brain, have given us insight into how people think, learn, and see the world. People who have strong left-brain tendencies are more likely to be logical, to see the parts rather than the whole, and to prefer to do activities step by step. They are also more analytical, realistic, and verbal than their right-brained companions. The right-brain preference is to see the whole picture rather than the details, to work out of sequence, and to bring ideas together.

The Myers-Briggs Type Indicator® (MBTI), on the other hand, is a personality assessment that provides you with information about how you prefer to think and act. For example, one dimension of the personality test asks you how outgoing, or extroverted, you are in certain situations or how reserved, or introverted, you are in social settings. These questions indicate whether you are Extroverted (E) or Introverted (I). Both left-brain/right-brain inventories, or samples of the complete inventories, as well as the MBTI, can be found in books and online sources.

Other inventories, such as the Dunn and Dunn Learning Styles Assessment and the PEPS Learning Styles Inventory, focus not only on how a person prefers to take in information, but also on a person's social and

©Fotolia

Kinesthetic learning involves using your hands or body to master a concept.

environmental learning preferences. These types of inventories provide a thorough view of how you prefer to learn, including the temperature of the room, the amount of light and sound, or the preference for moving about as you learn.

Regardless of which learning theory leads you to greater personal insight, as stand-alone models they are somewhat insignificant unless you *use* the information to benefit your situation. The purpose of this learning plan inventory is to provide you with a basic understanding of the factors that impact your learning preferences so that you can use this information to create an individualized and flexible learning plan for the various tasks and assignments that you will experience while you are in college. Ultimately, greater personal understanding and self-knowledge leads to action, and this learning plan inventory provides you with not only information about how you prefer to learn but also the roadmap for the journey to completing tasks and goals successfully.

There are many ways of analyzing yourself and creating a plan of action for your work in college, but no single inventory, assessment, or work plan will completely reflect the exceptional person you are or your unique circumstances; in other words, no matter what inventory you take or what you learn about how you prefer to learn, the results are not the final verdict on your abilities and potential.

The goal, then, of this learning plan is to provide you with an adaptable, flexible model for putting your learning style preference into action. It also gives you a roadmap for accomplishing the many goals that you will set for yourself. Additionally, it can serve as a place to start when faced with situations that require you to work outside your learning preference comfort zone. For example, what will you do, as a morning learner, when faced with completing an important project late at night? Or how will you, as an individual learner, fare when required to collaborate with classmates on an assignment?

As you read about the characters whose stories begin certain chapters, reflect on how you would act in a situation and consider how you would meet similar challenges—this is one way to move outside your learning preference comfort zone.

Although the characters are fictional, representative of many different college students, their stories ring true because they are based on real-life situations that you may face. Reflecting on who you are and how you will get where you want to go will help you create your own story of success.

Learning Styles Relate to Career Choices

Discovering your learning style preference and your personality type will definitely help you set realistic short-term and long-term goals. For example, confirming that you have a read/write learning preference and you work well with deadlines and stay organized may help you realize that your long-term goal of being a writer will work well with who you are and how you learn and work. However, identifying your style and type should not limit your choices or keep you from working on areas of your learning style and personality that may be weaker or get less attention. If you are a strong visual learner, but you are taking a class that relies on listening effectively and critically, you should use that opportunity to become a better listener and improve your aural learning style by following the listening tips. Likewise, if you work better alone and have a strong kinesthetic learning

---

IT'S IN THE SYLLABUS

Your professors' syllabi contain clues about how the content will address learning style preferences. For example, a syllabus for biology may include a description of a kinesthetic class project that will involve creating a 3-D model of DNA replication.

- What learning styles will be addressed through the assignments in your classes this semester?
- Which assignments do you think will be the most challenging for you to complete?
- Which assignments are the most intriguing? Why?

Q

My learning style preferences are kinesthetic and visual, but most of my classes seem to benefit students whose preferences are read/write and aural. I feel as though my professors should provide more opportunities for students like me. What can I do?

A

Your professors will teach you in the manner that they believe is most effective for learning the content, so it is best to find ways to adapt your preference to their teaching styles. Here are a few more tips for making your preference work for you:

- Find a classmate who complements your learning style preference and study together.

- "Translate" the material into your learning style preference. For example, if your professor lectures on the Kreb's cycle, it may be helpful to find or create diagrams and other visual representations of the material to be included in your written notes.

- Be open to developing your least preferred learning styles by embracing the way your professor teaches.

style preference, choosing a career as a computer technician may play to your strengths, but you may also find yourself working with others collaboratively and communicating frequently in writing and verbally. See Exhibit 1-1 for examples of careers and majors as they connect to learning style preferences.

Whatever your learning style strength and personality preferences are, consider how other styles and types will factor into your short-term and long-term educational goals. Then, look for opportunities to strengthen those less-developed sides of your learning style and personality so that you are more comfortable in a variety of situations and so that you are a well-rounded person.

The VARK Questionnnaire (Version 7.1)

Copyright Version 7.1 (2011) is held by Neil D. Fleming, Christchurch, New Zealand. Used with permission.

The following inventory allows you to answer the question that Neil Fleming asks: "How do you learn best?" When completing the inventory, choose the answer which best explains your preference and circle the letter(s) next to it. Circle more than one if a single answer does not match your perception. Leave blank any question that does not apply.

EXHIBIT 1-1   Learning Style Preferences, Majors, and Careers

Learning Style Preference	College Majors	Careers
VISUAL	Art, graphic design, architecture, video production	Art teacher, artist, graphic designer, architect, interior designer, video producer
AURAL	Music, communications, counseling	Musician, music educator, marketing director, public relations director, counselor
READ/WRITE	English, writing, journalism, communications, public relations, marketing	Copy editor, writer, journalist, public relations director, grant writer, policy writer
KINESTHETIC	Sciences, sociology, computer technology, culinary arts, theater	Nurse, doctor, therapist, networking specialist, computer technician, thespian, director

1. You are helping someone who wants to go to your airport, town center, or railway station. You would:
   A. go with her.
   B. tell her the directions.
   C. write down the directions.
   D. draw or give her a map.

2. You are not sure whether a word should be spelled 'dependent' or 'dependant'. You would:
   A. see the words in your mind and choose by the way they look.
   B. think about how each word sounds and choose one.
   C. find it in a dictionary.
   D. write both words on paper and choose one.

3. You are planning a holiday for a group. You want some feedback from them about the plan. You would:
   A. describe some of the highlights.
   B. use a map or website to show them the places.
   C. give them a copy of the printed itinerary.
   D. phone, text, or email them.

4. You are going to cook something as a special treat for your family. You would:
   A. cook something you know without the need for instructions.
   B. ask friends for suggestions.
   C. look through the cookbook for ideas from the pictures.
   D. use a cookbook where you know there is a good recipe.

5. A group of tourists want to learn about the parks or wildlife reserves in your area. You would:
   A. talk about, or arrange a talk for them about parks or wildlife reserves.
   B. show them internet pictures, photographs, or picture books.
   C. take them to a park or wildlife reserve and walk with them.
   D. give them a book or pamphlets about the parks or wildlife reserves.

6. You are about to purchase a digital camera or mobile phone. Other than price, what would most influence your decision?
   A. Trying or testing it.
   B. Reading the details about its features.
   C. It is a modern design and looks good.
   D. The salesperson telling me about its features.

7. Remember a time when you learned how to do something new. Try to avoid choosing a physical skill, e.g., riding a bike. You learned best by:
   A. watching a demonstration.
   B. listening to somebody explaining it and asking questions.
   C. diagrams and charts—visual clues.
   D. written instructions—e.g,. a manual or textbook.

8. You have a problem with your heart. You would prefer that the doctor:
   A. gave you a something to read to explain what was wrong.
   B. used a plastic model to show what was wrong.
   C. described what was wrong.
   D. showed you a diagram of what was wrong.

9. You want to learn a new program, skill or game on a computer. You would:
    A. read the written instructions that came with the program.
    B. talk with people who know about the program.
    C. use the controls or keyboard.
    D. follow the diagrams in the book that came with it.

10. I like websites that have:
    A. things I can click on, shift, or try.
    B. interesting design and visual features.
    C. interesting written descriptions, lists, and explanations.
    D. audio channels where I can hear music, radio programs, or interviews.

11. Other than price, what would most influence your decision to buy a new non-fiction book?
    A. The way it looks is appealing.
    B. Quickly reading parts of it.
    C. A friend talks about it and recommends it.
    D. It has real-life stories, experiences, and examples.

12. You are using a book, CD, or website to learn how to take photos with your new digital camera. You would like to have:
    A. a chance to ask questions and talk about the camera and its features.
    B. clear, written instructions with lists and bullet points about what to do.
    C. diagrams showing the camera and what each part does.
    D. many examples of good and poor photos and how to improve them.

13. Do you prefer a teacher or a presenter who uses:
    A. demonstrations, models, or practical sessions.
    B. question and answer, talk, group discussion, or guest speakers.
    C. handouts, books, or readings.
    D. diagrams, charts, or graphs.

14. You have finished a competition or test and would like some feedback. You would like to have feedback:
    A. using examples from what you have done.
    B. using a written description of your results.
    C. from somebody who talks it through with you.
    D. using graphs showing what you had achieved.

15. You are going to choose food at a restaurant or cafe. You would:
    A. choose something that you have had there before.
    B. listen to the waiter or ask friends to recommend choices.
    C. choose from the descriptions in the menu.
    D. look at what others are eating or look at pictures of each dish.

16. You have to make an important speech at a conference or special occasion. You would:
    A. make diagrams or get graphs to help explain things.
    B. write a few key words and practice saying your speech over and over.
    C. write out your speech and learn from reading it over several times.
    D. gather many examples and stories to make the talk real and practical.

The VARK Questionnaire Scoring Chart

Use the following scoring chart to find the VARK category that each of your answers corresponds to. Circle the letters that correspond to your answers. For example, if you answered B and C for question 3, circle V and R in the question 3 row.

Question	A Category	B Category	C Category	D Category
3	K	Ⓥ	Ⓡ	A

Scoring Chart

Question	A Category	B Category	C Category	D Category
1	K	A	R	V
2	V	A	R	K
3	K	V	R	A
4	K	A	V	R
5	A	V	K	R
6	K	R	V	A
7	K	A	V	R
8	R	K	A	V
9	R	A	K	V
10	K	V	R	A
11	V	R	A	K
12	A	R	V	K
13	K	A	R	V
14	K	R	A	V
15	K	A	R	V
16	V	A	R	K

Calculating Your Scores

Count the number of each of the VARK letters you have circled to get your score for each VARK category.

Total number of Vs circled =	
Total number of As circled =	
Total number of Rs circled =	
Total number of Ks circled =	

60-SECOND PAUSE

After completing the learning style inventory and considering the different theories about intelligences and learning preferences, what are some learning-related insights that you have discovered about yourself? How can you apply these insights to your college experience?

Concept Review and Reinforcement

Key Terms

human relations 3
organizational effectiveness 4
self-understanding 9
self 9
public self 10
private self 10

feedback 10
peer evaluations 11
developmental opportunity 11
Johari Window 12
open area 13
hidden area 13

blind area 13
unknown area 13
human relations movement 14
scientific management 15
Hawthorne Effect 15
virtual office 20

Summary

Human relations is the art and practice of using systematic knowledge about human behavior to improve personal, job, and career effectiveness. From the standpoint of management, human relations is important because it contributes to organizational effectiveness. Treating employees with respect and paying them fairly contributes to developing an efficient and creative organization.

Major benefits of studying human relations include the following:

- Acquiring information about human behavior
- Developing skills in dealing with people
- Coping with job problems
- Coping with personal problems
- Capitalizing on opportunities

Work and personal life often influence each other in several ways, as follows:

- Mood influences job satisfaction, but the effect passes quickly.
- Job satisfaction influences the mood at home, with more emotional employees more likely to experience this relationship.
- A high level of job satisfaction tends to spill over to your personal life. Conversely, an unsatisfactory personal life could lead to negative job attitudes.
- Your job can affect physical and mental health. Severely negative job conditions may lead to a serious stress disorder, such as heart disease.
- The quality of relationships with people at work and in one's personal life influence each other.
- Certain skills (such as the ability to listen) contribute to success at work and in one's personal life.

- How we behave at work is closely related to how we behave at home.

To be effective in human relationships, you must first understand yourself. Six sources of information that contribute to self-understanding are as follows:

1. General information about human behavior
2. Informal feedback from people
3. Feedback from superiors
4. Feedback from coworkers
5. Feedback from self-examination exercises
6. Looking at the self through the Johari Window

Be aware of the self-evaluation traps of highlighting your shortcomings and unrealistically overevaluating your competence. Cultural differences help explain some of the differences in underevaluation versus overevaluation.

The human relations movement was a concentrated effort to become more sensitive to the needs of employees and to treat them in a more humanistic manner. Along with the indirect influence of scientific management, the movement was supported directly by four historic influences:

1. Scientific management applied scientific methods to increase worker productivity.
2. The Hawthorne studies showed that concern for workers can increase their performance as much as or more than improving physical working conditions.
3. Employers used the threat of unionization, in which management employed human relations techniques to deter workers from joining a labor union.
4. The philosophy of industrial humanism, in which motivation and emotional factors are important.

Many of the pioneering ideas described in the history of human relations are still relevant, partly because human nature has not undergone major changes. An example of a pioneering idea in use is that Theory Y has prompted managers to think through which leadership style works best with which employees.

Human relations knowledge and skill will help you deal with major challenges in the workplace, as follows:

- Emphasis on teamwork and collaboration
- High expectations for personal productivity

- Dealing with workplace diversity and globalization
- Emphasis on employee creativity and innovativeness
- Being part of the virtual workplace and telecommuting
- Increased emphasis on skill acquisition and less on upward mobility

The major factors influencing job performance and behavior are related to the employee, manager, job, and organization.

Questions for Discussion and Review

1. Why do you think good human relations skills are so important for supervisors who direct the work activities of entry-level workers?
2. Give an example of a business executive, politician, athletic coach, or professor who you think has exceptional human relations skills. On what basis did you reach your conclusion?
3. Give an example from your own experience of how work life influences personal life and vice versa.
4. How might a person improve personal life to the extent that the improvement would also enhance job performance?
5. How might a person improve his or her job or career to the extent that the improvement would actually enhance personal life?

6. Of the five sources of information about the self described in this chapter, which one do you think is likely to be the most accurate? Why?
7. Imagine yourself as a manager or small-business owner. How might you apply the Hawthorne effect to increase the productivity of workers reporting to you?
8. In what way might the chief diversity officer mentioned in this chapter being four feet tall enhance the credibility of her position?
9. How do you think having good human relations skills and knowledge might add to your job security in a competitive workplace?
10. In your current job, or any previous one, which set of factors had the biggest impact on your performance and behavior—those related to the employee, manager, job, or organization? How do you know?

The Web Corner

The Dale Carnegie organization has long been associated with teaching human relations effectiveness. The company stemmed from the work of Dale Carnegie, who many years ago popularized the idea of "winning friends and influencing people." Visit www.dalecarnegie.com to understand what type of skills Dale Carnegie teaches. Compare the course listing to subjects listed in the table of contents in this text. What similarities do you see?

Internet Skill Builder

The Importance of Human Relations Skills in Business

One of the themes of this chapter and the entire book is that human relations skills are important for success in business. But what do employers really think? To find out, visit the Web sites of five of your favorite companies, such as www.apple.com or www.ge.com. Go to the employment section and search for a job that you might qualify for now or in the future. Investigate which human relations or interpersonal skills the employer mentions as a requirement, such as "Must have superior spoken communication skills." Make up a list of the human relations, or interpersonal, skills you find mentioned. What conclusions do you reach from this exercise?

Developing Your Human Relations Skills

Human Relations Application Exercises

Applying Human Relations Exercise 1-1

Learning about Each Other's Human Relations Skills

A constructive way of broadening your insights about human relations skills is to find out what other people perceive as their strengths in dealing with others. Toward this end, each class member comes to the front of the class, one by one, to make a two-minute presentation on his or her best ability in dealing with people. To help standardize the presentations, each student answers the following question: "What I do best with people is _____."

In this exercise, and all other class presentation exercises contained in the text, students are asked to share only those ideas they would be comfortable in sharing with the class. Here, for example, you might be very good at doing something with people about which you would be embarrassed to let others know.

As the other students are presenting, attempt to concentrate on them and not be so preoccupied with your presentation that you cannot listen. Make note when somebody says something out of the ordinary. When the presentation is over, the class will discuss answers to the following questions:

1. What was the most frequent human relations capability mentioned?
2. To what extent do classmates appear to be exaggerating their human relations skills?
3. What omissions did you find? For example, were there any important human relations skills you thought a few students should have mentioned but did not?

Applying Human Relations Exercise 1-2

My Human Relations Journal

A potentially important aid in your development as a person with effective human relations skills is to maintain a journal or diary of your experiences. Make a journal entry within 24 hours of carrying out a significant human relations action or failing to do so when the opportunity arose. You therefore will have entries dealing with human relations opportunities both capitalized on and missed. Here is an example: "A few of my neighbors were complaining about all the vandalism in the neighborhood. Cars were getting dented and scratched, and lamplights were being smashed. A few bricks were thrown into home windows. I volunteered to organize a neighborhood patrol. The patrol actually helped cut back on the vandalism." Or, in contrast, given the same scenario: "I thought that someone else should take care of the problem. My time is too valuable." (In the first example, the key human relations skill the person exercised was leadership.)

Also include in your journal such entries as feedback you receive on your human relations ability, good interpersonal traits you appear to be developing, and key human relations ideas about which you read.

Review your journal monthly, and make note of any progress you think you have made in developing your human relations skills. Also consider preparing a graph of your human relations skill development. The vertical axis can represent skill level on a 1 to 100 scale, and the horizontal axis might be divided into time internals, such as calendar quarters.

Human Relations Case Study 1-1

We Can't Afford Good Human Relations around Here

Tammy Horton was happy to be hired by Bradbury Foods as a supervisor in the main food processing plant. It was apparent to her that being a supervisor so soon after graduation from career school would be a real boost to her career. After about a month on the job, Tammy began to make some critical observations about the company and its style of management.

To clarify issues in her own mind, Tammy requested a meeting with Marcus Green, plant superintendent. The meeting between Horton and Green included a conversation of this nature:

Marcus: Have a seat, Tammy. It's nice to visit with one of our new supervisors. Particularly so when you didn't say you were facing an emergency that you and your boss couldn't handle.

Tammy: (*nervously*) Marcus, I want to express my appreciation for your willingness to meet with me. You're right, I'm not facing an emergency, and I am not here to complain about my boss. But I do wonder about something. That's what I came here to talk to you about.

Marcus: That's what I like to see—a young woman who takes the initiative to ask questions about things that are bothering her.

Tammy: To be truthful, I am happy here and I'm glad I joined Bradbury Foods. But I'm curious about one thing. As you may know, I majored in business at my career college. A few of the courses I took emphasized using human relations knowledge and skills to manage people—you know, kind of psychology on the job. It seems like the way to go if you want to keep employees productive and happy. Here at Bradbury it seems that nobody uses human relations knowledge and skills. I know that we're a successful company. But some of the management practices seem out of keeping with the times. The managers make all the decisions. Everybody else listens and carries out orders. Even professionals on the payroll have to use time recording devices for checking in

and checking out. I've been here for almost two months and I haven't even heard the term "human relations" used once.

Marcus: Oh, I get your point. You're talking about using human relations around here. I know all about that. The point you are missing, Tammy, is that human relations is for big, profitable companies. That stuff works great when business is good and profit margins are high. But around here business is so-so, and profit margins in the food business are thinner than a potato chip. Maybe someday when we get fat and profitable we can start using human relations. In the meantime, we've all got a job to do.

Tammy: I appreciate your candid answer, Marcus. But when I was in career school, I certainly heard a different version of why companies use human relations.

Case Questions

1. What is your evaluation of Marcus's contention that human relations knowledge is useful primarily when a firm is profitable?
2. To what extent should Tammy be discouraged?
3. What should Tammy do next about her concerns about the application of human relations knowledge at Bradbury?
4. Based on your experiences, how representative of most managers is Marcus's thinking?

Human Relations Case Study 1-2

Is This Any Way to Run a Trucking Company?

J. A. Frate Inc. tries to make sure its most dedicated drivers feel valued and want to stay for the long haul. The company was founded by CEO R. Douglas Jennings, who says he has always run J. A. Frate with the goal of treating employees as fairly and kindly as possible.

Managers hire only experienced truck drivers—those with at least two years on the job—and those who dress and act professionally, Mr. Jennings says. The company then motivates its fifty-some drivers to do their best by giving recognition and prizes to those who show special

effort. Each month the company's Driver Recognition Committee selects "Drivers of the Month" and usually divvies $200 in Wal-Mart gift certificates among them. The recognition is based on a point system where drivers can be docked points for issues such as damaged freight, tardiness, or sloppy log books.

Each year, one driver is designated "Driver of the Year" and wins a larger prize. Joe Rhamey, a driver who's worked with J. A. Frate since 1991, won in 2006 and 2007. Last year, the company bought a new truck tractor for him to drive but added about $4,000 of embellishments that drivers usually don't get, such as satellite radio, power windows, and chrome wheels. "They just come up with these things, and you think, 'Wow, that's nice,'" says Rhamey, who is fifty-four.

Employees are also encouraged to suggest changes, with the top three suggestions each quarter winning $100, $50, and $25 respectively. All of these efforts pay off in employee retention. The average tenure of current employees is 7.3 years.

Here is how management at J. A. Frate handled a particularly challenging predicament: Soon after the September 11, 2001, terrorist attacks, the company lost two big clients and laid off six drivers—the only layoffs in its thirty-seven-year history. The board of directors then asked remaining employees to vote on taking a 10 percent pay cut, promising to reinstate their normal wages after three months. The majority of employees voted for the cut.

Within six months, the company rehired all the drivers it had laid off and reinstated their pre–September 11 wages. In 2006, it reimbursed the missed income to all employees who had taken the 10 percent pay cut, as well as those who had been laid off.

Case Questions

1. What does this case tell you about the importance of good human relations in a basic industry like trucking?
2. Why bother spending company money giving frills like chrome wheels, power windows, and satellite radio to a trucker? Isn't the trucker already getting paid to do a job?
3. Why might giving recognition to truck drivers, such as the "Drivers of the Month" award, be especially effective with members of this occupational group?
4. Think of all the money executives at J. A. Frate have given to employees in gift certificates and back pay. Is this any way to run a trucking company?

Source: Abridged from Kelly K. Spors, "Top Small Workplaces 2008: J. A. Frate Inc.," *Wall Street Journal*, October 13, 2008, p. R5.

Human Relations Role-Playing Exercise

Kindness and Recognition

Here a role-playing (or role- assuming) exercise will be presented to provide practice in implementing a specific human relations skill or technique. The role-plays will typically be presented in front of others for about five to ten minutes. A natural and easy way of carrying out most of these role-plays is for you to get a general idea of the role and then spontaneously say and do what you think a person in that role might do and say. For many of the role-plays, it will be helpful for you to read the relevant text material to assist you in refining your skill. For these two introductory role-plays, just rely on whatever knowledge and skills you already have.

Scenario 1: Kindness at the Not-for-Profit Agency One person plays the role of Sandy Bellows who is presented with what appears to be a way-off-base suggestion from a staff member. The staff member suggests that their organization should raise more funds by requiring each person who works at the agency to be assigned a monthly collection quota. The money would be collected from anybody in their network, including family members, friends, neighbors, and work associates. The staff members who failed to meet quota for three consecutive months would be eligible to be fired. One person plays the role of the staff member who makes the suggestion. Another person plays the role of Bellows, who will reject the suggestion with kindness. Run the conversation for about six minutes.

Scenario 2: Giving Recognition to a Trucker Getting back to Case Study 1-2, one person plays the role of a supervisor at J. A. Frate, the trucking company. While at headquarters he runs into Billy Joe, who has stopped by to fill out some forms for the human resources department. The supervisor is aware that Billy Joe achieved better than average performance last month and would like to give him appropriate recognition. But Billy Joe was certainly not the *top* performer among the truck drivers. Another student plays the role of Billy Joe, who feels somewhat underappreciated and would like some recognition. The two role-players carry out an on-the-spot recognition session rather than meeting in a cubicle or conference room.

For both scenarios, observers rate the role-players on two dimensions, using a 1 to 5 scale from very poor to very good. One dimension is "effective use of human relations techniques." The second dimension is "acting ability." A few observers might voluntarily provide feedback to the role-players in terms of sharing their ratings and observations. The course instructor might also provide feedback.

Class Activity: The Unique People

Most of the self-assessment quizzes and human relations exercises presented throughout this book are performed by students working individually or in small groups. At the end of selected chapters we may present an additional activity geared toward enhanced human relations knowledge or skill that is to be performed by the entire class, often interacting with each other. The unit of contribution might be you working alone, but at some point the contributions become collective.

Our first class activity is geared toward reinforcing the idea that part of effective human relations is to recognize that people are different in many ways, stemming from their group characteristics, culture, personality, problem-solving ability, experiences, and interests, among many other factors. Each student in the class, or only those who volunteer, come up to the front of the class one at a time to make a one-minute presentation about any way in which he or she is unique. Here are three statements of uniqueness among an infinite number of possibilities: "I graduated number one in my high school class of fifty-seven students." "I was born and raised in China, but I don't like to eat in Chinese restaurants. I prefer Applebee's and Outback Steakhouse." "I rigged up my house to be smart. I can use my BlackBerry to start the air-conditioning or the oven in my house from miles away."

After the unique aspects of each class member are presented, volunteers might offer feedback to participants by completing the following statements:

1. "What really surprised me was _____."
2. "What made me really think positively about _____ was the fact that he (or she) _____."
3. "I really learned something about human relations today. Now I know that _____."

REFERENCES

1. Steven Kent, "Happy Workers Are the Best Workers," *Wall Street Journal*, September 6, 2005, p. A20.

2. Jeffery Pfeffer, *The Human Equation* (Boston: Harvard Business School Press, 1998), p. 59; Pfeffer, "Producing Sustainable Competitive Advantage through the Effective Management of People," *Academy of Management Executive*, November 2005, pp. 95–108.

3. Timothy A. Judge and Remus Ilies, "Affect and Job Satisfaction: A Study of Their Relationship at Work and Home," *Journal of Applied Psychology*, August 2004, pp. 661–673.

4. "Making Relationships Work: A Conversation with Psychologist John M. Gottman," *Harvard Business Review*, December 2007, pp. 45–50.

5. C. R. Snyder, "So Many Selves," *Contemporary Psychology*, January 1988, p. 77.

6. Cited in Etienne Benson, "The Synaptic Self," *Monitor on Psychology*, November 2002, p. 40.

7. Joseph Luft, *Group Process: An Introduction to Group Dynamics* (New York: Mayfield Publishing Company/ McGraw-Hill, 1984); Luft, *Of Human Interaction* (Palo Alto, CA: National Press, 1969); Suzanne C. De Janasz, Karen O. Dowd, and Beth Z. Schneider, *Interpersonal Skills in Organizations* (New York: McGraw-Hill, 2002), pp. 31–32.

8. Saul Kassin, *Psychology*, 3rd ed. (Upper Saddle River, NJ: Prentice Hall, 2001), p. 74.

9. Research summarized in Tori DeAngelis, "Why We Overestimate Our Competence," *Monitor on Psychology*, February 2003, p. 61.

10. Ibid.

11. Robert Kreitner, *Management*, 5th ed. (Boston: Houghton Mifflin, 1992), pp. 51–52.

12. Edward G. Wertheim, "Historical Background of Organizational Behavior." Retrieved March 15, 2006, from: http:// web.cba.neu.edu/~Wertheim/introd/history.htm

13. Elton Mayo, *The Human Problems of Industrial Civilization* (New York: Viking Press, 1960).

14. James A. F. Stoner and R. Edward Freeman, *Management*, 4th ed. (Upper Saddle River, NJ: Prentice Hall, 1989), p. 49.

15. Kreitner, *Management*, p. 50.

16. Alan B. Krueger, "Job Satisfaction Is Not Just a Matter of Dollars," *New York Times*. Retrieved December 8, 2005, from: www.nytimes.com

17. "Union Members Summary," *Bureau of Labor Statistics News* Retrieved January 25, 2008, from: www.bls.gov/news

18. Kreitner, *Management*, p. 62.

19. Douglas McGregor, *The Human Side of Enterprise* (New York: McGraw-Hill, 1960), pp. 33–48.

20. Susan Berfield, "After the Layoff, the Redesign," *Business Week*, April 14, 2008, p. 56.

21. Cliff Edwards, Kenji Hall, and Ronald Grover, "Sony Chases Apple's Magic," *Business Week*, November 10, 2008, p. 51.

22. Vanessa O'Connell, "Stores Count Seconds to Cut Labor Costs," *Wall Street Journal*, November 17, 2008, pp. A1, A15.

23. David Welch and Nandini Lakshman, "My Other Car Is a Tata," *Business Week*, January 14, 2008, p. 33.

24. Ann Pomeroy, "A Passion for Diversity," *HR Magazine*, March 2008, p. 49. The other information about Merck & Co. is from page 48 of the same source.

25. Jane McGregor, "Artful Discounts," *Business Week*, October 20, 2008, p. 59.

26. Simona Covel, "Making a Virtual Company a Reality," *Wall Street Journal*, January 10, 2008, p. B4.

27. Cindy Krischer Goodman, "Telecommuting: Driving Down the Cost of Working," *Miami Herald*, June 25, 2008. Available at: www.miamiherald.com

28. Susan Ladika, "When Learning Lasts a Lifetime," *HR Magazine*, May 2008, pp. 56–60.

Team Building

Ann Livermore, head of Hewlett-Packard's storage and servers, software and services businesses, has faced decisions at her company that might have sent some executives heading for the door. But despite deals that cut into her territory, she keeps her focus on the big picture, on the challenges at hand, and on new opportunities for growth. It's all part of knowing that "business is a team sport," she says.

That sentiment isn't common among business leaders these days. Many senior executives are more focused on their individual well-being than on furthering their company goals. They're quick to jump to new employers when they don't feel appreciated.

Some outside H-P had speculated that Livermore was unhappy about relinquishing part of her portfolio after the company announced plans to acquire Electronic Data Systems, an

Objectives

1. Explain the difference between a traditional team and a virtual team.
2. Understand the advantages and disadvantages of teams.
3. Identify various team member roles.
4. Apply interpersonal-related tactics for effective team play.
5. Apply task-related tactics for effective team play.

IT outsourcing company. She says that she's staying put. "This isn't about me," she said in an interview. "It's about what is best for H-P. It makes sense to combine all outsourcing businesses—and with a merger this big for EDS to report directly to Mark (Mark Hurd, former CEO of H-P)."[1]

The attitude of the executive just described illustrates a spirit of teamwork that can help a company prosper. The modern organization depends on teamwork throughout the company. Many firms rely more on teamwork than on individuals acting alone to accomplish work. To be successful in the modern organization, it is therefore necessary to be an effective team player. You have to work smoothly with other members of the team to accomplish your goals. Teamwork is more important as people work their way up through the organization. Executives, such as CEOs, preach teamwork but tend to dominate meetings and make more decisions by themselves.[2] (Ann Livermore might be an exception.)

The challenges a team member faces come to light when the true nature of a team is recognized. A **team** is a special type of group. Team members have complementary skills and are committed to a common purpose, a set of performance goals, and an approach to the task. In other words, the members of a team work together smoothly, and all pull in the same direction. A workplace team should be more like an effective athletic team than a group of individuals out for individual glory.[3]

This chapter gives you the information, insights, and preliminary practice necessary to develop effective teamwork skills. Self-Assessment Quiz 2-1 will help you assess your current mental readiness to be a contributing team member.

team

A small number of people with complementary skills who are committed to a common purpose, set of performance goals, and approach for which they hold themselves mutually accountable.

FACE-TO-FACE VERSUS VIRTUAL TEAMS

LEARNING OBJECTIVE 1

All teams in the workplace have the common element of people working together cooperatively and members possessing a mix of skills. No matter what label the team carries, its broad purpose is to contribute to a *collaborative workplace* in which people help each other achieve constructive goals. The idea is for workers to collaborate (a high level of cooperation) rather than to compete with or prevent others from getting their work done.

As teams have become more common in the workplace, effort has been directed toward specifying the skills and knowledge a person needs to function effectively on a team. Self-Assessment Quiz 2-2 presents a representative listing of team skills as perceived by employers.

Although many different types of teams exist, a useful distinction is between the traditional teams in which workers share the same physical space and virtual teams whereby the team members rarely see each other in person.

Face-to-Face (Traditional) Teams

The best-known workplace team is a group of workers who take some of the responsibility for managing their own work. Face-to-face teams are used in a wide variety of activities,

Team Player Attitudes

Directions: Describe how well you agree with each of the following statements, using the following scale: disagree strongly (DS); disagree (D); neutral (N); agree (A); agree strongly (AS). Circle the number in the appropriate column.

		DS	D	N	A	AS
1.	I am at my best when working alone.	5	4	3	2	1
2.	I have belonged to clubs and teams ever since I was a child.	1	2	3	4	5
3.	It takes far too long to get work accomplished with a group.	5	4	3	2	1
4.	I like the friendship of working in a group.	1	2	3	4	5
5.	I would prefer to run a one-person business than to be a member of a large firm.	5	4	3	2	1
6.	It's difficult to trust others in the group on key assignments.	5	4	3	2	1
7.	Encouraging others comes to me naturally.	1	2	3	4	5
8.	I like the give-and-take of ideas that is possible in a group.	1	2	3	4	5
9.	It is fun for me to share responsibility with other group members.	1	2	3	4	5
10.	Much more can be accomplished by a team than by the same number of people working alone.	1	2	3	4	5

Total Score _____

Scoring and Interpretation: Add the numbers you circled to obtain your total score.

41–50 You have strong positive attitudes toward being a team member and working cooperatively with other members.

30–40 You have moderately favorable attitudes toward being a team member and working cooperatively with other members.

10–29 You prefer working by yourself to being a team member. To work effectively in a company that emphasizes teamwork, you may need to develop more positive attitudes toward working jointly with others.

including producing motorcycles, telephone directories, a major component for a large computer, or launching a new product. Team members interact with other frequently rather than doing their work in isolation from one another.

Members of a traditional team typically work together on an ongoing, day-by-day basis, thus differentiating it from a task force or a committee. The team is often given total responsibility for or "ownership" of an entire product or service, such as producing a telephone directory. At other times, the team is given responsibility for a major chunk of a job, such as building an airplane engine (but not the entire airplane).

A major hurdle in forming a true team is to help employees overcome the attitude reflected in the statement "I'm not paid to think." Teams often rely less on supervisors and more on the workers assuming more responsibilities for managing their own activities.

As with all teams, mutual trust among members contributes to team effectiveness. A study conducted with business students, however, showed that if the members trust each other too much, they may not monitor (check up on) each other's work enough. As a result, group performance will suffer. This problem of too much trust surfaces primarily when the team members have individual assignments that do not bring them into frequent contact with each other.[4] An example of an individual, or autonomous, project would be preparing a statistical report that would later be given to the group.

Virtual Teams

virtual team

A small group of people who conduct almost all of their collaborative work by electronic communication rather than face-to-face meetings.

Some teams conduct most of their work by sending electronic messages to each other rather than conducting face-to-face meetings. A **virtual team** is a small group of people who conduct almost all of their collaborative work by electronic communication rather than by face-to-face meetings. E-mail, including IM (instant messaging), is the usual medium

Team Skills

A variety of skills are required to be an effective member of various types of teams. Several business firms use the skill inventory here to help guide team members toward the competencies they need to become high-performing team members.

Directions: Review each team skill listed, and rate your skill level for each one using the following classifications:

    S = strong (capable and comfortable with effectively implementing the skill)

    M = moderate (demonstrated skill in the past)

    B = basic (minimum ability in this area)

    N = not applicable (not relevant to the type of work I do)

	Skill level (S, M, B, or N)
Communication skills	
Speak effectively	_____
Foster open communications	_____
Listen to others	_____
Deliver presentations	_____
Prepare written communication	_____
Self-management skills	
Act with integrity	_____
Demonstrate adaptability	_____
Engage in personal development	_____
Strive for results	_____
Display a commitment to work	_____
Thought process skills	
Innovate solutions to problems	_____
Use sound judgment	_____
Analyze issues	_____
Think "outside the box"	_____
Organizational skills	
Know the business	_____
Use technical/functional expertise	_____
Use financial/quantitative data	_____
Strategic (broad business perspective) skills	
Recognize "big picture" impact	_____
Promote corporate citizenship	_____
Focus on customer needs	_____
Commit to quality	_____
Manage profitability	_____

Interpretation: There is no scoring key for this questionnaire. Its purpose is to raise your awareness of the types of skills that are required to be a successful team member in business.

for sharing information and conducting meetings. *Groupware* is another widely used approach to conducting an electronic meeting. Using groupware, several people can edit a document at the same time, or in sequence. Desktop videoconferencing, such as a webcam, is another technological advance that facilitates the virtual team.

Most high-tech companies make some use of virtual teams and electronic meetings. Strategic alliances in which geographically dispersed companies work with each other are ideally suited for virtual teams. It is less expensive for the field technician in Iceland to hold an electronic meeting with her counterparts in South Africa, Mexico, and California than it is to bring them all together in one physical location. Virtual teams are sometimes the answer to the challenge of hiring workers with essential skills who do not want to relocate. Because the members of a virtual team might be working in different countries, they are often considered to be multicultural teams.

With team members geographically dispersed, precise communications are all the more important for virtual teams. The virtual team members usually need a formal document outlining the objectives, job responsibilities, and team goals. Another communication problem takes place when the virtual team is composed of both in-house workers and those in remote locations. The office-bound members become jealous of the seemingly cushy setup enjoyed by the telecommuters. One solution to this problem is for every member of the team to be given a chance to prove that he or she can work off-site.[5] Another consideration is that the work should be distributed fairly among office-bound workers and virtual team members. Last-minute assignments are often handed to the first in-house worker the manager sees.[6]

Establishing trust is a major challenge in a virtual team because the team members have to rely on people they never see to carry out their fair share of the workload, and to exchange reliable information. Trust is also needed in terms of what information should be shared outside of the team. For example, if the team is behind schedule on a project, can each member be trusted not to inform outsiders about the problem? For example, one virtual team had an external communication norm that prohibited team members from conveying negative information to anyone outside the team.[7]

Despite the efficiency of virtual teams, there are times when face-to-face (or at least telephone) interaction is necessary to deal with complex and emotional issues. Negotiating a new contract between management and a labor union, for example, is not well suited to an electronic meeting.

> "Virtual teams need to know that their coworkers are 'real people.' It's the personal information they learn from one another that will foster the social ties that allow collaboration to occur naturally."
>
> —Tammy Burch, CEO of Virtual Concepts International in Milford, Michigan.

THE ADVANTAGES AND DISADVANTAGES OF TEAMS AND TEAMWORK

LEARNING OBJECTIVE 2

synergy

A situation in which the group's total output exceeds the sum of each individual's contribution.

Groups have always been the building blocks of organizations. Yet groups and teams have recently grown in importance as the basic unit for organizing work. In an attempt to cope with numerous changes in the outside world, many organizations have granted teams increased independence and flexibility. Furthermore, teams are often required to work more closely with customers and suppliers.

The increased acceptance of teams suggests that group work offers many advantages. Nevertheless, it is useful to specify several of these advantages and also examine the potential problems of groups. Being aware of these potential pitfalls can often help a person avoid them. These same advantages and disadvantages also apply to group decision making.

Advantages of Group Work and Teamwork

Group work and group decision making offer several advantages over individual effort. Because so much of what is accomplished in organizations is done by groups, it may appear that groups and teams have many advantages. However, the importance of this topic warrants mentioning a few of the advantages of groups, teams, and group decision making.

Synergy. If several knowledgeable people are brought into the decision-making process, a number of worthwhile possibilities may be uncovered. It is also possible to gain **synergy**, whereby the group's total output exceeds the sum of each individual's contribution. For example, it would be a rare person working alone who could build a racing car. At the same time, groups and teams are the building block of the larger organization.

Work Accomplishment and High Productivity. Without groups, including teams, an organization could not get its work accomplished. Clarence Otis, Jr., the CEO of Darden Restaurants (which includes the Olive Garden, Red Lobster, and Bahama Breeze), says that the thrust of his leadership is to build the team because the team accomplishes so much of the work.[8]

A major justification for relying on teams in the workplace is that under the right circumstances, they can enhance productivity and profitability. The right circumstances include an atmosphere that promotes teamwork and financial bonuses for high-performing teams. A classic example is American steel maker Nucor Corp. The company is committed to the spirit of teamwork, and bonuses for teams of steelworkers average 170 percent to 180 percent. Since Nucor had implemented its team incentive plan in 1966, the company has been profitable each quarter through 2009 despite foreign competition. Also, the company has increased the dividend to shareholders for 37 consecutive years.[9]

A broad perspective about the advantages of groups is that because of groups and teams, large organizations can be built that provide useful goods and services to the world. For example, a company such as Apple, Inc., or Johnson & Johnson is only possible because of group effort. Furthermore, the existence of large organizations, including business firms, colleges, universities, and hospitals, helps advance civilization.

Acceptance and Commitment. Group decision making is also helpful in gaining acceptance and commitment. The argument is that people who contribute to making a decision will feel some ownership about implementing the decision. Under these conditions, it becomes more difficult to object to a decision because your contribution is included in the decision. At times, managers will deliberately ask for input into a decision they have already made as a manipulative way of gaining acceptance for and commitment to the decision.

Avoidance of Major Errors. Team members often evaluate each other's thinking, so the team is likely to avoid major errors. An advertising specialist was developing an advertising campaign to attract seniors to live in a retirement community. The proposed ads had photographs of senior citizens engaged in playing shuffleboard, visiting the pharmacy, and sleeping in a hammock. Another team member on the project pointed out that many seniors perceive themselves to be energetic and youthful. Ads emphasizing advanced age might therefore backfire. A successful advertising campaign was then developed that featured seniors in more youthful activities, such as jogging and dancing.

Increased Job Satisfaction. Working in teams and groups also enhances the job satisfaction of members. Being a member of a work group makes it possible to satisfy more needs than working alone. Among these needs are affiliation, security, self-esteem, and self-fulfillment.

A major reason that groups and teams contribute to worker satisfaction is that many people find working in groups to be a natural way of life. In school, sports, and the community, they have been accustomed to working collaboratively and therefore feel more comfortable in group than in individual effort.

Disadvantages of Group Work and Teamwork

Group activity has some potential disadvantages for both individuals and the organization, as described in the following paragraphs. Some of these disadvantages serve as alerts for preventing problems.

Time Wasting. Teams and other groups often waste time because they talk too much and act too little. Committees appear to suffer from more inaction than teams. Abigail Johnson, president of Fidelity Employer Services Division, says that committees are not effective decision makers. "They have tended to be slow and overly risk averse. Even worse, I believe, they can drain an organization of talent, because the group can only be as good as the average."[10]

Pressures toward Conformity. A major problem is that members face pressures to conform to group standards of performance and conduct, as just implied. Some teams might shun a person who is much more productive than his or her coworkers. Also, to be liked by coworkers, as well as avoiding conflict, a group member will sometimes agree with the opinion of other group or team members. Group members will often use the same jargon, whether or not it is precise. For example, workers at Microsoft refer to e-mail as "mail," thereby snubbing postal mail.

Conformity in dress and appearance is also apparent in many work groups. You might want to examine a photo of Google, Microsoft, or Apple employees and observe how much conformity in dress you find. Conformity in dress, however, is not much of a disadvantage except when a group member is dissatisfied because of the pressure to dress in the same manner as coworkers.

Self-Assessment Quiz 2-3 gives you an opportunity to think about your tendencies toward conformity.

Shirking of Individual Responsibility (Social Loafing). Shirking of individual responsibility is another problem frequently noted in groups. Unless work is assigned carefully to each team member, an undermotivated person can often squeeze by without contributing his or her fair share to a group effort. **Social loafing** is the psychological term for shirking individual responsibility in a group setting. The social loafer risks being ostracized (shunned) by the group but may be willing to pay the price rather than to work hard. Loafing of this type is sometimes found in groups such as committees and project teams. Have you ever encountered a social loafer on a group project at school?

Fostering of Conflict. At their worst, teams and other groups foster conflict on the job. People within the work group often bicker about such matters as doing a fair share of the undesirable tasks within the department. Cohesive work groups can also become xenophobic (fearful of outsiders). As a consequence, they may grow to dislike other groups and enter into conflict with them. A customer service group might put considerable effort into showing up a sales group because the latter makes promises to customers that the customer service group cannot keep. For example, a sales representative might promise that a customer can get a loaner if his or her equipment needs repair, although customer service has no such policy.

Groupthink. A well-publicized disadvantage of group decision making is **groupthink**, a deterioration of mental efficiency, reality testing, and moral judgment in the interest of group solidarity. Simply put, groupthink is an extreme form of consensus. The group atmosphere values getting along more than getting things done. The group thinks as a unit, believes it is impervious to outside criticism, and begins to have illusions about its own invincibility. As a consequence, the group loses its powers of critical analysis. [11] Groupthink appears to have contributed to several of the major financial scandals of the previous decade. Members of top management got together to vote themselves huge bonuses just before filing bankruptcy for their company. Several of the executives, including a few from Enron Corporation, were later sent to prison for their outrageous decisions.

Two conditions are important for overcoming the potential disadvantages of teams and groups.[12] First, the members must strive to act like a team following some of the suggestions given in the upcoming pages. Second, the task given to the group should require collective effort instead of being a task that could better be performed by individuals. For example, an international business specialist would probably learn to conjugate verbs in a foreign language better by working alone than on a team. What is your opinion on this issue? Figure 2-1 presents more information about key factors associated with effective work teams and groups. The more of these factors that are present, the more likely it is that a given team or group will be productive.

TEAM MEMBER ROLES

A major challenge in learning to become an effective team member is to choose the right roles to occupy. A **role** is a tendency to behave, contribute, and relate to others in a particular way. If you carry out positive roles, you will be perceived as a contributor to team effort. If you neglect carrying out these roles, you will be perceived as a poor contributor.

The Conformity Quiz

Directions: Circle the extent to which each of the following statements describes your behavior or attitude: agree strongly (AS); agree (A); neutral (N); disagree (D); disagree strongly (DS). You may have to respond in terms of any team or group experience you have had if you are not currently a member of a work team, a class project team, or a sports team. Consider that having someone who is familiar with your behavior and attitudes helps you respond accurately.

		AS	A	N	D	DS
1.	I rarely question the decision reached by the team.	5	4	3	2	1
2.	Whatever the group wants is fine with me.	5	4	3	2	1
3.	My clothing distinguishes me from the other members of the team.	1	2	3	4	5
4.	I consider myself to be one of the gang.	5	4	3	2	1
5.	I rarely express disagreement during a group discussion.	5	4	3	2	1
6.	I routinely have lunch with other members of the team.	5	4	3	2	1
7.	My teammates sometimes complain that I think too independently.	1	2	3	4	5
8.	My preference is to piggyback on the ideas of others rather than contributing the ideas of my own.	5	4	3	2	1
9.	When I notice that the other members of the team make the same error in speech, I will copy them rather than sound different.	5	4	3	2	1
10.	I am often the first person to get up at the scheduled ending of the meeting.	1	2	3	4	5
11.	I do almost all of my creative thinking for the team task when I'm with the team.	5	4	3	2	1
12.	I'm particularly careful not to criticize an idea submitted by the team leader.	5	4	3	2	1
13.	The number of hours I work per week corresponds closely to the number worked by my teammates.	5	4	3	2	1
14.	When I think it is necessary, I bring information to the group conflicting with the path we are following.	1	2	3	4	5
15.	I would rather keep my mouth closed than point out weaknesses in a teammate's ideas.	5	4	3	2	1
16.	I've been called a maverick on more than one occasion by teammates.	1	2	3	4	5
17.	I encourage team members to express doubts about proposed solutions to problems.	1	2	3	4	5
18.	I invite criticism of my ideas.	1	2	3	4	5
19.	When the team laughs at a comment, I laugh too even if I don't think the comment was funny.	5	4	3	2	1
20.	Most of my social life centers on activities with my teammates.	5	4	3	2	1

Interpretation: Calculate your score by adding the numbers you have circled, and use the following guide:

80–100 You are a high-conforming individual who readily goes along with the team without preserving your individuality. In an effort to be liked, you might be overcompromising your thinking.

40–79 You have probably achieved the right balance between following group norms (standards of conduct) and expressing your individuality. With actions and attitudes like this, you are on your way to becoming a good team player, yet also in a position to attain individual recognition.

20–29 You are highly individualistic, perhaps to the point of not working smoothly in a team setting. Be careful that you are not going out of your way to be a nonconformist, thereby interfering with your ability to be an effective team player.

Skill development: Examine your responses to the 20 questions because the response might give you a clue to needed development, often just by making a subtle change within your control. Here are two examples: If you answered agree strongly or agree to question 8, you might work toward contributing ideas of your own. If you answered disagree or disagree strongly to question 14, you might work toward helping the team think more critically about the path it is following.

FIGURE 2-1 Key Characteristics of Effective Teams and Work Groups

- The group has collective efficacy, or a belief that it can handle the assigned task.
- The team has clear-cut goals linked to organizational goals so that group members feel connected to the entire organization. However, the group does not have so many goals that confusion results. Goals include having a mission that helps explain what the group is attempting to accomplish.
- Group members are empowered so that they learn to think for themselves rather than expecting a supervisor to solve all the difficult problems. At the same time, the group believes it has the authority to solve a variety of problems without first obtaining approval from management.
- Group members are assigned work they perceive to be challenging, exciting, and rewarding. As a consequence, the work is self-rewarding.
- Members depend on one another to accomplish tasks, and work toward a common goal. At the same time, the group believes in itself and that it can accomplish an independent task.
- Diversity exists within the group, including differences in education, experience, and cultural background. Different backgrounds lead to more creative problem solving. Also, the differences prompt more discussion and analysis.
- Members receive extensive training in technical knowledge, problem-solving skills, and interpersonal skills.
- Members receive part of their pay related to team or group incentives rather than strictly based on individual performance.
- Group size is generally about 6 people, rather than 10 or more.
- Team members have good intelligence and personality factors, such as conscientiousness and pride that contribute to good performance.
- There is honest and open communication among group members and with other groups in the organization.
- Members have the philosophy of working as a team—6 brains, not just 12 hands.
- Members are familiar with their jobs, coworkers, and the work environment. This experience adds to their expertise. The beneficial effects of experience may diminish after awhile because the team needs fresh ideas and approaches.
- The team has emotional intelligence in the sense that it builds relationships both inside and outside the team. Included in emotional intelligence are norms that establish mutual trust among members, a feeling of group identity, and group efficacy.
- Stronger performing group members assist weaker performing group members accomplish their task, particularly when the performance of the "weakest link" in the group is key for group performance.

Sources: Alexander D. Stajkovic, Dongseop Lee, and Anthony J. Nyberg, "Collective Efficacy, Group Potency, and Group Performance: Meta-Analysis of their Relationships, and Test of a Mediation Model," *Journal of Applied Psychology,* May 2009, p. 815; Stanley M. Gulley, Kara A. Incalcaterra, Aparna Joshi, and J. Matthew Beaublien, "A Meta-Analysis of Team Efficacy, Potency, and Performance: Interdependence and Level of Analysis as Moderators of Observed Relationships," *Journal of Applied Psychology,* October 2002, pp. 819–832; Stephen R. Covey, "Secrets Behind Great Teams," *USA Weekend,* July 11–13, 2008, p. 7; Katherine W. Phillips, Katie A. Liljenquist, and Margaret A. Neale, "Is the Pain Work the Gain? The Advantages and Liabilities of Agreeing With Socially Distinct Newcomers," *Personality and Social Psychology Bulletin,* March 2009, pp. 336–350; Shawn L. Berman, Vanessa Urch Druskat, and Steven B. Wolff, "Building the Emotional Intelligence of Groups," *Harvard Business Review,* March 2001, pp. 80–90; Claus W. Langred, "Too Much of a Good Thing? Negative Effects of High Trust and Individual Autonomy in Self-Managing Work Teams," *Academy of Management Journal,* June 2004, pp. 385–389; Bernhard Weber and Guido Hertel, "Motivation Gains of Inferior Group Members: A Meta-Analytical Review," *Journal of Personality and Social Psychology,* No. 6, 2007, pp. 973–993.

Self-Assessment Quiz 2-4 will help you evaluate your present inclinations toward occupying effective roles as a team member. In this section, we describe a number of the most frequently observed positive roles played by team members.[13] We will also mention a group of negative roles. The description will be followed by an activity in which the roles can be practiced.

Team Player Roles

Directions: For each of the following statements about team activity, check *mostly agree* or *mostly disagree*. If you have not experienced such a situation, imagine how you would act or think if placed in that situation. In responding to the statements, assume that you are taking the questionnaire with the intent of learning something about yourself.

	Mostly agree	Mostly disagree
1. It is rare that I ever miss a team meeting.	_____	_____
2. I regularly compliment team members when they do something exceptional.	_____	_____
3. Whenever I can, I avoid being the note taker at a team meeting.	_____	_____
4. From time to time, other team members come to me for advice on technical matters.	_____	_____
5. I like to hide some information from other team members so that I can be in control.	_____	_____
6. I welcome new team members coming to me for advice and learning the ropes.	_____	_____
7. My priorities come first, which leaves me with very little time to help other team members.	_____	_____
8. During a team meeting, it is not unusual for several other people at a time to look toward me for my opinion.	_____	_____
9. If I think the team is moving in an unethical direction, I will say so explicitly.	_____	_____
10. Rarely will I criticize the progress of the team even if I think such criticism is deserved.	_____	_____
11. It is typical for me to summarize the progress in a team meeting, even if not asked.	_____	_____
12. To conserve time, I attempt to minimize contact with my teammates outside our meetings.	_____	_____
13. I intensely dislike going along with a consensus decision if the decision runs contrary to my thoughts on the issue.	_____	_____
14. I rarely remind teammates of our mission statement as we go about our work.	_____	_____
15. Once I have made up my mind on an issue facing the team, I am unlikely to be persuaded in another direction.	_____	_____
16. I am willing to accept negative feedback from team members.	_____	_____
17. Just to get a new member of the team involved, I will ask his or her opinion.	_____	_____
18. Even if the team has decided on a course of action, I am not hesitant to bring in new information that supports another position.	_____	_____
19. Quite often I talk negatively about one team member to another.	_____	_____
20. My teammates are almost a family to me because I am truly concerned about their welfare.	_____	_____
21. When it seems appropriate, I joke and kid with teammates.	_____	_____
22. My contribution to team tasks is as important to me as my individual work.	_____	_____
23. From time to time, I have pointed out to the team how we can all improve in reaching our goals.	_____	_____
24. I will fight to the last when the team does not support my viewpoint and wants to move toward consensus.	_____	_____
25. I will confront the team if I believe that the members are thinking too much alike.	_____	_____

Total Score _____

(Continued)

According to the role theory developed by R. Meredith Belbin and his group of researchers, there are nine frequent roles occupied by team members. All of these roles are influenced to some extent by an individual's personality.

1. **Creative problem solver.** The creative problem solver is imaginative, and unorthodox. Such a person solves difficult problems. A potential weakness of this role is that the person tends to ignore fine details and becomes too immersed in the problem to communicate effectively.

2. **Resource investigator.** The resource investigator is extraverted, enthusiastic, and communicates freely with other team members. He or she will explore opportunities and develop valuable contacts. A potential weakness of this role is that the person can be overly optimistic and may lose interest after the initial enthusiasm wanes.

3. **Coordinator.** The coordinator is mature, confident, and a natural team leader. He or she clarifies goals, promotes decision making, and delegates effectively. A downside to occupying this role is that the person might be seen as manipulative and controlling. Some coordinators delegate too much by asking others to do some of the work they (the coordinators) should be doing.

4. **Shaper.** The shaper is challenging, dynamic, and thrives under pressure. He or she will use determination and courage to overcome obstacles. A potential weakness of the shaper is that he or she can be easily provoked and may ignore the feelings of others.

5. **Monitor-evaluator.** The monitor-evaluator is even tempered, engages in strategic (big picture and long-term) thinking, and makes accurate judgments. He or she sees all the options and judges accurately. A potential weakness of this role occupant is that he or she might lack the drive and the ability to inspire others.

6. **Team worker.** The team worker is cooperative, focuses on relationships, and is sensitive and diplomatic. He or she is a good listener who builds relationships, dislikes confrontation, and averts friction. A potential weakness is that the team worker can be indecisive in a crunch situation or crisis.

7. **Implementer.** The implementer is disciplined, reliable, conservative, and efficient. He or she will act quickly on ideas, and convert them into practical actions. A potential weakness is that the implementer can be inflexible and slow to see new opportunities.

8. **Completer-Finisher.** The completer-finisher is conscientious and eager to get the job done. He or she has a good eye for detail, and is effective at searching out errors. He or she can be counted on for finishing a project and delivering on time. A potential weakness is that the completer-finisher can be a worrier and reluctant to delegate.

9. **Specialist.** The specialist is a single-minded self-starter. He or she is dedicated and provides knowledge and skill in rare supply. A potential weakness of the specialist is that he or she can be stuck in a niche with little interest in other knowledge and may dwell on technicalities.

The weaknesses in the first nine roles point to problems the team leader or manager can expect to emerge, and therefore an allowance should be made. Belbin refers to these potential problems as *allowable weaknesses* because an allowance should be made for them. To illustrate, if a team worker has a tendency to be indecisive in a crisis, the team should not have high expectations of the team worker when faced with a crisis. Team workers will be the most satisfied if the crisis is predicted and decisions involving them are made before the pressure mounts.[14]

Another perspective on team roles is that team members will sometimes engage in *self-oriented roles*. Members will sometimes focus on their own needs rather than those of the group. The individual might be overly aggressive because of a personal need, such as wanting a bigger budget for his or her project. The individual might hunger for recognition or power. Similarly the person might attempt to dominate the meeting, block others from contributing, or serve as a distraction. One of the ploys used by distracters recently is to engage in cell phone conversations during a meeting, blaming it on "those people who keep calling me."

The many roles just presented overlap somewhat. For example, the implementer might engage in specialist activities. Do not be concerned about the overlap. Instead, pick and choose from the many roles as the situation dictates—whether or not overlap exists. Skill-Building Exercise 2-1 gives you an opportunity to observe these roles in action. The behavior associated with the roles just described is more important than remembering the labels. For example, remembering to be creative and imaginative is more important than remembering the specific label "creative problem solver."

GUIDELINES FOR THE INTERPERSONAL ASPECTS OF TEAM PLAY

The purpose of this and the following section is to help you enhance your effectiveness as a team player by describing the skills, actions, and attitudes required to be an effective team player. You can regard these behaviors (the collective term for skills, actions, and attitudes) as goals for personal improvement. Identify the actions and attitudes for which you need the most improvement, and proceed accordingly with self-development.

One convenient method for classifying team activities in the pursuit of goals is to categorize them as people-related or task-related. Remember, however, that the categorization of people- versus task-related activities is not entirely accurate. For example, if you are challenging your teammates with a difficult goal, are you focusing more on the people (offering them a motivational challenge) or the task (achieving the goal)? We begin first with people-related actions and attitudes, (see also Figure 2-2) followed in the next section by task-related actions and attitudes.

BACK TO THE OPENING CASE

A key aspect of Ann Livermore being a good team player was to not care about experiencing a decrease in her power and authority because her company acquired a large outsourcing firm. She said that her main concern was the prosperity of her employer, H-P. In crediting Livermore for her team spirit, recognize that Livermore already has had an outstanding career and was once a candidate to become CEO of H-P. She still has enough responsibility left to satisfy her needs for power and influence. A person still pursuing loftier positions might not have such a strong team spirit.

Team Member Roles

A team of approximately six people is formed to conduct a 20-minute meeting on a significant topic of their choosing. The possible scenarios follow:

Scenario A: Management Team. A group of managers are pondering whether to lay off one-third of the workforce in order to increase profits. The company has had a tradition of caring for employees and regarding them as the company's most precious asset. However, the CEO has said privately that times have changed in our competitive world, and the company must do whatever possible to enhance profits. The group wants to think through the advisability of laying off one-third of the workforce, as well as explore other alternatives.

Scenario B: Group of Sports Fans. A group of fans have volunteered to find a new team name to replace "Redskins" for the local basketball team. One person among the group of volunteers believes that the name "Redskins" should be retained because it is a compliment, rather than an insult to Native Americans. The other members of the group believe that a name change is in order, but they lack any good ideas for replacing a mascot team name that has endured for over 50 years.

Scenario C: Community Group. A community group is attempting to launch an initiative to help battered adults and children. Opinions differ strongly as to what initiative would be truly helpful to battered adults and children. Among the alternatives are establishing a shelter for battered people, giving workshops on preventing violence, and providing self-defense training. Each group member with an idea strongly believes that he or she has come up with a workable possibility for helping with the problem of battered people.

While the team members are conducting their heated discussion, other class members make notes on which team members carry out which roles. Students should watch for the different roles as developed by Belbin and his associates, as well as the self-oriented roles. For example, students in the first row

might look for examples of the plant. Use the role worksheet that follows to help make your observations. Summarize the comment that is indicative of the role. An example would be noting in the shaper category: "Linda said naming the team the 'Washington Rainbows' seems like too much of an attempt to be politically correct."

Creative Problem Solver _____

Resource Investigator _____

Coordinator _____

Shaper _____

Monitor-Evaluator _____

Team Worker _____

Implementer _____

Completer-Finisher _____

Specialist _____

Self-Oriented Roles _____

Understanding team member roles will contribute to working effectively as a member of a team. However, a foundation contributor to effective team play is recognizing individual differences and having good communication skills. The same two factors are fundamental for effectiveness in any setting involving interaction between and among people. Here is an example of how recognizing individual differences and having effective communication skills can help in a team setting: Max and Beth are teammates, and Max notices that Beth is shy and somewhat sullen. (He observes individual differences.) Max gives Beth a playful fist in the air, and says, "Come on Beth, we need your contribution in the 10 o'clock meeting. You have one of the sharpest minds on the team, and you're hiding it from us." With such warm encouragement, Beth then has the courage to contribute more to the morning meeting.

Trust Team Members

The cornerstone attitude of an outstanding team player is to trust team members, including the leader. Working on a team is akin to a small-business partnership. If you do not believe that the other team members have your best interests at heart, it will be difficult for you to share opinions and ideas. You will fear that others will make negative statements behind your back.

FIGURE 2-2   Interpersonal Aspects of Team Play

1. Trust team members.
2. Display a high level of cooperation and collaboration.
3. Recognize the interests and achievements of others.
4. Give and receive helpful criticism.
5. Share the glory.
6. Take care not to rain on another person's parade.

Trusting team members also includes believing that their ideas are technically sound and rational until proven otherwise. Another manifestation of trust is taking risks with others. You can take a risk by trying out one of their unproved ideas. You can also take a risk by submitting an unproved idea and not worrying about being ridiculed.

One of the goals of offsite training is to help team members trust each other. As is familiar to most readers, such trust builders include falling into each other's arms, rappelling up a wall, racing down rapids in a raft, and dangling from cables over gorges.[15]

Display a High Level of Cooperation and Collaboration

Cooperation and collaboration are synonymous with teamwork. If you display a willingness to help others by working cooperatively with them, you will be regarded as a team player. If you do not cooperate with other team members, the team structure breaks down. Collaboration at a team level refers to working jointly with others to solve mutual problems. Although working with another person on a given problem may take longer than working through a problem alone, the long-term payoff is important. You have established a climate favorable to working on joint problems where collective action is necessary. Sharing success stories with each other about what worked in the past is another useful approach to collaboration.[16]

Achieving a cooperative team spirit is often a question of making the first move. Instead of grumbling about poor teamwork, take the initiative and launch a cooperative spirit in your group. Target the most individualistic, least cooperative member of the group. Ask the person for his or her input on an idea you are formulating. Thank the person, and then state that you would be privileged to return the favor.

Another way of attaining good cooperation is to minimize confrontations. If you disagree with the opinion of another team member, patiently explain the reasons for your differences and look for a workable way to integrate both your ideas. A teammate might suggest, for example, that the team stay until midnight to get a project completed today. You have plans for the evening and are angered by the suggestion. Instead of lashing out at your teammate, you might say, "I agree we need to put in extra time and effort to get the job done. But why can't we spread out this extra effort over a few days? In this way those of us who cannot work until midnight this evening can still contribute."

A side advantage of cooperation within the group is that the part of the brain associated with pleasure is activated when people cooperate. According to team building specialist Anna Maravelas, "It is intrinsically rewarding for human beings to pull together."[17]

Skill-Building Exercise 2-2 is a widely used technique for demonstrating the importance of cooperation and collaboration.

SKILL-BUILDING EXERCISE 2-2

The Scavenger Hunt

The purpose of this teamwork exercise is to demonstrate the importance of cooperation and collaboration in accomplishing a task under pressure. The class is divided into teams of about five students. How much time you can devote to the task depends upon your particular class schedule. The instructor will supply each team with a list of items to find within a prescribed period of time—usually about 35 minutes. Given the time constraints, the group will usually have to conduct the hunt on campus. Following is a representative list of items to find in an on-campus scavenger hunt:

- A piece of chalk
- A tie
- A brick
- A cap from a beer bottle
- A pocket knife
- A flash drive

When the group returns within 30 minutes, hold a public discussion about what you learned about teamwork and what insights you acquired.

Recognize the Interests and Achievements of Others

A fundamental tactic for establishing yourself as a solid team player is to actively recognize the interests and achievements of others. Let others know you care about their interests. After you make a suggestion during a team meeting, ask: "Would my suggestion create any problems for anybody else?" or "How do my ideas fit into what you have planned?"

Recognizing the achievements of others is more straightforward than recognizing interests. Be prepared to compliment any tangible achievement. Give realistic compliments by making the compliment commensurate with the achievement. To do otherwise is to compromise your sincerity. For example, do not call someone a genius just because he or she showed you how to compute an exchange rate from one currency to another. Instead, you might say, "Thank you. I am very impressed by your knowledge of exchange rates."

A technique has been developed to enable the entire team to recognize the interests and achievements of others. Playing the anonymous praise game, each team member lists what he or she admires about a specific coworker. The team leader collects the responses and sends each team member the comments made about him or her. Using this technique, team members see a compilation of praise based on how coworkers perceive them. The anonymous praise game helps overcome the hesitancy some people have to praise another person face-to-face.[18]

Give and Receive Helpful Criticism

The outstanding team player offers constructive criticism when needed, but does so diplomatically. To do otherwise is to let down the team. A high-performance team demands sincere and tactful criticism among members. No matter how diplomatic you are, keep your ratio of criticism to praise small. Keep two time-tested principles in mind. First, attempt to criticize the person's work, not the person. It is better to say, "The conclusion is missing from your analysis" than "You left out the conclusion." (The latter statement hurts because it sounds like your teammate did something wrong.)

Another key guideline for criticism is to ask a question rather than to make a declarative statement. By answering a question, the person being criticized is involved in improving his or her work. In the example at hand, it would be effective to ask, "Do you think your report would have a greater impact if it contained a conclusion?" In this way, the person being criticized contributes a judgment about the conclusion. The person has a chance to say, "Yes, I will prepare a conclusion."

Criticism works both ways, so the effective team player is willing to accept helpful criticism, such as "You are speaking too fast for several of our team members for whom English is their second language." Becky Blalock, the vice president and chief information officer (CIO) of the electric utility the Southern Company, regards being open to feedback as one of the core principles of teamwork.[19]

Share the Glory

An effective team player shares praise and other rewards for accomplishment even if he or she is the most deserving. Shared praise is usually merited to some extent because teammates have probably made at least some contribution to the achievement that received praise. For example, if a team member comes up with a powerful suggestion for cutting costs, it is likely that somebody else in the group sparked his or her thinking. Effective examples of sharing glory are easy to find. Think back to watching athletes and other entertainers who win a title or an award. Many of them are gracious enough to share the glory. It has become almost standard practice for an award-winning coach or player to say, "I never would have accomplished what I did if I hadn't played with such a great group of people."

Take Care Not to Rain on Another Person's Parade

As teamwork specialist Pamela Lovell observes, we all have achievements and accomplishments that are sources of pride. Belittling the achievements of others for no legitimate reason brings about tension and anger. Suppress your feelings of petty jealousy.[20] An example would be saying to someone who is proudly describing an accomplishment,

FIGURE 2-3   Task Aspects of Team Play

1. Provide technical expertise (or knowledge of the task).
2. Assume responsibility for problems.
3. See the big picture.
4. Believe in consensus.
5. Focus on deadlines.
6. Help team members do their jobs better.
7. Be a good organizational citizen.

"Don't take too much credit. It looks to me like you were at the right place at the right time." If you support teammates by acknowledging their accomplishments, you are more likely to receive their support when needed.

GUIDELINES FOR THE TASK ASPECTS OF TEAM PLAY

The task aspects of team play also make a key contribution to becoming an effective team player. Here we describe seven major task-related tactics (see Figure 2-3). As mentioned earlier, a task aspect usually has interpersonal consequences.

Provide Technical Expertise (Or Knowledge of the Task)

Most people are selected for a work team primarily because of their technical expertise. *Technical* refers to the intimate details of any task, not just tasks in engineering, physical science, and information technology. The sales promotion specialist on a product development team has technical expertise about sales promotion, whether or not sales promotion requires knowledge of engineering or computers.

As team consultant Glenn Parker observes, to use your technical expertise to outstanding advantage you must have the willingness to share that expertise.[21] Some experts perceive their esoteric knowledge as a source of power. As a consequence, they are hesitant to let others share their knowledge for fear of relinquishing power. It is also necessary for the technical expert to be able to communicate with team members in other disciplines who lack the same technical background. The technical person who cannot explain the potential value of his or her contribution may fail to receive much attention.

An analysis of 72 studies based on more than 17,000 individuals in a variety of work settings lends credibility to the belief that information sharing is beneficial to teams. A major finding of the analysis is that team performance is enhanced when team members share information not commonly shared by all team members. A somewhat distressing side finding of the study is that many teams do not share information when the sharing is most needed. An example of information being most needed is when the other team members are not aware of the useful information possessed by the other members.[22]

Assume Responsibility for Problems

The outstanding team player assumes responsibilities for problems. If a problem is not yet assigned to anybody, he or she says, "I'll do it." One team member might note that the true progress on the team's effort is blocked until the team benchmarks (compares itself) with other successful teams. The effective team player might say, "You are right, we need to benchmark. If it's okay with everybody else, I'll get started on the benchmarking project tomorrow. It will be my responsibility." Taking responsibility must be combined with dependability. The person who takes responsibility for a task must produce, time after time.

See the Big Picture

Effective team players need to think conceptually, or see the big picture. A trap in team effort is that discussion can get bogged down in small details and the team might lose sight of what it is trying to accomplish. The team player (including the team leader) who can help the group focus on its broader purpose plays a vital role. The following case history illustrates what it means to see the big picture.

A group of retail sales associates and customer service representatives were sent to a one-day seminar about customer service training. The group was sent to training because customer service ratings at their store were below the level store executives thought was acceptable. During the lunch breaks, the conversation quickly turned to the fact that the coffee was not as hot as desired, the snacks were mediocre, the restrooms were too far from the meeting room, and the presenter had a phony smile and told goofy jokes. Next came a few complaints about a couple of the PowerPoint slides having too much detail.

Alyssa, an experienced sales associate, stepped in with a comment. She noted, "I think all of you have valid complaints, but your points are minor. We are here to learn how to improve customer service. If we want our store to survive, and earn bigger bonuses, we have to learn what we can to help us do our jobs better. Whether or not you like our trainer's smile or jokes, he is trying to be helpful." The group returned after lunch with a more determined effort to focus on the purpose of the seminar—picking up ideas to improve customer service.

Believe in Consensus

consensus

General acceptance by the group of a decision.

A major task-related attitude for outstanding team play is to believe that consensus has merit. **Consensus** is general acceptance of a decision by the group. Every member may not be thrilled about the decision, yet they are unopposed and are willing to support the decision. Believing that consensus is valuable enables you to participate fully in team decisions without thinking that you have sacrificed your beliefs or the right to think independently. To believe in consensus is to believe that the democratic process has relevance for organizations and that ideal solutions are not always possible.

Focus on Deadlines

A notable source of individual differences among work group members is how much importance they attach to deadlines. Some work group members may regard deadlines as a moral contract, to be missed only in case of emergency. Others may view deadlines as an arbitrary date imposed by someone external to the group. Other work group members may perceive deadlines as moderately important. Differences in perception about the importance of deadlines influence the group's ability to meet deadlines.[23]

Keeping the group focused on the deadline is a valuable task behavior because meeting deadlines is vital to team success. Discussing the importance of the deadlines is helpful because of the varying attitudes about deadlines that are likely to be found among group members.

Help Team Members Do Their Jobs Better

Your stature as a team player will increase if you take the initiative to help coworkers make needed work improvements. Helping other team members with their work assignments is a high-level form of cooperation. Make the suggestions in a constructive spirit rather than displaying an air of superiority. Identify a problem that a coworker is having, and then suggest alternatives he or she might be interested in exploring. Avoid saying to team members that they "should" do something, because many people become defensive when told what they should do. The term *should* is usually perceived as a moral judgment given to one person by another, such as being told that you should save money, should learn a second language, or should improve your math skills.

Be a Good Organizational Citizen

A comprehensive way of carrying out the task aspects of team play (as well as relationship aspects) is to help out beyond the requirements of your job description. Such extra-role activity is referred to as organizational citizenship behavior—working for the good of the organization even without the promise of a specific reward. As a result of many workers being good organizational citizens, the organization functions more effectively in such ways as improved product quantity and quality.[24] Good citizenship on the job encompasses many specific behaviors, including helping a coworker with a job task and refraining from complaints or petty grievances. A good organizational citizen would carry out such specific acts as picking up litter in the company parking lot, and turning out lights when they are not in use. He or she would also bring a reference to the office that could help a coworker solve a job problem. Most of the other team player tactics described here are related to organizational citizenship behavior.

Two experiments, one with business students and one with managers, suggested that organizational citizenship behavior is even more important when people depend on each other to accomplish a task.[25] An example is filling an order with components from different departments. Given that most tasks on a team are interdependent, organizational citizenship behavior is quite important for effective teamwork.

A recent synthesis of studies about the type of team processes described in this chapter supports the relevance of such actions by team members. (A team process is essentially an action taken by one or more team members.) A group of researchers examined the results of a variety of team member processes in 147 different samples of workers. The major conclusion reached was that teamwork processes are positively associated with both team member performance and satisfaction.[26] You can therefore have some assurance that if you engage in the activities described in this chapter, your efforts will help increase performance and satisfaction.

Skill-Building Exercise 2-3 will help you integrate the many suggestions presented here for developing teamwork skills.

SKILL-BUILDING EXERCISE 2-3

Habitat for Homeless People

Organize the class into teams of about six people. Each team takes on the assignment of formulating plans for building temporary shelters for homeless people. The task will take about one hour and can be done inside or outside the class. The dwellings you plan to build, for example, might be two-room cottages with electricity and indoor plumbing.

During the time allotted to the task, formulate plans for going ahead with Habitat for Homeless People. Consider dividing up work by assigning certain roles to each team member. Sketch out tentative answers to the following questions:

1. How will you obtain funding for your venture?
2. Which homeless people will you help?
3. Where will your shelters be located?
4. Who will do the actual construction?

After your plan is completed, evaluate the quality of the teamwork that took place within the group. Specify which teamwork

skills were evident and which ones did not surface. Search the chapter for techniques you might use to improve teamwork. The skills used to accomplish the habitat task could relate to the team skills presented in Self-Assessment Quiz 2-2, the interpersonal aspects of team play, the task aspects of team play, or some team skill not mentioned in this chapter. Here is a sampling of the many different skills that might be relevant in this exercise:

- Speaks effectively
- Listens to others
- Innovates solutions to problems
- Thinks outside the box
- Displays a high level of cooperation and collaboration
- Provides knowledge of the task
- Sees the big picture
- Focuses on deadlines

Self-Assessment Quiz 2-1 gave you an opportunity to think through the extent to which you really enjoy, or are interested, in teamwork. Being part of a close-knit team is important for many types of work, but there is always room for some people who prefer to work alone doing analytical or creative work. For example, at Microsoft Corp. the office layout gives space to people who want to work alone and not be distracted by other people. Self-Assessment Quiz 2-2 follows up your interests and attitudes about teamwork with an opportunity to review your skills. Interest and skills are not the same. A given individual who likes the idea of skydiving might lack the eye-hand coordination to pull the cord under pressure, and therefore would be a disaster as a skydiver.

If you have the attitudes for teamwork, another subtle factor about teamwork can influence your effectiveness. As measured in Self-Assessment Quiz 2-3, your level of conformity can influence your effectiveness. Too much or too little conformity can detract from your effectiveness. Self-Assessment Quiz 2-4 takes you even further into the intricacies of teamwork by measuring your tendency to play positive team roles. With few exceptions, a person needs to focus on positive team roles to be a successful team member.

Concept Review
and Reinforcement

Key Terms

team 37
virtual team 38
synergy 40

social loafing 42
groupthink 42

role 42
consensus 52

Summary

To be successful in the modern organization, it is necessary to be an effective team player. Team members have complementary skills and are committed to a common purpose. All teams have some elements in common. Teams can be broadly classified into face-to-face versus virtual types. A virtual team does most of its work electronically instead of in face-to-face meetings.

Groups and teams offer such advantages as (1) gaining synergy, (2) work accomplishment and high productivity, (3) gaining increased acceptance of and commitment to decisions, (4) avoidance of major errors, and (5) increased job satisfaction.

Groups and teams also have disadvantages, such as (1) time wasting, (2) pressures toward conformity, (3) shirking of individual responsibility, (4) fostering of conflict, and (5) groupthink. The latter refers to making bad decisions as a by-product of strong consensus. Key characteristics of effective work groups are outlined in Figure 2-1.

An important part of being an effective team player is to choose effective roles. The roles studied here are: creative problem solver, resource investigator, coordina-tor, shaper, monitor-evaluator, team worker, implementer, completer-finisher, and specialist. Self-oriented roles are less effective and detract from group productivity. Understanding roles does not supplant the need for recognizing individual differences and communicating well.

Guidelines for effectively contributing to the interpersonal aspects of team play include (1) trusting team members, (2) displaying a high level of cooperation and collaboration, (3) recognizing the interests and achievements of others, (4) giving and receiving helpful criticism, (5) sharing the glory, and (6) taking care not to rain on another person's parade.

Guidelines for effectively contributing to the task aspects of team play include (1) providing technical expertise, (2) assuming responsibility for problems, (3) seeing the big picture, (4) believing in consensus, (5) focusing on deadlines, and (6) helping team members do their jobs better.

A synthesis of research studies demonstrates that the types of teamwork processes described here are positively associated with both team member performance and satisfaction.

Questions for Discussion and Review

1. What do executives really mean when they say that "business is a team sport"?

2. From your perspective, what would be the satisfactions and frustrations of being a member of a virtual team?

3. How do team members know when they have achieved synergy?

4. What should the other team members do when they uncover a social loafer?

5. How can the *monitor-evaluator* role backfire for a person?
6. Assume that you are a team member. What percentage of your pay would you be willing to have based on a group reward? Explain your reasoning.
7. Many retail companies, banks, and medical offices require customer-contact employees to wear the same uniform. In what ways might these uniforms enhance teamwork?

8. A number of companies have sent employees to a team-building exercise in which they prepare a gourmet meal. Why would preparing a gourmet meal help build teamwork?
9. The "little picture" in studying this chapter is learning details about teamwork skills. What is the "big picture"?
10. How can a person achieve individual recognition yet still be a team player?

The Web Corner

http://www.timeanalyzer.com/lib/teamroles.htm
(Belbin's team roles to improve team performance.)

http://www.quintcareers.com/team_player_quiz.html
(Take the quiz, "Are You a Team Player: A Quintessential Careers Quiz.")

Internet Skill Builder: Becoming a Better Team Player

The purpose of this exercise duplicates the major purpose of the chapter—finding practical suggestions for improving your teamwork skills. Visit several Web sites that deal with enhancing teamwork skills from the standpoint of the individual, not the manager. An example of such a Web site is www.confidencecenter.com. Write down at least three concrete suggestions you find, and compare these suggestions to those made in this chapter. If the opportunity arises, practice one of these skills in the next 10 days and observe the results.

Developing Your
Human Relations Skills

Leah Puts on Her Team Player Face

Leah was happy to find a position as a scanning technician at a business process outsourcing company, Expert Resource, Inc. A major part of the Expert's business was converting paperwork related to human resource management into digital form. Clients would mail their forms, such as medical claims, to Expert. Scanning technicians would then insert the claim forms into large scanning machines to make the conversion to digital. Clients would then have digital instead of paper documents for health claims and other human resource records.

The scanning technicians had to interact with other employees in several ways. Many of the claims received contained illegible identifying information, so they had to be sent to a security department that attempted to obtain the proper identification for the forms. The scanning technicians were expected to help level the workload among the technicians. For example, if one of the technicians was overwhelmed, and another was caught up, the latter was supposed to help out the former. Also, the company frequently held small celebrations in the office. A typical celebration would be to hold a brunch in honor of a new employee joining the company.

Leah believed that if she performed well in her position as scanning technician, she would be eligible for promotion to the information technology department. Eventually being promoted to a supervisor position was also within the realm of possibility. Leah also recognized that having good skills and speed in scanning documents were not sufficient to be promoted to a supervisory position. Her size-up of the situation was that being a good team player would be required to be considered for promotion. Leah then set out to develop the reputation of being a good team player.

The next Monday morning, Leah arrived at the office with a box of donuts that she placed in the break room, with a note attached that said, "Enjoy your coffee or tea this morning with a treat from your coworker Leah." Several of the other scanning technicians thanked Leah; however, one technician said to her, "Why did you bring us donuts? You're not our supervisor."

A week later, Leah implemented another tactic designed to boost her reputation as a team player. She sent an e-mail to the other technicians informing them that they were free to send her an e-mail or an IM anytime they were overloaded with documents to scan. Leah said that she would help the overloaded coworker so long as she was caught up on her own work.

A week later Lean reflected, "I think I am developing a reputation as a good team player, but I can't give up yet. I think I know a way to really cement being regarded as a strong team player." Leah then wrote an e-mail to the other scanning technicians, as well as her supervisor. The e-mail read in part.

"We all know that it takes a village to raise a child. But did you also know that it takes a group of friendly and cooperative coworkers to get a scanning technician up to speed? I want to thank you all for your cooperation and friendliness. You have been very helpful to me."

Case Questions

1. How effective do you think Leah's initiatives are in helping her develop a reputation as a strong team player?
2. If you were Leah's supervisor, how would you react to the e-mails she sent to the group?
3. What advice might you offer Leah to help her advance her reputation as a team player?

Ruth Waves a Red Flag

Carlos is the team leader of a cost-reduction team within a well-established baked-goods company that produces bakery products under its own label, as well as private labels for grocery-store chains such as Giant and Win-Dixie. Top-level management formed the team to arrive at suggestions for reducing costs throughout the organization. A transcript of one of the meetings is presented next.

Carlos: We've been gathering information for a month now. It's about time we heard some specific suggestions.

Jack: At the top of my list is cutting pension benefits. Our pension payments are higher than the minimum required by law. Our medical benefits are way above average. If we cut back on pension benefits, no current employees would be adversely affected.

Melissa: I like your analysis, Jack. No sense risking laying off employees just to keep retirees happy.

Jordan: We should make absolutely certain there are no legal complications here. Then we can sharpen our cost-cutting knives and dig right in.

Gunther: I'd support cutting pension benefits. It would probably reduce expenses more dramatically than the ways I have uncovered.

Carlos: There seems to be consensus so far that we should consider making recommendations about cutting pension benefits. Ruth, what do you think?

Ruth: I think it is much too early to reach consensus on such a sensitive issue. Cutting pension benefits would create panic among our retirees. Out older employees would be screaming as well. We'll have an avalanche of negative publicity in the media.

Jordan: Hold on, Ruth. I said the team should first check out this idea with the legal department.

Ruth: Just because cutting pension benefits could squeeze by legally doesn't mean that it's a good idea. We haven't examined the negative ramifications of cutting pension benefits. Let's study this issue further before word leaks out that we're taking away the golden egg.

Carlos: Maybe Ruth has a point. Let's investigate this issue further before making a recommendation.

Case Questions

1. What role, or roles, is Ruth occupying on the cost-reduction team?
2. How effective does she appear to be in her role?
3. What role, or roles, is Jack occupying on the cost-reduction team?
4. How effective does he appear to be in his role?
5. How effective is Carlos in his role as a team leader?

REFERENCES

1. Carol Hymowitz, "H-P's Ann Livermore Keeps Eye on 'Team'," *The Wall Street Journal,* June 2, 2008, p. B.
2. Conference Board report cited in "CEO Leadership Skips Teamwork, Article Says," Rochester, New York, *Democrat and Chronicle,* February 17, 2002, p. 1E.
3. Jon R. Katzenbach and Douglas K. Smith, "The Discipline of Teams," *Harvard Business Review,* March–April 1993, p. 112.
4. Claus W. Langfred, "Too Much Trust a Good Thing? Negative Effects of High Trust and Individual Autonomy in Self-Managing Teams," *Academy of Management Journal,* June 2004, pp. 385–399.
5. "Shepherding Communications When the Flock Is Scattered," *Flexible Workplace Management,* sample issue, 2001.
6. "Bridge Gaps with Remote Workers," *Manager's Edge,* July 2008, p. 1.
7. Arvind Malhotra, Ann Majchrzak, and Benson Rosen, "Leading Virtual Teams," *Academy of Management Perspectives,* February 2007, p. 62.
8. Cited in Adam Bryant, "Ensemble Acting, in Business," *The New York Times* (www.nytimes.com), June 7, 2009.
9. Matt Bolch, "Rewarding the Team," *HR Magazine,* February 2007, pp. 91–93; www.wikiinvest.com, December 4, 2009.
10. "When Committees Spell Trouble: Don't Let Individuals Hide Within a Group," *WorkingSMART,* August 1998, p. 1; Ross Kerber, "For Abigail Johnson, a Leadership Test," *The Boston Globe* (boston.com), August 21, 2007, p. 1.
11. Irving L. Janus, *Victims of Groupthink: A Psychological Study of Foreign Policy Decisions and Fiascos* (Boston: Houghton Mifflin, 1972); Glen Whyte, "Groupthink Reconsidered," *Academy of Management Review,* January 1989, pp. 40–56.
12. Martha A. Peak, "Treating Trauma in Teamland," *Management Review,* September 1997, p. 1.
13. "R. Meredith Belbin," in *Business: The Ultimate Resource* (Cambridge; MA: Perseus, 2002), pp. 966–967; Belbin, *Management Teams* (London: Elsevier Butterworth-Heinemann, 2003); Belbin® Team-Roles, *http://www.belbin.com/belbin-teamroles.htm.*
14. From a review of Meredith Belbin, *Management Teams,* by Colin Thomson appearing in *http://www.accountingweb.co.uk.,* accessed April 14, 2004.
15. Jeffrey m. O'Brien, "Team Building in Paradise," *Fortune,* May 26, 2008, pp. 112–122.
16. Romanus Wolter, "Get Team-Focused," *Entrepreneur,* February 2009, p. 124.
17. Cited in "Gather Round, People!" *Entrepreneur,* September 2009, p. 21.
18. "Fly in Formation: Easy Ways to Build Team Spirit," *WorkingSMART,* March 2000, p. 6.
19. "Score a Perfect '10' on Teamwork," *Manager's Edge,* May 2006, p. 1.
20. Pamela Lovell, "Healthy Teams Display Strong Vital Signs," *Teamwork,* sample issue, the Dartnell Corporation, 1997.
21. Glenn M. Parker, *Cross-Functional Teams: Working with Allies, Enemies, & Other Strangers* (San Francisco: Jossey-Bass, 1994), p. 170.
22. Jessica R. Mesmer-Magnus and Leslie A. DeChurch, "Information Sharing and Team Performance: A Meta-Analysis," *Journal of Applied Psychology,* March 2009, pp. 535–546.
23. Mary J. Waller et al., "The Effect of Individual Perceptions of Deadlines on Team Performance," *Academy of Management Review,* October 2001, p. 597.
24. Mark G. Ehrhant and Stefanie E. Naumann, "Organizational Citizenship Behavior in Work Groups: A Group Norms Approach," *Journal of Applied Psychology,* December 2004, pp. 960–974.
25. Daniel G. Bachrach, Benjamin C. Powell, Elliot Bendoly, and R. Glenn Richey, "Organizational Citizenship Behavior and Performance Evaluations: Exploring the Impact of Task Interdependence," *Journal of Applied Psychology,* January 2006, pp. 193–201.
26. Jeffrey A. LePine et al., "A Meta-Analysis of Teamwork Processes: Tests of a Multidimensional Model and Relationships with Team Effectiveness Criteria," *Personnel Psychology,* Summer 2008, pp. 273–307.

Professional Presence and Interviewing

CONDUCTING A JOB SEARCH

The vast majority of workers have to conduct a job search at various times in their careers. Job searches are conducted to find employment in a firm the job seeker is not already working for, or sometimes to find a new position within one's own firm. When job openings are on short supply, job search skills are especially important. Even during the most prosperous of times, when jobs are in ample supply, learning more about conducting a job search is useful. It can help you land an excellent position. Included in the job search are job-hunting tactics and preparing a résumé and cover letter.

1. Demonstrate strategies to implement when invited to interview.
2. Conduct company and job-specific research for interview preparation.
3. Prepare a *personal commercial* to sell skills and tie them to a target job.
4. Identify pre-interview preparation activities including creating an *interview portfolio* and practice interview questions.
5. Demonstrate how to behave during technology-based interviews.
6. Explain key areas of employee rights and how to respond to discriminatory questions.
7. Describe specific statements and behaviors to exhibit at the close of an interview and job offer.
8. Discuss salary negotiation strategies.
9. Describe and discuss the importance of professional behavior.
10. State the impact dress can have on others' perception of you.
11. Demonstrate a professional introduction and handshake.
12. Demonstrate appropriate professional behavior in business dining situations.
13. Recognize and apply the appropriate use of technology in business/social situations.
14. Utilize professional *etiquette* in appropriate business situation.

Job-Hunting Tactics

Most people already have usable knowledge about how to find a job, and information about job hunting is abundant. Some of the ideas discussed next will therefore be familiar; some will be unfamiliar. We recommend using this list of tactics as a checklist to ensure that you have not neglected something important. Also, it is important to search for employment systematically. It is easy to overlook the obvious when job hunting because your emotions may cloud your sense of logic.

Identify Your Job Objectives.   An effective job search begins with a clear perception of what kind of position (or positions) you want. If you express indecision about the type of work you seek, the prospective employer will typically ask in a critical tone, "What kind of work are you looking for?" Your chances of finding suitable employment increase when several different types of positions will satisfy your job objectives. Assume that one person who majored in business administration is only willing to accept a position as an office manager in a corporation. Another person with the same major is seeking a position as (1) an office manager; (2) a management trainee in a corporation; (3) an assistant manager in a retail store, restaurant, or hotel; (4) a sales representative; (5) an assistant purchasing agent; or (6) a management analyst. The second person has a much better chance of finding a suitable position.

Be Aware of Qualifications Sought by Employers.   What you are looking for in an employer must be matched against what an employer is looking for in an employee. If you are aware of what employers are seeking, you can emphasize those aspects of yourself when applying for a position. For example, applicants for almost any type of position should emphasize their information technology skills. Job interviewers and hiring managers do not all agree on the qualifications they seek in employees. Nevertheless, a number of traits, characteristics, skills, and accomplishments are important to many employers. Self-Assessment Quiz 3-1 summarizes these qualifications in a way that you can apply to yourself as you think about your job hunt.

Qualifications Sought by Employers

Directions: Following is a list of qualifications widely sought by prospective employers. After reading each qualification, rate yourself on a 1 to 5 scale by circling the appropriate number: 1 = very low, 2 = low, 3 = average, 4 = high, 5 = very high.

1.	Appropriate education for the position under consideration and satisfactory grades	1	2	3	4	5
2.	Relevant work experience	1	2	3	4	5
3.	Communication and other interpersonal skills	1	2	3	4	5
4.	Motivation and energy	1	2	3	4	5
5.	Problem-solving ability (intelligence) and creativity	1	2	3	4	5
6.	Judgment and common sense	1	2	3	4	5
7.	Adaptability to change, including ability to take on tasks not directly part of your field of expertise.	1	2	3	4	5
8.	Emotional maturity (acting professionally and responsibly)	1	2	3	4	5
9.	Teamwork (ability and interest in working in a team effort)	1	2	3	4	5
10.	Positive attitude (enthusiasm about work and initiative)	1	2	3	4	5
11.	Emotional intelligence (ability to deal with own feelings and those of others)	1	2	3	4	5
12.	Customer service orientation (wanting to meet customer needs)	1	2	3	4	5
13.	Information technology skills	1	2	3	4	5
14.	Willingness to continue to study and learn about the job, company, and industry	1	2	3	4	5
15.	Likableness and sense of humor	1	2	3	4	5
16.	Dependability, responsibility, and conscientiousness (including good work habits and time management)	1	2	3	4	5
17.	Willingness and ability to work well with coworkers and customers from different cultures	1	2	3	4	5
18.	Behaves ethically toward customers and company employees and obeys laws and regulations	1	2	3	4	5
19.	Can relate well to customers (even if not in formal customer contact position)	1	2	3	4	5
20.	Able to use social networking sites for business purposes	1	2	3	4	5

Interpretation: Consider engaging in some serious self-development, training, and education for items on which you rated yourself low or very low. If you accurately rated yourself as 4 or 5 on all the dimensions, you are an exceptional job candidate.

Identify Your Skills and Potential Contribution. The job market is skill-based. Employers typically seek out job candidates with tangible skills (including interpersonal skills) that can be put to immediate use in accomplishing work. Job-relevant skills you might identify include all of those listed in Self-Assessment Quiz 3-1. The cornerstone of a job search should be a thorough list of assets and accomplishments, because they point to useful skills and abilities you can use to help the employer.

A successful candidate for a customer service position at a telecommunications company told the interviewer, "I know I can help your customers with their software and hardware problems. I worked at the technical support center at college, and my friends and family members are forever coming to me with their computer problems. I even get long-distance calls for help. Give me a chance to help your customers." (Notice that the candidate implied that he or she had good listening skills.)

Develop a Comprehensive Marketing Strategy. A vital job-finding strategy is to use multiple approaches to reach the right prospective employer. This is particularly true when the position you seek is in short supply. A comprehensive marketing strategy is also useful because the job search can be framed as a plan for marketing yourself to prospective employers. The more channels you use, the greater the probability of being successful.

Among the many approaches employers use to recruit candidates are employee referrals, newspaper ads, job boards, employer Web sites, social networking Web sites, college and professional school recruitment, job fairs, temporary help firms, walk-ins, unsolicited résumés and phone calls, and government employment services. Even if some approaches to job finding are not the most effective, they all work some of the time. For example, some people think that newspaper ads are obsolete, yet all big-city newspapers, as well as *The Wall Street Journal,* advertise many interesting and high-paying positions.

Part of a comprehensive marketing strategy is to use a multi-track approach to job finding. Executive coach Donna Rawady suggests that you might prepare three different résumés focused on the contribution you would bring to each position.[1] You could then use the multiple-résumé approach for each approach to job finding, such as employer Web sites and job fairs.

Multiple approaches to finding a job can also include **extreme job hunting,** an offbeat way of attracting an employer's attention, with a small probability of success. Three examples follow: (1) Joshua Perskey, an investment banker, handed out his résumé while wearing a sandwich board that read, "Experienced M. I. T. Grad for Hire." (2) James A. Williamson III, a new business graduate, taped his résumé inside the taxi cab he was driving because he could not find a marketing position. (3) Peggy Greco printed a T-shirt announcing her availability for private-duty nursing. She then wore the T-shirt while riding her bicycles through wealthy neighborhoods.[2] These approaches led to considerable publicity, which in turn led to landing a job through personal contacts.

Skill-Building Exercise 3-1 provides an opportunity to think through the realities of extreme job hunting.

extreme job hunting

An offbeat way of attracting an employer's attention, with a small probability of success.

Use Networking to Reach Company Insiders. The majority of successful job campaigns stem from personal contacts. Employers rely heavily on referrals from employees to fill positions, even though many good positions are also announced publicly, such as through Web sites, classified ads, and employment agencies. In regard to job hunting, networking is contacting friends and acquaintances and building systematically on these relationships to create a still wider set of contacts that might lead to employment. Formal mechanisms to develop network contacts have been introduced in recent years, such as bar parties in metropolitan areas devoted just to making job contacts. Social networking sites sometimes lead to useful contacts, and some people join social networking sites so that they can help strangers find a suitable position. Nevertheless, most of the contacts one develops on Web sites such as Twitter and Facebook are much weaker than in-person contacts. The social networking contact becomes more useful if it leads to an in-person contact.

SKILL-BUILDING EXERCISE 3-1

Extreme Job Hunting

Assemble into brainstorming groups of about five people. The task is to dream up extreme approaches to job hunting that could possibly work for someone. It is best to choose a target position that would be in the realm of possibility for many members of the class. For example, it would probably be more useful to extreme job hunt for a marketing assistant position than for one as an astronaut or movie actor. After you have assembled a list of about six methods of extreme job hunting, appoint a team leader who will present your findings to the class. The team leader can also be the person in the group who records the ideas.

As you listen to all the team leaders present, including the person from your own group, think through which of these techniques might actually be helpful in a job hunt.

Figure 3-1 presents a list of potential network contacts. In addition, a skill-building exercise about networking as a method of career advancement, including a job search, is presented toward the end of this chapter.

The networking technique is so well known today that it suffers from overuse. It is therefore important to use a tactful, low-key approach with a contact. For example, instead of asking a person in your network to furnish you a job lead, ask that person how someone with qualifications similar to yours might find a job. In addition, guard against taking up a large portion of a busy person's workday, for instance, by insisting on a luncheon meeting.

Another way of reaching company insiders is to write dozens of e-mail messages or hard-copy letters to potential employers. A surprisingly large number of people find jobs by contacting employers directly. Most large company Web sites have a section allocated to inviting job inquiries as part of the employee recruitment program. Prepare a prospective employer list, including the names of executives to contact in each firm. The people who receive your letters and e-mail messages become part of your network. A variation of this approach is to develop a 30-second telephone presentation of your background. After you have researched firms that may have opportunities for you, call them and make your pitch. However, voicemail systems usually make it difficult to speak directly to your target person.

Use Multiple Online Approaches. The Internet is a standard avenue for job hunting, even for middle-management and executive positions. Sources of job leads on the Internet include general job boards, specialty job boards, company Web sites, and social networking Web sites.

With a job board (or job search site), the job seeker can post a résumé or scroll through hundreds of job opportunities. A number of job board Web sites are résumé database services because they give employers access to résumés submitted by job hunters. Many position announcements on the Internet require the job seeker to send a résumé by attached file. A few position announcements still request that the résumé be sent by fax or paper mail.

Figure 3-2 lists some of the leading job boards, and dozens of others can be found quickly with an Internet job search. Job boards post positions both field and geographic region. Specialty job boards, such as those listed in Figure 3-2, are preferred by some job seekers and employers because these boards are less flooded with positions and applicants. An Internet search will quickly reveal any specialty job site in your field.

FIGURE 3-1   Potential Sources of Network Contacts

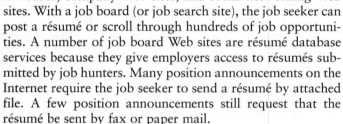

- Coworkers and previous employers
- Friends and neighbors
- Faculty and staff
- Graduates of any schools you have attended
- Former employers
- Present employers (assuming you hold a temporary position)
- Professional workers such as bankers, brokers, and clergy
- Political leaders at the local level
- Members of your club or athletic team
- Community groups, churches, temples, and mosques
- Trade and professional associations
- Student professional associations
- Career fairs
- People met in airports and on airplanes
- People met in aerobic classes and health clubs
- People you get to know through Internet social networks

FIGURE 3-2   General and Specialty Job Boards

Leading General Job-Search Web Sites
www.CareerBuilder.com
www.Monster.com
www.HotJobs.Yahoo.com
www.Job.com
www.Indeed.com

Examples of Specialized Job-Search Web Sites
www.Dice.com (technology positions)
www.SalesAnimals.com (sales positions)
www.Healthcaresource.com (health care positions)
www.cruisejobfinder.com (cruise and hospitality positions)

Many managers prefer the employment section of their Web site over commercial job boards. Some of the more advanced company job sites, such as GE, present possible career paths for people who enter the company in the position sought. Many employers believe that the best way to find good job candidates is to advertise on Web sites where these candidates are likely to be spending considerable time, such as Facebook or LinkedIn. Job boards also have a presence on social networking sites, as do recruiting firms. HotJobs has an application form on the social networking site Facebook. The potential applicant can send an e-mail or instant message to a particular posting.

Hundreds of people every day land jobs they first learned about through a job board or company Web site, so this approach offers some promise. A caution is that job hunting on the Internet can lead to a false sense of security. Using the Internet, a résumé is cast over a wide net, and hundreds of job postings can be explored. As a consequence, the job seeker may think that he or she can sit back and wait for a job offer to come through e-mail. In reality, the Internet is just one source of leads that should be used in conjunction with other job-finding methods, especially personal contacts that might lead to an interview. Remember also that thousands of other job seekers can access the same job opening, and many of the positions listed have already been filled. Be aware also that scam artists posing as employment agencies might post job openings on the Internet. After making you a tentative offer, the scammer writes that you must now send him or her your social security and bank account numbers so that your application can be processed completely. You then become a victim of identity theft.

Skill-Building Exercise 3-2 will give you an opportunity to learn firsthand about job hunting on the Internet.

SKILL-BUILDING EXERCISE 3-2

Job Hunting on the Internet

Job hunting on the Internet can be a rewarding or frustrating experience, depending on your skill in navigating job search Web sites and the availability of positions for a person with your qualifications. Use several job boards to locate a position opening for the following three persons:

Position 1: You. Find a position listed on the Internet that would appear to be an excellent fit for you at this time in your career.

Position 2: Sales Representative, Fluent in English and Mandarin Chinese. Attempt to find an opening for an industrial sales representative or retail sales position that requires the applicant to be fluent in English and Mandarin Chinese.

Position 3: Sports Administrator. Attempt to find an opening for a sports administrator, typically a person who does administrative work for a professional sports team. Set a time limit for your surfing, perhaps 60 minutes. If you are working in a team, each team member can search for one position. Share with each other your approaches and job boards that appear to achieve the best results.

Establishing your own Web site or blog, with résumé included, will sometimes attract an employer who conducts an Internet search for potential candidates. For example, recruiting specialists often spend several hours per week scanning blogs for new talent or additional information about candidates already interviewed. A blog is most likely to attract a recruiter's attention if it relates to work in your contemplated field, such as explaining how you helped your employer save energy.

Smile at Network Members and Interviewers, and Be Enthusiastic. Assuming that you have the right qualifications, the simple act of smiling can be an effective job-hunting technique. Remember to smile as you hand your business card to a potential network member. One reason that smiling is effective at any stage of the job search is that it helps build a relationship, however brief. If you use a webcam or video as part of your job search, smile on camera. Closely related to smiling is to display enthusiasm and excitement when speaking to people who can help you land a position. Conducted properly, a job search should be exciting and invigorating, and you should express these emotions to your contacts.[3] The excitement and invigoration stem from each small step you take leading to your goal of finding suitable employment.

Smooth Out Rough Spots in Your Background. About 95 percent of employers routinely conduct background investigations of prospective employees. A background investigation by a firm hired for the purpose could include speaking to neighbors and coworkers about your reputation. In addition, the investigator may delve into your driving record, check for criminal charges or convictions, survey your credit record, and find out whether you have had disputes with the government about taxes. The information just mentioned is used to supplement reference checks because so many employers are hesitant to say anything negative about past employees. The information uncovered through the background check is often compared to the information presented on your résumé. A discrepancy between the two sends up an immediate red flag.

A job seeker's credit history has gained importance as part of a background investigation. Rightfully or wrongfully, many otherwise qualified candidates are rejected because of a poor credit history. Whether or not the law is usually followed, U.S. law requires companies to get permission from applicants to run credit checks. Applicants should also be given the opportunity to respond.[4] Concerns about hiring someone with a poor credit record include (a) worries that finances will interfere with his or her concentration, (b) the person is unreliable in general, or (c) that being in dire need of money, he or she might steal from the company. Under ideal circumstances, an employer would give the applicant a chance to explain a poor credit history. For example, many reliable people have poor credit records because their medical bills went into collection while they waited for an insurance company to pay, or were victims of identity theft.[5]

Any job seeker who has severe negative factors in his or her background cannot readily change the past. Yet the job seeker can receive copies of a credit bureau report to make sure that it is fair and accurate. If inaccuracies exist, or certain credit problems have been resolved, the credit report might be changed in the applicant's favor. Or, bring up the negative credit rating during an interview to present your side of the story. Perhaps you had cosigned a loan for a friend who fell behind on his or her payments. It might also be possible to obtain a more favorable reference from an employer by making a polite request. A third step can be to request a copy of the consumer report, which is a report of your reputation based on interviews with coworkers, neighbors, and others. It is often possible to have deleted damaging information that is incorrect or exaggerated.

Another way to learn about what public information exists about you is to place your own name into a couple of search engines. Sometimes another person with the same name as yours—particularly if many people have the same name as you—might have been involved in criminal activity, so be prepared to defend yourself! *Googling* candidates has become standard practice to uncover both positive and negative information about job applicants. Going one step further, many employers search social Web sites like MySpace and Facebook to see if the candidate has engaged in outrageous behavior such as swimming in a public fountain while under the influence of alcohol—and then bragged about the episode on the social networking Web site.

Have you mastered interview techniques?	True	False
1. Arriving more than ten minutes early to the office where your interview is to take place is considered unprofessional.	❏	❏
2. It is best to have a draft of a post-interview thank-you note written prior to an interview.	❏	❏
3. The same amount of pre-interview preparation should be made for an Internet and/or telephone interview as is made for a traditional face-to-face interview.	❏	❏
4. Employers expect a job candidate to ask valid questions during interviews.	❏	❏
5. When offered a job, it is acceptable to negotiate a salary for entry-level positions.	❏	❏

If you answered "true" to the majority of these questions, congratulations. You are already aware of successful interview techniques and are ready to successfully interview.

THE INTERVIEW

You've conducted a targeted job search, and created and distributed your résumé, and now it is time to interview. A successful interview involves more than dressing sharp. It includes advance preparation; confidence; and a strategy to be used before, during, and after this important meeting. During an interview, an employer is looking to hire the best person to represent his or her company. Your goal is to communicate visually and verbally that you are the right person for the job. A job search takes work, takes time, and can sometimes be frustrating. Do not get discouraged if you do not get an interview or job offer on your first try. The purpose of this chapter is to provide you the skills and confidence to secure a good job in a reasonable time period.

THE INVITATION TO INTERVIEW

There is a strategy to successful interviews, and it starts as soon as you receive an invitation to interview. Most interview invitations are extended by phone or electronic mail. Therefore, regularly check and respond to both phone and electronic messages. This is a good reminder to maintain a professional voice-mail message and e-mail address. When you are invited to interview, attempt to identify with whom you will be interviewing. You may be meeting with one person or a group of individuals. Your first interview may be a pre-screening interview where a human resource representative or some other representative from the company briefly meets with you to ensure you are qualified and the right fit for the job.

Ask how much time the company has scheduled for the interview. If possible, identify how many applicants are being called for interviews. Although this is a lot of information to secure, if you are friendly, respectful, and professional, most companies will share this information. Attempt to arrange your interview at a time that puts you at an advantage over the other candidates. The first and last interviews are the most memorable, so try to be the first or last interview. If you are given a choice of times to interview, schedule your interview in the morning. People are much more alert at that time, and you will have a greater advantage of making a favorable and memorable impression. If this is not possible, try to be the last person interviewed prior to the lunch break or the first person interviewed immediately after the lunch break. Be aware that sometimes you will have no say in when your interview is scheduled. Do not make demands when scheduling your interview. Politely ask the interview scheduler if it is possible for him or her to tell you who will be conducting the interview. Finally, note the name of the individual who is assisting you in arranging the interview. This will allow you to contact him or her should you need information and also allow you to personally thank him or her if you meet on the day of the interview. The goal is to secure as much information as possible prior to the interview so you are prepared.

COMPANY-SPECIFIC RESEARCH

Prior to your interview, conduct research on the company and the specific position for which you are applying. Many candidates ignore this step, thinking it is unnecessary or takes too much time. Planning better prepares you for your interview, increases your confidence, and provides you a greater advantage over other candidates. Learn as much as you can about the company's leadership team, strategy, and any current event that may have affected the company. Review the company web and social network sites if available, or conduct a general Internet search to read blogs and other posts related to the company. Note products the company produces, identify the company's key competitors, and note any recent community activities or recognized accomplishments the company has been involved with.

In addition to the Internet, other sources for securing company information include company-produced brochures/literature, industry journals, and interviews with current employees and business leaders. Job-specific information is easily gathered by conducting a quick search on the O*Net database using the position title as your key word. This database of occupational information which will be mentioned in the next chapter, provides key information by job title.

The pre-interview research will assist you during your job interview. Identify as much as you can about the company, its administrators, and the department of your target job. Not only will you have an advantage in the interview, but you will know if this company is the right fit for you and your career goals. Use the company-specific research information to tailor your résumé, cover letter, and interview responses. This provides you an advantage over others who do not research the company.

In your interview, mention specific information about the company. This shows you have conducted research. For example, a popular interview question is, "Why do you want to work for this company?" If you have conducted research, be specific in your answer and respond with information that reflects your research. For example, say, "Your company has been green-conscious in the last two years, which is an area I, too, believe is important," instead of saying, "I have heard it is a great company."

Cory's friend Tomasz was excited about an interview he would be having in a week. When Tomasz was sharing his excitement with Cory, Cory asked him if he had conducted research on the company. Tomasz said he really didn't need to conduct research because the company was pretty well known. Cory explained that it was important to conduct research beyond general knowledge to make sure Tomasz stood out from the other candidates. Cory and Tomasz conducted an extensive Internet search on the target company, and Tomasz discovered useful information that Tomasz was able to use throughout his interview. After a successful interview, Tomasz thanked Cory and told Cory that the research prior to his interview gave him a lot of confidence that ultimately helped him secure the job.

THE PERSONAL COMMERCIAL

personal commercial

A brief career biography that conveys one's career choice, knowledge, skills, strengths, abilities, and experiences.

Prepare a **personal commercial** that sells your skills and ties these skills to the specific job for which you are interviewing. A personal commercial is a brief career biography that conveys your career choice, knowledge, skills, strengths, abilities, and experiences that make you uniquely qualified for the position for which you are applying. Include your interest in the targeted position, and use this personal commercial at the beginning or end of an interview. The purpose of the commercial is to sell your skills in a brief statement.

Communicating Key Information

If you were alone in an elevator with the hiring manager of your target job, what key pieces of information would you communicate about yourself as you rode from the fifth floor to the first floor?

Your goal is to sell yourself and match your skills to fit the company needs by adapting them to the requirements for each target job. Your personal commercial is essentially your "sales pitch" that communicates your key and unique knowledge, skills, and abilities that make you the right choice for your target job.

Do not include marital status, hobbies, or other personal information in your personal commercial. Identify your personal qualifications for a target job. This information can be used to create a career objective for your résumé. Use this information in your personal commercial. When you write your personal commercial make it reflect your personality. Include your interest in your chosen career, activities related to the career, the skills you have acquired, and why you have enjoyed learning these skills. Your personal commercial should take no more than two minute to deliver. The following is an example of a personal commercial.

Use your personal commercial during your interview when asked, "Tell me about yourself." If you are not given this instruction during the interview, include your personal commercial at the end of the interview. Practice delivering your commercial in front of a mirror.

THE INTERVIEW PORTFOLIO

An **interview portfolio** is a small folder containing relevant documents that are taken to an interview. Use a professional looking business portfolio or paper folder with pockets

interview portfolio
A folder to be taken on an interview that contains photocopies of documents and items relevant to a position.

Personal Commercial Example

Since I can remember, I have been interested in math, numbers, and counting money. In junior high, I started myself on a budget and kept track of saving and spending. By high school I knew I wanted to become an accountant.

After finishing my classes at our local community college, I started working as an account clerk for a hospital. In addition to my regular duties, I was able to attend conferences and workshops where I expanded my knowledge and skills in different areas of accounting.

I am a recent college graduate from State University, where I received a bachelor's of science in accounting. With the additional education, I utilized these new skills and knowledge to work with general ledgers, accounts payable, and accounts receivable. I plan to apply my abilities and improve constantly.

With my experience as an Account Clerk, I have developed soft skills including how to deal with customers and coworkers in good and bad situations. In addition to the skills I have obtained working with MAS 90, I am proficient in MS Word and Excel. I have basic skills with Access, Outlook, and PowerPoint.

My goal is to become a CPA. Your company will benefit from my work ethic, which is to give 100 percent of my ability to all clients and provide them the confidence they need for someone handling their money. My values include integrity and innovation. I am organized, dedicated, responsible, punctual, and willing to learn. I believe I am the best candidate for this position. Since your company is committed to clients and the community, I would like to be a part of your team.

Starting a Personal Commercial

Identify key points to include in your personal commercial.

_____

_____

_____

_____

_____

_____

for your interview portfolio. Include copies of items pertinent to the position for which you are applying. Original documents (unless required) should not be given to the employer, only photocopies. Have the following items in your interview portfolio: copies of résumé, cover letter, reference list, generic application, and personal commercial. Also, include a calendar, note paper, a pen, and personal business cards. Print copies of your résumé, cover letter, and references on résumé paper. Copies of other items such as skill or education certificates and recent performance evaluations may be included if the information is relevant to the job. Keep your interview portfolio on your lap during the interview. Place your personal commercial on the top of your portfolio for easy access. Do not read the commercial. You may glance at it if you become nervous and forget what to say.

PRACTICE INTERVIEW QUESTIONS

Another activity when preparing for an interview is to practice interview questions. Table 3-1 identifies common interview questions, the purpose of each question, and an appropriate way to answer each question. Review this list and begin creating appropriate responses to each question. Whenever you are answering interview questions, be honest and provide examples of specific skills and experiences that support your answers and meet the key requirements of the target job. The more real-life examples you provide, the more you demonstrate your experience and skill level to the employer. Anyone can say, "I can handle stress on a busy day"; however, by providing a specific example of how you handled stress on a busy day, you have demonstrated how you realistically handle stress.

Practice answering interview questions in front of a mirror, and, if possible, create a practice interview video of yourself answering common interview questions. Critically analyze your responses to see if you are appropriately answering the questions, selling your key skills, and projecting a professional image. Also check for nervous gestures. Doing this will better prepare you for an interview and help increase your self-confidence.

Talk It Out

Identify the most difficult questions to answer, and formulate appropriate responses that sell your skills.

PRE-INTERVIEW PRACTICE

Prior to the day of your interview, visit the interview location, pre-plan your interview wardrobe, ensure your interview portfolio is up-to-date, and prepare post-interview thank-you notes.

Conduct a "practice day" prior to the day of your interview. If possible, drive or find transportation to the interview location. Ideally, do this on the same hour as your scheduled interview to identify potential transportation problems including traffic and parking. Once at the site, walk to the location where the interview will be held. This will enable

TABLE 3-1 Common Interview Questions

Question	Answer	Do Not
Tell me about yourself.	Use your personal commercial modified to the job description.	Do not divulge where you were born, hobbies, or other personal information.
What are your strengths?	Include how your strengths meet the job requirements and how they will be an asset to the company.	Do not include strengths that are not related to the job. Do not include personal information (e.g., "I'm a good mother").
Tell me about a time you failed.	Use an example that is not too damaging. Turn it into a positive by including the lesson learned from your mistake.	Do not exclude the lesson learned from the failure. Do not place blame for why the failure occurred.
Tell me about a time you were successful.	Use an example that relates to the job for which you are applying.	Do not take full credit if the success was a team effort.
How do you handle conflict?	Use an example that is not too damaging. Include how the conflict was positively resolved.	Do not provide specifics on how the conflict occurred, and do not use a negative example or place blame on others.
Would you rather work individually or in a team? Why?	State that you prefer one or the other and why, but relate your answer to the job requirements.	Do not state that you will not work one way or the other.
Why do you want this job?	Convey career goals and how the job supports your current skills. Include company information learned through research.	Do not state money or benefits in your response.
How do you deal with stress?	Share positive stress reducers.	Do not state that stress does not affect you. Do not use negative examples.
What is your greatest weakness?	Use a weakness that will not damage your chance of getting the job. Explain how you are minimizing your weakness or are turning it into a strength (e.g., "I'm a perfectionist, but I don't allow it to interfere with getting my job done on time").	Do not state, "I don't have any."
Where do you want to be in five years?	Share your career goals.	Do not say you want the interviewer's job.
Tell me about a time you displayed leadership.	Use a specific example, and try to relate the example to the needed job skills.	Do not appear arrogant.

you to become comfortable and familiar with your surroundings and let you know how much time you will need to arrive at the interview on time. Do not go into the specific office, just the general area. Make note of the nearest public restroom so you can use it the day of the interview to freshen up prior to your meeting.

Ensure that your interview attire is clean and professional prior to the day of the interview. Dress at a level above the position for which you are interviewing. For example, if you are interviewing for an entry-level position, dress like you are interviewing for a supervisor position. Check that your clothes are spotless and fit appropriately and your shoes are clean. Women, if relevant, it is a good idea to have an extra pair of nylons available in case of snags or tears. Ensure that your hair and fingernails are professional and appropriate for an interview. If necessary, get a haircut prior to your interview. Use little or no perfume/aftershave and keep jewelry to a minimum. Cleanliness is important.

Prior to the interview, customize your interview portfolio for the target job. Place your portfolio in a place where you will not forget it when you leave your home.

Purchase a package of simple but professional thank-you notes. The evening before your interview, write a draft thank-you note on a blank piece of paper. Keep your

Thank-You Note

Write a draft thank-you note.

thank-you note brief, only three to four sentences. In the note, thank the interviewer for his or her time. State that you enjoyed learning more about the position, are very interested in the job, and look forward to hearing from the interviewer soon. This draft note will be used as a foundation for notes you will be writing immediately after your interview. Place the draft note, the package of thank-you notes, and a black pen alongside your interview portfolio to take with you.

THE DAY OF THE INTERVIEW

Be well rested and have food in your stomach prior to leaving your home for the interview. Look in the mirror to check your appearance and clothing. Your clothes should fit properly and project a professional image. If you smoke, refrain from smoking prior to the interview. The smell may be a distraction to the interviewer.

Plan to arrive at your destination fifteen minutes early. This provides time to deal with unforeseen traffic and/or parking issues. If there is a public restroom available, go to the restroom and freshen up. Check your hair, clothing, and makeup, if applicable. Turn off your phone, and if you are chewing gum, throw it away. Enter the specific meeting location five minutes prior to your scheduled interview. This is where your interview unofficially begins. First impressions matter, and any interaction with representatives of the organization must be professional.

Immediately upon entering the interview location, introduce yourself to the receptionist. Offer a smile and a handshake, and then clearly and slowly state your name. For example, "Hi, I'm Cory Kringle, and I am here for a 9:00 a.m. interview with Ms. Dancey for the accounting clerk position." If you recognize the receptionist as the same individual who arranged your interview appointment, make an additional statement thanking the individual for his or her assistance. For example, "Mrs. Wong, were you the one that I spoke with on the phone? Thank you for your help in arranging my interview." Be sincere in your conversation, and convey to the receptionist that you appreciate his or her efforts. The receptionist will most likely ask you to have a seat and wait to be called into the interview. Take a seat and relax. While you are waiting, use **positive self-talk**. Positive self-talk is a mental form of positive self-reinforcement. It helps remind you that you are qualified and deserve both the interview and the job. Mentally tell yourself that you are prepared, qualified, and ready for a successful interview. Review your personal commercial, your qualifications, and the key skills you want to convey in the interview.

Cory's friend Shelby had been asked to interview with one of her target companies. Shelby really wanted the job but was afraid she was not going to do well during her interview. Cory worked with Shelby the evening before the interview by role-playing

positive self-talk

A mental form of positive self-reinforcement that helps remind you that you are qualified and deserve both the interview and the job.

interview questions and reviewing Shelby's company research. The next day, when Shelby arrived for the interview, she arrived early, thanked the receptionist, and took a seat. As Shelby waited to be called in to the interview, she began getting extremely nervous. Remembering Cory's tips, Shelby briefly closed her eyes and used positive self-talk to improve her attitude, increase her confidence, and calm her nerves. After doing this, she felt more confident when called into the office to begin the interview.

THE INTERVIEW

During an interview, communicate confidence. Your primary message during the interview will be how your knowledge, skills, and abilities will be assets to the company. When you are called to interview, stand up and approach the individual who called your name. If it is not the receptionist who called you, extend a smile and a handshake, then clearly and slowly state your name. For example, "Hi, I'm Cory Kringle. It's nice to meet you." Listen carefully to the interviewer's name so you will remember it and use it during the interview. He or she will escort you to an office or conference room where the interview will take place. If you enter a room and there is someone in the room that you have not met, smile, extend a handshake, and introduce yourself. Once in the room, do not be seated until you are invited to do so. When seated, if possible, write down the names of the individuals you have just met. Inject the interviewer's name(s) during the interview. Although you may be offered something to drink, it is best to decline the offer so there is nothing to distract you from the interview. If you are sitting in a chair that swivels, put your feet flat on the floor to remind yourself not to swivel. If you forgot to turn off your phone and it rings during the interview, do not answer the phone. Immediately, apologize to the employer and turn it off.

The interview may be conducted different ways. It may involve only one person, it may involve several individuals, it may involve testing, or it may be a combination of interviewing and testing. Testing activities must be job-related, such as typing tests for office work, lifting for a warehouse position, or demonstrating other skills that are included in the job requirements and/or job duties. If the interview is taking place in an office, look around the room to get a sense of the person who is conducting the interview, assuming it is his or her office. This provides useful information for conversation, should it be necessary. Depending on the time available and the skills of the interviewer(s), you may first be asked general questions, such as, "Did you have trouble finding our office?" The interviewer is trying to get you to relax. During the interview, pay attention to body language—both yours and that of the individual conducting the interview. Sit up straight, sit back in your chair, and try to relax. Be calm but alert. Keep your hands folded on your lap or ready to take notes, depending on the situation. If you are seated near a desk or table, do not lean on the furniture. Make eye contact, but do not stare at the interviewer.

If you are given the opportunity to provide an opening statement, share your personal commercial. If you are not able to open with your personal commercial, include it in an appropriate response or use it at the end of the interview. When asked a question, listen carefully. Take a few seconds to think and digest what information the interviewer truly wants to know about your skill sets. Formulate an answer. Interview answers should relate back to the job qualifications and/or job duties. Your goal is to convey to the interviewer how your skills will assist the company in achieving success. Keep your answers brief but complete. Sell your skills and expertise by including a specific but short example. Whenever possible, inject information you learned about the company during your research.

PHONE- AND OTHER TECHNOLOGY-BASED INTERVIEWS

In some situations, your first interview may take place over the phone. Phone interviews may occur without prearrangement, while others are scheduled. During your job search, consistently answer your phone(s) in a professional manner and keep your interview portfolio in an accessible place. If a company calls and asks if it is a good time to speak with you and it is not, politely respond that it is not a good time and ask if you can reschedule the call. Try to be as accommodating as possible to the interviewer.

Those being interviewed by phone should follow these tips:

- *Be professional and be prepared.* Conduct the interview in a quiet room. Remove all distractions, including music, pets, television, and other individuals from your quiet area. Company research, personal examples, and the use of your personal commercial are just as important to inject into the phone conversation as during a face-to-face interview. Just as in a face-to-face interview, take notes and ask questions.

- *Be concise with your communication.* Those conducting the interview are not able to see you; therefore, they are forming an impression of you by what you say and how it is stated. Speak clearly and slowly, and do not interrupt. Smile while you speak, and speak with enthusiasm. Use proper grammar and beware of "ums" and other nervous verbal phrases. If you stand while conducting your phone interview, you will keep alert, focused, and more aware of your responses.

- *Be polite.* Exercise good manners. Do not eat or chew gum during your interview. It is not appropriate to use a speaker phone when being interviewed, nor is it polite to take another call, or tend to personal matters. Your attention should be completely focused on the interview. When the conversation is over, ask for the job, and thank the interviewer for his or her time.

Due to a tight economy, it is becoming increasingly common for interviews to take place through video chat venues such as Skype, WebEx, and Google Talk. An individual participating in a video chat interview needs a computer, a web cam, and a reliable Internet connection. When taking part in a video chat interview, the participant will receive a designated time and specific instructions on where and how to establish the connection. In addition to following the phone interview tips, the interviewer needs to prepare and treat the video chat interview as if it were a face-to-face interview. Therefore,

- *Plan ahead.* Research the venue you will be using to address any unforeseen issues. Identify where you will conduct the interview and what technology is required. If possible, arrange a pre-interview trial to ensure all equipment works properly and you know how to use it (including your volume and microphone).

- *Dress professionally.* You will be in plain view of the interviewer, so visual impressions matter.

- *Maintain a professional environment.* Conduct your interview in a quiet and appropriate location. A bedroom, public place, or outside location is not appropriate.

- *Speak to the camera.* Focus on the web cam as if it were the interviewer's face. Feel free to ask questions, take notes, and use hand gestures. While it may be more difficult to communicate, make every effort to not only project your personality, but, more importantly, sell your knowledge, skills, abilities, and unique qualifications. As with a traditional face-to-face interview, your job is to connect with the interviewer.

INTERVIEW METHODS AND TYPES OF INTERVIEW QUESTIONS

one-on-one interview

An interview that involves a one-on-one meeting between the applicant and a company representative.

There are several common types of interviews. These include one-on-one interviews, group interviews, and panel interviews. **One-on-one interviews** involve a one-on-one meeting between the applicant and a company representative. The company representative is typically either someone from the human resource department or the immediate supervisor of the department with the open position. **Group interviews** involve several applicants interviewing with each other while being observed by company representatives. The purpose of a group interview is to gauge how an individual behaves in a competitive and stressful environment. In a group interview situation, practice positive human relation and communication skills toward other applicants. Listening and communicating that you are the best candidate is critical to a successful group interview. If another applicant is first asked a question and you are immediately asked the same question, do not repeat what the other applicant said. If you agree with the first applicant's response, state, "I agree with Ms. Bell's response and would like to add that it's also important to…," and then elaborate or expand on the first applicant's response. If you do not agree with the first applicant's response, state, "I believe…," and then confidently provide your response. Do not demean other applicants. Be professional, do not interrupt, and behave like a leader. Be assertive, not aggressive.

Panel interviews involve the applicant meeting with several company employees at the same time. During a panel interview, make initial eye contact with the person asking the question. While answering the question, make eye contact with the other members of the interview panel. Whenever possible, call individuals by name.

The three general types of interview questions are structured, unstructured, and behavioral. **Structured interview questions** address job-related issues where each applicant is asked the same question(s). An example of a structured question is, "How long have you worked in the retail industry?" The purpose of a structured interview question is to secure information related to a specific job. An **unstructured interview question** is a probing, open-ended question. The purpose of an unstructured interview question is to identify if the candidate can appropriately sell his or her skills. An example of an unstructured interview question is, "Tell me about yourself." When you are asked to talk about yourself, state your personal commercial. This is where you begin using the interview portfolio. Whenever possible, pull job samples from your interview portfolio if you are referring to a specific skill. Relate answers back to the job for which you are applying. **Behavioral interview questions** are questions that ask candidates to share a past experience related to a workplace situation. An example of a behavioral question is: "Describe a time you motivated others." Prior to answering the question, take a moment to formulate your answer. Use an example that puts you in a positive light and utilizes key skills that are necessary for your target job.

DISCRIMINATION AND EMPLOYEE RIGHTS

Title VII of the Civil Rights Act was created to protect the rights of employees. It prohibits employment discrimination based on race, color, religion, sex, or national origin. Other federal laws prohibit pay inequity and discrimination against individuals forty years or older, individuals with disabilities, and individuals who are pregnant. This does not mean that an employer must hire you if you are a minority, pregnant, forty or older, or have a disability. Employers have a legal obligation to provide every qualified candidate equal opportunity to interview. Their job is to hire the most qualified candidate. Unfortunately, some employers ask interview questions that can be discriminatory. Discriminatory questions are illegal. Table 3-2 was taken from the California Department of Fair Employment and Housing to provide examples of acceptable and unacceptable employment inquiries.

If an interviewer asks you a question that is illegal or could be discriminatory, do not directly answer the question; instead, address the issue. For example, if the interviewer states, "You look Hispanic—are you?" Your response should not be "Yes" or "No." Politely smile and say, "People wonder about my ethnicity. What can I tell you about my qualifications for this job?" Also, do not accuse the interviewer of asking an illegal question or say, "I will not answer that question because it is illegal." Most employers do not realize they are asking illegal questions. However, some employers purposely ask inappropriate questions. In this case, you need to decide if you want to work for an employer who intentionally asks illegal questions. If employers are behaving inappropriately during an interview, one would wonder how they will treat the applicant after he or she is hired.

group interview

An interview that involves several applicants interviewing with each other while being observed by company representatives.

panel interview

An interview that involves the applicant meeting with several company employees at the same time.

structured interview question

A type of interview question that addresses job-related issues where each applicant is asked the same question.

unstructured interview question

A probing, open-ended interview question intended to identify if the candidate can appropriately sell his or her skills.

behavioral interview question

Interview question that asks candidates to share a past experience related to a specific workplace situation.

Talk It Out

Role-play an interview. During the interview, ask one legal question and one illegal question. Practice answering the illegal question with confidence but in a non-offensive manner.

TABLE 3-2 Illegal Interview Questions

Acceptable	Subject	Unacceptable
Name	**Name**	Maiden name
Place of residence	**Residence**	Questions regarding owning or renting
Statements that employment is subject to verification if applicant meets legal age requirement	**Age**	Age Birth date Date of attendance/completion of school Questions that tend to identify applicants over forty
Statements/inquiries regarding verification of legal right to work in the United States	**Birthplace, citizenship**	Birthplace of applicant or applicant's parents, spouse, or other relatives Requirements that applicant produce naturalization or alien card prior to employment
Languages applicant reads, speaks, or writes if use of language other than English is relevant to the job for which applicant is applying	**National origin**	Questions as to nationality, lineage, ancestry, national origin, descent or parentage of applicant, applicant's spouse, parent, or relative
Statement by employer of regular days, hours, or shifts to be worked	**Religion**	Questions regarding applicant's religion Religious days observed
Name and address of parent or guardian if applicant is a minor. Statement of company policy regarding work assignment of employees who are related	**Sex, marital status, family**	Questions to indicate applicant's sex, marital status, number/ages of children or dependents Questions regarding pregnancy, child birth, or birth control Name/address of relative, spouse, or children of adult applicant
Job-related questions about convictions, except those convictions that have been sealed, expunged, or statutorily eradicated	**Arrest, criminal record**	General questions regarding arrest record

Know and protect your rights. It is inappropriate to disclose personal information about yourself during an interview. Avoid making any comment referring to your marital status, children, religion, age, or any other private issue protected by law.

TOUGH QUESTIONS

Life is unpredictable and sometimes results in situations that can be embarrassing or difficult to explain during a job interview. These situations may include a negative work experience with a previous employer, time gaps in a résumé, or a prior felony conviction. The following information provides the proper response to interview questions related to these difficult situations.

Some job seekers have had negative work-related experiences that they do not want to disclose during an interview. Disclosing such information could be potentially devastating to a job interview if it is not handled properly. Some of these experiences include being fired, having a poor performance evaluation, or knowing that a former manager or teacher will not provide a positive reference if called. Perhaps you behaved in a negative manner prior to leaving your old job.

If you did have a difficult circumstance and are not asked about the situation, you have no need to disclose the unpleasant event. The only exception to this rule is if your current or former boss has the potential to provide a negative reference. If this is the situation, tell the interviewer that you know you will not receive a positive reference from him or her and request that the interviewer contact another manager or coworker who will provide a fair assessment of your performance.

Being honest and factual is the best answer to any difficult question. If you were fired, performed poorly, or left in a negative manner, state the facts, but do not go into great detail. Tell the interviewer that you have matured and realize that you did not handle the situation appropriately. Add what lesson you have learned. Do not speak poorly of your current or previous employer, boss, or coworker. It is also important to not place blame by stating who was right or wrong in your negative workplace situation.

It is common for an individual to have time gaps in a résumé as a result of staying at home to raise a young child, care for an elderly relative, or continue his or her education. Those who have gaps in their résumé may need to be prepared to explain what they did during the time gap. Identify a key skill you sharpened during your time gap and relate this experience to a key skill necessary for your target job and industry. For example, if you stayed at home to care for an elderly relative and are asked about the time gap, explain the situation without providing specific details, and then share how the experience improved your time management and organizational skills in addition to improving your awareness of diverse populations including the elderly and disabled.

If you have a felony record, you may be asked about your conviction. As with other difficult interview questions, be honest and factual in your response. Explain the situation, and tell the interviewer that you are making every attempt to start anew and are committed to doing your very best. Sell your strengths, and remember to communicate how your skills will help the company achieve its goals. Your self-confidence and honesty will be revealed through your body language and eye contact. Be sincere. Depending on the type and severity of your offense, it may take more attempts to secure a job than during a typical job search. You may also need to start at a lower level and/or lower pay than desired. The goal is to begin to reestablish credibility. Do not give up. Each experience, be it positive or negative, is a learning experience.

CLOSING THE INTERVIEW

After the interviewer has completed his or her questioning, you may be asked if you have any questions. Having a question or closing statement prepared for use at the close of your interview demonstrates to your prospective employer that you have conducted research on the company. A good question refers to a current event that has occurred within the company. For example, "Ms. Dancey, I read about how your company employees donated time to clean up the ABC school yard. Is this an annual event?" A statement such as this provides you one last opportunity to personalize the interview and demonstrate that you researched the company. This is also a good time to share any relevant information you have in your portfolio.

Do not ask questions that imply you did not research the company or that you care only about your needs. Inappropriate questions include questions regarding salary, benefits, or vacations. These questions imply that you care more about what the company can do for you than what you can do for the company. However, it is appropriate to ask what the next steps will be in the interview process, including when a hiring decision will be made.

Questions You *May* Ask the Interviewer

1. Does your company have any plans for expansion?
2. What type of formal training does your company offer?
3. What is the greatest challenge your industry is currently facing?
4. What is the next step in the interview process?
5. What are the required work days and hours of the position?
6. When will you be making a hiring decision?

Questions You *Should Not* Ask During an Interview

1. How much does this job pay?
2. How many sick days do I get?
3. What benefits will I get?
4. What does your company do?
5. How long does it take for someone to get fired for poor performance?

After the interviewer answers your general questions, make a closing interview statement. Restate your personal commercial and ask for the job. An example of a good closing statement is to restate your personal commercial and add: "Once again, thank you for your time, Ms. Dancey. As I stated at the beginning of our meeting, I feel I am qualified for this job based upon my experience, knowledge, and demonstrated leadership. I would like this job and believe I will be an asset to XYZ Company." The purpose of the job interview is to sell you and your skills. A sale is useless if you do not close the sale.

After you make your closing statement, the interviewer will signal that the interview is over. He or she will do this either through conversation or through body language, such as standing up and walking toward the door. Prior to leaving the interview, hand the interviewer your personal business card and ask the interviewer for a business card. You will use this business card for the interview follow-up. As you are handed the card, shake the interviewer's hand using a firm shake and eye contact, and thank him or her for his or her time and state that you look forward to hearing from him or her. Remember to continue communicating confidence, friendliness, and professionalism to every company employee you encounter on your way out of the building.

When you leave the building, retrieve your draft thank-you note. Modify your draft thank-you note to include information that was shared during your interview. Handwrite a personalized thank-you note to each individual who interviewed you. Use your finest handwriting and double-check your spelling and grammar. Refer to the business card(s) you collected for correct name spelling. After you have written your note, hand deliver it to the reception area and ask the receptionist to deliver the notes. Your goal is to make a positive last impression and stand out from the other candidates.

AFTER THE INTERVIEW

After delivering your thank-you notes, congratulate yourself. If you did your best, you should have no regrets. Prior to leaving the company property, make notes regarding specific information you learned about your prospective job and questions you were asked during the interview. Through the excitement of an interview, you may forget parts of your meeting if you do not immediately write notes. Write down what you did right and areas in which you would like to improve. This is a good time for you to evaluate your impressions of the company and determine if it is a company where you will want to work. This information will be helpful in the future.

SALARY NEGOTIATION

Soon after your initial interview, you should hear back from the company. At that point, you may be called in for a second interview or may receive a job offer. A job offer may be contingent upon reference and background checks. This will be a good time to contact the individuals on your reference list to provide them an update on your job search and ensure your references are prepared to respond appropriately to the individual conducting your reference check.

If you are a final candidate for the job, the interviewer may ask you about your salary requirements. In order to negotiate an acceptable salary, first conduct research and compare your research to the salary range that was included in the job announcement. Check job postings and conduct online research to determine local and regional salaries. When conducting your salary research, attempt to match the job description as closely as possible to that of the job for which you are applying. Depending on your experience, start a few thousand dollars higher than your desired starting salary and do not forget to consider your experience and/or lack of experience. Some companies do not offer many benefits but offer higher salaries. Other companies offer lower salaries but better benefits. Weigh these factors when determining your desired salary. Prior to stating your salary requirement, sell your skills. For example, "Ms. Dancey, as I mentioned in my initial interview, I have over five years' experience working in a professional accounting office and an accounting degree; therefore, I feel I should earn between $55,000 and $65,000." If you are offered a salary that is not acceptable, use silence and wait for the interviewer to respond. This minute of silence may encourage the employer to offer a higher salary.

Cory's friend Kenny was invited to a second interview. Prior to the interview, Cory and Kenny prepared for potential questions and situations Kenny might encounter during the interview. In their practice, Cory asked Kenny about his starting salary. Kenny said he did not care; he would just be happy to get a job. Cory reminded Kenny that he needed to sell his skills and go into the interview with a desired target salary. Cory and Kenny then conducted an Internet search of both local and statewide jobs that were similar to the one Kenny wants. Kenny was surprised that starting salaries were much higher than he expected. Fortunately, the next day, when the interviewer asked Kenny about his desired starting salary, Kenny was prepared to answer.

PRE-EMPLOYMENT TESTS, SCREENINGS AND MEDICAL EXAMS

Pre-employment tests are assessments that are given to potential employees as a means of determining if the applicant possesses the desired knowledge, skills, or abilities required for the job. Pre-employment tests can be giving during the application process, during the interview process, or prior to receiving a job offer. Some employers require applicants to take online pre-employment tests. Some tests may require lifting, others are skills-based, while others measure listening or logic. Legally, pre-employment tests must be job-related. Depending on the type of test, you may be given the results immediately. In other cases, you may need to wait for the results. If you pass the employment test(s), you will be invited to proceed with the interview process. It is common for employers to have applicants who did not pass a pre-employment test to wait a predetermined period prior to reapplying.

Employers may also conduct pre-employment screenings and medical exams. The most common pre-employment screenings include criminal checks, education verification, driver's license history, security checks, employment checks, credit checks, and reference checks. The number and type of pre-employment screenings performed will be based upon how relevant the check is to the job you will be performing. Legally, employers can require medical exams only after a job offer is made. The exam must be required for all applicants for the same job, and the exam must be job-related. Employers are not allowed to ask disability questions related to pre-employment screenings and medical exams. Common medical exams include vision and strength testing. Employers may also require pre-employment drug tests.

An employer legally cannot conduct these checks without your permission. Most employers will secure your permission in writing when you complete an employment application or when you are a finalist for the position.

WHEN YOU ARE NOT OFFERED THE JOB

A job search is similar to a full-time job. It takes time and can sometimes be discouraging. If you are not called in for an interview or fail to receive a job offer, do not be discouraged.

When you are not invited to interview, evaluate your résumé and cover letter. Check for typographical or grammatical errors. Make sure you have listed important skills that reflect the needs of your target job. Have someone who knows you and your skills—and whom you trust—review your cover letter and résumé. Many times, a fresh perspective will catch obvious errors or opportunities for improvement.

If you are invited to interview but do not receive a job offer, do not be discouraged. Remember to make every experience a learning experience. Sit down and carefully review each step in the interview process and grade yourself. Consider your pre-interview preparation, your interview-day appearance, your interview answers, your ability to interject company research into each interview answer, and your overall attitude. Any area that did not receive an "A" grade is an area poised for improvement.

There are several steps you can take to increase the probability for success in your next interview. Consider your overall appearance. Make sure you convey professionalism. Ensure that your clothes are clean and fit properly. Have a hairstyle that is flattering and well kempt. Check that your fingernails and jewelry are appropriate and do not distract from your personality and job skills.

WORKPLACE DOS AND DON'TS

Do tailor your résumé and personal commercial to the needs of your targeted employer	*Don't* have unprofessional introductions on your voice-mail message
Do try to schedule your interview at a time that puts you at an advantage over the other candidates and secure information that better prepares you for the interview	*Don't* make demands with the individual scheduling the interview
Do learn as much as you can about the company, its strategy, and its competition	*Don't* forget to include your research information in your interview answers
Do practice interview questions and formulate answers that highlight your skills and experience	*Don't* show up to an interview unprepared
Do remember that your interview begins the minute you step onto company property	*Don't* let your nerves get the better of you in a job interview
Do know how to handle inappropriate questions that may be discriminatory	*Don't* answer an illegal question. Instead address the issue

Mentally review job interview questions that were asked and the responses you provided. Every answer should communicate how your skills will assist the target company in achieving success. Review the amount of company research you conducted. Did you feel amply prepared, or did you simply research the bare minimum? If you felt you did conduct the appropriate amount of research, evaluate whether you fully communicated your research to the interviewer.

Assess your body language and attitude. Stand in front of a mirror and practice your answers to difficult and/or illegal questions. If possible, have a friend videotape you and provide an honest evaluation of your appearance, attitude, and body language. Check for nervous gestures, and keep practicing until you are able to control these nervous habits.

Finally, be honest about your overall performance. Did you ask for the job? Did you immediately send a thank-you note to your interviewer(s)? Sell your skills through your mannerisms, answers, and attitude. Your goal is to stand out above the other candidates.

HOW-DO-YOU-RATE

How proper are you?	True	False
1. You do not have to shake someone's hand if you already know the person.	❑	❑
2. Visible tattoos, nose rings, or lip rings, if tasteful, are now acceptable in a professional business situation.	❑	❑
3. If you are invited to a business meal, you may order anything on the menu.	❑	❑
4. Sending a handwritten thank-you note is no longer necessary.	❑	❑
5. It is now acceptable business practice to read a text message during business meetings.	❑	❑

If you answered "true" to two or more of these questions, it is time to begin actively practicing business etiquette. While business protocol may vary in some industries, it is best to lean toward a conservative, traditional approach until you are confident of acceptable industry standards.

EXECUTIVE PRESENCE

Employees represent their company. Therefore, the way you communicate, dress, and behave, both inside and outside the company, contributes to others' perception of you and your company. Consistently demonstrating proper etiquette and protocol in business, dining, and social situations results in positive business relationships. The way you look and behave is a reflection of the organization for which you work. **Executive presence** is defined as having the attitude of an executive. Projecting an executive presence demonstrates to employers that they have hired a new employee with knowledge regarding appropriate workplace behavior.

executive presence
Having the attitude of an executive.

Many of our parents taught us early in life that good manners, such as smiling and saying please and thank you in social situations, create positive relationships. Those successful at work understand the basics regarding expected professional behavior on topics including attire, business protocol, social etiquette, dining, and the appropriate use of technology. You will encounter many social situations at work. Knowing how to behave in professional social situations will help you be more successful in workplace relationships. Some of this information may be new to you, and you may feel awkward when you first implement these positive behaviors.

Define Your "Frame"

What does your frame look like? Be honest.

Is it trendy, outdated, professional, or inconsistent?

_____

Does it complement your desired appearance as a professional?

_____

If your current frame is not yet professional, what changes need to occur?

_____

_____

INFLUENCES OF DRESS IN A PROFESSIONAL ENVIRONMENT

appearance

How you look.

Both your maturity and the importance you place on your job are reflected in the way you behave and dress at work. Because impressions are often made in the first few minutes of meeting someone, individuals rarely have time to even speak before an impression is formed. The majority of first impressions are made through visual **appearance**, which is how you look. Coworkers, bosses, and customers form attitudes based on appearance. Appearance also has an impact on how you perform at work. If you dress professionally, you are more apt to act in a professional manner. The more casually you dress, the more casually you tend to behave. Think of your appearance as a frame. A frame is used to highlight a picture. You do not want the frame to be too fancy, because it will take away from the picture. You want a frame to complement the picture. The frame highlights not only your physical features, including your face, but also your attitude, knowledge, and potential.

One of the toughest transitions to make when entering the workplace is choosing appropriate dress. Dressing professionally does not have to conflict with current fashion trends. The trick is to know what is acceptable. A basic rule of thumb is to dress one position higher than your current position (i.e., dress like your boss). Doing so communicates that you are serious about your career and how you represent the company. Dressing professionally will assist you in projecting a favorable image at work and position you for job advancement.

dress code

An organization's policy regarding appropriate workplace attire.

Know your workplace dress policies, and understand that professional dress carries different meaning depending on both the industry and work environment. One of the first steps to determining appropriate attire for work is to identify your company's **dress code**. A dress code is a policy that addresses issues such as required attire, uniforms, hairstyle, undergarments, jewelry, and shoes. Dress codes vary by company depending on the industry, the specific work area, and health/safety issues. If your company has a mandatory uniform, the company dress code will be detailed. If a uniform is not required, identify what is and is not acceptable attire by reading the dress code policy, by observing what is practiced in the workplace, or by asking your supervisor. Some dress codes are vague, while others are specific. Work attire should pose no safety hazards. Unstable footwear that does not provide protection are not appropriate. Dangling jewelry that could be caught in equipment is also inappropriate for work. As previously stated, organizational dress policies exist for customer service, safety, and security reasons. Frequently, these policies are included in the employee handbook. If there is no policy, ask your boss if there is a formal dress code and secure a copy. An important cue to workplace attire is to observe how managers dress. Suits are not always the preferred attire in an office environment. In some situations, pants are acceptable for women, while in other situations they are not. Note that sweats (shirts and/or pants) are not appropriate for the traditional workplace.

Once you have identified what your organization considers proper attire, begin to create a **work wardrobe**. These are clothes that you primarily wear only to work and work-related functions. You need not invest a lot of money when building a work wardrobe. Start with basic pieces and think conservative. For women working in a traditional office environment, this attire includes a simple, solid skirt or pantsuit in a dark color and a blazer. Skirt length should not be above the knee. Pants should be worn with a matching blazer. For most office environments, men should select dark slacks, a matching jacket, and a tie. If you are just starting your job and cannot afford new clothing, these items can sometimes be found inexpensively at thrift and discount stores. If these items are purchased at a thrift store, inspect them for tears or stains and take them to the dry cleaner for cleaning and pressing. You will be surprised how professional these items look after they are cleaned and pressed. Select items that are made of quality fabrics that will not wear out quickly, fit properly, and are comfortable. As you begin to earn money, continue building your wardrobe and develop a style that conforms to both company policy and your taste.

work wardrobe

Clothes that are primarily worn only to work and work-related functions.

Talk It Out

Name local places where you can buy professional attire at a low cost.

CASUAL WORKDAYS AND SPECIAL EVENTS

Many companies allow **casual workdays**. These are days when companies relax their dress code. Unfortunately, some employees attempt to stretch the term casual. If your company has a casual workday, remember that you are still at work and should dress appropriately. Of course, you can wear jeans if jeans are the preferred attire; just adhere to the head-to-toe tips presented later in this chapter. Do not wear clothing that is tattered, stained, or torn (even if it is considered stylish). Avoid wearing shirts with sayings or graphics that may offend others. In general, it is best to dress modestly.

As you learn more about professional dress and expectations regarding professional attire, consider cultural and geographic differences and expectations. Globally, differing cultural expectations apply to workplace dress. In some countries, women must be completely covered from head to toe, while in other countries, women should not wear pants. "Business casual" for men on the East Coast of the United States may require a suit jacket, while "business casual" on the West Coast of the United States may allow for wearing khaki pants and a polo shirt. When conducting business in a geographic area different than yours (whether in your own country or abroad), research appropriate attire prior to your visit.

Your company may also host or invite you to attend a special function. Holiday parties and receptions are examples. In these situations, instead of daily work attire, more formal attire may be required. Just as with casual workdays, stick with the basics provided in the head-to-toe tips. Women, if appropriate, should wear something in a more formal fabric. Although you have increased freedom and flexibility regarding style and length, this is still a work-related function, so dress conservatively and not suggestively. Men, check ahead of time and see if tuxedos are preferred. For most semiformal occasions, a suit will suffice.

As a reward for being selected Employee of the Month, Cory was invited to attend a one-day conference luncheon with several managers from the company. Cory had not attended a function like this before and was a little nervous about how to dress and behave in this new business situation. Cory did some preparation and found that dress and behavior are as important in public situations as they are at work. Cory checked with others who had attended these functions and decided that dressing in formal business attire would be most appropriate. Cory made sure to shower, clean and trim fingernails, wear polished shoes, and not wear inappropriate jewelry. When entering the conference, Cory was glad to have conducted research, as nearly everyone was dressed in formal business attire.

casual workdays

Workdays when companies relax the dress code policy.

Talk It Out

Identify people in class who are wearing something appropriate for a casual workday.

TIPS FROM HEAD TO TOE

Regardless of the company's dress code, practice these basic hygiene rules:

- *Shower daily.* If needed, use deodorant. Use perfume, lotion, or cologne sparingly. Scent should not be overpowering.
- *Clothes should be clean and ironed, not torn or tattered, and should fit properly.*
- *Hair should be clean, well kempt, and a natural color.* Your hairstyle should reflect your profession. Fad hairstyles and unnatural color are inappropriate in many workplaces.
- *Practice good dental hygiene.* Brushing and flossing your teeth both in the morning and at bedtime, if not more often, not only ensures clean teeth and fresh breath, it also helps prevent tooth decay. Many public health clinics provide no-cost or low-cost dental care.
- *Hands and nails should be clean, well groomed, and trimmed.* Unnaturally long nails are inappropriate. Polish or artwork if allowed, should be neat and kept conservative.
- *Jewelry should be kept to a minimum.* Jewelry should complement your outfit. Do not wear anything that is distracting or makes noise.
- *Shoes should be in good condition.* Keep shoes polished and free of scuffs. Flip-flops are not appropriate for the workplace. Men's sock color should match shoe or pant color. Women, keep heels in good condition; repair or replace them as needed. Heels should not be too high. Nylons should be free of runs and snags.

A woman's outfit should reflect her style and personality—within reason. When dressing for work, your goal is to appropriately frame yourself in a manner that draws attention to your professional qualities (i.e., your brains and inner beauty). Additional tips for women include the following:

- *Makeup should be for day wear.* Makeup is appropriate for work. Makeup that makes people think you are going to a bar after work is not. Do not wear heavy eyeliner, eyeshadow in colors that draw attention, or lipstick in bold colors.
- *It is not acceptable to wear suggestive clothing.* Visible cleavage or bare midriffs are inappropriate for work. No matter the current fashion trends, undergarments (bras and panties) should not be visible. Skirts worn at work should be no shorter than knee length.

Just like a woman's outfit, a man's outfit should reflect his style and personality. For some positions, a suit may not be appropriate. The biggest wardrobe blunder men make is wearing clothing that is not clean and/or pressed. After checking your company's dress code, heed these unspoken rules regarding professional dress at work for men:

- *Shave and/or trim facial hair, including nose and ear hair.*
- *In an office environment, dress pants are the only pants that are professional.* With the exception of casual workdays, jeans are inappropriate. Baggy pants that reveal underwear are also inappropriate. Whenever possible, wear a neutral, plain belt that does not draw attention.
- *Shirts should be tucked in.* A polo shirt or a dress shirt with a tie is best. Shirts should not display excessive wear (check around the collar line for fraying or stains). Shirts with offensive logos or offensive phrases are inappropriate at work.
- *Hats should not be worn inside buildings except for religious purposes.*

JEWELRY, BODY PIERCING, AND TATTOOS

As with professional attire, you do not want to wear or display anything that brings unwanted attention to you in the workplace. While body art and piercings are becoming more common and acceptable in society, many companies have policies that prohibit visible

Talk It Out

When or when not is it appropriate for a woman to be sleeveless in a professional setting?

tattoos and/or visible body piercings beyond one in each ear. Body art and piercings are offensive to some individuals. Many people get a tattoo and/or body piercing to signify a special event, individual, or symbol. If you are considering getting a tattoo or body piercing, consider the long-term consequences of doing so. Relationships and situations change. Tattoos and some piercings are difficult and painful, if not impossible, to remove. While you may currently not care how society feels about your tattoo and/or piercing, you may regret your decision in the future. If you already have body art and/or piercing, it is recommended that you cover your tattoo with clothing, makeup, or other means until you are clear on your employer's policy regarding visible body art. Many companies also have strict policies on body piercings beyond earrings. Some piercings close quickly, so it may be impossible to remove the piercing during work hours. Other forms of piercings, such as microdermal piercings, cannot be easily removed. In these cases, determine which is more important—a job, or your body art and/or piercing. In general, follow these guidelines regarding jewelry, piercings, and tattoos:

- Nose rings, lip rings, and/or tongue rings are not professional and should not be worn in a professional setting. Any other body piercing/body jewelry should not be visible at work.
- More than two earrings worn on each ear is considered unprofessional.
- Earrings, chains, and other jewelry should not draw attention. This includes symbols or words that could be considered offensive to others.
- Body art (tattoos) should not be visible at work.

BUSINESS ETIQUETTE

In a modern workplace, human interaction is unavoidable. Our society has a standard of social behavior that is called **etiquette**. Typically, when individuals think of etiquette, they think it applies only to high society. This is not true. Socially acceptable behavior should penetrate all demographic and economic groups. Individuals wanting to succeed in the workplace need to heed this protocol and consistently utilize proper etiquette not only at work, but in all areas of their life.

etiquette
A standard of social behavior.

Before we study common areas of business etiquette, we need to define a few terms. Understanding these terms and integrating them into your daily routine will make it much easier to carry out the desired and appropriate workplace behavior. The first word is **courtesy**. When you display courtesy, you are exercising manners, respect, and consideration toward others. The second word is **respect**. Respect is defined as holding someone in high regard. This means putting others' needs before your own needs. Displaying both courtesy and respect toward others are the keys in becoming ladies and gentlemen at work.

courtesy
Exercising manners, respect, and consideration toward others.

respect
Holding someone in high regard.

Some of the first words most parents teach young children are *please* and *thank you*. Although they are not used as frequently as they should be, both are extremely valuable terms that can actually create power for you at work. Think about it; when someone says "please" and "thank you" to you, you are more likely to repeat a favor or gesture because your deed was acknowledged. When someone does something nice, verbally say "thank you." Not doing so makes you appear selfish and unappreciative. When you express thanks, individuals will be more likely to continue performing kind acts for you.

Talk It Out

Discuss ways you can be courteous and respectful in class.

Make it a habit to write a thank-you note when someone does something for you that takes more than five minutes or when someone gives you a gift. Write the note as soon as possible. Do not wait more than three days to write the thank-you note.

HANDSHAKES

A good handshake conveys confidence. Make a habit of greeting others in business situations with a professional handshake and friendly verbal greeting. Approach the individual you are greeting, make eye contact, smile, and extend your right hand as you verbalize a greeting. For example, "Hello Ms. Cao, my name is Talia. We met at last week's meeting. It's nice to see you again." Ms. Cao will extend her right hand. Your two hands should meet at the web (see Figure 3-3). Grip the other person's hand and gently squeeze and shake hands.

FIGURE 3-3 Proper Handshake

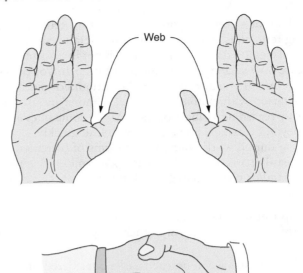

Web

SKILL-BUILDING EXERCISE 3-7

Shake Hands

With another person practice initiating an introduction, making sure to include a professional handshake. Rate the quality of the introduction and handshake on a scale of 1 to 5, with 5 being the best. Discuss what improvements should be made.

- Do not squeeze the other hand too firmly.
- Shake the entire hand and not just the other person's fingers. Doing so is insulting and implies that you feel you are better than the other person.
- Do not place your hand on top of the other person's hand or pat the hand. Doing so is insulting.
- If your palms are sweaty, discretely wipe your palm on the side of your hip prior to shaking.

A good handshake takes practice. As mentioned earlier, get into the habit of being the first to greet and introduce yourself to others. At first you may not feel comfortable, but practice makes perfect. The more frequently you initiate a good handshake, the more comfortable and confident you will become.

INTRODUCTIONS AND BUSINESS NETWORKING

An element of success in the workplace involves meeting new people. This process of meeting and developing relationships with individuals outside of one's immediate work area is referred to as **networking**. Networking is also commonly used in the job search process. In the workplace, creating a professional network is a useful tool for collaboration. In a business situation when you do not know someone in the room, increase your confidence by being the first to initiate a conversation. After you have introduced yourself, ask your new acquaintance about himself or herself. Learn about his or her job and find something you have in common. Keep the initial conversation focused on him

networking

Meeting and developing relationships with individuals outside one's immediate work area; the act of creating professional relationships.

or her. Your goal is to meet new people and create a positive impression so that if you see them again or contact them in the future, they will remember and have a favorable impression of you.

At times, you will be with individuals who do not know each other. When you are with two people who do not know each other and you know both people, it is your responsibility to introduce the two individuals to each other. Politely introduce the lower-ranking person to the higher-ranking person. For example, "Matt, this is Ryan McClaine, the president of our company." "Ryan, this is Matt Yu, my next-door neighbor." Apply this introduction rule to all social situations, including dining, meetings, receptions, and parties. Making introductions to others is an excellent form of networking. After you have introduced the two individuals, if possible, provide a piece of information about one of the individuals that creates a foundation for a conversation. For example, "Ryan, you and Matt attended the same college."

APPOINTMENTS

A daily function of business is making and keeping appointments. Appointments can occur in many forms, such as face-to-face meetings, over the phone, or through current technologies (e-mail, texting, or video chat). When setting meeting times, check regional time differences and clearly include the regional time zone abbreviation in your confirmation if you are located in different time zones. For example, "I look forward to meeting with you on Tuesday, April 21st, at 9 a.m. Pacific Standard Time (PST)."

Sometimes you will be required to work with receptionists and/or administrative assistants to schedule appointments. Be kind to the receptionist and/or administrative assistant. These individuals are the gatekeepers to their bosses; they control schedules and often wield great power in decisions. When scheduling an appointment, state your name, the purpose, and the desired date and time of the meeting. If possible, avoid scheduling appointments on Monday mornings; many people use Monday mornings to schedule their own week and are less likely to accommodate you. If you will be arriving late to an appointment, call and let the other party know you are running late. If you must cancel an appointment, do so immediately and apologize for any inconvenience. Do not just ignore an appointment.

If your meeting is to take place on the telephone, ensure you are holding the call in a quiet place where you will not have distracting background noise. Use a reliable phone connection. If your meeting requires Internet technologies, use a reliable connection and log in at least ten minutes early to ensure a proper connection. If your meeting involves video chat with a web camera, dress professionally and hold your meeting in a professional location. In general, an office or study is most appropriate. Due to confidentiality issues, problems with noise, and the need for a professional backdrop, do not use a public location.

When keeping an appointment (face-to-face or via technology), arrive or check in five minutes early. For face-to-face meetings, after you enter the office, greet the receptionist and politely introduce yourself. State whom you have an appointment with and the time of the meeting. When entering an office for a meeting, wait to be invited to sit down. At the close of any meeting, thank the other participants for their time. If you are in person, exchange business cards if appropriate and close with a final handshake.

DINING

In the workplace, you will encounter a variety of dining situations. Some dining experiences will be less formal than others. You will most likely come across some form of the table setting illustrated in Figure 3-4. Take time to study and review a common place setting to learn the proper location and use for utensils, plates, and cups. Apart from fast food, few college students are generally comfortable eating in a formal dining situation. Here are several rules of thumb regarding dining etiquette:

- As soon are you are seated, place your napkin on your lap. If you leave the table, place your napkin to the side of your plate, not on your chair.

FIGURE 3-4   Table Setting

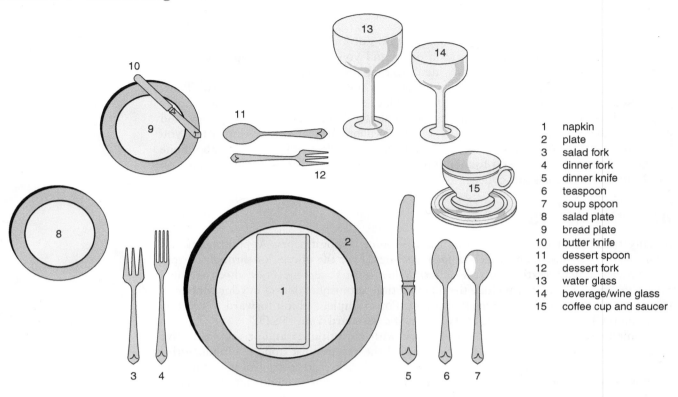

1   napkin
2   plate
3   salad fork
4   dinner fork
5   dinner knife
6   teaspoon
7   soup spoon
8   salad plate
9   bread plate
10 butter knife
11 dessert spoon
12 dessert fork
13 water glass
14 beverage/wine glass
15 coffee cup and saucer

- Do not discuss business matters until everyone has ordered. Table conversation should be positive and free of controversial subjects such as politics and religion.
- Utensils are set to be used in order of necessity. As your courses are served, start with the outside utensil and work in, toward the plate. The utensils set at the top of the plate are for your dessert.
- When serving coffee, water, tea, or any other beverage available at the table, first offer and serve others at your table.
- Do not order anything expensive or messy.
- Do not order alcohol unless others at your table first order an alcoholic beverage. Abstaining from alcohol is the most desired behavior. If you choose to drink, limit consumption to one drink.
- When bread is available, first offer bread to others at your table before taking a piece.
- Place your bread on the bread plate (located at the top left corner of your dinner plate). Place your serving of butter on the bread plate. Do not butter the entire piece of bread at one time. Tear a piece of bread and butter only that piece of bread before eating.
- Do not take the last piece of bread or appetizer unless it is first offered to others at your table.
- When your meal arrives, do not begin eating until everyone at your table has been served. If everyone receives their meals except you (you are the last to be served), give others at your table permission to begin eating without you so that their food does not get cold. Eat your meal at the same pace as others at the table.
- Do not eat your meal with your fingers unless your main course is meant to be eaten without utensils.

- Be kind and polite to the staff and servers.

- Burping and slurping are inappropriate while dining. If you accidentally burp or slurp, immediately apologize and say "excuse me." Also, chew with your mouth closed.

- When you are finished eating, place your knife and fork together, with the blade facing in and the tines up. When you are only resting and you do not want the server to take your plate away, cross your utensils with the tines facing down.

- It is inappropriate to use a mobile communication device while dining. If you must take a call or text, excuse yourself from the table.

When Cory arrived at the conference, Cory was glad to be dressed professionally. Everyone was dressed in business attire. As Cory was introduced to others, Cory was sure to make eye contact, smile, and properly shake hands. Cory also collected many business cards while networking. During the meal, Cory was careful to follow dining etiquette. At work the next day, Cory immediately wrote a thank-you note to the managers who invited Cory to the event. At the end of the day, Cory's manager called Cory and let Cory know what a great impression Cory made at the conference. Several colleagues had mentioned to Cory's manager how impressed they were with Cory's professionalism. Cory realized that conducting a little research and being professional was well worth the effort.

A common activity in business involves attending social functions. Many invitations request an RSVP, which is French for *répondez s'il vous plaît* (i.e., please respond). As soon as you receive an invitation, send a reply—whether it is an acceptance to attend or a regret that you cannot attend. Not acknowledging the invitation and failing to respond is rude.

When you attend a social function, remember that you are attending it to meet and network with other professionals. Do not focus on the food; focus on the networking opportunities.

- As with dining situations, refrain from or limit the consumption of alcohol.

- If you choose to eat, serve yourself a small plate of hors d'oeuvres and move away from the food table.

- Hold your hors d'oeuvres in your left hand, leaving your right hand free to shake hands and greet others.

- If there are name badges, wear one placed neatly on your right shoulder. If you must handwrite your own name badge, print your first and last name clearly.

- Do not talk with food in your mouth.

OTHER ETIQUETTE BASICS

At first glance, business etiquette can be a bit overwhelming. However, with practice, business etiquette becomes habit. When in doubt, mimic what the most polished person in the room is doing. Be aware of your surroundings and watch and learn from those whom you admire. The following is a final list of etiquette tips to assist you in becoming one of the most admired and respected individuals in the workplace.

- *Have a pleasant attitude.* In addition to saying "please" and "thank you," do not underestimate the value of a simple smile and eye contact. If you have a positive attitude, it will be reflected in your demeanor. When encountering people in the hallways, elevators, and/or meeting rooms, smile, make eye contact, and greet them.

- *Knock before entering an office.* Do not enter an office or private workspace such as a cubicle until you are invited. If the individual you want to see normally has his or her door open, do not disturb the individual when the door is closed. The exception is for an emergency or urgent situation needing his or her attention—but

Talk It Out

Share common dining and social situations that make you uncomfortable, and identify how best to deal with these situations.

Web Quiz

Rate your workplace etiquette. Use the following website, or find another etiquette web quiz.

http://www.usatoday .com/img/content/flash/ getiquettequiz/flash.htm apologize for interrupting. If the door is open but the individual is with someone else, politely wait your turn.

- *Put others first.* When you are with colleagues and you are taking turns (in line, to order, etc.), allow your colleagues to go first. Doing so shows respect and courtesy.
- *Apologize when necessary.* Everyone is human. Therefore, everyone makes mistakes. When you realize that you may have said or done something hurtful to someone, apologize immediately. Relating to conflict and negotiation, apologizing is not a sign of weakness. Apologizing is a sign of strength and maturity. Even if you are not certain if you have offended someone, apologize to avoid any potential misunderstandings. However, do not unnecessarily and continually apologize. Doing so not only gives you the appearance of being needy and insecure, more importantly you are not being assertive and possibly not standing up for your rights in an unoffending manner.
- *Do not use profanity.* The use of profanity is not appropriate in the workplace. Even if others in your presence use profanity, do not assume everyone is comfortable with the bad language. Conversations should be professional, respectful, and free of profanity.
- *Avoid dominating a conversation.* There is a key to carrying on a successful conversation: listening. When you are an active listener, you value the information the other individual is providing. Too frequently, individuals dominate a conversation with their own personal accounts. In general, this is not appropriate. This behavior becomes annoying to the listener when you turn the conversation to yourself. Next time you are in a conversation, listen to how many times you state the words *me*, *I*, and *my*. Try to minimize the use of these words in your conversation.

WORKPLACE DOS AND DON'TS

Do wear professional clothes to work	*Don't* wear sweats, flip flops, or suggestive apparel at work
Do shower and make sure you are always clean	*Don't* overdo the cologne (or any body sprays)
Do make eye contact and offer a gentle but firm handshake	*Don't* grasp just the fingers when shaking hands
Do follow formal dining etiquette at work-related functions	*Don't* reach, grab, or overload your plate at the hors d'oeuvres table
Do say "please" and "thank you" when appropriate	*Don't* assume that the other person knows you are thankful for his or her act of kindness

Concept Review and Reinforcement

Key Terms

extreme job hunting 63
personal commercial 68
interview portfolio 69
positive self-talk 72
one-on-one
  interview 74
group interview 75
panel interview 75

structured interview
  question 75
unstructured interview
  question 75
behavioral interview
  question 75
executive presence 81
appearance 82

dress code 82
work wardrobe 83
casual workdays 83
etiquette 85
courtesy 85
respect 85
networking 86

Summary

Recommended job-hunting tactics include the following:

1. Identify your job objectives.
2. Be aware of qualifications sought by employers.
3. Identify your skills and potential contribution.
4. Develop a comprehensive marketing strategy.
5. Use networking to reach company insiders.
6. Use multiple online approaches.
7. Smile at network members and interviewers and be enthusiastic.
8. Smooth out the rough spots in your background.

Job hunting almost always requires a résumé. A length of one page is recommended for a less experienced person, and two pages for a more experienced person. Résumés should emphasize skills and accomplishments. Be aware of the problems of identity theft and scams associated with online résumés. Video résumés can be important, as well as creative formats. A résumé should almost always be accompanied by a cover letter explaining how you can help the organization and why you are applying for this particular job.

Summary of Key Concepts Regarding Interview Techniques:

- Create and modify your personal commercial and adapt it to the requirements of your target job.
- Review common interview questions and formulate answers as part of your interview preparation

- Conduct a pre-interview practice to ensure you are prepared the day of the interview
- During your interview, communicate how your knowledge, skills, and abilities will be assets to the company
- Understand the laws that protect employees from discrimination in the interviewing and hiring process
- Be prepared to confidently handle gaps in employment and other difficult interview questions
- Know how to sell yourself and professionally ask for the job at the close of an interview

Summary of Key Concepts Regarding Etiquette/Dress:

- Projecting an executive presence is important in demonstrating knowledge of basic workplace behavior.
- The majority of first impressions are made through visual appearances.
- Both your maturity and the importance you place on your job are reflected in the way you behave and dress at work.
- Begin to create a work wardrobe today.
- Visual body art/piercing and body rings/jewelry are offensive to some individuals and are not appropriate in a professional work environment. Consider the long-term consequences of getting a tattoo or piercing.

- Follow business etiquette protocol and consistently utilize it in all areas of your life.
- Make a habit of thanking individuals either verbally or in writing.

- Appropriate etiquette at social functions and while dining is as important as professional behavior at work.

Questions for Discussion and Review

1. During a labor shortage (when there are more positions open than qualified applicants), why is it still important to have good job search skills?
2. Describe the type of success you or several of your friends and family members have had in conducting a job search through the Internet.
3. In what ways might video résumés both help and hinder a company attain the goal of having a diverse workforce?
4. Why is a vertical career path still the dream of so many workers?
5. Imagine that you are friends with a 24-year-old NBA player who has to quit playing professional basketball because of injuries to both knees. What advice would you offer this man to restart his career in another field?
6. Give an example from your own life in which you behaved as if you were a proactive personality.
7. How does talent and expertise contribute to career advancement?
8. How might a person use a webcam to help build and sustain a network?
9. Assume that you are attempting to create a personal brand. What key features about yourself would you feature in your personal brand?
10. What is the most useful idea you picked up from this chapter about either conducting a job campaign or managing your career? Explain your reasoning.

The Web Corner

http://www.JobHuntersBible.com
(Career guru Dick Bolles provides suggestions for using the Internet to help in the job search.)

http://www.Vault.com
(Wealth of information about career advancement, job finding, and occupational profiles)

http://www.mentoringgroup.com
(Suggestions for having a good mentoring relationship)

Internet Skill Builder: Finding a Job Efficiently

So many job boards exist on the Internet that conducting a Web-based job search can be baffling. A direct approach is to visit Yahoo! Hot Jobs (on the front page of www.Yahoo.com) and enter three specific job titles of interest to you. You will be directed to loads of job opportunities closely matching the job titles you entered. It may be helpful to enter variations of the same job title, such as both "office manager" and "administrative assistant." Your assignment is to identify five jobs for which you appear to be qualified. Even if you have no interest in conducting a job search, it is informative to be aware of job opportunities in your field. Seek answers to the following questions:

1. Do I appear to have the qualifications for the type of job I am seeking?
2. Is there a particular geographic area where the job or jobs I want are available?
3. How good are opportunities in my chosen field?

Web Links regarding Interview Techniques:

http://www.onetcenter.org/

http://jobstar.org/electra/question/sal-req.cfm

http://www.collegegrad.com/intv

http://www.careercc.com/interv3.shtml

http://interview.monster.com

http://www.rileyguide.com/interview.html

Web Links regarding Etiquette/Dress:

http://www.ravenwerks.com/practices/etiquette.htm

If You Were the Boss

1. What kind of information should you share with your current staff members as they prepare to interview a new employee?

2. How would you handle a prospective employee who disclosed inappropriate information during the job interview?

3. You are the manager of a bank, and one of your employees comes in on a Monday morning with a pierced tongue and purple hair. What should you do?

4. You have just hired a new employee who clearly has no concept of business etiquette. What specific steps would you take to teach your new employee how to behave professionally?

Developing Your Human Relations Skills

Interpersonal Relations Case 3-1

The Brand Called Brandy

As Brandy Barclay navigated the challenging highways toward her job interview in Los Angeles, she rehearsed in her mind the importance of communicating that she is a unique brand. "I have to get across the idea that I am special, even if my brand is not as well established as Godiva Chocolates or Dr. Pepper. This administrative assistant position at the hotel and resort company will be a good way to launch my career and brand."

An excerpt of her job interview with the hiring manager Gloria Gomez follows:

Gomez: Welcome Brandy, I am pleased that you made it through the online job application and the telephone screening interview. Tell me again why you would like to join our hotel company as an administrative assistant.

Barclay: Oh, I really don't want to join you as an administrative assistant. I would prefer a vice president job, but I have to start somewhere. (Smiling) Seriously, I like the hotel field. It fits my brand called Brandy. I am a great support person, and a great people person. I'm so unique because I'm great with details and great with people.

Gomez: Tell me specifically what key strengths would you bring to this job?

Barclay: As found in my brand called Brandy, I am high info tech and high touch. I'm a whiz at Microsoft Office Suite, and I'm sweet with people. Kind of catchy, don't you think? Come to think of it, have you seen my business card? It contains loads of details about my skills and strengths on the back. The card is laminated so it will last, and it contains my photo, and even is like a hologram with a 3-D look.

Gomez: Yes, Brandy, I do have your card. You gave one to the receptionist, and she gave it to me. And why do you keep referring to yourself as a brand? Is this just a gimmick to get you noticed?

Barclay: Being a brand is the modern way to tell you that Brandy Barclay is one of a kind. I've got a skill set that is hard to beat. Besides, I want to build a reputation fast that will propel me to the top as an executive in the hotel field.

Gomez: On your trip to the top, what do you plan to do for us as an administrative assistant?

Barclay: I will live up to the brand called Brandy by getting the job done big time. Just ask me to do something, and it will be done. Don't forget I will be building my brand image while in this beginning assignment.

Gomez: Now let's talk about details like the job assignment, salary, and benefits.

Barclay: Fine with me. We have to deal with the mundane at some point.

Case Questions

1. How effectively is Brandy Barclay presenting herself as a brand?
2. What suggestions can you offer Barclay for presenting herself as a brand more effectively?
3. What suggestions can you offer Barclay for conducting herself better during her next job interview?

Interpersonal Relations Case 3-2

Networking in Evanston

Jason, age 31, is an office administrator at a medical supplies company in Evanston, Illinois, located outside Chicago. He enjoys the medical supply field because he perceives the business as an efficient method of distributing medical supplies to settings, such as hospitals, medical clinics, and hospices where they are vitally needed.

Jason has long been interesting in advancing his career by making contacts that could help him in such ways as being recommended for a bigger position, learning new skills and technology, and bringing in business for his company. Although Jason is not in sales he believes that all professional employees have a responsibility to promote the company. One Sunday morning while reading the business section of the newspaper, he learned that a newly formed networking group, the Evanston Professionals, would be holding its first meeting that Friday at an upscale restaurant, starting at 5 p.m. Admission was $15.

Jason thought, "Here is an opportunity made for me. I'll send the event organizer an e-mail this morning, and pay at the door. I'll bring loads of business cards, and wear my sharpest business casual attire." (The announcement specified business casual as the dress code.) Jason showed up precisely at 5 p.m. for the event, and registered at the door. He told the woman at the front table, "I'm Jason and I'm here to meet some great folks."

Jason purchased a glass of Chardonnay, and then made his first move. He spotted a woman wearing a Coach bag, leading him to conclude that she must have a good position. Jason's opening line was, "Hi, I'm Jason, a key office administrator in the medical supply field. Here's my card with a condensed résumé on the back. I'm not specifically looking for a job, but I would never turn down a great opportunity. Be in touch with me if you want to learn more."

The woman wearing the Coach bag replied, "Thanks for coming over, I hope you have a nice evening."

Jason then spotted a hospital administrator, Baxter, he recognized from the past. He approached the administrator and said, "Hello Baxter. I'm glad we're both attending the opening event for this networking group. Here's how you can help me. If you know about any really interesting job openings let me know. Also, if you are using any new business processes for your hospital that work well, let me know. I can visit you at work to learn all about them."

Baxter replied, "I hear you Jason. See you later."

Jason then thought, "So far, my networking approach is not working so well. Maybe I should try the personal touch before I get into professional areas." He next approached a woman dressed in a red blouse, slacks, and high heels. Jason's opening line was,

"Hello there, stylish Evanston Professional. You look fabulous. I love red on a woman, and high heels please me also. Are you married? Here's my card."

With an icy stare, the woman replied, "I thought this was a professional networking event, not a place to hit on people."

Case Questions

1. What suggestions can you offer Jason for improving his networking effectiveness?
2. What important ground rule for networking is Jason violating?
3. What, if anything, is Jason doing right in terms of career networking?

Activities

Activity 3-1

Identify a local company for which you would like to interview. Using the following table, conduct a thorough targeted job search on this company. Answer as many of the questions as possible.

1. Company name	
2. Company address	
3. Job title	
4. To whom should the cover letter be addressed?	
5. What are the job requirements?	
6. Is this a full-time or part-time job?	
7. What are the hours/days of work?	
8. What are the working conditions?	
9. Is there room for advancement?	
10. What kind of training is offered?	
11. What other positions at this company match my qualifications?	
12. What are the average starting salaries (benefits)?	
13. Is traveling or relocation required?	
14. Where is the business located (home office, other offices)?	
15. What are the products or services that the employer provides or manufactures?	
16. What is the mission statement?	
17. What kind of reputation does this organization have?	
18. What is the size of the employer's organization relative to the industry?	
19. What is the growth history of the organization for the past five, ten, or fifteen years?	
20. How long has the employer been in business?	
21. Who is the employer's competition?	

Activity 3-2

Write a statement to use during an invitation to an interview that will help you secure all relevant interview information.

_____

_____

Activity 3-3

Using information obtained in your target company research (Activity 3-1), write three common interview questions and answers. Integrate relevant company information in your answers.

Question	Answer
1.	
2.	
3.	

Activity 3-4

Conduct a salary search for a target job. Identify the salary range. Using your research data, write out a statement you could use to negotiate a higher salary.

Lowest Salary	Highest Salary
$	$
Salary Negotiation Statement	

Activity 3-5

Assume you are starting a new job as an accounting clerk next week. You need a work wardrobe and are limited to a $50 budget. Make a list of what you need and could buy to get you through your first week of work. Include the cost.

What You Need to Buy	Cost
	$
Total Cost	$50

Prior to being faced with this scenario, what items can you purchase today to begin building your professional wardrobe?

Activity 3-6

Imagine you are at a business reception and you do not know anyone else in the room. Role-play formal introductions with a classmate, and then evaluate your partner's performance by identifying strengths and weaknesses.

STUDENT NAME	
Strengths	**Weaknesses**

STUDENT NAME	
Strengths	**Weaknesses**

Activity 3-7

Visit a (non-fast-food) restaurant to practice proper dining etiquette. While you are doing so, identify five acts of inappropriate behavior others are exhibiting and explain why this behavior is not professional.

Inappropriate Behavior	Why Behavior Is Not Professional
1.	
2.	
3.	
4.	
5.	

Sample Exam Questions

1. The purpose of a/an _____ is to identify _____ and identify companies for which you would like to work.

2. In addition to finding out with whom you will be interviewing, identify how much _____ _____ the company has scheduled and _____ are being called in to _____.

3. Prior to your interview, _____.

4. If possible, prior to the interview day, _____.

5. When asked a difficult question, be _____ and _____.

6. The majority of first impressions are made by _____.

7. One of the first steps to determining appropriate attire for work is to identify _____.

8. Provide five tips for women for dressing professionally from head to toe. _____, _____, _____, _____, _____.

9. Provide five tips for men for dressing professionally from head to toe. _____, _____, _____, _____, _____.

10. A standard of social behavior is called _____.

11. When someone does something nice for you, you should _____.

12. A good handshake conveys _____.

13. Provide five rules of thumb regarding dining etiquette. _____, _____, _____, _____.

REFERENCES

1. Donna Rawady, "Market Yourself Across Multiple Tracks," *Democrat and Chronicle* (Rochester, New York), October 18, 2009, p. 2E.
2. Joann S. Lublin, "Lessons of Extreme Job Hunting," *The Wall Street Journal,* September 1, 2009, pp. D1, D4.
3. "Kat & Dale Talk Jobs," King Features Syndicate, April 14, 2002.
4. "Checking Credit of Job Candidates Drives Concerns about Civil Rights," *Christian Science Monitor,* January 19, 2007.
5. Chris Pentila, "Risky Business," *Entrepreneur,* September 2003, pp. 78–79.

Interview Techniques

"How to Stand Out from the Crowd and Kick-Start Your Own Recovery," *U.S. News & World Report* 147 (May 2010): 14–16.

National Association of Colleges and Employers, Bethlehem, PA, www.Jobweb.com

Skorkin, A. The Main Reason Why You Suck at Interviews: Lack of Preparation. *Lifehacker.com,* http://lifehacker.com/5710712/the-main-reason-why-you-suck-at-interviews-lack-of-preparation December 10, 2010.

Garrison, S., Gutter, M., and Spence, L. Managing in Tough Times: Building Your Assets by Volunteering. Department of Family, Youth and Community Sciences, Florida Cooperative Extension Service, Institute of Food and Agricultural Sciences, University of Florida. October 2009, http://edis.ifas.ufl.edu/fy1107#FOOTNOTE_1

Etiquette/Dress

The Emily Post Institute, Burlington, VT, www.emilypost.com

Wayne, T. "Why Etiquette Schools Are Thriving," *Bloomberg Business Week* (October 14, 2010).

Fisher, A. "Is Cubical Etiquette an Oxymoron?" *CNNMoney* (October 22, 2010).

McAfee, A. "Mistakes Millennials Make at Work," *Harvard Business Review* (August 30, 2010).

"Discovering Hats, a New Generation Brims with Anxiety Over Etiquette," *Wall Street Journal* (August 11, 2010).

Schrage, M. "Why Your Looks Will Matter More," *Harvard Business Review* (April 22, 2010).

Tillotson, K. "Manners Mean More in Tough Job Market," *Minneapolis Star Tribune* (March 22, 2010).

CHAPTER 4

Resumes and Cover Letters

Choose a job you love, and you will never have to work a day in your life.

Confucius

Objectives

1. Utilize the *self-discovery* process to identify the right career
2. Conduct a *targeted job search,* including a realistic job preview
3. Determine the *cost of living* in your desired work location
4. Ensure a professional *electronic image*
5. Create a *job search portfolio*
6. Identify references to be used in your job search
7. Identify sources for job leads
8. Demonstrate appropriate behaviors for the application process
9. Define *networking* and create a professional *network*
10. Identify the steps for building a résumé package
11. Write a career objective or personal profile
12. Distinguish between a *functional résumé* and a *chronological résumé*
13. Identify personal *soft skills, job-specific skills,* and *transferable skills*
14. Create a winning *résumé*
15. Write a *cover letter*

HOW-DO-YOU-RATE

	Are you job search savvy?	True	False
1.	It is best to attend a job fair alone.	☐	☐
2.	It is acceptable to distribute personal business cards at social functions.	☐	☐
3.	It is not necessary to share personal information such as a birthdate and Social Security number during a job search.	☐	☐
4.	A job search portfolio is a foundation for the interview portfolio.	☐	☐
5.	Most realistic job leads are found through informal networks.	☐	☐

If you answered "true" to three or more of these questions, congratulations—you are well on your way to finding the job of your dreams. Knowing how the job search process works, creating a job search plan, and properly utilizing job search tools pave the way to job search success.

THE JOB SEARCH

An effective job search is the key to finding a great job. A successful job search involves creating a plan, conducting research, and taking action. Doing so takes time, organization, communication, and professionalism (all key skills you have developed throughout this text). This chapter is designed to help you create a job search strategy. A successful job search strategy identifies what type of job you will be looking for, what tools and resources you will need, and how these tools and resources are best used. The ultimate goal of a job search is to secure an interview that paves the way toward obtaining the job of your dreams.

CHOOSING THE RIGHT CAREER

Creating a job search plan begins with choosing the right career. This involves **self-discovery.** Self-discovery is the process of identifying key interests and skills built upon your career goals. Knowing your key selling points and linking these with your career goals will assist

self-discovery

The process of identifying key interests and skills built upon career goals.

you in landing a job you will enjoy. The process of a career self-discovery includes identifying key interests and accomplishments from your work, educational, and personal experiences. A method for identifying key interests is creating an accomplishments worksheet. This is done by inventorying skills you have acquired from either your work or nonwork experience. Education and nonwork experience such as volunteerism are career-building experiences. The following trigger words assist you in identifying accomplishments:

Trigger Words

Adapted	Developed	Organized
Addressed	Earned	Planned
Analyzed	Established	Projected
Arranged	Financed	Recommended
Assisted	Implemented	Risked
Built	Increased	Saved
Calculated	Instructed	Staffed
Chaired	Installed	Taught
Cleaned	Introduced	Typed
Coached	Investigated	Updated
Communicated	Learned	Won
Coordinated	Located	Wrote
Created	Managed	
Determined	Motivated	

SKILL-BUILDING EXERCISE 4-1

Complete the Following Accomplishments Worksheet

Prior to answering each question, review the trigger words. Whenever possible, quantify your answers by documenting how many, how often, and how much. Do not worry if you cannot answer every question. The purpose of this exercise is to begin identifying accomplishments.

Question

1. What have you done in your career or career-building activities that you are most proud of?

2. List something that you have achieved at work or school.

3. What tasks have you performed at work and in career-building activities?

4. What results have you produced from the tasks performed?

5. List three things that demonstrate your ability to produce results.

6. What have you done that shows an ability to successfully work with people?

7. What else have you accomplished professionally or educationally that makes you proud?

8. What extracurricular activities have you been involved with?

9. List special skills or foreign languages you speak or write.

10. What areas of interest do you have?

Your Response (Quantify Your Answers)

Your accomplishments will be used to identify the right career, and they will also provide an excellent foundation when you begin to build your résumé.

After you have completed your accomplishments worksheet, reread your responses. They will most likely reveal a targeted career of interest to you.

A second means of identifying key skills and jobs of interest is to take a career assessment. Common career assessment tools include the Golden Personality Type Indicator, the Myers-Briggs Type Indicator, and the Strong Interest Inventory. Many college career centers offer these assessments, as do various online sources.

Conducting a realistic job preview identifies day-to-day and common tasks that are performed and required for a specific job. This common human resource management practice is used on job finalists prior to a job offer to ensure the candidate is fully aware of both the positive and negative aspects of a specific job. Be proactive and conduct your own realistic job preview. Identify any additional education or other requirements. For example, if you are a felon, you may not work in some areas of health care and education. There are other careers that require a clean DMV or credit history. Thoughtfully researching and understanding what is required to secure and succeed in a desired job early in the career exploration process will save time and money if the wrong career is selected.

CAREER OBJECTIVE AND PERSONAL PROFILE

A foundation for both your job search strategy and building a winning résumé is to write a career objective or personal profile. A **career objective** is an introductory written statement for individuals with little or no work experience. A **personal profile** is an introductory written statement for individuals with professional experience related to their target career. These statements are used on a résumé to relate to the target career and/or employer, briefly introduce key skills, and express interest in a position. The responses from your completed accomplishments worksheet and career assessment provide a good summary of your current career goal based upon the knowledge, skills, and abilities you possess. Use this information as a foundation to create a statement that briefly and professionally describes you and your career goals. Depending on the layout of your résumé, this information will either have the heading "Career Objective" or "Personal Profile." This statement will be the first item listed on your résumé.

As mentioned earlier, a career objective is an introductory written statement for individuals with little or no work experience. This is a brief statement that will include your interest in a specific position, a brief one-line description of your skills related to the position, and how your skills can benefit your target employer. The career objective is the only place on a résumé where it is acceptable to use the words "I" and "my."

Examples of Career Objectives

Objective: *Seeking a position with an established accounting firm where I can utilize and apply my current accounting and computerized skills toward the excellence of Bell Company.*

Objective: *To obtain an Account Clerk position at Bell Company, where I can demonstrate and increase my general accounting skills to contribute to the success of the company.*

Those with extensive work experience will utilize a personal profile. In creating a personal profile, review your key skills and accomplishments and group these items into general categories. Also identify key qualities you possess that are required for your target job. Take this information and turn it into a two- to three-sentence statement that provides a snapshot of your professional qualifications in a manner that sells your knowledge, skills, and abilities.

Talk It Out

Review your completed accomplishments worksheet. What career area do you believe suits your skills and previous experiences?

Web Quiz

Take the Career Planner Quiz to get a snapshot of your target job or find another career website.

http://careerpath.com/career-tests/?lr=cbmsn&siteid=cbmsnchcpath

career objective

An introductory written statement used on a résumé for individuals with little or no work experience.

personal profile

An introductory written statement used on a résumé for individuals with professional experience related to their target career.

An Example of a Personal Profile

Personal Profile: *Highly professional and detail-oriented accounting professional with demonstrated leadership and success in the areas of payroll, collections, and project management. Excellent analytical, communication, computer, and organizational skills. Bilingual (English/Spanish).*

INDUSTRY RESEARCH

One step toward a successful job search is research. When a job fits your personality and skills, you will more likely succeed. A satisfying career comes from working at a company that reflects your values and performing a job you enjoy. In chapter 7 you will create goals for your career. Conducting industry research will reinforce that you have made the right career decision to support your life plan. In order to determine what type of industry you will research, identify industries that require your key skills. You may realize there is more potential for jobs that require your key skills than you thought.

Once you have identified industries requiring your skills, begin identifying specific jobs in these industries. Note the different job opportunities that exist within each industry. In addition, look at various job titles. Being aware of the various job titles you qualify for allows you more flexibility when job searching. After determining industries and job titles that fit your skills, identify the environments available, including where the jobs are located and specifically what type of work environment you desire.

For example, if you finished college with a business degree, you begin by conducting industry research on the skills you have acquired. Many different industries need employees with a business background, such as health care, educational institutions, and manufacturing. Once you have determined which industry or industries you would like to work for, you can begin reviewing job titles that fit the skills you have acquired in college, such as financial analyst, general accountant, marketing assistant, or human resource generalist. After identifying specific job titles that match your skill sets, decide what type of work environment you desire. If you select health care, you may have the choice of working in a hospital, a clinic, or a private physician's office.

Conducting industry and work environment research will provide you information that will make your job search easier and more successful. Instead of sending out hundreds of résumés in hopes of securing just any job, target companies that are a good match with your life plan, your skills, and your desired work environment.

THE TARGETED JOB SEARCH

targeted job search

Job search process of discovering positions for which you are qualified in addition to identifying specific companies for which you would like to work.

After you have a clearly defined career objective and have identified jobs that suit your personal and career goals, it is time to begin a targeted job search. A **targeted job search** leads you through the process of discovering open positions for which you are qualified, in addition to identifying specific companies for which you would like to work.

Part of a job search is to determine in what city you want to work. If your job search is limited to your local area, you will be restricted to local employers. If you are willing to commute outside of your area, determine how far you are willing to commute (both directions) on a daily basis. If you wish to move out of the area, identify what locations are most appealing. Should you desire to move to a new location, do not forget to consider the cost of living in your desired location. The **cost of living** is the average cost of basic necessities such as housing, food, and clothing. For example, it is much more expensive to live in Manhattan, New York, than it is to live in Cheyenne, Wyoming. While a job in Manhattan may pay a lot more than a job in Cheyenne, living expenses typically justify the higher salary.

cost of living

Average cost of basic necessities such as housing, food, and clothing for a specific geographic area.

Identify Target Employers

Identify your target work location and three companies/employers in your target location that may be of interest to you.

1.

2.

3.

PREPARATION

With the popularity of social networking sites, your personal life has a greater chance of being exposed in the job search process. Ensure you have a favorable **electronic image**. An electronic image is the image formed when someone is communicating with you and/or researching you through electronic means. This involves conducting an Internet search on you through personal pages and search engines. Since the majority of information on the Internet is public information, an increasing number of employers are conducting web searches on potential employees to gain a better perspective of the applicant's values and lifestyle. With today's overabundance of electronic social networking and information sites, personal blogs, and other file-sharing services, ensure that defamatory photos, writings, or other material will not be a barrier in your job search. When conducting an Internet search on yourself, remove any information that portrays you in a negative light. If you are actively involved in social networking sites, carefully evaluate any personal information that is contained on the sites of your friends. If negative information is contained on sites of your friends, explain your job search plans and politely ask them to remove the potentially harmful information.

An additional step toward ensuring a clean electronic image is to maintain a professional e-mail address. Sending a potential employer an e-mail from the address "prty2nite" is not the image you want to project. If necessary, establish a new e-mail address that utilizes some form of your name or initials to maintain a clean and professional electronic image. Two final considerations in maintaining a professional electronic image are the maintenance of a professional voice mail message and the avoidance of text slang in all written communication. Your job search strategy will involve extensive communication with employers and other individuals who will assist you with your job search. Interaction with these parties needs to be professional.

JOB SEARCH PORTFOLIO

A **job search portfolio** is a collection of paperwork used for job searches. Some items from your job search portfolio will become a part of your interview portfolio. You will use the items you collect for your job search portfolio to keep you organized and prepared while searching for a job.

It is best to have a three-ring binder with tabs to keep all paperwork organized and protected. Do not punch holes in original documents. Place original documents in plastic notebook protectors. When you begin collecting items for your portfolio, keep the original and at least two copies of each item available at all times. These copies will be transferred to your interview portfolio when needed.

Because many of today's job searches occur over the Internet, it is also recommended you create an electronic job search portfolio. An **electronic job search portfolio** is a computerized folder that contains electronic copies of all job search documents. For your electronic job search file, scan copies of all documents you will be keeping in your hard-copy portfolio.

---

electronic image

The image formed when someone is communicating and/or researching you through electronic means such as personal web pages and search engines.

Talk It Out

What type of photos, writings, or materials do you think are inappropriate for a potential employer to see?

job search portfolio

A collection of paperwork needed for job searches and interview.

electronic job search portfolio

A computerized folder that contains electronic copies of all documents kept in hard-copy job search portfolio.

When you share documents with potential employers and others over the Internet, these electronic documents will be sent as attachments.

A useful networking and introduction tool is a personal business card. A personal business card is a small card that contains contact information including your name, mailing and e-mail addresses, and phone number. It is a good practice to share your personal business card with anyone you meet, especially in networking, informational interview, and mentoring encounters. Doing so makes it easier for your new acquaintance to remember you and contact you in the future. Personal business cards are inexpensive and valuable networking tools and need not be professionally printed. Templates are available on the web and can easily be printed on cardstock paper, or you can purchase special business card packages online or at an office supply store. When designing a personal business card, ensure it contains all relevant contact information and reflects a professional image. Use an easy-to-read font style. Do not include fancy graphics, pictures, or too many words. Simple is better.

The following is a list of items to keep in your job search portfolio. Some of these items and their purpose will be discussed in this chapter.

Item	Description
Network list	A list of professional relationships used for job contacts
Personal business cards	Cards with personal contact information used to share for job leads
Résumé	A formal profile that is presented to potential employers
Cover letter	Introduces a résumé
Reference list	A list of individuals who will provide a professional reference
Letters of recommendation	A written professional reference to verify work experience and character
Transcripts	Documents that verify education. Have both official (sealed) and copies available. Sealed transcripts may be required
Current state licenses	Documents that verify the ability to practice certain professions
Awards, certificates, work samples	Documents that demonstrate proficiency in specific skills
Completed generic application	Generic job application that makes information readily available
Copy of ID and/or driver's license	A valid ID and proof of ability to drive (if driving is a job requirement)
Copy of recent DMV record (if relevant to your career)	Used to ensure a safe driving record
Personal commercial	Statement that assists with interview
Small calendar, note pad, pen	To track important dates and make notes
Performance appraisals from previous jobs	Proof of positive work performance

Many careers that involve driving require a copy of your driving history. This information is secured by contacting your local Department of Motor Vehicles (DMV). If you have a poor driving record, check with your local DMV to identify how long this history stays on your record. Those with a blemished driving history may have a tougher time securing a job in a field that involves driving. When sharing your DMV record, as with all other portfolio items, provide only a copy (unless otherwise required) and maintain the original in your job search portfolio.

EMPLOYMENT APPLICATIONS

Keep a completed generic employment application in your job search portfolio so you have required information readily available. If you have a smart phone, store this information on your device for quick and easy retrieval. When completing the application in its entirety, do not list your Social Security number or birth date. This information is not given to a prospective employer until you are a finalist for a job to protect against the potential of age discrimination and/or identity theft. Let the employer know you will supply this information upon hire.

An employment application is a legal document. When completing the application, read the fine print prior to signing the document. Commonly, at the end of the application, there will be a statement that grants the potential employer permission to conduct reference and various background checks, including a credit check if the information is relevant to the job for which you are applying. Fully understand why this background information is necessary and how it will be used in the hiring process. If you do not fully understand the statements on the application, clarify these statements prior to signing the application.

It is common for employers to request that the applicant complete an employment application and submit this document along with the résumé package. If you submitted only a cover letter and résumé, you may be asked to complete an application after you have been interviewed. Some employment applications can now be completed through a kiosk located at a worksite. Applications may also be downloaded, completed, and submitted directly from a target company's website. A keyboarded employment application is best. If keyboarding the application is not possible, complete the application by printing neatly in black ink. In some instances, after you have completed an online application, you may be asked to take a pre-employment test as part of the application process.

PERSONAL REFERENCES AND RECOMMENDATIONS

Create a list of professional references that a potential employer can contact to verify your work experience and personal character. References are not to be included on your résumé. References are listed on a separate page. Do not send your reference list with your résumé unless it is requested by the employer. However, have a copy available to share if the employer requests references during the interview. Prior to including individuals on your reference list, ask each person if he or she is willing to serve as a reference. Be sure each person on this list will provide a positive reference. Have at least three names to submit as references. Include each reference's name, contact phone number, business mailing address, relationship, and e-mail address. References can be past or present employers and supervisors, coworkers, instructors, or someone with whom you have volunteered. Do not use relatives, friends, or religious leaders unless you have worked or volunteered with or for them.

In addition to reputable references, it is wise to have at least three **letters of recommendation**. A letter of recommendation is a written testimony from another person that states that you are credible. Letters of recommendation need to reflect current job skills, accomplishments, and positive human relations skills and should be no older than one year. Letters of recommendation can be from past or present employers, coworkers, instructors, or someone you worked for as a volunteer. It is common and acceptable to have someone write a formal letter of recommendation and serve as a personal reference.

letters of recommendation

A written testimony from another person that states that a job candidate is credible.

In addition to routinely updating your résumé, keep your references list updated. Provide references relevant to your career. Occasionally check with your references and verify if they are still willing to serve as references. Keep these individuals current on your job search status and career goals.

List Your References

List three people you can use as references. Then list three people you can ask to write you a letter of recommendation. Include their relationship to you.

Reference	Relationship
1.	
2.	
3.	

Letter of Recommendation	Relationship
1.	
2.	
3.	

SOURCES OF JOB LEADS

There are many sources for job leads. Do not wait for potential employers to find you. Actively search association and employer sites of targeted industries. The most obvious job lead is directly from a targeted company. It is also acceptable to personally visit the target company's human resource department for current job announcements. If you do not have a targeted company but have a location where you would like to work, conduct an Internet search using the target city and target position as key search words. Search for associations in your targeted industry. They may offer online job banks. Many employers now post job announcements on social networking and corporate websites. Check online message boards and popular job search sites. Also, conduct key-word searches on community message boards. Keep track of the sites you are utilizing for your job search and monitor activity. Many larger cities and counties offer one-stop centers for job seekers. These government-funded agencies provide job-seeker assistance and serve as a link between job seekers and local employers. Other job sources include job fairs, newspaper advertisements, industry journals, and current employees who work in your targeted industry and/or company. Most individuals rely on posted job positions. However, many jobs are unsolicited (not advertised to the general public). The way to become aware of these unsolicited jobs is to use your professional network. The larger your professional network, the more you will become aware of unannounced job leads. A discussion on how to create and utilize a professional network is presented later in this chapter. Once you have established a network, inform network members of your desire for a job and ask for potential job leads.

Treat all face-to-face job search situations, including distributing your résumé, meeting a potential network contact, or visiting a company to identify open positions, as if you are going to an interview. Dress professionally, go alone, have extra copies of your résumé, display confidence, and bring your interview portfolio. In networking situations where there are many job seekers, such as a job fair, be polite and professional in your interactions with everyone. Do not interrupt or be rude to other job seekers. Take the lead in introducing yourself to company representatives. Sell your skills and confidently ask the company representative if he or she has an open position requiring your skills. Your goal in such a situation is to favorably stand out from the crowd, share your résumé, and arrange an interview. There are situations where applicants are invited to "on the spot" interviews. Your professional appearance and interview portfolio will show that you are prepared. Dressing casually and/or having a child or friend in tow will communicate unprofessionalism to a potential employer.

If you are unable to find a job lead, send an unsolicited cover letter and résumé to your target company either electronically or through traditional mail. When sending an unsolicited résumé, send two copies: one to the human resource manager, and the other to the manager of your target job. Prior to sending your résumé, call the company to secure the names of both individuals. Ensure you have identified the correct spelling and gender for the individuals to whom you will be sending your résumé. Sending two résumés to the same company increases the opportunity of securing an interview. The targeted department manager will most likely read and file your résumé for future reference. The human resource manager will also review your résumé and may identify other jobs for which you are qualified.

NETWORKING

During the time you will be looking for a job or advanced position, establishing a professional network is important—as is maintaining this network throughout your career. **Networking** is the act of creating professional relationships. Think of networking as a connection device. The purpose of creating a professional network is to have a resource of individuals whom you can call upon for professional assistance and/or advice. While the intent of this discussion is to utilize a professional network for job search purposes, a professional network is also a useful tool for collaborating and assisting others.

Professional networking is necessary throughout a job search. There are two primary forms of networking. The first form is the traditional method, which involves face-to-face interaction. The second method utilizes social media. Traditional networking involves interacting with and meeting as many people as possible who work or know someone who works in your targeted industry. There are many formal networking opportunities for job seekers, including attending association meetings, service clubs, and conferences or trade shows. Additionally, many college career centers provide networking events for students to interact with local employers. Job fairs, volunteer fairs, and trade shows are excellent venues for professional networking. The key to successful networking is to begin creating a network before you need one. This provides you time to develop your networking skills, increase your confidence, and identify which venues work best. Many college recruiters enjoy meeting students a year prior to graduation. Students who are networking early in their job search convey organization, planning, and strategic skills, which are skills highly desired by employers.

Developing a professional network is easy. You inform one person that you are looking for a job. That person informs others, then those people inform others, and soon you

networking

Meeting and developing relationships with individuals outside one's immediate work area; the act of creating professional relationships.

FIGURE 4-1 Networking

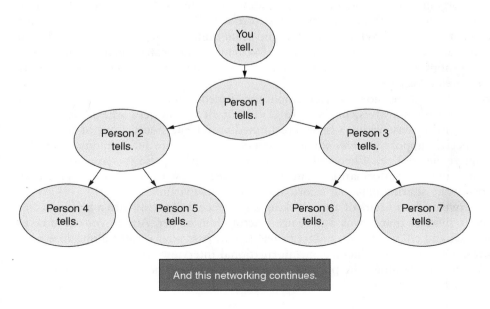

have many people who know that you are searching for a job. View Figure 4-1 to see how a network grows.

Almost every person you know may be a part of your network, including coworkers, supervisors, instructors, family, and friends.

Cory has been working as an account clerk for a year. During this year, Cory has acquired new accounting skills, has learned new software packages, and has graduated with an accounting degree. Cory begins by telling supervisors and coworkers what skills and education have been acquired. In addition, Cory mentions the new skills and software packages learned over the last year and shares future goals. Cory then tells family members and friends the same information. This is the beginning of Cory's professional network. Cory creates a network list and begins tracking and updating these people. Cory will continue to update the people on the network list about new skills acquired and job search progress.

When engaging in traditional networking, remember that the success of one's networking attempts begin with a positive attitude. Review what you have learned in previous chapter of this text regarding professional behavior. First and foremost, believe in yourself and your abilities. Be confident and willing to approach and initiate an introduction with strangers. People are drawn to positive people. When actively networking, dress professionally, because first impressions matter. Have both your personal business card and a brief statement of your key skills to informally share with anyone you meet. When you share a business card, ask for one in return. Obtaining the card provides you the opportunity to follow up. Also use the information from your new contact's business card to update your network list. Practice the art of introducing yourself in a positive and professional manner, beginning with a professional handshake. Listen carefully to the name of the individual you are meeting. After the handshake, exchange business cards. Prior to telling your new contact about you and your job search, ask about him or her. Get the individual to talk about where he or she works, what he or she does, and what he or she enjoys about the job. Use this time to build rapport. At the appropriate time, tell the individual about you and your job search. As your conversation continues, watch for body-language cues. If the person is engaged, he or she will make direct eye contact and turn his or her body toward you. If the person does not want to visit too long, he or she will look away and/or turn his or her body away from you. Utilize these cues to either continue the visit or politely thank him or her for the visit and end the conversation.

While it is common to have food and beverages available at formal networking events, it is best to refrain from eating and drinking until you have met your desired network contacts. Practice proper etiquette by not overindulging in food items. You are in attendance to meet people, not to eat. It is always best to refrain from drinking alcohol.

There are also other methods to expand your network, such as volunteering for community organizations. Volunteering provides a chance to meet people in different organizations and learn about new positions throughout the community. Volunteering is an excellent venue to develop leadership and team-building skills, network, and, most importantly, give back to your community. Join clubs and professional organizations. Attend workshops, conferences, and seminars to meet people from corporations that are in your targeted career field.

Current technologies now provide ample social media outlets to not only post your résumé to targeted industries, but also to create an electronic network. Some popular online professional networking venues are LinkedIn and Facebook. Both of these venues have special support services for job seekers, but there are many industry-specific networking venues online. When utilizing a social networking site for your job search, ensure that your career information is current and consistent with your résumé. However, be cautious when sharing personal information over these venues.

Within twenty-four hours of a networking experience, follow up with a brief message telling the individual that it was a pleasure meeting him or her. Attach your résumé to your message, and tell your new contact to feel free to pass your résumé along to others. If you are interested in conducting an informational interview with your new contact, do not attach your résumé. The purpose of your message will be to not only thank the individual for his or her time, but also to ask for and arrange an informational interview.

Talk It Out

What is appropriate and inappropriate information to share when creating an online network?

Identify Your Current Network

Where have you met people who you can include in your professional network?

1. _____

2. _____

3. _____

An **informational interview** is when a job seeker meets with a business professional to learn about a specific career, company, or industry. You are not asking for a job during an informational interview. You are only expanding your professional network. During an informational interview, ask the business professional questions about targeted careers, hiring, and the culture of the company. By meeting and talking with business professionals, you have increased your professional network. When you network, do not be afraid to ask those with whom you network for additional contacts who may be able to assist you. Networking involves giving and taking. If you read an industry-related article, attend a conference, or are working on a project that may interest someone in your network, share the information and demonstrate how you can be of value to them.

Create and maintain a network list. A **network list** is an easily accessible list of all network contacts' names, industries, addresses, and phone numbers so you can contact each person for quick reference. Provide each contact who is actively assisting with your job search a copy of your most current résumé. Keep all contacts on your network list updated throughout your job search. When keeping in contact with members of your network, be sensitive to their time. Do not annoy them or be inconsiderate in your interactions. Ensure that your network contact list is up-to-date. Find and consistently utilize a database system that is convenient for you. Most individuals use an electronic database, while some still prefer a traditional address book. Whatever you use, keep it current. If you find a job, immediately remove job search postings and inform members of your network who were actively assisting you with your search for a job.

Networking for both business and job search purposes is work, but the effort reaps tremendous benefits if done appropriately. Every few months, review your professional network list. If there is someone with whom you have not recently connected, contact him or her to say hello and keep him or her updated on your career and growth plans.

informational interview

When a job seeker meets with a business professional to learn about a specific career, company, or industry.

network list

An easily accessible list of all professional network contacts' names, industries, addresses, and phone numbers.

PROTECTING YOUR PRIVACY

The job search process involves sharing personal information. Be cautious and share only personal information with reputable sources or you may become a target for identity theft. If you are applying for a job and have never heard of the employer, conduct research to verify that the employer is legitimate. As stated earlier, do not share your birth date or Social Security number with any employer until after you are a finalist for the job.

Cory's friend Terry was looking for a job. Terry found a job on an online classified job site that sounded legitimate. The employer asked that Terry submit a résumé online. Within a few days after sharing his résumé, Terry received an e-mail telling him that he was a finalist for the job. The only step left in the process was for Terry to forward a copy of his credit report. Although Terry was desperate for a job, he thought this was a little strange, so he asked Cory what Cory thought of the situation. Cory conducted an Internet search for Terry and could not find any evidence that the company Terry was applying to even existed. Cory asked Terry if he completed an application that gave the potential employer permission to view Terry's credit information, and Terry said no. Cory and Terry agreed that sharing personal information with an unknown company was not a good idea.

KEEPING THE RIGHT ATTITUDE

Throughout this text, you have learned how to be successful in the workplace. The importance of maintaining a positive attitude throughout your career cannot be stressed enough. This holds true during your job search. The job search process is a lot of work and can sometimes be frustrating. Do not get discouraged if you do not get an interview or job offer on your first try. In tight job markets, it may take many interviews before receiving a job offer. To maintain a healthy attitude during this time of transition, follow these tips when looking for a job:

1. *Stay positive:* Start each day with a positive affirmation. Speaking aloud, tell yourself that you are a talented and great person who deserves a good job (and believe what you say). Your attitude is reflected in your actions. If you allow negative elements to influence your job search, you will be at a disadvantage.

2. *Stay active:* Create a daily and weekly "to do" list. Every day, check the websites of your targeted industries, associations, and companies in addition to checking relevant job sites. Schedule time for industry and company research, as well as time for networking. A job search is a job in itself. You do not want to be an unproductive employee in the workplace, so begin creating good work habits now by making the most of your time in a job search.

3. *Keep learning:* Use job search down time to learn or develop a skill. As with your routine industry and company research and daily review of targeted job postings, schedule learning time. Identify a skill that will assist you when you are offered a job. Finances do not have to be a barrier to learning new skills. There are many free tutorials available on the Internet. Topics to consider include computer skills, writing skills, or any skill specific to your chosen industry.

4. *Stay connected:* Although it is natural to not want to socialize with others when discouraged, the job search period is the time when you most need to be in the presence of others. In addition to keeping your current network updated on your job search, identify further reasons to communicate with your network. Consistently work on expanding your network by attending association meetings and events, volunteering, and scheduling informational interviews. Plan at least one meeting and/or activity each day. As opposed to sitting around the house waiting for the phone to ring, dressing professionally and networking every day will contribute to your maintaining a positive outlook.

5. *Stay focused:* During this time of transition, manage your professional job search, your personal health, and your environment. Manage your professional job search by maintaining an up-to-date calendar with scheduled follow-up activities relating to your job search. Because a job search is a stressful experience, practice healthy stress management techniques, including a proper diet, regular exercise, and positive self-talk. Invest a portion of your time in something of interest other than your job search. Consider volunteering for an organization of special interest to you. Doing so will provide a mental break, provide possible new network contacts, and provide you the satisfaction of helping others. Managing your personal environment involves making wise choices regarding personal finances. Be cautious and conservative with your money. Make thoughtful purchases and avoid emotional spending. Finally, surround yourself with individuals who are positive and supportive of you and your efforts.

If you are currently working and you begin looking for a new job, keep your job search confidential. If you are listing your supervisor as a reference, let him or her know you are looking for a new job and briefly explain why. Do not quit your current job before accepting a new job. Also, do not bad-mouth your company or anyone who works for your current or former employer(s).

WORKPLACE DOS AND DON'TS

Do keep your original job search documents in a portfolio	*Don't* give employers your original documents and expect them to be returned to you
Do keep a network list and keep the people on your list updated	*Don't* be annoying or inconsiderate of your network contacts' time
Do realize that a targeted job search takes time	*Don't* get discouraged if you do not get an interview or job offer on your first try
Do explore various sources of job leads, including your personal network, the Internet, and industry journals	*Don't* limit your job leads to one source

HOW-DO-YOU-RATE

	Test your resume expertise	True	False
1.	Paper résumés are not necessary in today's electronic age.	☐	☐
2.	Career objectives are used on all resumes.	☐	☐
3.	Unique skills such as being bilingual or serving in the military can lead to discrimination and should not be listed on a formal résumé.	☐	☐
4.	Using a word-processing résumé template is best when creating a résumé.	☐	☐
5.	If I have a job gap on my résumé it is acceptable to make up a job to fill in the gap.	☐	☐

If you answered "true" to at least two questions, use the information and tools in this chapter to improve your chances of creating and utilizing a winning résumé.

BUILDING YOUR RÉSUMÉ PACKAGE

Before an employer meets you, they first view your résumé package. A résumé package includes a résumé and a cover letter. Your résumé needs accents package needs to efficiently and effectively sell your skills and communicate how your attributes are unique compared to those of all the other candidates vying for your target job. A **résumé** is a formal written profile that presents a person's knowledge, skills, and abilities to potential employers. Your résumé is an important job search tool that should be continually updated throughout your career. You may not be planning to find a new job or get promoted today, but a time will come when a current résumé is needed. Do not wait until that time to create or update your résumé. As you increase your job skills and accomplishments, add these new skills and experiences to your résumé.

When you begin to create your résumé, you will quickly discover that there are various types of résumés and résumé formats. You may also receive conflicting advice as to how the perfect résumé should look and what it should include. The appropriate type of résumé used depends upon your work experience. A well-written résumé makes it easy for potential employers to quickly and easily identify your skills and work experience.

This chapter will present the tools for creating a professional résumé and cover letter. As you go through the process of constructing your résumé package, make every word, the visual presentation, and the information sell your skills and career accomplishments. There are five steps toward building a winning résumé:

- *Step One:* Career Objective/Personal Profile
- *Step Two:* Gathering Information
- *Step Three:* Proper Layout
- *Step Four:* Skills, Accomplishments, and Experience
- *Step Five:* The Final Résumé

STEP ONE: CAREER OBJECTIVE/PERSONAL PROFILE

The first step in developing a winning résumé is to write a career objective or personal profile. A career objective is a statement that presents your key skills in a brief statement for individuals with little or no work experience. A personal profile is used for individuals with more extensive career experience. Create a career objective or personal profile. Use your career objective or personal profile as the foundation for your résumé. Make your career objective or personal profile specific to the job for which you are applying.

SKILL-BUILDING EXERCISE 4-5

Your Career Objective or Personal Profile

Write a career objective or personal profile.

_____

_____

_____

_____

_____

_____

STEP TWO: GATHERING INFORMATION

The second step in building a résumé is to create a draft document with key headings. This step involves collecting and merging all relevant information into one document. Begin identifying and listing the following information into an electronic document:

1. *Education.* List schools, dates, degrees, certificates, credentials, GPA, licenses, and other relevant education information, including military experience.
2. *Skills.* List all skills you possess.
3. *Employment.* Starting with the most recent job, list the employer, dates of employment (month and year), job title, and responsibilities.
4. *Languages.* List all foreign languages, fluency levels, and if you can read, speak, and/or write the foreign language.
5. *Honors and Awards.* List any honors and awards you have received at school, work, or from the community.
6. *Professional/Community Involvement.* List volunteer work and community service projects. Include any leadership role you took in these activities.

Note that when compiling information to include in your résumé, there is no personal information listed. Personal information including birth date, marital/child status, ethnicity, or religion should not be included on a résumé. It is also inappropriate to list hobbies or include photographs. There are laws that protect employees from discrimination in hiring and advancement in the workplace, and employers should not be aware of personal information unless it is relevant to the job for which you are applying. Older job seekers should not list the date of graduation on a résumé as it could be used for age discrimination.

SKILL-BUILDING EXERCISE 4-6

Gather Information

Complete the following table:

Education (list most recent first)			
School Name	City, State	Dates	Degree, Certificate, Credential, Licenses
Skills			
Employment (list most recent first)			
Employer	Employment Dates	Job Title	Duties

Languages		Fluency (Read, Write, and/or Speak)

Honors and Awards	Dates	Place

Professional/Community Involvement	

functional résumé layout

A résumé layout that emphasizes relevant skills when related work experience is lacking.

Functional Résumé Layout see Figure 4-2 on page 127

Functional Résumé Example with Minimal Career Work Experience, see Figure 4-3 on page 128

Functional Résumé Example without Career Work Experience, see Figure 4-4 on page 129.

chronological résumé layout

A résumé layout used by those with extensive career experience that emphasizes related work experience, skills, and significant accomplishments.

Chronological Résumé Layout, see Figure 4-5 on page 130

Chronological Résumé Example with Degree, see Figure 4-6 on pages 131–132

Chronological Résumé Example with No Degree, see Figure 4-7 on pages 133–134

Talk It Out

Which résumé layout is best for your situation? Why?

STEP THREE: PROPER LAYOUT

The third step in developing a successful résumé is to identify and arrange your information in the proper résumé layout. If you are at the start of your career and/or do not have extensive work experience, create a résumé using the **functional résumé layout.** This layout is used to emphasize relevant skills when you lack related work experience. A functional résumé focuses on skills and education. When writing a functional résumé, list your career objective, relevant skills, and education before any work experience. Include only your high school in the education section if you are using a functional layout and have not yet graduated from college. Most functional résumés are only one page in length. Refer to Figure 4-2 for the functional résumé layout, and see Figures 4-3 and 4-4 for examples of a functional résumé with and without career-related work experience.

Those with extensive career experience should use a **chronological résumé layout.** In the chronological layout, note that the career objective is replaced with a personal profile. General skills emphasized in a personal profile are key skill sets. These skill sets will be used as subheadings in the professional experience section on a chronological résumé. The chronological layout presents related work experience, skills, and significant accomplishments under each respective skill set subheading. When writing a personal profile, include key general skills and key qualities desired by your target employer. Specific skills will be detailed under each respective professional experience subheading. Share major accomplishments and responsibilities from each position. Include important activities you have accomplished in your job. If necessary, add a second page to your résumé. A chronological layout best highlights, communicates, and sells specific job skills and work accomplishments. Refer to Figure 4-5 for the chronological résumé layout, and see Figures 4-6 and 4-7 for examples of chronological résumés.

For both functional and chronological résumé layouts, present employment history and education in reverse time order (most recent job first). When listing work history, bold your job title, not the place of employment. When listing dates of employment, use only month and year. Be consistent in how dates are listed on the résumé.

When you have determined which résumé layout is best for your current situation, electronically arrange the information you have compiled into the correct résumé layout. Avoid résumé templates. Résumé templates can be difficult to update, modify, and personalize.

STEP FOUR: SKILLS, ACCOMPLISHMENTS, AND EXPERIENCE

Once you have electronically arranged your information into the correct layout, it is time to move to the fourth step in developing your résumé. This involves detailing the information listed in your skills, work experience, and professional accomplishments. Work experience includes learned skills, job duties, and accomplishments. Professional accomplishments communicate specific activities you achieved beyond your job duties. Whenever possible, quantify your skills, responsibilities, and professional accomplishments. Do not assume the reader will know what you have done. As you insert professional accomplishments and responsibilities into your electronic file, include both job-specific skills and transferable skills. **Job-specific skills** are those that are directly related to a specific job or industry. If you were to change careers, job-specific skills would probably not be useful. For example, if you are a medical billing clerk who knows how to use a specific software program such as Medical Manager, you will not need to use this skill if you become a preschool teacher.

job-specific skills

Skills that are directly related to a specific job or industry.

Transferable skills are skills that are transferred from one job to the next. If you change careers, you will still be able to use (transfer) these skills in any job. For example, if you are a medical billing clerk, you may have learned customer service skills from consistent contact with patients and must practice being positive when dealing with customers. If you become a preschool teacher, the customer service skill of being positive is transferable to the children in your classroom. Employers need employees with job-specific skills and transferable skills, so list both types on your résumé. The term **soft skills** refers to the people skills necessary when working with others in the workplace. Employers want employees that are reliable, team players, good communicators, and able to get along well with others.

transferable skills

Skills that can be transferred from one job to another.

soft skills

People skills that are necessary when working with others in the workplace.

When listing work experience on your résumé, include the job title, company name, city, and state where the company is located, and the duties of the position. When listing job duties, be specific with common workplace skills, such as computer skills. The term computer skills can be too general and typically includes many different areas: networking, programming, applications, data processing, and/or repair. An employer needs to know what specific computer skills you possess. For example, inform the employer of your computer skill level (e.g., basic, intermediate, or advanced) with a specific software. When listing your skills, first list the skills relevant to your target job. If you are bilingual include this information in your résumé. Let the employer know what second language you read, write, or only speak that second language.

Résumés do not normally contain complete sentences. They contain statements that sell your skills, qualifications, and work experience. Except for the career objective on a functional résumé, the words "I" and "my" should not appear.

SKILL-BUILDING EXERCISE 4-7

Detail Your Skills

List as many job-specific and transferable skills as possible. If you do not have any job-specific skills, list the job skills you will have after finishing your schooling.

Job-Specific Skills (Related to Your Career Job)	Transferable Skills (Can Be Used in Any Job)
1.	1.
2.	2.
3.	3.
4.	4.
5.	5.

When applying for a specific position, identify the key knowledge, skills, and abilities the employer desires. General information regarding a specific position will be listed in the job announcement. If possible, secure a copy of the job description. If this is not possible, use the target job information or conduct an occupational quick search on the O*Net database. This database of occupational information was developed for the U.S. Department of Labor and provides key information by job title. Match the key knowledge, skills, and abilities required for your target job with the knowledge, skills, and abilities you possess. Then emphasize this information on your résumé.

Organize your skills and work experience by first listing the key skills required for your target job. When communicating your skills, experience, and accomplishments, write with energy. Use action verbs, also referred to as **power words**. Power words are action verbs that describe your accomplishments in a lively and specific way. For example, instead of stating "started a new accounts receivable system," use "developed a new accounts receivable system that reduced turnaround time by 20 percent." Power words are listed in Table 4-1 and Table 4-2.

power words

Action verbs that describe your accomplishments in a lively and specific way.

SKILL-BUILDING EXERCISE 4-8

Accomplishments

Refer back to the accomplishments worksheet you completed in Skill-Building Exercise 4-1. Review these accomplishments and turn them into powerful action statements. Quantify whenever possible.

Choose Your Top Five Accomplishments   **Change to Powerful Action Statements**

1.

2.

3.

4.

5.

TABLE 4-1   Skills Power Words

Sample Power Statements for Skills
• Ideal oral and written communications skills
• Understanding of office practices and procedures; ability to operate fax machine, copy machine, and ten-key machine; ability to enter data; ability to effectively interpret policies and procedures; work well under the pressure of deadlines; establish and maintain a positive working relationship with others; ability to communicate
• Accurate typing skills at _____ wpm
• Experienced with Microsoft Office, including Word, Excel, Access, PowerPoint, and Outlook
• Excellent English grammar, spelling, and punctuation skills
• Accurately proofread and edit documents
• Strong attention to detail
• Accurately follow oral and written instructions
• Excellent attendance and punctuality record
• Maintain confidentiality
• Positive attitude, motivated, and organized

TABLE 4-2 Experience Power Words

Sample Power Statement for Work Experience

- Prepared reports and other materials requiring independent achievement
- Enjoy working in a flexible team situation
- Established and maintained positive and effective working relationships
- Planned, scheduled, and performed a variety of clerical work
- Maintained office equipment and supplies
- Proofread forms and materials for completeness and accuracy according to regulations and procedures
- Processed and prepared materials for pamphlets, bulletins, brochures, announcements, handbooks, forms, and curriculum materials
- Provided training of temporary or new employees
- Maintained department files and records
- Demonstrated ability to receive incoming calls and route them efficiently
- Processed purchase requisitions, ordered and distributed supplies, and maintained inventory control
- Responsibly planned and conducted meetings

STEP FIVE: COMPLETE THE RÉSUMÉ

Prior to finalizing your résumé, ensure that you have added all information identified in steps one through four to your electronic document. As you finalize your résumé, check for information that too frequently is forgotten or not presented appropriately. This is the fifth step in finalizing the information on your résumé. The top of your résumé is called the **information heading**. An information heading contains relevant contact information including name, mailing address, city, state, ZIP code, contact phone, and e-mail address. Include your complete and formal name, including a middle initial if you have one. When listing your e-mail address, remove the hyperlink so the print color is consistent. If your current e-mail address is unprofessional, secure an address that is professional. Include only one contact phone number. Whatever number is listed should be active and have a professional voice-mail message. Check the spelling and numbers for accuracy. Spell out the names of streets. If you use abbreviations, check for appropriate format, capitalization, and punctuation.

information heading
A résumé heading that contains relevant contact information including name, mailing address, city, state, ZIP code, contact phone, and e-mail address.

Immediately after your information heading is the career objective or personal profile created in step one. Review this opening statement to ensure it introduces the reader to who you are and motivates him or her to learn more about your specific knowledge, skills, abilities, and key accomplishments.

In step three, you determined whether a functional or chronological résumé layout was appropriate for your situation. Review the respective layout for proper order and refer to the sample résumés. Confirm that your experience and education are listed chronologically (most recent first). Keep your résumé consistent in its setup, including all periods or no periods at the end of each line, line spacing, alignment of dates, date format, bold/italics, upper- and lowercase words, and underlines. Be consistent with word endings and the use of tense in each section (e.g., *-ing* and *-ed)*. Also be consistent with the use of the postal abbreviation for your state (e.g., the state is *CA*, not *Ca.*, not *Ca*, not *C.A*). When your draft résumé is complete, spell-check and proofread the document to ensure it is free of typographical errors and inconsistencies.

As for proper résumé layout and design, underlines, bold, and italic print are acceptable for emphasis but should not be overdone. Do not use bullets throughout your résumé; use bullets only to emphasize key skills. Use easy-to-read fonts and sizes. Times New Roman or Arial are most common. Apart from your name on the information heading of your résumé, do not use more than two different font sizes, preferably 12 to 14 points. Do not use different color fonts, highlights, or graphics on your résumé; use only black ink. It is not appropriate to include personal information such as a photograph of yourself,

Tailored Package, see
Figure 4-12 on page 139

your birth date, marital status, Social Security number, or hobbies. It is also no longer appropriate to state, "References Available Upon Request" at the close of your résumé. Professional references should be on a separate sheet and provided only when requested. Refer to figure 4-12 for proper format for a professional reference list.

Check to ensure your résumé is presented professionally, is free of errors, and does not contain unnecessary or inappropriate information. Print the résumé in black ink on 8½ × 11–inch, letter-sized paper. Laser print is ideal. Double-sided résumés are not appropriate. If your résumé is more than one page, place your name at the top of each page after page one. Proper résumé paper is cotton-fiber, 24-pound white (not bond or card stock) paper of good quality. Colored paper, especially if dark, is both difficult to read and does not photocopy well. Do not use fancy paper stocks or binders. Do not staple your résumé or other job search documents. Since résumés are frequently photo-copied, stapled résumés and other job search documents may be torn in the process.

When you have completed your résumé and believe it is ready for distribution, have several individuals whom you trust review it for clarity, consistency, punctuation, grammar, typographical errors, and other potential mistakes. Remember that complete sentences are not necessary and, with the exception of your career objective, the words "I" or "my" should not be used. Your résumé must create a positive, professional visual image and be easy to read.

SHARING YOUR RÉSUMÉ

As you begin to share your completed résumé with both potential employers and members of your professional network, you may have the option of presenting your résumé on résumé paper (traditional hard copy) or electronically (online) as an attachment. Résumés printed on résumé paper are designed to be used for face-to-face job searches. Regardless of which method you choose, the first step is to perfect your traditional (hard-copy) résumé, as this document contains key information you will need to share with all potential employers. When converting a traditional (hard-copy) résumé into an online version, consider content. When forwarding a résumé to an employer or posting your résumé online, such as on a job board, consider key words that reflect your target job. When employers and job boards receive résumés, the résumés are commonly dropped into a database or résumé tracking system that allow recruiters to search for potential applicants based on key words and phrases that match the position they are trying to fill. Sometimes, when posting an online résumé, you may be required to cut and paste sections from your traditionally formatted résumé. During this process, you may lose the formatting. Do not worry. Visual appeal is not an issue for this process and formatting does not matter. You are merely dropping your information into a database. Your focus should be on utilizing key words and phrases that sell your skills and quantify your accomplishments.

The second consideration when converting a traditional résumé to an online version is sending it as an attachment while preserving formatting. If you are sending your résumé electronically as an attachment, it is best to send it either as a Microsoft (MS) Word file or as a portable document file (.pdf). Doing so ensures that the résumé layout is properly maintained through the file transfer. Sending your résumé as a .pdf file also ensures that those who do not use the same word processing software as you are able to read the file.

Most colleges and career centers now have electronic job boards that allow students to upload their résumés for recruiters and employers to view. There are also many niche job boards specific to industries. Another popular means of sharing an electronic résumé is through social media sites. Just be certain that you are posting your information on valid business sites and not personal sites. As with a traditional job search, keep track of and monitor all activity with your online search.

When posting your résumé online, always date your resume and update it every two to three months. Most employers won't view online résumés that are more than six months old. Guard your personal information by posting your résumé only on reputable job search sites. Just as with a hard-copy résumé, protect your identity and do not include personal information of any kind, including photographs, marital status, birth dates, or your Social Security number.

Check for Inconsistencies

Circle the fifteen inconsistency errors on the following résumé.

1100 EAST FAVOR AVENUE • POSTVILLE, PA 16722
PHONE (555) 698-2222 • E-MAIL AERIE@PBCC.COM

AMANDA J. ERIE

OBJECTIVE

Seeking a position as an Administrative Assistant where I can utilize my office skills

SUMMARY OF QUALIFICATIONS

- Computer software skills include Microsoft Word, Excel, Outlook, Access, and PowerPoint
- Knowledge of Multi-line telephone system, filing, data entry, formatting of documents and reports, and operation of office equipment.
- Excellent interpersonal skills and polished office etiquette.
- written and oral communication skills
- Typing skills at 50 WPM
- Bilingual in English/Spanish (speaking)

EDUCATION

Reese Community College, Postville, PA Currently pursuing AA Degree in Office Occupations.

Calvin Institute of Technology, Cambridge, OH Office Technology Certificate Spring 2010

WORK AND VOLUNTEER EXPERIENCE

01/11 – Present   *Rigal Entertainment Group*   Postville, CA
Usher – Responsible for ensuring payment of services. Answer customer inquiries. Collect and count ticket stubs.

11/07 – 02/09   Lablaws   Cambridge, OH
Cashier – Operated cash register, stocking, assisting customers

01/07 – 04/07   Jolene's Diner   Cambridge, OH
Server – Provided customer service by waiting tables, cleaned, and operated cash register

In some instances employers, will request that an **electronic formatted résumé** be submitted. Electronic formatted résumés are résumés that are submitted in American Standard Code for Information Interchange (ASCII) format. Once the employer receives your electronic formatted résumé, the résumé is added to a specialized database/software that routinely scans résumés based on key words (qualifications/skills) for specific jobs. The résumé is used to match key words contained in your résumé with specific jobs. Therefore, on this type of résumé, list as many key words as possible related to your target job. For electronic formatted résumés, visual appeal is not an issue. Electronic formatted résumés use Times New Roman font size 10 to 14. An electronic formatted résumé should be left-justified. Avoid tabs and centering. Headings should be in all capital letters. Hard returns must be used instead of word wrap. Avoid bold, italics, underlines, graphics, percent signs, and foreign characters. Also avoid boxes, horizontal and vertical lines, solid/hollow bullets, and table and column formatting.

Content for electronic formatted résumés include having your name at the top of the page on its own line. Standard address formatting (as when addressing a letter) should be used. Use key words specific to your desired job category and/or when communicating your knowledge, skills, and abilities. Work experience dates should have beginning

electronic formatted résumés

Résumés that are submitted in American Standard Code for Information Interchange (ASCII) format.

and ending dates on the same line. Use asterisks or dashes (no bullets or boxes of any kind) and list each telephone number on its own line (no parentheses around area codes). Date your electronic résumé. Just as with hard-copy résumés, do not include personal information of any kind, including photographs, marital status, birth dates, or your Social Security number. See Figure 4-8 for an example of an electronic formatted résumé.

Electronic Résumé Example, see Figure 4-8 on page 135

COVER LETTERS

cover letter

A letter that introduces your résumé.

A **cover letter** is often the first impression a potential employer will have of you. It serves as an introduction to your résumé. Employers use cover letters as screening tools.

When writing a cover letter, use a friendly but professional tone. Use complete sentences and proper grammar. When tailoring your cover letter, include information about the target company that communicates to the employer you have conducted research on the company. In a cover letter, communicate how your key skills, experience, and accomplishments can meet the employer's needs. This is accomplished by identifying the skills and qualifications the target employer is requesting in the job announcement and/or job description and matching these needs with your key skills and qualifications. Let the employer know what you can offer the company, not what you want from the company. In the paragraph where you are communicating your key skills and experience, refer the reader to the attached résumé. Do not duplicate what is already listed on your résumé; instead, emphasize your experience and key skills. Although it is acceptable to utilize the words "I and my" in a cover letter, be careful to not begin most of your sentences with the word "I". Instead, focus the attention toward the employer. This puts the company first and makes its needs more important. Attempt to begin a sentence with what the company will receive with your skills. For example:

Instead of writing, "*I* am proficient in Word,"

Write, "*Your* company will benefit from my proficiency in Word."

Address the cover letter to a specific person. This should be the person who will be making the hiring decision. Do not address your cover letter to a department, the company name, or "to whom it may concern." Call the company and ask for a specific name and title, identifying the appropriate spelling and gender. If you have conducted research and still cannot secure a specific name, use a subject line instead of a salutation. For example, instead of writing, "To Whom It May Concern," write, "Subject: Account Clerk Position." If you have talked to a specific person at your target company, refer to the previous communication. Include the specific position you are seeking in your cover letter and how you learned about the job opening. At the end of your cover letter, request an interview (not the job). Do not write that you look forward to the employer contacting you. Display initiative by stating that you will follow up on your request for an interview within the next week. Include an enclosure notation for your résumé and close courteously.

Use the proper business-letter format for your cover letter. Each word and paragraph in your cover letter must have a purpose. Your goal is to communicate how your knowledge, skills, abilities, and accomplishments fill a targeted company's needs and make the reader want to review your résumé. The cover-letter setup in Figure 4-9 and sample cover letters in Figures 4-10 and 4-11 will help you create a winning cover letter.

Cover Letter Setup, see Figure 4-9 on page 136

Cover Letter Example 1, see Figure 4-10 on page 137

Cover Letter Example 2, see Figure 4-11 on page 138

Print your cover letter on the same type of paper used for your résumé. Copy the information heading you created for your résumé and use it on your cover letter. This creates a consistent and professional visual appeal for your résumé package. Avoid making common mistakes, including typographical or grammatical errors, forgetting to include a date, or forgetting to sign the cover letter. Complete and grammatically correct sentences must be used on a cover letter. As with your résumé, have someone you trust proofread your letter before you send it to a potential employer. Any error communicates a lack of attention to detail. Even minor errors have the potential to disqualify you from securing an interview.

TAILORING YOUR RÉSUMÉ AND COVER LETTER

Tailor your résumé and cover letter specifically to each job and company for which you are applying. Carefully review the target job announcement. If possible, secure a copy of the job description from the company's human resource department if it is not available or attached to the job posting. Identify key job skills that the position requires, and highlight the company needs with your skills. As you learned in step four of creating your résumé, utilize the O*Net website to identify key skills for your targeted position. If necessary, rearrange the order of the information presented on your résumé so that the key skills required for your target position are presented first. On your cover letter, emphasize your specific qualifications that match those required for the open position. Figure 4-12 provides an example of a résumé and cover letter tailored to a specific job announcement.

Tailored Package, see Figure 4-12 on page 139–142

Although mentioned earlier, it cannot be stressed enough that a daytime phone number and e-mail address need to be listed on both the cover letter and résumé. Because most invitations for job interviews occur over the phone, your phone voice-mail and/or message machine need to be professional. Do not include musical introductions or any other greeting that would not make a positive first impression to a potential employer. Maintain a professional e-mail address to use in your job search.

Cory's friend Rebecca was a practical joker. Cory enjoyed calling Rebecca because her voice-mail message started with a joke or had some strange voice and/or music. However, the last time Cory called Rebecca, Cory noticed that Rebecca's message was normal. The next time Cory saw Rebecca, Cory asked Rebecca why her voice message was suddenly so serious. Rebecca explained that she had recently applied for a job and had been selected to interview. However, she was embarrassed because when the interviewer called to arrange the appointment, the interviewer left a message and also suggested that Rebecca change her voice-mail message to a more professional message.

TIPS FOR EX-OFFENDERS

If you have served time in prison and are now attempting to reenter the workforce, you are to be congratulated for wanting to move forward with your life. Others have made poor choices in their past, and you have made restitution for yours. Be honest with the potential employer.

On your résumé, include all jobs you have held and skills you learned while incarcerated. List the correctional facility in place of the employer for these jobs. List all education, including degrees and courses you received while incarcerated. Include the educational institution that provided the training.

The employment application is a legal document. At the bottom of this document, applicants sign a statement that affirms that all information provided on the application is true. Therefore, you must not lie. If, after being hired, your employer discovers that you have lied on the application, you may be immediately terminated. The majority of applications ask if you have been convicted of a felony. Please note that arrests are not convictions. If you have been convicted of a felony, check "Yes." The application should also have a space to write a statement after the felony question. Do not leave this space blank. In this space, write, "Will explain in detail during interview."

WORKPLACE DOS AND DON'TS

Do keep your résumé updated with skills and accomplishments	*Don't* wait until the last minute to update your résumé
Do change your résumé format after you have gained work experience	*Don't* use outdated reference names and letters
Do use the correct format for your résumé	*Don't* send out a résumé or cover letter that has not been proofread by someone you can trust
Do check your résumé and cover letter for errors before sending them to employers	*Don't* forget to sign your cover letter

FIGURE 4-2 Functional Résumé Layout

YOUR NAME (16 point, bold)
Your Address (12 or 14 point, bold)
City, State ZIP
Phone Number (Include Area Code)
E-Mail Address (Remove Hyperlink)

Horizontal line optional and thickness varies

OBJECTIVE Headings can be on the left or centered, 12- or 14-point font, and uppercase or initial cap.
Format headings the same throughout the resumé.
Keep spacing equal between each section.

QUALIFICATIONS (OR SKILLS)
- Relate to target job, all job-related skills and transferable skills
- Most relative to the job are listed first
- Bullet (small round or small square only) these items to stand out

> Emphasize skills and education. List your skills and education before any work experience.

EDUCATION
You may list before qualifications
Do not list high school if you have graduated from college
Include the dates and align to the right
List schools in chronological order, most recent attended first

WORK EXPERIENCE
Include: *Name of Company* and City, State—No Addresses
Job title bolded, if part-time, dates employed (month, year)
List the jobs in chronological order, most recent first align dates to the right
Align dates to the right
List the duties, responsibilities, and achievements
Be consistent in your setup
Use the same tense throughout (*ed* or *ing*)
Do not use complete sentences or *I, me,* or *my*

OTHER CAPABILITIES
Optional items in this section may not be directly related to the job but may interest the employer such as honors or awards.

> **Keep in mind**
> - Watch periods, punctuation
> - Watch spelling
> - Use a regular font, no color, 12-point font (except heading)
> - Use résumé paper, no dark or bright colors
> - Do not use full sentences or *I, me,* or *my*
> - References are not necessary; you will have a separate sheet with references
> - Do not use graphics

Suzie S. Kringle

1234 Tolearn Avenue, Meadeville, PA 16335
555-555-5555
skringle05@careerssuccess.lns

OBJECTIVE

To obtain a position as a Junior Accountant with Owen Company where I can utilize my general accounting skills in a dynamic company.

SKILLS

- Knowledgeable and accurate in general ledger and journal posting
- Basic software knowledge of QuickBooks
- Knowledge of account receivables and account payables
- Experienced with Microsoft Office, including Word, Excel, Access, PowerPoint, and Outlook
- Ten-key at 150 cspm
- Type 50 wpm accurately
- Excellent English grammar, spelling, and punctuation skills
- Accurately follow oral and written instructions
- Strong attention to detail
- Positive attitude, motivated, and organized

EDUCATION

State University, Meadeville, PA   5/12
Bachelor of Science Degree in Business, Accounting

Meadeville City College, Meadeville PA   5/10
Associate in Arts Degree in Business, Certificate of Completion in Account Clerk Program

WORK EXPERIENCE

S and L Accounting   Edinboro, PA   1/10–present
Account Clerk
Assist the Accountant by answering telephone, bookkeeping, data entry in Excel and QuickBooks, verifying totals, making copies, faxing, and other clerical duties when needed.

Bret's Hamburger Haven   Edinboro, PA   1/07–12/09
Cashier/Food Service
Worked as a team member to assist customers with food orders, cleaned, handled cash, and trained new employees.

FIGURE 4-4   Functional Résumé Example without Career Work Experience

HEIDI H. KRINGLE

**1234 Tolearn Avenue, Meadeville, PA 16335
555-555-5555   hkringle02@careersuccess.lns**

OBJECTIVE

To obtain a position as an Office Assistant with Austin Office Supplies that will enable me to utilize my current skills and education.

QUALIFICATIONS

- Type 50 wpm
- Experienced with Microsoft Office, including Word, Excel, Access, PowerPoint, and Outlook
- Accurately proofread and edit documents
- Knowledge of records management
- Positive telephone skills
- Excellent oral and written communications skills
- Positive attitude, motivated, and organized
- Excellent customer services skills

EDUCATION/CERTIFICATION

2010–2012	Meadeville City College	Meadeville, PA

Associate of Art Degree, Business & Technology
Clerical Administration Certificate
GPA 3.9, Dean's list

EXPERIENCE

06/2009–present	Fine Linens by Jen	Meadeville, PA

Cashier
Responsibilities include: providing customer service, cashiering, placing merchandise on the floor, helping return go backs, processing merchandise on the floor, stocking merchandise in back/stockroom, training new hires.

02/2003–05/2009	Jerry's Burger Place	Meadeville, PA

Cashier/Counter Person
Responsibilities included: assisted guests with their orders, ensured a safe and clean work environment, and assisted other team members as needed.

FIGURE 4-5 Chronological Résumé Layout

YOUR NAME (16 point, bold)

Your Address (12 or 14 point, bold) ■ **City, State ZIP** ■ **Phone Number** (Include Area Code)
E-Mail Address (Remove Hyperlink)

PERSONAL PROFILE:

Include key skill sets. Headings can be on the left or centered, 12- or 14-point font, and uppercase or initial cap. Format headings the same throughout the resumé.
Keep the spacing equal between each section.

PROFESSIONAL EXPERIENCE:

Group key skills, experience, and accomplishments under each major skill set heading.

First Skill Set Subheading

- Communicate experience, and key accomplishments relating to your first skill set subheading
- Using power words, quantify as much as possible
- Include duties, responsibilities, and achievements

> Emphasize key skill sets and accomplishments. List work experience before education and employment history.

Second Skill Set Subheading

- Relate statements to target job. Communicate both job-related skills or transferable skills
- Accomplishments and experience most relative to target job are listed first
- Bullet (small round or small square only) accomplishments and experience to stand out

Third Skill Set Subheading

- Be consistent in setup
- Use same tense throughout (ed or ing)
- Do not use complete sentences or I, me, or my

> **Keep in mind**
> - Watch punctuation, and spelling
> - Can be one or two pages. If two pages, place name on second page
> - Use a regular font, no color, 12-point font (except heading)
> - Do not use full sentences or *I, me,* or *my*
> - Do not use graphics
> - Align bullets to the right

WORK HISTORY:

Name of Company and City, State—No Addresses—
dates employed (month, year)
Job title (bold title, NOT employer)
List jobs in chronological order with most recent date first

EDUCATION:

Do not list high school
Include the years attended, areas of study, and degrees earned
List schools in chronological order, most recent attended first

PROFESSIONAL AFFILIATIONS/CERTIFICATIONS:

List professional memberships including the name of the organization, status (member, board member, etc.) and dates of membership. Also include any certifications or community service activities that are relevant to the target job.

FIGURE 4-6   Chronological Résumé Example with Degree

PEARL B. KRINGLE, CPA

1234 Tolearn Avenue ▲ Meadeville, PA 16335 ▲ 555.555.5555
pbkringle@careerssuccess.lns

PROFILE:
Highly experienced, personable, and detail-oriented Certified Public Accountant with expertise and demonstrated leadership in the areas of accounting, computer information systems, and quantitative analysis.

PROFESSIONAL EXPERIENCE:

Accounting
- Audit cash, investments, payables, fixed assets, and prepaid expenses for small business enterprises, corporations, and not-for-profit organizations.
- Collect and analyze data to detect deficient controls, extravagance, fraud, or noncompliance with laws, regulations, and management policies.
- Prepare detailed reports on audit findings, report to management about asset utilization and audit results, and recommend changes in operations and financial activities.
- Inspect account books and accounting systems for efficiency, effectiveness, and use of accepted accounting procedures to record transactions.
- Examine and evaluate financial and information systems, recommending controls to ensure system reliability and data integrity.
- Confer with company officials about financial and regulatory matters.

Computer Information Systems
- Developed information resources, providing data security/control, strategic computing, and disaster recovery.
- Consulted with users, management, vendors, and technicians to assess computing needs and system requirements.
- Stayed abreast of advances in technology and forwarded research and recommendations to ensure company and respective clients were utilizing proper and most efficient tools and information systems.
- Met with department heads, managers, supervisors, vendors to solicit cooperation and resolve problems.
- Provided users with technical support for computer problems.

Quantitative Analysis
- Assembled computerized spreadsheets, draw charts, and graphs used to illustrate technical reports.
- Analyzed financial information to produce forecasts of business, industry, and economic conditions for use in making investment decisions.
- Maintained knowledge and stayed abreast of developments in the fields of industrial technology, business, finance, and economic theory.
- Interpreted data affecting investment programs, such as price, yield, stability, future trends in investment risks, and economic influences.

FIGURE 4-6   Chronological Resumé Example with Degree page 2 (*continued*)

PEARL B. KRINGLE, CPA

Page Two

- Monitored fundamental economic, industrial, and corporate developments through the analysis of information obtained from financial publications and services, investment banking firms, government agencies, trade publications, company sources, and personal interviews.
- Recommended investments and investment timing to companies, investment firm staff, or the investing public.
- Determined the prices at which securities should be syndicated and offered to the public.
- Prepared plans of action for investment based on financial analyses.

WORK HISTORY:

Coopers & Lion, LLP, Alltown, PA   May 2010–present
Auditor

Mitchell Ho, CPA, Atlanta, GA   May 2007–April 2010
General Accountant

U.S. Department of Labor, Atlanta, GA   January 2005–February 2007
Program Assistant

Grace's Burger Palace, Riverside, GA   August 2001–December 2004
Server

EDUCATION AND LICENSE:

Masters of Computer Information Systems
Georgia State University, Atlanta, GA   August 2012

Certified Public Accountant – State of Georgia   May 2010

Bachelor of Science in Accounting
Heather Glenn College, Heather Glenn, NC   May 2007

PROFESSIONAL AFFILIATIONS:

American Institute of Certified Financial Accountants
Beta Alpha Psi Fraternity
National Association of Black Accountants

FIGURE 4-7   Chronological Résumé Example with No Degree

Steven Mark Kringle

1234 Tolearn Avenue ■ Meadeville, PA 16335 ■ 555.555.5555
smkringle@careersuccess.lns

PERSONAL PROFILE

Results and efficiency focused professional with experience in sales/vendor relations, inventory/ warehousing, and management/supervision. Proven ability in relationship management with demonstrated and consistent increase in sales over a five-year period. Inventory expertise includes streamlined operations, improved productivity, and favorable inventory ratio utilization for wholesale food supplier. Management ability to create goal-driven teams, groom leaders, and facilitate the creation of a learning organization.

PROFESSIONAL EXPERIENCE

Customer Service Orientation ■ Innovative Risk Taker ■ Excellent Quantitative Skills ■ Purchasing, Inventory Planning & Control ■ Supply Chain Management ■ Warehouse Operations ■ Process Improvement ■ Cost Containment ■ Hiring, Staffing & Scheduling Safety Training ■ Excellent Computer Knowledge

Sales/Vendor Relations

- Through the establishment of vendor relationships, schedule product installations, exchanges, buy-backs or removals of equipment or other assets including supplier networks and agent contacts in order to meet customer expectations for private soda company. Have grown sales territory from two county area to tri-state contract area over four-year period.

- Source and facilitate delivery of product (e.g., beverage equipment, parts, point of sale material, return of assets) for retail suppliers. Sales complaints are consistently .05% per year, while sales volume and customer satisfaction rates are the highest of all sales team and consistently grow.

- Research and resolve issues for customers, business partners, and Company associates in order to expedite service, installations, or orders using information systems and working with supply chain partners.

- Create and maintain partnerships with customers, clients or third party service providers (e.g., contract service/installation agents, distributors) by establishing common goals, objectives, and performance target requirements in order to improve customer service and satisfaction.

- Created troubleshooting equipment process which allows retail suppliers to receive immediate response on service issues (e.g., beverage vending, dispensing) via telephone or Internet to minimize customer down time and service cost.

FIGURE 4-7 Chronological Résumé Example with No Degree (*continued*)

Steven Mark Kringle

Page Two

Inventory/Warehousing

- Responsible for maintaining customer contact to confirm service or orders including accuracy, service follow up, equipment service confirmation, product delivery confirmation, and routine service scheduling for local foodservice broker.

- Received, recorded, and responded to customer or consumer inquiries/feedback using specially designed database which documented best practices from nationwide foodservice association in an effort to provide improved service, order accuracy, and optimized supply chain efficiency. Information was collected, analyzed, and reported to all members of the supply chain for feedback and control purposes.

- Processed orders for goods and services with food service business partners, customers, suppliers, and company associates, either through direct telephone contact or electronic means, to increase speed and accuracy of order transactions and improve loss prevention systems.

Management/Supervision

- Developed and trained team members on inventory control, customer service, and safety for local foodservice provider. Program was so successful customers within the company supply chain requested and received training. To date, over 500 individuals have received custom training.

- Supervised cross-functional team of 100 including order technicians, outside repair personnel, transportation associates, warehouse attendants, and loss prevention specialists.

- As assistant-manager for college-town restaurant, assisted in the hiring, training, scheduling, and performance evaluation of staff for small soda company and local food service supplier.

<u>WORK HISTORY</u>

Christopher Cola Company, Susanville, NE   2007–2012
Vendor Relations Associate

Joshua Food Service, Pocatoe, NE   2005–2007
Warehouse Manager

Nick-Mike Ribs 'N Stuff, Pocatoe, NE   2003–2005
Assistant Restaurant Manager

<u>EDUCATION/PROFESSIONAL DEVELOPMENT</u>

University of Nebraska, Lincoln, NE   2009–2012
Business Management/Marketing

FIGURE 4-8   Electronic Resumé Example

AUTUMN S. KRINGLE
1234 TOLEARN AVENUE,
MEADEVILLE, PA 16335
555-555-5555
askringle@careersuccess.lns

OBJECTIVE

Bookkeeper

KEY WORD SUMMARY

Bookkeeping skills, financial management, accounting, receivables and payroll, organized, data entry, communication skills, problem solving, responsible, team player, computer skills.

EDUCATION

City College: City, WA
2012
Associate Degree in Accounting

COURSES OF STUDY
----
* Intro to Accounting
* Intro to Business
* MS Office
* Workplace Communication
* Office Accounting
* Business Law
* Intro to Marketing

COMPUTER SKILLS
----
* Microsoft Office: Word, Excel, Access, PowerPoint
* WordPerfect
* Internet

WORK EXPERIENCE

Yang Enterprises: Fresno, CA
2010 – Present
Bookkeeping Assistant: Responsible for assisting accounting department with payroll, budgets, planning, and forecasting, purchasing, and managing accounts.

FIGURE 4-9   Cover Letter Setup

Date of Letter

Employer's Name, Title
Company Name
Address
City, State Zip

Dear Mr./Ms./Dr.:

First Paragraph. Give the reason for the letter, the position for which you are applying, and how you learned of this position. Note any previous contact you may have had with the employer.

Second Paragraph. Tell why you are interested in the position, the organization, and its products or services. Indicate any research you have done on the position and/or the employer.

Third Paragraph. Refer to the attached resumé and highlight relevant aspects of your resumé. Emphasize the skills mentioned in the advertisement or on the job description. Provide specific reasons why the organization should hire you and what you can do to contribute to the organization's success.

Last Paragraph. Indicate your desire for an interview, and offer flexibility as to the time and place. Thank the employer for his or her consideration and express anticipation in meeting him or her. Include a phone number and e-mail address for contact.

Sincerely,

(Do not forget to sign your cover letter)

Your Name
Your Address
City, State Zip

Enclosure

FIGURE 4-10   Cover Letter Example 1

September 25, 2015

Owen Corporation
Attention Brandon Owen
435 East Chesny Street
Meadeville, PA 16335

Dear Mr. Owen:

As a recent accounting graduate of State University, Meadeville, I was delighted to learn from your web site of the available Junior Accountant position. The purpose of this letter is to express a strong interest in becoming an Owen Company Accountant at your Meadeville facility. In addition to possessing a B.S. degree in Business, Accounting, I am responsible and consider myself a leader.

Owen Company sponsors a variety of community services and employee recognition programs, which I have read a great deal about. Your company has earned my respect, as it has from much of the community for your involvement in the after-school programs in Meadeville Unified School District.

As you will see on the attached resumé, Owen Company would benefit from the skills I have learned throughout college. These include: general ledger and journal posting; Microsoft Word, Excel, and Access programs; Quickbooks; and accurate ten-key (150 cspm). In addition, I also offer a superior work ethic, strong communicative abilities, attention to detail, and a keen interest in upgrading my skills.

I am confident that my skills and abilities will make me an ideal candidate for a position in this field. I would appreciate an opportunity to meet with you to discuss how my skills can meet the needs of Owen Company. I will contact you by phone within the week to discuss the possibility of an interview.

Sincerely,

Suzie Kringle

Suzie Kringle
1234 Tolearn Avenue
Meadeville, PA 16335

Enclosure

FIGURE 4-11   Cover Letter Example 2

HEIDI H. KRINGLE

1234 Tolearn Avenue, Meadeville, PA 16335
555-555-5555   hshore02@careersuccess.lns

September 21, 2015

Mr. Jared Bill
Austin Office Supplies
1122 Friendly Road
Meadeville, PA 93725

Dear Mr. Bill:

I recently spoke with Gene Armstrong, an employee at your company, and he recommended that I send you a copy of my resumé. Knowing the requirements for the position and that I am interested in working at this type of establishment, he felt that I would be an ideal candidate for your office assistant position.

My personal goal is to be a part of an organization such as yours that wants to excel in both growth and profit. I would welcome the opportunity to be employed at Austin's Office Supplies since this is the largest and best-known office supply company in the city. Your company has a reputation of excellent products and service.

Austin's Office Supplies would benefit from someone such as I who is accustomed to a fast-paced environment where deadlines are a priority and handling multiple jobs simultaneously is the norm. As you can see on the attached resumé, my previous jobs required me to be well organized, accurate, and friendly. I enjoy a challenge and work hard to attain my goals. Great customer skills are important in a business such as yours.

Nothing would please me more than to be a part of your team. I would like very much to discuss with you how I could contribute to your organization with my office skills and my dependability. I will contact you next week to arrange an interview. In the interim, I can be reached at 555-555-5555.

Sincerely,

Heidi H. Kringle

Heidi H. Kringle

Enclosure

FIGURE 4-12   Tailored Package—Page 1 Job Announcement

ACCOUNT CLERK – position #022394   full time, permanent posit

The current vacancy is a full-time position at Viau Technical College.

Definition: Under direction performs a wide variety of entry-level accounting/busines office work.

Compensation: Starts at $3,176 per month. Full-time permanent positions provide an attractive benefit package which include health, dental, and vision coverage for the employee and eligible dependents, as well as life insurance and disability coverage for employees.

Experience: Entry-level experience performing general accounting duties.

Education: Formal or informal education equivalent to completion of an Associate Degree in accounting.

Examples of Duties: Performs a wide variety of duties including but not limited to: basic accounting work; verifying, balancing, and posting/recording accounting informati< verifying and preparing invoices, checks, correspondence, and statistical information; proof-reading; and filing. Calculates, prepares, and reconciles various financial reports. Entering and retrieving data from computer system as needed. Assigning and/or reviewil the work of other employees and students. May perform other related duties as needed.

Required Knowledge and Abilities:
Knowledge of sequence of procedures in the accounting cycle, analysis, use, and interpretation of accounting and financial data; and modern office practices. Knowledge of and ability to employ proper English usage, spelling, grammar, and punctuation. Skil make deposits, process checks, and reconcile accounts; employ mathematical and statisti< techniques sufficient to maintain district records; keyboard; utilize word processing software, email, online calendaring, and data entry/retrieval from database programs; and create and utilize spreadsheets. Ability to assign, monitor, and/or review the work of others; receive and follow instructions and appropriately interact with students, staff, faculty, and the public; and learn and apply college and district policies and procedures.

Selection Process: The selection process will include screening to ensure applicatior are complete and meet all minimum qualifications. This process will also include a written test of knowledge and abilities (35% weight), a performance test (35% weight), a an oral appraisal board interview (30% weight). Of those candidates achieving a passir score on the first test, only the 30 highest scoring candidates, plus ties, will be invited the performance exam. Of those candidates achieving a passing score on the performar exam, only the 15 highest scoring candidates, plus ties, will be invited to the oral appraisal board interview. Passing score is 75% out of 100% on each testing section.

FIRST EXAM IS TENTATIVELY SCHEDULED FOR SATURDAY, JUNE 20, 2015.

To move forward in the selection process, you must complete an online application through our web site at www.viaucommunitycollege.com. Resumes may also be submitted by mail, in person, or by emailing to job@viaucommunitycollege.com.

Filing Deadline: 4:30 p.m., Monday, June 1, 2015.

FIGURE 4-12   Tailored Package—Page 2 Resumé (*continued*)

Jolene M. Kringle

1234 Tolearn Avenue ■ Meadville, PA ■ 555.555.5555
jmkringle@careersuccess.lns

Objective

Highly motivated, responsible, and ethical individual seeks an entry-level accounting position with Viau Technical College in an effort to apply newly acquired general business and accounting skills. Experienced in basic accounting procedures, operational efficiencies, and logistics.

Key Skills & Qualifications

- Strong math and analytical skills
- Data entry
- Bilingual (Spanish–speak and write)
- Works well in group environments
- Excellent grammatical and English usage
- Proficient in MAS 90 and Quickbooks

- Demonstrate leadership
- Maintain records and filing
- Strong attention to detail
- Experience with balancing and posting
- Accurately proofread and edit documents
- Proficient in Word, Excel, Access, Outlook

Education

Hill Valley Technical College, Clarkville, PA   01/10–06/12
Associate of Arts Degree, Accounting

Work Experience

El Montes Restaurant, Reedville, PA   12/08–present
Bookkeeper/Server
Perform bookkeeping functions for small family business including creation and analysis of financial statements, cash/banking functions, and communication with CPA firm. Implemented electronic accounting and inventory system which saved the company an estimated $50K. Serve as Lead Server for evening staff. In addition to exemplary customer service and cashier duties, responsibilities include inventory control, and training of new staff training in both customer service and food safety/handling for busy Mexican food restaurant.

Freshwide Marketing, Lewis, PA   05–09/08, 09, 10
Quality Control Clerk (*seasonal*)
Received and counted stock items and recorded data. Monitored fruit and produce as it arrived or was shipped from cold storage for twenty independent fruit growers. Verified inventory computations by comparing them to physical counts of stock, and investigated discrepancies or adjusted errors. Stored items in an orderly and accessible manner in cold storage and warehouse.

Starlight Produce, Lewis, PA   06/06–09/08
Shipping Manifest Clerk
As a shipping clerk for regional fruit packer, prepared, monitored, and facilitated orders for shipping to over fifty clients throughout the United States. Duties included examining contents and comparing with records, such as manifests, invoices, or orders, to verify accuracy of incoming or outgoing shipment. Prepared documents, such as work orders, bills of lading, and shipping orders to route materials. Determined shipping method for materials, using knowledge of shipping procedures, routes, and rates.

FIGURE 4-12 Tailored Package—Page 3 Cover Letter (*continued*)

Jolene M. Kringle

1234 Tolearn Avenue ■ Meadeville, PA 16335 ■ 555.555.5555

jmkringle@careersuccess.lns

April 21, 2015

Monique Marshall, Director
Human Resource Department
Viau Community College
60157 S. Holbrook
Viau, PA 12150

RE: Account Clerk Position #022394

Dear Ms. Marshall:

It is with great excitement that I am submitting the following application package for consideration of your current full time Account Clerk Position posted on the Viau Community College web site. Viau Community College has a legacy of quality and excellence in education and nothing would please me more than to apply my newly acquired accounting education to your organization.

As you can see on the attached resumé, your company will benefit from my demonstrated leadership in the areas of general accounting, business, and computer applications. Excelling in the creation and quantitative analysis of basic financial statements, I am familiar with both the installation and utilization of common accounting software programs. At my current job, interaction with both the company owners and the company's contracted CPA firm is a weekly required activity which has greatly improved my communication and presentation skills. In my opinion, diversity is a valuable asset and I enjoy utilizing my fluency in speaking Spanish when interacting with customers. I consider myself an ethical and responsible individual with excellent verbal and written communication skills.

It would be a privilege to have the opportunity to discuss how my knowledge, skills, and professional experience can contribute to the continued success of the Viau Community College. I will contact you within the next week to follow-up on my application materials. In the interim, I can be reached at 555-555-5555 or via e-mail at jmkringle@careersuccess.lns.

Sincerely,

Jolene M. Kringle

Jolene M. Kringle

Enclosures

FIGURE 4-12 Tailored Package—Page 4 Reference List (*continued*)

Jolene M. Kringle

1234 Tolearn Avenue ■ Meadeville, PA 16335 ■ 555.555.5555

jmkringle@careersuccess.lns

Professional Reference List

Name	Relationship	Phone	E-mail	Mailing Address
Autumn Hart	Former Accounting Instructor, Hill Valley Technical College	555.555-1111	atmnhrt@hillvalley.scl	123 Hillvalley Clarkville, PA
Gloria Montes	Owner, El Montes Restaurant	555.555-1112	gloria@eatelmontes.fat	5432 Food Ct. Reedville, PA
Gary Solis	Floor Manager, Freshwide Marketing	555.555-1113	solisg@freshwide.fruit	2220 Tulare Lewis, PA
Patty Negoro	Office Manager, Starlight Produce	555.555-1114	pattyn@starlight.sun	444 Adoline Lewis, PA

Concept Review and Application

Key Terms

self-discovery 103
career objective 105
personal profile 105
targeted job search 106
cost of living 106
electronic image 107
job search portfolio 107
electronic job search portfolio 107

letters of recommendation 109
networking 111
informational interview 113
network list 113
résumé 116
functional résumé layout 118
chronological résumé layout 118
job-specific skills 119

transferable skills 119
soft skills 119
power words 120
information heading 121
electronic formatted résumés 123
cover letter 124

Summary

- The career objective or personal profile is a brief statement that sells your key skills and relates to your self-discovery
- A targeted job search leads you through the process of identifying open positions for which you are qualified, in addition to identifying companies for which you would like to work
- Ensure you have a professional electronic image while job searching
- Professional networking is the act of creating professional relationships
- In addition to people you already know, develop additional network contacts through various sources of job leads
- Creating and maintaining a job search portfolio will keep you organized and prepared during the job search process

- Create a list of professional references for employers
- A winning résumé makes it easy for potential employers to quickly and easily identify your skills and experience
- Update your résumé with new skills and accomplishments at least once a year
- Include both job-specific skills and transferable skills on your résumé
- Use the correct résumé layout for your career work experience
- A cover letter is most often an employer's first impression of you
- Check that your résumé and cover letter are free of typographical and grammatical errors
- Share your résumé electronically as a .pdf file to ensure the résumé layout is maintained

If You Were the Boss

1. What information would you supply to a job seeker during an informational interview with you?

2. If you discovered that one of your top interview candidates had an unprofessional website, what would you do?

3. What would you look for first when reviewing a résumé?

4. What would your reaction be if you were reading a cover letter that had several typing and grammar errors?

The Web Corner

http://www.rileyguide.com/network.html#netprep

http://jobsearch.about.com/od/networking

http://www.truecareers.com

http://www.weddles.com/associations/index.cfm

http://money.cnn.com/magazines/fortune/rankings/

http://www.glassdoor.com/index.htm

www.onetcenter.org/

http://resume.monster.com

http://jobstar.org/tools/resume/index.htm

http://jobsearch.about.com/od/networking

Activities

Create a reference list with at least three names; include the following information.

Reference 1

Name

Job title

Place of employment

Address

Telephone number

E-mail address

Relationship (why is he or she a reference?)

Reference 2

Name

Job title

Place of employment

Address

Telephone number

E-mail address

Relationship (why is he or she a reference?)

Reference 3

Name

Job title

Place of employment

Address

Telephone number

E-mail address

Relationship (why is he or she a reference?)

Activity 4-2

Using the following network table to create a networking list.

NETWORK TABLE				
Network List				
Name	Address	Phone No.	E-Mail Address	Last Date of Contact

Activity 4-3

Using an Internet job site or other job sources, identify three specific job titles that match your career goals and current qualifications.

Job Titles
1.
2.
3.

Design a personal business card.

Secure a job application online or from a local employer. With the exception of your signature, complete the application. Include this document in your job search portfolio.

Conduct an Internet search to identify five new power words to include in your résumé.

1. _____

2. _____

3. _____

4. _____

5. _____

Activity 4-7

Search for a job you would like to have when you graduate, and fill in the following information that will be used to tailor your résumé and create a cover letter.

Position for which you are applying	
How you learned about the job	
Any contact you have had with the employer or others about the job	
Why are you interested in this job?	
Why are you interested in this company?	
What products or services are provided?	
List relevant skills related to the job description	
List reasons this company should hire you	
Indicate your desire for an interview	
Indicate your flexibility for an interview (time and place)	

Activity 4-8

Using a word-processing program and the steps and/or exercises from this chapter, create a résumé for the job you found in Activity 4-7.

Activity 4-9

Using a word processing program and the information from this chapter, create a cover letter for the job you found in Activity 4-7.

Activity 4-10

Change the résumé from activity 4-8 to an electronic formatted résumé.

Sample Exam Questions

1. The act of creating professional relationships is referred to as _____.

2. The following people could be included in a professional network:

   _____,

   _____,

   _____,

   _____, and

   _____.

3. One of the most obvious job sources is utilizing your _____.

4. Keep your phone message _____.

5. The process of identifying your key interests and skills built upon career goals is known as

   _____.

6. The _____ or _____ is an introductory written statement at the beginning of a résumé.

7. A _____ is an image formed when someone is researching you through a computer search.

8. An employment application is a _____.

9. Update your résumé at least _____.

10. If you are starting a new career, create a résumé using the _____.

11. A/An _____ résumé format emphasizes your related work experience and skills.

12. _____ skills are those that are directly related to a specific job.

13. _____ skills are transferable from one job to the next.

14. Use _____ words whenever possible in your résumé; they describe your accomplishments in a lively and specific way.

15. The _____ is an introduction to your résumé.

REFERENCES

Jim Blasingame, "There Are No Handshakes 'In the Clouds,'" *The Wall Street Journal* (Special Advertising Feature), October 13, 2009, B5.

Ritch Sorenson, Grace DeBord, and Ida Ramirez, *Business and Management Communication: A Guide Book,* 4th edition (Upper Saddle River, NJ: Prentice Hall, 2001), pp. 6–10.

Steven Pinker, *The Stuff of Thought* (New York: Viking, a Member of Penguin Group (USA), Inc., 2007).

Linda Talley, "Body Language: Read It or Weep," *HR Magazine,* July 2010, p. 64.

Talley, "Body Language," p. 65.

Jeffrey Jacobi, *The Vocal Advantage* (Upper Saddle River, NJ: Prentice Hall, 1996).

Quoted in Joyce M. Rosenberg, "Don't Take Voice Message for Granted," Associated Press, February 21, 2006.

Eric Kress, "The Unintended Word," *HR Magazine* August 2006. p. 51.

Research presented in "We Can Measure the Power of Charisma," *Harvard Business Review,* January–February 2010, p. 34.

Benice Atufunwa, "The Art of Effective Communi-cation," *Black Enterprise,* November 2009, p. 47.

An of empathy in both humans and other animals is Frans de Waal, *The Age of Empathy* (New York: Harmony, 2009).

Robert Lee Hotz, "How Your Brain Allows You to Walk in Another's Shoes," *The Wall Street Journal,* August 17, 2007, p. B1.

Jared Sandberg, "'It Says Press Any Key. Where's the Any Key?'" *The Wall Street Journal,* February 20, 2007, p. B1.

Paul Hemp, "Death by Information Overload," *Harvard Business Review,* September 2009, p. 83.

Mark Henricks, "Can We Talk? Speaking Up about the Value of Dialogue," *Entrepreneur,* January 1998, p. 82.

Sharon Lund O'Neil, "An Empowered Attitude Can Enhance Communication Skills," *Business Education Forum,* April 1998, pp. 28–30.

Frank Luntz, "Words That Pack Power," *Business* Week, November 3, 2008, p. 106; Roberta H. Karapelsl and Vanessa D. Arnold, "Speaker's Credibility in Persuasive Work Situations," *Business Education* Forum, December 1997, pp. 24–26; Interview by Alyssa Danigelis, "Like, Um, You Know," *Fast Company,* May 2006, p. 99.

Jean Mausehund and R. Neil Dortch, "Communications—Presentation Skills in the Digital Age," *Business Education Forum,* April 1999, pp. 30–32.

"Avoid Words That Mar Your Image," *Administrative Professional Today,* January 2009, pp. 1–2.

For more details, see Brian Fugere, Chelsea Hardaway, and Jon Warshawsky, *Why Business People Speak Like Idiots* (New York: Free Press, 2005).

Joann Baney, *Guide to Interpersonal Communication* (Upper Saddle River, NJ: Pearson/Prentice Hall, 2004), p. 7.

Quoted in Jessica Shambora, "Stop Talking and Start Listening," *Fortune,* November 9, 2009, p. 24.

Daniel Araoz, "Right Brain Management (RBM): Part 2," *Human Resources Forum,* September 1989, p. 4.

Cited in Matthew S. Scott "Five Keys to Effective Listening," *Black Enterprise,* March 2005, p. 113.

Ideas from Marshall Goldsmith cited in "Eliminate Bad Words," *Manager's Edge,* special issue, 2008, p. 5.

Quoted in Mimi Whitefield, "Listen Up—Your Job Could Depend on It," *Miami Herald* (www.miamiherald.com), April 20, 2009.

The information in this section is from Holly Weeks, "Taking the Stress Out of Stressful Conversations," *Harvard Business Review,* July–August 2001, pp. 112–119. The quote is from p. 117.

Deborah Tannen, *Talking from 9 to 5* (New York: William Morrow, 1994); Tannen, "The Power of Talk: Who Gets Heard and Why," *Harvard Business Review,* September–October 1995, pp. 138–148; Daniel J. Canary and Kathryn Dindia, *Sex Differences and Similarities in Communication* (Mahwah, NJ: Erlbaum, 1998), p. 318; John Gray, *Men Are from Mars, Women Are from Venus* (New York: HarperCollins, 1992).

CHAPTER 5

Communication

Rock star Bono was visiting then-Senator Jesse Helms's Capitol Hill office to enlist his help in the global war against AIDS. Bono had all the facts and figures at his fingertips, and he launched into a detailed appeal based on these data. He was, in essence, speaking to Helms the same way he had recently spoken to executives and technical experts at the many foundations and corporations he had approached about the issue. But within a few minutes, Bono sensed that he was losing Helms's attention, and he instinctively changed his pitch.

Objectives

1. Explain the basic communication process.
2. Explain the relationship-building aspect of interpersonal communication.
3. Describe the nature and importance of nonverbal communication in the workplace.
4. Identify roadblocks to communication.
5. Know how to build bridges to communication.
6. Overcome many gender communication barriers.
7. Enhance your listening skills.
8. Describe the formal channels of communication within organizations.

Knowing that Helms was a deeply religious man (and drawing on his own born-again Christian values), Bono began speaking of Jesus Christ's concern for the sick and the poor. He argued that AIDS should be considered the twenty-first-century equivalent of leprosy, an affliction cited in many Bible stories of the New Testament. Helms immediately sat up and began listening, and before the meeting was over he had promised to become the Senate champion for Bono's cause.[1]

Whether or not you believe that combating AIDS is a worthy cause, or believe in Christian values, the story about Bono's conversation with Helms sends a key message about personal communication effectiveness. You have to understand your listener's viewpoint and interests to get through to him or her—or even to get the person to listen.

Effective communication skills are also important for many other reasons. Communication is so vital that it has been described as the glue that holds organizations and families together. Most job foul-ups and personal relationship disputes are considered to be a result of communication problems. Furthermore, to be successful in work or personal life, you usually have to be an effective communicator. You can't make friends or stand up against enemies unless you can communicate with them. And you can't accomplish work through others unless you can send and receive messages effectively.

In this chapter we explain several important aspects of interpersonal communication, such as the communication process and overcoming various communication barriers. Many factors contribute to enhanced communication, leading in turn to more effective human relations. Explanation should also lead to skill improvement. For example, if you understand the steps involved in getting a message across to another person, you may be able to prevent many communication problems.

HOW DOES COMMUNICATION TAKE PLACE?

LEARNING OBJECTIVE 1

A convenient starting point in understanding how people communicate is to look at the steps involved in communicating a message. **Communication** is the sending and receiving of messages. A diagram of how the process takes place is shown in Figure 5-1. The theme of the model is that two-way communication involves three major steps and that each step is subject to interference or noise. Assume that Crystal, a customer, wishes to inform Tony, a used-car sales representative, that she is willing to make an offer of $8,000 on a used car. The price tag on the car is $8,750.

communication

The sending and receiving of messages.

Step One. *Sender encodes the message.* **Encoding** is the process of organizing ideas into a series of symbols, such as words and gestures, designed to communicate with the receiver. Word choice has a strong influence on communication effectiveness. The better a person's grasp of language, the easier it is for him or her to encode. Crystal says, "Tony, this car obviously is not in excellent condition, but I am willing to give you $8,000 for it."

Step Two. *Sender chooses one or more channels.* The message is sent via a communication channel or medium, such as voice, telephone, paper, e-mail, or messaging. It is important to select a medium that fits the message. It would be appropriate to use the spoken word to inform a coworker that he swore under his breath at a customer. It would be less appropriate to send the same message through e-mail. Many messages on and off the job are sent nonverbally through the use of gestures and facial expressions. For example, a smile from a superior during a meeting is an effective way of communicating the message "I agree with you." Crystal has chosen the oral medium to send her message.

Step Three. *Receiver decodes the message.* In **decoding**, the receiver interprets the message and translates it into meaningful information. Decoding is the process of understanding a message. Barriers to communication are most likely to surface at the decoding step. People often interpret messages according to their psychological needs and motives. Tony wants to interpret Crystal's message that she is very eager to purchase this car. Therefore, he may listen attentively for more information demonstrating that she is interested in purchasing the car. Effective decoding is also dependent on the receiver understanding the words chosen by the sender. Breadth of vocabulary as well as cultural factors can influence the interpretation of a word or phrase. For example, if Crystal says the car is "bad," she could mean that the car is in poor condition or that it is wonderful, depending on her vernacular.

FIGURE 5-1 The Communication Process

When sending a message to another person, one has to take into account potential barriers to communication. Feedback from the receiver helps clarify if the message has been sent as intended.

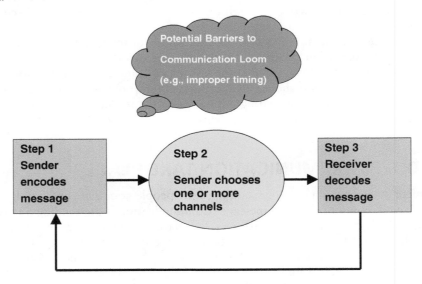

Feedback helps sender evaluate effectiveness of message.

Decoding the message leads naturally to action—the receiver does something about the message. If the receiver acts in the manner the sender wants, the communication has been successful. If Tony says, "It's a deal," Crystal had a successful communication event. Many missteps can occur between encoding and decoding a message. **Barriers to communication** or unwanted interference or **noise** can distort or block a message. If Crystal has an indecisive tone and raises her voice at the end of her statement, it could indicate that she is not really serious about offering a maximum of $8,000 for the car.

HOW DOES INTERPERSONAL COMMUNICATION RELATE TO RELATIONSHIP BUILDING?

Another way of understanding the process of interpersonal communication is to examine how communication is a vehicle for building relationships. According to Texas Tech business communication professors Rich Sorenson, Grace De Bord, and Ida Ramirez, we establish relationships along two primary dimensions: dominate– subordinate and cold– warm. In the process of communicating, we attempt to *dominate or subordinate*. When we dominate, we attempt to control communication. When we subordinate, we attempt to yield control, or think first of the wishes and needs of the other person. Dominators expect the receiver of messages to submit to them; subordinate people send a signal that they expect the other person to dominate.[2]

LEARNING OBJECTIVE 2

We indicate whether we want to dominate or subordinate by the way we speak or write, or by the nonverbal signals we send. The dominator might speak loudly or enthusiastically, write forceful messages filled with exclamation points, or gesture with exaggerated, rapid hand movements. He or she might write a harsh e-mail message, such as, "It's about time you started taking your job seriously and put in some real effort."

In the subordinate mode, we might speak quietly and hesitantly, in a meek tone, being apologetic. A subordinate person might ask, "I know you have better things on your mind than to worry about me, but I was wondering when I can expect my reimbursement for travel expenses?" In a work setting we ordinarily expect people with more formal authority to have the dominant role in conversations. However, in more democratic, informal companies, workers with more authority are less likely to feel the need to dominate conversations.

The *cold–warm dimension* also shapes communication because we invite the same behavior that we send. Cold, impersonal, negative messages evoke similar messages from others. In contrast, warm verbal and nonverbal messages evoke similar behavior from others. Getting back to the inquiry about the travel-expense check, here is a colder-versus-warmer response by the manager:

Colder: Travel vouchers really aren't my responsibility. You'll just have to wait like everybody else.

Warmer: I understand your problem. Not getting reimbursed on time is a bummer. I'll follow up on the status of your expense check sometime today or tomorrow.

The combination of dominant and cold communication sends the signal that the sender of the message wants to control and to limit, or even withdraw from, a personal relationship. A team leader might say that she cannot attend a Saturday morning meeting because she has to go out of town for her brother's wedding. A dominant and cold manager might say, "I don't want to hear about your personal life. Everyone in this department has to attend our Saturday meeting."

Subordinate actions combined with warm communication signal a desire to maintain or build the relationship while yielding to the other person. A manager communicating in a warm and subordinate manner in relation to the wedding request might say, "We'll miss you on Saturday morning because you are a key player in our department, but I recognize that major events in personal life sometimes take priority over a business meeting."

FIGURE 5-2 Communication Dimensions of Establishing a Relationship

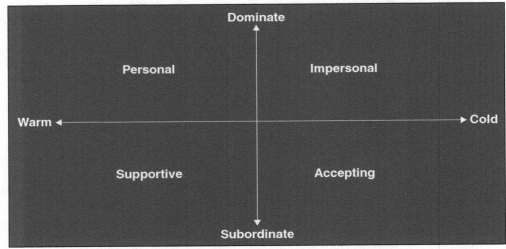

Source: Adapted with permission from Rich Sorenson, Grace De Bord, and Ida Ramirez, *Business and Management Communication: A Guide Book,* 4th ed. (Upper Saddle River, NJ: Prentice Hall, 2001), p. 7.

Figure 5-2 summarizes how the dual dimensions of dominate–subordinate and cold–warm influence the relationship-building aspects of communication. Rather than regarding these four quadrants of relationships as good or bad, think of your purposes. In some situations you might want to dominate and be cold, yet in most situations you might want to submit a little and be warm in order to build a relationship. For example, being dominant and cold might be necessary for a security officer who is trying to control an unruly crowd at a sporting event.

Observe that the person in the quadrant *dominate–cold* has an impersonal relationship with the receiver, and the person in the *warm–subordinate* quadrant has a supportive relationship with the receiver. Being *dominant and warm* leads to a personal relationship, whereas as being *subordinate and cold* leads to an accepting relationship. The combinations of *dominate–cold* and *warm–subordinate* are more likely to produce the results indicated.

WHAT IS NONVERBAL COMMUNICATION (SENDING AND RECEIVING SILENT MESSAGES)?

LEARNING OBJECTIVE 3

nonverbal communication

Using the body, voice, or environment in numerous ways to help get a message across.

So far we have been considering mostly spoken communication. But much of the communication among people includes nonspoken and nonwritten messages. These nonverbal signals are a critical part of everyday communication. As a case in point, *how* you say "thank you" makes a big difference in the extent to which your sense of appreciation registers. In **nonverbal communication,** we use our body, voice, or environment in numerous ways to help put a message across. Sometimes we are not aware how much our true feelings color our spoken message.

One problem of paying attention to nonverbal signals is that they can be taken too seriously. Just because some nonverbal signals (such as yawning or looking away from a person) might reflect a person's real feelings, not every signal can be reliably connected with a particular attitude. Jason may put his hand over his mouth because he is shocked. Lucille may put her hand over her mouth because she is trying to control her laughter about the message, and Ken may put his hand over his mouth as a signal that he is pondering the consequences of the message. Here we look at eight categories of nonverbal communication that are generally reliable indicators of a person's attitude and feelings.

Environment or Setting

Where you choose to deliver your message indicates what you think of its importance. Assume that your supervisor invites you over for dinner to discuss something with you. You will think it is a more important topic under these circumstances than if it were brought up when the two of you met in the supermarket. Other important environmental cues include room color, temperature, lighting, and furniture arrangement. A person who sits behind an uncluttered large desk, for example, appears more powerful than a person who sits behind a small, cluttered desk.

Few people in an organization have the authority to control the physical factors of room color, temperature, and lighting, but there are exceptions. An office or building painted gray in the interior might suggest an impersonal, strictly business atmosphere. A business owner who keeps the temperature at 62°F during cold months or 75°F during warm months communicates a message of frugality.

Distance from the Other Person

How close you place your body relative to another person's also conveys meaning when you send a message. If, for instance, you want to convey a positive attitude toward another person, get physically close to him or her. Putting your arm around someone to express interest and warmth is another obvious nonverbal signal. However, many people in a work setting abstain from all forms of touching (except for handshakes) because of concern that touching might be interpreted as sexual harassment. Cultural differences must be kept in mind in interpreting nonverbal cues. A French male is likely to stand closer to you than a British male, even if they had equally positive attitudes toward you. A set of useful guidelines has been developed for estimating how close to stand to another person (at least in many cultures).[3] They are described here and diagrammed in Figure 5-3.

Intimate distance covers actual physical contact to about eighteen inches. Usually, it is reserved for close friends and loved ones or other people you feel affectionate toward. Physical intimacy is usually not called for on the job, but there are exceptions. For one, confidential information might be whispered within the intimate distance zone.

Personal distance covers from about one and a half to four feet. In this zone it is natural to carry on friendly conversations and discussions. When people engage in a heated argument, they sometimes enter the personal distance zone. One example is a baseball coach getting up close to an umpire and shouting in his face.

Social distance covers from four to twelve feet and in general is reserved for interaction that is businesslike and impersonal. We usually maintain this amount of distance between ourselves and strangers, such as retail sales associates.

Public distance covers from twelve feet to the outer limit of being heard. This zone is typically used in speaking to an audience at a large meeting or in a classroom, but a few insensitive individuals might send ordinary messages by shouting across a room. The unstated message suggested by such an action is that the receiver of the message does not merit the effort of walking across the room.

People sometimes manipulate personal space in order to dominate a situation. A sales representative might move into the personal or intimate circle of a customer simply to intimidate him or her. Many people become upset when you move into a closer circle than that for which a situation calls. They consider it an invasion of their personal space, or their "territorial rights."

Posture

Certain aspects of your posture communicate a message. Leaning toward another individual suggests that you are favorably disposed toward his or her message. Leaning backward communicates the opposite. Openness of the arms or legs serves as an indicator of liking or caring. In general, people establish closed postures (arms folded and legs crossed) when speaking to people they dislike. Standing up straight generally indicates

FIGURE 5-3 Four Circles of Intimacy

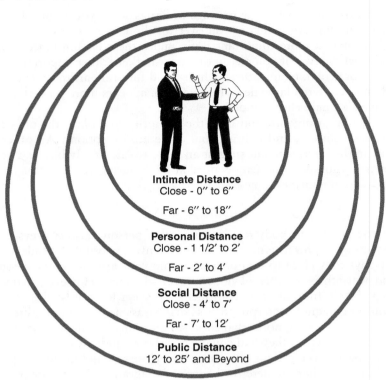

Intimate Distance
Close - 0″ to 6″

Far - 6″ to 18″

Personal Distance
Close - 1 1/2′ to 2′

Far - 2′ to 4′

Social Distance
Close - 4′ to 7′

Far - 7′ to 12′

Public Distance
12′ to 25′ and Beyond

high self-confidence. Stooping and slouching could mean a poor self-image. In any event, there is almost no disadvantage to standing up straight.

Related to posture are the nonverbal signals sent by standing versus sitting. Sitting down during a conversation is generally considered to be more intimate and informal than standing. If you do sit down while conversing, be sure to stand up when you wish the conversation to end. Standing up sends a message to the other person that it is time to leave. It also gives you the chance to be more attentive and polite in saying good-bye.

Hand Gestures

An obvious form of body language is hand gestures. Hand gestures are universally recognized as conveying specific information to others within the same culture. If you make frequent hand movements, you will generally communicate a positive attitude. If you use few gestures, you will convey dislike or disinterest. An important exception here is that some people wave their hands vigorously while arguing. Some of their hand movements reflect anger. Another example is that open-palm gestures toward the other person typically convey positive attitudes. Many hand gestures have culture-specific meanings. An off-color example follows:

> In many cultures holding your hand in front of you as if pushing something away tells the other person to stop—you have had enough. In West Africa, the same gesture means "There are different men who could be your father," thereby insulting the receiver's mother.[4]

It is often said that gestures speak louder than words, because if there is a discrepancy between words and gestures, the receiver will usually take your gestures more seriously. In general more weight is given to nonverbal cues than verbal cues when a discrepancy exists between the two.[5]

Imagine that you have been interviewed for a job you really want. At the close of the interview, the interviewer looks at you with a solemn face, and his arms are crossed with his hands tucked under his armpits. He says in a monotone, "We will get back to you soon." Most likely, you will continue your job search.

Facial Expressions and Eye Contact

When used in combination, the head, face, and eyes provide the clearest indications of attitudes toward other people. Lowering your head and peering over your glasses, for instance, is the nonverbal equivalent of the expression "You're putting me on." As is well known, maintaining eye contact with another person improves communication with that person. To maintain eye contact, it is usually necessary to correspondingly move your head and face. Moving your head, face, and eyes away from another person is often interpreted as a defensive gesture or one suggesting a lack of self-confidence. Would you hire a job candidate who didn't look at you directly? Yet again, cultural differences can influence the meaning of eye contact. In some Asian cultures, looking down rather than maintaining eye contact is a sign of respect.

The face is often used as a primary source of information about how we feel. We look for facial clues when we want to determine another person's attitude. You can often judge someone's current state of happiness by looking at his or her face. The expression "sourpuss" attests to this observation. Happiness, apprehension, anger, resentment, sadness, contempt, enthusiasm, and embarrassment are but a few of the emotions that can be expressed through the face.

Voice Quality

More significance is often attached to the *way* something is said than to *what* is said. A forceful voice, which includes a consistent tone without vocalized pauses, connotes power and control. Closely related to voice tone are volume, pitch, and rate of speaking. Anger, boredom, and joy can often be interpreted from voice quality. Anger is noted when the person speaks loudly with a high pitch and at a fast rate, with irregular inflection. Boredom is indicated by a monotone. Joy is often indicated by loud volume, high pitch, fast rate, upward inflection, and regular rhythm.

Avoiding an annoying voice quality can make a positive impact on others. The research of Jeffrey Jacobi, voice coach and founder of Jacobi Voice, provides some useful suggestions. A while back he surveyed a nationwide sample of one thousand men and women and asked, "Which irritating or unpleasant voice annoys you the most?" His results are still valid today. The most irritating quality was a whining, complaining, or nagging tone.

Jacobi notes that we are judged by the way we sound. He also contends that careers can be damaged by voice problems, such as those indicated in the survey. "We think about how we look and dress. And that gets most of the attention. But people judge our intelligence much more by how we sound than how we dress."[6] Self-Assessment Quiz 5-1 provides more details about his findings.

Personal Appearance

Your external image plays an important role in communicating messages to others. Job seekers show recognition of this aspect of nonverbal communication when they carefully groom for a job interview. People pay more respect and grant more privileges to people they perceive as being well dressed and attractive. The meaning of being well dressed depends heavily on the situation and the culture of the organization. In an information technology firm, neatly pressed jeans, a stylish T-shirt, and clean sport shoes might qualify as being well dressed. The same attire worn in a financial service firm would qualify as being poorly dressed. In recent years, more formal business attire has made a comeback, as reflected in more space in department stores being devoted to suits for men and women.

Voice Quality Checkup

The study of voice quality (cited in the text) ranked voice quality, in decreasing order of annoyance, as follows:

- Whining, complaining, or nagging tone—44.0 percent
- High-pitched, squeaky voice—15.9 percent
- Mumblers—11.1 percent
- Very fast talkers—4.9 percent
- Weak and wimpy voice—3.6 percent
- Flat, monotonous tone—3.5 percent
- Thick accent—2.4 percent

Ask yourself and two other people familiar with your voice if you have one or more of the preceding voice-quality problems. If your self-analysis and feedback from others does indicate a serious problem, get started on self-improvement. Record your voice and attempt to modify the biggest problems. Another avenue of improvement is to consult with a speech coach or therapist.

Tattoos and body piercing represent another aspect of personal appearance that sends a strong nonverbal message. The message that tattoos and body piercing send, however, depends to a large extent on the values and preferences of the receiver. A positive message sent by visible tattoos and piercing is that the individual is cool, modern, fashionable, and youthful in outlook. A negative message is the person with visible tattoos and piercing is immature, daring, and nonconscientious. As the percentage of people wearing visible tattoos and body piercing continues to increase, less significance will probably be attached to them. For example, about thirty years ago when a man appeared in the office wearing a pierced earring, it was considered shocking. Today, the same behavior is unremarkable—at least to many people.

Common sense and research indicate that a favorable personal appearance leads to higher starting salaries and, later, salary increases. One study showed that people perceived to be physically attractive tend to receive salaries 8 to 10 percent higher. A possible explanation offered for the results is that employers might attribute other positive attributes to employees they perceive as physically attractive.[7]

Nonverbal Communication and Airport Security

An advanced workplace application of nonverbal communication is to help combat drug trafficking and terrorism. The art of spotting nervous or threatening behavior has gained respect among airport security officials. Since the terrorist attacks on September 11, 2001, the Federal Bureau of Investigation (FBI) started teaching nonverbal behavior analysis to all new FBI recruits. In the past, passengers were selected to be interrogated mostly on the basis of what they looked like, such as a negative ethnic stereotype. Customs agents are now trained to observe what people do and to ask pointed questions when suspicious nonverbal behavior surfaces. Among the indicators of suspicious behavior are darting eyes, hand tremors, a fleeting style, and an enlarged carotid artery (indicating the rapid blood flow associated with anxiety). Failure to make eye contact with the customs official is a strong red flag.[8]

Behavior detection officer is the term given to airport security officers who specialize in detecting nonverbal signs of stress, fear, and deception. Part of the officer's responsibility is to roam a major airport and watch for anyone who seems nervous or out of place, or is acting suspiciously. Particularly suspicious are passengers traveling without bags, sweating, and constantly checking people passing by, especially those with badges and guns. Facial movements detecting a lie, such as rapid eye movements, are also regarded as suspicious.

Other suspicious nonverbal communication cues are passengers avoiding eye contact or veering away when police approach. Suspicious-appearing people are routinely brought in for questioning, but nonverbal behavior alone is not sufficient evidence to be charged with attempting a crime.[9]

The American Civil Liberties Unions objects to nonverbal behavior detection because it is easy to find these negative nonverbal behaviors if you look for them. The many flight cancellations and delays, for example, trigger many passengers into looking stressed and suspicious.

WHAT ARE SOME FREQUENT ROADBLOCKS TO COMMUNICATION?

LEARNING OBJECTIVE 4

Communication rarely proceeds as effectively as we would like. Many different factors filter out a message on its way to the intended receiver, shown as potential barriers in Figure 5-1. In this section we look at some of the human roadblocks to communication. If you are aware of their presence, you will be better able to overcome them.

Routine or neutral messages are the easiest to communicate. Communication roadblocks are most likely to occur when a message is complex, is emotionally arousing, or clashes with the receiver's mental set. An emotionally arousing message would deal with such topics as job security or money. A message that clashes with a receiver's mental set requires that person to change his or her familiar pattern of receiving messages. The next time you order a meal in a restaurant, order dessert first and an entrée second. The server will probably not "hear" your dessert order because it deviates from the normal ordering sequence. The roadblocks or barriers described here are as follows:

1. Limited understanding of people
2. One-way communication
3. Different interpretation of words (semantics)
4. Credibility of the sender and mixed signals
5. Distortion of information
6. Different perspectives and experiences
7. Emotions and attitudes
8. Communication overload
9. Improper timing
10. Poor communication skills
11. Cultural and language barriers

Limited Understanding of People

If you do not understand people very well, your communication effectiveness will be limited. To take a basic example, if you frame your message in terms of what can be done for you, you may be in trouble. It's much more effective to frame your message in terms of what you can do for the other person. Suppose a person in need of money wants to sell food supplements to a friend. Mentioning financial need is a very self-centered message. It could be made less self-centered:

Very self-centered. "You've got to buy a few food supplements from me. I can't meet my credit card payments."

Less self-centered. "Would you be interested in purchasing a few food supplements that would bring you more energy and help you live longer? If your answer is yes, I can help you."

Limited understanding of people can also take the form of making false assumptions about the receiver. The false assumption serves as a communication roadblock. A supervisor might say to a telemarketer (a person who sells over the phone), "If you increase sales by 15 percent, we will promote you to lead telemarketer." When the telemarketer does not work any harder, the supervisor thinks the message did not get across. The false assumption the supervisor made was that the telemarketer wanted a position with supervisory responsibility. What false assumptions have you made lately when trying to communicate with another person?

Limited understanding of another person can sometimes be attributed to cultural differences. For example, a supervisor might send a message to Kim, a South Korean American in her group, that she can win an Employee of the Month award if she increases her productivity by 5 percent. Kim does not receive the message well because according to her cultural beliefs, it is negative behavior to stand out from the group. (After Kim assimilates more into the American culture, she will most likely receive the message more clearly.)

One-Way Communication

Effective communication proceeds back and forth. An exchange of information or a transaction takes place between two or more people. Person A may send messages to person B to initiate communication, but B must react to A to complete the communication loop. One reason written messages sometimes fail to achieve their purpose is that the person who writes the message cannot be sure how it will be interpreted. One written message that is subject to many interpretations is, "Your idea is of some interest to me." (How much is *some*?) Face-to-face communication helps clarify meanings.

Instant messaging helps overcome the one-way barrier because the receiver reacts immediately to your message. An example: "You said ship the first batch only to good customers. Who do you consider to be a *good* customer?" Ten seconds later comes the reply: "A good customer bought at least $4,000 worth of goods last year and is up-to-date on payments." Three seconds later, the first person writes, "Got it." E-mail is also widely used to clarify messages and engage in two-way communication.

A quick way to bring about the exchange of information necessary for two-way communication is to ask a question. An example here would be, "Are you clear on what I mean by a *good customer*?"

Different Interpretation of Words (Semantics)

semantics

The study of the meaning and changes in the meaning of words or symbols.

Semantics is the study of the meaning and changes in the meaning of words or symbols. These different meanings can create roadblocks to communication. Often the problem is trivial and humorous; at other times, semantic problems can create substantial communication barriers. Consider first an example of trivial consequence.

Two first-time visitors to Montreal, Quebec, entered a restaurant for dinner. After looking over the menu, the husband suggested they order the shrimp cocktail entrées. He said to his wife, "A whole shrimp dinner for $11.95 Canadian is quite a deal. I guess it's because Montreal is a seaport." When the entrées arrived, the visitors were sadly disappointed because they were the size of an *appetizer*.

The husband asked the server why the entrées were so small in Montreal. With a smile, the server replied, "You folks must be Americans. In French-speaking countries, the entrée is the beginning of the meal, like the word *enter*. In the United States, it's just the reverse—the entrée is the main meal. Are you now ready to order your main meal?"

Of greater consequence is the use of a word or term without thorough explanation that could cause people to act in an unintended direction. An example is for a manager to use the term *restructure* when speaking to employees or outsiders. Four common interpretations of the word are the following: (1) refinance the company debt, (2) declare bankruptcy, (3) change the organization structure, or (4) lay off many workers. A negative consequence of not knowing the true meaning of the term would be for a competent employee to seek employment elsewhere because he or she feared being laid off.

Credibility of the Sender and Mixed Signals

mixed signals

Type of message in which the sender might recommend one thing to others yet behave in another way.

The more trustworthy the source or sender of the message, the greater the probability that the message will get through clearly. In contrast, when the sender of the message has low credibility, many times it will be ignored. Communications can also break down for a subtle variation of low credibility. The disconnect occurs from **mixed signals**, a type of message in which the sender might recommend one thing to others yet behave in another way himself or herself. A team leader might tell others that a tidy worker is a productive worker. However, his or her own cubicle contains a four-month supply of empty soft-drink cans, and old papers consume virtually every square inch of his or her desk.

Mixed signals also refers to sending different messages about the same topic to different audiences. For example, company representatives might brag about the high quality of the company's products in public statements. Yet on the shop floor and in the office, the company tells its employees to cut costs whenever possible to lower costs.

Distortion of Information

A great problem in sending messages is that people receiving them often hear what they want to hear. Without malicious intent, people modify your message to bolster their self-esteem or improve their situation. An incident that occurred between Danielle and her supervisor is fairly typical of this type of communication roadblock. Danielle asked her supervisor when she would be receiving a salary increase. Regarding the request as far-fetched and beyond the budget at the time, Danielle's supervisor replied, "Why should the company give you a raise when you are often late for work?"

Danielle *heard* her supervisor say, "If you come to work on time regularly, you will receive a salary increase." One month later, Danielle said to her supervisor that she had not been late for work in a month and should now be eligible for a raise. Her supervisor replied, "I never said that. Where did you get that idea?"

Different Perspectives and Experiences

People perceive words and concepts differently because their experiences and vantage points differ. On the basis of their perception of what they have heard, many Latino children believe that the opening line of the "Star-Spangled Banner" is "José, can you see . . ." (note that few children have *seen* the national anthem in writing). Cultural differences create different perspectives and experiences, such as workers from Eastern cultures tending to have high respect for authority. A worker from India might more readily accept a message from the boss than would his or her counterpart from California or Sweden. In the last two places, workers have a more casual attitude toward authority.

Emotions and Attitudes

Have you ever tried to communicate a message to another person while that person is emotionally aroused? Your message was probably distorted considerably. Another problem is that people tend to say things when emotionally aroused that they would not say when calm. Similarly, a person who has strong attitudes about a particular topic may become emotional when that topic is introduced. The underlying message here is try to avoid letting strong emotions and attitudes interfere with the sending or receiving of messages. If you are angry with someone, for example, you might miss the merit in what that person has to say. Calm down before proceeding with your discussion or attempting to resolve the conflict. Emotional intelligence makes a key contribution in this situation.

Communication Overload

A major communication barrier facing literate people is being bombarded with information. **Communication overload** occurs when people are so overloaded with information that they cannot respond effectively to messages. As a result, they experience work stress. Workers at many levels are exposed to so much printed, electronic, and spoken information that their capacity to absorb it is taxed. The problem is worsened when low-quality information is competing for your attention. An example is a flashing pop-up ad informing you that you have just won a free laptop computer, and all you have to do is follow a link to claim your prize. The human mind is capable of processing only a limited quantity of information at a time. Workers who intentionally multitask, such as reading instant messages and filling in a spreadsheet at the same time, aggravate the problem of communication overload.

communication overload
Phenomenon that occurs when people are so overloaded with information that they cannot respond effectively to messages.

Improper Timing

Many messages do not get through to people because they are poorly timed. You have to know how to deliver a message, but you must also know *when* to deliver it. Sending a message when the receiver is distracted with other concerns or is rushing to get somewhere is a waste of time. Furthermore, the receiver may become discouraged and therefore will not repeat the message later.

The art of timing messages suggests not to ask for a raise when your boss is in a bad mood or to ask a new acquaintance for a date when he or she is preoccupied. However, do ask your boss for a raise when business has been good, and do ask someone for a date when you have just done something nice for that person and have been thanked.

Poor Communication Skills

A message may fail to register because the sender lacks effective communication skills. The sender might garble a written or spoken message so severely that the receiver finds it impossible to understand. Also, the sender may deliver the message so poorly that the receiver does not take it seriously. A common deficiency in sending messages is to communicate with low conviction by using *wimpy* words, backpedaling, and qualifying. Part of the same idea is to use affirmative language, such as saying "when" instead of "if." Also, do not use phrases that call your integrity into question, such as "to be perfectly honest" (implying that you usually do not tell the truth).[10] To illustrate, here are three statements that send a message of low conviction to the receiver: "I think I might be able to finish this project by the end of the week." "It's possible that I could handle the assignment you have in mind." "I'll do what I can."

Another communication skill deficiency that can serve as a communication barrier is to have a regional accent so strong that it detracts from your message. Your regional accent is part of who you are, so you may not want to modify how you speak. Nevertheless, many public personalities, business executives, and salespeople seek out speech training or speech therapy to avoid having an accent that detracts from their message.[11] Also, at high-level positions people typically want to be universal in their appeal. You may notice that commentators on national television usually speak in a universal, rather than regional, manner.

Communication barriers can result from deficiencies within the receiver. A common barrier is a receiver who is a poor listener. Improving listening skills is such a major strategy for improving communication skills that it receives separate mention later in this chapter.

> "You can have brilliant ideas; but if you can't get them across, your ideas won't get you anywhere."
>
> —Lee Iacocca, former Chrysler chairman and Ford CEO

Cultural and Language Barriers

Communication barriers in work and personal life can be created when the sender and receiver come from different cultures and are not fluent in each other's language. Quite often cultural differences and language differences exist at the same time. A cultural difference creating a barrier to communication often takes this form: A supervisor from a culture that emphasizes empowering (giving power to) employees is giving instructions to an employee from a culture that believes the boss should make all the decisions. In response to a question from the subordinate, the supervisor says, "Do what you think is best." The subordinate has a difficult time understanding the message because he or she is waiting for a firm directive from the boss.

A language communication barrier is sometimes amusing, such as an American worker complimenting another by saying, "You have been working like a dog" on this project. The second person might interpret the comment as suggesting he or she must be punished to work hard. At other times language barriers cause accidents. Many foreign-language-speaking construction workers in the United States encounter accidents because they do not clearly understand the instructions about danger.

A notable problem with language barriers has stemmed from the practice of *off-shoring* (sending overseas) customer service and call center positions to India, as well as Mexico and the Philippines. For Mexicans and Filipinos, English is usually their second language so they have an accent unfamiliar to many Americans. Although English might be the primary or strong second language of Indian workers, it is not a type of English familiar to many Americans. As a result, many Americans who are not familiar with the accents of English-speaking Indians will say, "I can't understand the person who is trying to help me." Many of these people hang up in frustration. Several U.S.-based telecommunication companies have therefore reestablished customer service centers in the United States.

To help overcome cultural and language barriers, many companies invest considerable time and money in cross-cultural training.

WHAT ARE SOME WAYS TO BUILD BRIDGES TO COMMUNICATION?

LEARNING OBJECTIVE 5

With determination and awareness that communication roadblocks and barriers do exist, you can become a more effective communicator. It would be impossible to remove all barriers, but they can be minimized. The following nine techniques are helpful in building better bridges to communication.

1. Appeal to human needs, and time your messages.
2. Repeat your message, using more than one channel.
3. Have an empowered attitude, and be persuasive.
4. Discuss differences in frames of reference.
5. Check for comprehension and feelings through feedback.
6. Minimize defensive communication.
7. Combat communication overload.
8. Use mirroring to establish rapport.
9. Engage in small talk and constructive gossip.

Appeal to Human Needs, and Time Your Messages

People are more receptive to messages that promise to do something for them. In other words, if a message promises to satisfy a need that is less than fully satisfied, you are likely to listen. The person in search of additional money who ordinarily does not hear low tones readily hears the whispered message, "How would you like to earn $500 in one weekend?"

Timing a message properly is related to appealing to human needs. If you deliver a message at the right time, you are taking into account the person's mental condition at the moment. A general principle is to deliver your message when the person might be in the right frame of mind to listen. The right frame of mind includes such factors as not being preoccupied with other thoughts, not being frustrated, being in a good mood, and not being stressed out. (Of course, all this severely limits your opportunity to send a message!)

Repeat Your Message, Using More than One Channel

You can overcome many roadblocks to communication by repeating your message several times. It is usually advisable not to say the same thing so as to avoid annoying the listener with straight repetition. Repeating the message in a different form is effective in another way: The receiver may not have understood the message the way in which it was first delivered. Repetition, like any other means of overcoming communication roadblocks, does not work for all people. Many people who repeatedly hear the message "text messaging while driving is dangerous" are not moved by it. It is helpful to use several methods of overcoming roadblocks or barriers to communication.

A generally effective way of repeating a message is to use more than one communication channel. For example, follow up a face-to-face discussion with an e-mail message or phone call or both. Your body can be another channel or medium to help impart your message. If you agree with someone about a spoken message, state your agreement and also shake hands over the agreement. Can you think of another channel by which to transmit a message?

Have an Empowered Attitude, and Be Persuasive

A positive attitude helps a person communicate better in speaking, writing, and nonverbally. Being positive is a major factor in being persuasive, as mentioned previously in avoiding wimpy words. *Empowerment* here refers to the idea that the person takes charge of his or her own attitude.[12] Developing a positive attitude is not always easy. A starting point is to see things from a positive perspective, including looking for the good in people and their work. If your work is intrinsically motivating, you are likely to have a positive attitude. You would then be able to communicate about your work with the enthusiasm necessary. Figure 5-4 summarizes key ideas about persuasive communication, a topic most readers have most likely studied in the past.[13] If you can learn to implement most of the nine suggestions, you are on your way toward becoming a persuasive communicator. In addition, you will need solid facts behind you, and you will need to make skillful use of nonverbal communication.

Discuss Differences in Frames of Reference

frame of reference

Model, viewpoint, or perspective.

Another way of understanding differences in perspectives and experiences is to recognize that people often have different frames of reference that influence how they interpret events. A **frame of reference** is a model, viewpoint, or perspective. When two people with different frameworks look at a situation, a communication problem may occur. For instance, one person may say, "I have just found the *ideal* potential mate." To this person, an *ideal* mate would be a person who was kind, caring, considerate, in good health, gainfully employed, and highly ethical. The listener may have a perception of an *ideal* potential mate as someone who has a superior physical appearance and is wealthy (a traditional stereotype). Until the two people understand each other's frame of reference, meaningful communication about the prospective mate is unlikely. The solution to this communication clash is to discuss the frame of reference by each side defining the perception of an *ideal* mate.

Check for Comprehension and Feelings through Feedback

Don't be a hit-and-run communicator. Such a person drops a message and leaves the scene before he or she is sure the message has been received as intended. It is preferable to ask for feedback. Ask receivers for their understanding or interpretation of what you said. For example, you might say after delivering a message, "What is your understanding of our agreement?" Also use nonverbal indicators to gauge how well you delivered your message. A blank expression on the receiver's face might indicate no comprehension. A disturbed, agitated expression might mean that the receiver's emotions are blocking the message.

A comprehension check increases in importance when possible cultural and language barriers exist. A simple direct inquiry about comprehension is often effective, such as, "Is what I said okay with you" or "Tell me what I said." A friendly facial expression should accompany such feedback checks, otherwise your inquiry will come across like a challenge.

In addition to looking for verbal comprehension and emotions when you have delivered a message, check for feelings after you have received a message. When a person speaks, we too often listen to the facts and ignore the feelings. If feelings are ignored, the true meaning and intent of the message are likely to be missed, thus creating a communication barrier. Your boss might say to you, "You never seem to take work home." To clarify what your boss means by this statement, you might ask, "Is that good or bad?" Your boss's response will give you feedback on his or her feelings about getting all your work done during regular working hours.

When you send a message, it is also helpful to express your feelings in addition to conveying the facts. For example, "Our customer returns are up by 12 percent [fact], and

FIGURE 5-4 Key Principles of Persuasive Communication

1. *Know exactly what you want.* First clarify ideas in your mind.
2. *Never suggest an action without describing its end benefit.* Explain how your message will benefit the receiver.
3. *Get a yes response early on.* It is helpful to give the persuading session a positive tone by establishing a "yes pattern" at the outset.
4. *Use powerful words.* Sprinkle your speech with phrases like "bonding with customers," and "vaporizing the competition."
5. *When you speak, begin with your headline—the most important point.* After the headline, provide more information as needed. To come up with the right headline, imagine what you would say if you had only ten minutes to deliver your message. An environmental specialist might begin a message to management with, "My new program will help us save the planet."
6. *Minimize raising your pitch at the end of sentences.* Part of being persuasive is not to sound unsure and apologetic.
7. *Back up conclusions with data.* You will be more persuasive if you support your spoken and written presentations with solid data, but do not become an annoyance by overdoing it.
8. *Minimize "wimp" phrases.* (As discussed earlier in this chapter.)
9. *Avoid or minimize common language errors.* Do not say "could care less," when you mean "couldn't care less," or "orientated" when you mean "oriented."
10. *Avoid overuse of jargon and clichés.* To feel "in" and cool, many workers rely heavily on jargon and clichés, such as referring to their "fave" (for *favorite*) product or that "At the end of the day," something counts. It is also helpful to minimize the use of catchphrases like *bottom line*, *quantum leap,* and *cutting edge.* The problem is that if you make frequent use of overused expressions, you may give the impression of not thinking critically.
11. *Frame your position in the direction you want.* Describe in a positive way the option you want the receiver to choose, or describe in a negative way the option you don't want the receiver to choose. For example, if you want to convince others of the advantages of global outsourcing, you might refer to it as *seeking wage rates that will make us competitive.* If you want to convince others of the disadvantages of global outsourcing, you might refer to it as *shipping jobs from our country overseas.*

I'm quite disappointed about those results [feelings]." Because feelings contribute strongly to comprehension, you will help overcome a potential communication barrier.

Minimize Defensive Communication

Distortion of information was described previously as a communication barrier. Such distortion can also be regarded as **defensive communication,** the tendency to receive messages in such a way that our self-esteem is protected. Defensive communication is also responsible for people sending messages to look good. For example, when criticized for achieving below-average sales, a store manager might shift the blame to the sales associates in her store. Overcoming the barrier of defensive communication requires two steps. First, people have to acknowledge the existence of defensive communication. Second, they have to try not to be defensive when questioned or criticized. Such behavior is not easy because of **denial,** the suppression of information we find uncomfortable. For example, the store manager previously cited would find it uncomfortable to think of herself as being responsible for below-average performance.

defensive communication

Tendency to receive messages in such a way that one's self-esteem is protected.

denial

The suppression of information one finds uncomfortable.

Combat Communication Overload

You can decrease the chances of suffering from communication overload by such measures as carefully organizing and sorting information before plunging ahead with reading. Speed-reading may help, provided that you stop to read carefully the most relevant information. Or you can scan through hard-copy reports, magazines, and Web sites looking for key titles and words that are important to you. Recognize, however, that many subjects have to be studied carefully to derive benefit. It is often better to read thoroughly a few topics than to skim through lots of information.

Being selective about your e-mail and Internet reading goes a long way toward preventing information overload. Suppose you see an e-mail message titled "Car Lights Left on in Parking Lot." Do not retrieve the message if you distinctly remember having turned off your lights or you did not drive to work. E-mail programs and Internet search software are available to help users sort messages according to their needs. You can help prevent others from suffering from communication overload by being merciful in the frequency and length of your messages. Also, do not join the ranks of pranksters who send loads of jokes via e-mail and who widely distribute their personal blogs.

A useful way of combating information (or communication) overload when making a decision is to aim for the *flat maximum*. This point takes place where you have gotten rid of dead weight and can choose any of the remaining options because they are pretty much equal.[14] An example would be in purchasing a new laptop computer. After having eliminated five models that do not fit your requirements, perhaps you would regard the other models as equally useful. When you have stopped processing information and have made your decision, your mind will be clearer to receive other messages.

Use Mirroring to Establish Rapport

mirroring

Form of nonverbal communication to overcome communication barriers by subtly imitating another; used to improve rapport with another person.

Another approach to overcoming communication barriers is to improve rapport with another person. A form of nonverbal communication, called **mirroring,** can be used to establish such rapport. To mirror someone is to subtly imitate that individual. The most successful mirroring technique for establishing rapport is to imitate the breathing pattern of another person. If you adjust your own breathing rate to someone else's, you will soon establish rapport with that person. Mirroring sometimes takes the form of imitating the boss in order to communicate better and win favor. Many job seekers now use mirroring to get in sync with the interviewer. Is this a technique you would be willing to try?

Mirroring takes practice to contribute to overcoming communication barriers. It is a subtle technique that requires a moderate skill level. If you mirror (or match) another person in a rigid, mechanical way, you will appear to be mocking that person. And mocking, of course, erects rather than tears down a communication barrier.

Engage in Small Talk and Constructive Gossip

The terms *small talk* and *gossip* have negative connotations for the career-minded person with a professional attitude. Nevertheless, the effective use of small talk and gossip can help a person melt communication barriers. Small talk is important because it contributes to conversational skills, and having good conversational skills enhances interpersonal communication. Trainer Randi Fredeig says, "Small talk helps build rapport and eventually trust. It helps people find common ground on which to build conversation."[15] A helpful technique is to collect tidbits of information to use as small talk to facilitate work-related or heavy-topic conversation in personal life. Keeping informed about current events, including sports, television, and films, provides useful content for small talk.

Being a source of positive gossip brings a person power and credibility. Workmates are eager to communicate with a person who is a source of not-yet-verified developments. Having such inside knowledge enhances your status and makes you a more interesting communicator. Positive gossip would include such tidbits as mentioning that the company will be looking for workers who would want a one-year assignment in Europe or that more employees will soon be eligible for profit-sharing bonuses. In contrast, spreading negative gossip will often erode your attractiveness to other people.[16]

HOW DO YOU OVERCOME GENDER BARRIERS TO COMMUNICATION?

Another strategy for overcoming communication barriers is to deal effectively with potential cultural differences. Two types of cultural differences are those related to gender (male versus female role) and those related to geographic differences. Of course, not everybody agrees that men and women are from different cultures. Here we describe gender differences, whereas cultural differences are a separate topic.

LEARNING OBJECTIVE 6

Despite the movement toward equality of sexes in the workplace, substantial interest exists in identifying differences in communication style between men and women. The basic difference between women and men, according to the research of Deborah Tannen, professor of sociolinguistics at Georgetown University, is that men emphasize and reinforce their status when they talk, whereas women downplay their status. As part of this difference, women are more concerned about building social connections.[17] People who are aware of these differences face fewer communication problems between themselves and members of the opposite sex.

As we describe these differences, recognize that they are group stereotypes. Individual differences in communication style are usually more important than group styles (men versus women). Here we will describe the major findings of gender differences in communication patterns.[18]

1. Women prefer to use conversation for rapport building. For most women, the intent of conversation is to build rapport and connections with people. It has been said that men are driven by transactions, whereas women are driven by relations. Women are therefore more likely to emphasize similarities, to listen intently, and to be supportive.

2. Men prefer to use talk primarily as a means to preserve independence and status by displaying knowledge and skill. When most men talk, they want to receive positive evaluations from others and maintain their hierarchical status within the group. Men are, therefore, more oriented to giving a *report*, whereas women are more interested in establishing *rapport*.

3. Women want empathy, not solutions. When women share feelings of being stressed out, they seek empathy and understanding. If they feel they have been listened to carefully, they begin to relax. When listening to the woman, the man may feel blamed for her problems or that he has failed the woman in some way. To feel useful, the man might offer solutions to the woman's problem.

4. Men prefer to work out their problems by themselves, whereas women prefer to talk out solutions with another person. Women look on having and sharing problems as an opportunity to build and deepen relationships. Men are more likely to look on problems as challenges they must meet on their own. Similarly men are more hesitant to ask questions when faced with a problem, and women gather information by asking questions. The communication consequence of these differences is that men may become uncommunicative when they have a problem.

5. Men tend to be more directive and less apologetic in their conversation, whereas women are more polite and apologetic. Women are therefore more likely to frequently use the phrases "I'm sorry" and "thank you," even when there is no need to express apology or gratitude. Men less frequently say they are sorry, because they perceive communications as competition, and they do not want to appear vulnerable.

6. Women tend to be more conciliatory when facing differences, whereas men become more intimidating. Again, women are more interested in building relationships, whereas men are more concerned about coming out ahead.

7. Men are more interested than women in calling attention to their accomplishments or hogging recognition. One consequence of this difference is that men are more likely to dominate discussions during meetings. Another consequence is that women are more likely to help a coworker perform well. In one instance, a sales representative who had already made her sales quota for the month turned over an excellent prospect to a coworker. She reasoned, "It's somebody else's turn. I've received more than my fair share of bonuses for the month."

8. **Women are more likely to use a gentle expletive, whereas men tend to be harsher.** For example, if a woman locks herself out of the car, she is likely to say, "Oh dear." In the same situation, a man is likely to say, "Oh _____." (Do you think this difference really exists?)

(Here we could be dealing with both a sex and generational difference, with recent generations of women being more likely to swear than previous generations.)

The use of expletives is more consequential than simply a difference in communication style. Many people feel uncomfortable, and even harassed, when hearing expletives in the workplace. A constructive counterapproach to the expletive user is to express your discomfort and politely ask for the person to refrain from swearing in your presence. An example of this approach is as follows:

> You make me feel uncomfortable when you use expletives in my presence. I'm not challenging your right to swear, but I just wish you could avoid swearing in front of me.

Another counterapproach is to repeat what the expletive user just said, so the person will understand the inappropriateness of the swearing. Precede the statement just made with, "You just referred to one of our coworkers as a "_____ son of a _____."

How can this information just presented help overcome communication problems on the job? As a starting point, remember that gender differences often exist. Understanding these differences will help you interpret the communication behavior of people. For example, if a male coworker is not as polite as you would like, remember that he is simply engaging in gender-typical behavior. Do not take it personally.

A woman can remind herself to speak up more in meetings because her natural tendency might be toward holding back. She might say to herself, "I must watch out to avoid gender-typical behavior in this situation." A man might remind himself to be more polite and supportive toward coworkers. The problem is that, although such behavior is important, his natural tendency might be to skip saying thank you.

Men and women should recognize that when women talk over problems, they might not be seeking hard-hitting advice. Instead, they may simply be searching for a sympathetic ear so they can deal with the emotional aspects of the problem.

A general suggestion for overcoming gender-related communication barriers is for men to improve communication by listening with more empathy. Women can improve communication by becoming more direct.

HOW CAN YOU ENHANCE YOUR LISTENING SKILLS?

LEARNING OBJECTIVE 7 Improving your receiving of messages is another part of developing better face-to-face and telephone communication skills. Unless you receive messages as they are intended, you cannot perform your job properly or be a good companion. Listening is a particularly important skill for anybody whose job involves solving problems for others because you need to gather information to understand the nature of the problem. Improving employee listening skills is important because insufficient listening is extraordinarily costly. Listening mistakes lead to reprocessing letters and e-mail messages, rescheduling appointments, reshipping orders, and recalling defective products. Effective listening also improves interpersonal relationships because people listen to feel understood and respected. Self-Assessment Quiz 5-2 gives you the opportunity to think through possible listening traps you may have developed. The accompanying in Practice illustrates how being a good listener can enrich the lives of others.

A fundamental reason so many people do not listen well is because of the difference between the average speed of talking and the average speed of processing information. Humans speak at an average pace of 110 to 200 words per minute. In contrast, they can understand or process information in the range of 400 to 3,000 words per

Listening Traps

Communication specialists have identified certain behavior patterns that interfere with effective hearing and listening. After thinking carefully about each trap, check how well the trap applies to you: not a problem, or need improvement. To respond to the statements accurately, visualize how you acted when you recently were in a situation calling for listening.

	Not a Problem	Need Improvement
1. **Mind reader.** You will receive limited information if you constantly think, "What is this person really thinking or feeling?"	❑	❑
2. **Rehearser.** Your mental rehearsals for "Here's what I'll say next" tune out the sender.	❑	❑
3. **Filterer.** You engage in selective listening by hearing only what you want to hear. (Could be difficult to judge because the process is often unconscious.)	❑	❑
4. **Dreamer.** You drift off during a face-to-face conversation, which often leads you to an embarrassing, "What did you say?" or "Could you repeat that?"	❑	❑
5. **Identifier.** If you refer everything you hear to your experience, you probably did not really listen to what was said.	❑	❑
6. **Comparer.** When you get sidetracked sizing up the sender, you are sure to miss the message.	❑	❑
7. **Derailer.** You change the subject too quickly, giving the impression that you are not interested in anything the sender has to say.	❑	❑
8. **Sparrer.** You hear what is said but quickly belittle or discount it, putting you in the same class as the derailer.	❑	❑
9. **Placater.** You agree with everything you hear just to be nice or to avoid conflict By behaving this way, you miss out on the opportunity for authentic dialogue.	❑	❑

Interpretation:

If you checked "Need Improvement" for five or more of the above statements, you are correct—your listening needs improvement! If you checked only two or fewer of the above traps, you are probably an effective listener and a supportive person.

Source: Reprinted with permission from *Messages: The Communication Skills Book* (Oakland, CA: New Harbinger Publications, 1983).

minute.[19] As a result, the mind tends to wander while listening to the slow pace of the sender talking.

Active Listening

A major component of effective listening is to be an **active listener.** The active listener listens intensely, with the goal of empathizing with the speaker. **Empathy** means understanding another person's point of view. If you understand the other person's paradigm, you will be a better receiver and sender of messages. Empathy does not necessarily mean that you sympathize with the other person. For example, you may understand why some people are forced to beg in the streets, but you may have very little sympathy for their plight.

active listener

Person who listens intensely, with the goal of empathizing with the speaker.

empathy

Understanding another person's point of view.

Big Success Tony Wainwright Listened Well

Barry Farber, top-rated sales, management, and motivation speaker, reflects fondly about a person he admired, in these terms: "I met Tony Wainwright, chairman of a $2.5 billion corporation, author, playwright, incredible philanthropist, and one of the world's foremost salespeople. He became my greatest mentor and one of my best friends.

"Tony passed away not long ago. I miss him every day. Shortly after he died, I began to wonder: What set him apart from the other people who tried to do what he did but failed? As I thought about Tony's life—not just his sales life, but about everything he did—I realized that what made him great was his uncanny ability to listen. He listened—truly listened to everyone he met.

"When you had a conversation with Tony, he made you feel as if your ideas were worth their weight in gold. (Not that everything you said was right—if you were on the wrong track, he would let you know.) He would make you feel special, as if you were the most important appointment he had in his life, and his only purpose was to find out what was on your mind. Then he'd tell you how you could make your idea 20 times larger than anything you'd conceived. His belief in you was so strong that you had to believe it, too. That's what made him such a great salesperson: He sold you on yourself."

Source: Abridged from Barry Farber, "All Ears? Sales Success: In Business and in Life, Learning to Listen Is One of the Most Important Skills You Can Develop," *Entrepreneur*, April 2004, pp. 83–84.

Accepting the Sender's Figure of Speech   A useful way of showing empathy is to accept the sender's figure of speech. By so doing, the sender feels understood and accepted. Also, if you reject the person's figure of speech by rewording it, the sender may become defensive. Many people use the figure of speech "I'm stuck" when they cannot accomplish a task. You can facilitate smooth communication by a response such as, "What can I do to help you get unstuck?" If you respond with something like, "What can I do to help you think more clearly?" the person is forced to change mental channels and may become defensive.[20]

paraphrase

Repeating in one's own words what a sender says, feels, and means.

Feedback and Paraphrasing   As a result of listening actively, the listener can feed back to the speaker what he or she thinks the speaker meant. Feedback of this type relies on both verbal and nonverbal communication. Feedback is also important because it facilitates two-way communication. To be an active listener, it is also important to **paraphrase,** or repeat in your own words what the sender says, feels, and means. In your paraphrasing, avoid rewording a person's figure of speech so long as that phrase is acceptable to you. You might feel awkward the first several times you paraphrase. Therefore, try it with a person with whom you feel comfortable. With some practice, it will become a natural part of your communication skill kit. Here is an example of how you might use paraphrasing:

Other Person: I'm getting ticked off at working so hard around here. I wish somebody else would pitch in and do a fair day's work.

You: You're saying that you do more than your fair share of the tough work in our department, and it's ticking you off.

Other Person: You bet. Here's what I think we should be doing about it. . . .

Life coach Sophronia Scott advises that, after you have paraphrased, it is sometimes helpful to ask the person you listened to whether your impression of what he or she said is correct. Your goal is not to make others repeat themselves but to extend the conversation so you can obtain more useful details.[21]

Minimize Distractions   If feasible, keep papers and your computer screen out of sight when listening to somebody else. Having distractions in sight creates the temptation to glance away from the message sender. Avoid answering a cell telephone call unless you are anticipating an emergency call. At the start of your conversation, notice the other person's eye color to help you establish eye contact. (But don't keep staring at his or her eyes!) A major technique of active listening is to ask questions rather than making conclusive statements. Asking questions provides more useful information. Suppose a teammate is late with data you need to complete your analysis. Instead of saying, "I must have your input by Thursday afternoon," try, "When will I get your input?"

Allow Sender to Finish His or Her Sentence Be sure to let others speak until they have finished. Do not interrupt by talking about you, jumping in with advice, or offering solutions unless requested. Equally bad for careful listening is finishing the sentence of a receiver. Almost all people prefer to complete their own thoughts, even though there are two curious traditions that run counter to this idea. One is that business partners who have been working together for many years, and understand each other well, have a tendency to finish the other partner's sentence. Couples in personal life behave similarly. Also, have you noticed how when you start to enter a phrase into a major search engine, suddenly you are given about ten choices that are not necessarily what you are planning to write? (Of course, this is responding to writing and not really listening, but the overtaking of your thinking is the same.)

Minimize Words That Shut Down Discussion A key part of listening is to keep the conversation flowing. According to executive coach Marshall Goldsmith, an especially useful approach to keep conversation going in most work situations is for the listener to minimize certain negatively toned words that frequently shut down conversation. When you say, "no," "but," or "however," you effectively shut down or limit the conversation. No matter what words follow, the sender receives a message to the effect, "You are wrong and I am right." Even if you say, "I agree, but..." the shut-down message still comes through. The other person is likely to get into the defensive mode.[22]

After the person has finished talking, there are times it will be appropriate to say, "no," "but," or "however." Assume, for example, that a worker says to the business owner that the company should donate one-third of its profits to charity each year. The owner might then reply, "I hear you, but if we give away all that money, our profits will be too slim to grow the business."

Avoid the Need to Lie or Fake When You Have Not Been Paying Attention A consequence of active listening is that you will avoid the need to pretend that you have been paying attention. Performance management coach Joe Takash suggests that you,

> Remind yourself that other people can sense if you're not listening. Force yourself to be honest and admit that you didn't catch everything that was said. That means asking the other person to repeat or requesting clarification. In this way you're being honest rather than deceitful—and deceit kills results-producing relationships fast.[23]

Personal Communication Style

In this chapter we have described many aspects of how people communicate, including gender-specific tendencies. How you combine verbal and nonverbal communication becomes part of your **personal communication style,** or your unique approach to sending and receiving information. Your personal communication style is a major component of your personality because it differentiates you from others. Hundreds of styles are possible, including the following:

- Katherine speaks loudly, smiles frequently, and moves close to people when speaking. Her communication style might be described as aggressive.

- Oscar speaks softly, partially covers his mouth with his hand while talking, and looks away from others. His communication style might be defined as passive or wimpy.

- Tim speaks rapidly, uses a colorful vocabulary, smiles frequently, and makes sweeping gestures. His communication style might be defined as flamboyant.

personal communication style

Verbal and nonverbal communication style for a unique approach to sending and receiving information.

WHAT ARE THE FORMAL CHANNELS OF COMMUNICATION WITHIN ORGANIZATIONS?

formal communication channels

The official pathways for sending information inside and outside an organization.

Messages in organizations are sent over both formal (official) and informal (unofficial) channels. **Formal communication channels** are the official pathways for sending information inside and outside an organization. The primary source of information about formal channels is the organization chart. It indicates the channels the messages are supposed to follow. By carefully following an organization chart, an entry-level worker would know how to transmit a message to someone in the executive suite. Formal communication channels are often bypassed through information technology. Using e-mail, instant messaging, and company blogs, anybody can send a message to anybody else in the organization. During an emergency, workers are also likely to bypass formal channels, such as a technician telephoning the plant manager directly about a chemical spill.

Relatively recent formal channels of communication include company blogs, social networks, intranets, and webinars, as well as procedures for crisis management. We also look at communication directions.

Web sites have now become the premier formal crisis communication channel. Formal channels during a crisis are necessary for informing employees about a disaster, work assignments, health services and grief counseling, and assistance in returning to work. Other formal communication channels during a crisis include television or radio.

Company Blogs as Formal Channels

The company blog (or, more precisely, a Web log or journal) is a widely used formal mode of communication, paralleling the use of blogs in private life. Blogs originated by consumers are often used to complain about products or services and less often to compliment a company. Blogs were first used by business to communicate with customers in a personal, direct manner and perhaps form a bond with them. The blog can provide customers with a behind-the-scenes look at the company.[24] A company can also use a blog to defend its side of the story in the face of criticism. Today, about 10 percent of major business corporations have entered the *blogosphere.*

The blog communicates business information but with a soft, human touch. For example, a product manager for bicycle helmets might write,

> *Just the other day, I heard from a mother of a six-year-old in our housing development. Little Jason complained about having to wear a helmet simply to ride his tricycle around the neighborhood. But then he was hit lightly by a car and thrown five feet. He escaped with a few scratches and bruises but no head injury. I'm so happy for Jason and so thankful to our fine staff who built that bike helmet to get the job done.*

The company blog can also be used to communicate with employees in a relaxed, casual tone. Employees, as well as customers, can interact with the Web log by providing comments that can be a source of valuable feedback to management and communicated directly to other visitors to the site. Blogs are also useful for communicating about shared projects, as a substitute for cutting back on large numbers of shared e-mail messages. Publishing company Ziff Davis found that by encouraging employees to use internal blogs, group e-mails were reduced from about one hundred per day to one per week. A company spokesperson said, "We've saved a month in a four-month software project, and everyone is on the same page."[25]

An individual who establishes a blog on his or her own to chat about the employer creates an *informal* rather than a formal channel—when the blog is not authorized by the company. Several years ago, Whole Foods Market Inc. amended its company code of conduct to restrict Internet postings by company officials. Based on problems created by the CEO with his anonymous blogs, the revised code bars executives and directors from posting messages about Whole Foods, its competitors, or vendors that are not sponsored by the company.[26]

Bloggers who publish negative information about their employer, or publish unprofessional photos of themselves, are liable to being fired. The rationale behind these firings is that the employee is making unwarranted use of his or her association with the company. To prevent problems of negativity appearing on personal blogs by employees, many companies now establish guidelines, such as "no disclosure of negative information about the company," "no nude photos," or "no profanity."

A general guideline for the use of offensive blogs is that a person's First Amendment right to free speech is not protected if it defames a company or divulges trade secrets on a Web posting. As explained by Nancy Flynn, executive director of the ePolicy Institute, "You could find yourself on the wrong side of a civil lawsuit."[27]

Social Networking Web Sites, Intranets, and Webinars

Formal communication channels in the workplace have kept pace with Internet-based communication technology. An important implication of this development is that workers at all levels are expected to use these channels to send and receive messages and to work collaboratively with each other. Here we describe three key Internet-based workplace communication channels: social networking Web sites, intranets, and webinars.

Social Networking Web Sites   As a majority of workers have become members of social networking Web sites such as MySpace, Facebook, LinkedIn, and Twitter, these sites have become natural channels for members of the same company to communicate. Twitter is used for brief messages of up to 140 characters, such as "Jogged today. Feel great." Because of their more widespread membership, MySpace and Facebook are more likely to be used as official workplace communication channels. Also, Facebook and MySpace have networks dedicated to companies or coworkers. Nevertheless, Twitter is becoming quite competitive in the workplace.

Social networking technologies on the job are quite similar to their use in personal life. Members are allowed to create profiles of themselves and link up with others in a virtual community.[28] The focus on the workplace site, however, is to communicate work-related messages. The sites are also useful for workers offering support to each other, such as encouraging another Facebook member when he or she is facing a challenging problem. Another official use of social networking by corporations is for recruiting workers, with many companies posting positions on these sites. Also, site members can pass along recruiting information to their network friends.

Yet another business application of social networks is to connect workers looking for mentors with more experienced workers who are available for mentoring. Members create profiles, ask questions of potential mentors, and arrange for in-person meetings. The same software has a "praise" tab, enabling site members to write quick notes of appreciation to each other.

Social networking sites also have an application that rests at the border between a formal and informal communication channel. For example, all employees might be encouraged to join Facebook so they can network with each and build their working relationships. Facebook becomes a virtual watercooler. In the words of Jeremy Burton, CEO of Serena Software Inc., "Social networking tools like Facebook can bring us back together, help us to get to know each other as people, help us understand our business and our products, and help us better serve our customers."[29]

A concern about social networking sites in the workplace is that they facilitate spending time on nonwork matters, such as pausing to watch a coworker's surfing video instead of reviewing his or her input. Nestlé USA has created a social network with its own firewall. Employees can post content related to nutrition and health but are prohibited from using the site for dating or selling products or services.[30] Another problem is that the same social networking site that displays a professional presence might present unprofessional images and content.

Assume that your vice president of finance sends you a finance message from her Facebook page. Will you take her seriously when her page also includes photos of her mud wrestling in a bikini? (This is the reason that many companies implement a company-specific social networking site rather than a public site.)

The accompanying Human Relations in Practice presents an example of the successful application of a social networking site in the workplace.

intranet

A company version of the Internet with the basic purpose of giving employees a central place to find what they need amidst a sea of digital information.

Intranets An **intranet** is essentially a company version of the Internet with the basic purpose of giving employees a central place to find what they need amidst a sea of digital information.[31] The intranet serves as a useful communication channel because updated information is readily available to workers, and the information is centralized, curent, and correct. For example, an employee might want to know the company's per diem allowance for meals while traveling. Instead of having to send an e-mail to the boss or human resources department, the employee can search the intranet.

The intranet is also used for much more than a file for routine information. More advanced uses include posting a video displaying a new product or service, describing the company's stand on a particular environmental issue, or posting a motivational message from the CEO. The company might also post a vision statement focusing on its exciting plans for the future. Another useful purpose is to use the intranet as a storage place for the minutes of meetings.

An intranet can also have a wiki feature in which workers are encouraged to add information of their own to certain content, similar to Wikipedia. Employee interaction of this type is helpful when those adding input are well informed and serious. The wiki approach facilitates worker collaboration, including the modification of documents as needed. The on-the-spot modification replaces sending hundreds of e-mails with attachments back and forth. To guard against misinformation being circulated, the company restricts which content allows for employee interaction. For example, the company cannot allow employees to modify per diem meal allowances.

For intranets to work well as a formal communication channel, they must have the same features of a useful commercial Web site, such as being able to find the information you need readily.

Some company intranets have added a human touch by adding such features as a phone book, menus from the company cafeteria, a classified ad section, and a dating site.

HUMAN RELATIONS IN PRACTICE

Alpine Access Uses Social Networking to Get Work Accomplished

When Denver-based Alpine Access wanted to provide a place for its home-based customer service representatives to trade ideas, it turned to a method usually reserved for college students and other young people.

"To meet the needs of our employees, we wanted to provide a watercooler in a virtual way," said David Parkhurst, director of client operations for Alpine Access. "It's a trend where people use technology to get what they need from one another rather than the traditional, institutional organization."

Alpine has about 7,500 home-based operators in the U.S. who take calls for a number of corporations, such as Office Depot and J. Crew. Parkhurst said the company wanted to unify all its workers, offering them a common online space to trade ideas and socialize.

Community builds morale, so Alpine enlisted the help of HiveLive Inc., a Boulder-based company that develops social networking platforms for businesses. Within 45 days of launching the Web-based HiveLive application at Alpine, 1,500 people were using it. Now employees are trading photos and recipes, and have even set up a classified marketplace to buy and sell items.

"Web 2.0 and social networks, blogs, wikis, tags, all shifted the way we connect and share with each other," said John Kembel, co-founder and chief executive of HiveLive. "Either from a competitive point of view or the effectiveness of doing business with each other, people realize they need to bring different communication tools to the business."

Source: Excerpted from Kimberly S. Johnson, "Work, Connected by Social Networking, *Denver Post* (denverpost.com), February 11, 2008.

Again, we see how a formal communication channel can also serve an informal, social purpose.

Webinars   Another formal communication channel is a web-based method of holding a seminar, referred to as a **webinar**. The speaker sends information to participants, who can interact with the conference presenter by computer. Collaboration is possible through such means as asking and answering questions. A telephone hookup is also typically used, including a speakerphone so many people at the same time can tune in on the information flow. Slides are displayed throughout the presentation.

The participants in the webinar often are working alone, yet they can be gathered in groups at one or more locations. The meetings can include PowerPoint presentations and streaming videos. Chat is another possible feature, so participants can react to the points raised by other participants.

Webinars as a formal communication channel are efficient and save travel costs and time, but, as with some other forms of communication technology, they have a limited human touch. For example, it is more difficult to inspire a worker with a message to his or her computer screen than an in-person message complete with many nonverbal cues.

webinar

A web-based method of holding a seminar.

Concept Review and Reinforcement

Key Terms

communication 153
encoding 154
decoding 154
barriers to communication
  (or noise) 155
nonverbal communication 156
semantics 162

mixed signals 162
communication overload 163
frame of reference 166
defensive communication 167
denial 167
mirroring 168
active listener 171

empathy 171
paraphrase 172
personal communication style 173
formal communication channels 174
intranet 176
webinar 177

Summary

Communication is the sending and receiving of messages. Therefore, almost anything that takes place in work and personal life involves communication. The steps involved in communication are sending, transmission over a channel, and decoding.

Communication is a vehicle for building relationships. We establish relationships along two primary dimensions: dominate–subordinate and cold–warm.

- In the process of communicating, we attempt to dominate or subordinate.
- We indicate whether we want to dominate or subordinate by the way we speak or write or by nonverbal signals we send.
- The four combinations of dominate–subordinate and cold–warm lead to different types of relationships—impersonal, accepting, supportive, or personal.

Nonverbal communication, or silent messages, are important parts of everyday communication. Nonverbal communication includes the following:

- Environment or setting in which the message is sent
- Distance from the other person
- Posture
- Hand gestures
- Facial expressions and eye contact
- Voice quality
- Personal appearance

An advanced application of nonverbal communication is to help combat drug trafficking and terrorism by spotting nervous or threatening behavior.

Roadblocks to communication are most likely to occur when messages are complex or emotional or clash with the receiver's mental set. Communication roadblocks include the following:

- Limited understanding of people
- One-way communication
- Semantics
- Credibility of the sender and mixed signals
- Distortion of information
- Different perspectives and experiences
- Emotions and attitudes
- Communication overload
- Improper timing
- Poor communication skills
- Cultural and language barriers

Strategies to overcome communication roadblocks include these:

- Appealing to human need and timing your messages
- Repeating your message using more than one channel
- Having an empowered attitude and being persuasive
- Discussing differences in paradigms
- Checking for comprehension and feelings
- Minimizing defensive communication
- Combating communication overload
- Using mirroring to establish rapport
- Engaging in small talk and constructive gossip

Some opinion and evidence exists about gender differences in communication style. For example, women prefer to use conversation for rapport building, and men prefer to use talk primarily as a means to preserve independence and status by displaying knowledge and skill. Understanding gender differences will help you interpret the communication behavior of people.

Improving your receiving of messages is another part of developing better communication skills. Unless you receive messages as intended, you cannot perform your job properly or be a good companion. A major component of effective listening is to be an active listener. The active listener uses empathy and can feed back to the speaker what he or she thinks the speaker meant.

Active listening also involves:

- Accepting the sender's figure of speech
- Feedback and paraphrasing
- Minimizing distractions
- Allowing the sender to finish his or her sentences
- Minimizing words that shut down discussion

How you combine verbal and nonverbal communication becomes your personal communication style.

Questions for Discussion and Review

1. Based on Figure 5-1, describe one way in which you could use interpersonal communication to build a better relationship.

2. How can knowing the three major steps in communication help a person communicate more effectively?

3. Many people contend they communicate much more formally when on the job and much more informally (including using a more limited vocabulary) when among family members and friends. What do you see as the potential advantages and disadvantages of using two communication styles?

4. Why is nonverbal communication so important for the effectiveness of a manager or sales representative?

5. What can a person do to send more positive nonverbal communication signals with his or her handshake?

6. Assume that a person who is intent on a career in business chooses to have several tattoos. Which type of tattoo is likely to send the most positive message about his or her maturity and seriousness?

7. Shortly after experienced IT executive Carol Bartz, age sixty, was appointed as the new CEO of Yahoo! Inc., she made the following comments: "Let's give Yahoo! some frickin' breathing room," and "I promise to get outward looking and kick some butt."[23] What is your evaluation of this type of communication style for an Internet company executive?

8. Based on your own observations, identify a term or phrase in the workplace that creates semantic problems.

9. So what if differences in communication patterns between men and women have been identified? What impact will this information have on your communication with men and women?

10. How would you rate the persuasive communication skills of the current president of the United States? Have you any suggestions as to how the president could improve?

The Web Corner

Effective listening:
www.womensmedia.com/seminar-listening.html

Exploring nonverbal communication:
http://nonverbal.ucsc.edu/

INTERNET SKILL BUILDER

Infoplease offers some practical suggestions for improving your listening skills that both support and supplement the ideas offered in this chapter. Infoplease divides listening into three basic steps: hearing, understanding, and judging. Visit the site at www.infoplease.com/homework/listeningskills1.html. The Web site includes a video of a person offering a service that will enable you to earn money as a public speaker. What is your opinion of this man's persuasiveness and credibility? What is you opinion of the effectiveness of his nonverbal communication?

Developing Your Human Relations Skills

Human Relations Application Exercises

Applying Human Relations Exercise 5-1

I Want a Raise

The purpose of this exercise is to practice your persuasive skills using a topic of interest to many people—obtaining a salary increase. One by one, students make a presentation in front of the class, presenting a persuasive argument as to why they merit a salary increase. The instructor will decide whether to use a handful of volunteers or the entire class. The audience represents the boss. The student will first explain his or her job title and key responsibilities. (Use your imagination here.) Next, make a three-minute convincing argument as to why you merit a salary increase and perhaps indicate how much you want. You will probably have about 15 minutes to prepare, inside or outside of class.

After the presentations, volunteers will offer feedback on the effectiveness of selected presentations. During the presentations of the other students, make a few notes about the presenter's effectiveness. You may need a couple of minutes between presenters to make your notes. Consider these factors:

- Overall, how convincing was the presenter? If you were the boss, would you give him or her the requested salary increase?
- Which techniques of persuasion did he or she use?
- What aspect of the presentation was unconvincing or negative?

What lessons did you take away from this exercise about persuasive communication?

Applying Human Relations Exercise 5-2

Active Listening

Before conducting the following role-plays, review the suggestions for active listening in this chapter. The suggestion about paraphrasing the message is particularly relevant because the role-plays involve emotional topics.

The Cost-Cutting Coworker

One student plays the role of a coworker who has just been appointed as the cost-cutting coordinator for the department. The cost cutter has decided to explain his or her new responsibilities to coworkers one at a time before calling a group meeting. He or she wants to emphasize how everybody has an important role in saving the company money, even in such minor initiatives as copying on two sides of a sheet of paper and not throwing out pencils until they are less than three inches long. The second worker decides to listen intently to the first worker. Other class members will rate the second student on his or her listening ability.

The Failed Nurse

One student plays the role of a coworker who has just been notified that she has failed her licensing exam to become a registered nurse (RN). She now faces being dismissed from the hospital because she has failed to obtain her license for the second time. She worries about what she will be able to do to earn a living. Another student plays the role of a coworker she corners to discuss his problems. The second worker decided to listen intently to her problems but is pressed for time. Other class members will rate the second student on his or her listening ability.

When evaluating the active listening skills of the role-players, consider using the following evaluating factors, on a scale of 1 (low) to 5 (high):

Evaluation Factor	Rating 1 2 3 4 5
1. Maintained eye contact	
2. Showed empathy	
3. Paraphrased what the other person said	
4. Focused on other person instead of being distracted	
5. Asked questions	
6. Let other person speak until he or she was finished	

Total Points: _____

Human Relations Class Activity

How Good Should Our Communication Skills Be?

"How good do my communication skills have to be to succeed in the workplace?" is a question on the minds of many career-oriented people. The purpose of this exercise is to observe the verbal and nonverbal communication skills of people who appear to have succeeded in their careers. The class in its entirety will observe a business leader or sports leader, such as a coach or an athletic director, being interviewed on television. Business channels and sports channels might be a good source of material, as might YouTube. Larry King is another potential source of useful interviews. The transmission can be real time or previously recorded, and it should last approximately five to ten minutes.

As you observe the leader (or perhaps two leaders) on television or on the Internet, grade the person or persons on two dimensions: verbal communication skills and nonverbal communication skills. Use a standard A though F system. Back up your grading with a few written comments, such as "Great eye contact with the interviewer," or "Dull, unanimated person. Put me to sleep." Also, attempt to answer the following questions:

1. What kind of impact is the presenter having on your classmates? To answer this question, take a few quick peeks around the room during the presentation, and observe the nonverbal communication of your classmates.

2. To what extent would this person be a good communications role model for me?

3. What, if any, communication tips did I learn from the person or persons in the interview(s)?

A couple of minutes after the grading and written observations are completed, the class will discuss some of the student observations. Be alert to whether consensus exists about the quality of the communications skills observed.

Human Relations Case Study 5-1

The Scrutinized Team Member Candidate

HRmanager.com is a human resources management firm that provides human resource services such as payroll, benefits administration, affirmative action programs, and technical training to other firms. By signing up with HRmanager, other firms can outsource part or all of their human resources functions. During its seven years of operation, HRmanager has grown from three to fifty employees and last year had total revenues of $21 million.

Teams perform most of the work, led by a rotating team leader. Each team member takes an eighteen-month turn at being a team leader. CEO and founder Jerry Clune regards the four-person new ventures team as vital for the future of the company. In addition to developing ideas for new services, the team members are responsible for obtaining clients for any new service they propose that Clune approves. The new ventures team thus develops and sells new services. After the service is launched and working well, the sales group is responsible for developing more clients.

As with other teams at HRmanager, the team members have a voice as to who is hired to join their team. In conjunction with Clune, the new ventures team decided it should expand to five members. The team posted the job opening for a new member on an Internet recruiting service, ran classified ads in the local newspaper, and also asked present employees for referrals. One of the finalists for the position was Gina Cleveland, a 27-year-old business graduate. In addition to interviewing with Clune and the two company vice presidents, Cleveland spent a half day with the new ventures team, breakfast and lunch included. More than two hours of that time was spent in a team interview in which Gina sat in a conference room with the four team members.

The team members agreed that Cleveland appeared to be a strong candidate on paper. Her education and experience were satisfactory, her résumé was impressive, and she presented herself well during a telephone-screening interview. After Cleveland completed her time with the new ventures team, Lauren Nielsen, the team leader, suggested that the group hold a debriefing session. The purpose of the session would be to share ideas about Cleveland's suitability for joining the team.

Nielsen commented, "It seems like we think that Gina is a strong candidate based on her credentials and what she said. But I'm a big believer in nonverbal communication. Studying Gina's body language can give us a lot of valuable information. Let's each share our observations about what Gina's body language tells us she is *really* like. I'll go first."

Lauren: I liked the way Gina looked so cool and polished when she joined us for breakfast. She's got all the superficial movements right to project self-confidence. But did anybody else notice how she looked concerned when she had to make a choice from the menu? She finally did choose a ham-and-cheese omelet, but she raised her voice at the end of the sentence when she ordered it. I got the hint that Gina is not very confident.

I also noticed Gina biting her lips a little when we asked her how creative she thought she was. I know that Gina said she was creative and gave us an example of a creative project she completed. Yet nibbling at her lips like that suggests she's not filled with firepower.

Michael: I didn't make any direct observations about Gina's being self-confident or not, but I did notice something that could be related. I think Gina is on a power trip, and this could indicate high or low self-confidence. Did anybody notice how Gina put her hands on her hips when she was standing up? That's a pure and clear signal of somebody who wants to be in control. Her haircut is almost the same length and style as most women who've made it to the top in *Fortune* 500 companies.

Another hint I get of Gina's power trip is the way she eyed the check in the restaurant at lunch. I could see it in her eyes that she really wanted to pay for the entire team. That could mean a desire to control and show us that she is very important.

Do we want someone on the team with such a strong desire to control?

Brenda: I observed a different picture of Gina based on her nonverbal communication. She dressed just right for the occasion—not too conservatively, not too far business casual. This tells me she can fit into our environment. Did you notice how well groomed her shoes were? This tells you she is well organized and good at details. Her attaché case was a soft, inviting leather. If she were really into power and control, she would carry a hard vinyl or aluminum attaché case. I see Gina as a confident and assertive person who could blend right into our team.

Larry: I hope that because I'm last, I'm not too influenced by the observations that you three have shared so far. My take is that Gina looks great on paper but that she may have a problem in being a good team player. She's too laid-back and distant. Did you notice her handshake? She gave me the impression of wanting to have the least possible physical contact with me. Her handshake was so insincere. I could feel her hand and arm withdrawing from me as she shook my hand.

I also couldn't help noticing that Gina did not lean much toward us during the roundtable discussion. Do you remember how she would pull her chair back ever so slightly when we got into a heavy discussion? I interpreted that as a sign that Gina does not want to be part of a close-knit group.

Lauren: As you have probably noticed, I've been typing as fast as I can at my laptop, taking notes on what you have said. We have some mixed observations here, and I want to summarize and integrate them before we make a decision. I'll send you an e-mail with an attached file of my summary observations by tomorrow morning. Make any changes you see fit and get back to me. After we have finished evaluating Gina carefully, we will be able to make our recommendations to Jerry.

Case Questions

1. To what extent are new ventures team members making an appropriate use of nonverbal communication to size up Gina Cleveland?

2. Which team member do you think made the most realistic interpretation of nonverbal behavior? Why?

3. Should Lauren, the team leader, have told Gina in advance that the team would be scrutinizing her nonverbal behavior? Justify your answer.

Human Relations Case Study 5-2

The Financial Services Coach

Kristine Florentine is an account representative (stockbroker) at a branch office of a financial services firm. Her manager, Chad Olsen, is concerned that Kristine is 25 percent below quota in sales of a new hedge mutual fund offered by the company. (In the past, hedge funds were only for the wealthiest investors.) Chad sets up an appointment with Kristine to spur her to achieve quota. The conversation proceeds, in part, in this manner:

Chad: My most important responsibility is to help team members work up to their potential. I wanted to get together with you today to see if there is any way I can help you. During the past quarter you were 25 percent below quota in your sales of the new hedge fund.

Kristine: I know that I am under quota, but I can't help it. It's tough pushing a hedge fund these days. Our clients are becoming conservative, and they don't want to jump into an investment they don't understand well and is associated with taking a high risk.

Chad: Why don't your clients understand the hedge fund?

Kristine: It's a fund that the average investor does not understand. The information I send them is pretty complicated for a layperson.

Chad: What steps could you take to make this hedge fund easier for our clients and prospects to understand?

Kristine: Maybe I could work up a thirty-second presentation that would give a nice overview of the hedge fund. This would enable me to make a quick pitch over the telephone. I could get back with more details by email.

Chad: Now you're making good sense. But I'm disappointed that an intelligent person like you didn't think of that before. Do you have a self-confidence problem when it comes to making quota on a new product?

Kristine: Most people would have a self-confidence problem if they were going through what I am these days. It's not that easy concentrating on my work.

Chad: I don't like to hear excuses, but I'll make an exception this time. What are you going through that makes it difficult for you to concentrate on your work, Kristine?

Kristine: My sister and I are pretty close, and she's in big trouble. I mean *big* trouble. She was down on her luck, so she started dealing drugs. I warned her. My folks warned her, but she wouldn't listen. She got busted recently and faces a ten-year prison term.

Chad: Sorry to hear about your sister. But can't you keep things in perspective? You weren't involved in her drug dealing, were you?

Kristine: What's really dragging me down is that my sister used to tell me that I was her role model. Some role model. Her life is ruined.

Chad: Now I understand why you are so down. However, let's meet again real soon to talk about your sales on the hedge fund.

Case Questions

1. Identify the strengths in Chad's listening technique.

2. Identify the areas for improvement in Chad's listening technique.

3. How effective is Chad as a coaching style of manager?

Human Relations Role-Playing Exercise

Listening to Kristine's Tale of Woe

The case about the financial services coach serves as the scenario and the story line for this role-play. One student plays the role of Kristine, who believes that her distress about her sister's personal problem is a valid reason for her below-average performance. Her hope is that her boss, Chad, will listen carefully to her tale of woe and be empathetic. She will try to get Chad to listen more attentively to her. Another person plays the role of Chad, who is quite work oriented. He is willing to listen to an employee's personal problems, but he believes that his most important role is to focus on business results.

For both scenarios, observers rate the role-players on two dimensions, using a 1 to 5 scale from very poor to very good. One dimension is "effective use of human relations techniques." The second dimension is "acting ability." A few observers might voluntarily provide feedback to the role-players in terms of sharing their ratings and observations. The course instructor might also provide feedback.

REFERENCES

1. "'The Art of Woo': Selling Your Ideas to the Entire Organization, One Person at a Time," Knowledge@Wharton (www.knowledgeatwharton.com), October 17, 2007, p. 1.

2. Rich Sorenson, Grace De Bord, and Ida Ramirez, *Business and Management Communication: A Guide Book,* 4th ed. (Upper Saddle River, NJ: Prentice Hall, 2001), pp. 6–10.

3. Edward T. Hall, "Proxemics—A Study of Man's Spatial Relationships," in *Man's Image in Medicine and Anthropology* (New York: International Universities Press, 1963); Pauline E. Henderson, "Communication without Words," *Personnel Journal,* January 1989, pp. 28–29.

4. Brochure for Executive Advantage program, Washington, DC, offered by Letitia Baldrige, 1997, p. 6.

5. Nick Morgan, "How to Become an Authentic Speaker," *Harvard Business Review,* November 2008, p. 116.

6. Jeffrey Jacobi, *The Vocal Advantage* (Upper Saddle River, NJ: Prentice Hall, 1996).

7. Genviève Coutu-Bouchard, "L'effet Pygmalion," *Montréal Campus,* April 24, 2002, p. 11.

8. Ann Davis, Joseph Pereira, and William M. Bulkeley, "Silent Signals: Security Concerns Bring New Focus on Body Language," *Wall Street Journal,* August 15, 2002, pp. A1, A6;

9. Del Quentin Wilber and Ellen Nakashima, "They Don't Like Your Looks," *Washington Post,* September 19, 2007, p. DO1.

10. "Weed Out Wimpy Words," *WorkingSMART,* March 2000, p. 2; George Walther cited in "Power Up Your Persuasiveness," *Executive Leadership,* July 2003, p. 1.

11. Joe Neumaier, "Sweet Sounds of Success: Dialect Coach Sam Chwat Accents Hollywood's Best," *USA Weekend,* July 12–14, 2002, p. 12.

12. Sharon Lund O'Neill, "An Empowered Attitude Can Enhance Communication Skills," *Business Education Forum,* April 1998, pp. 28–30.

13. Several of the ideas are from "Six Ways to Be More Persuasive," *Manager's Edge,* November 2008, p. 3; Charles Harrington Elster, "Cubicle Conversation," *Wall Street Journal,* July 23, 2008, p. A15; "Talk in Headlines," *Manager's Edge,* April 2008, p. 8. For more details about point 9 in Figure 5-4, see Brian Fugere, Chelsea Hardaway, and Jon Warshawsky, *Why Business People Speak like Idiots* (New York: Free Press, 2005); Jessica E. Vascellaro, "Yahoo Chief to Deliver More Straight Talk," *Wall Street Journal,* January 26, 2009, p. A2.

14. Chris Pentila, "I Know Too Much!" *Entrepreneur,* February 2007, p. 83.

15. Quoted in Jacquelyn Lynn, "Small Talk, Big Results," *Entrepreneur,* August 1999, p. 30.

16. Nancy B. Kurland and Lisa Hope Pelled, "Passing the Word: Toward a Model of Gossip and Power in the Workplace," *Academy of Management Review,* April 2000, pp. 428–438.

17. Deborah Tannen, *Talking from Nine to Five* (New York: William Morrow, 1994).

18. Deborah Tannen, *You Just Don't Understand* (New York: Ballantine, 1990); John Gray, *Men Are from Mars, Women Are from Venus* (New York: HarperCollins, 1992); Deborah Tannen, "The Power of Talk: Who Gets Heard and Why," *Harvard Business Review,* September–October 1995, pp. 138–148; Laurie Arliss, *Gender Communication* (Englewood Cliffs, NJ: Prentice Hall, 2005).

19. One source of this widely quoted statistic is Jared Sandberg, "Bad at Complying? You Might Just Be a Very Bad Listener," *Wall Street Journal,* September 25, 2007, p. D1.

20. Daniel Araoz, "Right-Brain Management (RBM): Part 2," *Human Resources Forum,* September 1989, p. 4.

21. Cited in "Five Keys to Effective Listening," *Black Enterprise,* March 2005, p. 113.

22. Ideas from Marshall Goldsmith cited in "Eliminate Bad Words," *Manager's Edge,* special issue, 2008, p. 5.

23. Quoted in Mimi Whitefield, "Listen Up—Your Job Could Depend on It," *Miami Herald* (www.miamiherald.com), April 20, 2009.

24. Rich Sorenson, Grace De Bord, and Ida Ramirez, *Business and Management Communication: A Guide Book,* 4th ed. (Upper Saddle River, NJ: Prentice Hall, 2001), pp. 6–10.

25. Edward T. Hall, "Proxemics—A Study of Man's Spatial Relationships," in *Man's Image in Medicine and Anthropology* (New York: International Universities Press, 1963); Pauline E. Henderson, "Communication without Words," *Personnel Journal,* January 1989, pp. 28–29.

26. Brochure for Executive Advantage program, Washington, DC, offered by Letitia Baldrige, 1997, p. 6.

27. Nick Morgan, "How to Become an Authentic Speaker," *Harvard Business Review,* November 2008, p. 116.

28. Jeffrey Jacobi, *The Vocal Advantage* (Upper Saddle River, NJ: Prentice Hall, 1996).

29. Genviève Coutu-Bouchard, "L'effet Pygmalion," *Montréal Campus,* April 24, 2002, p. 11.

30. Ann Davis, Joseph Pereira, and William M. Bulkeley, "Silent Signals: Security Concerns Bring New Focus on Body Language," *Wall Street Journal,* August 15, 2002, pp. A1, A6;

31. Del Quentin Wilber and Ellen Nakashima, "They Don't Like Your Looks," *Washington Post,* September 19, 2007, p. DO1.

Self-Esteem and Attitude

Scott Gould went from trader to waiter—by choice. Growing up in Florida, Gould enjoyed working in restaurants as a waiter and bartender. But he also liked working with numbers; and after graduating from the University of Florida, he went into finance. He got a job as a fixed income trader in 2000, and later raised money to invest in new markets and helped develop avenues for investors. He learned to do research and listen to customers. Every client wanted something a little different with respect to risk.

On the morning of September 11, 2001, Gould was working in his office near the World Trade Center. He evacuated after the first plane hit. As he walked down 36 flights of stairs, he saw the second plane flying into the tower. It made him reevaluate his career. "I had to think,

1. Describe the nature, development, and consequences of self-esteem.
2. Explain how to enhance self-esteem.
3. Describe the importance of self-confidence and self-efficacy.
4. Pinpoint methods of enhancing and developing your self-confidence.
5. Explain how emotional intelligence contributes to effective human relations.
6. Understand the components of attitudes and how they are acquired and changed.
7. Appreciate the importance of positive attitudes.
8. Pinpoint why organizational citizenship behavior is so highly valued in the workplace.
9. Understand the nature of happiness and how it can be acquired and enhanced.

'Do I love what I'm doing?' and I couldn't answer yes," he says. "It's not like I hated going to work, but we spend so much time working and it wasn't exciting and I wasn't running to the office on Monday morning."

Gould kept thinking back to how he had liked working at restaurants. As a trader, he had taken clients regularly to Del Frisco's, a steakhouse in Midtown Manhattan. On a whim, he called a manager he knew and asked for a job. And, he was told that there was an opening as a server. He handed in his notice the next day, and started at Del Frisco's in August 2002. Three months later, he moved behind the bar for another three months.

"Obviously coming here as a guest two months earlier and then becoming a waiter—it wasn't insulting but it messes with your pride a little," he says. "I think if you can get over the pride factor of taking a step down and understand that sometimes you take a step backwards to eventually take three steps forward, it is more than worth it."

In February 2003, Gould got a big break. A sommelier (wine specialist) was leaving, and he was offered the chance to step in by David O'Day, the director of wine for Del Frisco's Restaurant Group. O'Day says Gould's financial background helped him work with customers. Some of them wanted to talk about a $40 bottle of wine and others asked about a $4,000 bottle. Gould was comfortable working with both. In November 2007, he was promoted to general manager of the restaurant, a big popular place with 475 seats. He now oversees 17 managers and 250 employees.

Gould says he has brought the listening skills he learned during his finance days onto the restaurant floor, and the hectic pace of trading helps him stay calm during crises now. One Sunday night in fall 2007, the ventilation system stopped working, causing the room to over-heat and the kitchen sprinklers to go off.

There were inches of water on the kitchen floor, a fire department on the way and 300 diners waiting to eat. "I went from table to table with my cell phone in one hand and a Zagat's in the other, asking people what their second choice was," Gould said. (Zagat is an online restaurant directory.) He tried to stay calm, thinking that if he panicked, so would his staff.

"Instead," he says, "For months people came back and said, 'I was here on that Sunday night. That was so crazy.'"[1]

The story about the career-switching Wall Street trader illustrates many human relations topics covered in this book. Our focus, however, is how high self-esteem and self-confidence enabled Scott Gould to do the type of work he really loved. For example, his strong self-esteem enabled him to shift down to a server's job temporarily without worrying about status. Gould's self-confidence helped him recognize that he could move upward in the restaurant, and also help him stay cool under pressure.

Many other people you will meet in this book score high in self-esteem and self-confidence—otherwise they would never have been so successful. In this chapter, we focus on two of the biggest building blocks for more effective human relations: the nature and development of self-esteem and self-confidence. The development of both self-esteem and self-confidence includes refining certain skills.

THE MEANING OF SELF-ESTEEM, ITS DEVELOPMENT AND CONSEQUENCES

LEARNING OBJECTIVE 1

Understanding the self from various perspectives is important because who you are and what you think of you influence many different facets of your life both on and off the job. A particularly important role is played by **self-esteem,** the overall evaluation people make about themselves whether positive or negative.[2] A useful distinction is that our self-concept is what we *think* about ourselves whereas self-esteem is what we *feel* about ourselves.[3] People with positive self-esteem have a deep-down, inside-the-self feeling of their own worth. Consequently, they develop a positive self-concept. Before reading further, you are invited to measure your current level of self-esteem by doing Self-Assessment Quiz 6-1. We look next at the development of self-esteem and many of its consequences.

SELF-ASSESSMENT QUIZ 6-1

The Self-Esteem Checklist

Indicate whether each of the following statements is Mostly True or Mostly False as it applies to you.

		Mostly True	Mostly False
1.	I am excited about starting each day.		
2.	Most of any progress I have made in my work or school can be attributed to luck.		✓
3.	I often ask myself, "Why can't I be more successful?"	✓	
4.	When my manager or team leader gives me a challenging assignment, I usually dive in with confidence.	✓	
5.	I believe that I am working up to my potential.	✓	
6.	I am able to set limits to what I will do for others without feeling anxious.	✓	
7.	I regularly make excuses for my mistakes.	✓	
8.	Negative feedback crushes me.		✓
9.	I care very much how much money other people make, especially when they are working in my field.	✓	
10.	I feel like a failure when I do not achieve my goals.	✓	
11.	Hard work gives me an emotional lift.		
12.	When others compliment me, I doubt their sincerity.		
13.	Complimenting others makes me feel uncomfortable.		
14.	I find it comfortable to say, "I'm sorry."		✓
15.	It is difficult for me to face up to my mistakes.		✓
16.	My coworkers think I am not worthy of promotion.		
17.	People who want to become my friends usually do not have much to offer.		✓
18.	If my manager praised me, I would have a difficult time believing it was deserved.		✓

(Continued)

19. I'm just an ordinary person.

20. Having to face change really disturbs me.

21. When I make a mistake, I have no fear owning up to it in public.

22. When I look in the mirror, I typically see someone who is attractive and confident.

23. When I think about the greater purpose in my life, I feel like I am drifting.

24. When I make a mistake, I tend to feel ashamed and embarrassed.

25. When I make a commitment to myself, I usually stick to it with conviction and await the rewards that I believe will come from it.

Scoring and Interpretation: The answers in the high self-esteem direction are as follows:

1. Mostly True	8. Mostly False	15. Mostly False	22. Mostly True
2. Mostly False	9. Mostly False	16. Mostly False	23. Mostly False
3. Mostly False	10. Mostly False	17. Mostly False	24. Mostly False
4. Mostly True	11. Mostly True	18. Mostly False	25. Mostly True
5. Mostly True	12. Mostly False	19. Mostly False	
6. Mostly True	13. Mostly False	20. Mostly False	
7. Mostly False	14. Mostly True	21. Mostly True	

20–25 You have very high self-esteem. Yet if your score is 25, it could be that you are denying any self-doubts.

14–19 Your self-esteem is in the average range. It would probably be worthwhile for you to implement strategies to boost your self-esteem (described in this chapter) so that you can develop a greater feeling of well-being.

0–13 Your self-esteem needs bolstering. Talk over your feelings about yourself with a trusted friend or with a mental health professional. At the same time, attempt to implement several tactics for boosting self-esteem described in this chapter.

Questions:

1. How does your score on this quiz match your evaluation of your self-esteem?

2. What would it be like being married to somebody who scored 0 on this quiz?

Source: Statements 21–25 are based on information in the National Association for Self-Esteem, "Self-Esteem Self-Guided Tour – Rate Your Self-Esteem," http://www.self-esteem–nase.org/jssurvey.shtml, accessed May 6, 2005, pp. 1–4.

How Self-Esteem Develops

Part of understanding the nature of self-esteem is to know how it develops. Self-esteem develops and evolves throughout our lives based on interactions with people, events, and things.[4] As an adolescent or adult, your self-esteem might be boosted by a key accomplishment. A 44-year-old woman who was studying to become licensed practical nurse (LPN) said that her self-esteem increased when she received an A in a pharmacology course. Self-esteem can also go down in adulthood by means of a negative event such as being laid off, and not being able to find new employment.

Early life experiences have a major impact on self-esteem. People who were encouraged to feel good about themselves and their accomplishments by family members, friends, and teachers are more likely to enjoy high self-esteem. Early life experiences play a key role in the development of both healthy self-esteem and low self-esteem, according to research synthesized at the Counseling and Mental Health Center of the University of Texas.[5] Childhood experiences that lead to healthy self-esteem include

- being praised
- being listened to
- being spoken to respectfully
- getting attention and hugs
- experiencing success in sports or school

In contrast, childhood experiences that lead to low self-esteem include

- being harshly criticized
- being yelled at or beaten
- being ignored, ridiculed, or teased
- being expected to be "perfect" all the time
- experience failures in sports or school
- often being given messages that failed experiences (losing a game, getting a poor grade, and so forth) were failures of their whole self.

A widespread explanation of self-esteem development is that compliments, praise, and hugs alone build self-esteem. Yet many developmental psychologists seriously question this perspective. Instead, they believe that self-esteem results from accomplishing worthwhile activities and then feeling proud of these accomplishments. Receiving encouragement, however, can help the person accomplish activities that build self-esteem.

Leading psychologist Martin Seligman argues that self-esteem is caused by a variety of successes and failures. To develop self-esteem, people need to improve their skills for dealing with the world.[6] Self-esteem therefore comes about by genuine accomplishments, followed by praise and recognition. Heaping undeserved praise and recognition on people may lead to a temporary high, but it does not produce genuine self-esteem. The child develops self-esteem not from being told he or she can score a goal in soccer but from scoring that goal.

In attempting to build the self-esteem of children and students, many parents and teachers give children too many undeserved compliments. Researchers suggest that inappropriate compliments are turning too many adults into narcissistic praise-junkies. As a result, many young adults feel insecure if they do not receive compliments regularly.[7]

As mentioned above, experiences in adult life can influence the development of self-esteem. David De Cremer of the Tilburg University (Netherlands) and his associates conducted two studies with Dutch college students about how the behavior of leaders and fair procedures influence self-esteem. The focus of the leaders' behavior was whether he or she motivated the workers/students to reward *themselves* for a job well done, such as a self-compliment. Procedural fairness was measured in terms of whether the study participants were given a voice in making decisions. Self-esteem was measured by a questionnaire somewhat similar to Self-Assessment 6-1 in this chapter. The study questionnaire reflected the self-perceived value that individuals have of themselves as organizational members.

The study found that self-esteem was related to procedural fairness and leadership that encourages self-rewards. When leadership that encouraged rewards was high, procedural fairness was more strongly related to self-esteem. The interpretation given of the findings is that a leader/supervisor can facilitate self-esteem when he or she encourages self-rewards, and uses fair procedures. Furthermore, fair procedures have a stronger impact on self-esteem when the leader encourages self-rewards.[8] A takeaway from this study would that rewarding yourself for a job well done, even in adult life, can boost your self-esteem a little.

The Consequences of High Self-Esteem

High self-esteem has many positive consequences for people, as well as a few potential negative ones. Table 6-1 outlines these consequences, and they are described in the

TABLE 6-1   Several Consequences of High Self-Esteem

1. Career success, including a high income
2. Good mental health
3. Profiting from feedback
4. Organizational success
5. Trying too hard to preserve one's status (negative consequence)

following paragraphs. Low-self esteem would typically have a negative impact on the first three factors. People with low self-esteem are likely to have less career success, poorer mental health, and profitless from feedback. Also, an organization populated with low self-esteem workers would be less successful. Yet on the positive side of low self-esteem, it would not lead to trying too hard to preserve one's status.

Career Success. No single factor is as important to career success as self-esteem, as observed by psychologist Eugene Raudsepp. People with positive self-esteem understand their own competence and worth, and have a positive perception of their ability to cope with problems and adversity.[9]

As part of a larger study of personal characteristics and career success, the University of Florida psychology professors Timothy A. Judge, Chalice Hurst, and Lauren S. Simon studied the impact of *core self-evaluation.* Core self-evaluation is a personality trait representing the favorability of a person's overall self-concept. The self-evaluation includes self-esteem, belief in self-control of events in one's life, self-confidence, and emotional stability. Three hundred participants were studied over a 10-year period. One of the many findings in the study was that people with a higher core self-evaluation tended to have higher incomes. Two other factors studied, general mental ability and physical attractiveness, were also found to have a positive relationship with income from employment. A partial explanation of these findings was that being smart and physically attractive contributed to having high self-esteem.[10]

Good Mental Health. One of the major consequences of high self-esteem is good mental health. People with high self-esteem feel good about themselves and have a positive outlook on life. One of the links between good mental health and self-esteem is that high self-esteem helps prevent many situations from being stressful. Few negative comments from others are likely to bother you when your self-esteem is high. A person with low self-esteem might crumble if somebody insulted his or her appearance. A person with high self-esteem might shrug off the insult as simply being the other person's point of view. If faced with an everyday setback, such as losing keys, the high self-esteem person might think, "I have so much going for me, why fall apart over this incident?"

Positive self-esteem also conributes to good mental health because it helps us ward off being troubled by feelings of jealousy, and acting aggressively toward others because of our jealousy. Particularly with adolescents, lower self-worth leads to jealousy about friends liking other people better.[11]

Profiting from Feedback. Although people with high self-esteem can readily shrug off undeserved insults, they still profit well from negative feedback. Because they are secure, they can profit from the developmental opportunities suggested by negative feedback.

Organizational Success. Workers with high self-esteem develop and maintain favorable work attitudes and perform at a high level. These positive consequences take place because such attitudes and behavior are consistent with the personal belief that they are competent individuals. Mary Kay Ash, the legendary founder of a beauty products company, put it this way: "It never occurred to me I couldn't do it. I always knew that if I worked hard enough, I could." Furthermore, research has shown that high self-esteem individuals value reaching work goals more than do low-self-esteem individuals.[12]

The combined effect of workers having high self-esteem helps a company prosper. Long-term research by Nathaniel Branden, as well as more recent studies, suggests that self-esteem is a critical source of competitive advantage in an information society. Companies gain the edge when, in addition to having an educated workforce, employees have high self-esteem, as shown by such behaviors as the following:

- Being creative and innovative
- Taking personal responsibility for problems
- A feeling of independence (yet still wanting to work cooperatively with others)
- Trusting one's own capabilities
- Taking the initiative to solve problems[13]

Behaviors such as these help workers cope with the challenge of a rapidly changing workplace where products and ideas become obsolete quickly. Workers with high self-esteem are more likely to be able to cope with new challenges regularly because they are confident that they can master their environment.

Potential Negative Consequences. High self-esteem can sometimes have negative consequences, particularly because individuals with high self-esteem work hard to preserve their high status relative to others. When people with high self-esteem are placed in a situation where undermining others helps them maintain their status, they will engage in behaviors that diminish others. In one study, it was shown that high self-esteem individuals who are also a little neurotic (somethwat emotionally unstable) will often engage the following undermining behaviors: criticizing group members in front of others, intentionally ignoring others, talking down to other group members, going back on their word, giving others the silent treatment, belittling others, and not listening to people.[14]

According to economist Robert H. Frank of Cornell University, our own reference group has the biggest impact on self-esteem. He writes: "When you see Bill Gates' mansion, you don't actually aspire to have one like it. It's who is local, who is near you physically and who is most like you—your family members, coworkers and hold high school classmates—with whom you compare yourself. If someone in your reference group has a little more, you get a little anxious."[15]

> " Self-esteem is key to succeeding in the business world. You can maintain high self-esteem by facing problems, avoiding excesses, defining clear goals and associating with positive people. May high self-esteem and success be yours! "
> —TigerByte,
> www.helium.com.

LEARNING OBJECTIVE 2

ENHANCING SELF-ESTEEM

Improving self-esteem is a lifelong process because self-esteem is related to the success of your activities and interactions with people. Following are approaches to enhancing self-esteem that are related to how self-esteem develops. (See Figure 6-1.) Each of these

FIGURE 6-1   Methods of Enhancing Self-Esteem

- Create high self-esteem living space
- Legitimate accomplishments
- Be aware of personal strengths
- Model people with high self-esteem
- **Self-esteem**
- Rebut the inner critic
- Find people who boost your self-esteem
- Minimize detracting from fellings of complectence
- Practice self-nurturing

approaches has a skill component, such as learning to avoid situations that make you feel incompetent. In addition to working on skills to enhance self-esteem, it is helpful to maintain a constructive attitude. A representative statement to keep in mind as you work on self-esteem enhancement is as follows:[16]

> *"I am a very special, unique and valuable person. I deserve to feel good about myself."*

Attain Legitimate Accomplishments

To emphasize again, accomplishing worthwhile activities is a major contributor to self-esteem (as well as self-confidence) in both children and adults. Social science research suggests this sequence of events: Person establishes a goal; person pursues the goal; person achieves the goal; person develops esteem-like feelings.[17] The opposite point of view is this sequence: Person develops esteem-like feelings; person establishes a goal; person pursues the goal; person achieves the goal. Similarly, giving people large trophies for mundane accomplishments is unlikely to raise self-esteem. More likely, the person will see through the transparent attempt to build his or her self-esteem and develop negative feelings about the self. What about you? Would your self-esteem receive a bigger boost by (1) receiving an A in a course in which 10 percent of the class received an A or by (2) receiving an A in a class in which everybody received the same grade?

Be Aware of Personal Strengths

Another method of improving your self-esteem is to develop an appreciation of your strengths and accomplishments. A good starting point is to list your strengths and accomplishments on a word processing document or paper. This list is likely to be more impressive than you expected.

You can sometimes develop an appreciation of your strengths by participating in a group exercise designed for such purposes. A group of about seven people meet to form a support group. All group members first spend about 10 minutes answering the question, "What are my three strongest points, attributes, or skills?" After each group member records his or her three strengths, the person discusses them with the other group members.

Each group member then comments on the list. Other group members sometimes add to your list of strengths or reinforce what you have to say. Sometimes you may find disagreement. One member told the group, "I'm handsome, intelligent, reliable, athletic, self-confident, and very moral. I also have a good sense of humor." Another group member retorted, "And I might add that you're unbearably conceited."

Skill-Building Exercises 6-1 and 6-2 provide additional ways of developing self-esteem, both of which focus on appreciation of strengths.

SKILL-BUILDING EXERCISE 6-1

Reinforcing a Positive Self-Image

To do this exercise, you will need a piece of paper and a pencil or pen or a word processor, and a timer or clock. Set a timer for 10 minutes or note the time on your watch, cell phone, or a clock. Write your name across the top of the document. Then write everything positive and good you can think of about yourself. Include special attributes, talents, and achievements. You can use single words or sentences. You can write the same things over and over if you want to emphasize them. Your ideas do not have to be well organized. Write down whatever comes to mind. You are the only one who will see this document. Avoid using any negative words. Use only positive ones.

When the 10 minutes are up, read the document over to yourself. You may feel sad when you read it over because it is a new,

different, and positive way of thinking about yourself. Your document will contradict some of the negative thoughts you have had about yourself. Those feelings will diminish as you reread this document. Read the document over again several times. Print the document if written by computer, and put it in a convenient place, such as in your pocket, purse, wallet, or your bedside table. Read it over at least once a day to keep reminding yourself of how great you are! Find a private space and read it aloud. If you have a good friend or family member who is supportive, read it to that person. Maybe your confidant can think of a positive attribute that you have missed.

Source: Adapted from "Building Self-esteem: A Self-Help Guide," *http://mentalhealth.samhsa.gov/*, accessed September 7, 2007.

The Self-Esteem Building Club

You and your classmates are invited to participate in one of the most humane and productive possible skill-building exercises, membership in the "self-esteem building club." Your assignment is for three consecutive weeks to help build the self-esteem of one person. Before embarking upon the exercise, review the information about self-esteem development in the chapter. One of the most effective tactics would be to find somebody who had a legitimate accomplishment, and give that person a reward or thank you. Record carefully what the person did, what you did, and any behavioral reactions of the person whose self-esteem you attempted to build. An example follows, written by a 46-year-old student of human relations:

> Thursday night two weeks ago, I went to the athletic club to play racquetball. Different than usual, I had a date after the club. I wanted to look good, so I decided to wear my high school class ring. The ring doesn't have much resale value, but I was emotionally attached to it, having worn it for special occasions for 28 years. I stuffed the ring along with my watch and wallet in my athletic bag.
>
> When I was through with racquetball, I showered, and got dressed. My ring was missing from my bag even though my wallet and watch were there. I kind of freaked out because I hate to lose a prized possession. I shook

the bag out three times, but no luck. Very discouraged, I left my name, telephone number, and e-mail address at the front desk just in case somebody turned in the ring. I kept thinking that I must have lost the ring when I stopped at the desk to check in.

> The next morning before going to class, I got a phone call from a front-desk clerk at the club. The clerk told me that Karl, from the housekeeping staff, heard a strange noise while he was vacuuming near the front desk. He shut off the vacuum cleaner immediately, and pulled out my ring. To me Karl was a hero. I made a special trip to the club that night to meet with Karl. I shook his hand, and gave him a ten-dollar bill as a reward. I also explained to Karl what a difference he had made in my mood. I told him that honest, hardworking people like him who take pride in their work make this world a better place. It made my day when Karl smiled and told me it was a pleasure to be helpful.

Your instructor might organize a sharing of self-esteem building episodes in the class. If the sharing does take place, look for patterns in terms of what seemed to work in terms of self-esteem building. Also, listen for any patterns in failed attempts at self-esteem building.

Rebut the Inner Critic

Another early step in attaining better self-esteem is to rebut your inner critic—the voice inside you that sends negative messages about your capabilities. Rebutting critical statements about you might also be considered another way of appreciating your strengths. Two examples of rebutting your inner critic follow:[18]

> **Your unfairly harsh inner critic says:** "People said they liked my presentation, but it was nowhere as good as it should have been. I can't believe no one noticed all the places I messed up. I'm such an imposter."
>
> **Your reassuring rebuttal:** "Wow, they really liked it. Maybe it wasn't perfect, but I worked hard on that presentation and did a good job. I'm proud of myself. This was a great success."
>
> **Your harsh inner critic makes leaps of illogic:** "He is frowning. He didn't say anything, but I know it means that he doesn't like me!"
>
> **Your rebuttal that challenges the illogic:** "Okay, he's frowning, but I don't know why. It could have nothing to do with me. Maybe I should ask."

The above are but two examples of the type of putdowns we often hear from our inner critic. To boost your self-esteem in spite of such criticism, you need to develop the skill of rebuttal by rebutting your inner critic frequently.

Practice Self-Nurturing

Although you may be successful at pointing to your strengths and rebutting the inner voice that puts you down, it is also helpful to treat yourself as a worthwhile person. Start to challenge negative experiences and messages from the past by nurturing and caring for yourself in ways that show how valuable, competent, deserving, and lovable you really are. Self-nurturing is often referred to as treating yourself well or spoiling yourself. Here are two suggestions for self-nurturing, both of which involve a modest amount of skill development.

- **Administer self-rewards for a job well done.** When you have carried out an activity especially well in relation to your typical performance, reward yourself in a small, constructive way. You might dine at a favorite restaurant, take an afternoon off to go for a nature walk, or spend an hour at a Website you usually do not have the time to visit.

- **Take good care of yourself mentally and physically.** Make sure that you get enough sleep and rest, eat nutritious foods, avoid high-bacteria environments such as a public keyboard unless you use a bacteria spray, and participate in moderate physical exercise. Even taking an extra shower or bath can give you a physical and mental boost. The suggestions just mentioned are also part of stress management.

Real estate agent Laura provides a helpful example of how self-nurturing can help bolster self-esteem. While watching her son play soccer at 4 in the afternoon, she was asked by another soccer parent, "How's business?" Laura replied, "I haven't made a deal in two weeks, but I know times will get better. So for now, I'm enjoying myself watching Todd [her son] play his little heart out. Afterwards we are going for pizza, and a few video games. My soul will be energized again."

Minimize Settings and Interactions That Detract from Your Feelings of Competence

Most of us have situations in work and personal life that make us feel less than our best. If you can minimize exposure to those situations, you will have fewer feelings of incompetence. The problem with feeling incompetent is that it lowers your self-esteem. Suppose, for example, Sally is a very poor golf player, and intensely dislikes the sport. She is better off excusing herself from a small group of people at the office who invite her to a golf outing. A problem with avoiding all situations in which you feel lowly competent is that it might prevent you from acquiring needed skills. Also, it boosts your self-confidence and self-esteem to become comfortable in a previously uncomfortable situation. In Sally's case perhaps she can eventually learn to play golf better, and then she will be mentally prepared to participate in golf outings.

Get Help from Others

Self-esteem is strongly shaped by how others perceive us, so getting help from other is major step a person can take to improve his or her self-esteem. However, getting help from others can also be difficult. People with low self-esteem often do not ask for help because they may not think they are worthy of receiving help. Yet help from others is effective in overcoming the negative messages received from others in the past.

Asking for support from friends can include such basic steps as these: (1) Ask friends to tell you what they like about you or think that you do well. (2) Ask someone who cares about you to listen to your complain about something without offering a solution to your problem. (3) Ask for a hug. (4) Ask someone who loves you to remind you that he or she does.

Getting help from teachers and other helps can include these steps: (1) Ask professors or tutors for help with work you find challenging. (2) If you lack self-confidence in certain areas, take classes or attempt new activities to increase your competence. An increasing number of retired people today are taking classes in such subjects as computer utilization and digital photography to help catch up with younger people whose skills have challenged their self-esteem.[19]

Another way of getting help from others is to talk and socialize frequently with people who can boost your self-esteem. Psychologist Barbara Ilardie says that the people who can raise your self-esteem are usually those with high self-esteem themselves. They are the people who give honest feedback because they respect others and themselves. Such high self-esteem individuals should not be confused with yes-people who agree with others just to be liked. The point is that you typically receive more from strong people than weak ones. Weak people will flatter you but will not give you the honest feedback you need to build self-esteem.[20]

For many people with low self-esteem, casual help with others will not increase self-esteem. In these situations, discussing low self-esteem with a mental health specialist might be the most effective measure.

Model the Behavior of People with High Self-Esteem

Observe the way people who believe to have high self-esteem stand, walk, speak, and act. Even if you are not feeling so secure inside, you will project a high self-esteem image if you act assured. Raudsepp recommends, "Stand tall, speak clearly and with confidence, shake hands firmly, look people in the eye and smile frequently. Your self-esteem will increase as you notice encouraging reactions from others."[21] (Notice here that self-esteem is considered to be about the same idea as self-confidence.)

Choose your models of high self-esteem from people you know personally, as well as celebrities you might watch on television news and interview shows. Observing actors on the large or small screen is a little less useful because they are guaranteed to be playing a role. Identifying a teacher or professor as a self-esteem model is widely practiced, as is observing successful family members and friends.

Create a High Self-Esteem Living Space

A panel of mental health specialists recommends that to enhance your self-esteem you should make your living space that honors the person you are.[22] Whether you live in a single room, a small apartment, or a large house, make that space comfortable and attractive for you. If you have a clean, inviting living space, others are likely to treat you with more respect, which will contribute to your self-esteem. If you share your living space with others, dedicate some space just for you—a place where you can keep your things and know that they will not be disturbed and that you can decorate any way you choose.

Your living space is part of your self-image, so you may want to ask yourself if your living space projects the right self-image. Also, you arrange your living space to fit your preferences you will feel better about yourself.

How a Manager Helps Build the Self-Esteem of Group Members

Above we mentioned that leaders who are fair and who encourage self-rewards contribute to the self-esteem of subordinates. There are many other actions and attitudes of managers that help group members enhance their self-esteem. Many of these approaches are related to suggestions for enhancing self-esteem just mentioned. For example, a manager who provides subordinates with an opportunity to accomplish challenging tasks, and then rewards them appropriately will help bolster their self-esteem. Also, if the manager has high self-esteem, he or she can be your person to model in terms of developing high self-esteem.

Giving subordinates positive feedback about legitimate accomplishments is a powerful approach to enhancing their self-esteem. When accomplishments are out of the ordinary, they can be celebrated through such means as public recognition electronically or during a face-to-face meeting. Accurately assessing the strengths and skill sets of subordinates will often point them in the direction of accomplishing tasks that will boost self-esteem. Helping subordinates develop new skills by coaching can be quite useful in developing their self-esteem.

Skill-Building Exercise 6-3 presents an easy, non-time-consuming activity for enhancing your self-esteem. Should the exercise not have a remarkable impact on your self-esteem, at least it will have no damaging emotional consequences.

SKILL-BUILDING EXERCISE 6-3

The Self-Esteem Calendar

Find a calendar or daily planner on paper or on the computer, with large blank spaces for each day. Schedule into each day a small activity that you enjoy doing such as "watching YouTube to look for videos about people I know personally," "jogging through my neighborhood," "texting a few people I care about," "reading the classified ads in *The Wall Street Journal*," or "hugging somebody I love." Now make a commitment to check your enjoy-life calendar every day, and follow through to make sure that you engaged in the activity you entered into the calendar. The accumulation of small, enjoyable activities should boost your self-esteem a little because you will feel better about yourself.

Source: Adapted from "Building Self-Esteem: A Self-Help Guide," *Health* (athealth.com/Consumer/disorder/self-esteem.html, p. 7).

THE IMPORTANCE OF SELF-CONFIDENCE AND SELF-EFFICACY

LEARNING OBJECTIVE 3

Although self-confidence can be considered part of self-esteem (or almost its equivalent), it is important enough to study separately. Self-efficacy is confidence in your ability to carry out a specific task in contrast to generalized self-confidence. Various studies have shown that people with a high sense of self-efficacy tend to have good job performance, so being self-confident is important for your career. They also set relatively high goals for themselves.[23] Self-confidence has also long been recognized as a trait of effective leaders. A straightforward implication of self-efficacy is that people who think they can perform well on a task do better than those who think they will do poorly.

Research by college professors and psychological consultants George P. Hollenbeck and Douglas T. Hall suggests that our feelings of self-confidence stem from five sources of information.[24] The first source is the *actual experience, or things we have done*. Having done something before and succeeded is the most powerful way to build self-confidence. If you successfully inserted a replacement battery into your watch without destroying the watch, you will be confident to make another replacement.

The second source of self-confidence is the *experiences of others, or modeling*. You can gain some self-confidence if you have carefully observed others perform a task, such as resolving conflict with a customer. You might say to yourself, "I've seen Tracy calm down the customer by listening and showing sympathy, and I'm confident I could do the same thing." The third source of self-confidence is *social comparison, or comparing yourself to others*. If you see other people with capabilities similar to your own perform a task well, your will gain in confidence. A person might say to himself or herself, "If that person can learn how to work with enterprise software, I can do it also. I'm just as smart."

The fourth source of self-confidence is *social persuasion, the process of convincing another person*. If a credible person convinces you that you can accomplish a particular task, you will often receive a large enough boost in self-confidence large enough to give the task a try. If the encouragement is coupled with guidance on how to perform the task, your self-confidence gain will be higher. So the boss or teacher who says, "I know you can do it, and I'm here to help you," knows how to build self-confidence.

The fifth source of information for making a self-confidence judgment is *emotional arousal, or how we feel about events around us and manage our emotions*. We rely somewhat on our inner feelings to know if we are self-confident enough to perform the task. Imagine a person standing on top of a high mountain ready to ski down. However, he or she is trembling and nauseous with fear. Contrast this beginner to another person who simply feels mildly excited and challenged. Skier number one has a self-confidence problem, whereas skier number two has enough confidence to start the descent. (Have your emotional sensations ever influenced your self-confidence?)

The more of these five sources of self-confidence are positive for you, the more likely your self-confidence will be positive. A subtle point about self-confidence is that being too low in self-confidence is a problem yet being too high is also a problem. The overly self-confident person may not listen carefully to the suggestions of others, and may be blind to criticism.

Self-Assessment Quiz 6-2 provides some insight into your level of self-confidence.

TECHNIQUES FOR DEVELOPING AND ENHANCING YOUR SELF-CONFIDENCE

LEARNING OBJECTIVE 4

Self-confidence is generally achieved by succeeding in a variety of situations. A confident civil engineering technician may not be generally self-confident unless he or she also achieves success in activities such as forming good personal relationships, navigating complex software, writing a letter, learning a second language, and displaying athletic skills.

Although this general approach to self-confidence building makes sense, it does not work for everyone. Some people who seem to succeed at everything still have lingering self-doubt. Low self-confidence is so deeply ingrained in this type of personality that success in later life is not sufficient to change things. Following are seven specific strategies and tactics for building and elevating self-confidence, as outlined in Figure 6-2. They will generally work unless the person has deep-rooted feelings of inferiority. The tactics and strategies are arranged approximately in the order in which they should be tried to achieve best results.

Develop a Solid Knowledge Base

A bedrock strategy for projecting self-confidence is to develop a knowledge base that enables you to provide sensible alternative solutions to problems. Intuition is very important, but working from a base of facts helps you project a confident image. Formal education is an obvious and important source of information for your knowledge base. Day-by-day absorption of information directly and indirectly related to your career is equally important. A major purpose of formal education is to get you in the right frame of mind to continue your quest for knowledge. In your quest for developing a solid knowledge base to project self-confidence, be sensitive to abusing this technique. If you bombard people with quotes, facts, and figures, you are likely to be perceived as an annoying know-it-all.

A solid knowledge base contributes to self-confidence also because the knowledge facilitates engaging in conversation with intelligent people. A weak counterargument is that having information stored in your brain is no longer important because information is so accessible online. When in a gathering of people, you could then use a smart phone to access some facts to talk about. Such behavior is unlikely to help a person project a confident, intelligent image.

FIGURE 6-2   Boosting Your Self-Confidence

Bounce back from setbacks and embarrassments

Develop solid knowledge base

Use positive self-talk

Strive for peak performance

Self-confidence

Avoid negative self-talk

Develop explanatory style of optimists

Set high self-expectations (Galeta effect)

Use positive visual imagery

BACK TO THE OPENING CASE

Scott Gould, the fixed-income trader turned manager of a luxury restaurant, used his self-confidence to help propel him toward an ideal position for himself. He needed self-confidence to move from server to bartender in a New York restaurant with the most demanding clientele. Gould then needed even more self-confidence to think that his knowledge and love for wines would enable him to work as a sommelier in the same restaurant. He was then self-confident enough to tackle the job of being the manager of a Del Frisco restaurant, only seven years after beginning as a server. Furthermore, Gould's high self-confidence facilitated his being able to cope with the pressures of managing an upscale restaurant.

Use Positive Self-Talk

A basic method of building self-confidence is to engage in **positive self-talk,** saying positive things about yourself. The first step in using positive self-talk is to objectively state the incident that is casting doubt about self-worth.[25] The key word here is *objectively*. Terry, who is fearful of poorly executing a report-writing assignment, might say, "I've been asked to write a report for the company, and I'm not a good writer."

The next step is to objectively interpret what the incident *does not* mean. Terry might say, "Not being a skilled writer doesn't mean that I can't figure out a way to write a good report or that I'm an ineffective employee."

Next, the person should objectively state what the incident *does* mean. In doing this, the person should avoid put-down labels, such as "incompetent," "stupid," "dumb," "jerk," or "airhead." All these terms are forms of negative self-talk. Terry should state what the incident does mean: "I have a problem with one small aspect of this job."

The fourth step is to objectively account for the cause of the incident. Terry would say, "I'm really worried about writing a good report because I have very little experience in writing along these lines."

The fifth step is to identify some positive ways to prevent the incident from happening again. Terry might say, "I'll get out my textbook on business communications and review the chapter on report writing" or "I'll enroll in a course or seminar on business report writing."

The final step is to use positive self-talk. Terry imagines his boss saying, "This report is really good. I'm proud of my decision to select you to prepare this important report."

Positive self-talk builds self-confidence and self-esteem because it programs the mind with positive messages. Making frequent positive statements or affirmations about the self creates a more confident person. An example would be, "I know I can learn this new equipment rapidly enough to increase my productivity within five days."

Business coach Gary Lockwood emphasizes that positive self-talk is also useful for getting people past difficult times. "It's all in your head," he said. "Remember you are in charge of your feelings. You are in control of your attitude." Instead of berating yourself after making a mistake, learn from the experience and move on. Say to yourself, "Everyone makes mistakes," "Tomorrow is another day," or "What can I learn from this?"[26]

Despite the many advantages of positive self-talk, as with optimism, there can be times when thinking too positively can create problems. Negative thoughts are often useful in alerting us to potential problems, and prompting us to develop a plan of correction. Imagine that Lisa is job hunting, and that she has urgent need of employment. She has a promising interview, and her positive thinking prompts her to think, "There is no doubt that I will receive an offer real soon." Her positive thinking blocks her from continuing her job search. When the offer in question does not come through, Lisa has lost momentum in her job search. In the words of author John Derbyshire, we must be "vigilantly realistic" toward against the potential dangers of positive thinking.[27]

Avoid Negative Self-Talk

As implied, you should minimize negative statements about yourself to bolster self-confidence. A lack of self-confidence is reflected in statements, such as "I may be stupid but . . .," "Nobody asked my opinion," "I know I'm usually wrong, but . . .," and "I know I don't have as much education as some people, but. . . ." Self-effacing statements like these serve to reinforce low self-confidence.

It is also important not to attribute to yourself negative, irreversible traits, such as "idiotic," "ugly," "dull," "loser," and "hopeless." Instead, look on your weak points as areas for possible self-improvement. Negative self-labeling can do long-term damage to your self-confidence. If a person stops that practice today, his or her self-confidence may begin to increase.

Use Positive Visual Imagery

Assume you have a situation in mind in which you would like to appear confident and in control. An example would be a meeting with a major customer who has told you by e-mail that he is considering switching suppliers. Your intuitive reaction is that if you cannot handle his concerns without fumbling or appearing desperate, you will lose the account. An important technique in this situation is **positive visual imagery,** or picturing a positive outcome in your mind. To apply this technique in this situation, imagine yourself engaging in a convincing argument about why your customer should retain your company as the primary supplier. Imagine yourself talking in positive terms about the good service your company offers and how you can rectify any problems.

Visualize yourself listening patiently to your customer's concerns and then talking confidently about how your company can handle these concerns. As you rehearse this moment of truth, create a mental picture of you and the customer shaking hands over the fact that the account is still yours.

Positive visual imagery helps you appear self-confident because your mental rehearsal of the situation has helped you prepare for battle. If imagery works for you once, you will be even more effective in subsequent uses of the technique.

Set High Expectations for Yourself (the Galatea Effect)

If you set high expectations for yourself and you succeed, you are likely to experience a temporary or permanent boost in self-confidence. The **Galatea effect** is a type of self-fulfilling prophecy in which high expectations lead to high performance. Similar to positive self-talk, if you believe in yourself you are more likely to succeed. You expect to win, so you do. The Galatea effect may not work all the time, but it does work some of the time for many people.

Workplace behavior researchers D. Brian McNatt and Timothy A. Judge studied the Galatea effect with 72 auditors within three offices of a major accounting firm over a three-month period. The auditors were given letters of encouragement to strengthen their feelings of self-efficacy. Information in the letters was based on facts about the auditors, such as information derived from their résumés and company records. The results of the experiment showed that creating a Galatea effect bolstered self-efficacy, motivation, and performance. However, the performance improvement was temporary, suggesting that self-expectations need to be boosted regularly.[28]

Develop the Explanatory Style of Optimists

According to the research and observations of consultant and trainer Price Pritchett, optimism is linked to self-confidence. Explaining events in an optimistic way can help preserve self-confidence and self-esteem. When experiencing trouble, optimists tend to explain the problems to themselves as temporary. Bad events are expected to be short-lived, and optimists look to the future when times will be better. Another aspect of optimists' explanatory style protects their self-confidence. Rather than condemn themselves for failures, they look for how other factors or circumstances have contributed to the problem. Optimists then do not take all the blame for a problem, but look to external factors to help explain what went wrong.

Interpreting difficulties in this way gives the optimists a sense of control. Instead of looking at the unfortunate situation as hopeless, they have faith in their ability to deal with the problem.[29] Suppose an optimist purchases a computer workstation that comes packed in a box with many parts along with directions. A problem arises is that some of the screws and dowels do not fit, and the directions are unclear. A pessimist might suffer a drop in self-confidence and self-esteem, saying "What a fool I am. I can't even assemble a piece of office furniture." In contrast, the optimist might say, "I'm doing something wrong here, and I will get a buddy to help show me my mistake. But the manufacturer can also be blamed. The instructions are terrible, and all the parts may not fit together." In this way, the optimist does not take such a big hit to self-confidence and self-esteem.

Strive for Peak Performance

A key strategy for projecting self-confidence is to display **peak performance,** or exceptional accomplishment in a given task. The experience is transient but exceptionally meaningful. Peak performance refers to much more than attempting to do your best. Experiencing peak performance in various tasks over a long period of time would move a person toward self-actualization.[30] To achieve peak performance, you must be totally focused on what you are doing. When you are in the state of peak performance, you are mentally calm and physically at ease. Intense concentration is required to achieve this state. You are so focused on the task at hand that you are not distracted by extraneous events or thoughts. To use an athletic analogy, you are *in the zone* while you are performing the task. In fact, many sports psychologists and other sports trainers work with athletes to help them attain peak performance.

The mental state achieved during peak performance is akin to a person's sense of deep concentration when immersed in a sport or hobby. On days when tennis players perform way above their usual game, they typically comment, "The ball looked so large, I could read the label as I hit it." On the job, focus and concentration allow the person to sense and respond to relevant information coming both from within the mind and from outside stimuli. When you are at your peak, you impress others by responding intelligently to their input. While turning in peak performance, you are experiencing a mental state referred to as *flow.*

Building Your Self-Confidence and Self-Efficacy

Most people can use a boost to their self-confidence. Even if you are a highly confident individual, perhaps there is room for building your feelings of self-efficacy in a particular area, such as a proud and successful business owner learning a new skill such as editing digital photos or speaking a foreign language. For this, skill-building exercise enhances your self-confidence or self-efficacy in the next two weeks by trying out one of the many suggestions for self-confidence building described in the text.

As part of planning the implementation of this exercise, think about any area in which your self-confidence could use a boost. A candid human relations student, who was also a confident cheerleader, said, "Face it. I'm terrible at PowerPoint presentations. I put up so many details on my slides that the audience is trying to read my slides instead of looking at me. I have to admit that my PowerPoint presentation consists mostly of my reading my slides to the audience. I'm much better at cheerleading." So this student studied information in her human relations text about making better graphic presentations. She revamped her approach to using her slides as headlines and talking points. She tried out one presentation in class, and one for at her church. She received so many compliments about her presentations that now she has much higher self-efficacy with respect to PowerPoint presentations.

Your instructor might organize a sharing of self-confidence building episodes in the class. If the sharing does take place, look for patterns in terms of what seemed to work in terms of self-confidence or self-efficacy building. Also, listen for any patterns in failed attempts at self-confidence building.

Although you are concentrating on an object or sometimes on another person during peak performance, you still have an awareness of the self. You develop a strong sense of the self, similar to self-confidence and self-efficacy, while you are concentrating the task. Peak performance is related to self-confidence in another important way. Achieving peak performance in many situations helps you develop self-confidence.

Skill-Building Exercise 6-4 gives you the opportunity to work on enhancing your self-confidence.

Bounce Back from Setbacks and Embarrassments

Resilience is a major contributor to personal effectiveness. Overcoming setbacks also builds self-confidence, as implied from the description of the explanatory style of optimists. An effective self-confidence builder is to convince yourself that you can conquer adversity such as setbacks and embarrassments, thus being resilient. The vast majority of successful leaders have dealt successfully with at least one significant setback in their careers, such as being fired or demoted. In contrast, crumbling after a setback or series of setbacks will usually lower self-confidence. Two major suggestions for bouncing back from setbacks and embarrassments are presented next.

Get Past the Emotional Turmoil.   Adversity has enormous emotional consequences. The emotional impact of severe job adversity can rival the loss of a personal relationship. The stress from adversity leads to a cycle of adversity followed by stress, followed by more adversity. A starting point in dealing with the emotional aspects of adversity is to *accept the reality of your problem*. Admit that your problems are real and that you are hurting inside.

A second step is *not to take the setback personally*. Remember that setbacks are inevitable so long as you are taking some risks in your career. Not personalizing setbacks helps reduce some of the emotional sting. If possible, *do not panic*. Recognize that you are in difficult circumstances under which many others panic. Convince yourself to remain calm enough to deal with the severe problem or crisis. Also, *get help from your support network*. Getting emotional support from family members and friends helps overcome the emotional turmoil associated with adversity.

Find a Creative Solution to Your Problem.   An inescapable part of planning a comeback is to solve your problem. You often need to search for creative solutions. Suppose a person faced the adversity of not having enough money for educational expenses. The person might search through standard alternatives, such as applying for financial aid, looking for more lucrative part-time work, and borrowing from family members. Several students have solved their problem more creatively by asking strangers to lend them money as intermediate-term investments. An option the investors have is to receive a payback based on the future earnings of the students.

A useful approach to finding a creative solution to your problem is to use response-oriented thinking that focuses on finding answers. A resilience program developed by Joshua D. Margolis of the Harvard Business School and Paul G. Stoltz, the founder of a global research and consulting firm, includes finding answers to then four following questions:

1. What features can I improve or potentially improve?
2. What sort of positive impact can I personally have on what happens next?
3. How can I contain the negatives of the situation and generate currently unseen positives?
4. What can I do to begin addressing the problem now?[31]

It is highly recommended that you write down answers to these questions rather than merely thinking about them. Writing offers people more command over an adverse situation than does mere reflection. A plausible reason is that writing down something is an early step in developing an action plan. Getting back to the person concerned about educational expenses, he or she might write down in response to question 4, "What do I or my family members own that I might be able to sell over eBay that would raise a little cash to get me started?"

SELF-ASSESSMENT QUIZZES IN OVERVIEW

The two self-assessment quizzes presented in this chapter support each other well. Self-Assessment Quiz 6-1 is a self-esteem checklist. People who score high on the Self-Esteem Checklist should theoretically score high on Self-Assessment Quiz 6-2, How Self-Confident Are You? The reason is that self-esteem and self-confidence are closely related and may be part of the same concept. An exception is that some people might like themselves even though they are not particularly self-confident in many situations. Perhaps their attitude is, "So who cares if I am not self-confident? I like me anyway."

WHAT IS EMOTIONAL INTELLIGENCE?

LEARNING OBJECTIVE 5

How effectively people use their emotions has a major impact on their success. The term *emotional intelligence* has gathered different meanings, all relating to how effectively a person makes constructive use of his or her emotions. John D. Mayer, a professor of psychology at the University of New Hampshire, along with Yale psychology professor Peter Saloey, originated the concept of emotional intelligence. Mayer explained that from a scientific (rather than a popular) viewpoint, **emotional intelligence** is the "ability to accurately perceive your own and others' emotions; to under- stand the signals that emotions send about relationships; and to manage our own and others' emotions."[32] A person with high emotional intelligence would be able to engage in such behaviors as sizing up people, pleasing others, and influencing them.

emotional intelligence

The ability to accurately perceive emotions, to understand the signals that emotions send about relationships, and to manage emotions.

Key Components of Emotional Intelligence

Four key factors included in emotional intelligence are as follows:[33]

1. **Self-awareness.** The ability to understand your moods, emotions, and needs as well as their impact on others. Self-awareness also includes using intuition to make decisions you can live with happily. (A person with good self-awareness knows whether he or she is pushing other people too far.)

2. **Self-management.** The ability to control one's emotions and act with honesty and integrity in a consistent and acceptable manner. The right degree of self-management helps prevent a person from throwing temper tantrums when activities do not go as planned. Effective workers do not let their occasional bad moods ruin

self-awareness

The ability to understand moods, emotions, and needs as well as their impact on others; self-awareness also includes using intuition to make decisions you can live with happily.

their day. If they cannot overcome the bad mood, they let coworkers know of their problem and how long it might last. (A person with low self-management would suddenly decide to drop a project because the work was frustrating.)

3. **Social awareness.** Includes having empathy for others and having intuition about work problems. A team leader with social awareness, or empathy, would be able to assess whether a team member has enough enthusiasm for a project to assign him or her to that project. Another facet of social skill is the ability to interpret nonverbal communication, such as frowns and types of smiles.[34] (A supervisor with social awareness, or empathy, would take into account the most likely reaction of group members before making a decision affecting them.)

4. **Relationship management.** Includes the interpersonal skills of being able to communicate clearly and convincingly, disarm conflicts, and build strong personal bonds. Effective workers use relationship management skills to spread their enthusiasm and solve disagreements, often with kindness and humor. (A worker with relationship management skill would use a method of persuasion that is likely to work well with a particular group or individual.)

Emotional intelligence thus incorporates many of the skills and attitudes necessary to achieve effective interpersonal relations in organizations. Many topics in human relations, such as resolving conflict and helping others develop, and positive political skills, would be included in emotional intelligence. Figure 6-3 outlines and illustrates how emotional intelligence relates many other topics in human relations.

Tests of emotional intelligence typically ask you to respond to questions on a 1 to 5 scale (never, rarely, sometimes, often, consistently). For example, indicate how frequently you demonstrate the following behaviors:

I can laugh at myself.	1 2 3 4 5
I help others grow and develop.	1 2 3 4 5
I watch carefully the nonverbal communication of others.	1 2 3 4 5

Self-Assessment Quiz 6-3 gives you an opportunity to measure your emotional intelligence.

Consequences of High and Low Emotional Intelligence

Demonstrating good emotional intelligence is impressive because it contributes to performing well in the difficult arena of dealing with feelings. A worker with good emotional intelligence would engage in such behaviors as (a) recognizing when a coworker needs help but is too embarrassed to ask for help, (b) dealing with the anger of a dissatisfied customer, (c) recognizing that the boss is facing considerable pressure also, and (d) being able to tell whether a customer's "maybe" means "yes" or "no."

Another positive consequence of emotional intelligence is that if you know how to project positive emotion you will spread that positive feeling to others in your immediate

---

SELF-ASSESSMENT QUIZ 6-3

What Is Your Emotional Intelligence?

Psychologists have developed various measures of emotional intelligence. The EQ (Emotional Quotient) test, found by visiting www.myskillsprofile.com, deals with sixteen emotional competencies. The feedback report provides a chart of your emotional competencies together with a detailed description of your profile. An advantage of this quiz is that it is based on the work of two of the original researchers in emotional intelligence, not the later popularizers of the concept.

FIGURE 6-3 **The Link between Emotional Intelligence and Other Topics in Human Relations**

Chapter Number	Illustrative Links to the Emotional Intelligence (EI)
1. Human Relations and You	To understand yourself well, the self-awareness aspect of EI is essential.
2. Self-Esteem and Self-Confidence	Self-esteem focuses heavily on understanding your feelings, which makes EI quite important.
3. Self-Motivation and Goal Setting	Some aspects of self-motivation involve being able to read your own emotions. The self-management aspect of EI contributes to self-discipline.
4. Emotional Intelligence, Attitudes, and Happiness	EI is linked to attitudes because they have an emotional content. You need to understand your own emotions and feelings to be happy.
5. Values and Ethics	Values are colored with emotions, so understanding emotions helps develop your values. An important test of being ethical is to understand how you would feel if your behavior were made public. EI helps you understand these feelings.
6. Problem Solving and Creativity	Emotions and intuition contribute heavily to problem solving and creativity, so having good EI can be an asset.
7. Personal Communication Effectiveness	Personal communication includes relationship building, such as being supportive of others. A key part of EI is relationship building. Dealing with emotions and attitudes is also a contributor to overcoming barriers to communication.
8. Communication in the Workplace	Behaving effectively in meetings includes being able to understand the impact you are making on others and also reading the emotions of others. Both skills are part of EI.
9. Getting Along with Your Managers, Coworkers, and Customers	Managing relationships is one of the major components of EI. The social awareness aspect of EI includes having empathy for others, which is helpful in developing workplace relationships.
10. Managing Conflict	The relationship-management aspect of EI includes disarming conflict, so your emotional intelligence will help you deal with conflict. Also, being able to read the emotions of others will help you resolve conflict.
11. Becoming an Effective Leader	Several researchers believe that EI is the most important trait and characteristic of an effective leader. Your EI will also help you develop good relationships with subordinates.
12. Motivating Others and Developing Teamwork	When attempting to motivate others, it is helpful to understand their emotions and feelings and identify their major needs. Also, if your EI is good, you will be able to more readily praise others.
13. Diversity and Cross-Cultural Competence	A major contributor to effective cross-cultural relations is to have the cultural sensitivity to size up your environment and then act appropriately. Having cultural sensitivity and empathy is part of EI.
14. Getting Ahead in Your Career	Having good EI will help you build the relationships you need to succeed, such as during a job interview and with network members. Also, appropriate etiquette can contribute to career advancement, and EI helps you size up which standards of behavior are expected.
15. Learning Strategies, Perception, and Lifespan Changes	EI can help in such ways as having the self-awareness to understand your learning style and being able to recognize the subtle changes you need to make at various stages of life. Strong EI can also help you sharpen your perception because you will be able to recognize potential emotional biases.
16. Developing Good Work Habits	An important part of having good work habits is to understand your potential tendencies toward procrastination. The self-awareness aspect of EI is a major contributor to this type of self-reflection.
17. Managing Stress and Personal Problems	To understand how stress from work and personal life might be affecting you, you have to be able to read your emotions. Dealing well with personal problems also requires enough EI to read your emotions.

emotional contagion

The automatic and unconscious transfer of emotions between individuals based on cues the one person observes in another.

workplace. **Emotional contagion** is the automatic and unconscious transfer of emotions between individuals based on cues the other person observes. The contagion takes place because people have a tendency to mimic and synchronize the facial expressions, sounds, postures, and movements of another person. As a result of the mimicking, the second person experiences the emotion of the first person.[35] Here is how you might use emotional contagion to solve a human relations problem: You are the team leader of a group of discouraged, disgruntled, and downtrodden people working in a distribution center of a large online retailer. You hear regular complaints such as, "We get treated like prison labor in a third-world country," "The computer systems keeps going down so we can't get our work done on time," "Even the Rollerblades management gives us to scoot around the center are in drastic need of repair." From time to time you tell the group to cheer up, but your words are not taken seriously.

Being skilled at emotional intelligence, you give emotional contagion a try. You enlist the help of the most cheerful member of the group, Willy, to duplicate your act so the effects of emotional contagion will be doubled. You and your confederate Willy come to work smiling, expressing positive thoughts, standing up straight, and making fist-to-fist contact with anybody who says something positive. Soon the positive mood and actions of you and Willy begin to rub off a little on other teammates. The mood becomes positive enough to start working on problems instead of simply moaning and complaining.

A review of many studies concluded that employees with low emotional intelligence are more likely than their high-emotional-intelligence counterparts to experience negative emotional reactions to job insecurity, such as high tension. Furthermore, workers with low emotional intelligence are more likely to engage in negative coping behaviors, such as expressing anger and verbally abusing an immediate supervisor for the organization failing to provide job security.[36]

Acquiring and Developing Emotional Intelligence

Many people believe that emotional intelligence can be acquired and developed, much like a person can learn to become more extraverted or learn to control his or her temper. Many consultants offer training programs for helping employees develop emotional intelligence, and school systems throughout North America provide students some training in emotional intelligence. Elkhonon Goldberg, a clinical professor of neurology at New York University School of Medicine, explains that emotional intelligence can be learned to a degree, much like musical talent or numerical ability can be developed. Having the right natural talent, however, is an important starting point. The combination of biological endowment (such as being aware of your emotions) and training will enable most people to enhance their emotional intelligence.[37]

Given that emotional intelligence is composed of different components, to acquire and develop such ability would usually require working on one component at a time. For example, if a person had difficulty in self-management, he or she would study and be coached in an aspect of self-management such as anger control. Training in anger management is widespread today because so many people have difficulty in managing their anger. Skill-Building Exercise 6-1 presented later in the chapter provides a step-by-step approach to the development of emotional intelligence.

Concerns and Cross-Cultural Considerations

A criticism of the idea of emotional intelligence is that it might simply be part of analytical (or traditional) intelligence. For example, if you can read the feelings of other people, aren't you just being smart? Another concern is that the popularized concept of emotional intelligence has become so broad it encompasses almost the entire study of personality. Emotional intelligence has become an all-inclusive term for many ideas about human behavior that were studied before and since the popularization of the term. Yet when emotional intelligence is regarded as a series of skills that can be developed, it has more scientific backing.[38]

As with all dimensions of human relations, in some situations it will be helpful to be aware of possible cross-cultural differences in what constitutes effective emotional intelligence. For example, an overt display of emotion might be more effective in a meeting conducted in Mexico City than London, because the typical Mexican businessperson is more open in expressing emotion than his or her typical British counterpart.

WHAT ARE THE COMPONENTS OF ATTITUDES, AND HOW ARE THEY ACQUIRED AND CHANGED?

"You've got an attitude," said the supervisor to the store associate, thus emphasizing the importance of attitude to job performance. For mysterious reasons, the term *attitude* in colloquial language often connotes a *negative* attitude. More accurately, an **attitude** is a predisposition to respond that exerts an influence on a person's response to a person, a thing, an idea, or a situation. Attitudes are an important part of human relations because they are linked with perception and motivation. For example, your attitude toward a coworker influences your perception of how favorably you evaluate his or her work, and you will be better motivated if you have a positive attitude toward your work. Having and displaying positive attitudes will also help you build better relationships with coworkers, managers, and customers.

Our study of attitudes includes the components of attitudes, how attitudes are acquired, how they are changed, the importance of positive attitudes, how companies attempt to enhance positive attitudes and job satisfaction, and organizational citizenship behavior.

Components of Attitudes

Attitudes are complex, having three components, as shown in Figure 6-4. The **cognitive component** refers to the knowledge or intellectual beliefs an individual might have about an object (an idea, a person, a thing, or a situation). A market researcher might have accumulated considerable factual information about statistics (such as sampling procedures) and software for running data. The researcher might, therefore, have a positive attitude toward statistics.

The feeling or **affective component** refers to the emotion connected with an object or a task. The market researcher mentioned might basically like statistical analysis because of some pleasant experiences in college associated with statistics. The **behavioral component** refers to how a person acts. The market researcher might make positive statements about statistical methods or emphasize them in his or her reports.

LEARNING OBJECTIVE 6

attitude

A predisposition to respond that exerts an influence on a person's response to a person, a thing, an idea, or a situation.

cognitive component

(of attitude) The knowledge or intellectual beliefs an individual might have about an object (an idea, a person, a thing, or a situation).

affective component

(of attitude) The emotion connected with an object or a task.

behavioral component

(of attitude) How a person acts.

FIGURE 6-4   The Three Components of Attitudes

Observe that the three components of attitudes influence each other and that the attitude toward a subject, person, object, or thing is the combined effect of the cognitive, affective, and behavioral components.

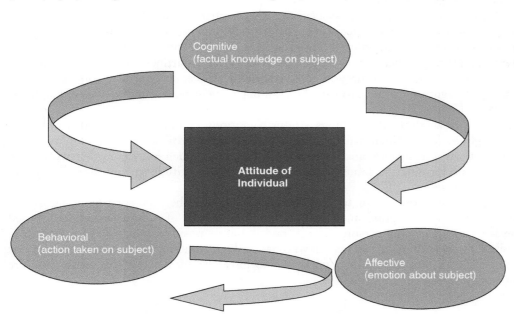

The cognitive, affective, and behavioral aspects of attitudes are interrelated. A change in one of the components will set in motion a change in one or more of the others. If you have more facts about an object or process (cognitive), you form the basis for a more positive emotional response to the object (affective). In turn, your behavior toward that object would probably become more favorable. For example, if you have considerable information about the contribution of feedback to personal development, you might have a positive feeling toward feedback. When receiving feedback, therefore, you would act favorably.

At times, people do not experience the type of consistency previously described and feel compelled to search for consistency. **Cognitive dissonance** is the situation in which the pieces of knowledge, information, attitudes, or beliefs held by an individual are contradictory. When a person experiences cognitive dissonance, the relationship between attitudes and behaviors is altered. People search for ways to reduce internal conflicts when they experience a clash between the information they receive and their actions or attitudes. The same process is used when a person has to resolve two inconsistent sets of information.

A typical example of cognitive dissonance on the job might occur when a worker believes that the report she submits to team members is of high quality; her teammates, however, tell her the report is flawed and requires substantial revisions. To reduce the dissonance, the worker might conveniently ignore the criticism. Or the worker might reason that she is the resident expert on the topic of the report, and her teammates, therefore, are not qualified to judge the merits of her report.

How Attitudes Are Formed

Attitudes usually are based on experience. Assume that you visited a convenience store, and you left your wallet on the counter without realizing it. Your wallet contained your credit cards, debit cards, driver's license, $150 in cash, and personal items. On returning home you receive a phone call from the clerk, informing you that he is holding your wallet for you. You most likely develop an immediate positive attitude toward the convenience store, the clerk, and perhaps toward other people of his ethnic group. Next we look more closely at the processes underlying attitude formation.[39]

A starting point in developing attitudes is to receive direct instruction from another individual. A friend whose opinion you respect tells you that e-filing of income tax is fast, efficient, and modern. You might quickly have a positive attitude toward e-filing. Similarly, you might develop a positive attitude through modeling the behavior of another person. You have seen that your trusted friend e-files her income tax, so you develop a positive attitude toward e-filing.

Conditioning, or making associations, also contributes to attitude formation, as in the example of the convenience store. The attitudes that we develop based on conditioning or associations usually develop after at least several exposures. You might develop a favorable attitude toward the human resources (HR) department if you asked for help several times, and each time you received useful advice. In contrast, you might have developed negative attitudes toward HR if a department representative was unhelpful at each visit.

The way we think about things, or our *cognitions*, can influence attitude formation. You might be quite content with your salary and benefits provided by your employer. You then visit www.salary.com and discover that you make much less than other workers in your city performing the same work. As a result, your attitude toward your salary and benefits plunges.

The deepest contributor to attitude formation could be a person's standing on the personality trait of optimism. People with a high degree of optimism are predisposed toward viewing events, persons, places, and things as positive, which in turn leads to a positive attitude. In contrast, people who have a high standing on pessimism will harbor many negative attitudes. Many workers who have chronically low job satisfaction are pessimistic at the core. [40]

The Importance of Positive Attitudes

Positive attitudes have always been the foundation of effective human relations, as reflected in the writings of Dale Carnegie, the pioneer of the popular (rather than scientific) approach to human relations. A sampling of Carnegie's wisdom is presented in Figure 6-5. In recent years positive attitudes have also become of interest to human relations specialists, as reflected in the fields called positive psychology and positive organizational studies. A major thrust of these fields is to enhance our experiences of enjoyment of work, as well as love and play. The assumption is that when employees are in a positive mood, they are typically more creative, better motivated to perform well, and more helpful toward coworkers. [41]

A worker who consistently maintains a *genuine* positive attitude will accrue many benefits. Being genuine is important because people with good emotional intelligence can readily detect a phony smile used as a cover-up for anger. Assuming the worker with a positive attitude backs it up with good performance, he or she is more likely to (a) be liked by customers, (b) close more sales, (c) receive good performance reviews, (d) receive favorable work assignments, and (e) be promoted.

A mild note of caution is that there is a negative side to workers being too positive. As analyzed by Judge and Ilies, putting on a happy face can lead to stress, burnout, and job dissatisfaction. Workers who have an unrealistically positive self-concept might become self-centered and manipulative and think they deserve more attention and rewards than other workers.[42] Also a little negativity and cynicism is helpful in jobs such as auditor, budget analyst, tax accountant, and store detective. Sometimes being suspicious and negative contributes to a job role.

How Attitudes Are Changed

In general, attitudes can be changed by reversing the processes by which they were formed. Yet, we can look at the process of attitude change more specifically. First, we might receive information from a source we trust. A manager might have negative attitudes toward the value of employee training but then reads in a reliable business magazine that IBM spends more than $4,000 per employee annually on training. As a consequence, the manager develops a more favorable attitude toward training. A person might also be reconditioned to bring about attitude change. A small-business owner might

FIGURE 6-5   The Wisdom of Dale Carnegie

The name Dale Carnegie is synonymous with a popularized approach to human relations. Carnegie (1888–1955) authored several best sellers, including *How to Win Friends and Influence People*, first published in 1937. More than 50 million copies of Carnegie's books have been printed, and they have been published in thirty-eight languages. Nine of Carnegie's suggestions for becoming a positive, friendlier person follow:

1. Don't criticize, condemn, or complain.
2. Give honest, sincere appreciation.
3. Arouse in the other person an eager want.
4. Become genuinely interested in other people.
5. Smile.
6. Remember that a person's name is to that person the sweetest and most important sound in any language.
7. Be a good listener. Encourage others to talk about themselves.
8. Talk in terms of the other person's interests.
9. Make the other person feel important—and do it sincerely.

Source: Dale Carnegie's Golden Book, Dale Carnegie Training, www.dalecarnegie.com, undated.

have a negative attitude toward e-filing income taxes because of the need to learn new skills combined with a fear of lack of security. After trying e-filing for two consecutive years because of being almost forced to by the law, the business owner receives refunds promptly and find the process not really so complicated. So her attitude toward e-filing becomes reconditioned in a positive direction.

Another way to change attitudes is to learn to look at the positive or negative aspect of situations, if you are a pessimist or optimist, respectively. A pessimistic person should concentrate on searching for the positive elements of a situation, such as a supervisor saying to himself or herself, "Okay, this employee is a pill, but maybe there is something good about him."

In contrast, a naturally optimistic person might learn to say, "I tend to fall in love with the credentials of most job candidates. So maybe I should scrutinize this candidate more carefully."

Looking at the positive aspects of a situation to change your attitude is often a question of where you choose to focus your attention. What we see tends to shape how we feel. Suppose you dislike your job. The way to change your attitude is to write down every single thing you like about your job, even something small, like the free espresso. It is also helpful to maintain a list of anything positive that happens to you during the workday. An example might be, "Today Laura showed me how to position my mouse over a false e-mail address to uncover the true address. I found that interesting." Keep in mind also that you are being paid, and without paid work a person cannot live independently.[43]

How Companies Encourage Positive Attitudes and Job Satisfaction

From the standpoint of management it is beneficial for employees to have positive attitudes and job satisfaction. These two emotional states contribute to better customer service, less absenteeism and tardiness, less turnover, and often higher productivity. The logic is that satisfied employees will lead to satisfied customers, resulting in a more profitable business. Much of the effort of human resource professionals is aimed at making employees more content. Among the hundreds of possible company initiatives to foster positive attitudes and high job satisfaction among employees are flexible working hours, recognition awards, company picnics, financial bonuses, time off for birthdays, on-site haircuts, and on-premises child-care centers. Following are three specific examples of companies voted among the 100 Best Companies to Work For (as evaluated by *Fortune* magazine) to enhance employee attitudes and satisfaction:[44]

Genentech, South San Francisco (biotechnology products). Employees receive free doggie day care, onsite farmer's market, and parties every Friday night. The company matches 401(k) payments 100 percent up to 5 percent of pay. (A 401(k) is a retirement fund contributed to by the employee and often the employer, with the balance being the property of the individual.)

W. L. Gore & Associates, Newark, Delaware (Gore-Tex fabrics, guitar strings, dental floss). To encourage job satisfaction as well as innovation, there are no bosses, job titles, or organization charts. Instead there are sponsors, team members, and leaders. The company attempts to hire candidates who are driven by opportunity rather than a job title or its associated status. Highly engaged employees are referred to as "passionate champions."

Principal Financial Group, Des Moines, Iowa (financial products). The company has a new, state-of-the-art child-care center. Employees can buy extra time off, and the majority receives retirement benefits of 100 percent of their income. During the financial upheaval in 2008, CEO Larry Zimpleman sent weekly e-mails to keep employees up-to-date and reassure them that the company was healthy.

The accompanying Human Relations in Practice provides an example of the steps a company will take to keep employees satisfied and why company leadership thinks keeping employees satisfied is important.

Job Satisfaction Counts at Advertising, Marketing, and Public Relations Agency

At Dixon Schwabl, an advertising, marketing, and public relations agency based in Victor, New York, creativity forms the corner-stone of the business. As a result, its seventy-seven employees are encouraged to share imaginative ideas in various forums. Six years ago when the company moved to its new office, employees were asked what they wanted in the space, and true to the company's extroverted culture, they didn't hold back.

Among employees' suggestions: windows that open, thermostat controls in each office, a giant slide, a fireplace in the conference room, and a padded "primal scream" room. The final design incorporates every idea, CEO Lauren Dixon says proudly.

"We never make a decision without putting it on the table for everyone's approval," Dixon says. "You might think our clients are number one, but really it's our employees. If we make our employees number one, they'll make our clients number one."

In its twenty-first year, Dixon Schwabl topped the *HR Magazine* annual list of the "Best Small Companies to Work For"

in America. Leaders and employees of the privately held company, which has been on the list for four years, work hard to live its values of integrity, teamwork, fun, creativity, and community.

Company leaders have earned a reputation for listening to and valuing employees' opinions, offering the staff freedom and flexibility on the job, and providing benefits such as a generous health-care package and nutrition programs, profit sharing, and an array of training opportunities.

Questions

1. What factors in the job environment at Dixon Schwabl appear to be contributing to employee job satisfaction?
2. Why should company leaders care if its employees have "fun" on the job?
3. Put on your accounting hat. Explain whether a "padded primal scream room" is a good investment of company money.

Source: Abridged from Desda Moss, "Catering to a Creative Workforce," *HR Magazine,* July 2008, pp. 33–34.

Although companies invest considerable money in satisfying employees, a good deal of job satisfaction stems from positive interpersonal relationships in the work environment. A comprehensive study about job satisfaction was conducted with 540 people in a variety of positions, including teachers, physicians, and construction workers. The nature of the work, such as having a variety of interesting tasks to perform, contributed to job satisfaction. A bigger impact on job satisfaction, however, stemmed from frequent interaction with others, office friendship, and receiving emotional support from supervisors and coworkers.[45]

Organizational Citizenship Behavior

An employee attitude highly valued by employers is **organizational citizenship behavior (OCB)**—the willingness to go beyond one's job description to help the company, even if such an act does not lead to an immediate reward. Being a good organizational citizen is also tied in with values, because the person who goes beyond the job description to help others most likely has a strong work ethic and values helping others. Several examples of good organizational citizenship follow:

organizational citizenship behavior (OCB)

The willingness to go beyond one's job description to help the company, even if such an act does not lead to an immediate reward.

- Melissa helps an employee in another department with a currency exchange problem because she has skill in this area, but Melissa's job does not involve working with currency exchange.

- Jeff is walking into the company from the company parking lot. He notices that a few beer bottles have been scattered on the lot. Worried about possible flat tires to employee vehicles, Jeff collects the bottles and disposes of them properly. He does not tell anybody about his good deed.

- Penelope, a gifted information technology person, is walking down the isle toward her cubicle. She notices a worker from another department with a panicked look on his face as he stares into his computer monitor. Penelope asks if there is anything she can do to help and proceeds to transfer valuable data from a corrupted file to a new file for the employee in panic.

Organizational citizenship behavior is so important to organizations that this set of attitudes has been the subject of many studies. A general finding has been that as a result of many workers being good organizational citizens, the organization functions more effectively in such ways as improved product quantity and quality.[46]

The personal support dimension of OCB will help you understand how citizenship behavior contributes directly to effective human relations in the workplace. **Personal support** refers to assisting others in the workplace through the use of interpersonal skills. As outlined in Figure 6-6, and presented next, the personal support dimension has four components, or subdimensions.[47] The three examples presented above involve a mixture of personal support and task-related assistance. Here is the difference: Penelope, just mentioned, is providing personal support when she helps the frustrated computer user calm down. She provides task-related assistance when she transfers the data to a new file.

1. **Helping.** Person-focused helping includes self-esteem maintenance and other more personal problem-solving behaviors. Penelope would be engaged in self-esteem maintenance if she said to the man she was helping, "Don't feel bad; even Bill Gates and Steve Jobs have trouble with corrupted files." Helping behavior contributes to organizational effectiveness when the help is of high technical quality. If Penelope calms down the man she is trying to help but does not help him with the corrupted file, not much has been accomplished for the organization.

2. **Courtesy.** In general, courtesy involves showing consideration and tact in interpersonal relationships. Although courtesy might be regarded as expected behavior on the job, many workers are rude and discourteous toward each other. Being courteous therefore stands out as part of organizational citizenship behavior. An example of courteous behavior during a department meeting would be to listen intently to the presenter without engaging in other activities, even if the person bored you.

3. **Cooperating.** A person who cooperates on the job willfully contributes time, effort, and resources to accomplish joint tasks. As a member of a team, you are expected to cooperate. In terms of citizenship behavior, cooperating includes accepting the suggestions of work associates, following their lead, and placing team objectives over personal interests. Included also in cooperation is informing others of events or requirements that may affect them. Cooperation is mostly clearly part of OCB when you go out of your way to cooperate with people outside of your immediate work unit. An example would be sending a job-relevant Web link to someone in another department.

FIGURE 6-6   The Four Components of the Personal Support Dimension of Organizational Citizenship Behavior

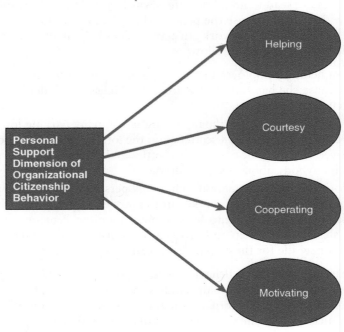

4. **Motivating.** As related to organizational citizenship behavior, motivating behaviors include applauding the achievements and successes of coworkers, encouraging them when they face adversity, and helping them overcome setbacks. Expressing confidence in coworkers, and perhaps supervisors, is also part of the motivating component of personal support. In the example of Melissa presented above, she might have to encourage the person she is helping to study more about currency exchange. In sum, you are a good organizational citizen if you are helpful, courteous, cooperative, and motivational, even if these behaviors are not part of your job description.

WHAT IS HAPPINESS, AND HOW CAN IT BE ACQUIRED AND ENHANCED?

LEARNING OBJECTIVE 7

When asked "What is the most important thing in life?" most people respond, "Happiness." Research and opinion on the topic indicate that people can take concrete steps to achieve happiness. Planning for happiness is possible because it appears to be about 40 percent under people's control. Happier people have better physical health, achieve more career success, work harder, and are more caring and socially engaged. Misery can lead to self-obsession and inactivity.[48] Based partially on the importance of happiness for well-being, there has been a surge of writing and study about happiness in recent years. A course about positive psychology has become the most popular course at Harvard University, and at least one hundred other colleges and universities offer similar courses.[49]

Our approach to the unlimited topic of understanding how to achieve happiness involves a model of happiness, a listing of keys to happiness, and the five principles of psychological functioning.

The Spheres of Life and Happiness

A practical way of understanding happiness is that it is a byproduct of having the various components of life working in harmony and synchrony. To understand this approach, visualize about six gears with teeth, spinning in unison. As long as all gears are moving properly (and no teeth are broken), a state of equilibrium and fluid motion is achieved. Similarly, imagine that life has six major components. The exact components will differ among people. For most people, the components would be approximately as follows:

1. Work and career
2. Interpersonal life, including loved ones and romantic life
3. Physical and mental health
4. Financial health
5. Interests and pastimes, including reading, surfing the Internet, and sports
6. A spiritual life or belief system, including religion, science, or astrology

When you have ample satisfactions in all six spheres, you achieve happiness. However, when a deficiency occurs in any of these six factors, your spheres are no longer in harmony, and dissatisfaction or unhappiness occurs. Yet sometimes if you are having problems in one sphere, satisfaction in the other spheres can compensate temporarily for a deficiency in one. For the long range, a state of happiness depends on all six spheres working in harmony. In short, work and personal life are mutually supportive. Figure 6-7 presents the spheres-of-life model of happiness.

People vary as to how much importance they attach to each sphere of life. A person with intense career ambitions, for example, might place less weight on the interests sphere than would a more leisure-oriented person. However, if any of these spheres are grossly deficient, total happiness will not be forthcoming. Another source of variation is that the importance people attach to each sphere may vary according to the stage of life. If you are a full-time student, for example, you might need just enough money to avoid worrying about finances. However, after about ten years of full-time career experience, your expenses might peak. You would then attach more importance to the financial sphere.

66 Don't worry, be happy. 99
— Bobby McFerrin, jazz vocalist and classical conductor.

FIGURE 6-7 The Spheres-of-Life Model of Happiness

The Keys to Happiness

If you are aware of known contributors to happiness, you might be able to enhance your happiness. Fortunately there is some consistency in information about what makes people happy. Here we summarize and synthesize a wide range of research and opinion on the keys to happiness.[50]

Give High Priority to the Pursuit of Happiness.   Having the intention or goal of being happy will enhance your chances of being happy. A key principle is to discover what makes you happy and make the time to pursue those activities, as spending time doing what you enjoy contributes directly to happiness. University of California–Riverside psychology professor Sonja Lyubormirsky has researched routines to help people become happy by focusing on happiness, thereby systematically pursuing happiness. Her research shows that you need to put intentional effort into becoming happier. If people think about happy life events every day for three days, within four weeks they are happier than they were before they started this routine.[51] If you are going through a particularly unhappy period, you may have to stretch to think of a few happy life events. For example, did anybody pay you a compliment about anything you did or said recently? Did you help anybody recently who thanked you for your kindness?

Develop and Maintain Friendships with Happy People.   New evidence indicates that getting connected to happy people improves a person's own happiness. Nicholas Christakis, a professor of medical sociology at Harvard Medical School, and James Fowler, a political scientist at the University of California–San Diego, surveyed the emotional state of about 5,000 people and the 50,000 social ties they shared. Happiness level, or emotional state, was measured at various points. Happiness was measured by asking people how often during the past week they could say, (a) I enjoyed life, (b) I was happy, (c) I felt hopeful about the future, and (d) I felt that I was just as good as other people.

The study found that happiness is contagious. If a participant's friend was happy, that participant was 15 percent more likely to be happy. If the friend of a participant's friend was happy, the original participant was 10 percent more likely to be happy. The happiness chain even extended further out, with a happy friend of a friend, of a friend giving a 5.6 percent boost to the original participant's happiness.

Another key finding was that people with the most social connections, including friends, spouses, neighbors, and relatives, were also the happiest. Each additional person in your network makes you happier. Spouses and other live-in partners who are happy increase the likelihood of their partners being happy by 8 percent. Happy siblings living nearby boosted life satisfaction 14 percent, and happy neighbors increased happiness levels by 34 percent.

The "friends" in this study were mostly traditional friends, not the type of "friends" you contact on social networks like MySpace and Facebook. Yet the study also found that people who are smiling on their Facebook photos tend to cluster together, forming an online social circle.[52]

Develop a Sense of Self-Esteem. Self-love must precede love for others. High self-esteem enables one to love and be loved. Developing a good self-image leads to the self-esteem required for loving relationships. An early contributor to the importance of thinking positively about oneself was Emile Coué, a French psychologist. He made a name for himself in the twentieth century by teaching that mental health could be achieved by repeating the sentence, "Every day and in every way I'm becoming better and better."[53]

A feeling of self-worth is important because it helps prevent being overwhelmed by criticism. An important part of developing self-esteem is to not want financial success more than other things. Insecure people seek society's approval in the form of purchasing consumer goods and accumulating investments. (In this way the person might be admired by others.) The accompanying Core Self-Evaluation Scale is a scientifically developed instrument that gives you an opportunity to assess how positively you think about yourself.

Work Hard at What You Enjoy and Achieve the Flow Experience. To achieve happiness, it is necessary to find a career that fits your most intense interests. In addition, it helps to achieve regularly the flow experience of total involvement in what you are doing at the moment. Happiness stemming from flow is powerful because it is not dependent on favorable external circumstances, such as recognition or love. The individual creates the happiness that follows from flow. Hard work contributes to happiness in another important way. A fundamental secret of happiness is accomplishing things and savoring what you have accomplished. Happiness researcher David T. Lyken argues that happiness is available to anyone who develops skills, interests, and goals that he or she finds meaningful and enjoyable.[54] A log cabin dweller who lived off the land and whose goal was to be close to nature would therefore be happier than a wealthy person in a luxurious house who was not leading the lifestyle he or she wanted.

Appreciate the Joys of Day-to-Day Living. A major obstacle to happiness is **hedonic adaptation**—the tendency to adapt to regard exciting new aspects of life as routine after a while.[55] Imagine a person who wants a luxurious lifestyle finally purchases a fiftieth-story condominium penthouse overlooking a harbor. At first the view is breathtaking, yet after a while looking at the harbor becomes routine. To overcome the hedonic adaptation you therefore have to learn to appreciate the joys of day-to-day living. The essence of being a happy person is to savor what you have right now. As Benjamin Franklin said, "Happiness is produced not so much by great pieces of good fortune that seldom happen as by the little advantages that occur every day."

Part of the same key to happiness is the ability to live in the present without undue worry about the future or dwelling on past mistakes. Be on guard against becoming so preoccupied with planning your life that you neglect to enjoy the happiness of the moment.

Be Fair, Kind, and Helpful, and Trust Others. The Golden Rule is a true contributor to happiness. It is also important to practice charity and forgiveness. Helping others brings personal happiness. Knowing that you are able to make a contribution to the welfare of others gives you a continuing sense of satisfaction and happiness. Related to fairness and kindness is trust of others. Happy people have open, warm, and friendly attitudes.

hedonic adaptation

The tendency to adapt to regard exciting new aspects of life as routine after a while.

The Core Self-Evaluation Scale

Below are several statements about you with which you may agree or disagree. Using the response scale below, indicate your agreement or disagreement with each item by placing the appropriate number on the line preceding that item.

1	2	3	4	5
Strongly Disagree	**Disagree**	**Neutral**	**Agree**	**Strongly Agree**

1. _____ I am confident I get the success I deserve.
2. _____ Sometimes I feel depressed.
3. _____ When I try, I generally succeed.
4. _____ Sometimes when I fail, I feel worthless.
5. _____ I complete tasks successfully.
6. _____ Sometimes, I do not feel in control of my work.
7. _____ Overall, I am satisfied with myself.
8. _____ I am filled with doubts about my competence.
9. _____ I determine what will happen in my life.
10. _____ I do not feel in control of my success in my career.
11. _____ I am capable of coping with most of my problems.
12. _____ There are times when things look pretty bleak and hopeless to me.

_____ **Total Score**

Scoring and Interpretation:

The scoring for items 1, 3, 5, 7, 9, and 11 proceeds as follows: 5, 4, 3, 2, 1 to indicate a positive attitude toward yourself. The scoring for questions 2, 4, 6, 8, 10, and 12 proceeds as follows: 1, 2, 3, 4, 5 to indicate a positive attitude toward yourself. Add all your scores to attain your total score. The higher the score, the more positive your attitude toward yourself. Scores of 48 and higher suggest a very positive attitude, scores between 37 and 47 suggest a neutral attitude, and scores between 12 and 35 indicate a negative attitude toward yourself. The mean score for several different groups of people, including working adults and students, is 45.

Source: Timothy A. Judge, Amir Erez, Joyce E. Bono, and Carl J. Thoresen, "The Core Self-Evaluation Scale: Development of a Measure," Personnel Psychology, Summer 2003, p. 315. This measure is nonproprietary (free) and may be used without permission.

Have Recreational Fun in Your Life. A happy life is characterized by fun, zest, joy, and delight. When you create time for fun (in addition to the fun in many kinds of work), you add an important element to your personal happiness. But if you devote too much time to play, you will lose out on the fun of work accomplishments. In choosing fun activities, avoid overplanning. Because novelty contributes to happiness, be ready to pursue an unexpected opportunity or to try something different.

Learn to Cope with Grief, Disappointment, Setbacks, and Stress. To be happy, you must learn how to face problems that occur in life without being overwhelmed or running away. It is also important to persevere in attempting to overcome problems rather than to whine or engage in self-pity. Once you have had to cope with problems, you will be more able to appreciate the day-to-day joys of life. An example of an everyday problem that ranks high on the misery list is lengthy commutes to work, by private or public transportation.[56] If you cannot change the length of the commute for now, find ways to make commuting more enjoyable, such as finding a radio station that provides information useful for your professional growth or is simply enjoyable.

Live with What You Cannot Change. Happiness guru Martin Seligman says that attempting to change conditions unlikely to change sets us up for feeling depressed about failing. Weight loss is a prime example. Nineteen out of twenty people regain weight they lost. It is, therefore, better to worry less about weight loss and concentrate on staying in good physical condition by engaging in moderate exercise. Good condition contributes much more to health than does achieving a weight standard set primarily to achieve an aesthetic standard. You can then concentrate on being happy about your good physical condition instead of being unhappy about your weight.[57]

Energize Yourself through Physical Fitness.   Engage in regular physical activity, such as dancing or sports that make you aerobically fit. Whether it is the endorphins released by exercise, dopamine released by the excitement, or simply the relaxed muscles, physical fitness fosters happiness. Another important part of energizing yourself is to attain adequate rest. Happy people invest time in revitalizing sleep and solitude.

Satisfy Your Most Important Values.   Based on a survey of more than six thousand individuals, social psychologist Steven Reiss concluded that people cannot find lasting happiness by aiming to have more fun or seeking pleasure. Instead, you have to satisfy your basic values or desires and take happiness in passing. To increase your value-based happiness, you have to first identify your most important desires and then gear your life toward satisfying these values. Among these key values are curiosity, physical activity, honor, power, family, status, and romance.[58] For example, if power and romance are two of your basic values, you can achieve happiness only if your life is amply provided with power and romance. Religion also fits into the realm of values, and religious people tend to be happier than nonreligious people.[59]

To attain happiness by living your values, you first have to know what your values are. Physician and happiness counselor Russ Harris suggests that you answer the following question to identify your key values: "Imagine you could wave a magic wand to ensure that you would have the approval and admiration of everyone on the planet, forever. What, in this case, would you choose to do with your life?"[60]

Earn Enough Money to Avoid Feeling Miserable.   The role of money as a contributor to happiness is the subject of endless debate. Money cannot buy happiness, but having enough money to purchase the things that make you happy is important. Whether an iPod or a penthouse condominium with a view of the water would make you happy, they both require money—even though the amounts differ. However, the pursuit of money for its own sake is less likely to contribute to happiness.

According to Arthur C. Brooks, a professor at the Syracuse University Maxwell School of Public Affairs, some research by economists suggests that people with a lot of money tend to express a higher degree of subjective happiness than people with very little. Data from the National Opinion Research Center indicate that people in the top 20 percent income bracket are about 50 percent more likely to say they are "very happy" than people in the bottom 20 percent. Those in the higher bracket are also about half as likely to say they are "not too happy."[61, 62]

Another consideration is that not being able to pay for what you consider a necessity may lead to low self-esteem and unhappiness. Even if a person does not equate money with happiness, having a car repossessed or a house foreclosed contributes to at least a temporary state of unhappiness. Yet despite this obvious truth, many people in poor countries are happy. For example, surveys taken over a twenty-year period indicate that the Inuit people of northern Greenland score an average of 5.8 on a scale of 1 to 7 in response to a question about life satisfaction. Survey respondents on the list of the *Forbes* magazine wealthiest 400 also averaged 5.8 on the same scale.[63] People in rich countries are not consistently happier than people in poor countries. Yet the underlying principle could be the same. As long as you have enough money to pay for what you consider to be necessities, money is not a factor in your happiness.

Lead a Meaningful Life.   Most of the principles previously stated, as well as the spheres-of-life happiness model, all point toward the conclusion that having a meaningful life is a major contributor to happiness. A meaning or an important purpose helps a person get through periodic annoyances that temporarily lower happiness. Seligman says that the ultimate level of happiness is the meaningful life. It consists of identifying your core strengths and then using them in the services of something you perceive to be bigger than you are.[64] For example, if you are a greeting card designer and you perceive that you are contributing to improved personal relationships, you are likely to be happy.

The Five Principles of Psychological Functioning

According to clinical psychologist Richard Carlson, the best way to achieve inner serenity (or happiness) is to follow the five principles of psychological functioning.[65] These principles act as guides toward achieving a feeling of inner happiness. The first is *thinking*, which creates the psychological experience of life. Feelings come about only after you thought about something or somebody. If you think of another person as attractive, it will lead to a warm feeling toward that person. People who learn to direct their thinking in positive directions will contribute to their own happiness. Remember that you produce your own thoughts.

The second principle is *moods*, meaning that the positive or negative content of your thinking fluctuates from moment to moment and day to day. Practice ignoring your low (bad) moods rather than analyzing them, and you will see how quickly they vanish. Developing this skill will contribute substantially to healthy psychological functioning. The third principle is *separate psychological realities*. Because each person thinks in a unique way, everyone lives in a separate psychological reality. Accept the idea that others think differently from you, and you will have much more compassion and fewer quarrels. As a result, you will be happier. Also, if you accept the principle of separate realities, you will waste less time attempting to change people. At the same time, others will like you more, thus contributing to your happiness.

The fourth principle of psychological functioning is *feelings*. Combined with emotions, feelings are a built-in feedback mechanism that tells us how we are doing psychologically. If your feelings turn negative suddenly, you know that your thinking is dysfunctional. It is then time to make a mental readjustment. If you feel discontented, for example, it is necessary to clear the head and start thinking positively. As a consequence, you will experience contentment and happiness. A key point is that the person will maintain a sense of well-being as long as he or she does not focus on personal concerns.

The fifth principle is *the present moment*. Learning to pay attention to the present moment and to your feelings enables people to live at peak efficiency without the distraction of negative thinking. Much like the flow experience, the present moment is where people find happiness and inner peace. Carlson advises, "The only way to experience genuine and lasting contentment, satisfaction, and happiness is to learn to live your life in the present moment."[66]

Concept Review and Reinforcement

Key Terms

self-esteem 188
positive visual imagery 200
peak performance 201
emotional intelligence, 203
self-awareness 203
self-management 204
social awareness 204

relationship management 204
emotional contagion 206
attitude 207
cognitive component
    (of attitude) 207
affective component
    (of attitude) 207

behavioral component
    (of attitude) 207
cognitive dissonance 208
organizational citizenship behavior
    (OCB) 211
personal support 212
hedonic adaptation 215

Summary

Self-esteem refers to the overall evaluation people make about themselves. People with high self-esteem develop a positive self-concept. Self-esteem develops from a variety of early-life experiences. People who were encouraged to feel good about themselves and their accomplishments by key people in their lives are more likely to enjoy high self-esteem. Of major significance, self-esteem also results from accomplishing worthwhile activities, and then feeling proud of these accomplishments. Praise and recognition for accomplishments also help develop self-esteem.

Self-esteem has many important consequences, as follows: career success, including a high income; good mental health; profiting from feedback, and organizational success. One of the links between good mental health and self-esteem is that high self-esteem helps prevent many situations from being stressful. Workers with high self-esteem develop and maintain favorable work attitudes and perform at a high level. A company with high self-esteem workers has a competitive advantage.

High self-esteem can sometimes have negative consequences such as undermining others to preserve one's own status. Our own reference group has the biggest impact on self-esteem. Self-esteem can be enhanced in many ways: (a) attain legitimate accomplishments, (b) be aware of your personal strengths, (c) rebut the inner critic, (d) practice self-nurturing, (e) minimize settings and interactions that detract from your feelings of competence, (f) get help from others including talking and socializing frequently with people who boost your self-esteem, (g) model the behavior of people with high self-esteem, and (h) create a high self-esteem living space. The manager can play an important role in helping build the self-esteem of group members, such as giving positive feedback for legitimate accomplishments.

Various studies have shown that people with a high sense of self-efficacy tend to have good job performance, so self-confidence is important for your career. Our feelings of self-confidence stem from five sources of information: actual experiences, or things that we have done; experiences of others, or modeling; social comparison, or comparing yourself to others; social persuasion, the process of convincing another person; and emotional arousal, or how we feel about events around us and manage our emotions.

A general principle of boosting your self-confidence is to experience success (goal accomplishment) in a variety of situations. The specific strategies for building self-confidence described here are: (a) develop a solid knowledge base, (b) use positive self-talk, (c) avoid negative self-talk, (d) use positive visual imagery, (e) set high expectations for yourself (the Galatea effect), (f) develop the explanatory style of optimists, (e) strive for peak performance, and (f) bounce back from setbacks and embarrassments.

Emotional intelligence generally refers to how effectively a person makes constructive use of his or her emotions. The four key components of emotional intelligence are

1. Self-awareness (understanding the self)
2. Self-management (emotional control)
3. Social awareness (includes empathy and intuition)
4. Relationship management (includes interpersonal skills)

Demonstrating good emotional intelligence is impressive because it contributes to performing well in the difficult area of dealing with feelings. Another positive consequence of emotional intelligence is that if you know how to project positive emotion you will spread those positive feelings to others in the workplace. In some situations it will be helpful to be aware of possible cross-cultural differences in what constitutes effective emotional intelligence.

The combination of biological endowment and training will enable most people to enhance their emotional intelligence.

Attitudes are complex, having three components

1. Cognitive (knowledge or beliefs)
2. Affective (emotional)
3. Behavioral (how a person acts)

Cognitive dissonance occurs when the three components are not consistent with each other. Attitudes are formed based on experience, including receiving instruction from another person, conditioning, and cognitions (the way we think about something). The trait of optimism versus pessimism influences attitudes strongly. A worker who maintains a genuine positive attitude will accrue many benefits, yet being too positive can have disadvantages.

Attitudes can be changed by reversing the process by which they were formed. Looking at the positive or negative aspect of a situation can also lead to attitude change. From the standpoint of management it is beneficial for employees to have positive attitudes and job satisfaction. Much of job satisfaction stems from good interpersonal relationships in the workplace. Organizational citizenship behavior is highly valued by employers because such attitudes can lead to improved product quality and quantity. Personal support is one aspect of organizational citizenship behavior and includes helping, courtesy, cooperating, and motivating.

Planning for happiness appears to be about 40 percent under a person's control. A practical way of understanding happiness is that it is a byproduct of having the spheres of life working in harmony and synchrony. For most people these spheres would be the following:

- Work and career
- Interpersonal life, including romance
- Physical and mental health
- Financial health
- Interests and pastimes
- Spiritual life or belief system

Contributors or keys to happiness include the following:

- Giving priority to happiness
- Developing and maintaining friendships with happy people
- Self-esteem
- Working hard at things enjoyed, and achieving the flow experience
- Appreciation of the joys of day-to-day living
- Fairness, kindness, helpfulness, and trust
- Recreational fun
- Coping with grief, disappointment, setbacks, and stress
- Living with what you cannot change
- Energizing yourself through physical fitness
- Satisfying your most important values
- Earning enough money to avoid feeling miserable

According to Richard Carlson, the best way to achieve inner serenity (or happiness) is to follow the five principles of psychological functioning.

- First is thinking which brings about feelings.
- Second is moods, including the idea that you can ignore bad moods.
- Third is separate psychological realities, meaning that each person thinks in a unique way.
- Fourth is feelings, which can be turned from negative to positive.
- Fifth is the present moment, which is where people find happiness and inner peace.

1. Why does holding an important job contribute to a person's self-esteem?

2. A study by economists indicated that workers with higher levels of self-esteem tended to be more productive. What would be an explanation for this finding?

3. Exercises to boost self-esteem and self-confidence often emphasize focusing on your positive qualities. Why might it also be important to be aware of your weak points to develop self-esteem?

4. The criticism is often heard that the American emphasis on building the self-esteem of children has resulted in a generation of young adults who expect to be strongly praised by their bosses, no matter what they accomplish. What is your opinion of this criticism?

5. When you meet another person, on what basis do you conclude that he or she is self-confident?

6. What positive self-talk can you use after you have failed on a major assignment?

7. In what way does your program of studies contribute to building your self-esteem and self-confidence?

8. Many pharmaceutical firms actively recruit cheerleaders as sales representatives to call on doctors to recommend their brand of prescription drugs. The firms in question say that cheerleaders make good sales reps because they are so self-confident. What is your opinion on this controversial issue?

9. For what type of job might a worker having low self-esteem and self-confidence actually be an asset?

10. Interview a person whom you perceive to have a successful career. Ask that person to describe how he or she developed high self-esteem. Be prepared to discuss your findings in class.

11. What has one of your professors or instructors done recently to demonstrate good emotional intelligence in dealing with students?

12. Describe what a business executive, entertainer, or well-known athlete has done recently to demonstrate low emotional intelligence. Explain your reasoning.

13. Suppose the vast majority of company managers had high emotional intelligence. How might this fact give the company a competitive advantage?

14. Imagine yourself as a manager or team leader. What could you do to make positive use of emotional contagion with the people in your group?

15. How is a person supposed to maintain a positive attitude when major things in life are going wrong, such as a job loss, a personal bankruptcy, a broken relationship, or the premature death of a loved one?

16. What are some of the skills a person needs to acquire to become happy?

17. How do your "spheres of life" compare with those in Figure 6.6-6.7?

18. When you are happiest, are you more productive professionally/academically?

19. Why might being very happy prompt some people to become less competitive in their careers?

20. Happiness researchers agree that having a high income is not necessarily associated with happiness. Yet at the same time activities that bring happiness, such as dining in restaurants, or taking vacations with friends and family, require considerable money. How does a person resolve this conflict?

The Web Corner

www.athealth.com/Consumer/disorders/self-esteem.html
(Measuring and building your self-esteem)

www.self-confidence.co.uk
(Developing your self-confidence)

www.mindtools.com/selfconf.html
(The difference between self-confidence and low self-confidence)

Internet Skills Builder: Learning More about Your Self-Esteem

The Self-Esteem Checklist in this chapter gave you one opportunity to assess you self-esteem. To gain additional insights into your self-esteem, visit www.more-selfesteem.com. Go to "quizzes" under Free Resources, and take the self-esteem test. How does your score on this quiz compare to your score on *The Self-Esteem Checklist*? If your level of self-esteem as measured by the two quizzes is quite different (such as high versus low), explain why this discrepancy might occur.

Emotional intelligence:

www.emotionalintelligence.com; www.eiconsortium.org

The Happiness Test:

www.pathwaytohappiness.com/happiness_test.htm

Positive attitudes:

www.attitudeiseverything.com.

Positive Psychology Center:

www.ppc.sas.upenn.edu

Internet Skill Builder: Daily Doses of Happiness on the Web

Visit www.thehappyguy.com to receive your "daily dose of happiness." This site offers you happiness quotes and suggestions for self-actualization. The "Happy Guy" promises to help you achieve such ends as becoming inspired about life, discovering the meaning of happiness, and achieving personal growth. After trying out this program of happiness and personal growth, you be the judge. Have you made strides toward becoming happier? Do you feel any better emotionally? What impact do the Daily Happiness mugs have on your personal well-being? Be happy!

Developing Your Human Relations Skills

The Confetti Man

Nick Jablonski works for a manufacturer of property maintenance and recreational vehicles such as lawnmowers, snow blowers, and all-terrain vehicles. The company prospers even during downturns in the economy. This is true because when economic conditions are worrisome many people invest more money in taking care of their property and enjoying themselves close to home instead of traveling. Nick holds the job title, "celebrations assistant." The more traditional part of his job is to organize company events like picnics, sales meetings, and shareholder meetings.

When asked to explain the celebrations assistant part of his job in more detail, Nick replied with a smile:

My job is to help workers throughout the company celebrate accomplishments that help the company reach its goals. I'll give you a couple of examples. Suppose I learn that a production technician has exceeded quota on inserting dashboards on riding mowers, I will visit the factory floor and help the technician celebrate. Sometimes I will attach a smiley face to his or her work area. I might shake his or her hand or pat the person on the back. Yet to be dramatic, I will shower the person with confetti.

Just last week I was told by her supervisor that one of our customer service reps was working on the phone with a woman suffering from arthritis. The customer was having a difficult time starting one of our lawnmowers. The rep stayed on the phone twenty minutes with the lady until she could pull the start cord correctly. The customer was so pleased that she wrote a letter to the CEO praising the helpfulness of the rep.

My response was to visit the customer service rep's area and have a little celebration. Not only did I throw two bags of confetti, I blew a fog horn. I could tell the rep became a little embarrassed because she blushed. Yet I knew that I really boosted her self-esteem.

When Jablonski was asked why his work as a celebrations assistant boosted worker self-esteem, he answered as follows: "My job is to make our employees feel good about themselves. My smiley faces, my encouraging message, and especially my confetti throwing make people feel great. If people feel great about themselves and their accomplishments, their self-esteem heads north. It's that simple."

Case Questions

1. To what extent do you think that the celebrations assistant is really boosting the self-esteem of workers?
2. Assume that Nick is successful in boosting worker self-esteem. How might this help the company?
3. Advise the CEO of the company in question as to whether having a celebrations assistant on the payroll is a good investment of company money.

Source: Several facts in this case are based on Jeffrey Zaslow, "The Most-Praised Generation Goes to Work," *The Wall Street Journal*, April 20, 2007, pp. W1, W7.

Homeboy Industries Helps Ex-Cons Go Green

When Albert Ortega was released from prison, he was determined to turn his life around. So he went green. Ortega sports tattoos of an Aztec warrior on his back, a dragon on his chest, and the name of his former gang rings his biceps. Drug trafficking kept him locked up for most of the past seven years, he says. But after serving his last term, he heard about a solar installation course. "I wanted a new way of life," says the tall, brawny 34-year old. "Solar puts me on the cutting edge."

In the race to train America's "green collar" workforce, a group composed mostly of former Los Angeles gang members on parole is an early participant. Their training is funded by Homeboy Industries, a Los Angeles nonprofit that helps people with criminal pasts find employment.

For years, Homeboy Industries put former felons to work at a bakery and café it runs in East Los Angeles. A few summers ago, founder Greg Boyles, a Jesuit priest, was approached by a supporter about the idea of preparing them for the green economy. "I leapt at the opportunity," says Father Boyle.

Homeboy joined forces with the East Los Angeles Skills Center, a public vocational school that offers a hands-on program to teach the design, construction, and installation of solar panels. The center created an intensive course for Homeboy. "I loved the idea of doing something for these guys," says Brian Hurd, the senior instructor who designed it. "My best student ever in a construction course was a Homeboy referral who needed a second chance." Homeboy participants are paid an hourly wage of $8. The class meets for two months, weekdays from 9 A.M. to 3 P.M.

"I was so motivated, I would fall asleep with the books on my bed," says Ortega. Determined to get into the course, he phoned or visited Father Boyle for two weeks, until he was asked to take a drug test. Ortega passed and was offered a spot in the class. "I knew I was good at wir-ing," says Ortega, who once installed car-stereo systems. "I was always good at math."

Manuel Delgado, 42, who dropped out of high school, said he struggled at first. But four weeks into the class, he's doing "real good," he says. "I got 76% on my last math test." Another student, Jessica Espinoza, 23, says she couldn't find a job after being locked up for two years because she helped a felon escape from a courthouse. "The minute they saw I went to jail, employers didn't give me the time of day," she says. "Hopefully I can take what this school gave me and make a career in this new industry."

Doug Lincoln, 61, who once managed luxury car dealerships, was offered admission in the Homeboy course after he inquired about a faster-paced class. On hearing it was mainly for ex-cons, he said, "I thought it was a joke." Now, Lincoln is about to graduate. He plans to start a solar-panel installation firm and hire some of his former classmates. "These guys are more motivated than hundreds of employees I've managed in the car business," he says.

Ortega recently passed an examination that qualifies him to install solar panels nationwide. He says he has already been approached by employers. But he says he is waiting until when he is off parole before starting work, because until then he can't travel out of Los Angeles County. When that happens, he says, "I'll be just another citizen."

Several of his classmates who completed the course are already working, earning about $15 an hour. Experienced installers can make about $30 an hour. Phillip Hartley, general manager of Phat Energy, a Los Angeles solar company, has hired several Homeboy graduates. The Los Angeles Unified School District plans to start hiring some graduates of the program to install 50 megawatts of solar power units on its campuses. "Being former gang members doesn't preclude them from building a career in solar technology," says Veronica Soto, a school district director.

Human Relations Application Exercises

Case Questions

1. Why might an ex-con enrolled in the Homeboy solar-panel building program have a self-esteem problem?
2. In what way might the Homeboy solar-panel training program be building the self-esteem and self-confidence of its students?
3. What suggestions can you offer for the staff at Homeboy to do an even better job of building the self-esteem and self-confidence of its students?
4. Should the instructor for the solar-panel installation class give high grades in math to all the students, just to raise their self-esteem? Explain your reasoning.

Source: Miriam Jordan, "A New Gang Comes to Los Angeles: Solar-Panel Installers," *The Wall Street Journal*, February 14–15, 2009, pp. A1, A9.

Applying Human Relations Exercise 6-1

Enhancing Your Emotional Intelligence

A realistic starting point in improving your emotional intelligence is to work with one of its four components at a time, such as the empathy aspect of social awareness. A complex behavior pattern or trait such as emotional intelligence takes considerable time to improve, but the time will most likely be a good investment. Follow these steps:

1. Begin by obtaining as much feedback as you can from people who know you. Ask them if they think you understand their emotional reactions and how well they think you understand them. It is helpful to ask someone from another culture or someone who has a severe disability how well you communicate with him or her. (A higher level of empathy is required to communicate well with somebody much different from you.) If you work with customers, ask them how well you appear to understand their position.

2. If you find any area of deficiency, work on that deficiency steadily. For example, perhaps you are not perceived as taking the time to understand a point of view quite different from your own. Attempt to understand other points of view. Suppose you believe strongly that only people with lots of money can be happy. Speak to a person with a different opinion and listen carefully until you understand that person's perspective.

3. At a minimum of a few weeks later, obtain more feedback about your ability to empathize. If you are making progress, continue to practice.

4. Prepare a document about your skill development. Describe the steps you took to enhance your empathy, the progress you made, and how people react differently to you now. For example, you might find that people talk more openly and freely with you now that you are more empathetic.

5. Then repeat these steps for another facet of emotional intelligence. As a result you will have developed another valuable interpersonal skill.

Applying Human Relations Exercise 6-2

Achieving Happiness

The following exercises will help you develop attitudes that contribute mightily to happiness.

1. Start the day off right. Begin each day with five minutes of positive thought and visualization. Commit to this for one week. When and how do you plan to fit this into your schedule?

_____

_____

_____

2. Make a list of five virtues in which you believe. Examples would include patience, compassion, and helping the less fortunate.

_____

_____

_____

3. Each week, for the next five weeks, incorporate a different virtue into your life. On a simple index card, write this week's virtue in bold letters, such as "helping the less fortunate." Post the card in a prominent place. After you have completed one incident of helping the less fortunate, describe in about ten to twenty-five words what you did. Also record the date and time.

_____

_____

_____

4. Look for good things about new acquaintances. List three students, customers, or coworkers you have just met. List three positive qualities about each.

_____

_____

_____

5. List the positive qualities of fellow students or coworkers you dislike or have trouble working with. Remember, keep looking for the good.

_____

_____

_____

6. Think of school assignments or job tasks you dislike, and write down the merits of these tasks. Identify the benefits they bring you.

_____

_____

_____

7. Look at problems as opportunities. What challenges are you now facing? In what way might you view them that would inspire and motivate you?

_____

_____

_____

Source: Adapted from Stu Kamen, "Turn Negatives into Positives," Pryor Report Success Workshop, May 1995, pp. 1–2.

Human Relations Class Activity

The World's Happiest Person

Hundreds of thousands of articles and Web sites have been devoted to the subject of the world's happiest, man, woman, or person. Class time and resources most likely prohibit you from searching the globe for that person, but you and your classmates can search for that person in your classroom. If you are taking this course online, the work can be accomplished by e-mail or course Web site.

After about five minutes of reflection, each class member should decide whether he or she is totally happy, or almost totally happy. Several class members who feel that they might qualify for the title of World's Happiest Person (at least who comes closest within this classroom) volunteer to explain why to the rest of the class. Candidates for the Happiest Person category will make about a three-minute presentation of precisely why they feel so happy. As you listen to these presentations, attempt to identify any of the principles of happiness covered in this chapter.

After the presentations are completed, spend a few minutes looking for trends to arrive at a few conclusions. For discussion points, you might complete these sentences:

1. All the happy people seem to think that _____.
2. I notice that each candidate for the World's Happiest Person seemed to _____.
3. A difference I noticed between me and the volunteers (or between me and the rest of the volunteers) is that _____.
4. In terms of the candidates smiling, I noticed that _____.

The conclusions you reach can become information for class discussion. Look to see if many class members arrived at similar conclusions—perhaps in response to the four questions.

Human Relations Case Study 6-1

The Very Positive Kelly Malibu

Kelly Malibu, twenty-seven, is the manager of Deco, a woman's store that features clothing with an art deco design. Deco is one of several specialty retail stores owned by Max and Mary Lowenstein. When the store opened three years ago, Malibu was hired as the manager. Max Lowenstein said, "Kelly was a wonderful fit. She had retailing in her blood, having worked at women's stores since age seventeen. She also had supervisory experience and is so upbeat. Our one concern was that she might be too nice to be a tough boss when needed."

Malibu is responsible for merchandising. Twice a year she makes trips to New York to buy designs imported from Asia in bulk, and she also purchases some clothing online. Malibu contends that the most difficult part of her responsibilities is dealing with employees and customers. "When I deal with vendors, things usually go pretty smoothly," she says. "The vendors are usually trying to please me. We sometimes haggle a little bit about price, but we can usually work out a deal. We have the occasional dispute about returning merchandise that we cannot sell. I know that some big retailers insist on a generous return policy."

"My attitude is that our vendors are themselves small outfits operating on slim margins. So I hate to cut too deeply into their profits. If we can't sell a few dresses at Deco unless we practically give them away, it's as much my fault as that of the manufacturer or distributor. I guessed wrong on what our clientele wants. Max and Mary don't agree with my philosophy 100 percent, but they do respect my right to manage the store as I see fit."

Malibu notes that keeping her store associates productive and happy can be a challenge. Deco has two full-time associates and three part-time associates. One challenge is that her part-time associates make frequent requests for a change of schedule to fit their personal life or school demands. A recent Columbus Day was a good example of this problem.

She says, "Columbus Day is usually one of our best days outside of the holiday season. So I wanted to make sure we had two part-time sales associates on board to supplement the two full-time associates." Three days before Columbus Day, Tracy, one of the part-timers, told her she had to complete a mammoth project for her computer science class, so she wouldn't be able to work that day. "My instinct was to tell Tracy that if she couldn't be here on Columbus Day, she could set sail for another job. Then I thought of my own experiences in college. A computer science project can suck up all your mental energy and make it difficult to concentrate on anything else. So I let Tracy off the hook.

"Kim, another one of our associates, said she would be out of town for her brother's wedding. She had given me two month's notice about the wedding, so I couldn't insist that she be here. Bruce, another one of our associates, said he couldn't work on Columbus Day because he would be running a marathon. My first thoughts were to tell Bruce that running a marathon was no excuse for missing work. However, as I thought it through I realized that completing a marathon would add considerably to Bruce's self-esteem. As a result, I simply wished Bruce the best of luck in the marathon. I know that Bruce appreciated my understanding.

"That left me with one sales associate, Nicki, who could work on Columbus Day. I made up for one of the missing sales associates with my mom, who isn't a bad last-minute substitute.

"My biggest hassle with customers is when they want to see the manager because of a dispute with the associate about a return. You know that quite often they bought the dress, blouse, or suit with the intention of using it for a special occasion and then returning it for a full refund. I usually go along with the return as a way of building customer goodwill. But I have my limits. No returns when clothing has food or perspiration stains."

Case Questions

1. In what way does Malibu demonstrate empathy?
2. In what way does Malibu demonstrate a positive attitude?
3. To what extent do you think Malibu would be a more effective manager if she were less empathic and positive?

Human Relations Role-Playing Exercise

Empathizing with Tracy

Human Relations Case Study 6-1 serves as the background information and storyline for this role-playing exercise. One person plays the role of Kelly Malibu, the store manager of Deco. She has made her staffing plans for Columbus Day, in anticipation of heavy store traffic over the holiday. Kelly wants to have two part-timers on board to supplement the two full-time associates. Three days before Columbus Day, Tracy, one of the part-timers, told her that she has to complete a mammoth project for her computer science class, so she wouldn't be able to work that day. Another student plays the role of Tracy, who wants her job at Deco, but she also wants to receive a good grade in her computer science class.

Kelly wants to demonstrate good emotional intelligence, including empathy and emotional control, yet she also wants the store to be properly staffed. Tracy expects Kelly to understand her predicament.

For both scenarios, observers rate the role-players on two dimensions, using a 1 to 5 scale from very poor to very good. One dimension is "effective use of human relations techniques." The second dimension is "acting ability." A few observers might voluntarily provide feedback to the role-players in terms of sharing their ratings and observations. The course instructor might also provide feedback.

Human Relations Case Study 6-2

Alex Explodes in Anger

Alex worked as an accountant in the fraud investigation unit of the welfare department of a state government. He said that one of the things he liked about his job was that he was indirectly helping people in need. Although he was not dealing directly with welfare clients, he helped the state uncover fraud in providing financial assistance to hordes of people. Alex reasoned that when fraudulent applications for public assistance are uncovered, more money is available for families that really need the money. One such case

Alex helped uncover involved a woman making $30,000 per year selling stolen electronics goods on her Web site, yet she claimed to be unemployed.

Although Alex did not have major problems with his coworkers and management, he incurred some difficulties. He would become quite irritated when his work was interrupted by an e-mail message or a phone call from a work associate. He would often respond in writing: "I can't answer you now. I'm busy with something important." By phone he would respond in an abrupt tone: "Call me later. I'm busy now."

One day Alex came to work in a particularly bad mood. He smashed the bumper on his car by backing into a two-foot-high guard rail in a parking lot, he had a fight with his girlfriend, and his favorite NFL team was eliminated from the playoffs. The same day, Alex was due for a performance and salary review. Marilyn, his supervisor, told him that he would not be receiving merit pay because he was a poor team player. (Merit pay is a bonus for good performance beyond a cost-of-living adjustment.) Alex became red in the face and explained that he was one of the most valuable people in the agency because his detection of fraud saved the agency over $500,000 during the past year. Alex left the evaluation interview without even saying thank you or goodbye to Marilyn.

Before leaving the office, Alex sent an e-mail to Marilyn with distribution to every e-mail account in the agency, with the subject line, "Getting Ripped Off." The rest of the e-mail explained in a couple of hundred words how much he had contributed to the agency and how because of office politics he was not receiving merit pay.

Still feeling mistreated when he returned home, Alex made in the following entry in his blog:

Our investigation unit should be investigated itself. I have personally found five instances in which state funds are being diverted to personal use. Did you know that our director uses a state limousine for trips to race tracks and gambling casinos? Did you know that three of the officials in our department ran up a $650 tab at a fancy restaurant and charged it to the state as a business expense?

Two hours after Alex arrived at the office the next morning, Marilyn and the agency head came to his cubicle to tell Alex he was immediately suspended from his job because of insubordination. Also, a strong recommendation was being made to the state review board that he be fired and never allowed to work for the state again. As he left the office, Alex said angrily, "Don't you guys believe in free speech?"

Case Questions

1. Which aspects of low emotional intelligence did Alex display?
2. How justified is Alex's suspension along with the recommendation for termination?
3. You be the career coach: What can Alex do to patch the problems he has created with his career?

REFERENCES

1. Dawn Fallik, "A Finance Executive Walks Away to Work His Way up from Waiter," *The Wall Street Journal,* September 22, 2009, p. D7.

2. Michelle K. Duffy, Jason D. Shaw, Kristin L. Scott, and Bennett J. Tepper, "The Moderating Roles of Self-Esteem and Neuroticism in the Relationships Between Group and Individual Undermining Behavior," *Journal of Applied Psychology,* September 2006, p. 1067.

3. April O'Connell, Vincent O'Connell, and Lois-Ann Kuntz, *Choice and Change: The Psychology of Personal Growth and Interpersonal Relationships,* 7th edition (Upper Saddle River, NJ: Pearson/Prentice Hall, 2005), p. 3.

4. "Better Self-Esteem," www.utexas.edu/student/cmhc/booklets/selfesteem/selfest.html, 1999, p. 2.

5. Ibid.

6. Cited in Randall Edwards, "Is Self-Esteem Really All that Important?" *The APA Monitor,* May 1995, p. 43.

7. Research reported in Jeffrey Zaslow, "The Most-Praised Generation Goes to Work," *The Wall Street Journal,* April 20, 2007, p. W7.

8. David De Cremer et al., "Rewarding Leadership and Fair Procedures as Determinants of Self-Esteem," *Journal of Applied Psychology,* January 2005, pp. 3–12.

9. Eugene Raudsepp, "Strong Self-Esteem Can Help you Advance," *CareerJournal.com (The Wall Street Journal),* August 10, 2004.

10. Timothy A. Judge, Charlice Hurst, and Lauren S. Simon, "Does It Pay to Be Smart, Attractive, or Confident (or All Three)? Relationships Among General Mental Ability, Physical Attractiveness, Core Self-Evaluation, and Income," *Journal of Applied Psychology,* May 2009, pp. 742–755. The definition of core self-evaluation is from Christian J. Resick, et al., "The Bright-Side and the Dark-Side of CEO Personality: Examining Core Self-Evaluations, Narcissism, Transformational Leadership, and Strategic Influence," *Journal of Applied Psychology,* November 2009, p. 1367.

11. Research reported in Melissa Dittman, "Study Links Jealousy with Aggression, Low Self-Esteem," *Psychology Today,* February 2005, p. 13.

12. Jon L. Pierce, Donald G. Gardner, Larry L. Cummings, and Randall B. Dunman, "Organization-Based Self-Esteem: Construct Definition, Measurement, and Validation," *Academy of Management Journal,* September 1989, p. 623.

13. Nathaniel Branden, *Self-Esteem at Work: How Confident People Make Powerful* Companies (San Francisco: Jossey-Bass, 1998); Timothy A. Judge and Joyce E. Bono, "Relationship of Core Self-Evaluations Traits—Self-Esteem, Generalized Self-Efficacy, Locus of Control, and Emotional Stability—With Job Satisfaction and Job Performance: A Meta-Analysis," *Journal of Applied Psychology,* February 2001, pp. 80–92.

14. Duffy et al., "The Moderating Role of Self-Esteem and Neuroticism," 2006, p. 1069.

15. Quoted in Carlin Flora, "The Measuring Game: Why You Think You'll Never Stack Up," *Psychology Today,* September/October 2005, p. 44.

16. "Building Self-Esteem: A Self-Help Guide," *Health* (athealth.com/Consumer/disorder/self-esteem.html), p.1.

17. Research mentioned in book review by E. R. Snyder in *Contemporary Psychology,* July 1998, p. 482.

18. "Better Self-Esteem," pp. 3–4.

19. Ibid, pp. 4–5.

20. Cited in "Self-Esteem: You'll Need It to Succeed," *Executive Strategies,* September 1993, p. 12.

21. Raudsepp, "Strong Self-Esteem Can Help You Advance."

22. "Building Self-esteem: A Self-Help Guide," *http://mentalhealth.samhsa.gov/,* p. 2, accessed September 7, 2007.

23. Marilyn E. Gist and Terence R. Mitchell, "Self-Efficacy: A Theoretical Analysis of Its Determinants and Malleability," *Academy of Management Review,* April 1992, pp. 183–211.

24. George P. Hollenbeck and Douglas T. Hall, "Self-confidence and Leader Performance," *Organizational Dynamics,* Issue 3, 2004, pp. 261–264.

25. Jay T. Knippen and Thad B. Green, "Building Self-Confidence," *Supervisory Management,* August 1989, pp. 22–27.

26. Quoted in "Entrepreneurs Need Attitude: Power of Being Positive Can Help You to Succeed In Spite of Setbacks," *Knight Ridder,* September 16, 2002.

27. John Derbyshire, *We Are Doomed* (New York: Crown Forum, 2009).

28. D. Brian McNatt and Timothy A. Judge, "Boundary Conditions of the Galatea Effect: A Field Experiment and Constructive Replication," *Academy of Management Journal,* August 2004, pp. 550–565.

29. Price Pritchett, *HardOptimism: Developing Deep Strengths for Managing Uncertainty, Opportunity, Adversity, and Change* (Dallas, TX: Pritchett, 2004), p. 16.

30. Frances Thornton, Gayle Privette, and Charles M. Bundrick, "Peak Performance of Business Leaders: An Experience Parallel to Self-Actualization Theory," *Journal of Business and Psychology,* Winter 1999, pp. 253–264.

31. Joshua D. Margolis and Paul G. Stoltz, "How to Bounce Back from Adversity," *Harvard Business Review,* January–February 2010. pp. 91–92.

32. Quoted in "Leading by Feel: Be Realistic," *Harvard Business Review*, January 2004, p. 28.

33. Daniel Goleman, Richard Boyatzis, and Annie McKee, "Primal Leadership: The Hidden Driver of Great Performance," *Harvard Business Review*, December 2001, pp. 42–51.

34. David A. Morand, "The Emotional Intelligence of Managers: Assessing the Construct Validity of a Nonverbal Measure of 'People Skills,'" *Journal of Business and Psychology*, Fall 2001, pp. 21–23.

35. Stefanie K. Johnson, "I Second That Emotion: Effects of Emotional Contagion and Affect at Work on Leader and Follower Outcomes," *Leadership Quarterly*, February 2008, p. 2.

36. Peter J. Jordan, Neal M. Ashkanasy, and Charmine E. J. Hartel, "Emotional Intelligence as a Moderator of Emotional and Behavioral Reactions to Job Insecurity," *Academy of Management Review*, July 2002, pp. 361–372.

37. "Leading by Feel: Train the Gifted," *Harvard Business Review*, January 2004, p. 31.

38. This is one of the major themes from Kevin R. Murphy, ed., *A Critique of Emotional Intelligence: What Are the Problems and How Can They Be Fixed?* (Mahwah, NJ: Lawrence Erlbaum, 2006).

39. Based to some extent on information synthesized in Dodge Fernald, *Psychology* (Upper Saddle River, NJ: Prentice Hall, 1997), pp. 562–563.

40. L. A. Burke and L. A. Witt, "Personality and High-Maintenance Employee Behavior," *Journal of Business and Psychology*, Spring 2004, pp. 349–363.

41. Timothy A. Judge and Remus Ilies, "Is Positiveness in Organizations Always Desirable?" *Academy of Management Executive*, November 2004, 152.

42. Ibid., pp. 153–155.

43. Judith Sills, "Take This Job and Love It," *Psychology Today*, November/December 2008, pp. 58–59.

44. "The 100 Best Companies to Work for 2008," pp. 61–94; Robert Levering and Milton Moskowitz, "The 100 Best Companies to Work for 2009: And the Winners Are . . ." *Fortune*, February 2, 2009, pp. 67–78.

45. Frederick P. Morgeson and Stephen E. Humphrey, "The Work Design Questionnaire (WDQ): Developing and Validating a Comprehensive Measure for Assessing Job Design and the Nature of Work," *Journal of Applied Psychology*, November 2006, pp. 1321–1339.

46. Mark C. Ehrant and Stefanie E. Nauman, "Organizational Citizenship Behavior in Work Groups: A Group Norms Approach," *Journal of Applied Psychology*, December 2004, pp. 960–974.

47. Nicole M. Dudley and Jose M. Cortina, "Knowledge and Skills That Facilitate the Personal Support Dimension of Citizenship," *Journal of Applied Psychology*, November 2008, pp. 1249–1270.

48. Research reported in "So What Do You Have to Do to Find Happiness?" *Sunday Times Magazine*, available at www.timesonline.co.uk, October 2, 2005; Amy Novotney, "The Happiness Diet: Sonjya Lyubomirsky Argues that Limiting Overthinking Can Improve Our Emotional Well-Being," *Monitor on Psychology*, April 2008, pp. 24–25.

49. Carlin Flora, "The Pursuit of Happiness," *Psychology Today*, January/February 2009, pp. 60–69.

50. The major sources of information for this list are Mihaly Csikzentmihalyi, "Finding Flow," *Psychology Today*, July/August 1997, pp. 46–48, 70–71; Flora, "The Pursuit of Happiness," pp. 60–69; Richard Corliss, "Is There a Formula for Joy?" *Time*, January 20, 2003, pp. 72–74; David G. Meyers, "Pursuing Happiness," *Psychology Today*, available at www.psychologytoday.com/articles; retrieved March 1, 2006; Martin Seligman, *What You Can Change and What You Can't* (New York: Knopf, 1994).

51. Cited in Novotney, "The Happiness Diet," p. 24.

52. Study cited in Alice Park, "The Happiness Effect. How Emotions and Even Behaviors Can Spread Like an Epidemic," *Time*, December 22, 2008; Maggie Fox, "Happiness Is Contagious, Study Finds," *Scientific American*, www.sciam.com. Accessed December 5, 2008.

53. Quoted in George Melloan, "The Rich Are Getting Richer, but So Are Others," *Wall Street Journal*, December 23, 2003, p. A15.

54. David T. Lykken, *Happiness: What Studies on Twins Show Us about Nature, Nurture, and Happiness Set Point* (New York: Golden Books, 1999), p. 67.

55. Jonathan Clements, "The Pursuit of Happiness: Six Experts Tell What They've Done to Achieve It," *Wall Street Journal*, December 6, 2006, p. D1.

56. Clements, "The Pursuit of Happiness," p. D1.

57. Martin Seligman, "Don't Diet, Be Happy," *USA Weekend*, February 4–6, 1994, p. 12.

58. Steven Reiss, "Secrets of Happiness," *Psychology Today*, January/February 2001, pp. 50–52, 55–56.

59. Corliss, "Is There a Formula for Joy?" p. 74.

60. Quoted in Flora, "The Pursuit of Happiness," p. 69.

61. Arthur C. Brooks, "Money Buys Happiness," *Wall Street Journal*, December 8, 2005, p. A16.

62. Jonathan Clements, "Money and Happiness: Here's Why You Won't Laugh All the Way to the Bank," *Wall Street Journal*, August 16, 2006, p. D1.

63. Sharon Begley, "Wealth and Happiness Don't Necessarily Go Hand in Hand," *Wall Street Journal* (Science Journal), August 13, 2004, p. B1.

64. Quoted in Corliss, "Is There a Formula for Joy?" p. 74.

65. Richard Carlson, *You Can Be Happy No Matter What: Five Principles Your Therapist Never Told You*, revised edition (Novato, CA: New World Library, 1997).

66. Ibid., p. 71.

Goal Setting and Motivation

THE IMPORTANCE OF PERSONAL GOAL SETTING

Everyone has dreams. These dreams may be for a college degree, a better life for loved ones, financial security, or the acquisition of material items such as a new car or home. Goal setting is the first step toward turning a dream into a reality. This important process provides focus and identifies specific steps that need to be accomplished. It is also a common practice used by successful individuals and organizations. A **goal** is a target. Think of a goal as a reward at the top of a ladder. Goals typically come in two forms: short-term goals and long-term goals. To reach a long-term goal, you need to progress up each step of the ladder. Each step contributes to the achievement of a goal and supports your personal values. More difficult goals typically take longer to achieve. Goals provide focus; increase self-concept; and help overcome procrastination, fear, and failure.

goal
A target.

INFLUENCES OF GOALS

When you set and focus on goals, career plans become more clear and meaningful. They motivate you to continue working to improve yourself and help you achieve, not just hope for, what you want in life.

Consider Cory's goals. At twenty-two years of age, Cory had only a high-school education. After working as a service clerk since graduating from high school, Cory decided to go to college to become a Certified Public Accountant (CPA). Cory's long-term goal is to finish college in five years. Self-supporting and having to work, Cory set a realistic goal to obtain an associate degree in accounting within three years. After achieving that goal, Cory found a good job, has a good income, and has more self-confidence. Still committed to becoming a CPA, Cory needs to earn a bachelor's degree and has set a goal to do that within two years. This is motivating Cory to perform well.

In Cory's example, as one goal was reached, Cory became more motivated and self-confident enough to set a higher goal. Achieving goals results in continually striving for improvement.

Goals can and should be set in all major areas of your life, including personal, career, financial, educational, and physical. Goals help maintain a positive outlook. They also contribute to creating a more positive perception of you and will result in improved human relations with others.

Talk It Out

Discuss one goal that can be set for this class.

HOW TO SET GOALS

As explained earlier, achieving short- and long-term goals is like climbing a ladder. Imagine that there is a major prize (what you value most) at the top of the ladder. The prize can be considered your long-term goal, and each step on the ladder is a progressive short-term goal that helps you reach the major prize.

Long-Term Career Goal

Write your long-term career goal.

_____

_____

_____

Set short-term and long-term goals and put them in writing. **Long-term goals** are goals that will take longer than a year to accomplish, with a realistic window of up to ten years.

To set a goal, first identify what you want to accomplish in your life. Write down everything you can think of, including personal, career, and educational dreams. Next, review the list and choose which items you most value. In reviewing your list, ask yourself where you want to be in one year, five years, and ten years. The items you identified are your long-term goals. Keep each goal realistic and something you truly want. Each goal should be challenging enough that you will work toward it but it should also be attainable. There should be a reason to reach each goal. Identify why each goal is important to you. This is a key step toward setting yourself up for success. Identify both opportunities and potential barriers toward reaching these goals. Remember Cory's goal to be a CPA? Cory believes becoming a CPA represents success. It is important to Cory, and it is a realistic goal that can be reached.

Short-term goals are goals that can be reached within a year's time. Short-term goals are commonly set to help reach long-term goals. Businesses often refer to short-term goals as **objectives,** because they are short-term, measurable, and have specific time lines. Short-term goals can be achieved in one day, a week, a month, or even several months. As short-term goals are met, long-term goals should be updated.

Just like long-term goals, short-term goals (objectives) must be realistic, achievable, and important to you. They need to be measurable so you know when you have actually reached them.

An additional long-term goal for Cory is to buy a car one year after graduation. Cory has set several short-term goals, one being to save a specific amount of money each month. To do this, Cory needs to work a certain number of hours each week. Cory also needs to be specific about the type of car, whether to buy used or new, and whether he needs to take out a loan. The answers to these questions will determine if the time frame is realistic and how much Cory needs to save every month.

A popular and easy goal-setting method is the SMART method. SMART is an acronym for "specific, measurable, achievable, relevant, and time-based." Clearly identify what exactly you want to accomplish and, if possible, make your goal quantifiable. This makes your goal specific. Also, make your goal measurable. Identify how you know when you have achieved your goal. Keep your goal achievable but not too easily attainable nor

long-term goal

A target that takes longer than one year to accomplish.

short-term goals

Goals that can be reached within a year's time (also called objectives).

objectives

Short-term goals that are measurable and have specific time lines that occur within one year.

Short-Term Goals

Using your long-term career goal from Skill-Building Exercise 7-1, identify at least three short term goals.

_____

_____

_____

SMART Goals

Rewrite the goals into SMART goals.

_____

_____

_____

SMART goal

A goal that is specific, measurable, achievable, relevant, and time-based.

too far out of reach. A good achievable goal is challenging, yet attainable and realistic. Relevant personal goals have meaning to its owner. The goal should belong to you, and you should have (or have access to) the appropriate resources to accomplish the goal. Finally, **SMART goals** are time-based. Attaching a specific date or time period provides a time frame for achieving the goal. For example, instead of writing, "I will become a manager in the future," write, "I will become a manager with a top accounting firm by the beginning of the year 2018." After you have written a goal, give it the SMART test to increase its probability for success.

After you have written your goals in a positive and detailed manner, there are a few additional aspects of goal setting to consider. These include owning and being in control of your goals.

Owning the goal ensures that the goal belongs to you. You should decide your goals, not your parents, spouse, significant other, friends, relatives, or anyone else who may have influence over you. For example, if Cory goes to college because it is a personal dream to be a CPA, that goal will be accomplished. However, if Cory becomes a CPA because it was Cory's parents' idea to be a CPA, this would not be Cory's goal and it would make it harder to accomplish this goal.

Control your goal by securing the right information necessary to accomplish it. Know what resources and constraints are involved, including how you will be able to use resources and/or get around constraints. If your goal is related to a specific career, identify what attaining it will require in regard to finances, education, and other matters. Clarify the time needed to reach these goals by writing them as short-term or long-term goals. Referring back to the concept of locus of control, remember that not every factor is within your control. Therefore, be flexible and maintain realistic control over your goal.

GOALS AND MOTIVATION

Some attitudes and values are held more strongly than others. Likewise, some goals are pursued more strongly than others. If goals are to be achieved, they must be specific and realistic.

Figure 7-1 shows the relationship between values and goals. Once a goal has been identified, values provide the impetus—the start—toward its attainment. A person fulfills a desire or a need by engaging in goal-seeking behavior—leading, one hopes, to goal achievement. The seeking of goals requires energy, commitment, and motivation. As the figure shows, not all goals are reached; some have to be reformulated or dropped. Accordingly, flexibility is one of the most important characteristics of goal setting. Knowing when to

FIGURE 7-1 Interactive Values–Goals Model

let go of unrealistic or unattainable goals is an important step in the management process. Goals should be constantly re-evaluated and updated. If goals are not fully committed to (and are not exciting and compelling), they have little chance of being attained. Here are some pointers to remember when you set goals:

- What benefits will attaining this goal bring to my life?
- What will I be able to do once this goal is achieved?
- How will this goal benefit others?
- How will I feel when I achieve this goal?

Goals Versus Habits

Goals are things people are trying to accomplish. Not all behaviors are goal-directed or goal-activated; some are simply basic survival behaviors or habits.

Habits are repetitive, often unconscious, patterns of behavior. Confucius said that "the nature of men is always the same; it is their habits that separate them." In other words, habits are unique to the individual. They can be either good or bad. Whining and overeating are bad habits. Treating others with respect and being courteous are good habits. Goals encompass more than just the fulfillment of immediate wants and needs. For example, graduating from law school is a goal, but eating a hamburger is not—it is the fulfillment of a need, hunger.

habits
Repetitive, often unconscious, patterns of behavior.

Goal Attributes

Not all goals are created equal; each has certain characteristics or attributes.

For example, goals vary in

- *Intensity:* Commitment, how much the goal is desired
- *Complexity:* Interrelationships, how many other goals are related to this goal
- *Priority:* How important the goal is
- *Resource Use:* How much the goal is going to cost (energy, money) and how many resources will be put into this goal versus other pursuits
- *Timing:* How long it will take to attain the goal

These goal attributes are demonstrated by the behaviors of Roger and Stephanie. Roger, a 22-year-old, worked for eight years during high school and college and saved every penny to buy a BMW. Stephanie, also a 22-year-old, made finding the best job her top priority during her senior year in college and put that goal before everything else. Roger and Stephanie directed their attention, developed strategies, mobilized effort, and persisted until they reached their goals. Both were highly goal-driven.

Goals provide a sense of purpose and direct behavior toward a positive end result (e.g., a BMW, a job). Although goals are generally regarded as positive, problems can surface when goal conflict occurs in families or other groups. Conflict develops when goals compete with or subvert each other. If a family's goal is to eat a leisurely Sunday dinner together, conflict may arise if the teenage children would rather skip dinner and spend the afternoon with their friends.

Types of Goals

For purposes of discussion, it is useful to categorize goals. Among the ways goals can be categorized are the following:

- *By time:* short-term, intermediate, or long-term
- *By role:* personal, professional, societal, or familial
- *By type:* primary or secondary

Each category will be discussed in the following sections.

Striving for goals has often been compared to climbing a mountain.

Source: Dorling Kindersley Media Library.

Goals and Time. In terms of time required for attaining, goals can be separated into short-term, intermediate, and long-term goals.

- Short-term goals usually take less than three months to accomplish.
- Intermediate goals can usually be achieved in three months to one year.
- Long-range goals usually take more than one year to achieve.

A fall-semester college junior may have a short-term goal of finishing current course-work, an intermediate goal of finishing the year, and a long-term goal of graduating. College students are assumed to be long-term planners. For example, job recruiters typically ask college interviewees, "What do you plan to be doing five years from now?" With this question, the recruiter finds out whether the student has thought ahead, is a realistic planner, and is ambitious.

For some, goal setting is a luxury reserved for the wealthy and the better educated. Certainly, setting long-term goals implies a secure future or at least one partially under control. Low-income families do not always have the resource base to think beyond fulfilling daily needs and short-term goals. In terms of Maslow's hierarchy of needs, they are concerned with the physiological and safety levels of the hierarchy. For them, planning six months in advance would be a luxury. At the other extreme are celebrities who may have managers or agents, who plan their schedules five years or more in advance.

Goals and Roles. Another way to categorize goals is by role. In this typology, goals can be personal, professional, societal, or familial. Personal goals include such things as learning how to swing dance, ski, skydive, or ride a horse. Professional goals are related to one's job or career; they might include improving skills like using computers, writing a contract, or conducting an interview. You achieve career success when you reach the goals you have set for yourself. Because the goals are individually defined, they vary among individuals. For some, success is defined by titles, awards, frequent promotions, or salary increases; for others, these are less important, and success is defined by completion of difficult projects, for example. One way to envision success is to pay attention to the winners in a field—who they are and what they do—with special focus on those with continued success rather than a singular moment of glory.

Societal goals are commonly held by the greater society; they include such goals as having a full-time job by a certain age, marrying, having children, and retiring. Familial goals are related to being a son, daughter, parent, or other family member. At any one time, a person might be achieving personal and professional goals while considering or reacting to societal or familial goals.

An individual can have one or two goals, or dozens. People who are professionally oriented may have many career goals and may ignore personal goals. Other people may have no professional or career goals (their job is simply something they do to earn money, so they go home at five o'clock and forget about it) and are interested only in personal or family goals. Management comes into play because goals must be prioritized and strategies developed.

What is most important? How do people go about getting what they want?

Goals by Type: Primary and Secondary Goals. Goals can also be categorized as primary and secondary. For example, if a person's primary goal is to attain a college degree, then his or her secondary goals would include being accepted into a college, passing courses, and completing graduation requirements. Secondary goals are smaller; they motivate and collectively add up to the primary goals.

Setting Goals

The beneficial effect of goal setting on task performance is one of the most validated concepts in psychology. Simply stated, people accomplish more when they set goals. Studies of survivors of concentration camps found that those who had a purpose for living and well-defined goals were better able to withstand deprivation, including starvation and torture, than those without goals. Many of the survivors said that their main goal was to see their family again.

To be helpful, goals should have certain characteristics. First, goals must be reasonable, attainable, and within the resources of the goal setter. For example, a person who wants to buy a house must have the resources to make a down payment and meet the monthly payments. Saying that goals should be realistic and attainable does not mean that they should be easy to accomplish. Indeed, goals should present some challenge for the goal setter.

Goals should also be clearly formed. When asked about his formula for success, J. Paul Getty, one of the richest men in the world, said, "Rise early. Work late. Strike oil." The importance of having clear, specific goals cannot be overemphasized. The goal of buying a new car is too vague because it cannot be visualized. The goal of buying a certain type of car in one year is effective, however, because it allows the mind to form a specific picture of the car and focuses attention on actions and a time frame for achieving the goal. When the person sees advertisements for that particular car or passes one in a parking lot, her decision to try to buy that car will be reinforced. Of course, during the year she may decide on another model, but at least initially, visualizing a specific car can be helpful. Goals provide an avenue for freedom, a sense of control, and, as noted before, a sense of direction and purpose.

REACHING GOALS MEANS SETTING GOALS

The most successful people are those who set goals—for their career, for their self-development, and for their personal life. A manageable way to set goals is to first set your goals for the next 3 years or more and then to break these goals into smaller chunks.

Studies show that articulating significant goals leads to an increase in a person's effort and thus success (Hamner & Harnett, 1974; Locke, 1968). Further, this success leads to higher self-esteem, which contributes to future success!

Setting goals is critical, and here are some questions to consider: First, why are you setting a goal? Is your goal a personal one, a performance goal for the course, or a long-term goal, such as completing your degree?

Think about a day when you woke up and had no idea of what you wanted to accomplish. Did you accomplish anything? More often than not, the answer to that question is no. Explore what you want: is it earning an A, reaching for a better work/life balance, or just improving your participation in class? Then divide each goal into smaller, more immediately manageable parts and plan how you will attain each one. You may feel more comfortable setting mostly short-term goals or you may prefer to take the long view, but whatever you do, have goals.

Have you ever ended a day after completing all your goals and felt fantastic and invigorated? If the answer is yes, it is probably because you accomplished your goals and you felt successful.

Steps in Goal Setting

When setting a goal, follow the **SMART** model: Specific, Measurable, Attainable, Realistic, and Timely. For example, you had set the goal of *acquiring an education* or you would not be in school.

Let's apply the **SMART** model to that goal:

Goal:	Acquire an education
Specific:	Gain an associate's degree within 2 years of beginning a program
Measurable:	Measure by assessing whether the degree is complete within 2 years
Attainable:	Do you have the resources in place to pursue this goal?
Realistic:	Is this a realistic goal at this time in your life, given what you have going on?
Timely:	Two years is normally what would be required to complete an associate's degree, so this is a realistic time frame.

The preceding list outlined a long-term goal. Now break the goal into smaller parts:

Goal:	Finish 30 credits my first year (you fill in the following sections)
Specific:	
Measurable:	
Attainable:	
Realistic:	
Timely:	

Now break the goal into smaller parts:

Goal:	Finish my first class within 3 months
Specific:	
Measurable:	
Attainable:	
Realistic:	
Timely:	

Finally, *even more* specifically: with a grade of no less than a B

Goal:	Finish my first class within 3 months
Specific:	
Measurable:	
Attainable:	
Realistic:	
Timely:	

Here's the bottom line: You know how you eat an elephant: one bite at a time. Set your goals, determine the reasons for them, and then establish manageable subgoals.

When each of us started our academic programs, we had no idea if we could complete them. But we were motivated and we set goals. Each of us decided we would complete one class at a time. And here we are, finished with the programs.

For more information on setting goals, do an online search for *SMART* and *goal setting*. Many wonderful resources are available to you. There are also additional goal worksheets found at the back of the book.

Optimism, Goals, and Well-Being. In *Authentic Happiness* Martin Seligman, a past president of the American Psychological Association and professor of psychology at the University of Pennsylvania, says that happiness and optimism are essential for a good and successful life. He is a leader in the positive psychology movement, which looks at what is right with people rather than at what is wrong. **Optimism** is a tendency or a disposition to expect the best outcome or to think hopefully about a situation. According to Seligman, flexible optimism—optimism with its eyes open—provides limitless benefits. He adds that habits of thinking and living need not go on forever; in other words, people are not stuck with their pasts, but can learn from them. The kinds of phrases associated with optimism include a person saying or thinking

optimism

A tendency or a disposition to expect the best outcome or to think hopefully about a situation.

- "I'm usually lucky."
- "I'm talented."
- "My rival is no good."
- "I'm smart."
- "I'm good at lots of things."
- "I give everything my best shot."
- "I have a lot to look forward to."

In pursuit of understanding the linkages between health and illness, other researchers have explored the relationship between optimism and general well-being. *An optimist is more likely to think that goals are reachable.* A study by scientists at the

Mayo Clinic in Rochester, Minnesota, revealed that optimists had 19 percent greater longevity, in terms of their expected life span, than did pessimists (Danner, Snowdon, & Friesen, 2001).

A Harris poll revealed that Americans are happier and more optimistic about their future than are most Europeans. Within Europe, the percentage of people who were very satisfied with their lives varied from 64 percent in Denmark to 26 percent in Finland. Those in between included people in the Netherlands, Luxembourg, Sweden, United Kingdom, Ireland, and Austria. More Irish and Swedish respondents, than the Americans, to the telephone poll said their lives had improved more in the last five years. The most optimistic European country was Spain. Germany and the Mediterranean countries indicated that they were less happy and optimistic than Northern Europeans [1]. Not all evidence comes from surveys. In anecdotal evidence, curators at a New York retrospective exhibition of works by Matisse and Picasso noted that the colorful, cheerful works of Matisse drew far more visitors than did Picasso's (Goodale, 2003).

Importance of Challenge. The novelist F. Scott Fitzgerald said, "Vitality shows in not only the ability to persist but the ability to start over." Starting over is a challenge. Goals need to be reset. How does a person choose the goals to pursue? The study of management assumes that if someone devotes the required resources, plans well, and makes the sacrifices necessary, almost anything is achievable. Consequently, people should aim high and set goals that force them to do their best. By creating a challenge, goals affect performance by directing attention, mobilizing effort, increasing persistence, and motivating strategy development.

Anthony, who is single and 25, listed his goals for the next five years as follows:

- *Career/work:* Own a fitness center
- *Home:* Have a nice apartment
- *Personal:* Date someone seriously, have lots of friends
- *Leisure:* Work out every day

Do Anthony's goals seem realistic for someone who works full-time in a gym and has a college degree in nutrition and fitness? How much does it cost to open a fitness center? To rent an apartment? What secondary goals does he need to accomplish to reach his primary goal of owning a center? Anthony's goal of owning a fitness center has created a very real challenge for him and forced him to develop strategies to achieve it. Anthony's strategies include learning all he can from the gym where he now works before opening his own fitness center and fulfilling his secondary goals of paying off his college loans and credit cards and saving money.

Plans for Attaining Goals. Once goals are set, a plan for achieving them must be developed. Planning includes all managerial activities that determine results and the appropriate means to achieve those results. It involves the following four steps:

1. Set specific goals and prioritize them.
2. State the goals clearly and positively. For example, "I will be a nonsmoker by January 1"—not "I will stop smoking." "I will lose five pounds"—not "I will lose weight."
3. Forecast possible future events and the resources that will be needed to deal with them. This entails determining both the level of material resources that will be needed and the amount of effort that will be required.
4. Implement the plan by following through with goal-directed activity.

Note that the planning process begins with prioritizing goals. Prioritizing involves ranking goals by the degree of commitment to them. Commitment is the sense of obligation one feels toward the goal. If a goal is not enticing or inspiring, something is wrong, and the goal will not serve its function of motivating the person to put in greater effort.

Prioritizing forces people to decide what they really want and how they are going to get it.

A new year-eve tradition in many countries is to make resolutions, which are types of goals. About 23 percent of new year resolutions are broken in the first week, 45 percent by the end of January (Norcross & Prochaska, 1998). People fail to keep their resolutions because their willpower is not enough, they haven't chosen realistic resolutions, and they fail to devise a plan to work on them every day. Even the smallest step makes a difference in the long run.

Obstacles to Goal Achievement.   Crises happen. All the goal setting in the world cannot stop unplanned events from altering the course of resource use. Obstacles to achieving goals include, but are not limited to, the following: time, parents, family, rules, peers, social customs, demands, imagination, money, health, and natural disasters (e.g., hurricanes, tornadoes, floods).

Obstacles alone do not determine the fate of human goal-seeking behavior. Instead, the way people perceive and react to obstacles will determine whether they will reach their goals. One way to overcome obstacles is to divide larger goals into smaller ones, which allows a person to make progress a little at a time. It also helps to find a trusted, nonjudgmental friend who is willing to discuss about one's goals and periodically check on how projects are going.

Monitoring one's progress by marking deadlines on a calendar is useful as well. Everyone should also be aware of when roadblocks are likely to occur. Is it at the start of projects? In the middle? At the end?

Resilience is defined as the ability to overcome obstacles and to achieve positive outcomes even after experiencing extreme difficulties. Individual traits associated with resilience include intelligence, competence, a good-natured temperament, internal locus of control, and self-esteem. Researchers also note that relationships can help protect a person from stress and promote positive growth. In other words, resilience—although an inner ability (involving courage and fortitude)—is helped and accentuated by strong, encouraging relationships. Parents play an important role in helping children learn how to be resilient.

Renee Spencer (2000) found a number of studies indicating that one supportive adult can provide good outcomes for children coping with poverty, problems at school, malnutrition, separation from a parent, marital discord at home, divorcing parents, and mental illness of parents. David Elkind, a Tufts University professor emeritus and author of *The Hurried Child*, says that teens experience what he calls "an imaginary audience," a feeling that others are watching and evaluating them. There are so many changes going on in teens' lives that they tend to over-magnify other peoples' judging of them. They are often sensitive and self-absorbed during these years. He believes that parents can help during these trying times, while their children are making transitions to the next stage. The reason why this is especially important is that the teens are laying the groundwork for how they will deal with future life transitions when they are on uncertain social ground.

Finally, goals need to be re-evaluated. Resistance to goals may mean that it is time to change them or to take a break. Pursuing goals requires energy.

CRITICAL THINKING

Joel Haber, author of *Bullyproof Your Child for Life,* says that a resilient child knows how to handle letdowns. To boost resilience, he says, first show you understand the child's feelings and then ask what he or she has done to rebound. Brainstorm together how to deal with bullying situations and setbacks. Do you remember any bullying situations or disappointments that you or your friends experienced? What steps were taken to bounce back? How long did it take?

Needs for Achievement: The n Ach Factor. People can make themselves miserable trying to set impossible goals such as earning a million dollars in a year or insisting that everyone be happy every minute of a family vacation. Healthy goals are a little out of reach, but they are not impossible dreams. Compromise and flexibility rule the day.

In a classic study, David McClelland, a Harvard psychologist, stressed that individuals vary in their need for achievement, which he called "n Ach" (McClelland, 1961). He found that each individual has a different level of motivation for overcoming obstacles, desiring success, and expending effort to seek out difficult tasks and do them well as quickly as possible. He emphasized that the achievement motive can be expressed as a desire to perform in terms of a standard of excellence or to be successful in competitive situations. *You can choose to act in ways that help you achieve goals.*

A person possessing high n Ach takes moderate risks, not high risks as one might assume. This phenomenon can be demonstrated by the ring-toss game. Low achievers will stand very near the peg and drop the rings over it or stand far away and wildly throw the ring. High achievers will carefully calculate the exact distance from the peg that will challenge their abilities, yet will give them a chance for success. Thus, low achievers take a low or high risk, and high achievers take a moderate risk. Research indicates that this pattern holds true in most walks of life and for children as well as for adults.

Lifestyles, Goals, and Feedback. Each person has a basic notion of what he or she wants in the way of food, shelter, and companionship; these basic needs evolve into a more complicated set of needs, which combine to form a lifestyle. Likewise, goals often start simple and evolve into more complicated notions. A recent college graduate might want a job, any job, to get started and then, as time goes by, develop a more specific definition of what a good job is.

Forming short-term goals is a way to conserve the time and energy needed to reach long-term goals. Short-term goals have the advantage that they can be completed fairly rapidly, giving a sense of accomplishment. An author, for example, might write newspaper and magazine articles during the same time period she is writing a novel so that she always has something in process, in the mail, or in print.

Individuals and families need feedback to determine whether their goals are viable or need to be changed. Goals are generally thought of as positives in life, but they can be self-defeating if they are too difficult. Goals can also have a negative effect if they cause people to be so single-minded that they do not see other possible goals or courses of action that might be better. Both depression over failure to be an overnight success and single-minded focus on today without a thought of the future can be self-defeating. Listening to feedback helps keep goals realistic and on track.

College Students' Values, Goals, and Life Outcomes

Psychologists conducted a fascinating study of college yearbook photos. They compared the actual life outcomes of women students whose photos showed a genuine smile, called the "Duchenne smile" (named after its discoverer Guillaume Duchenne), with those of women whose photos showed an inauthentic smile, called the Pan American smile. In the Duchenne smile the corners of the mouth turn up, and the skin around the corners of the eyes crinkles (like crow's feet). The muscles that control these functions are connected, and it is difficult to voluntarily control them. The Pan Am smile is a fake smile named after flight attendants posing in advertisements for a now-defunct airline.

Dacher Kelter and LeeAnne Harker (2001) of the University of California, Berkeley, found that the women with a Duchenne smile were more likely to be married, to stay married, and to experience more personal well-being over a 30-year period. Others questioned whether the results had more to do with good looks than with the smile itself, so the investigators went back and rated how pretty each of the women seemed. They found that looks had nothing to do with good marriages or life satisfaction. It turns out that a genuinely smiling woman was simply more likely to be well-wed and happy (Seligman, 2002).

College students' values, goals, and life outcomes have been the subject of many studies. Researchers have found that, overall, college men and women have similar goal and value

The happiest college students surround themselves with family and friends.

Source: Corbis RF.

orientations. For many students, the college years serve as a transition stage between living at home with parents and living on their own—a physical and emotional bridge between childhood and adulthood. Studies have shown that a close family relationship leads to more successful adjustments to college life for students.

Because college is a transitory stage, goal instability is not unusual during the college years. For example, students may change their majors and career choices many times. Thus, goal instability is common for college students and can even be helpful, but it can also be uncomfortable for the individual experiencing it. Nearly one-third of college freshmen do not return for their sophomore year and the numbers on this are much higher for community colleges than for four-year colleges. The main reasons they do not return are job opportunities, financial circumstances, and personal situations.

Although college students have the same array of values as the general population, the media and social scientists over the years have attempted to categorize the general typology of college students by decade or by generation. For example, students of the 1950s have been described as conservative and conforming, as holders of traditional values who had only slight concern for societal problems. After graduation, a typical student from these years went on to become the join organizations and businesses grew incredibly. Many obeyed the laws and fulfilled obligations, as they strove to get ahead. In this decade, significant advances occurred in civil rights.

The late 1960s and the early 1970s are considered years of unrest and change, characterized by the advent of the peace movement, the women's liberation movement, and other societal causes. College students challenged traditional ways of doing things, questioned material gain, and extolled the virtues of individual rights and freedom. Values changed on campuses, exemplified by the widespread introduction of coeducational dormitories and the end of dress codes and curfews.

In the 1980s, the college culture moved back to material goals; students flooded business schools and became more egocentric and less committed to broad sociopolitical change. The students of the 1980s grew up during the downsizing of certain businesses; they saw or experienced social and personal insecurities. As a result, they became more savvy and more skeptical (Stoneman, 1998). A shift that occurred in the 1980s is that since 1982 more women than men have received bachelor's degrees and this trend continues today.

How will current students compare with those of previous generations? One trend is the growing concern over crime in the greater society and on college campuses. Another trend is the increasing acceptance of fragmentation and extreme individuality. As a counterpoint, some studies report a return to social engagement and involvement by college students. What do you think? Are college students becoming more socially engaged? Do they have lots of friends? Do they do a lot of volunteer or service work? Or, is it going the other way? One wonders because there are indications of increased disengagement experienced in many areas of life: political apathy, retreat from church attendance, eroding union membership, and the decline of bridge clubs, dinner parties, Rotary clubs, volunteering, and blood donation (Putnam, 2000). College students are often at the forefront of new thought and action. They can change the direction of the greater society.

Students of the 1990s enjoyed the benefits of a strong economy and a thriving labor market. They had more money than their predecessors. Colleges realized that standard dormitory style living was becoming less attractive to students.

In the 21st century, many colleges in the United States and other countries built or renovated dormitories to allow for more single rooms with bathrooms ensuite, which means each room has its own bathroom, or shared suites with fewer students per suite; others allowed privatized on-campus apartments. The ups and downs of the economy affected the amount of choice in the job market, although, as always, some majors led to more job opportunities than others. In 2003, The Association of American Medical Colleges reported that more women than men applied to and were accepted at medical schools for the first time ever.

Through intensive orientation programs, parents' weekends, and other such activities, campuses are trying to build a sense of community and purpose that meets students' needs. It appears that the happiest people (college students or anyone else) *"surround themselves with family and friends, don't care about keeping up with the Joneses next door, lose themselves in daily activities, and most important, forgive easily"* (Elias, 2002, p. A1).

The next section on motivation has enormous implications for college students. How do they stay in college and keep studying so that they reach their goal of a college degree? Motivation is a combination of individual qualities and parental and society's reaction or support.

Motivation

"The biggest human temptation is . . . to settle for too little," says Thomas Merton, an American monk and spiritual writer. Thomas Edison and his staff tried 3,000 ways to perfect a lightbulb before they found one that worked. A motivated person has to take risks and overcome obstacles to achieve goals. The word "motivation" comes from the Latin word *movere* (to move). In management, **motivation** refers to movement toward goals or other desired outcomes and also to vigor, drive, persistence, creativity, direction, and sustained energy. One of the goals of nurturing children is to build each child's strengths and virtues as well as helping them find a niche where their positive traits can develop to the fullest. For example, in the 2008 Olympics, the parents of one of the gold medal winners in gymnastics mortgaged their house three times to pay for her coaching. They were definitely motivated, as was their daughter.

Motivated individuals work hard. Motivation is shown through tasks, in mastery, in practice, and in public performances, such as piano recitals, debates, or sports events. Motivated individuals develop exceptional qualities usually through an investment of time, staying in the field as long as it takes to build expertise. They keep going despite setbacks. How they do this is one of the puzzles in the study of human excellence.

motivation

Movement toward goals or other desired outcomes.

Expertise is "the characteristics, skills, and knowledge that distinguish experts from novices and less experienced people. In some domains there are objective criteria for finding experts, who are consistently able to exhibit superior performance for representative tasks in a domain. For example, chess masters will almost always win chess games against recreational chess player in chess tournaments, medical specialists are far more likely to diagnose a disease correctly than advanced medical students, and professional musicians can perform pieces of music in a manner that is unattainable for less skilled musicians" (Ericsson, Charness, Feltovich, & Hoffman, 2006, p. 3).

Motivation is not just a personal or family construct; it is the driving force behind companies and organizations. Car salespeople try to sell a certain number of cars per month to reach a quota. Real estate salespeople try to sell enough houses in a year to be on the "million dollar seller list." Girl Scouts try to sell enough boxes of cookies to go to camp. Goal setting's potential for improving productivity is so well established that it is rarely questioned as a management technique.

Motivation is a process rather than an end state. The process begins with an unsatisfied need that creates tension. This tension drives a person to undertake a search for resources or information. Hence, the person does not feel satisfied until her or his need is fulfilled or the goal attained. Internal and external factors contribute to the motivation to achieve goals.

Intrinsic motivation involves the underlying causes and the internal need for competence and self-determination. It refers to the pleasure or value a person derives from the content of work or activity. If a student works hard in school, the satisfaction he or she derives from learning and mastering a subject provides the intrinsic motivation to keep learning. **Extrinsic motivation** involves forces external to the individual—environmental factors such as titles, raises, preferred offices, promotions, and other forms of rewards. For a student, extrinsic motivators include "A" grades, the honor roll, the dean's list, the honor society, scholarships, and other forms of recognition for academic performance.

A study by Regina Conti asked 110 adults about their summer projects: which ones they wanted to do (primarily intrinsically motivated) and which ones they had to get done (primarily extrinsically motivated). The results showed that projects that participants had to do as compared with those they wanted to do were started and finished more often and had more time devoted to them each week (Conti, 2000). Is this finding surprising to you? It actually adds to the procrastination literature by suggesting that extrinsic motivation is essential to getting things done. Summer projects such as those for self-improvement or enjoyment are most likely to be put off.

Both intrinsic and extrinsic motivation are important for goal achievement. Children need to experience both types. They should feel good about learning (intrinsic), and they should also feel that their efforts are recognized by others (extrinsic). In the home, the family members who do housework should feel good about living in a clean house and about having their cleaning efforts noticed and appreciated by other family members.

One of the unsolved mysteries of life is why some people have more intrinsic motivation than others. These people work hard regardless of the number and quality of external rewards. Are the answers in genetics? In early childhood experiences? In work experiences? In temperament? Psychologists and others are searching for the answers

expertise

The ability to perform tasks successfully and dependably.

intrinsic motivation

The underlying causes of and the internal need for competence and self-determination. The pleasure or value a person derives from the content of work or activity.

extrinsic motivation

Outside rewards or motivation.

to these questions. Often the intrinsically motivated individual values mastery, or values the learning process over achievement of outcomes. The tennis champion Monica Seles described her intrinsic motivation:

> I really never enjoyed playing matches, even as a youngster. I just love to practice and drill and that stuff. I just hate the whole thought that one [player] is better than the other. It drives me nuts. (Vecsey, 1999, p. D1)

Far more is known about the working of extrinsic motivation than about intrinsic motivation. For example, extrinsic rewards are most effective if

- They are specific.
- They are given immediately after a good work performance.
- They are valued by the receiver.
- They are equitable.

What one person perceives as a reward may not be perceived as desirable by another. For example, a trip at the company's expense to a convention might be valued by one employee, but considered a burden by another. As another example, a child who does not like candy will not view a candy bar as a reward. Rewards should be appropriate to the individual and at the same time be perceived as equitable by the family or organization.

Concept Review and Reinforcement

E-Resources

Many Web sites, some interactive, discuss values, happiness, and attitudes. An ongoing study of authentic happiness including a Signature Strengths Survey can be found at **www.authentichappiness.org**. The main polling organizations report regularly on the state of values and attitudes in the United States and in other countries. As more companies (the primary financial supporters of the polling organizations) sell globally, the polling organizations have found that they need to collect more values and attitude data internationally. Government agencies and politicians also use data from polling organizations.

Key Terms

goal 232
long-term goal 233
short-term goals 233
objectives 233
SMART goal 234

habits 235
optimism 239
suggested activity 241
resilience 241
motivation 244

expertise 245
intrinsic motivation 245
extrinsic motivation 245

Summary

Values, attitudes, and goals are three of the most important concepts in the management process. Values are principles that guide behavior. They stand for what is worthwhile, preferred, and consistent. Sometimes there is a gap between values and actual behavior. Environmental conditions affect behavior. A value chain is the glue that holds families together, in time and in space. Value chain analysis is borrowed from business and refers to organizations that have a shared vision and value set.

Families play a fundamental role in the formation and transmission of values. Parents, as the primary socializers of children, greatly influence their children's values. Goals are end results, the things people are working toward.

Motivation and optimism are important elements in achieving goals. Researchers study motivation in many fields from sports to chess and are interested in what drives individuals to perform at high levels. Is it intrinsic (inward) versus extrinsic (outside rewards, praise, recognition) motivation or a combination?

Attitudes are states of mind or feelings, likes and dislikes, about some matter. They often occupy a middle ground between values and goals.

A value or goal change recently evidenced is the growing number of people in their 20s, married or not, buying houses, a sign of settling down and establishing roots. This trend may be a symbol of optimism, an area studied by many psychologists including Martin Seligman. A Harris poll revealed that Americans are generally happier with their lives and more optimistic about their futures than are Europeans, although results vary depending on the individual nation within Europe.

When two people date or become close friends, they try to find out about each other's values, attitudes, and goals, especially the one's they have in common. Do they enjoy the same activities? Do they have similar or compatible views about leisure, work, religion, and politics? Do they have similar reactions to situations and people?

Selecting one's life goals is a complex task, which is easier for people who have been raised in a supportive environment. Whether an individual family is supportive depends to a great extent on how much energy and enthusiasm family members invest in each other, especially in each other's goals. The family that encourages children's development by attending school plays and sporting events, music recitals, award ceremonies, and science and history fairs is a family that recognizes and rewards hard work, performance, and achievement. To be achievable, goals should be clear, realistic, and challenging, but not overwhelming.

Most importantly, goals should be flexible. The motivation process starts with an unsatisfied need or unmet demand that creates tension and results in a satisfied need and reduced tension. Goals give direction to life, and values serve as a guide. However, goals cannot be set without consideration of resource availability.

Questions for Discussion and Review

1. According to the book *The Necessary Revolution: How Individuals and Organizations are Working Together to Create a Sustainable Future*, businesses form value chains, a shared commitment to goals built around time and space. Likewise, families form multigenerational value chains. Describe a shared value in your family which has endured over time.

2. Women have outnumbered men on college campuses since 1979 and on graduate campuses since 1984. This has resulted in more women than men receiving bachelor's degrees every year since 1982. Why do you suppose this happens?

3. What does Henry David Thoreau mean when he says, "My life is like a stroll upon the beach, as near the ocean's edge as I can go." How does this statement relate to the ideas in the chapter?

4. Why does Martin Seligman say that optimism is essential for achieving goals?

5. What is the difference between intrinsic and extrinsic motivation? Which one do researchers know more about? Why?

Sample Exam Questions

1. The _____ identifies who you believe controls your future.

2. _____ is an individual's perception of how he or she views himself or herself, while _____

   _____ is one's belief of how others view him or her.

3. When one understands one's own _____ and

   _____, it is much easier to understand reactions to others' actions.

4. A/An _____ affects group performance,

   which, in turn, impacts organizational performance.

5. Dealing with negative baggage involves _____ your past,

   _____, and moving _____

   _____.

6. Past influences shape our _____

7. Goals need to be set so you can become _____.

8. Long-term goals are set to be reached after _____.

9. Short-term goals should usually be reached _____.

10. _____ help you reach long-term goals.

11. When setting a goal, there must be a time frame; it must be _____

    _____ and _____.

12. _____ will help you decide what needs

to be done and in what order.

13. To give up one thing for another is known as a/an _____.

14. Goals should be challenging but _____.

15. It is important to put goals into _____.

16. When creating a life plan, consider the following three areas:

_____

_____

_____

Career Goal Setting   By (Student Name)

This writing assignment guides you through the process of creating goals. Remember that these goals must be realistic, attainable, important to you, and measurable. Be as specific as possible in every paragraph.

Identify and write your five-year and one-year career goals here. Identify what kind of job and what title you want, in what city you want to work, whom you want to work for, and why you chose this goal. Use the SMART method.

Five-Year Goal

Paragraph 1:	*In five years, I want to be . . .*

One-Year Goal(s)

Paragraph 2:	*In order to reach my five-year goal, I need to set the following sho rt-term goals:* Identify necessary steps to reach your five-year goal. Be specific with activities, resources, and time frames.
Paragraph 3:	*I am currently…* What are you currently doing to reach these short-term goals? Be specific with activities, resources, and time frames.
Paragraph 4:	*I will know I have reached these goals when…* Goals must be measurable. How will you know when you have reached each short-term goal? Be specific with activities, resources, and time frames.
Paragraph 5:	*I need the following resources to reach my goal:* Identify physical, financial, emotional, and social resources and where they will come from.
Paragraph 6:	*My priorities for reaching my goals are:* Have priorities set for reaching your goals. Include your trade-offs and the areas where you may need to be flexible.

REFERENCES

Rotter, J. B. "Generalized Expectancies for Internal versus External Control of Reinforcement." *Psychological Monographs*, Vol. 80, No. 1 (1966): 1–28.

Taylor, M. "Does Locus of Control Predict Young Adult Conflict Strategies with Superiors? An Examination of Control Orientation and the Organizational Communication Conflict Instrument." *North American Journal of Psychology*, Vol. 12, No. 3 (2010): 445–458.

Anderson, C. R. and Schneider, C. E. "Locus of Control, Leader Behavior and Leader Performance among Management Students." *Academy of Management Journal*, Vol. 21, No. 4 (1978): 690–698, doi:10.2307/255709

Bandura, A. "Self-efficacy". In V. S. Ramachaudran (Ed.), *Encyclopedia of Human Behavior*, Vol. 4 (New York: Academic Press 1994), pp. 71–81.

Bandura, A. "Human Agency in Social Cognitive Theory." *American Psychologist*, Vol. 44, No. 9 (1989): 1175–1184.

"Work-Family Conflicts Affect Employees at All Income Levels," *HR Focus* 87 (April 2010): 9.

Golden, E. Organizational Renewal Associates. 1971. Golden LLC, May 2011, www.goldenllc.com

Isabel Briggs, M. Introduction to Type: A Guide to Understanding Your Results on the Myers-Briggs Type Indicator (Mountain View, CA: CPP, Inc., 1998).

O'Reilly, C. A., III, Chatman, J., and Caldwell, D. F. "People and Organizational Culture: A Profile Comparison Approach to Assessing Person-Organization Fit." *The Academy of Management Journal*, Vol. 34, No. 3 (September 1991): 487–516.

Hoel, H., Glasco, L., Hetland, J., Cooper, C. L., and Einarsen, S. "Leadership Styles as Predictors of Self-reported and Observed Workplace Bullying." *British Journal of Management*, Vol. 21, No. 2 (2010): 453–468.

Newhouse, N. "Implications of Attitude and Behavior Research for Environmental Conservation." *Journal of Environmental Education*, Vol. 22, No. 1 (Fall 1990): 26–32.

Doran, G. T. "There's a S.M.A.R.T. Way to Write Management's Goals and Objectives." *Management Review*, Vol. 70, No. 11 (AMA FORUM, 1981): 35–36.

Platt, G. "SMART Objectives: What They Mean and How to Set Them." *Training Journal* (August 2002): 23.

Ajzen, I., & Fishbein, M. (1980). *Understanding attitudes and predicting social behavior*. Englewood Cliffs, NJ: Prentice Hall.

Buck, S. (2003). Building capacity through leadership development programs. *Journal of Family and Consumer Sciences*, 95(3), 8–11.

Condor, B. (2002, September 3). Find your strengths, then your happiness. *Tallahassee Democrat*, p. 4D.

Consumer demand. (2003). Retrieved September 3, 2003, from http://www.sric-bi.com/consulting/ConsumerDmd.shtml.

Conti, R. (2000). Competing demands and complimentary motives: Procrastination on intrinsically and extrinsically motivated summer projects. *Journal of Social Behavior and Personality, 15* (5), 47–59.

Cravatta, M. (1997, November). Hanging on to students. *American Demographics*, 41.

Csikszentmihalyi, M. (1997). *Finding flow*. New York: Basic Books.

Danner, D., Snowdon, D., & Friesen, W. (2001). Positive emotions in early life and longevity: Findings from the nun study. *Journal of Personality and Social Psychology, 80*, 804–813.

de Lisser, E. (2002, September 24). One-click commerce: What people do now to goof off at work. *The Wall Street Journal*, pp. A1, A8.

Elias, M. (2002, December 9). What makes people happy.*USA Today*, p. A1.

Elkind, D. (1988). *The hurried child*. Reading, MA: Addison-Wesley.

Ericsson, K. A., Charness, N., Feltovich, P., & Hoffman, R. (2006). *The Cambridge handbook of expertise and expert performance*. New York: Cambridge University Press.

Goodale, G. (2003, July 3). Sunny side up. *Christian Science Monitor*. Retrieved from www.csmonitor.com.

Haber, J. (2007). *Bullyproof your child for life*. New York: Penguin.

Harman, W. (1998). *Global mind change* (2nd ed.). San Francisco: Berrett-Koehler.

Kelter, D., & Harker, L. (2001). Expressions of positive emotion in women's college yearbook pictures and their relationship to personality and life outcomes across adulthood. *Journal of Personality and Social Psychology, 80*, 112–124.

Kono, T., & Lynn, L. (2007). *Strategic new product development for the global economy*. New York: Palgrave Macmillan.

Leung, S. (2003, July 16). New kids on the block. *The Wall Street Journal*, p. B1.

Leung, S. (2003, October 1). A glutted market leaves food chains hungry for sites. *The Wall Street Journal*, p. A1.

McClelland, D. (1961). *The achieving society*. New York: Van Nostrand Reinhold.

McIntosh, W., Martin, L., & Jones, J. (1997). Goal beliefs, life events, and the malleability of people's judgments of their happiness. *Journal of Social Behavior and Personality, 12*(2), 567–575.

Norcross, J., & Prochaska, J. (1998). *Changing for good*. New York: Avon.

Putnam, R. (2000). *Bowling alone*. New York: Simon & Schuster.

Ray, P. (1997). The emerging culture. *American Demographics, 29–34*, 56.

Rokeach, M. J. (1973). *The nature of human values*. New York: Free Press.

Senge, P., Smith, B., Kruschwitz, N., Laur, J., & Schley, S. (2008). *The necessary revolution: How individuals and organizations are working together to create a sustainable future*. New York: Doubleday.

Seligman, M. (2002). *Authentic happiness*. New York: Free Press.

Spencer, R. (2000). *A comparison of national psychologies*. Project Report, No. 5, Wellesley, MA: Stone Center Working Paper Series.

Stoneman, B. (1998, December 4). Beyond rocking the ages: An interview with J. Walter Smith. *American Demographics*, 1–7.

Taylor, H. (2003, May 21). *Americans are far more optimistic and have much higher life satisfactions than Europeans*. Retrieved March 22, 2004, from http://www.harrisinteractive.com.

Vecsey, G. (1999, September 3). Seles feels windy blast from past. *New York Times*, p. D1.

Zaslow, J. (2003, February 6). Ready to pop the question? Hold off until you've done the interrogation. *The Wall Street Journal*, p. D1.

Allen, E & Seaman, J. (2010). Class differences: Online education in the United States. Babson Research Group.

Allen, I., Garrett, R., and Seaman, J. (2007). Blending in: The extent and promise of blended education in the United States. Retrieved March 5, 2011, from http://sloanconsortium.org/sites/default/files/Blending_In.pdf

American Library Association. (1998). Information literacy defined. Retrieved March 5, 2011, from http://www.ala.org/ala/mgrps/divs/acrl/standards/informationliteracycompetency.cfm#ildef

Annetta, L. (2006). Serious games: Incorporating videogames in the classroom. Retrieved November 23, 2010, from http://net.educause.edu/ir/library/pdf/eqm0633.pdf

Baikie, K., and Wilhelm, K. (2005). Emotional and physical health benefits of expressive writing. *Advances in Psychiatric Treatment, 11*, 338–346. Retrieved August 23, 2007, from http://apt.rcpsych.org/cgi/content/abstract/11/5/338

Betts, K. (2010, Winter). Online Education: Meeting Educational and Workforce Needs through Flexible and Quality Degree Programs. Retrieved May 18, 2011 from http://www.ijournalccc.com/articles/issue_24/betts-lynch.html

Brown, M., and Diaz, V. (2010). Blended learning: A report on the ELI focus session. Retrieved March 5, 2011, from http://net.educause.edu/ir/library/pdf/ELI3023.pdf

Bureau of Labor Statistics. (1999). 1999 Education requirements and job growth. Retrieved December 9, 2004, from http://www.bls.gov/opub/ted/1999/Dec/wk1/art02.htm

Bureau of Labor Statistics. (2004). Projected employment in high-paying occupations requiring a bachelor's or graduate degree. Retrieved March 12, 2005, from http://www.bls.gov/opub/ted/2004/mar/wk3/art03.htm

Bureau of Labor Statistics. (2011), Introduction, p. 20. http://www.bls.gov

Carnevale, D. (2005). Employers still prefer traditional degrees over online learning, study finds. *The Chronicle of Higher Education, 52* (5), A43.

Center for Media Literacy. *Vision & Mission*. Retrieved March 5, 2011, from http://www.medialit.org/about-cml

Dictionary.com Unabridged. (vol. 1.1). (2007). Random House, Inc. Retrieved June 3, 2007, from http://dictionary.reference.com/browse/plagiarism

Framework for 21st Century Learning. (2004). Retrieved November, 23, 2010, from http://www.p21.org/index.php?option=com_content&task=view&id=254&Itemid=120

Gardner, H. (1983). *Frames of mind: The theory of multiple intelligences*. New York: Basic Books.

Gross, R. (1999). *Peak learning*. New York: Tarcher/Penguin.

Hamner, W., and Harnett, D. (1974). Goal setting, performance, and satisfaction in an interdependent task. *Organizational Behavior and Human Performance, 12*, 217–230.

Hill, L. (2001). Learning styles: An examination of learning styles and my personal discovery of my own. Retrieved June 6, 2007, from http://www.authorsden.com/visit/viewarticle.asp?id=1421

IES National Center for Education Statistics—Fast Facts. (n.d.). Retrieved March 5, 2011, from http://nces.ed.gov/fastfacts/display.asp?id=80

Internet Tutorials: Boolean searching on the Internet: A primer in Boolean logic. (n.d.). Retrieved August 23, 2007, from http://www.internettutorials.net/boolean.html

Kerka, S. (1996). Journal Writing and Adult Learning. ERIC Digest No. 174. ERIC Clearinghouse on Adult Career and Vocational Education. Retrieved August 23, 2007, from http://www.ericdigests.org/1997–2/journal.htm

Locke, E. (1968). Towards a theory of task motivation and incentives. *Organizational Behavior and Human Performance, 3*, 157–189.

Myers & Briggs Foundation. (n.d.). Retrieved June 3, 2007, from http://www.myersbriggs.org

Nagel, D. (2010). The future of e-learning is more growth. The Journal. Retrieved February 26, 2011 from http://thejournal.com/articles/2010/03/03/the-future-of-e-learning-is-more-growth.aspx

Nagel, D. (2011). Online learning set for explosive growth as traditional classrooms decline. Retrieved February 27, 2011, from http://campustechnology.com/articles/2011/01/26/online-learning-set-for-explosive-growth-as-traditional-classrooms-decline.aspx

Nagel, D. (2010). The future of e-learning is more growth. *The Journal*. Retrieved February 26, 2011 from http://thejournal.com/articles/2010/03/03/the-future-of-e-learning-is-more-growth.aspx

National Center for Education Statistics. (n.d.). Retrieved June 15, 2007, from http://nces.ed.gov

Ragan, L. Best practices in online teaching—pulling it all together—teaching blended learning courses. Retrieved March 5, 2011, from http://cnx.org/content/m15048/latest/

Rhodes, J. (1998). Vision, reading, and computer uses: An interview with distinguished optometrists. Retrieved June 25, 2007, from http://webword.com/interviews/williams.html

Rowland, G., Lederhouse, A., and Satterfield, D. (2004). Powerful learning experiences within coherent learner groups. *Performance Improvement Quarterly, 17* (2), 46–65. Retrieved June 15, 2007, from ProQuest. http://onlinelibrary.wiley.com/doi/10.1111/j.1937–8327.2004.tb00307.x/abstract

The Sloan Consortium. (2007). Retrieved June 15, 2007, from http://www.sloan-c.org *Trends in blended learning research report 2006*. (2006). Retrieved March 5, 2011, from http://www.elearningguild.com/research/archives/index.cfm?id=102&action=viewonly

Using wildcards. (n.d.). Retrieved June 15, 2007, from http://apps.caes.uga.edu/impact/searchhelp.cfm

Ethics and Values

Touring the grounds of Electronic Recylers International in Fresno, California, is unnerving, like an unarmed walk through a prison yard. Tattooed, muscular men tear apart computers with hammers and electric grills. A guy with a gang insignia etched on his neck hoists a monitor over his head. Another rips the face off an old television with his bare hands. Machines chomp and grind gadgets and cell phones, spitting out shards of metal, plastic, and glass. Sharp edges and ex-cons are everywhere you look.

But ERI Chief Executive John S. Shegerian strolls comfortably through the place, dressed in a three-piece suit, green tie, cufflinks, and Rolex. Like a lot of like-minded businessmen these days, he espouses the importance of doing good while making a profit. "I believe you can recycle everything," he says, "including lives."

LEARNING
Objectives

After reading and studying this chapter and doing the exercises, you should be able to

1. Recognize the importance of ethical behavior for establishing good interpersonal relationships in organizations.
2. Describe why the character trait of virtuousness contributes to being ethical in the workplace.
3. Identify job situations that often present ethical dilemmas.
4. Use a systematic method for making ethical decisions and behaving ethically.

Shegerian aims to be the biggest among the 700 or so electronic recyclers in the United States. He's already a leader in California, which in 2006 banned all electronics from its landfills. Electronics can contain toxins such as cadmium, mercury, and chromium. ". . ."

"Electronics are the fastest-growing solid waste stream in the world," he says. ". . ."

At a big enough scale, Shegerian hopes to stanch the flow of electronic waste exported to poor countries overseas. Over the next three years, Americans will throw out maybe 110 million computers, 80 million television sets, and 350 million cell phones. The majority of electronics recyclers don't even bother recycling this waste. They just ship it to India, Southeast Asia, China, and Africa. Organizations such as Basel Action Network and Greenpeace say the workers in those countries are often children making pennies a day. They troll mounds of garbage in search of computers and TVs. Lacking proper tools to tear open computer shells, they burn the plastic to get to the valuable stuff inside, breathing noxious fumes. They dip circuit boards in acid and melt lead in the same pans they use to cook their meager meals. They toss any remains back on the pile, where toxins seep into water supplies. ". . ."

Shegerian wants to open his next few recycling centers in rusty, neglected neighborhoods. It's all very much in keeping with his drive to rehabilitate whatever he comes in contact with: people, places, things. One-third of ERI's 200 full- and part-time employees are in its "second chance" program, which includes ex-cons and former addicts. It so happens these workers have a 17% turnover rate, half that of other employees.[1] ". . ."

character trait

An enduring characteristic of a person that is related to moral and ethical behavior.

The scenario just described illustrates that some business people make it their mission in life to engage in activities that will help the environment as well as downtrodden people. As such they are being highly ethical on the job, as well as being socially responsible. (We are making the value judgment here, that preserving the environment and helping to rehabilitate ex-cons are ethical acts. Some people might disagree.)

People performing all types of work need a good sense of ethics (and etiquette) to be successful. Also, you often need to have an ethical reputation to get the job you want. *Ethics* refers to moral choices, or what is good and bad, right and wrong, just and unjust, and what people should do. Ethics is the vehicle for turning values into action. If you value fair play, you will do such things as giving honest performance evaluations to members of your group.

We study ethics here because a person's ethical code has a significant impact on his or her interpersonal relationships. This chapter's approach will emphasize the importance of ethics, common ethical problems, and guidelines for behaving ethically. Self-Assessment Quiz 8-1 gives you the opportunity to examine your ethical beliefs and attitudes.

The Ethical Reasoning Inventory

Directions: Describe how well you agree with each of the following statements, using the following scale: disagree strongly (DS); disagree (D); neutral (N); agree (A); agree strongly (AS). Circle the number in the appropriate column.

		DS	D	N	A	AS
1.	When applying for a job, I would cover up the fact that I had been fired from my most recent job.	5	4	3	2	1
2.	Cheating just a few dollars in one's favor on an expense account is okay if a person needs the money.	5	4	3	2	1
3.	Employees should report on each other for wrongdoing.	1	2	3	4	5
4.	It is acceptable to give approximate figures for expense account items when one does not have all the receipts.	5	4	3	2	1
5.	I see no problem with conducting a little personal business on company time.	5	4	3	2	1
6.	Just to make a sale, I would stretch the truth about a delivery date.	5	4	3	2	1
7.	I would fix up a purchasing agent with a date just to close a sale.	5	4	3	2	1
8.	I would flirt with my boss just to get a bigger salary increase.	5	4	3	2	1
9.	If I received $400 for doing some odd jobs, I would report it on my income tax return.	1	2	3	4	5
10.	I see no harm in taking home a few office supplies.	5	4	3	2	1
11.	It is acceptable to read the e-mail messages and faxes of coworkers, even when not invited to do so.	5	4	3	2	1
12.	It is unacceptable to call in sick to take a day off, even if only done once or twice a year.	1	2	3	4	5
13.	I would accept a permanent, full-time job even if I knew I wanted the job for only six months.	5	4	3	2	1
14.	I would first check company policy before accepting an expensive gift from a supplier.	1	2	3	4	5
15.	To be successful in business, a person usually has to ignore ethics.	5	4	3	2	1
16.	If I felt physically attracted toward a job candidate, I would hire that person over a more qualified candidate.	5	4	3	2	1
17.	On the job, I tell the truth all the time.	1	2	3	4	5
18.	If a student were very pressed for time, it would be acceptable to either have a friend write the paper or purchase one.	5	4	3	2	1
19.	I would be willing to put a hazardous chemical in a consume product if the product makes a good profit for the company.	5	4	3	2	1
20.	I would never accept credit for a coworker's ideas.	1	2	3	4	5

Total Score _____

Scoring and Interpretation: Add the numbers you have circled to obtain your total score.

90–100 You are a strongly ethical person who may take a little ribbing from coworkers for being too straitlaced.

60–89 You show an average degree of ethical awareness, and therefore should become more sensitive to ethical issues.

41–59 Your ethics are underdeveloped, but you at least have some awareness of ethical issues. You need to raise your level of awareness of ethical issues.

20–40 Your ethical values are far below contemporary standards in business. Begin a serious study of business ethics.

WHY BE CONCERNED ABOUT BUSINESS ETHICS?

LEARNING OBJECTIVE 1

When asked why ethics is important, most people would respond something to the effect that "Ethics is important because it's the right thing to do. You behave decently in the workplace because your family and religious values have taught you what is right and wrong." All this is true, but the justification for behaving ethically is more complex, as described next.[2]

A major justification for behaving ethically on the job is to recognize that people are motivated by both self-interest and moral commitments. Most people want to maximize gain for themselves (remember the expectancy theory of motivation?). At the same time, most people are motivated to do something morally right. As one of many examples, vast numbers of people donate money to charity, although keeping that amount of money for themselves would provide more personal gain.

Many business executives want employees to behave ethically because a good reputation can enhance business. A favorable corporate reputation may enable firms to charge premium prices and attract better job applicants. A favorable reputation also helps attract investors, such as mutual fund managers who purchase stock in companies. Certain mutual funds, for example, invest only in companies that are environmentally friendly. Managers want employees to behave ethically because unethical behavior—for example, employee theft, wasting time on the job, and lawsuits—is costly.

Behaving ethically is also important because many unethical acts are illegal as well, which can lead to financial loss and imprisonment. According to one estimate, the cost of unethical and fraudulent acts committed by U.S. employees totals $400 billion per year. A company that knowingly allows workers to engage in unsafe practices might be fined, and the executives may be held personally liable. Furthermore, unsafe practices can kill people. In recent years many people have perished in night club fires because there was only one door in operation, or unsafe pyrotechnics were on the premises. The financial scandals in recent years that resulted in major losses for millions of investors stemmed in part from financial managers making such risky investments that they were unethical. Securities were sold to the public that were based on loans to consumers with very poor credit ratings.

A subtle reason for behaving ethically is that high ethics increases the quality of work life. Ethics provides a set of guidelines that specify what makes for acceptable behavior. Being ethical will point you toward actions that make life more satisfying for work associates. A company code of ethics specifies what constitutes ethical versus unethical behavior. When employees follow this code, the quality of work life improves. Several sample clauses from ethical codes are as follows:

- Demonstrate courtesy, respect, honesty, and fairness.
- Do not use abusive language.
- Do not bring firearms or knives to work.
- Do not offer bribes.
- Maintain confidentiality of records.
- Do not harass (sexually, racially, ethnically, or physically) subordinates, superiors, coworkers, customers, or suppliers.

To the extent that all members of the organization abide by this ethical code, the quality of work life will improve. At the same time, interpersonal relations in organizations will be strengthened.

WHY WE HAVE SO MANY ETHICAL PROBLEMS

LEARNING OBJECTIVE 2

To become more skilled at behaving ethically, it is important to familiarize yourself with common ethical problems in organizations. Whether or not a given situation presents an ethical problem for a person depends to some extent on its **moral intensity**, or how deeply others might be affected.[3] A worker might face a strong ethical conflict about dumping mercury into a water supply but would be less concerned about dumping cleaning fluid. Yet both acts would be considered unethical and illegal. Here we first look at why being ethical is not as easy as it sounds. We then look at some data about the frequency of ethical problems and an analysis of predictable ethical temptations, and also examine the subtle ethical dilemma of choosing between rights.

moral intensity

In ethical decision making, how deeply others might be affected by the decision.

Why Being Ethical Isn't Easy

As analyzed by Linda Klebe Treviño and Michael E. Brown, behaving ethically in business is more complex than it seems on the surface for a variety of reasons.[4] To begin with, ethical decisions are complex. For example, someone might argue that hiring children for factory jobs in overseas countries is unethical. Yet if these children lose their jobs, many would starve or turn to crime to survive. Second, people do not always recognize the moral issues involved in a decision. The home-maintenance worker who finds a butcher knife under the bed might not think that he has a role to play in perhaps preventing murder. Sometimes language hides the moral issue involved, such as when the term "file sharing" music replaces "stealing" music.

Another complexity in making ethical decisions is that people have different levels of moral development. At one end of the scale, some people behave morally just to escape punishment. At the other end of the scale, some people are morally developed to the point that they are guided by principles of justice and want to help as many people as possible. The environment in which we work also influences whether we behave ethically. Suppose a restaurant owner encourages such practices as serving customers food that was accidentally dropped on the kitchen floor. An individual server is more likely to engage in such behavior to obey the demands of the owner—even though the server knows that dangerous bacteria may have attached to the food.

A fundamental reason that being unethical is not always easy is that some people have a predisposition to be unethical. The predisposition works almost like a personality trait, compelling certain people to be devious. A person with a **utilitarian predisposition** believes that the value of an act's outcomes should determine whether it is moral.[5] A server with this predisposition might be willing to serve food that dropped on the floor so long as no customer became sick or sued the restaurant. A small business owner with a utilitarian predisposition might be willing to sell fake luxury goods on the Internet so long as nobody complained and he or she was not caught. When asked about why he sold imitation watches, one vendor said, "What's the difference? My watches look like the real thing, and they tell time."

Another major contributor to ethical problems is the same factor that motivates people to do many things—acting out of self-interest. John Bogle, the founder and former chief executive of the Vanguard Groups of Mutual Funds, believes that self-interest contributed to the financial scandals of recent years. "But self-interest got out of hand. It created a bottom-line society in which success is measured in monetary terms. Dollars became the coin of the new realm. Unchecked market forces overwhelmed traditional standards of professional conduct, developed over centuries."[6] Another take on self-interest is that employee fraud intensifies during difficult financial times where workers are experiencing financial pressures in their personal lives. Among these frauds are check-forgery schemes, petty-cash thefts, and taking money from fabricated customer returns.[7] All of these schemes are illegal as well as unethical.

A Survey of the Extent of Ethical Problems

The ethical misdeeds of executives have received substantial publicity in recent years. However, ethical violations by rank-and-file employees are widespread, with stealing and sexual harassment making the list. Figure 8-1 presents data about unethical behavior noticed by employees. As found in other surveys, lying is another widespread ethical problem in the workplace. Lying to either employees or outsiders was observed by 31 percent of employees. These findings might suggest that workers are observant of ethical problems, and willing to note them on a survey.

Frequent Ethical Dilemmas

Certain ethical mistakes, including illegal actions, recur in the workplace. Familiarizing oneself can be helpful in monitoring one's own behavior. The next subsections describe a

FIGURE 8-1 Questionable Workplace Behavior as Reported by Employees

Despite a heightened emphasis on business ethics following scandals earlier this decade, a significant number of employees say they still witness questionable workplace behavior. Here is the percentage of employees who say they observed certain behaviors in the previous year, according to a survey of 2,852 workers by the Ethics Resource Center.

Lying to employees	19%
Engaging in conflicts of interest	16%
Lying to outside stakeholders	12%
Engaging in health and safety violations	11%
Producing poor product quality	9%
Stealing	9%
Sexual harassment	7%

Source: National Business Ethics Survey, Ethics Resource Center, Arlington, VA, 2009 survey. (www.ethics.org).

number of common ethical problems faced by business executives as well as by workers at lower job levels.[8] Figure 8-2 outlines these problems.

Illegally Copying Software. A rampant ethical problem is whether or not to illegally copy computer software. According to the Business Software Alliance, approximately 35 percent of applications used in business are illegal.[9] Figure 8-3 offers details about and insight into this widespread ethical dilemma.

Treating People Unfairly. Being fair to people means equity, reciprocity, and impartiality. Fairness revolves around the issue of giving people equal rewards for accomplishing equal amounts of work. The goal of human resource legislation is to make decisions about people based on their qualifications and performance—not on the basis

FIGURE 8-2 Frequent Ethical Dilemmas

Many ethical temptations face the individual on the job, forcing him or her to think through ethical issues practically every workday.

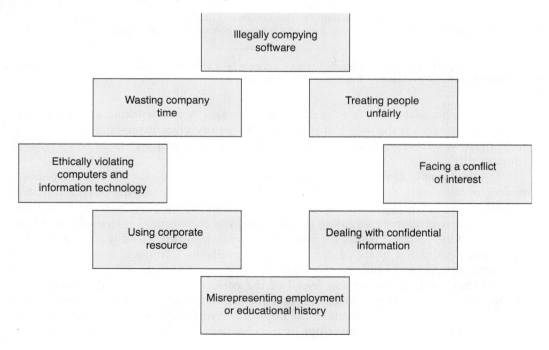

FIGURE 8-3 The Top Ten Reasons for Illegally Copying Software (and Why None of Them Are Good Enough)

A flagrant unethical and **illegal** job behavior is unauthorized copying of software. When confronted with software pirating, people are quick to rationalize their actions. Here are the top ten defenses of software pirates. (None of them are likely to hold up if you are caught.)

1. **I'm allowed to make a backup disk in case something happens to the original, so it must be okay to use it on another machine.** A backup is strictly a backup to be used on the same computer. The original should be safely locked away, and the copy should be stored away only as a backup.
2. **I didn't copy it—a friend gave it to me.** Technically you are right. You would not be guilty of illegally copying software in this case, although your friend would. However, since illegally copied software is regarded as stolen property, you are just as guilty as you would be for stealing it in the first place.
3. **My boss (or department head, or instructor) told me to. It's that person's problem.** The defense "I was just following orders" is a weak one. Complying with your boss's demands to commit an illegal act does not get you off the hook. You could be fired for obeying an order to commit a crime.
4. **I bought the software; shouldn't I be able to do what I want with it?** Software is seldom ever sold to individuals. What is sold is a license to use the software, not full rights to do what you want. When you break open the package, the law assumes that you have agreed to abide by those terms.
5. **It's not like I'm robbing somebody.** Software is intellectual property just like a song, a book, an article, or a trademark. You are taking bread from the table of software engineers when you copy their work.
6. **It's OK if you're using the software for educational purposes.** If education were a justification for theft, driving instructors would be able to steal cars with impunity. There is a doctrine of **fair use** that allows some limited use of written materials in classrooms without permission from the copyright holder.
7. **I needed it, but the price was unreasonably high. If I had to actually pay for it, there is no way I could ever afford it.** Software prices are high for the same reason the price of houses is high: both require a lot of highly skilled labor to create. You cannot steal a DVD player just because you cannot afford one.
8. **I didn't know it was illegal.** Unauthorized duplication of software is a felony in many states and provinces. State and federal laws provide for civil and criminal penalties if you are convicted. It would be difficult to convince a judge or jury that you had no idea that unauthorized copying was illegal.
9. **It's only illegal if you get caught.** Criminal behavior is illegal whether or not you are caught. If you do get caught illegally copying software, you could face fines, imprisonment, and/or civil penalties. Some educational institutions take disciplinary action against software pirates, including suspension.
10. **Oh, come on, everyone is doing it.** This excuse has been used to justify everything from speeding to lynching. The popularity of a criminal act does not make it legal.

Source: The Top Ten Reasons for Illegally Copying Software (and Why None of Them Are Good Enough). Rochester Institute of Technology. Reprinted with permission.

of demographic factors such as gender, race, or age. A fair working environment is where performance is the only factor that counts (equity). Employer–employee expectations must be understood and met (reciprocity). Prejudice and bias must be eliminated (impartiality).

Treating people fairly—and therefore ethically—requires a de-emphasis on political factors, or favoritism. Yet this ethical doctrine is not always easy to implement. It is human nature to want to give bigger rewards (such as fatter raises or bigger orders) to people we like.

A major contributor to treating people unfairly is cronyism, or giving jobs to people who have done personal favors for you. Often the unqualified friend is given a position when competent, and qualified candidates are available. Cronyism is often practiced in government, where heads of government agencies are sometimes appointed mostly because they are a supporter and friend of the person in power. Earl E. Devaney, the Interior Department's inspector general said at a hearing, "Simply stated short of a crime, anything goes at the highest levels of the Department of the Interior." Among the ethical charges were cronyism and cover-ups of incompetence.[10] Cronyism is also sometimes found in business, with buddies, relatives, and lovers often being chosen over more qualified workers for a variety of positions.

Sexually Harassing Coworkers. Sexual harassment is a source of conflict and an illegal act. Sexual harassment is also an ethical issue because it is morally wrong and unfair. All acts of sexual harassment flunk an ethics test. Before sexually harassing another person, the potential harasser should ask, "Would I want a loved one to be treated this way?"

Facing a Conflict of Interest. Part of being ethical is making business judgments only on the basis of the merits or facts in a situation. Imagine that you are a supervisor who is romantically involved with a worker within the group. When it comes time to assign raises, it will be difficult for you to be objective. A **conflict of interest** occurs when your judgment or objectivity is compromised. Conflicts of interest often take place in the sales end of business. If a company representative accepts a large gift from a sales representative, it may be difficult to make objective judgments about buying from the rep. Yet being taken to dinner by a vendor would not ordinarily cloud one's judgment. Another common example of a conflict of interest is making a hiring decision about a friend who badly needs a job, but is not well qualified for the position.

Blogging has created a new type of conflict of interest because many bloggers are paid for those kind, supposedly objective, comments they insert on the Internet about products and services. The Federal Trade Commission now requires bloggers to clearly disclose any payments or freebies they receive from companies for publishing reviews about their products or services. Penalties include a maximum fine of up to $11,000 per violation.[11]

Dealing with Confidential Information. An ethical person can be trusted by others not to divulge confidential information unless the welfare of others is at stake. Suppose a coworker tells you in confidence that she is upset with the company and is therefore looking for another job. Behaving ethically, you do not pass along this information to your supervisor even though it would help your supervisor plan for a replacement. Now suppose the scenario changes slightly. Your coworker tells you she is looking for another job because she is upset. She tells you she is so upset that she plans to destroy company computer files on her last day. If your friend does find another job, you might warn the company about her contemplated activities.

The challenge of dealing with confidential information arises in many areas of business, many of which affect interpersonal relations. If you learned that a coworker was indicted for a crime, charged with sexual harassment, or facing bankruptcy, there would be a temptation to gossip about the person. A highly ethical person would not pass along information about the personal difficulties of another person.

Misrepresenting Employment or Education History. Many people are tempted to distort in a positive direction information about their employment or education history on their job résumé, job application form, and during the interview. Distortion, or lying, of this type is considered to be unethical and can lead to immediate dismissal if discovered. Misrepresentation of credentials takes place at all job levels. Inflated credentials in the executive suite have been an embarrassment to many companies. A survey of 358 senior executives at 53 publicly traded companies has uncovered seven instances of inaccurate claims that an individual had received an academic degree. In recent years, misrepresentation of academic credentials has cost top corporate officials their positions at companies, including RadioShack Corp., vitamin maker Herbalife Ltd., and Usana Health Sciences, Inc.[12]

Using Corporate Resources. A corporate resource is anything the company owns, including its name and reputation. If Jake Petro worked for Ford Motor Company, for example, it would be unethical for him to establish a body shop and put on his letterhead and Web site, "Jake Petro, Manufacturing Technician, Ford Motor Company." (The card and Web site would imply that the Ford Motor Co. supports this venture.) Other uses of corporate resources fall more into the gray area. It might be quite ethical to borrow a laptop computer for the weekend from your employer to conduct work at home. But it

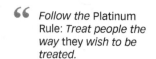
conflict of interest

A situation that occurs when a person's judgment or objectivity is compromised.

FIGURE 8-4   Eleven Commandments for Computer Ethics

1. Do not use a computer to harm other people. Avoid all obscene, defamatory, threatening, or otherwise harassing messages. Take precautions against others developing repetitive motion disorders.
2. Do not interfere with other people's computer work. (This includes intentionally spreading computer viruses.)
3. Do not snoop around in other people's files.
4. Do not use a computer to steal.
5. Do not use a computer to bear false witness.
6. Do not use or copy software for which you have not paid (see Figure 8-1).
7. Do not use other people's resources without authorization.
8. Do not appropriate other people's intellectual output.
9. Do not use the employer's computer for the personal promotion of commercial goods or services, unless granted permission by the employer.
10. Do think about the social consequences of the program you write.
11. Do use a computer in ways that show consideration and respect.

Source: Adapted and updated from Arlene H. Rinaldi and Florida Atlantic University, rinaldi@acc.fau.edu; "Code of Conduct for Computer and Network Use," *http://www.rit.edu/computerconduct.*

would be less ethical to borrow the laptop computer to prepare income taxes. In the latter case, you might be accused of using corporate resources for personal purposes. Loading personal software on company computers so that you can access your bank account and so forth also can be considered an ethical violation.

Ethically Violating Computers and Information Technology. As computers dominate the workplace, many ethical issues have arisen in addition to pirating software. One ethical dilemma that surfaces frequently is the fairness of tracking the Web sites a person visits and those he or she buys from. Should this information be sold, like a mailing list? The scams that appear on e-mail every day are another prime example of the unethical use of information technology. Another issue is the fairness of having an employee work at a keyboard for 60 hours in one week when such behavior frequently leads to repetitive motion disorder, vision problems, and back pain. Figure 8-4 lists some major ethical issues involved in computer use.

Wasting Company Time. Many workers waste company time in the pursuit of personal interests. Among these time wasters are making personal phone calls, shopping by phone or the Internet, visiting sports and pornography sites, talking about personal matters with coworkers, daydreaming, and spending long periods of time smoking outside the building. The problem has become so severe with cell phone calls and text messaging that many employers forbid the use of cell phones while working.

You may have observed that these common ethical problems are not always clear-cut. Aside from obvious matters such as prohibitions against stealing, lying, cheating, and intimidating, subjectivity enters into ethical decision making. Skill-Building Exercise 8-1 provides an opportunity to try out your ethical reasoning.

Choosing between Two Rights: Dealing with Defining Moments

defining moment

Choosing between two or more ideals in which one deeply believes.

Ethical decision making usually involves choosing between two options: one we perceive to be right and one we perceive to be wrong. A challenging twist to ethical decision making is to sort through your values when you have to choose between two rights, or two morally sound choices. Joseph L. Badaracco, Jr., uses the term **defining moment** to describe choosing between two or more ideals in which we deeply believe.[13] If you can learn to work through defining moments, your ethical skills will be enhanced. Let's first take a nonwork example to illustrate a defining moment.

The Ethics Game

Many companies teach ethics by asking small teams of employees to confront difficult scenarios such as those that follow. Discuss these ethical problems in teams. As you discuss the scenarios, identify the ethical issues involved.

Scenario 1: One of your assignments is to find a contractor to conduct building maintenance for your company headquarters. You invite bids for the job. High-Performance Cleaners, a firm staffed largely by teenagers from troubled families who have criminal records, bids on the job.

Many of these teenagers also have severe learning disabilities and cannot readily find employment. High-Performance Cleaners proves to be the second highest bidder. You:

A. advise High-Performance Cleaners that its bid is too high for consideration and that your company is not a social agency.

B. award the bid to High-Performance Cleaners and justify your actions with a letter to top management talking about social responsibility.

C. falsify the other bids in your report to management, making High-Performance Cleaners the low bidder—and thus the contract winner.

D. explain to High-Performance Cleaners that it lost the bid, but you will award the company a piece of the contract because of its sterling work with teenagers in need.

Scenario 2: You live in Texas, and your company sends you on a three-day trip to New York City. Your business dealings in the Big Apple will keep you there Wednesday, Thursday, and Friday morning. You have several friends and relatives in New York, so you decide to stay there until Sunday afternoon. Besides, you want to engage in tourist activities such as taking a boat tour around Manhattan and visiting Radio City Music Hall. When preparing your expense report for your trip, you request payment for all your business-related costs up through Friday afternoon, plus

A. your return trip on Sunday.

B. the return trip and the room cost for Friday and Saturday nights.

C. the return trip, one-half of your weekend food expenses, and two extra nights in the hotel.

D. the return trip and your food costs for the weekend (which you justify because you ate at fast-food restaurants on Wednesday, Thursday, and Friday).

Scenario 3: You are the leader of a self-managing work team in a financial services company. The work of your team has expanded to the point where you are authorized to hire another team member. The team busily interviews a number of candidates from inside and outside the company. The other team members agree that one of the candidates (Pat) has truly outstanding credentials. You agree that Pat is a strong candidate, yet you don't want Pat on the team because the two of you were emotionally involved for about a year. You think that working with Pat would disrupt your concentration and bring back hurtful memories. You decide to

A. tell the group that you have some negative information about Pat's past that would disqualify Pat for the job.

B. telephone Pat and beg that Pat find employment elsewhere.

C. tell the group that you agree Pat is qualified, but explain your concerns about the disruption in concentration and emotional hurt.

D. tell the group that you agree Pat is right for the position, and mention nothing about the past relationship.

Scoring and Observation: Scenario 1, about High-Performance Cleaners, raises dozens of ethical questions, including whether humanitarian considerations can outweigh profit concerns. Teams that chose "a" receive 0 points; "b", 20 points; "c", −10 points; "d", 10 points. (Answer "d" is best here because it would not be fair to give the bid to the second-highest bidder. However, you are still finding a way to reward the High-Performance Cleaners for its meritorious work in the community. Answer "c" is the worst because you would be outright lying.)

Scenario 2 raises ethical issues about using company resources. Teams that chose "a" receive 20 points; "b", −10 points; "c", −15 points; "d", 0 points. (Answer "a" is fairest because the company would expect to reimburse you for your roundtrip plus the expenses up through Friday afternoon. Answer "c" is the worst because it would be unjustified for you to be reimbursed for your vacation in New York.)

Scenario 3 raises issues about fairness in making selection decisions. Teams that chose "a" receive −20 points; "b", −10 points; "c", 15 points; "d", 0 points. (Answer "c" is the most ethical because you are being honest with the group about the reason you do not wish to hire Pat. Answer "a" is the most unethical because you are telling lies about Pat. Furthermore, you might be committing the illegal act of libel.)

Imagine yourself as a basketball referee in a league for boys 10 years old and younger. Luis, the smallest boy on the team, has a self-confidence problem in general, and he has not scored a basket yet this season. This is the final game of the season. The other team is ahead by 10 points with one minute to go. Luis lets fly with a shot that goes into the basket, but his right heel is on the line. If the goal is allowed, Luis will experience one of the happiest moments in his life, and his self-confidence might increase. You strongly believe in helping people grow and develop. Yet you also strongly believe in following the rules of sports. What should you do?

You may have recognized that a defining moment is a role conflict in which you have to choose between competing values. A CEO might deeply believe that she has an obligation

Dealing with Defining Moments

The toughest ethical choices for many people occur when they have to choose between two rights. The result is a defining moment, because we are challenged to think in a deeper way by choosing between two or more ideals. Working individually or in teams, deal with the two following defining moments. Explain why these scenarios could require choosing between two rights, and explain the reasoning behind your decisions.

Scenario 1: You are the manager of a department in a business firm that assigns each department a fixed amount of money for salary increases each year. An average-performing member of the department asks you in advance for an above-average increase. He explains that his mother has developed multiple sclerosis and requires the services of a paid helper from time to time. You are concerned that if you give this man an above-

average increase, somebody else in the department will have to receive a below-average increase.

Scenario 2: You are the team leader of an e-tailing (retail selling over the Internet) group. In recent months each team member has been working about 60 hours per week, with little prospect of the workload decreasing in the future. Since the e-tailing project is still losing money, higher management insists that one person be dropped from the team. One member of the team, Mildred, is willing to work only 45 hours per week because she spends considerable time volunteering with autistic children. Mildred's work is satisfactory, but her output is the lowest in the group because of her shorter number of working hours. You must make a decision about whether to recommend that Mildred be dismissed.

to the stockholders to make a profit, and also believe in being generous and fair toward employees. However, to make a profit this year she will be forced to lay off several good employees with long seniority. The CEO now faces a moment of truth. Badaracco suggests that the individual can work through a defining moment by discovering "Who am I?" You discover who you are by soul searching answers to three questions:

1. What feelings and intuitions are coming into conflict in this situation?
2. Which of the values that are in conflict are the most deeply rooted in my life?
3. What combinations of expediency and shrewdness, coupled with imagination and boldness, will help me implement my personal understanding of what is right?

Skill-Building Exercise 8-2 gives you an opportunity to deal with defining moments. The three questions just asked could help you find answers, but do not be constrained by these questions.

GUIDELINES FOR BEHAVING ETHICALLY

LEARNING OBJECTIVE 3

Following guidelines for ethical behavior is the heart of being ethical. Although many people behave ethically without studying ethical guidelines, they are usually following guidelines programmed into their minds early in life. The Golden Rule exemplifies a guideline taught by parents, grandparents, and kindergarten teachers. In this section, we approach ethical guidelines from five perspectives: (1) developing virtuousness, (2) following a guide to ethical decision making, (3) developing strong relationships with work associates, (4) using corporate ethics programs, and (5) following an applicable professional code of conduct.

Developing Virtuousness

A deep-rooted approach to behaving ethically is to have strong moral and ethical principles, or to be virtuous. A person of high virtue has good character, and genuine motivation and intentions. A major problem in becoming virtuous is to agree on what values constitute virtuousness. Management professor Edwin A. Locke has prepared a modern analysis of what values constitute virtue in a business environment.[14] Here we highlight his findings because they are representative of what constitutes virtuousness. Other observers might have a different list of virtuous values.

1. **Rationality** is a principle that leads to being virtuousness. Being rational includes taking reality (facts) seriously, thinking hard, thinking long range, and thinking of the consequences of one's actions. A rational parachute technician would not ship a defective

parachute just because it was close to quitting time, and he did not want to work late. And we hope that the manager is rational (and therefore ethical) when writing performance evaluations.

2. **Honesty**, the refusal to fake reality, is a value that contributes directly to ethical behavior. Being dishonest can also be illegal, such as when a company lies to the Internal Revenue Service about expenses it incurred or hides revenue when preparing a tax report. Dishonesty in terms of making false statements about the financial health of an enterprise has been one of the most frequent business frauds. Being caught lying can lead to dismissal at many employers. An example of such a lie would be blaming someone else for a mistake of your own. *Integrity* means loyalty to one's rational convictions, or sticking with one's principles. If you believe that favoritism is immoral, then you would not recommend that the company hire a friend of yours who you know to be unqualified.

3. **Independence** refers to the responsibility of using your own rational judgment rather than relying too heavily on the thinking of others. In personal life, being independent means not relying too heavily on others for permanent support. A worker with a strong value of independence would not readily go along with the thinking of the group if he or she had a better idea.

4. **Productivity** means creating, or obtaining through trade, the materials values your life requires. You are therefore virtuous if are productive on the job and contribute enough to be worth of your compensation. *Justice* refers to looking at the facts of the character and achievements of others and judging them objectively. To be just is to be fair, such as willing to pay somebody what they are worth, or pay a fair price for merchandise. When a big company executive "squeezes" a supplier to the point that the supplier can barely make a profit, the executive is not practicing justice.

5. **Forgiveness** is a virtue providing the breach of morality was not too severe, such as forging an employee who at a sandwich without paying when eating food without paying was not authorized. *Pride* in the context of virtues refers to working to perfect one's moral character. You would thus be proud because you are virtuous.

The above values that contribute to being virtuousness are useful in the study of human relations because they all translate into interpersonal skills, such as knowing how to be productive and treat people justly.

Following a Guide to Ethical Decision Making

A powerful strategy for behaving ethically is to follow a guide for ethical decision making. Such a guide for making contemplated decisions includes testing ethics. **Ethical screening** refers to running a contemplated decision or action through an ethics test. Such screening makes the most sense when the contemplated action or decision is not clearly ethical or unethical. If a sales representative were to take a favorite customer to Pizza Hut for lunch, an ethical screen would not be necessary. Nobody would interpret a pizza, salad, and a beer or soft drink to be a serious bribe. Assume, instead, that the sales rep offered to give the customer an under-the-table gift of $1000 for placing a large offer with the rep's firm. The sales representative's behavior would be so blatantly unethical that conducting an ethical screen would be unnecessary.

LEARNING OBJECTIVE 4

ethical screening
Running a contemplated decision or action through an ethics test.

Several useful ethical screens, or guides to ethical decision making, have been developed. A guide developed by Treviño and Nelson is presented here because it incorporates the basic ideas in other ethical tests.[15] After studying this guide, you will be asked to ethically screen three different scenarios. The eight steps to sound ethical decision making follow.

1. **Gather the facts.** When making an important decision in business, it is necessary to gather relevant facts. Ask yourself the following questions: "Are there any legal issues involved here?" "Is there precedent in our firm with respect to this type of decision?" "Do I have the authority to make this decision?" "Are there company rules and regulations governing such a decision?"

The manager of a child care center needed to hire an additional child care specialist. One of the applicants was a 55-year-old male with experience as a father and grandfather. The manager judged him to be qualified, yet she knew that many parents would not want their preschool children to be cared for by a middle-aged male. Many people perceive that a younger woman is better qualified for child care than an older man. The manager therefore had to gather considerable facts about the situation, including facts about job discrimination and precedents in hiring males as child care specialists.

Gathering facts is influenced by emotion, with the result that ethical decision making is not an entirely rational process.[16] We tend to interpret facts based upon our biases and preconceived notions. For example, if the child care center manager has heard negative information about middle-aged men who want to engage in child care, the manager might look hard for indicators that this candidate should be disqualified.

2. Define the ethical issues. The ethical issues in a given decision are often more complicated than a first glance suggests. When faced with a complex decision, it may be helpful to talk over the ethical issues with another person. The ethical issues might involve character traits such as being kind and caring and treating others with respect. Or the ethical issues might relate to some of the common ethical problems described earlier in the chapter. Among them are facing conflict of interest, dealing with confidential information, and using corporate resources.

The manager of the child care center is facing such ethical issues as fairness, job discrimination, and meeting the demands of customers at the expense of job applicants. The manager is also facing a diversity issue: Should the workforce in a child care center be culturally diverse, or do we hire only young women?

3. Identify the affected parties. When faced with a complex ethical decision, it is important to identify all the affected parties. Major corporate decisions can affect thousands of people. If a company decides to shut down a plant and outsource the manufacturing to a low-wage country, thousands of individuals and many different parties are affected. Workers lose their jobs, suppliers lose their customers, the local government loses out on tax revenues, and local merchants lose many of their customers. You may need to brainstorm with a few others to think of all the parties affected by a given decision.

The parties affected by the decision about hiring or not hiring the 55-year-old male include the applicant himself, the children, the parents, and the board of directors of the child care center. The government might also be involved if the man were rejected and filed charges of age and sex discrimination.

4. Identify the consequences. After you have identified the parties affected by a decision, the next step is to predict the consequences for each party. It may not be necessary to identify every consequence, yet it is important to identify the consequences with the highest probability of occurring and those with the most negative outcomes. The problem is that many people can be harmed by an unethical decision, such as not fully describing the possible side effects of a diet program.

Both short-term and long-term consequences should be specified. A company closing a plant might create considerable short-term turmoil, but in the long term the company might be healthier. People participating in a diet program might achieve their short-term objective of losing weight. Yet in the long term, their health might be adversely affected because the diet is not nutritionally balanced.

The *symbolic* consequences of an action are important. Every action and decision sends a message (the decision is a symbol of something). If a company moves manufacturing out of a community to save on labor costs, it means that the short-term welfare of domestic employees is less important than profit or perhaps the company surviving.

We return to the child care manager and the job applicant. If the applicant does not get the job, his welfare will be adversely affected. He has been laid off by a large employer and cannot find work in his regular field. His family will also suffer because he will not be able to make a financial contribution to the family. Yet if the man is hired, the child care center may suffer. Many traditionally minded parents will say, "Absolutely not. I do not want my child cared for by a middle-aged man. He could be a child molester." (It may be unethical for people to have vicious stereotypes, yet they still exist.) If the child care center does hire the man, the act will symbolize the fact that the owners of the center value diversity.

5. Identify the obligations. Identify the obligations and the reasons for each obligation when making a complex decision. The manufacturer of automotive brakes has an obligation to produce and sell only brakes that meet high safety standards. The obligation is to the auto manufacturer who purchases the brakes and, more important, to the ultimate consumer whose safety depends on effective brakes. The reason for the obligation to make safe brakes is that lives are at stake. The child care center owner has an obligation to provide for the safety and health of the children at the center. She must also provide for the peace of mind of the parents and be a good citizen of the community in which the center is located. The decision about hiring the candidate in question must be balanced against all these obligations.

6. **Consider your character and integrity.** A core consideration when faced with an ethical dilemma is how relevant people would judge your character and integrity. What would your family, friends, significant others, teachers, and coworkers think of your actions? To refine this thinking even further, how would you feel if your actions were publicly disclosed in the local newspaper or over e-mail? Would you want the world to know that you gave an under-the-table kickback or that you sexually harassed a frightened teenager working for you? If you would be proud for others to know what decision you made when you faced an ethical dilemma, you are probably making the right decision.

The child care center manager might ponder how she would feel if the following information were released in the local newspaper or on the Internet:

> The manager of Good Times Child Care recently rejected the application of a 55-year-old man for a child care specialist position. She said that although Mr. _____ was well qualified from an experience and personality standpoint, she couldn't hire him. She said that Good Times would lose too much business because many parents would fear that Mr. _____ was a child molester or pedophile.

7. **Think creatively about potential actions.** When faced with an ethical dilemma, put yourself in a creative-thinking mode. Stretch your imagination to invent several options rather than thinking you have only two choices—to do or not do something. Creative thinking may point toward a third, and even fourth, alternative. Imagine this ethical dilemma: A purchasing agent is told that if her firm awards a contract to the sales representative's firm, she will find a leather jacket of her choice delivered to her door. The purchasing agent says to herself, "I think we should award the contract to the firm, but I cannot accept the gift. Yet if I turn down the gift, I will be forfeiting a valuable possession that the company simply regards as a cost of doing business."

The purchasing agent can search for another alternative. She may say to the sales rep, "We will give the contract to your firm because your products fit our requirements. I thank you for the offer of the leather jacket, but instead I would like you to give the jacket to the Salvation Army."

A creative alternative for the child care manager might be to offer the applicant the next position that opened for an office manager or maintenance person in the center. In this way, she would be offering a qualified applicant a job, but placing him in a position more acceptable to parents. Or, do you feel this is a cop-out?

8. **Check your intuition.** So far we have emphasized the rational side of ethical decision making. Another effective way of conducting an ethical screen is to rely on your intuition. How does the contemplated decision feel? Would you be proud of yourself, or would you hate yourself if you made the decision? Imagine how you would feel if you took money from the handbag of a woman sleeping in the park. Would you feel the same way if you took a kickback, sold somebody a defective product, or sold an 80-year-old man an insurance policy he didn't need? How will the manager of the child care center feel if she turns down the man for the child care specialist position? In general, experienced workers rely more heavily on intuition when making ethical choices. The reason is that intuition is based largely on experience.[17] Rules for ethical behavior are important, yet often we have to follow our hunches. Experience and rules are not wasted because intuition includes both experienced and having studied rules in the past.

You are encouraged to use the guide for ethical decision making when you next face an ethical dilemma of consequence. Skill-Building Exercise 8-3 gives you an opportunity to practice using the eight steps for ethical decision making.

Ethical Decision Making

Working in small groups, take one or more of the following ethical dilemmas through the eight steps for screening contemplated decisions. If more than one group chooses the same scenario, compare your answers for the various steps.

Scenario 1: To Recycle or Not. Your group is the top management team at a large insurance company. Despite the movement toward digitizing all records, your firm still generates tons of paper each month. Customer payments alone account for truckloads of envelopes each year. The paper recyclers in your area claim that they can hardly find a market any longer for used paper, so they will be charging you just to accept your paper for recycling. Your group is wondering whether to recycle.

Scenario 2: The Hole in the Résumé. Emily has been working for the family business as an office manager for five years. Because the family business is being sold, Emily has started a job hunt. She also welcomes the opportunity to work in a larger company so that she could learn more about how a big company operates. As she begins preparing her job résumé, she ponders how to classify the year of unemployment prior to working at the family business. During that year, she worked a total of 10 weeks in entry-level jobs at three fast-food restaurants. Otherwise she

filled her time with such activities as walking in the park, watching daytime television shows, surfing the Internet, playing video games, and pursuing her hobby of visiting graveyards. Emily finally decides to tack that year onto the five years in the family business. She indicates on her résumé that she has been working six years at the family business. As Emily says, "It's a tight job market for office managers, and I don't want to raise any red flags." Evaluate the ethics of Emily's decision to fill in the year off from work, and perhaps offer her some advice.

Scenario 3: The High-Profit Toys. You are a toy company executive starting to plan your holiday season line. You anticipate that the season's hottest item will be Robo-Woman, a battery-operated crime fighter and superheroine. Robo-Woman should wholesale for $25 and retail for $45. Your company figures to earn $15 per unit. You receive a sales call from a manufacturing broker who says he can produce any toy you want for one-third of your present manufacturing cost. He admits that the manufacturer he represents uses prison labor in China, but insists that his business arrangement violates no law. You estimate you can earn $20 per unit if you do business with the manufacturing broker. Your decision is whether to do business with him.

Developing Strong Relationships with Work Associates

A provocative explanation of the causes of unethical behavior emphasizes the strength of relationships among people.[18] Assume that two people have close professional ties to each other, such as having worked together for a long time or knowing each other both on and off the job. As a consequence, they are likely to behave ethically toward one another on the job. In contrast, if a weak professional relationship exists between two individuals, either party is more likely to engage in an unethical relationship. The owner of an auto service center is more likely to behave unethically toward a stranger passing through town than toward a long-time customer. The opportunity for unethical behavior between strangers is often minimized because individuals typically do not trust strangers with sensitive information or valuables.

The ethical skill-building consequence of information about personal relationships is that building stronger relationships with people is likely to enhance ethical behavior. If you build strong relationships with work associates, you are likely to behave more ethically toward them. Similarly, your work associates are likely to behave more ethically toward you. The work associates I refer to are all your contacts, both internal and external customers.

Self-Assessment Quiz 8-2 provides an opportunity to think of the ethical aspects of your relationships with coworkers.

Using Corporate Ethics Programs

Many organizations have various programs and procedures for promoting ethical behavior. Among them are committees that monitor ethical behavior, training programs in ethics, and vehicles for reporting ethical violations. The presence of these programs is designed to create an atmosphere in which unethical behavior is discouraged and reporting on unethical behavior is encouraged.

Ethics hotlines are one of the best established programs to help individuals avoid unethical behavior. Should a person be faced with an ethical dilemma, the person calls a toll-free line to speak to a counselor about the dilemma. Sometimes employees ask questions to help interpret a policy, such as "Is it okay to ask my boss for a date?" or "Are

The Ethical Workplace Relationships Inventory

Directions: Describe how well you agree with each of the following statements, using the following scale: disagree strongly (DS); disagree (D); neutral (N); agree (A), agree strongly (AS). Circle the number in the appropriate column.

		DS	D	N	A	AS
1.	I would give a sexually suggestive hug to a team member who I thought was physically attractive.	5	4	3	2	1
2.	If I were asked to purchase pizza and soft drinks for the group, I would be willing to ask for more in reimbursement than I actually paid.	5	4	3	2	1
3.	If I were the manager of my group, I would be willing to put pressure on group members to purchase direct sales items from me, such as beauty and health products.	5	4	3	2	1
4.	I would be willing to recommend for promotion to supervisor a worker from a different racial group than my own.	1	2	3	4	5
5.	If I didn't get along with my manager or team leader, I would be willing to start a rumor that he or she was undergoing bankruptcy.	5	4	3	2	1
6.	To damage the reputation of a coworker I didn't like, I would be willing to write a negative blog about the company and sign his or her name.	5	4	3	2	1
7.	I like the idea of encouraging a coworker to complain about a mutual boss, and then report those negative comments back to the boss.	5	4	3	2	1
8.	If I were the team member who made a serious error on a project, I would quickly inform our team leader before the blame was placed on another team member.	1	2	3	4	5
9.	If I heard that a company executive was arrested in a domestic violence incident, I would immediately inform other employees.	5	4	3	2	1
10.	Stealing an idea from a coworker, and then taking credit for that idea is totally unacceptable under any circumstance.	1	2	3	4	5

Total Score _____

Scoring and Interpretation: Add the numbers you have circled to obtain your total score.

45–50 You are strongly ethical in your relationships with coworkers.

30–44 You show an average degree of ethical behavior in your workplace relationships and should therefore become more sensitive to ethical issues.

10–29 Your ethical values could lead you to develop a negative relationship with work associates, assuming that your unethical behavior is caught. Begin a serious study of business ethics.

we supposed to give senior citizen discounts to customers who qualify but do not ask for one?" At other times, a more pressing ethical issue might be addressed, such as "Is it ethical to lay off a worker just five months short of his qualifying for a full pension?"

Human resource professionals contend that no amount of training will ensure that employees will act ethically in every situation, particularly because ethics deals with subtle matters rather than strictly right or wrong. Deborah Haliczer, director of employee relations at Northern Illinois University, explains, however, that training is valuable in starting a useful dialogue about right and wrong behavior that employees could remember in murky situations.[19]

Wells Fargo & Co., a mammoth bank, emphasizes both a code of conduct and ethics training. Its Code of Ethics and Business Conduct specifies policies and standards for employees, covering a variety of topics from maintaining accurate records to participating in civic activities. Each year, employees also participate in ethics training. Any Wells Fargo employee may ask questions or report ethical breaches anonymously using an ethics hotline or dedicated e-mail address. The company will fire violators, dismissing

FIGURE 8-5 Representative Suggestions for Helping a Company Contribute to a Sustainable Environment

1. Conserve energy by adjusting thermostats to keep working areas cooler during cold months, and warmer during warm months.

2. Do what you can to encourage your company and coworkers to send to recycling centers no-longer-in-use electronic devices, such as desktop computers, laptop computers, cell phones, and personal digital assistants.

3. Spread the word about the environmental good that be accomplished from making new products from recycled goods, such as paving stones and park benches made from recycled bottles and tires. The entire re-manufacturing industry relies on the re-use of manufactured materials.

4. Do what you can to create a buzz about the possibilities of photovoltaic technology that is used to convert sunlight into clean energy. Alert influential people to energy-saving and money-saving solar heating systems, such as solar buildings that provide solar hot water and solar heating.

5. Place a lawn on the roof that can reduce its surface temperature by 70° F and internal temperatures by 15° F.

6. Carpool to work with at least three coworkers, and provide preferred parking spaces for carpoolers and hybrid or electric cars.

7. Campaign for a 4-day, 40-hour work week, which can save enormous amounts of energy by less commuting along with less heating and cooling of the workplace. (However, if the employees drive considerably on their day off and use more heating and cooling at home, much of the energy savings will be lost.)

8. Encourage employee use of mass transportation, and provide company shuttle busses from locations convenient to where employees live.

9. Offer employees at least $2,000 toward the purchase of a hybrid vehicle or electric car.

10. Turn off electronic machines when not in use unless starting and stopping them frequently uses more energy than leaving the machines turned on during working hours. Encourage the replacement of incandescent bulbs with fluorescent ones (providing the replacement bulb provides enough light for the purpose).

11. Recycle as many packages as possible and purchase products, such as office furniture and driveways, made from recycled products including vehicle tires. When possible, use old newspapers for packing material instead of new paper and plastic.

12. Use mugs instead of Styrofoam and set up bins to recycle aluminum cans and plastic bottles.

13. When constructing a new building, seek Leadership in Energy and Environmental Design (LEED) certification from the U.S. Green Building Council.

14. Provide bicycle racks and shows that enable employees to bike to work. Biking to work will save considerable energy as well as decrease carbon dioxide emissions.

15. Construct a system that captures rainwater to be reused for irrigation.

16. Grow as much vegetation on company premises as feasible, including celebrating special events by planting another tree. Use plants that are native to the region because native vegetation does not require as much maintenance, fertilizer, chemical sprays, or water.

17. Drink as much tap water as possible to minimize the use of bottled water, or filter tap water to one's specifications.

18. Combat litter and clutter in your work area and on company premises to help attain a pleasant, environmentally friendly atmosphere. Take such actions as alerting the company to exposed, rusted pipes, broken concrete in the parking lot, peeling paint, and broken fences.

19. Encourage people in your network not to drive at high speeds or sit in an idling vehicle while making phone calls or sending text messages. Encourage safe driving in general because vehicular accidents consume enormous amounts of energy, including tow trucks, salvage operations, and life-sustaining hospital stays. Also encourage them to walk to errands instead of driving, whenever feasible.

20. A general guideline is to use less stuff and less energy.

21. My suggestions. _____

Sources: Several of the ideas are from Ben Elgin and Brian Grow, "The Dirty Secret of Recycling Electronics," *Business* Week, October 27, 2008, pp. 040–044; Letita M. Aaron, "The Big Payback," *Black Enterprise*, May 2009, pp. 64–66; Michael Barbaro, "At Wal-Mart, Lessons in Self-Help," *The New York Times* (*nytimes.com*), April 5, 2007; Bryan Walsh, "Thank God It's Thursday," Time, September 7, 2009, p. 58; Melanie Warner, "Plastic Potion No. 9," *Fast* Company, September 2008, p. 88; Charles Lockwood, "Building the Green Way," *Harvard Business Review*, June 2006, pp. 129–137; David Roberts, "Another Inconvenient Truth," *Fast Company*, March 2008, p. 70; Tom Szaky, *Revolution in a Bottle* (New York: Portfolio, 2009).

Conducting an Environmental Audit

To create an environmentally friendly workplace, somebody has to take the initiative to spot opportunities for change. Organize the class into groups of about five, with one person being appointed the team leader. You might have to do the work outside of class because your assignment is to do an environmental audit of a workplace, including a nonprofit setting such as a place of worship, a school, or an athletic facility. If the audit is done during class time, evaluate a portion of the school, such as a classroom, an athletic facility, or the cafeteria. Your task is to conduct an environmental audit with respect to the energy efficiency and healthfulness of the workplace. Make judgments perhaps on a 1-to-10 scale plus comments about the following factors:

1. How energy efficient is the workplace in terms of such factors as building insulation, use of fluorescent lighting, heating and cooling, and use of solar panels?
2. How safe is the environment in terms of pollutants, and steps to prevent physical accidents?
3. How esthetic is the environment in terms of protecting against sight and sound pollution?

Summarize your findings and suggestions in a bulleted list of less than one page. Present your findings to classmates, and perhaps to a manager of the workplace. Classmates might comment on whether your findings will really improve the planet from an ecology standpoint.

---

about 100 people a year for misconduct ranging from conflicts of interest to cheating on incentive plans. Patricia Callahan, executive vice president and director of human resources at the bank, says, "I'm the biggest soft touch in the world. But when someone lies or cheats, you can't have people like that representing us to our customers, whose trust is all we have."[20]

The link between the programs just described and individual ethical skills is that these programs assist a worker's skill development. For example, if you become comfortable in asking about ethical issues, or turning in ethical violators, you have become more ethically skilled.

Being Environmentally Conscious

Another ethical skill is to be *green* or to do your job in helping sustain the physical environment. (*Green* derives from the idea that green vegetations such as trees and forests are a plus for the environment.) The reasoning behind this statement is that it is morally responsible to protect the environment. Do not be concerned with taking sides on the issue of global warming. Whether or not humans and the carbon dioxide emissions they create have contributed to global warming, the physical environment needs your help.

The skill of being environmentally conscious has two major components. First is to take as many steps as you can individually to help preserve the environment even in such small steps as carrying a reusable cloth bag to the grocery store, and not throwing a plastic bottle on a lawn. Second is to be an advocate for the environment by mentioning its importance at work. You might, for example, present data to management about how solar heating can save the company money in the long run, and how benches and walkways made from recycled tires and plastics are attractive and economical. Figure 8-5 gives you a starting point for contributing to a sustainable environment. You might want to add to this list with suggestions of your own, or those you find in the media and scientific articles.

You may need to use your communication persuasion skills to make an impact on the environment. And you will also need to use your positive political skills so that you will not be perceived as an environmental, tree-hugging, pest.

You are invited to do Skill-Building Exercise 8-4 to get started right away in improving the physical environment.

BACK TO THE OPENING CASE

John S. Sherigan, the CEO of Electronic Recyclers International, has chosen a path that most people would consider to be highly ethical. His company removes toxic waste from the environment, and he assists in the rehabilitation of former convicts. At the same time, the company, ERI, continues to prosper and grow. Sherigan is another example of "doing well by doing good."

Following an Applicable Professional Code of Conduct

Professional codes of conduct are prescribed for many occupational groups, including physicians, nurses, lawyers, paralegals, purchasing managers and agents, and real estate salespeople. A useful ethical guide for members of these groups is to follow the code of conduct for their profession. If the profession or trade is licensed by the state or province, a worker can be punished for deviating from the code of conduct specified by the state. The code of conduct developed by the profession or trade is separate from the legal code, but usually supports the same principles and practices. Some of these codes of conduct developed by the professional associations are 50 and 60 pages long; yet, all are guided by the kind of ethical principles implied in the ethical decision-making guide described earlier. Figure 8-6 presents a sampling of provisions from these codes of conduct.

Be Ready to Exert Upward Ethical Leadership

upward ethical leadership

The leadership displayed by individuals who take action to maintain ethical standards, although higher-ups engage in questionable moral behaviors.

A politically delicate situation can arise when a worker wants to behave ethically, yet he or she works for an unethical manager. He or she might worry that being ethical will lead to being reprimanded or job loss. The ethical person working for an unethical boss might feel that his or her values are being compromised, such as a virtuous credit card specialist being told to approve credit cards for people who will probably wind up paying many late fees. **Upward ethical leadership** is leadership displayed by individuals who take action to maintain ethical standards, although higher-ups engage in questionable moral behaviors.[21]

FIGURE 8-6   Excerpts from Professional Codes of Conduct

Professional Organization	Sample of Ethical Guidelines and Regulations
Institute of Management Accountants	1. Maintain an appropriate level of professional competence by ongoing development of their knowledge and skills. 2. Refrain from disclosing confidential information acquired in the course of their work and monitor their activities to assure the maintenance of that confidentiality. 3. Actual or apparent conflicts of interest and advise all appropriate parties of any potential conflict.
National Association of Legal Assistants	1. A legal assistant (paralegal) must not perform any of the duties that attorneys only may perform nor take any actions that attorneys may not take. 2. A legal assistant may perform any task which is properly delegated and supervised by an attorney, as long as the attorney is ultimately responsible to the client, maintains a direct relationship with the client, and assumes professional responsibility for the work product. 3. A legal assistant must protect the confidences of a client and must not violate any rule or statute now in effect or hereafter enacted controlling the doctrine of privileged communications between a client and an attorney.
National Association of Purchasing Management	1. Avoid the intent and appearance of unethical or compromising practice in relationships, actions, and communications. 2. Refrain from any private business or professional activity that would create a conflict between personal interests and the interest of the employer. 3. Refrain from soliciting or accepting money, loans, credits, or prejudicial discounts, and the acceptance of gifts, entertainment, favors, or services from present or potential suppliers which might influence, or appear to influence purchasing decisions.

Sources: Institute of Management Accountants Code of Ethics; National Association of Legal Assistants Professional Standards; National Association of Purchasing Management Principles and Standards of Purchasing Practice.

Confronting the Unethical Boss

One student plays the role of Fred, a manager who makes frequent business trips by airplanes. Fred also likes to fly frequently on vacation, and appreciates accumulating frequent-flyer miles. Company policy allows employees to keep the frequent-flyer miles they accumulate for work. So Fred will often take indirect trips to a destination to accumulate more air miles. For example, to fly to San Francisco, he will flew from Boston to Atlanta, and then to San Francisco. In this instance, he could have made a shorter trip by flying directly from Boston to San Francisco, or from Boston to Chicago to San Francisco. In general, the longer, indirect flights are more expensive.

Another person plays the role of Kelly, the office administrative assistant who sometimes helps Fred prepare his travel vouchers. Kelly, who has good knowledge of geography, notices this strange pattern of Fred taking indirect flights. She is also aware of company policy that permits employees to accumulate frequent flyer miles that are earned on business trips. Kelley is disturbed about what she perceives to be an inappropriate use of company resources—and therefore an ethical violation.

Kelly decides to discuss with Fred this most likely ethical violation. The role-play takes place in Fred's cubicle, and you can imagine how defensive Fred is going to be.

Run the role-play for about five minutes. For both scenarios, observers rate the role players on two dimensions, using a 1-to-5 scale from very poor to very good. One dimension is "effective use of human relations techniques." Observers look to see if Kelly can preserve her sense of ethics while not doing too much damage to her relationship with her boss, Fred. The second dimension is "acting ability." A few observers might voluntarily provide feedback to the role players in terms of sharing their ratings and observations. The course instructor might also provide feedback.

At the extreme, an employee might blow the whistle on the boss, and report the unethical behavior to top management or a government agency. An example would be telling the Consumer Protection Agency that your company was selling cribs that could trap a baby's head after your boss refused to accept your complaint.

The upward leadership approach would be to attempt to resolve the problem before going to the extreme of whistle blowing. The employee who spots the immoral or unethical behavior would use problem-solving and communication skills, along with conflict resolution skills. For example, the employee who spotted the potential head-trap problem might say to the boss, "I have a problem and I would like to discuss it with you." The employee would therefore be engaging the boss in helping solve the problem. Recognizing that you have less power than your boss, you would have to be diplomatic and nonaccusatory. It would be important to point to the problem (the possibility of an infant getting his or her head stuck) rather than accusing the boss of being unethical or immoral.

Skill-Building Exercise 8-5 gives you an opportunity to practice upward leadership skills for correcting unethical behavior.

SELF-ASSESSMENT QUIZZES IN OVERVIEW

Self-Assessment Quiz 8-1, The Ethical Reasoning Inventory, can be used as an alert to keep your ethical values in mind whenever faced with an ethical dilemma. Although you may study ethics and learn to use a guide to ethical decision making, your values will continue to exert a strong influence on your behavior. For example, if a person values the environment, he or she will not empty a car ashtray of cigarette butts on a parking lot pavement. If you know that your ethical values are in the low range, you will have to work extra hard to be ethical in work and personal life. Self-Assessment Quiz 8-2, The Ethical Workplace Relationships Inventory, is also about ethical reasoning but focuses on interpersonal relationships in the workplace. How ethically you relate to others is a major factor in building your ethical reputation.

Concept Review and Reinforcement

Key Terms

character trait 255
moral intensity 257

conflict of interest 261
defining moment 262

ethical screening 265
upward ethical leadership 272

Summary

Ethics refers to moral choices, or what is good and bad, right and wrong, just and unjust, and what people should do. Ethics turn values into action. A person's ethical code has a significant impact on his or her interpersonal relationships.

Understanding ethics is important for a variety of reasons. First, people are motivated by self-interest and a desire to be morally right. Second, good ethics can enhance business and avoid illegal acts. Third, having high ethics improves the quality of work life.

Being ethical isn't always easy for several reasons, including the complexity of ethical decisions, lack of recognition of the moral issues, poor moral development, and pressures from the work environment. Ethical violations in the form of lying are widespread in the workplace. Another problem is that some people have a utilitarian predisposition that tends toward unethical behavior. Self-interest drives many people toward unethical behavior.

Commonly faced ethical dilemmas include illegally copying software, treating people unfairly including cronyism, sexually harassing coworkers, facing a conflict of interest, dealing with confidential information, misrepresenting employment and educational history, using corporate resources, ethically violating computers and information technology, and wasting company time.

A challenging twist to ethical decision making is to sort through your values when you have to choose between two morally sound choices. A defining moment is when you have to choose between two or more ideals in which you deeply believe.

One strategy for behaving ethically is to develop virtuousness that includes rationality, honesty, independence, productivity, and forgiveness. A key strategy for behaving ethically is to follow the eight steps in making a contemplated decision:

1. Gather the facts.
2. Define the ethical issues.
3. Identify the affected parties.
4. Identify the consequences.
5. Identify the obligations (such as to customers and society).
6. Consider your character and integrity.
7. Think creatively about potential actions.
8. Check your intuition.

Another way to raise the level of ethical behavior is to form strong professional relationships with work associates. This is true because people tend to behave more ethically toward people who are close to them. At times using a corporate program such as an ethics hotline can help a person resolve ethical dilemmas. Being environmentally conscious contributes to ethical behavior. Following an applicable code of professional conduct, such as that for accountants, paralegals, and purchasing specialists, is another guide to behaving ethically. Upward leadership behavior can help you deal with the situation of maintaining ethical standards when the boss engages in questionable moral behavior.

Questions for Discussion and Review

1. To what extent does the owner of the electronics recycling business described in the chapter opener have an ethical obligation to tell customers that many of his employees have a prison record?

2. How can behaving ethically improve a person's interpersonal relationships on the job?

3. What would most likely be some of the specific behaviors of a manager who scored 20 points on the ethical reasoning inventory?

4. What is your opinion of the ethics of using the wi-fi access of other people, including business firms when you are not a customer, without asking permission?

5. What evidence can you present that coworkers or fellow students really care if you behave ethically?

6. Provide an example of an action in business that might be unethical but not illegal.

7. Virtually all accountants have studied ethics as part of their education, yet many business scandals involve accountants. What's their problem?

8. Based on your knowledge of human behavior, why do professional codes of conduct—such as those for doctors, paralegals, and realtors—not prevent all unethical behavior on the part of members?

9. Check out the Web site of a couple of major business corporations. What conclusion do you reach about whether an environmentally conscious (or green) person would fit in those companies?

10. What decision of ethical consequence have you made in the last year that you would not mind having publicly disclosed?

The Web Corner

http://www.ethics.org
(Ethics Resource Center)

http://www.ita.doc
(Information about sustainability and being green presented by the International Trade Administration of the U.S. Department of Commerce)

http://globalethicsuniversity.com
(An examination of many phases of business ethics)

Internet Skill-Builder: Learning from Ethical Role Models

One of the many ways of learning ethical skills is to get good ideas from ethical role models. For example, you might observe a professor who takes the initiative to change a grade upward because she later discovered a calculation error. This Internet skill-builder is more abstract than some others, so you might find it a little frustrating. Search for a few specific ways in which you can learn from an ethical role model. To illustrate, you might learn from a business executive, sports figure, or public servant you admire.

Developing Your Human Relations Skills

Is This Company Going Really "Going Out of Business"?

When Cyrus Hassankola moved to Dallas, Texas, a couple of years ago after successfully going out of business in several locales, he decided to settle down and go out of business permanently. "The response was good from day one," the carpet salesman says. Customers rooting through the stacks of oriental rugs in the store he opened on a busy road in North Dallas would sometimes say how sorry they were that he was going out of business. "We're not," Hassankola told them. "It's just the name of the store."

A business literally called "Going Out of Business" didn't sit well in some quarters, one of them the Texas Attorney General's office. So Hassankola—for a limited time only—has stopped going out of business. Now he's running "total liquidations" that "beat every going-out-of-business price." In his vocation, this is established practice. But the arrival of hard times has thrown the survival of the going-out-of-business model into doubt. Everybody else is slashing prices as if there's no tomorrow. Old-line going-out-of-businesses are lost in the crowd.

In 2000 Hassankola flew to the United States, found a green card sponsor and hit the road. He recounts steering rug stores out of business in Maryland, Tennessee, South Carolina, North Carolina, and Georgia. Tired of traveling, Hassankola move to Dallas and in late 2007 opened his extended-stay rug store. When he registered its name as "Going Out of Business," he doesn't recall any tax clerk or bank officer blinking. But when David Beasley caught sight of the sign, his eyes popped.

Beasly, 26, works for the Better Business Bureau. One morning he was cruising around Dallas in his Chevy Cavalier on a preposterous-sales hunt. The banner on an apartment complex read, "Free Rent." On a bedding showroom: "Nobody beats our prices." On a furniture outlet: "Bankruptcy liquidation."

"I understand the desire to stay in business," Beasley said as he drove along. "But you can't do it by going out of business."

Hassankola doubts Texas would have bugged him if Beasley hadn't gotten a TV station to show his "Going Out of Business" sign on local news. When the attorney general's office phoned to scold him, he dropped his "just-the-name-of-the-store" routine without a peep and regrouped.

He replaced the sign with "Cyrus Rug Gallery," and then let fly with a flier: "Due to the impending demolition and redevelopment of our premises, we are forced to sell at auction. *Let our loss be your gain.*" The demolition crisis went on for months. The wreckers didn't arrive. Lately, Hassankola has been hanging a "Liquidation Sale" banner out front.

Case Questions

1. What is your evaluation of the ethics of Cyrus Hassankola labeling his rug store, "Going Out of Business"?
2. What kind of ethical behavior can you really expect from somebody in the retail rug business?
3. What would you advise Hassankola to do to become more ethical and more profitable at the same time?

Source: Barry Newman, "In Texas, There's No Business Like 'Going Out of Business'," *The Wall Street Journal*, June 24, 2009, pp. A1, A2.

Am I Paid to Be My Manager's TV Repair Technician?

Karen worked for a division of a pharmaceutical company as a member of the technical support team. Among her many responsibilities were keeping the division's desktop computers, laptop computers, printers, and smart phones in working order. Gus, her manager, who had been with the company for about 10 years, had a general understanding of what the tech support staff was doing, but he was more of an administrator than a specialist in communication technology.

Several times in recent weeks, Gus complained to Karen and a few other team members about a problem he was having with a digital television set connected to an internal (rabbit ears) antenna. During a lunch break, he explained to Karen, "I'm going a little crazy. I have four television sets at home. The two big ones are satellite connected and they work just fine. I have a small set in the family room in the basement connected to rabbit ears, and the reception is reasonably good. I am picking up the digital signals with a few halts here and there, but I am getting the reception I need."

"The problem I have is with a relatively new set connected in our upstairs bedroom. I did the channel scan about one year ago, and I was getting the network channels I needed. A few weeks ago I stopped receiving the channels I needed. All that was left was HSN (Home Shopping Network). I must have done a channel scan twenty times to try to fix the problem. Plus, I rotated the antenna a few times. I called tech support at the manufacturer of my set, and the rep couldn't help. He told me to telephone the FCC (Federal Communication Commission). I did that, followed the rep's instructions, and still no signal."

Karen agreed that Gus was facing a frustrating problem, but that many people using antennas on their TV sets have lost reception since the conversion from analog to digital in 2009.

A week later, Gus spoke to Karen again about his TV reception woes. He then asked Karen, "How about you coming over after work some night to help straighten out my TV problem? My wife and I would really appreciate your help. You're a great tech fixer."

Karen pondered for a moment, thinking that Gus was making an unreasonable demand. She replied, "Gus, let me think about your request. I really don't know a lot about TV reception. Also, I am pretty much tied up after work for a couple of weeks."

With a frown on his face, Gus said, "Karen, I know you can help. Please don't let me down."

Case Questions

1. What do you see as any potential ethical issues in Gus' request that Karen attempt to fix his TV set reception problem?
2. What advice might you offer Karen for dealing with this problem?
3. How do Gus' demands fit into the category of expecting Karen to exhibit strong organizational citizenship behavior?

Dealing with an Unusual Request from the Boss

The case about the manager's request for tech support for this television set provides the background information for this role-play. The scenario is another meeting between Gus and Karen. One student plays the role of Gus who is now increasingly frustrated that he cannot get the reception he wants. Just last week he telephoned a television repair service, and was told politely that he should simply hook up the set to cable or satellite TV. But Gus and his wife do not want any more wires running through their house. So this time, Gus is more insistent that Karen come over to his house to fix the problem.

Another person plays the role of Karen who has thought through Gus's request some more, and she feels that his demand is both inappropriate and unethical. However, Karen still wants to maintain a good professional relationship with Gus.

Run the role-play for about five minutes. For both scenarios, observers rate the role players on two dimensions, using a 1-to-5 scale from very poor to very good. One dimension is "effective use of human relations techniques." The second dimension is "acting ability." A few observers might voluntarily provide feedback to the role players in terms of sharing their ratings and observations. The course instructor might also provide feedback.

REFERENCES

1. Erika Brown, "Rehab, Reuse, Recycle," *Forbes*, April 21, 2008, pp. 70, 72; "Electronic Recyclers International CEO John S. Shegarian Named Ernst & Young Entrepreneur of the Year 2008 Award Recipient in Northern California," www.businesswire.com, June 25, 2008.

2. Linda K. Treviño and Katherine A. Nelson, *Managing Business Ethics: Straight Talk about How to Do It Right* (New York: Wiley, 1995), pp. 24–35; O. C. Ferrell, John Fraedrich, and Linda Ferrell, *Business Ethics: Ethical Decision Making and Cases*, 4th ed. (Boston: Houghton Mifflin, 2000), pp. 13–16; Anita Bruzzese, "Tools Take Ethics to the Real World," Gannett News Service, May 16, 2005; Roger Parloff, "Wall Street: It's Payback Time," *Fortune*, January 19, 2009, pp. 56–69.

3. Thomas M. Jones, "Ethical Decision Making by Individuals in Organizations: An Issue Contingent Model," *Academy of Management Review*, April 1991, p. 391.

4. Linda Kelbe Treviño and Michael E. Brown, "Managing to Be Ethical: Debunking Five Business Ethics Myths," *Academy of Management Executive*, May 2004, pp. 69–72.

5. Scott J. Reynolds, "Moral Awareness and Ethical Predispositions: Investigating the Role of Individual Differences in the Recognition of Moral Issues," *Journal of Applied Psychology*, January 2006, p. 234.

6. John C. Bogle, "A Crisis of Ethic Proportions," *The Wall Street Journal*, April 21, 2009, p. A19.

7. Simona Covel, "Small Businesses Face More Fraud in Downturn," *The Wall Street Journal*, February 19, 2009, p. B5.

8. The basic outline for this section is from Treviño and Nelson, *Managing Business Ethics*, pp. 47–64.

9. Data reported in "McAfee Anti-Piracy Information," *http://www.networkassociates.com/us/antipircacy_policy.htm*, accessed January 6, 2010.

10. Edmund L. Andrews, "Interior Official Assails Agency for Ethics Slides," *The New York Times (nytimes.com)*, September 14, 2006.

11. "FTC: Bloggers Must Disclose Payments for Reviews," Associated Press, October 5, 2009.

12. Keith J. Winstein, "Inflated Credentials Surface in Executive Suite," *The Wall Street Journal*, November 13, 2008, p. B1.

13. Joseph L. Badaracco, Jr., "The Discipline of Building Character," *Harvard Business Review*, March–April 1998, pp. 114–124.

14. Edwin A. Locke, "Business Ethics: A Way Out of the Morass," *Academy of Management Learning & Education*, September 2006, pp. 328–330.

15. Treviño and Nelson, *Managing Business Ethics*, pp. 71–75.

16. Scott Sonenshein, "The Role of Construction, Intuition, and Justification in Responding to Ethical Issues at Work: The Sensemaking-Intuition Model," *Academy of Management Review*, October 2007, p. 1030.

17. Sonenshein, "The Role of Construction, Intuition," p. 1033.

18. Daniel J. Brass, Kenneth D. Butterfield, and Bruce C. Skaggs, "Relationships and Unethical Behavior: A Social Network Perspective," *Academy of Management Review*, January 1998, pp. 14–31.

19. Cited in Jean Thilmany, "Supporting Ethical Employees," *HR Magazine*, September 2007, p. 106.

20. "The Optima Awards: They've Got Game," *Workforce Management*, March 2005, p. 44.

21. Mary Uhl-Bien and Melissa K. Carsten, "Being Ethical When the Boss Is Not," *Organizational Dynamics*," Issue 2, 2007, p. 197.

Stress

Lynaia Lutes is taking time to focus. An account supervisor at a small Texas advertising and public relations agency, Lutes not long ago was a master of executing the details of work, without always focusing on strategy and long-term vision. Glued to her personal digital assistant, she shot off e-mails night and day, yet felt overwhelmed and sometimes did work that didn't pass muster with her bosses.

"A couple of times, I basically completed an assignment but didn't approach it strategically," admits Lutes. Now, taking the time to think and focus deeply has become one of Lutes' performance goals. And, she and the 14 other employees at the Blanchard Schaefer agency in Arlington are expected to make appointments with themselves just to contemplate, even daydream, for an hour. New on the premises, a "womb room," spartan and unwired, allows employees to retreat to let ideas flow without interruption.

"Our society has gotten to a place where we reward those who micromanage: Did I respond immediately on my BlackBerry; was I online at 11 p.m.", asserts agency president Ken Schaefer. "Having time to think is absolutely critical to creating good strategy. We view it as a competitive advantage."[1]

The account supervisor just described is attempting to become more productive by spending time thinking instead of responding to small messages of the moment. At the same time, she is attempting to get over the stressor of feeling overwhelmed. Although this book is primarily about interpersonal skills, information about managing stress and enhancing personal productivity is relevant. Having your work under control and not being stressed out enables you to focus better on interpersonal relationships.

The first half of this chapter deals with the nature of stress and how it can be managed, whereas the second half describes various approaches to improving personal productivity. The two topics are as closely related as nutrition and health. When you effectively manage stress, you can be more productive. And when your work is under control, you avoid the heavy stress of feeling overwhelmed. A useful thought to keep in mind is that many readers of

1. Explain many of the symptoms and consequences of stress, including burnout.
2. Describe personality factors and job factors that contribute to stress.
3. Manage your own stress effectively.
4. Reduce any tendencies you might have toward procrastination.
5. Identify attitudes and values that will enhance your productivity.
6. Identify work habits and skills that will enhance your productivity.
7. Pinpoint potential time wasters that drain your productivity.
8. Identify several positive and negative consequences of stress.
9. Describe key methods for managing the potential adverse effects of stress.

this book will become or are already **corporate athletes,** workers who engage in high-level performance for sustained periods.[2] To be a corporate athlete, you have to manage your energy and stress well, in addition to having good work habits and time management.

corporate athletes

Workers who engage in high-level performance for sustained periods.

UNDERSTANDING AND MANAGING STRESS

A major challenge facing any worker who wants to stay healthy and have good interpersonal relationships is to manage stress effectively. Although *stress* is an everyday term, a scientific definition helps clarify its meaning. **Stress** is an adaptive response that is the consequence of any action, situation, or event that places special demands on a person. Note that stress, as used here, refers to a reaction to the situation, not the situation or force itself. A **stressor** is the external or internal force that brings about the stress.

Individual differences in the perception of an event play a key role in determining what events are stressful. Giving a presentation to management, for example, is stressful for some people but not for others. Some people perceive a presentation as a threatening and uncomfortable experience, while others might perceive the same event to be an invigorating challenge.

The term *special demands* is also critical because minor adjustments, such as an ink cartridge that runs dry, are usually not perceived as stressful. Yet piling on of minor adjustments, such as having 10 small things go wrong in one day, is stressful. This is true because stress is additive: A series of small doses of stress can create a major stress problem.

This textbook's approach to understanding stress centers on its symptoms and consequences, personality and job factors that contribute to stress, and methods and techniques for stress management. Managing stress receives more emphasis because the same techniques can be used to combat a variety of stressors.

Symptoms and Consequences of Stress

The physiological changes that take place within the body in response to stress are responsible for most stress symptoms. These physiological changes are almost identical for both positive and negative stressors. Ski racing, romantic attraction, and being downsized can make you feel about the same physically. The experience of stress helps activate hormones that prepare the body to run or fight when faced with a challenge. This battle against the stressor is referred to as the **fight-or-flight response.** It helps you deal with emergencies.

The brain is the organ that decides whether a situation is stressful and produces the behavioral and physiological responses. Yet, the brain's response is based on personal experience and culture. Eating seal meat would rarely be stressful for an Eskimo, yet might be for a Floridian. The brain senses stress as damage to well-being and therefore sends out a signal to the body to cope. The brain is thus a self-regulating system that helps us cope with stressors.

LEARNING OBJECTIVE 1

fight-or-flight response

The body's physiological and chemical battle against a stressor in which the person tries to cope with the adversity head-on or tries to flee from the scene.

Physiological Reactions. The activation of hormones when the body has to cope with a stressor produces a short-term physiological reaction. Among the most familiar reactions is an increase in heart rate, blood pressure, blood glucose, and blood clotting. The stress hormone cortisol and other chemical responses to a stress can increase the cardiovascular function and the immune system in the short term. To help you recognize these symptoms, try to recall your internal bodily sensations the last time you were almost in an automobile accident or heard some wonderful news. Less familiar changes are a redirection of the blood flow toward the brain and large muscle groups and a release of stored fluids from places throughout the body into the bloodstream.

If stress is continuous and accompanied by these short-term physiological changes, annoying and life-threatening conditions can occur. Damage occurs when stress levels rarely subside. Eventually the immune system is suppressed, and memory is impaired. When the immune system is impaired, the severity of many diseases and disorders increases. For example, people whose stress level is high recover more slowly from colds and injuries, and they are more susceptible to sexually transmitted diseases.

A stressful life event usually leads to a high cholesterol level (of the unhealthy type) and high blood pressure. Other conditions associated with stress are cardiac disease, migraine headaches, ulcers, allergies, skin disorders, irritable bowel syndrome, and cancer. People under continuous negative stress, such as having severe family problems or having a life out of control, also age more quickly partially because of cell damage.[3] (Have you ever observed that stressed out friends of yours appear older looking than their chronological age?) A study of 812 Swedish workers conducted over a 25-year period found that work stress doubles the risk of dying from a heart attack. Seventy-three of the workers died from cardiac disease during the study. The major type of stress studied was having high work demands with little control over the work, combined with being underpaid.[4]

Stress symptoms vary considerably from one person to another. A general behavioral symptom of intense stress is for people to exaggerate their weakest tendencies. For instance, a person with a strong temper who usually keeps cool under pressure may throw a tantrum under intense pressure. Some common stress symptoms are listed in Figure 9-1.

Job Performance Consequences. Stress has both negative and positive consequences. **Hindrance stressors** are those stressful events and thoughts that have a negative effect on motivation and performance. Many of these have already been mentioned. In contrast, **challenge stressors** have a positive direct effect on motivation and performance.[5] A study with 215 employees across 61 offices of a state agency showed that when faced with challenge stressors, employees performed better on their regular tasks, citizenship behavior, and customer service. In contrast, performance on the three dimensions decreased when

hindrance stressors

Those stressful events that have a negative effect on motivation and performance.

challenge stressors

Stressful events that have a positive direct effect on motivation and performance.

FIGURE 9-1   A Variety of Stress Symptoms

Mostly Physical and Physiological	
Shaking or trembling	Mouth dryness
Dizziness	Upper and lower back pain
Heart palpitations	Frequent headaches
Difficulty breathing	Low energy and stamina
Chronic fatigue	Stomach problems
Unexplained chest pains	Constant craving for sweets
Frequent teeth grinding	Increased alcohol or cigarette consumption
Frequent nausea	Frequent need to eliminate
Mostly Emotional and Behavioral	
Difficulty concentrating	Anxiety or depression
Nervousness	Forgetfulness
Crying	Restlessness
Anorexia	Frequent arguments with others
Declining interest in sex	Feeling high strung much of the time
Frequent nail biting or hair tugging	Decrease in daily happiness

Note: Anxiety is a general sense of dread, fear, or worry not linked to a specific event, such as being anxious about your future.

FIGURE 9-2 **Relationship between Stress and Job Performance**

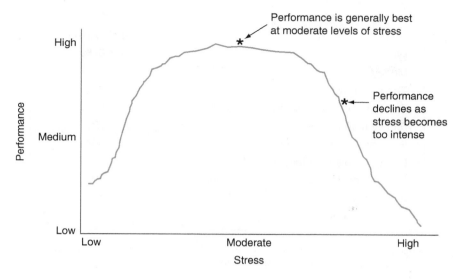

employees experienced hindrance stressors. An example of a challenge stressor was having high responsibility; having to deal with a lot of red tape to get the job done was an example of a hindrance stressor.[6]

The right amount of stress prepares us for meeting difficult challenges and spurs us on to peak intellectual and physical performance. An optimum level of stress exists for most people and most tasks. In general, performance tends to be best under moderate amounts of stress. If the stress is too great, people become temporarily ineffective; they may freeze or choke. Under too little stress, people may become lethargic and inattentive. Figure 9-2 depicts the relationship between stress and job performance. An exception to this relationship is that certain negative forms of stress are likely to lower performance even if the stress is moderate. For example, the stress created by an intimidating supervisor or worrying about radiation poisoning—even in moderate amounts—will not improve performance.

Job stress can also lower job performance indirectly because distressed workers are more likely to be absent from the job, thereby not accomplishing as much work. A study of 323 health service workers in the United Kingdom found that job-related psychological distress, particularly depression, was associated with more days absent, and a greater number of times absent.[7]

The optimum amount of stress is a positive force that is the equivalent of finding excitement and challenge. Your ability to solve problems and deal with challenge is enhanced when the right amount of adrenaline flows in your blood to guide you toward peak performance. In fact, highly productive people are sometimes said to be hooked on adrenaline.

Burnout and Stress.   One of the major problems of prolonged stress is that it may lead to **burnout**, a condition of emotional, mental, and physical exhaustion in response to long-term stressors. Burnout is also referred to as work exhaustion because fatigue is usually involved. Burned-out people are often cynical. Two other examples of burnout symptoms are irritability and impatience.

Burnout is a complex phenomenon with its causes centering on five factors. First is a feeling of limited autonomy or control in the workplace. Not being able to decide how to accomplish a task is significant, as well as having little say in choosing what tasks to do. Second is receiving insufficient recognition for accomplishments. Third is not having advancement opportunities and feeling stifled on the job. Fourth is having poor relationships with coworkers, including not getting much respect. Fifth is working in an organizational culture that is incompatible with your belief system, such as a vegetarian working for a poultry producer.[8] A recent study with Dutch workers suggests that having a charismatic leader can help reduce some of the problems that lead to burnout.[9] For example, a charismatic leader is likely to give ample recognition.

burnout

A condition of emotional, mental, and physical exhaustion in response to long-term stressors.

FIGURE 9-3 Cause of Stress among the General Population

Source of Stress	People Affected
Work	67%
Money	78%
The economy	75%
Relationships (spouse, kids, girl/boyfriend)	59%
Family responsibilities	58%
Personal health concerns	58%
Health problems affecting my family	61%
Housing costs (e.g., mortgage or rent)	59%
Job stability	58%
Personal safety	42%

Source: APA (American Psychological Association) Stress in America Survey, published in Michael Price, "The Recession is Stressing Men More than Women," *Monitor on Psychology*, July/August 2009, p. 10.

The key symptom of burnout is the distancing that occurs in response to work over-load. Burnout sufferers shift into a mode of doing the minimum as a way of protecting themselves. They start leaving work early and dehumanizing their clients, patients, or customers. People experiencing burnout may do their jobs, but their heart is not in it anymore.[10]

A synthesis of dozens of studies shows that burnout often damages the physical health of workers. Partly because burnout is a consequence of stress, burnout increases the risk for cardiovascular disease as much as well-known risk factors such as smoking, an elevated body mass index, and too much bad cholesterol. Other potential links between burnout and health problems include poor health behaviors and sleep disorder.[11]

Personality and Job Factors Contributing to Stress

LEARNING OBJECTIVE 2

Workers experience stress for many different reasons, including personal predispositions, factors stemming from the job, or the combined influence of both. If a person with an extreme negative predisposition has to deal with irate customers, he or she is most likely to experience substantial stress. Here we describe a sampling of important individual and organizational factors that contribute to job stress. Keep in mind, however, that a large number of potential stressors exist and that many of them overlap. For example, financial problems are a major source of stress, and they might contribute to relationship and health problems. Fighting about money harms relationships, and worrying about money can create health problems. Figure 9-3 lists some stressors facing the general population, and these sources of stress duplicate some of the stressors described in the following pages.

Personality Factors Predisposing People toward Stress.   Individuals vary considerably in their susceptibility to job stress based on their personality traits and characteristics. Four such factors are described next.

Low Perceived Control   A key factor in determining whether workers experience stress is how much they believe they can control a given adverse circumstance. **Perceived control** is the belief that an individual has at his or her disposal a response that can control the negative aspects of an event. A survey of over 100 studies indicated that people with a high level of perceived control had low levels of physical and psychological symptoms of stress. Conversely, people with low perceived control are more likely to experience work stress.[12]

Low Self-Efficacy   Self-efficacy, like perceived control, is another personal factor that influences susceptibility to stress. (Note that because self-efficacy is tied to a specific situation

perceived control

The belief that an individual has at his or her disposal a response that can control the negative aspects of an event.

it is not strictly a personality trait.) When workers have both low perceived control and low self-efficacy, the stress consequences may be much worse. However, having high self-efficacy softens the stress consequences of demanding jobs.[13] If you believe that you can successfully resolve a difficult problem, such as troubleshooting the reason for packages being sent to incorrect addresses, you will be less stressed.

Type A Behavior and Hostility   A person with **Type A behavior** is demanding, impatient, and overstriving and is therefore prone to negative stress. Type A behavior has two main components. One is the tendency to try to accomplish too many things in too little time. This leads the Type A individual to be impatient and demanding. The other component is free-floating hostility. Because of this sense of urgency and hostility, trivial things irritate these people. People with Type A behavior are aggressive and hardworking.

Type A personalities frequently have cardiac diseases, such as heart attacks and strokes, at an early age, but only certain features of the Type A personality pattern may be related to coronary heart disease. The heart attack triggers are hostility, anger, cynicism, and suspiciousness, as contrasted to impatience, ambition, and being work driven. In fact, hostility is more strongly associated with coronary heart disease in men than smoking, drinking, overeating, or high levels of bad (LDL) cholesterol.[14] A review of studies confirms that there is no significant association between Type A personalities and heart disease. However, there is a strong association between hostility and coronary heart disease. Hostility of the sort seen in habitual angry driving is also a heart disease risk factor.[15] Note that the heart attack triggers also make for strained interpersonal relationships.

Negative Affectivity   A major contributor to being stress prone is **negative affectivity**, a tendency to experience aversive emotional states. In more detail, negative affectivity is a pervasive disposition to experience emotional stress that includes feelings of nervousness, tension, and worry. The same disposition also includes such emotional states as anger, scorn, revulsion, guilt, self-dissatisfaction, and sadness.[16] Such negative personalities seem to search for important discrepancies between what they would like and what exists. Poor interpersonal relationships often result from the frequent complaining of people with negative affectivity.

Job Sources of Stress.   Almost any job situation can act as a stressor for some employees, but not necessarily for others. As just described, certain personality factors make it more likely that a person will experience job stress. Furthermore, other personal life stressors may spill over into the workplace, making it more likely that a person will experience job stress. In the words of human resource writer Pamela Babcock, "Employees' job-related anxieties such as deadline pressures and demanding bosses are compounded by recession-induced financial worries and domestic tensions that many workers find at home."[17] Six frequently encountered job stressors are outlined in Figure 9-4 and described below.

Role Overload Including Extreme Jobs   Having too much work to do, **role overload**, can create negative stress in two ways. First, the person may become fatigued and thus be less able to tolerate annoyances and irritations. Second, a person subject to unreasonable work demands may feel perpetually behind schedule, a situation that is itself a powerful stressor. Downsizing often creates overload because fewer people are left to handle the same workload as before. (If work is carefully streamlined, role overload is minimized.)

Work overload often takes the form of an **extreme job** in which the incumbent works at least 60 hours per week in a position that usually requires tight deadlines and heavy travel. Many of these jobs with long hours are found in information technology and financial services fields; yet, many business owners work comparable hours. The availability of work associates across the globe in different time zones facilitates extreme jobs. One financial analyst who immigrated to the United States from India reportedly works 120 hours per week, leaving only 48 hours for nonwork activities including sleep. Although many extreme job holders experience considerable job stress, many are exalted by the excitement and the high income.[18]

In extreme form, role overload can kill. For example, death from too much work is so common in Japan that the word *karoshi* has been coined to label the situation. In a celebrated case, a Toyota chief engineer worked up to 114 hours of overtime a month in

type a behavior

A behavior pattern in which the individuals is demanding, impatient, and overstriving, and therefore prone to negative stress.

negative affectivity

A tendency to experience aversive emotional states.

role overload

Having too much work to do.

extreme job

Job in which the incumbent works at least 60 hours per week in a position that usually requires tight deadlines and heavy travel.

FIGURE 9-4   Six Significant Sources of Job Stress

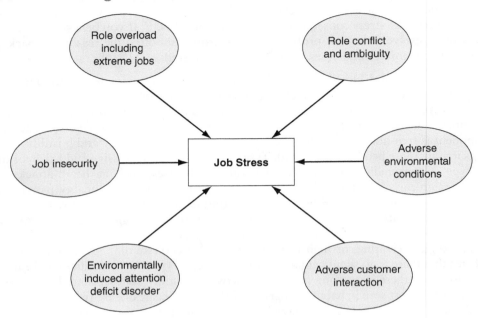

the six months before he died of heart failure. For decades, the Japanese government has been attempting without much success to set limits on hours of work, The consequenc es of role overload show up in claims for death and disability from overwork, and also in suicides attributed to work fatigue. Among 2,207 work-related suicides in Japanese companies in one year, the most frequent reason (672 suicides) was overwork.[19]

Role Conflict and Role Ambiguity   Role conflict is a major workplace stressor. People experience stress when they have to choose between two sets of expectations. Suppose an accountant is asked by her manager to state company earnings in a way that conflicts with the professional norms of accountants. If she complies with her manager, she will feel that she is betraying her profession. If she does not comply with her manager, she will enter into dispute with the manager. The woman is likely to experience job stress.

Role ambiguity is a condition in which the jobholder receives confusing or poorly defined expectations. Workers in many organizations are placed in situations in which they are unsure of their true responsibilities. Some workers who are placed on a work team experience role ambiguity because they are asked to solve many problems by themselves. It is less ambiguous to have the manager tell you what to do. Many people experience stress symptoms when faced with role ambiguity.

role ambiguity

A condition in which the job holder receives confusing or poorly defined expectations.

Adverse Environmental Conditions   A variety of adverse organizational conditions are stressors, as identified by the National Institute for Occupational Safety and Health (NIOSH). Among these adverse organizational conditions are unpleasant or dangerous physical conditions, such as crowding, noise, air pollutions, or ergonomic problems. Enough polluted air within an office building can create a sick building in which a diverse range of airborne particles, vapors, molds, and gases pollute the indoor environment. The result can be headaches, nausea, and respiratory infections as well as the stress created by being physically ill.[20]

Ergonomic problems refer to a poor fit between the physical and human requirements of a job. The demands of the modern workplace contribute to the development of musculoskeletal disorders. Working at a computer monitor for

prolonged periods of time can lead to adverse physical and psychological reactions. The symptoms include headaches and fatigue, along with eye problems. According to the Vision Syndrome Information Center, about 90 percent of people working on computers more than three hours a day have vision problems, with some 10 million a year seeking treatment. Common visual problems are dry eyes and blurred or double vision. Another vision-related problem is that people lean forward to scan the monitor, leading to physical problems such as back strain.

The repetitive-motion disorder most frequently associated with keyboarding and the use of optical scanners is **carpal tunnel syndrome**. The syndrome occurs when repetitive flexing and extension of the wrist causes the tendons to swell, thus trapping and pinching the median nerve. Carpal tunnel syndrome creates stress because of the pain and misery. About one in five computer users will suffer from carpal tunnel syndrome at some point.[21] A less publicized problem is a sore thumb (overuse syndrome) related to continuous use of the space bar and mouse. The "BlackBerry thumb" stems from using the thumb to type on the very small keyboard.

carpal tunnel syndrome
A condition that occurs when repetitive flexing and extension of the wrist causes the tendons to swell, thus trapping and pinching the median nerve.

The thoughts of having to permanently leave a job requiring keyboarding is another potential stressor. If ergonomic principles, such as erect posture, are incorporated into computer usage, these stress symptoms diminish. Office chairs developed in recent years allow for more flexibility of movement as workers shift rapidly between tasks such as moving toward the computer screen, placing feet on the desk, and then turning for a face-to-face conversation.[22]

Commuting to and from work is a major stressor for many people that could be classified as an adverse environmental condition. We emphasize *for many people* because individual differences again come into play. Some people enjoy driving, or being on a train or bus, for such reasons as the opportunity to listen to the radio or read. A study with New Jersey–New York commuters found that train rides of over one hour are particularly stressful for commuters. Longer commutes were associated with elevated cortisol (a stress hormone) poorer performance on a proofreading task given the study participants, and high levels of perceived commuting stress. The researcher also observed that for many workers commuting is the most stressful aspect of work.[23]

To avoid the stress of commuting in rush hour traffic, some workers leave home several hours before work, and then use the early arrival time to have breakfast, read the newspaper, or visit an athletic club near the work site.[24] Furthermore, a major reason many people work from home is to avoid the stresses associated with commuting.

Adverse Interaction with Customers and Clients and Emotional Labor   Interactions with customers can be a major stressor. Part of the problem is that the sales associate often feels helpless when placed in conflict with a customer. The sales associate is told that "the customer is always right." Furthermore, the store manager usually sides with the customer in a dispute with the sales associate. Unreasonable demands by clients and customers can also be stressful, such as customers who offer to buy a product or service below cost. During the Great Recession, many potential customers would frustrate car dealer sales reps by making offers 50 percent below sticker price, with an attitude of "take it or leave it." Being subjected to sexual harassment by clients and customers is another stressor widely experienced by store sales associates, especially young women.

Related to adverse customer interaction is the stressor of having to control the expression of emotion to please or to avoid displeasing a customer. Imagine having to smile at a customer who belittles you or your employer. Alicia A. Grandey, associate professor of psychology at Penn State University, defines **emotional labor** as the process of regulating both feelings and expressions to meet organizational goals.[25] The process involves both surface acting and deep acting. Surface acting means faking expressions, such as smiling, whereas deep acting involves controlling feelings, such as suppressing anger toward a customer you perceive to be annoying.

emotional labor
The process of regulating both feelings and expressions to meet organizational goals.

A study with 285 pairs of employees and customers suggests that deep acting, rather than maintaining an artificial smile, leads to better customer service.[26] As a result of the better customer service, it is possible that the customer will treat the associate better resulting in less stress for the latter.

Sales workers and customer service representatives often experience emotional labor because so often they have to fake facial expressions and feelings so as to please customers. Nevertheless, according to one study, the top five occupations in terms of emotional labor demands are (1) police and sheriff's patrol officers, (2) social workers, (3) psychiatrists, (4) supervisors of police and detectives, and (5) registered nurses. Bill and account collectors ranked 15![27]

Engaging in emotional labor for prolonged periods of time can lead to job dissatisfaction, stress, and burnout. Surface acting creates more dissatisfaction. A contributing cause is that faking expressions and emotions takes a physiological toll, such as the intestines churning. Workers who engage in emotional labor may also develop cardiovascular problems and weakened immune systems. The good news is that being extraverted helps reduce some of the stress associated with both surface acting and deep acting.[28] (Perhaps if you like people, you can better tolerate their unruly behavior.)

Environmentally Induced Attention Deficit Disorder   According to psychiatrist Edward Hallowell, many people suffer from an attention deficit disorder brought on by technology and activity overload. (The condition is similar to communication or information overload.) This problem appears to be a combination of the environment and the individual who chooses to overuse information technology devices. The symptoms of environmentally induced attention deficit disorder include frequently feeling rushed and impatient, being easily distracted, forgetfulness, and having little time for creative thought. In short, the person feels frazzled. A major cause of this type of attention deficit disorder is attempting to do more in less time.[29] Many of the suggestions about work habits and time management described later are useful in coping with environmentally induced attention deficit disorder.

Job Insecurity and Job Loss   Worrying about losing your job is a major stressor. Even when jobs are plentiful, having to search for another job and facing the prospect of geographic relocation are stressors for many people. Downsizing and corporate mergers (which usually result in downsizing) have contributed to job insecurity. The anticipation of layoffs among employees can increase negative stress and lower job performance. In addition, the survivors of a downsizing often experience pressure from the fear of future cuts, loss of friends, and worry about a sudden increase in workload.

Job loss is usually a more intense stressor than worrying about losing one's job. Losing a job often leads to the stressors of financial problems and relationship conflict. Some people who lose their job become so stressed and depressed that they commit suicide. An unfortunate example is that between 2006 and 2008, France Télécom laid off approximately 22,000 workers. Twenty-four laid off workers committed suicide, with the labor union blaming the layoffs for most of the suicides.[30] We hypothesize here that workers with good resources, such as supportive friends and family, good professional contacts, and effective job search skills are the least likely to commit suicide after job loss.

So which of the job stressors described have the most adverse effect on job performance? An analysis of 69 groups, comprising 35,265 employees indicated that role ambiguity and situational constraints are the most negatively related to job performance. A *situational constraint* refers to a situation in which conditions in an employee's job setting inhibit or constrain performance, such as improper machinery or inadequate supplies.[31] The job stressor, adverse environmental conditions, includes a few situational constraints.

Methods and Techniques for Stress Management

LEARNING OBJECTIVE 3 Unless stress is managed properly, it may lead to harmful long-term consequences, including disabling physical illness and career retardation. Managing stress refers to controlling stress by making it a constructive force in your life. Managing thus refers to both preventing and reducing stress. However, the distinction between methods of preventing and reducing stress is not clear-cut. For example, physical exercise not only reduces stress, it also contributes to a relaxed lifestyle that helps you prevent stress.

A key principle about managing stress is that you are less likely to experience distress from stressors if you have the right resources. Having the right personality characteristics such as high perceived control, high self-efficacy, and not being hostile helps ward off stress. External resources to help ward off negative stress include having a network of friends who provide support, an encouraging manager, and programs for helping distressed employees.[32] Assume, for example, that a worker is heavily stressed by a long rush hour commute. If the company provides flexible working hours that help decrease commuting during rush hour, the worker experience less of a hindrance stressor.

Coping with, or managing, stress includes hundreds of activities, with substantial individual differences in which technique is effective. Running is a case in point. For many people, running or jogging is an excellent method of stress reduction. Others find that running creates new stressors, such as aching knees, shin splints, dizziness from breathing in vehicle exhausts, and worrying about being hit by vehicles. In general, coping efforts involve cognitions and behaviors aimed at managing the stressor and its associated emotions. For example, you might have to decrease the troublesome elements in your job (such as role overload) and also deal with the tension generated by overwork. The following subsections describe eight methods for managing stress, including a list of everyday stress busters.

Eliminate or Modify the Stressor.

The most potent method of managing stress is to eliminate or modify the stressor giving you trouble. One value of relaxation techniques and tranquilizing medication is that they calm a person enough so that he or she can deal constructively with the stressor. A helpful way to attack the cause of stress is to follow the steps in problem solving and decision making. You clarify the problem, identify the alternatives, weigh the alternatives, and select one alternative. One difficulty, however, is that your evaluation of the real problem may be inaccurate. There is always a limit to self-analysis. For example, a person might think that work overload is the stressor when the true stressor is low self-efficacy.

A major strategy for modifying a stressor is to rethink your belief about a challenging situation. According to the **cognitive behavioral approach to stress management**, people learn to recognize how pessimistic and distorted thoughts of gloom and doom create stress. After recognition of the problem, the person learns to replace the overly pessimistic thinking with more realistic or optimistic thinking. Assume that Mandy is stressed about the prospects of losing her job. Using a cognitive-behavioral approach to stress management, she begins to think, "Would losing this job really be that bad? If this job folds, I could move to Denver where I've always wanted to live, and restart my career." Mandy is right on target because a synthesis of many studies found that cognitive-behavioral approaches are the most effective method of combating workplace stress.[33]

cognitive behavioral approach to stress management

A method by which people learn to recognize how pessimistic and distorted thoughts of gloom and doom create stress.

Get Appropriate Physical Exercise.

A moderate amount of physical exercise is a cornerstone of managing stress and achieving wellness. To manage stress, it is important to select an exercise program that is physically challenging but does not lead to overexertion and muscle and bone injury. Competitive sports, if taken too seriously, can actually increase stress. Aerobic exercises are most beneficial because they make you breathe faster and raise your heart rate. Walking is highly recommended as a stress reducer because it is inherently relaxing, and offers many of the benefits of other forms of exercise with a minimum risk of physical danger. Doing housework, yard work, and washing and waxing a vehicle are examples of everyday forms of gentle exercise that offer the side benefits of getting tasks accomplished. A major mental and emotional benefit of physical exercise stems from endorphins produced in the thalamus portion of the brain. The endorphins are associated with a state of euphoria referred to as "runner's high." Endorphins also work like pain killers, adding to their stress-reduction value.

Physical exercise directly reduces stress, and also reduces the risk of disorders that are both debilitating themselves, and as a result become intense stressors. As researched by the American College of Sports Medicine, among the benefits of exercise are (a) a 50 percent reduction in the incidence of diabetes, (b) a 40 percent reduction in the incidence of high blood pressure, (c) a 40 percent reduction in the risk of developing Alzheimer's disease, and (d) a decrease in depression as effective as Prozac or behavioral therapy.[34]

Millions of people seek to reduce and prevent stress through yoga, which is both physical exercise and a way of developing mental attitudes that calm the body and mind. One of yoga's many worthwhile goals is to solder a union between the mind and body, thereby achieving harmony and tranquility. Another benefit of yoga is that it helps people place aside negative thoughts that act as stressors. A caution about Yoga is that too much bending too soon can lead to injured hamstring muscles and torn blood vessels.

Rest Sufficiently. Rest offers benefits similar to those of exercise, such as stress reduction, improved concentration, improved energy, and better tolerance for frustration. Achieving proper rest is closely linked to getting proper exercise. The current interest in adult napping reflects the awareness that proper rest makes a person less stress prone and enhances productivity. A study was conducted of 23,681 healthy Greek adults over a six-year period, many of whom napped for about 30 minutes three times a week. Study participants who napped had 37 percent lower risk of dying from a heart attack than the people who did not. A criticism offered of this study is that the people who napped may also take better care of their bodies and mind in general.[35] The connection of this study to stress management is that many heart attacks are stress induced.

A growing number of firms have napping facilities for workers, and many workers nap at their desks or in their parked vehicles during lunch breaks. Naps of about 15 minutes duration taken during the workday are used both as energizers and as stress reducers. Napping can help a worker become less stressed as well as more productive. A rested brain is a more effective brain. To keep the effectiveness of workday napping in perspective, workers who achieve sufficient rest during normal sleeping hours have less need for a nap during working hours.[36]

Maintain a Healthy Diet. Another practical method of stress reduction and prevention is to maintain a well-balanced, and therefore healthy, diet. Nutritious food is valuable for physical and mental health, making it easier to cope with frustrations that are potential stressors. Some non-nutritious foods, such as those laden with caffeine or sugar, tend to enhance a person's level of stress. According to the Dietary Guidelines of the United States Department of Agriculture, a healthy diet is one that

- Emphasizes fruits, vegetables, whole grains, and fat-free or low-fat milk and milk products
- Includes lean meats, poultry, fish, beans, eggs, and nuts
- Is low in saturated fats, *trans* fats, cholesterol, salt (sodium), and added sugars.

These recommendations are for the general public over two years of age. Using MyPyramid, the government personalizes a recommended diet, taking into account our age, sex, and amount of physical exercise. Consult *http://www.mypyramid.gov*, as shown in Figure 9-5. Also, nutritionists highly recommend fibers found in whole-grain breads, rolls and cereals, and brown rice.

FIGURE 9-5 **Dietary Guidelines for Americans, developed by the U.S. Department of Agriculture**

The Food Groups

Grains

Vegetables

Fruits

Milk

Meat & Beans

Oils

Source: U.S. Department of Agriculture, *http://www.mypyramid.gov.*

Build a Support Network.   A **support network** is a group of people who can listen to your problems and provide emotional support. These people, or even one person, can help you through your difficult episodes. Members of your network can provide you with a sense of closeness, warmth, and acceptance that will reduce your stress. Also, the simple expedient of putting your feelings into words can be a healing experience. The way to develop this support network is to become a good listener so that the other person will reciprocate. A support network is therefore a method of stress management based squarely on effective interpersonal skills.

Practice Visualization and Meditation.   Perhaps the most effortless and enjoyable relaxation technique for managing stress is to visualize a pleasant experience, as explained in Skill-Building Exercise 9-1. Visualization, like so many stress-reduction techniques, including meditation, requires concentration. Concentrating helps slow down basic physiological processes, such as the heartbeat and dissipates stress. Visualization, meditation, prayer, and chanting all appear to offer such advantages as lowering heart rate, blood pressure, and oxygen consumption. These techniques also alleviate symptoms associated with such conditions as hypertension, insomnia, depression, and anxiety.[37] Forcing yourself to concentrate is also valuable because a key stress symptom is difficulty in concentrating.

Meditation is a relaxation technique used to quiet the mind, as well as to relieve stress, and is more complicated than simple visualization. (The well-known relaxation response is essentially a form of meditation.) A typical meditation technique proceeds as follows: Hold your back straight, and relax the body. Take three gentle breaths, breathing in and out through the nostrils. Let the respiration follow its natural flow. Your body breathes as if it was fast asleep, yet you remain vigilant. If you become distracted, simply let go of the thought, and return to the breath. It is helpful to count each inhale up to 21. Each time your mind wanders, return back to one. Practice meditating about 20 minutes a day, and meditate on the spot after a stressful event or thought.[38] The breathing part of meditation is so important that it is an everyday method of stress reduction itself.

Practice Everyday Methods of Stress Reduction.   The simple expedient of learning how to relax is an important method of reducing the tension and anxiety brought about by both challenge and hindrance stressors. Visualization of a pleasant experience is one such method. A sample of everyday suggestions for relaxation and other methods of stress reduction are presented in Figure 9-6. If you can accomplish these, you are less likely to need tranquilizing medication to keep you calm and in control. Your stress symptoms will ordinarily return, however, if you do not eliminate and modify the stressor. If the stress is an emotional conflict you do not see or understand, assistance from a mental health professional is recommended.

Now that you have studied various method of managing stress, reinforce your thinking by doing Skill-Building Exercise 9-2.

support network

A group of people who can listen to your problems and provide emotional support.

FIGURE 9-6   Stress Busters

- Take a deep breath and exhale slowly. Inhale and your heart beats faster. Exhale and your heart beats more slowly, and slow down the cardiac muscle.[31]
- Place your thumbs behind your ears and spread your fingers on the top of your head. Move your scalp back and forth gently by rotating your fingers for 15-20 seconds.
- Give in to your emotions. If you are angry, disgusted, or confused, admit your feelings. Suppressing your emotions adds to stress.
- Take a brief break from the stressful situation and do something small and constructive, such as washing your car, emptying a wastebasket, or getting a haircut.
- Get a massage, because it can loosen tight muscles, improve your blood circulation, and calm you down.
- Get help with your stressful task from a coworker, supervisor, or friend.
- Concentrate intensely on reading, surfing the Internet, a sport, or a hobby. Contrary to common sense, concentration is at the heart of stress reduction.
- Have a quiet place at home and have a brief idle period there every day.
- Take a leisurely day off from your routine.
- Finish something you have started, however small. Accomplishing almost anything reduces some stress.
- Stop to smell the flowers, make friends with a young child or elderly person, or play with a kitten or puppy.
- Strive to do a good job, but not a perfect job.
- Work with your hands, doing a pleasant task.
- Find somebody or something that makes you laugh, and have a good laugh.
- Minimize drinking caffeinated or alcoholic beverages, and drink fruit juice or water instead. Grab a piece of fruit rather than a can of beer.
- Help somebody less fortunate than you. The flood of good feelings will act like endorphins.

SKILL-BUILDING EXERCISE 9-2

Personal Stress Management Action Plan

Most people face a few powerful stressors in their work and personal life, but few people take the time to clearly identify these stressors or develop an action plan for remedial action. The purpose of this exercise is to make you an exception. Here is an opportunity to develop an inventory of your stressors, think through the problems they may be causing you, and develop action plans you might take to remedy the situation. Use the form below or create one with a word processing table or a spreadsheet.

Work or School Stressor	Symptoms This Stressor Is Creating for Me	My Action Plan to Manage This Stressor
1.		
2.		
3.		
Personal Life Stressor	Symptoms This Stressor Is Creating for Me	My Action Plan to Manage This Stressor
1.		
2.		
3.		

Seven days after preparing this work sheet, observe if any of your stress symptoms have diminished. Also, identify those stressors for which only a long-term solution is possible. One student reported that a major work stressor he faced is that he wanted to work in international business, and emphasize doing business with Italian fashion companies. Yet he was experiencing stress because he had almost zero knowledge of the Italian language or culture. (By the way, can you offer this man any suggestions?)

IMPROVING PERSONAL PRODUCTIVITY

Achieving personal productivity is more in vogue than ever. Companies strive to operate with smaller staffs than in the past by pushing workers to achieve higher productivity. Particularly during a recession, workers pressure themselves to produce more per hour of work because many of them fear for their jobs. At the same time, there is a movement toward simplifying personal life by reducing clutter and cutting back on tasks that do not add much to the quality of life. **Personal productivity** refers to the amount of resources, including time, you consume to achieve a certain level of output. We approach productivity improvement from four perspectives: (1) dealing with procrastination, (2) attitudes and values that enhance personal productivity, (3) work habits and skills that enhance personal productivity, and (4) overcoming time wasters.

personal productivity

The amount of resources, including time, you consume to achieve a certain level of output.

Dealing with Procrastination

The person who **procrastinates** delays action for no good reason on tasks that need to de done. Procrastination results in a gap between intention and action. A major reason why people procrastinate is that they want to feel good at the moment rather than reap future rewards. As such, procrastination is a form of impulsivity.[39] Why bother getting in touch with my boss to discuss my prospects for promotion when I can send a Tweet to 500 people right now?

procrastination

Delaying action on tasks that need to be done for no good reason.

Procrastination lowers productivity because it wastes time and many important tasks never get done. Another serious problem is that undone tasks rumble around in the back of your consciousness, thereby decreasing your concentration. Chronic procrastination can even lead to debt, divorce, and job loss. Even productive people sometimes procrastinate. If these people did not procrastinate, they would be even more productive.

Many people regard procrastination as a laughable weakness, particularly because procrastinators themselves joke about the problem. Yet procrastination has been evaluated as a profound, debilitating problem, with between 20 and 25 percent of working adults identifying themselves as chronic procrastinators.[40] Approximately 90 percent of college students report problems with overdue papers and delayed studying. About 25 percent are chronic procrastinators, and many of them drop out of school.[41] The enormity of the procrastination problem makes it worthwhile to examine methods for bringing it under control. Do Self-Assessment Quiz 9-1 to think through your own tendencies toward procrastination—and don't wait until tomorrow.

Choose from among the following suggestions for controlling procrastination, based on those that appear to best fit your type of procrastination. A combination of techniques is likely to be the most effective.

1. **Commit to what you want in life.** If you are not committed to something you want in life, you are likely to be chronic procrastinator. The reason is that it is difficult to prioritize and take action. (See the later discussion about a personal mission and work habits.)[42] Your commitment to what you want in life will often translate into forgoing short-term pleasure, such as stopping by a café, in order to finish a project due today.

2. **Calculate the cost of procrastination.** You can reduce procrastination by calculating its cost. You might lose out on obtaining a high-paying job you really want by not having your résumé and cover letter ready on time. Your cost of procrastination would include the difference in compensation between the job you do find and the one you really wanted. Another cost would be the loss of potential job satisfaction.

Procrastination Tendencies

Directions: Circle yes or no for each item:

1.	I usually do my best work under the pressure of deadlines.	Yes	No
2.	Before starting a project, I go through such rituals as sharpening every pencil, straightening up my desk more than once, and reading and responding to all possible e-mail.	Yes	No
3.	I crave the excitement of the "last-minute rush," such as researching and writing a paper right before the deadline.	Yes	No
4.	I often think that if I delay something, it will go away, or the person who asked for it will forget about it.	Yes	No
5.	I extensively research something before taking action, such as obtaining three different estimates before getting the brakes repaired on my car.	Yes	No
6.	I have a great deal of difficulty getting started on most projects, even those I enjoy.	Yes	No
7.	I keep waiting for the right time to do something, such as getting started on an important report.	Yes	No
8.	I often underestimate the time needed to do a project, and say to myself, "I can do this quickly, so I'll wait until next week."	Yes	No
9.	It is difficult for me to finish most projects or activities.	Yes	No
10.	I have several favorite diversions or distractions that I use to keep me from doing something unpleasant, such as a difficult homework assignment.	Yes	No

Total Yes Responses _____

Scoring and Interpretation: The greater the number of "yes" responses, the more likely it is that you have a serious procrastination problem. A score of 8, 9, or 10 strongly suggests that your procrastination is lowering your productivity.

3. **Follow the WIFO principle, which stands for "worst in, first out."**[43] If you tackle the worst task on your list first, doing the other tasks may function like a small reward. You get to do what you dislike the least by doing first what you dislike the most. WIFO is particularly effective when faced with a number of tasks simultaneously.

4. **Break the task into manageable chunks.** To reduce procrastination, cut down a task that seems overwhelming into smaller projects that seem less formidable. If your job calls for preparing an enormous database, begin by assembling some readily available information. Then take the next step by assembling another small segment of the database—perhaps all customers whose last names begin with Z. Think of your task as pulling together a series of small databases that will fit into a master database.

5. **Make a commitment to other people.** Try to make it imperative that you get something done on time by making it a commitment to one or more other people. You might announce to coworkers that you are going to get something accomplished by a certain date. If you fail to meet this date, you are likely to feel embarrassed.

6. **Remove some clutter from your mind.** Procrastination escalates when people have many unfinished projects in the back of their mind, draining their concentration. Having too much to do can freeze us into inaction. Just eliminating a few trivial items from your to-do list can give you enough mental energy to overcome procrastination on a few major tasks. This approach to overcoming procrastination requires that you apply enough self-discipline to take the first step. Notice the unfortunate cycle: Procrastination leads to poor concentration (as described above), and procrastination hampers concentration.

7. **Satisfy your stimulation quota in constructive ways.** If you procrastinate because you enjoy the rush of scrambling to make deadlines, find a more constructive way of using busyness to keep you humming. If you need a high level of stimulation, enrich your life with extra projects and learning new skills. The fullness of your

schedule will provide you the stimulation you had been receiving from squeezing yourself to make deadlines and reach appointments on time.[44]

8. **Eliminate tangible rewards you are giving yourself for procrastinating.** If you are procrastinating through socializing with coworkers, taking a walk to obtain a beverage, surfing the Internet, or any other pleasant experience—stop rewarding yourself. Just sit alone in your work area doing nothing while procrastinating. If you remove the pleasant activities from your stalling routine, you may be able to reduce procrastination.

Enhancing Personal Productivity through Attitudes and Values

LEARNING OBJECTIVE 5

Developing good work habits and time management practices is often a matter of developing the right attitudes toward your work and toward time. If, for example, you think that your schoolwork or job is important and that time is a precious resource, you will be on your way toward developing good work habits. In this section, we describe a group of attitudes, values, and beliefs that can help a person become more productive through better use of time and improved work habits.

Begin with a Mission and Goals.   A mission, or general purpose, propels you toward being productive. Assume that a person says, "My mission is to be an outstanding professional in my field and a loving, constructive spouse and parent." The mission serves as a compass to direct your activities, such as being well organized in order to accomplish more work and be highly valued by your employer. Goals are more specific than mission statements; they support the mission statement, but the effect is the same. Being committed to a goal also propels you toward good use of time. If you know that you can obtain the position in international business that you really want by mastering a second language, you are likely to work diligently on learning that language. Consultant Dean Fuhrman supports our point with this advice:

> If you really want to manage your time and get stuff done, have a burning life and work purpose that is a beacon for what you do. While they are useful, the lists, the shortcuts—all that stuff—pales in comparison to purpose for time management.[45]

Skill-Building Exercise 9-3 gives you the opportunity to establish a mission statement and supporting goals.

SKILL-BUILDING EXERCISE 9-3

Using a Mission Statement and Goals to Power Work Habits

People with a well-defined mission statement and supporting goals tend to have better work habits and time management than those who do not. The following exercise is designed to help you establish a mission statement and goals so that you will be energized to be more productive.

A. *Mission Statement:* To help develop your mission statement, or general purpose in life, ask yourself, "What are my five biggest wishes in life?" These wishes give you a hint to your purpose be-cause they point toward an ideal purpose in life. Feel free to think big, because mission statements tend toward being idealistic.

B. *Long-Range Goals to Support Mission Statement:* Now write down what long-range goals would support your mission statement. Suppose your mission statement related to "creating a better life for people who are disadvantaged." Your long-range goals might include establishing a foundation that would fund your efforts. You would also need to be successful enough in your career to get the foundation started.

C. *Intermediate-Range Goals to Support Long-Range Goals:* Write down the intermediate-range goals needed to support the long-range goals. You will probably need to complete your education, obtain broad experience, and identify a lucrative form of self-employment.

D. *Weekly Goals to Support Intermediate-Range Goals:* Write down what you have to do this week to help you complete your education, such as researching and writing a paper for a particular course, registering for courses for next term, and inquiring about career opportunities in your field.

E. *Today's Goals to Support Weekly Goals (My To-Do List):* Here's where your lofty purpose in life gets translated into reality. What do you have to do today to get that paper written? Do you need to get your car battery replaced, so you can get to the library, so you can write your paper, so you can graduate, so you can become rich, so you can ultimately help all those people who are disadvantaged? Get going.

Work Smarter, Not Harder.   People caught up in trying to accomplish a job often wind up working hard, but not in an imaginative way that leads to good results. Much time and energy are therefore wasted. A working-smart approach also requires that you spend a few minutes carefully planning how to implement your task. An example of working smarter, not harder, is to invest a few minutes of critical thinking before conducting a telemarketing campaign for home replacement windows. Develop a list of homeowners of houses of at least 15 years old. People with relatively new homes are poor prospects for replacing their windows.

A new perspective on working smarter, not harder, is to keep perfecting your skills through **deliberate practice**—strong effort to improve target performance over time. Practice alone does not lead to nearly as much improvement as thinking through what you have done to look for areas for improvement.[46] Feedback from others is also helpful. Assume that a loan officer at a bank signs off on loans to small business owners. She engages in deliberate practice by following the history of these loans to evaluate which business owners proved to be good risks, and those that proved to be poor risks. She frequently asks herself, "What did I miss here? "What did I do right here?" In this way, the loan officer is working smarter by honing her risk-evaluation skills.

Value Orderliness and Cleanliness.   An orderly desk, work area, briefcase, hard drive, or storage drive does not inevitably indicate an orderly mind. Yet, it does help most people become more productive because they can better focus their mind. Being surrounded by a collection of small, unfinished tasks interferes with your ability to focus on major tasks. Also, less time is wasted and less energy is expended if you do not have to hunt for information that you thought you had on hand. The central message of the best-seller *Getting Things Done* by David Allen is that to achieve maximum efficiency and relaxation is to clear clutter both outside and inside your mind.[47] One way of clearing clutter from your mind is to write down your tasks on to-do lists. If you are orderly, you clear clutter.

Knowing where information is and what information you have available is a way of being in control of your job. When your job gets out of control, you are probably working at less than peak efficiency. Valuing cleanliness improves productivity in several ways. According to the Japanese system, cleanliness is the bedrock of quality. Also, after you have thoroughly cleaned your work area, you will usually attain a fresh outlook.

As with any suggestions about human behavior, individual differences exist with respect to the impact of clutter on productivity. Internet guru Esther Dyson has a work area so cluttered that she gives the impression of being an exaggerated case of a person needing help from a personal productivity consultant. It has also been argued that focusing too much on tidiness might detract from creative thinking, and that many messy people, such as Albert Einstein, believe that a messy work area facilitates their creative thinking. To quote the great man, "If a cluttered desk is a sign of a cluttered mind, of what the, is an empty desk?"[48]

Value Good Attendance and Punctuality.   Good attendance and punctuality are expected of both experienced and inexperienced employees. You cannot be productive unless you are physically present in your work area. The same principle applies whether you work on company premises or at home. One exception is that some people can work through solutions to job problems while engaged in recreation. Keep in mind, too, that being late for or absent from meetings sends the silent message that you do not regard the meeting as being important. Also, being late for a meeting, whether face-to-face or virtual, is regarded quite negatively by many managers. Some managers even lock the door to the meeting room after the meeting has begun. Whether the person is late or absent for work, or just for a meeting, the behavior is interpreted by many as demonstrating irresponsibility.

Attain a Balance in Life and Avoid Being a Workaholic.   A productive attitude to maintain is that overwork can lead to negative stress and burnout. Proper physical rest and relaxation can contribute to mental alertness and an improved ability to cope with frustration. Many people do not achieve enough rest and relaxation as inferred from the avoidance of vacations. A recent survey by Right Management showed that 66 percent of 667 surveyed workers had not used all their vacation time in the year studied.[49] During a recession, the tendency increases to not take all the vacation time allotted to the employee.

The environmentally induced attention deficit disorder and extreme jobs described above represent a life out of balance. A strategy for preventing overwork is to strive for a balance in which you derive satisfaction from various spheres of life. Major spheres in addition to work include family life, romance, sports, the arts and music, faith, and intellectual growth.

A strongly recommended technique for attaining balance between work and other spheres of life is to learn how to say no diplomatically to your boss and family members.[50] For example, your boss might ask you to take on a project when you are already overloaded. It would be necessary to *occasionally* explain that you are so overloaded that you could not do a good job with the new assignment. And, you might have to *occasionally* turn down your family's or friend's request to take a weekend vacation when you face heavy work demands.

Neglecting the normal need for rest and relaxation can lead to **workaholism**, an addiction to work in which not working is an uncomfortable experience. Some types of workaholics are perfectionists who are never satisfied with their work and therefore find it difficult to leave work behind, and have no real hobbies outside of the office. In addition, the perfectionist-type workaholic may become heavily focused on control of people and information, leading to rigid behavior and strained interpersonal relationships. Many workaholics take laptops to bed, and leave their cell phones on during the night to catch any potential calls from distant time zones. However, some people who work long and hard are classified as achievement-oriented workaholics who thrive on hard work and are usually highly productive.[51] For example, a person with strong family values might nevertheless work 65 hours per week for one year while establishing a new business. In contrast, giving up on the income and status you are striving for to avoid working long hours may not be a good idea.

workaholism

An addiction to work in which not working is an uncomfortable experience.

Increase Your Energy. According to Tony Schwartz, the founder of the Energy Project in New York City, increasing your energy is the best way to get more done faster and better. Becoming more energetic leads to more productivity gains than merely working longer hours. Schwartz believes that energy has four wellsprings—the body, emotions, mind, and spirit. Rituals can be established to build energy in the four areas, highlighted as follows:

1. **Body.** Increasing bodily energy closely follows some of the guidelines for stress management described above. Proper nutrition, moderate physical exercise, adequate rest, and taking brief breaks form work all enhance a person's energy level.

2. **Emotions.** Positive emotions bring us much more energy than do negative ones. Being in the fight-or-flight mode too frequently lowers emotional energy. Deep abdominal breathing can help ward off negative emotion. A powerful ritual that helps generate positive emotion is to express appreciation to others. Overcoming the idea that you are a victim can also bring about positive energy.

3. **Mind.** To enhance mental energy, it is particularly important to minimize distractions that lead to constant multitasking. Switching to another task increases the amount of time required to complete the primary tasks by up to 25 percent, a phenomenon know as *switching time*.

We recognize, however, that you still have to live in a modern world. If you are preparing a report, and your boss sends you an urgent IM, or your sick parent or child sends you a text message, it is natural to be distracted away from your primary task. The sensible strategy is to minimize distractions, not eliminate them completely.

4. Spirit. Participating in activities that give you a sense of meaning and purpose, such coaching and mentoring others, boosts the energy of the spirit. Being attentive to your deeper needs, such as being concerned about human or animal welfare, can boost your effectiveness and satisfaction on the job.[52]

You may have observed that this energy program for business executives is quite similar to what you have been studying in relation to developing interpersonal skills.

Enhancing Personal Productivity through Work Habits and Skills

LEARNING OBJECTIVE 6

Overcoming procrastination and developing the right attitudes contribute to personal productivity. Effective work habits and skills are also essential for high productivity. Six key work habits and skills are described next. They represent a mixture of traditional productivity boosters and those geared toward information technology.

Prepare a To-Do List and Set Priorities. At the heart of every time management system is list making, whether the list is placed on an index card, in a leather-bound planner, or in a personal digital assistant, or smart phone. The to-do list is the basic tool for achieving your daily goals, which in turn helps you achieve bigger goals and your mission. Almost every successful person in any field composes a list of important and less important tasks that need to be done. Many business executives stick a to-do list in their jacket pocket each morning. Before you compose a useful list, you need to set aside a few minutes of quiet time every day to sort out the tasks at hand. This is the most basic aspect of planning.

The "Getting Things Done" system of time management guru David Allen is built on a base of a to-do list. First, you transfer all the tasks floating around in your head onto paper or into software, and sort them into a system of prioritized lists. Second, you take the items on the to-do lists (such as "sanitize the bakery") into "next actions," or necessary steps to accomplish the goal.[53] For the task in question, you might send an e-mail to a commercial cleaning company in your area.

As is well known, it is helpful to set priorities for items on the to-do list. A typical system is to use A to signify critical or essential items, B to signify important items, and C for the least important ones. Although an item might be regarded as a C (e.g., emptying the wood shavings from the electronic pencil sharpener), it still makes a contribution to your management of time and sense of well-being. Accomplishing anything reduces some stress. Also, many people obtain satisfaction from crossing off an item on their list, however trivial. If you are at all conscientious, small, unaccomplished items will come back to interfere with your concentration.

To-do lists contribute enormously to productivity, yet a to-do list may have to be revamped to meet the changing demands of the day. Marissa Mayer, vice president, Search Products and User Experience, at Google, explains that she keeps a task list in a text file. She uses the list as high-priority things to focus on. "But at Google things can change pretty fast. This morning I had my list of what I thought I was going to do today, but now I'm doing entirely different things," says Mayer.[54] As a result, she quickly prepares a new to-do list.

Preparing to-do lists should not become an end in itself, with so much time devoted to list making that accomplishing some of the tasks are neglected. The compulsive list maker sometimes neglects seeing the big picture of what needs to get done. Another danger is filling the to-do list with items you would have to accomplish anyway, such as "check e-mail" or "handle customer inquiry." The to-do list can become so long that it becomes an overwhelming task.

Streamline Your Work and Emphasize Important Tasks. As companies continue to operate with fewer workers than in the past despite prosperity, more unproductive work must be eliminated. Getting rid of unproductive work is part of *business process improvement* in which work processes are radically redesigned and simplified. Every employee is

> 66 Time is your most precious commodity. You students live as if you had infinite time. You can always make more money later. But you can't make more time. Time, like money, must be explicitly managed. 99
>
> —Paraphrased from comments made to his students by Randy Pausch, Professor of computer science at Carnegies Mellon University, and co-author of the best-seller, *The Last Lecture* (New York: Hyperion, 2008).[55] Before and after his death at age 47, Pausch attained a cult following.

expected to get rid of work that does not contribute to productivity or help customers. In general, to streamline your work, look for duplication of effort and waste. An example of duplication of effort would be to routinely send people e-mail and voicemail messages covering the same topic. An example of waste would be to call a meeting for disseminating information that could easily be communicated by e-mail.

Emphasizing important tasks means that you make sure to take care of A items on your to-do list. It also implies that you search to accomplish a few work activities that, if done well, would make a big difference in your job performance. Although important tasks may take less time to accomplish than many routine tasks, they can represent the difference between success and failure. Five minutes of telephone conversation with a major customer might do more good for your company than three hours of arranging obsolete inventory in the warehouse.

Concentrate on One Important Task at a Time Instead of Multitasking. While working on important tasks, concentrate on what you are doing. Effective executives and professionals have a well-developed capacity to concentrate on the problem or person facing them, however surrounded they are with other obligations. Intense concentration leads to crisper judgment and analysis and also minimizes major errors. Another useful by-product of concentration is that it helps reduce absentmindedness. If you really concentrate on what you are doing, the chances diminish that you will forget what you intended to do.

While concentrating on an important task, such as performing analytical work or writing a report, avoid multitasking, or performing more than one activity simultaneously. Common forms of multitasking include surfing the Internet or reading e-mail while engaged in a phone conversation with a coworker or customer. Both experimental evidence and opinion have accumulated that multitasking while performing important tasks leads to problems in concentration, along with significant errors—for most people. The information about mental energy described above applies here. Multitasking on routine tasks has less negative consequences, and can sometimes be a legitimate time saver. For example, waiting in line at the airport during business travel provides a good opportunity to review company documents or catch up on work-related news.

David E. Meyer, the director of the Brain, Cognition and Action Laboratory at the University of Michigan, notes that when people attempt to perform two or more related tasks at the same time or alternating rapidly—instead of doing them sequentially—two negative consequences occur. Errors increase substantially, and the amount of time to perform the task may double.[56] Also, according to recent research about the brain, few people can concentrate on more than four tasks at once.[57]

Multitasking has enormous potential negative consequences when the lives of others are at stake, such as when driving a car, truck, or flying an airplane. In a celebrated case, two Northwest airline pilots lost their job because they used their personal laptops while in flight. As a result, they lost track of their responsibilities, and neglected frantic messages from air-traffic controllers, and flew past their destination airport in Minneapolis. The two pilots failed to establish radio contact with controllers for 78 minutes, and overshot their destination by more than 100 miles.[58]

Place the potential dangers of multitasking on a personal level. Would you want a cardiac surgeon to operate on a loved one while she was receiving personal calls on her cell phone? Would you want your commercial airline pilot to be sending text messages to "friends" on a social network while he was flaying through a storm? (Using personal laptops while in flight is not reassuring either.)

BACK TO THE OPENING CASE

Lynai Lutes and her coworkers at the advertising agency in Arlington, Texas, are prospering. One of the reasons for their success is that they do not subscribe to the idea that workers at a small firm are too busy to spend time thinking, and instead must chase after details continuously. Instead, the group invests enough time in quiet reflection to find creative solutions for their clients. Also, the time devoted to concentrating on one major task helps reduce stress.

Stay in Control of Paperwork and Electronic Work. Although it is fashionable to complain about paperwork in responsible jobs, the effective career person does not neglect paperwork. (Paperwork includes electronic work, such as electronic mail and voice-mail.) Paperwork involves taking care of administrative details such as correspondence, invoices, human resource reports, expense reports, and inventory forms. A considerable amount of electronic work results in paperwork because many e-mail messages and attachments wind up being printed. Unless paperwork and electronic work are attended to, a person's job may get out of control. A small amount of time should be invested in paperwork every day. Nonprime time (when you are at less than your peak of efficiency but not overfatigued) is the best time to take care of paperwork.

An effective technique is to respond quickly to high-priority e-mail messages, and permanently delete those you will most likely not need to refer to again. Print and file only those e-mail messages of high importance to avoid being overwhelmed with piles of old messages. For many types of work, it is important to be able to access old e-mails. However, some workers complain (brag?) of having 6,000 e-mails in their inbox. In addition to clogging the servers, this large accumulation of e-mails is distracting, thereby lowering productivity. Old e-mails should be archived, and others moved to appropriate folders.[59]

Communicating by e-mail or telephone with coworkers in distant time zones creates special challenges in terms of staying in control of electronic work. Assume that Pedro working in Washington DC has clients in London who want to have telephone conferences at 9 a.m. their time. Pedro has to be on the phone at 3 a.m. his time, so it is best to make all his 3 a.m. calls one morning per week rather than having a life out of control because he has to be on the phone many mornings at 3 a.m.

Work Productively from Your Home Office or Virtual Office. A growing segment of the workforce works either full or part time from home or from a **virtual office**. Estimates vary considerably, but it appears that about 4 percent of corporate employees work primarily from the home. Such an office is a place of work without a fixed physical location from where the worker or workers communicate their output electronically. A virtual office might be in a car, train, airplane, or hotel room; on a park bench; or wherever the worker happens to be at the time. Many people adapt well to working at home and from virtual offices because they are self-starters and self-disciplined. Many other workers lack the self-discipline and effective work habits necessary to be productive outside of a traditional office. Following is a list of representative suggestions for being productive while working independently.[60]

- Act as if you work in a traditional office. Set specific working hours, get dressed, go outside the house for a few minutes, then return and get to work. Also, close your office at home or virtual office at some regular time. Otherwise, you are open for business all the time. If you work at home, establish a clear workspace and let your family and friends know when you cannot be disturbed.

- Stay in touch with teammates to enhance your team player skills and not lose out on important information that could lower your effectiveness (such as missing an appointment at the traditional office). Stay in touch with other workers also, such as visiting an office supply store or attending networking meetings. In this way, you will feel less isolated from the workforce—assuming feeling isolated is a problem for you.

- Minimize conducting your personal life at the same time as working (e.g., working while watching television, talking to neighbors, or shopping over the Internet).

- Schedule regular times for meals and snacks; otherwise, you will lose many minutes and gain many pounds taking food and beverage breaks.

The practice of working at home or from virtual offices is increasing rapidly, so these suggestions merit careful consideration. Several of the productivity ideas also fit the conventional office. Best Buy is attempting to foster the virtual office movement with its results-only work environment (ROWE). The idea is that workers are free to do whatever they want, wherever they want, so long as the work gets done.[61] Of course, sales associates do not fit this system because a worker cannot demonstrate HDTVs to customers while at an Internet café. Also, if part of your job is to help other workers in person, or answer their spontaneous questions, a virtual office is not an effective option.

Enhance Your Internet Search Skills.   An important job skill is searching the Internet for a variety of information. It follows that if you develop your Internet search skills, you will be more productive by obtaining the results you need within a reasonable time. First, it is helpful to rely on several search engines to seek needed information. Several meta-search engines claim to be so comprehensive that no other engine is required. Such claims are exaggerated, because the same search word entered into several different comprehensive engines will reveal a different list of sources. Millions of people believe that conducting an Internet search means only that you google your search term.

Second, give careful thought to the search word or phrase you use. The more specific you are, the better it is. Assume that you wanted to find software to enhance your productivity, and that you enter the word "software" into a search engine. You will probably receive a message indicating that approximately one billion entries have been located in response to your personal inquiry. You are better advised to use the search phrase "Software for increasing personal productivity."

Third, for many searches, framing the query as a phrase by enclosing it in quotation marks refines the number of hits (or sites) returned. Place quotation marks before and after the search word, such as "software for improving work habits." Fourth, if you don't find what you want in your initial search, reframe your question in another way or change the terms. How about "software for time management" or "computer programs for increasing personal efficiency"? Skill-Building Exercise 9-4 will help you make better use of the Internet to enhance your personal productivity.

Overcoming Time Wasters

LEARNING OBJECTIVE 7

Another basic thrust to improve personal productivity is to minimize wasting time. The average U.S. worker wastes 28 percent of the day with interruptions, such as checking e-mail, responding to an instant message, clicking on YouTube, or posting a personal message on Twitter or Facebook. The wasted time includes doing the task and recovery time, with the combination resulting in an estimated productivity drain of $650 billion per year.[62] Recognize, however, that answer the phone or responding to an e-mail with a legitimate work purpose is not an interruption—it is part of your job.

Many of the techniques already described in this chapter help save time, such as eliminating nonessential work. Whether or not an activity is a time waster depends on the purpose of the activity. Suppose you play computer solitaire for 10 minutes to reduce stress and then return to work refreshed and more productive. In contrast, another worker who spends 10 minutes playing solitaire just for fun is wasting time.

Figure 9-7 presents a list of common time wasters. Being aware of time wasters will help sensitize you to the importance of minimizing them. Even if you saved just 10 minutes per workday, the productivity gain over a year could be enormous.

To analyze whether you might be wasting time, do Skill-Building Exercise 9-5 Self-Assessment Quiz 9-2 gives you an opportunity to think through your tendencies toward a subtle type of time wasting.

FIGURE 9-7 Ways to Prevent and Overcome Time Wasting

1. Get your desk, as well as your work space (usually a cubicle or office) in order for good because sorting through disorder wastes so much time. Also, keep track of important names, places, and things to avoid wasting time searching for them.

2. Use a time log for two weeks to track time wasters. (See Skill-Building Exercise 9-5.)

3. Avoid the computer as a diversion from work, such as sending jokes back and forth to work members, playing video games, and checking out recreational Web sites during working hours.

4. Cluster together tasks such as returning phone calls or responding to e-mail messages. For example, in most jobs it is possible to be polite and productive by reserving two or three 15-minute periods per day for taking care of e-mail correspondence.

5. Socialize on the job just enough to build your network. Chatting with coworkers is a major productivity drain.

6. Be prepared for meetings by, for example, having a clear agenda and sorting through the documents you will be referring to. Make sure electronic equipment is in working order before attempting to use it during the meeting.

7. Set a time limit for tasks after you have done them once or twice.

8. Prepare a computer template for letters and computer documents that you send frequently. (The template is essentially a form letter, especially with respect to the salutation and return address.)

9. When you arrive at work, be ready to get started working immediately. Greet people quickly, avoid checking your personal e-mail, and shut off your cell phone.

10. Take care of as much e-mail correspondence as you can after you have finished your other work, unless a key part of your job is dealing with e-mail. It consumes substantial time.

11. Avoid perfectionism, which leads you to keep redoing a project. Let go and move on to another project.

12. Make use of bits of time—for instance, five minutes between appointments. Invest those five minutes in sending a work-related e-mail message or revising your to-do list.

13. Minimize procrastination, the number one time waster for most people.

14. Avoid spreading yourself too thin by doing too many things at once, such as having one project too many to handle. When you are overloaded, time can be wasted because of too many errors.

15. Manage interruptions by letting coworkers know when you are available for consultation, and when you need to work independently—except for emergencies. Respond to instant messages only if your job requires responding immediately. Batch your instant messages just as you would other e-mails.

Sources: Suggestion 1 is from Toddi Gutner, "Beat the Clock," *Business Week*, February/March 2008, p. 58; Suggestions 6, 7, and 7 are based on Stephen R. Covey with Hyrum Smith, "What If You Could Chop an Hour from Your Day for Things That Matter Most?" *USA Weekend*, January 22–24, 1999, pp. 4–5; suggestion 10 is from Anita Bruzzese, "Tips to Avoid Wasting Time," Gannet News Service, August 9, 2004. Support for suggestion 13 is found in Vince Thompson, "Make the Most of Your White Space," *jobs@UpLadder.com*, October 3, 2007. Data about the productivity drain of interruptions are analyzed in Quintus R. Jett and Jennifer M. George, "Work Interrupted: A Closer Look at the Role of Interruptions in Organizational Life," *Academy of Management Review*, July 2003, pp. 494–507.

SKILL-BUILDING EXERCISE 9-5

Maintaining a Time Log

An effective starting point to avoid wasting time is to identify how you spend the 168 hours you have each week (24 hours × 7 days). For two weeks, catalog all the time you spend, down to as much detail as you can tolerate. Include the large obvious items, as well as the small items that are easy to forget. Keep track of any activity that requires at least five minutes. Major items would include working, attending class, studying, reading, watching television, sleeping, eating, going places, and time with loved ones and friends (hanging out). Small items would include visiting the coffee shop or vending machine, purchasing gum, and clip-ping your nails. If you multitask, such as walking and listening to music, do not double-count the time.

When your time logs have been completed, search for complete wastes of time, or activities that could be shortened. You might find, for example, that you spend about 45 minutes per day in the pursuit and consumption of coffee. If you reduced that time to 30 minutes, you would have an additional 15 minutes per day that you could invest in your career. However, if coffee time includes forming alliances with people or maintaining relationships, maybe the 45-minute-per-day investment is worthwhile.

Tendencies toward Perfectionism

Directions: Many perfectionists hold some of the behaviors and attitudes described below. To help understand your tendencies toward perfectionism, rate how strongly you agree with each of the statements below on a scale of 0 to 4 by circling the appropriate number. 0 means disagree, 4 means agree.

1.	Many people have told me that I am a perfectionist.	0	1	2	3	4
2.	I often correct the speech of others.	0	1	2	3	4
3.	It takes me a long time to write an e-mail because I keep checking and rechecking my writing.	0	1	2	3	4
4.	I often criticize the color combinations my friends are wearing.	0	1	2	3	4
5.	When I purchase food at a supermarket, I usually look at the expiration date so that I can purchase the freshest.	0	1	2	3	4
6.	I can't stand when people use the term "remote" instead of "remote control" or "cell" instead of "cell phone."	0	1	2	3	4
7.	If a company representative asked me "What is your *social*," I would reply something like, "Do you mean my *social security number*?"	0	1	2	3	4
8.	I hate to see dust on furniture.	0	1	2	3	4
9.	I like the Martha Stewart's idea of having every decoration in the home just right.	0	1	2	3	4
10.	I never put a map back in the glove compartment until it is folded just right.	0	1	2	3	4
11.	Once an eraser on a pencil of mine becomes hard and useless, I throw away the pencil.	0	1	2	3	4
12.	I adjust all my watches and clocks so that they show exactly the same time.	0	1	2	3	4
13.	It bothers me that clocks on personal computers are often wrong by a few minutes.	0	1	2	3	4
14.	I clean the keyboard on my computer at least every other day.	0	1	2	3	4
15.	I organize my e-mail messages and computer documents into many different, clearly labeled files.	0	1	2	3	4
16.	You won't find old coffee cups or soft drink containers on my desk.	0	1	2	3	4
17.	I rarely start a new project or assignment until I have completed my present project or assignment.	0	1	2	3	4
18.	It is very difficult for me to concentrate when my work area is disorganized.	0	1	2	3	4
19.	Cobwebs in chandeliers and other lighting fixtures bother me.	0	1	2	3	4
20.	It takes me a long time to make a purchase such as a digital camera because I keep studying the features on various models.	0	1	2	3	4
21.	When I balance my checkbook, it usually comes out right within a few dollars.	0	1	2	3	4
22.	I carry enough small coins and dollar bills with me so that when I shop I can pay the exact amount without requiring change.	0	1	2	3	4
23.	I throw out any underwear or T-shirts that have even the smallest holes or tears.	0	1	2	3	4
24.	I become upset with myself if I make a mistake.	0	1	2	3	4
25.	When a fingernail of mine is broken or chipped, I fix it as soon as possible.	0	1	2	3	4
26.	I am carefully groomed whenever I leave my home.	0	1	2	3	4
27.	When I notice packaged goods or cans on the floor in a supermarket, I will often place them back on the shelf.	0	1	2	3	4
28.	I think that carrying around antibacterial cleaner for the hands is an excellent idea.	0	1	2	3	4

(Continued)

29. If I am with a friend, and he or she has a loose hair on the shoulder,   0   1   2   3   4
    I will remove it without asking.

30. I am a perfectionist.   0   1   2   3   4

Total Score _____

Scoring and Interpretation: Add the numbers you circled to obtain your total score.

91 or over You have strong perfectionist tendencies to the point that it could interfere with your taking quick action when necessary. Also, you may annoy many people with your perfectionism.

61–90 You have a moderate degree of perfectionism that could lead you to produce high-quality work and be a dependable person.

31–60 You have a mild degree of perfectionism. You might be a perfectionist in some situations quite important to you, but not in others.

0–30 You are not a perfectionist. You might be too casual about getting things done right, meeting deadlines, and being aware of details.

SELF-ASSESSMENT QUIZZES IN OVERVIEW

Self-Assessment Quiz 9-1 measures tendencies toward procrastination. Thinking about the extent of your procrastination, and overcoming excessive amounts, can help you develop career thrust. You might be able to get by procrastinating small tasks, but delaying the completion of large, complex tasks like preparing a budget or developing a report about customer service will eventually result in low performance. Self-Assessment Quiz 9-2 measures perfectionism which in large doses can lead to procrastination and not getting things done. However, like fat in the diet, a healthy dose of perfectionism is an asset because it can lead to high levels of performance. Oprah Winfrey and Donald Trump are both perfectionists without being obsessed over details.

Concept Review and Reinforcement

Key Terms

corporate athletes 281
fight-or-flight response 281
hindrance stressors 282
challenge stressors 282
burnout 283
perceived control 284
type a behavior 285
negative affectivity 285

role overload 285
extreme job 285
role ambiguity 286
carpal tunnel syndrome 287
emotional labor 287
cognitive behavioral approach to
   stress management 289
support network 291

personal productivity 293
procrastination 293
deliberate practice 296
workaholism 297
virtual office 300

Summary

A major challenge facing any worker who wants to stay healthy and have good interpersonal relationships is to manage stress effectively. Individual differences play a big role in determining whether an event will lead to stress. The physiological changes that take place within the body in response to stress are responsible for most of the stress symptoms. The fight-or-flight response is the battle against the stressor.

The activation of hormones, such as cortisol, when the body has to cope with a stressor produces short-term physiological reactions, including an increase in heart rate and blood pressure. When stress levels rarely subside, the physiological changes create damage. People under continual negative stress age quickly. Hindrance stressors have a negative effect on motivation and performance. However, the right amount of stress (challenge stressors) prepares us for meeting difficult challenges and improves performance. An optimum level of stress exists for most people and most tasks. In general, performance tends to be best under moderate amounts of stress.

One of the major problems of prolonged stress is that it may lead to burnout, a condition of emotional, mental, and physical exhaustion in response to long-term stressors. Feelings of having limited control and not being recognized are major contributors to burnout. Burnout also creates cynicism and a distancing from tasks and people. Workers who perceive the cause of burnout to be external are more likely to become less committed to the firm and more cynical. Burnout also damages the physical health of workers.

Four personality factors predisposing people toward stress are low perceived control, low self-efficacy, Type A behavior and hostility, and negative affectivity. The heart attack triggers associated with Type A behavior are hostility, anger, cynicism, and suspiciousness, with hostility having the biggest impact. Frequently encountered job stressors are role overload including extreme jobs, role conflict and ambiguity, adverse environmental conditions including carpal tunnel syndrome and long commutes, environmentally induced attention deficit disorder, and job insecurity and job loss. Another frequent job stressor is adverse interactions with customers and clients and emotional labor.

Managing stress refers to controlling stress by making it become a constructive force in your life. Coping with, or managing, stress includes hundreds of activities, with substantial individual differences in which technique is effective. Seven representative stress management methods are to eliminate or modify the stressor, get appropriate physical exercise, rest sufficiently, maintain a healthy diet, build a support network, practice visualization and meditation, and practice everyday methods of stress reduction.

Achieving high personal productivity on the job is more in demand than ever. A starting point in improving productivity is to minimize procrastination, an enormous problem for many people that can be approached as follows: Commit to what you want in life; calculate the cost of procrastination; follow the worst in, first out (WIFO) principle; break the task into manageable chunks; make a commitment to other people; remove some clutter from your mind; satisfy your stimulation quota in constructive ways; and eliminate rewards for procrastinating.

Developing good work habits and time management practices is often a matter of developing the right attitudes toward your work and toward time, as follows: (1) Begin with a mission and goals; (2) work smarter, not harder including the use of deliberate practice (3) value orderliness and cleanliness; (4) value good attendance and punctuality; (5) attain a balance in life and avoid being a workaholic, and (6) increase your energy (body, emotions, mind, and spirit).

Effective work habits and skills are essential for high productivity, including the following: (1) Prepare a to-do list and set priorities, (2) streamline your work and emphasize important tasks, (3) concentrate on one important task at a time instead of multitasking, (4) stay in control of paperwork and electronic work, (5) work productively from your home office or virtual office, and (6) enhance your Internet search skills.

Another basic thrust to improved personal productivity is to minimize time wasting. Whether or not an activity is a time waster depends on its purpose. Being aware of time wasters such as those presented in Figure 9-6 will sensitize you to the importance of minimizing them.

Questions for Discussion and Review

1. Why might it be true that people who love their work live much longer than people who retire early because they dislike working?

2. Why might having your stress under control improve your interpersonal relationships?

3. Give an example of adverse interaction with a customer that you have personally experienced, or that you have witnessed. What could the worker have done to decrease some of the stress in the situation?

4. Interview a person in a high-pressure job in any field. Find out whether the person experiences significant stress and what method he or she uses to cope with it.

5. Provide an example from your own or somebody else's life of how having a major goal in life can help a person be better organized.

6. Executives at Toyota, among many other Japanese companies, emphasize that clean work areas in the factory enhance productivity. What might explain this relationship between cleanliness and productivity?

7. Describe any way in which you have used information technology to make you more productive.

8. Use information in this chapter to explain how a person might be well-organized yet still not get very far in his or her career.

9. For many young corporate professionals, a date often consists of the two people getting together in his or her place to spend three hours doing office work on their laptop computers, followed by a take-out meal. What is your evaluation of this approach to boosting personal productivity?

10. With millions of workers making regular use of personal digital assistants and smart phones throughout the world, why hasn't productivity in organizations taken a dramatic leap forward?

The Web Corner

http://www.stress.org
(Institute for Stress Management)

http://stress.about.com
(Considerable information about stress plus several self-quizzes)

http://ub-counseling.buffalo.edu/stressprocrast.shtml
(Overcoming procrastination for students)

Internet Skill Builder: Getting Personal Help from Your Employer

Use your favorite search engines to learn about an Employee Assistance Programs (EAPs). After visiting several sights, answer these questions: (1) What type of help can an employee expect to receive from an EAP? (2) How does an EAP help with stress management? (3) Does the EAP counselor typically tell the company the nature of the problem facing the employee who sought assistance? (4) What benefits do companies expect from offering an EAP to employees? (5) What would I tell the company if I needed help with problems that are causing me severe stress?

Internet Skill Builder: What Are You Doing with Your Time?

Go to www.getmoredone.com/tabulator.html to find the Pace Productivity Tabulator. This interactive module enables you to enter the time you spend on 11 major activities (such as employment, eating, sleeping, and television watching) and compare your profile to others. You are also able to enter your ideal profile to see where you would like to be. You just follow the straightforward instructions. After arriving at your personal pie chart, ask yourself, "What have I learned that will enhance my personal productivity?"

Developing Your Human Relations Skills

Interpersonal Relations Case 9-1

Rachel Runs the Treadmill

Six thirty Tuesday morning, 38-year-old Rachel Mendez hops out of her bed while her husband Ben Mendez is still sleeping. Rachel's first stop is to wake up her nine-year-old daughter, and encourage her to start getting ready to meet the school bus on time. By 8 a.m. Rachel is in her car and on her way to her job as a business development specialist for a human resource outsourcing company. Her primary responsibility is to entice small- and medium-size companies to turn over most of their human resource functions to her firm.

Just as Rachel begins to manage her e-mail and plan her agenda for the day, she places her right hand about three inches to the right of her heart. Rachel can feel the tightness next to her heart, and in her left arm. She thinks to herself, "This feels like I'm going to have a heart attack, but it doesn't make sense for a woman my age to be a heart attack victim. But I'm happy that I have an appointment at the cardiology center on Thursday."

At the North Side Cardiology Center, Rachel is first interviewed by Nurse Practitioner Janet Trudeau before her interview with Dr. Harry Ching, the cardiologist. Trudeau first took a brief medical history, followed by an interview. Parts of the interview with Trudeau went as follows:

Trudeau: So tell me in more detail why you came to visit our cardiology center.

Mendez: I have these annoying chest pains next to my heart and in my left arm. The pains usually start when I am extremely aggravated and frustrated. I have the pains about once a day.

Trudeau: Do you ever faint or become light-headed during the pains?

Mendez: No, my problem is just the pains. I keep doing whatever I'm doing when the pain hits.

Trudeau: Tell me about the situations you find so aggravating and frustrating.

Mendez: I'm really stressing out. I have a ton of aggravations and worries. To begin my nine-year-old daughter Samantha has seizures. She is under treatment but the problem remains, and it's worrisome. I worry every day that Samantha will have a seizure and strike her head or get involved in an accident.

My work is also quite worrisome. I work mostly on commission selling human resource services. Our business has grown rapidly in the last few years, but we have kind of dried up the territory. I have to travel more to find new clients. My earnings are taking a turn downward despite the extra travel.

Trudeau: Are you the sole breadwinner in the family?

Mendez: No, my husband Alex is an assistant manager at a Ruby Tuesday restaurant, and he makes a modest living. But talking about aggravation, my husband is a decent guy but he gives me chest pains. I think he cares much more about professional sports, especially the NFL and the NHL than he does about Samantha and me. If he's watching a game, I can forget about talking about something serious.

And then, of course, Alex works the hours of a restaurant manager, which means that he is often working when I am not working, like on Saturdays and Sundays.

Trudeau: Any other major aggravations in your life?

Mendez: Yes, commuting on busy highways. I can feel my chest pains starting when I think of sitting still for 15 minutes during rush-hour traffic.

Trudeau: Thank you Rachel. I will be studying this information before your interview with Dr. Ching. Have a seat in the waiting room. He will be with you in about 10 minutes.

Later that day Mendez had an extensive cardiology exam, including an electrocardiogram. Dr. Ching informed her that despite the muscle tension she was experiencing, her heart was in excellent condition.

Case Questions

1. What sources of stress does Rachel Mendez appear to be facing?
2. What do you recommend Mendez do about the stressors she is facing?
3. Given that Mendez does not have a heart problem, should she be concerned about the stressors in her life? Explain your answer.
4. How might Mendez organize her work and her life better to feel that her life is less out of control?

Stress Busting at the Agriculture and Markets Group

The State Department of Agriculture and Markets was having a demanding year. The mission of the group is to inspect grocery stores for possible health violations, such as unsanitary conditions and the sale of tainted food and meats. The group had a record number of complaints to investigate partially because so many stores were purchasing packaged goods, products, and meats from bottom-price suppliers in order to trim costs. At the same time, the Department of Agriculture and Markets was on a mandated cutback in spending. As a result, a few of the inspectors who had quit could not be replaced. The remaining inspectors were therefore carrying a much heavier workload.

The reality of a heavier workload with fewer staff available to make on-site visits created a high-pressure work environment. Michelle and Trevor, two of the more junior inspectors, decided together that the group needed to find a good way of blowing off steam. Their plan was to organize a few "prankster nights." On the first such night, six inspectors from the office got together to have a few drinks after work. During the drinking session at a bar close to the office, Michelle and Trevor announced their plan to relieve stress in a big way by pulling off a major prank.

The prank was the "popcorning" often executed by professional basketball players. The group would purchase a massive amount of popcorn and stuff into the vehicle of their supervisor Alicia Gordon, who typically parked her car in a remote spot in the garage to the state building. The three group members will pull off the prank "popcorned" her sports car the next Monday during lunch hour.

Tuesday morning, every employee at the State Department of Agriculture and Markets received an e-mail explaining that a misdemeanor had been committed in the parking lot in the form of damaging Alicia's vehicle. The e-mail also stated that the cruel act had violated the rights of Alicia Gordon to a harassment-free work environment. Anyone who knew who could have committed the hostile act of damaging Gordon's vehicle was urged to reply immediately to the e-mail.

Michelle and Trevor quickly sent text messages to each other. Michelle wrote, "Can't Alicia take a joke? What's her problem?"

Trevor wrote back, "Maybe we did lower our stress. But I'm afraid our stress is going to bump up now."

Case Questions

1. What is your evaluation of the effectiveness of the stress-reduction techniques created by Michelle and Trevor?

2. What might have been a more effective method of the group from Markets and Agriculture to have used to decrease their stress?

3. What do you recommend Michelle, Trevor, and the rest of the group do with respect to taking responsibility for their prank?

REFERENCES

1. Maggie Jackson, "Quelling Distraction: Help Employees Overcome 'Information Overload.'" *HR Magazine*, August 2008, p. 43.

2. Cait Murphy, "The CEO Workout," *Fortune*, July 10, 2006, pp. 43–44.

3. Research reported in Christine Gorman, "6 Lessons for Handling Stress," *Time*, January 29, 2007, p. 82.

4. *British Medical Journal* study reported in "Trop de Stress au Travail Double le Risque de Mourir d'une Crise de Coeur," *Journal de Montréal*, 18 October, 2002, p. 7. (Too much work stress doubles the risk of dying from a heart attack.)

5. Jeffery A. Lapine, Nathan P. Podsakoff, and Marcie A. Lepine, "A Meta-Analytic Test of the Challenge-Stressor-Hindrance-Stressor Framework: An Explanation for Inconsistent Relationships among Stressors and Performance," *Academy of Management Journal*, October 2005, pp. 764–775.

6. J. Craig Wallace et al., "Work Stressors, Role-Based performance, and the Moderating Influence of Organizational Support," *Journal of Applied Psychology*, January 2009, pp. 254–262.

7. Gillian E. Hardy, David Woods, and Toby D. Wall, "The Impact of Psychological Distress on Absence from Work," *Journal of Applied Psychology*, April 2003, pp. 306–314.

8. Christina Maslach and Michael Leiter, *The Truth about Burnout* (San Francisco: Jossey-Bass, 1997). Research updated in interview, Emily Waters, "Burnout on the Rise: Recognizing the Unconventional Telltale Signs," *NY Workplace Examiner* (www.examiner.com), June 18, 2009.

9. Annebel H. B. De Hoog and Deanne N. Den Hartog, "Neuroticism and Locus of Control as Moderators of the Relationships of Charismatic and Autocratic Leadership with Burnout," *Journal of Applied Psychology*, July 2009, pp. 1058–1067.

10. Maslach and Leiter, *The Truth About Burnout*.

11. Research reported in Deborah. Smith Bailey, "Burnout Harms Workers' Physical Health through Many Pathways," *Monitor on Psychology*, June 2006, p. 11.

12. M. Afalur Rahim, "Relationships of Stress, Locus of Control, and Social Support to Psychiatric Symptoms and Propensity to Leave a Job: A Field Study with Managers," *Journal of Business and Psychology*, Winter 1997, p. 159.

13. Steve M. Jex, Paul O. Bliese, Sheri Buzell, and Jessica Primeau, "The Impact of Self-Efficacy on Stressor-Strain Relations: Coping Style as an Explanatory Mechanism," *Journal of Applied Psychology*, June 2001, pp. 401–409.

14. Jeffrey R. Edwards and A. J. Baglioni, Jr., "Relationships between Type A Behavior Pattern and Mental and Physical Symptoms: A Comparison of Global and Component Measures," *Journal of Applied Psychology*, April 1991, p. 276; related research reported in Etienne Benson, "Hostility Is among Best Predictors of Heart Disease in Men," *Monitor on Psychology*, January 2003, p. 15.

15. Research reviewed in Nadja Geipert, "Don't Be Mad: More Research Links Hostility to Coronary Risk," *Monitor on Psychology*, January 2007, pp. 50–51.

16. Peter Y. Chen and Paul E. Spector, "Negative Affectivity as the Underlying Cause of Correlations between Stressors and Strains," *Journal of Applied Psychology*, June 1991, p. 398.

17. Pamela Babcock, "Workplace Stress? Deal with It!" *HR Magazine*, May 2009, p. 68.

18. Sylvia Ann Hewlett and Carolyn Buck Luce, "Extreme Jobs: The Dangerous Allure of the 70-Hour Work Week," *Harvard Business Review*, December 2006, pp. 49–59.

19. Blaine Harden, "Japan's Overtime Proves to Be Killer," *Washington Post* syndicated story, July 16, 2008.

20. William Atkinson, "Causes of Workplace Stress," *HR Magazine*, December 2000, p. 107; Michele Conlin, "Is Your Office Killing You?" *Business Week*, June 5, 2000, pp. 114–128; "Sick Building Syndrome," *www.doctorfungus.org*, accessed January 22, 2007, p. 1.

21. The data on vision and carpal tunnel syndrome are from the Computer Vision Syndrome Center reported in Anita Bruzzese, "Computer Users often Strain Eyes," Gannett News Service, September 13, 2004; Christine A. Sprigg et al., "Work Characteristics, Musculoskeletal Disorders, and the Mediating Role of Psychological Strain: A Study of Call Center Employees," *Journal of Applied Psychology*, September 2007, pp. 1456–1466.

22. Christina Binkley, "Sitting Pretty When You're Hard at Work," *The Wall Street Journal*, June 11, 2009. pp. D1, D7.

23. Study reported in Deborah Smith Bailey, "Longer Train Commutes Are More Stressful, Study Finds," *Monitor on Psychology*, September 2006, p. 12.

24. Larry Copeland, "Drivers Rising Earlier to Beat the Traffic," *USA Today* syndicated story, September 16, 2007.

25. Alicia A. Grandey, "Emotion Regulation in the Workplace: A New Way to Conceptualize Emotional Labor," *Journal of Occupational Health Psychology*, 5; 1, 2000, pp. 95–110; Grandey, "When the 'Show Must Go On:' Surface Acting and Deep Acting as Determinants of Emotional Exhaustion and Peer-Related Service Delivery," *Academy of Management Journal*, February 2003, pp. 86–96.

26. Markus Groth, Thornsen Henning-Thurau, and Gianfranco Walsh, "Customer Reactions to Emotional labor: The Roles of Employee Acting Strategies and Customer Detection Accuracy," *Academy of Management Journal*, October 2009, pp. 958–974.

27. Theresa M. Glomb, John D. Kammeyer-Mueller, and Maria Rotundo, "Emotional Labor Demands and Compensating Wage Differentials," *Journal of Applied Psychology*, August 2004, p. 707.

28. Timothy A. Judge, Erin Fluegge Woolf, and Charlice Hurst, "Is Emotional Labor More Difficult for Some than Others? A Multilevel, Experience-Sampling Study," *Personnel Psychology*, Spring 2009, pp. 57–88.

29. Edward Hallowell, *CrazyBusy: Overstretched, Overbooked, and about to Snap—Strategies for Coping in a World Gone ADD* (New York: Ballantine Books, 2006); "Zen and the Art of Thinking Straight," *Business Week*, April 3, 2006, p. 116; Maggie Jackson, "Quelling Distraction: Help Employees Overcome 'Information Overload,'" *HR Magazine*, August 8, 2008, pp. 42–46.

30. "Executive Quits after Suicides at France Télécom," The Associated Press, October 6, 2009.

31. Simona Gilboa, Arie Shirom, Yitzhak Fried, and Cary Cooper, "A Meta-Analysis of Work Demand Stressors and Job Performance: Examining Main and Moderating Effects," *Personnel Psychology*, Summer 2008, pp. 227–271.

32. Jan de Jonge and Christian Dormann, "Stressors, Resources, and Strain at Work: A Longitudinal Test of the Triple-Match Principle," *Journal of Applied Psychology*, November 2006, pp. 1359–1374.

33. Katherine M. Richardson and Hannah R. Rothstein, "Effects of Occupational Stress Management Intervention Programs: A Meta-Analysis," *Journal of Occupational Health Psychology*, January 2008, pp. 69–93.

34. Data reported in Laura Landro, "The Hidden Benefits of Exercise," *The Wall Street Journal*, January 5, 2010, p. D1.

35. Lisa Belkin, "Some Respect, Please, for the Afternoon Nap," *The New York Times* (nytimes.com), February 25, 2007. p. 1.

36. Lea Winerman, "Sleep Deprivation Threatens Public Health, Says Research Award Winner," July/August 2004, p. 61.

37. Research reported in Sara Martin, "The Power of the Relaxation Response," *Monitor on Psychology*, October 2008, p. 33.

38. Katherine Ellison, "Mastering Your Own Mind," *Psychology Today*, October 2006, p. 75.

39. Stephen Kotler, "Escape Artists," *Psychology Today*, September/October 2009, pp. 73–75.

40. Data reported in Kotler, "Escape Artists," p. 75.

41. Maia Szalavitz, "Stand & Deliver," *Psychology Today*, July/August 2003, p. 50.

42. Cited in Kotler, "Escape Artists," p. 76.

43. Shale Paul, as cited in "Tips to Keep Procrastination Under Control," Gannet News Service, November 9, 1998.

44. Dru Scott, *How to Put More Time in Your Life* (New York: New American Library, 1980), p 1.

45. Quoted in Jana McGregor (Editor), "Making Every Hour Count," *Business Week*, September 1, 2008, p. 68.

46. Christopher Percy Collier, "The Expert on Experts," *Fast Company*, November 2006, p. 116.

47. David Allen, *Getting Things Done* (New York: Penguin, 2001, 2007).

48. Quoted in Adrian Wooldridge, "Why Clean Up Your Desk? Delight in Disorder Instead," *The Wall Street Journal*, January 2, 2007, p. D7. Book review of Eric Abrahamson and David Freedman, *A Perfect Mess* (New York: Little, Brown & Co., 2007).

49. João-Pierre Ruth, "Report: Employees Not Taking All Vacation Time," *NJBIZ* (www.njbiz.com), January 4, 2010.

50. Anne Fisher, "The Rebalancing Act," *Fortune*, October 6, 2003, p. 110; Andrea Kay, "Avoid 'Traps' to Gain the Free Time You Need," Gannet News Service, January 10, 2005.

51. Brenda Goodman, "A Field Guide To the Workaholic," *Psychology Today*, May/June 2006, p. 41.

52. Tony Schwartz, "Manage Your Energy, Not Your Time," *Harvard Business Review*, October 2007, pp. 63–74.

53. Jana McGregor, "Getting Serious about Getting Things Done," *Business Week*, September 1, 2008, p. 069.

54. "Secrets of Greatness: Marissa Mayer," *Fortune*, March 20, 2006, p. 68.

55. Quoted paraphrased from information in "You Can't Make More Time: Randy Pausch's Heart-Felt Views on Using Time to the Fullest," *Business Week*, August 25/September 1, 2008, p. 071.

56. The scientific information about multitasking is reviewed in Claudia Wallis, "The Multitasking Generation," *Time*, March 27, 2006, pp. 48–55. See also Joshua S. Rubinstein, David E. Meyer, and Jeffrey E. Evans, "Executive Control of Cognitive Processes in Task Switching," *Journal of Experimental Psychology—Human Perception and Performance*, vol. 26, January 2000, No. 4, pp. 763–769.

57. Research from the University of Oregon reported in "The Problem with Extreme Multitasking," *The Wall Street Journal*, February 12, 2008, p. B4.

58. Andy Pasztor, "Laptops Drive Pilots to Distraction," *The Wall Street Journal*, October 27, 2009, p. A3.

59. Ellen Joan Pollock, "How I Got a Grip on My Workweek," *Business Week*, April 6, 2009, p. 086.

60. Michelle Conlin, "Out of Sight, Yes. Out of Mind, No," *Business Week*, February 18, 2008, p. 060; Sue Shellenbarger, "When Working at Home Doesn't Work: How Companies Comfort Telecommuters," *The Wall Street Journal*, August 24, 2006, p. D1; E. Jeffrey Hill, Brent C. Miller, Sara P. Weiner, and Joe Colihan, "Influences of the Virtual Office on Aspects of Work/Life Balance," *Personnel Psychology*, Autumn 1998, pp. 667–683.

61. Cali Ressler and Jody Thomson, "Make Results Matter," *HR Magazine*, April 2009, pp. 77–79.

62. Survey cited in Maggie Jackson, "May We Have Your Attention Please?" *Business Week*, June 23, 2008, p. 055.

63. Rabi S. Bhagat, "Effects of Stressful Life Events on Individual Performance and Work Adjustment Processes within Organizational Settings: A Research Model," *Academy of Management Review*, October 1983, pp. 660–670.

64. "Building Self-Esteem." Retrieved May 23, 2006, from: www.ashland.com/education/self-esteem/best_shot.html

65. David Lazarus, "Suicide Hotlines See Rise in Calls as Economy Tanks," *Los Angeles Times* (www.latimes.com), December 24, 2008.

66. Research reported in Etienne Benson, "Hostility Is among Best Predictors of Heart Disease in Men," *Monitor on Psychology*, January 2003, p. 15.

67. Quoted in Nadja Geipert, "Don't Be Mad: More Research Links Hostility to Coronary Risk," *Monitor on Psychology*, January 2007, pp. 50–51.

68. Peter Y. Chen and Paul E. Spector, "Negative Affectivity as the Underlying Cause of Correlations between Stressors and Strains," *Journal of Applied Psychology*, June 1991, p. 398.

69. Paul E. Spector, Peter Y. Chen, and Brian J. O'Connell, "A Longitudinal Study of Relations between Job Stressors and Job Strains while Controlling for Prior Negative Affectivity and Strains," *Journal of Applied Psychology*, April 2000, p. 216.

70. Mark Goulston, *Get Out of Your Own Way at Work . . . and Help Others Do the Same* (New York: Putnam Adult, 2005); Andrew J. DuBrin, *Your Own Worst Enemy: How to Overcome Career Self-Sabotage* (New York: AMACOM, 1992).

71. Based on the work of Judith Wright, as reported in Julie Deardorff, "Soft Addictions: You Can Get Hooked in So Many Ways," *Chicago Tribune*, March 18, 2007.

72. Kevin Hogan, "Why Everything Goes to Hell . . . How to Stop Self-Sabotage, NOW and Forever!" www.kevinhogan.com/selfsabotage.htm, 2009.

73. Daniel Goleman, "Leadership That Gets Results," *Harvard Business Review*, March–April 2000, p. 80.

74. Robyn D. Clarke, "A Reason for Ranting," *Black Enterprise*, November 2005, p. 161.

Anger and Conflict

Jud, age thirty, is quite happy with his job as a construction supervisor at a construction engineering firm. The work is exciting and challenging, and in Jud's opinion offers him the opportunity to contribute some value to society. In Jud's words, "When you help construct something like an apartment building, you do some good for the world."

Suddenly, the tranquility in Jud's life changed. On the positive side he and his wife, Shannon, had their first baby, Quentin. After a three-month maternity leave, Shannon returned to work as a medical secretary. Jud and Shannon took turns dropping off Quentin at the day-care center and then picking him up at night. On days Quentin was ill, the couple each took a half-day off from work or had a relative care for Quentin.

On the negative side, one day Jud was told by his manager that he would be sent on a six-month assignment to a construction site three hundred miles away. The company would

After studying the information and doing the exercises in this chapter, you should be able to

1. Identify reasons why conflict between people takes place so often.
2. Pinpoint several helpful and harmful consequences of conflict.
3. Choose an effective method of resolving conflict.
4. Improve your assertion skills.
5. Improve your negotiating skill.
6. Develop anger management skills.

pay the travel expenses for one weekend trip home per month. Jud thought, "What do I do now? This assignment will throw my home life into turmoil. The father of an infant can't work out of town. Yet, if I turn down this assignment I might either be fired or regarded as being too inflexible for a career in management with the firm."

In anguish, Jud planned to discuss his conflict with Shannon that evening.

The situation just described illustrates a reality about the workplace. Conflict takes place frequently, and being able to manage it successfully enables the workers involved to function more peacefully, and the company to get more work done. **Conflict** is a condition that exists when two sets of demands, goals, or motives are incompatible. For example, if a person wants a career in retailing yet also wants to work a predictable eight-hour day with weekends off, that person faces a conflict. He or she cannot achieve both goals. A conflict can also be considered a dispute, feud, or controversy.

Our approach to studying conflict includes explaining why so much conflict exists, constructive approaches to resolving conflict, and the management of anger.

conflict

Condition that exists when two sets of demands, goals, or motives are incompatible.

WHY DOES SO MUCH CONFLICT EXIST?

Many reasons exist for the widespread presence of conflict in all aspects of life. All these reasons are related to the basic nature of conflict—the fact that not every person can have what he or she wants at the same time. As with other topics in this book, understanding conflict helps you develop a better understanding of why people act as they do. Here we describe eight key sources of conflict.

LEARNING OBJECTIVE 1

Competition for Limited Resources

A fundamental reason you might experience conflict with another person is that not everybody can get all the money, material, supplies, or human help they want. Conflict also ensues when employees are asked to compete for prizes, such as bonuses based on individual effort or company-paid vacation trips. Because the number of awards is so limited, the competition becomes intense enough to be regarded as conflict. Conflict stemming from limited resources has become prevalent as so many companies attempt to reduce expenses. Many units of the organization have to compete for the limited money available to hire new people or purchase new technology.

Another type of limited resource that leads to conflict is trade names. Several companies or individuals might believe that they have the right to use a particular trade name. Instead of being able to resolve the conflict themselves, they often resort to litigation.

Imagine that a woman named Tiffany Horowitz wants to open a jewelry store called "Tiffany." Unfortunately, the lawyers for Tiffany & Co. will tell her to change the name on the storefront and Web site immediately or be sued for trademark infringement. Similarly, Anheuser Busch, the American brewery that makes Budweiser beer, and the Czechoslovakian brewery Budjovick Budvar have been in dispute for over a hundred years on who has the right to sell their Bud. The two brewers are also in conflict about who can use a particular slogan. The American Bud is the "King of Beers," and the Czech Bud is the "Beer of Kings." Who wins this conflict varies across different countries.[1] Somehow the executives of these two companies cannot settle their differences over a bottle of beer.

Differences of Opinion on Work-Related Issues and Rights

A natural source of conflict in the workplace centers on differences of opinion about work-related issues, including whose idea will work the best. One member of the design team for a luxury sports car might insist the paneling should be composed mostly of wood. Another might say that the car could get by with plastic paneling, saving the company considerable money. The two members might therefore enter into conflict.

Conflict from differences of opinion can last a long time and can lead to dismissal from the employer. Sallie Krawcheck, the former head of Citigroup's wealth management unit, stepped down after months of conflict with the chief executive. One difference of opinion was that Krawcheck pushed Citigroup to reimburse clients whose investments were severely depleted. She argued that the reimbursement would be preferable to alienating highly profitable clients. Other managers resisted her position, contending that the clients should have recognized the risks associated with their investments.[2]

Conflict over rights will often take the form of one group or individual feeling that it has the right to engage in certain behavior despite a rule or custom denying that right. Smoking is forbidden in most workplaces, with some employers forbidding workers to smoke anywhere on the property—especially at a medical facility. The smokers who have to walk or drive about a half mile become quite upset with the nonsmokers who have blocked what they consider their right to smoke immediately outside of a building. A frequent conflict over custom is when some office workers believe they have the right to wear low-cut jeans and shirts that display their midriff to work, but the company officials say that such clothing is unacceptable.

Personality Clashes

Various value and personality differences among people contribute to workplace conflict. Many disagreements on the job stem from the fact that some people simply dislike each other. A **personality clash** is thus an antagonistic relationship between two people based on differences in personal attributes, preferences, interests, values, and styles. People involved in a personality clash often have difficulty specifying why they dislike each other. The end result, however, is that they cannot maintain an amiable work relationship. A strange fact about personality clashes is that people who get along well may begin to clash after working together for a number of years. Many business partnerships fold because the two partners eventually clash.

Aggressive Personalities, Including Bullies

Coworkers naturally disagree about topics, issues, and ideas. Yet some people convert disagreement into an attack that puts down other people and damages their self-esteem. As a result, conflict surfaces. **Aggressive personalities** are people who verbally and sometimes physically attack others frequently. Verbal aggression takes the form

personality clash

Antagonistic relationship between two people based on differences in personal attributes, preferences, interests, values, and styles.

aggressive personalities

People who verbally and sometimes physically attack others frequently of insults, teasing, ridicule, and profanity. The aggression may also be expressed as attacks on the victim's character, competence, background, and physical appearance. When people are verbally abused, they are put on the defensive, making them feel uncomfortable.[3]

Aggressive personalities are also referred to as *bullies*. Among their typical behaviors are interrupting others, ranting in a loud voice, and making threats. A typical attitude of a bullying boss is "My way or the highway," sending the message that the employee's suggestions are unwelcome. Aggressiveness can also take the extreme form of the shooting or knifing of a former boss or colleague by a mentally unstable worker recently dismissed from the company. Violence has become so widespread that homicide is the second-highest cause of workplace deaths, with about six hundred workplace homicides each year in the United States since 2000.[4] Most of these deaths result from a robbery or commercial crime. Many of these killings, however, are perpetrated by a disgruntled worker or former employee harboring an unresolved conflict. As companies have continued to reduce their workforce despite being profitable, these incidents have increased in frequency. The accompanying Human Relations in Practice describes how one well-known company deals with the problem of potential employee violence.

Culturally Diverse Teams and Factional Groups

Conflict often surfaces as people work in teams whose members vary in many ways. Ethnicity, religion, and gender are three of the major factors that lead to clashes in viewpoints. Differing educational backgrounds and work specialties can also lead to conflict. Workers often shut out information that doesn't fit comfortably with their own beliefs, particularly if they do not like the person providing the information. When these conflicts are properly resolved, diversity lends strength to the organization because the various viewpoints make an important contribution to solving a problem. Groups that are reminded of the importance of effective communication and taught methods of conflict resolution usually can overcome the conflict stemming from mixed groups.[5]

Another form of diversity occurs when groups contain different factions, such as those representing two different companies that merged. Often the factional group consists of two subgroups, each with several representatives, such as a cost-cutting task force consisting of three representatives each from marketing, operations, and finance. The potential for conflict within factional groups increases when the subgroups differ substantially in demographic characteristics such as age, gender, and educational levels.[6]

Competing Work and Family Demands

Balancing the demands of work and family life is a major challenge facing workers at all levels. Yet achieving this balance and resolving these conflicts is essential for being successful in career and personal life. The challenge of achieving balance is particularly intense for employees who are part of a two-wage-earner family. A heavy workload also intensifies the conflict because the person feel compelled to work long hours, including performing some work at home. Frequent business travel is another major contributor to work–family conflict.

Work–family conflict occurs when the individual has to perform multiple roles: worker, spouse or partner, and often parent. From the standpoint of the individual, this type of conflict can be regarded as work interfering with family life. From the standpoint of the employer, the same conflict might be regarded as family life interfering with work. Being a single parent can lead to even stronger work–family conflict when the other parent does not help manage unanticipated problems. An example would be managing the situation of a sick child not being able to attend school and refused from day care also because of the illness.

work–family conflict

Conflict that occurs when an individual has to perform multiple roles: worker, spouse or partner, and often parent.

Pitney Bowes Attempts to Stamp Out Employee Violence

Pitney Bowes, the Stamford, Conn., mail and messaging management-equipment company, has a help line that employees can call anonymously if they're concerned that a colleague is exhibiting erratic or angry behavior, or has a problem such as substance abuse or depression. "We felt, on balance, it's better for employees to know they can call with concerns instead of sitting at their desks scared to death," says Michele Coleman Mayes, senior vice president and general counsel. Human-resource executives discretely investigate the complaints.

In January 2007, a guard at a Pitney Bowes facility in Phoenix quit his job and a few days later returned to the workplace and shot his replacement. The guard worked for a company from which Pitney Bowes subcontracts security personnel.

The company now asks its subcontractors to do more-vigorous employee screenings.

The company also is offering managers training on how to identify signs of employee distress. "People bring all sorts of demons to work—from problems with spouses and kids to bipolar disease—that they shouldn't think they can solve on their own," says Ms. Mayes. Pitney Bowes has a staff physician that employees can consult and a program offering referrals to counselors.

If the employee is very distressed or potentially violent, a manager encourages counseling with a mental-health professional, and may suggest a transfer or a leave of absence or, as a last resort, may dismiss him or her. "We have to ask, 'What's in the best interests of all our employees?' because we're responsible for everyone's overall safety," says Ms. Mayes.

Source: Carol Hymowitz, "Bosses Have to Learn How to Confront Troubled Employees," *Wall Street Journal,* April 23, 2007, p. B1.

Attempting to meet work and family demands is a frequent source of conflict because the demands are often incompatible. Imagine having to attend your child's championship soccer game and then being ordered at the last minute to attend a late-afternoon meeting. As revealed in a study with working adults, another complication of work–family conflict is that when family life interferes with work, the person will often feel guilty. Guilt will be experienced also by some people who feel that work interferes with family life.[7] Feelings of guilt arise because the person might feel that when one is being paid for doing a job, the job should have higher priority than taking care of personal issues. Or the person might feel guilty because he or she believes that family remains a higher priority than work.

Some people attempt to resolve their work–family conflict by doing some work at family and personal events. Watch any Little League baseball game, high school tennis match, or youth soccer match, and you will see parents at the sidelines busily engaged with their BlackBerrys conducting work. Equally extreme is a recent trend for young people to do office work while on a date.

> A 36-year-old Los Angeles entrepreneur said her dates start like many other couple's. "We cook an amazing dinner, grab a little wine, and then we pull out our laptops and get some work done. Toiling side by side for hours, we laugh and have a great time." She says that working while on a date saves her from having no social life at all. "I probably wouldn't have left the house or office for a man if I couldn't bring my laptop along."[8]

The conflict over work versus family demands intensifies when the person is serious about both work and family responsibilities. The average American corporate professional works approximately fifty-five hours per week, including five hours on weekends. Adhering to such a schedule almost inevitably results in some incompatible demands from work versus those from family members and friends. Conflict arises because the person wants to work sufficient hours to succeed on the job yet still have enough time for personal life.

Cross-national differences based on culture can influence the extent to which workers experience work–family conflict. A study of 5,270 managers from twenty countries investigated how much work interfered with family life. Four clusters of countries were studied: the individualistic (Anglo) cluster versus three collectivistic (Asia, Eastern Europe, and Latin America). A collectivistic culture highly values the group. A finding was that work interfering with family life led to more dissatisfaction and intention to quit for people in individualistic than collectivistic societies. The researchers suggested that people in the collectivistic society might be more likely to remain loyal to the employer. Also, managers who value collectivism are more apt to respond to adverse conditions with greater affiliation toward coworkers.[9] A study with immigrant Latinos in the poultry-processing industry also suggested that workers with collectivistic beliefs experience less work–family conflict. For this group of Latinos, work is necessary and a vital method of ensuring family well-being.[10]

Micro-Inequities as a Source of Conflict

Growing attention is being paid to snubbing, or ignoring, others as a source of conflict. A **micro-inequity** is a small, semiconscious message we send with a powerful impact on the receiver. A micro-inequity might also be considered a subtle slight. Conflict occurs because a person's feelings are hurt, and he or she feels trivialized. Two examples of workplace micro-inequities follow:

- You check your messages on a cell phone, BlackBerry, or computer screen while a coworker is talking to you. (You are devaluing the other person's time and trivializing his or her importance.)
- A manager dismisses the first idea offered in a meeting by responding, "Okay, so who would like to get the ball rolling?" (The person who offered the idea feels like his or her suggestion is not even worth consideration and therefore has hurt feelings.)

Many companies, including IBM and Wells Fargo, offer training seminars to help managers avoid micro-inequities, including those already mentioned as well as such things as mispronouncing the names of subordinates and looking at a watch while someone else is talking.[11]

micro-inequity
Small, semiconscious message sent with a powerful impact on the receiver.

Cross-Generational Conflict

Differences in values across generations lead to differences in behavior. The following list presents three examples of potential work-related conflict across generations. The illustrations presented are stereotypes that apply to a *typical* member of each generation.

- **Preferred approach to communication.** Gen X members prefer to send text messages and use cell phones and IM. Gen Y members prefer e-mail, IM, and cell phones. Baby boomers prefer e-mail, cell phones, and face-to-face communication.
- **Approach to problem solving.** Gen X members prefer to form a team to brainstorm a solution, as well as use the Web and social networking for research. Gen Y members prefer to think up a list of solutions on their own, then call a meeting to discuss the alternative solutions. Baby boomers like to think about what has worked in the past and how it can be replicated. Then they call a meeting to discuss possible alternatives.
- **Requirement for being respected.** Gen X members want to have their ideas valued by coworkers. Gen Y members want to have their professionalism and growing knowledge valued. Baby boomers want to have their decades of work experience and input still valued.[12]

Sexual Harassment: A Special Type of Conflict

Many employees face conflict because they are sexually harassed by a supervisor, coworker, or customers. **Sexual harassment** is an unwanted sexually oriented behavior in the workplace that results in discomfort or interference with the job. It can include an action as violent as rape or as subdued as telling a sexually toned joke. The word *unwanted* is important for understanding sexual harassment. When workers enjoy or welcome sexual behavior, such as joking and flirting, that behavior is not considered harassment.[13] Customers and clients, as well as members of a person's own organization, can be the

sexual harassment
Unwanted sexually oriented behavior in the workplace that results in discomfort or interference with the job.

source of harassment. Sexual harassment creates conflict because the harassed person has to make a choice between two incompatible motives. One motive is to get ahead, keep the job, or have an unthreatening work environment. But to satisfy this motive, the person is forced to sacrifice the motive of holding on to his or her moral values or preferences. For example, a person might say, "I want a raise, but to do this, must I submit to being fondled by my boss?" Here we focus on the types and frequency of sexual harassment and guidelines for dealing with the problem.

Types, Frequency, and Effects of Harassment Two types of sexual harassment are legally recognized. Both are violations of the Civil Rights Acts of 1964 and 1991 and are, therefore, a violation of your rights. Union contracts also prohibit sexual harassment. In quid pro quo sexual harassment, the individual suffers loss (or threatened loss) of a job benefit as a result of his or her response to a request for sexual favors. The demands of a harasser can be blatant or implied. An implied form of quid pro quo harassment might take this form: A manager casually comments to one of his or her employees, "I've noticed that workers who become very close to me outside of the office get recommended for bigger raises."

The other form of sexual harassment is hostile-environment harassment. Another person in the workplace creates an intimidating, hostile, or offensive working environment. No tangible loss or psychological injury has to be suffered under this form of sexual harassment.

A major problem in controlling sexual harassment in the workplace is that most workers understand the meaning and nature of quid pro quo harassment but are confused about what constitutes the hostile-environment type. For example, some people might interpret the following behaviors to be harassing, whereas others would regard them as friendly initiatives: (a) calling a coworker "sweetie" and (b) saying to a subordinate, "I love your suit. You look fabulous."

An employee who is continually subjected to sexually suggestive comments, lewd jokes, or requests for dates is a victim of hostile-environment harassment. When the offensive behavior stems from customers or vendors, it is still harassment. Although the company cannot readily control the actions of customers or vendors, the company may still be liable for such harassment. According to several legal decisions, it is a company's job to take action to remedy harassment problems involving employees.

Surveys as well as the opinions of human resource professionals suggest that somewhere between 50 and 60 percent of women are sexually harassed at least once in their careers. One study documented what has been observed in the past: Women in male-dominated organizations, such as a construction company, tend to be harassed more frequently than women in female-dominated organizations, such as a community service center. The same study found that women in male-dominated organizations who had relatively masculine personalities were sexually harassed the most. A "masculine" personality would include being highly aggressive and cold rather than warm.[14]

Aside from being an illegal and immoral act, sexual harassment has negative effects on the well-being of its victims. The harassed person may experience job stress, lowered morale, severe conflict, and lowered productivity.

The negative effects of sexual harassment toward women were documented by University of Calgary psychology professors Chelsea R. Willness and Kibeom Lee and business professor Piers Steel. The researchers analyzed data from forty-one studies involving nearly seventy thousand respondents. Sexual harassment experiences were associated with the negative outcomes of

- Decreased job satisfaction
- Lower commitment to the employer
- Withdrawing from work, such as being absent more frequently, escapist drinking, and a desire to quit
- Decreased productivity for both the individual and the work group

- Physical and mental health problems
- Symptoms of post-traumatic stress disorder

The negative effects in the list were more likely to occur when the climate (or culture) was more tolerant of sexual harassment.[15] To draw a stereotype not intended to offend male workers, it might be part of the climate in certain male-dominated industries for male workers to harass their female counterparts. For example, "flashing" women is considered to be part of the hazing ritual for recently hired women workers in certain male-dominated manufacturing settings.

Guidelines for Preventing and Dealing with Sexual Harassment   A starting point in dealing with sexual harassment is to develop an awareness of the types of behavior that are considered sexual harassment. Often the difference is subtle. Suppose, for example, you placed copies of two nudes painted by Renoir, the French painter, on a coworker's desk. Your coworker might call that harassment. Yet if you took that same coworker to a museum to see the originals of the same nude paintings, your behavior would usually not be classified as harassment. This example illustrates that the setting of the words or behavior influences whether they are harassing. College courses in understanding and dealing with pornography have grown in popularity, and these courses often show adult (sexually explicit) films as part of the curriculum.[16] If an accounting professor in a college of business showed the same films to accounting students, he or she would most likely be charged with sexual harassment.

Education about the meaning of sexual harassment is therefore a basic part of any company program to prevent sexual harassment. The situation and your tone of voice, as well as other nonverbal behavior, contribute to perceptions of harassment. For example, the statement "You look wonderful" might be perceived as good natured versus harassing, depending on the sender's voice tone and facial expression.

The easiest way to deal with sexual harassment is to speak up before it becomes serious. The first time it happens, respond with statements such as, "I won't tolerate that kind of talk," "I dislike sexually oriented jokes," or "Keep your hands off me." Write the harasser a stern letter shortly after the first incident. Confronting the harasser in writing dramatizes your seriousness of purpose in not wanting to be sexually harassed. If the problem persists, say something to the effect of, "You're practicing sexual harassment. If you don't stop, I'm going to exercise my right to report you to management." Don't leave any room for doubt that the behavior or words you heard were unwelcome. Recurring incidents should be reported to the immediate manager, a higher-level manager, or a human resources official. When the harasser is the manager, of course, reporting the incident to him or her is ineffective. In the typical situation, the employer will keep the information it gathers as confidential as possible, consistent with state, provincial, and federal laws. Both the accused and the complainant will have a chance to present the case.

Whether you are the accused employee, the complaining one, or a potential witness, confidentiality is crucial in dealing with accusations of harassment. Two people have their reputations on the line, and you may not have all the facts.

A recommended approach to dealing with continuing harassment from the same person or persons is to maintain a dated log of the incidents. If the incidents are severe, such as unwanted groping or hugs, a copy of the log might be sent to a high-level manager in the company and a human resources professional. The principle here is that any type of documentation is better than none when dealing with a workplace issue of legal consequences.[17]

Guidelines for Dealing with False Accusations of Sexual Harassment   Many workers, especially men, will be falsely charged with sexual harassment for such reasons as revenge related to another issue, a desire to get attention, or a misunderstanding of what constitutes sexual harassment. At the extreme, some women believe that if a man disagrees with them it is because he devalues the opinion of women. As such, he is engaging in sexism, which could be interpreted as sexual harassment. Next in frequency of false accusations of sexual harassment by women against men are false accusations by men against men. A remote third category is men falsely accusing women of harassment.

A strategy for a man defending against false accusations of sexual harassment is to establish the reputation of never engaging in sexual harassment. Among the possibilities here are (a) open no pornographic Web sites at work, (b) never touch women or men in the workplace except for a handshake or an occasional sideways hug in a group setting, (c) do not confer with a woman (or perhaps a man) face-to-face unless the door is open to an office or cubicle, and (d) don't make sexually toned comments or tell sexually oriented jokes.

When falsely charged of sexual harassment, the person should present a detailed account of his or her side of the story and point out that false accusations can be considered libel. The testimony of any witness to the alleged incident would also be helpful.

THE GOOD AND BAD SIDES OF CONFLICT

LEARNING OBJECTIVE 2 Conflict over significant issues is a source of stress. We usually do not suffer stress over minor conflicts such as having to choose between wearing one sweater or another. Like stress in general, we need an optimum amount of conflict to keep us mentally and physically energetic. Handled properly, moderate doses of conflict can be beneficial. Some of the benefits that might arise from conflict can be summarized around the following key points. Figure 10-1 outlines the positive as well as the negative consequences of conflict.

1. **Talents and abilities may emerge in response to conflict.** When faced with a conflict, people often become more creative than they are in a tranquil situation. Assume that your employer told you that it would no longer pay for your advanced education unless you used the courses to improve your job performance. You would probably find ways to accomplish such an end.

2. **Conflict can help you feel better because it satisfies a number of psychological needs.** By nature, many people like a good fight. As a socially acceptable substitute for attacking others, you might be content to argue over a dispute on the job or at home.

3. **As an aftermath of conflict, the parties in conflict may become united.** Two battling supervisors may become more cooperative toward each other in the aftermath of confrontation. A possible explanation is that the shared experience of being in conflict with each other *sometimes* brings the parties closer.

4. **Conflict helps prevent people in the organization from agreeing too readily with each other, thus making some very poor decisions.** Groupthink is the situation that occurs when group members strive so hard to get along that they fail to critically evaluate each other's ideas.

Despite the positive picture of conflict just painted, it can also have detrimental consequences to the individual, the organization, and society. These harmful consequences of conflict make it important for people to learn how to resolve conflict:

1. **Prolonged conflict can be detrimental to some people's emotional and physical well-being.** As a type of stress, prolonged conflict can lead to such problems as heart disease and chronic intestinal disorders. President Lyndon B. Johnson suffered his first heart attack after an intense argument with a young newspaper reporter.

2. **Relationships damaged by conflict can have consequences that impede individual, group, and organizational performance.** When coworkers have a falling out, the repercussions for the people in conflict as well as coworkers can include emotional strain, poor listening, reduced information processing, distraction from work tasks, and a lowering of commitment and satisfaction. As a result, performance suffers for the individual, group, and organization.[18]

3. **People in conflict with each other often waste time and energy that could be put to useful purposes.** Instead of fighting all evening with your roommate, the two of you might

FIGURE 10-1   The Good and Bad Sides of Conflict

Conflict between people and groups can have both positive and negative consequences.

Interpersonal Conflict

Positive Consequences

- Talents and abilities emerge

- Need satisfaction leads to good feelings

- Unity after conflict

- Prevents premature agreement and poor decisions

Negative Consequences

- Poor well-being

- Wasted time and energy

- Financial and emotional costs

- Fatigue

- Self-interest dominates

- Workplace violence

fix up your place. Instead of writing angry e-mail messages back and forth, two department heads might better invest that time in thinking up ideas to save the company money.

4. The aftermath of extreme conflict may have high financial and emotional costs. Sabotage—such as ruining machinery or destroying a company database—might be the financial consequence. At the same time, management may develop a permanent distrust of many people in the workforce, although only a few of them are saboteurs.

5. Too much conflict is fatiguing, even if it does not cause symptoms of emotional illness. People who work in high-conflict jobs often feel spent when they return home from work. When the battle-worn individual has limited energy left over for family responsibilities, the result is more conflict. (For instance, "What do you mean you are too tired to visit friends?" or "If your job is killing your interest in having friends, find another job.")

6. People in conflict will often be much more concerned with their own interests than with the good of the family, organization, or society. An employee in the shipping department who is in conflict with his supervisor might neglect to ship an order. And a gang in conflict with another might leave a park or beach strewn with broken glass.

7. Workplace violence erupts, including the killing of managers, previous managers, coworkers, customers, as well as spouses and partners. Intense conflict can release anger, leading to aggressive behavior and violence. Disgruntled employees, such as those recently fired, may attempt revenge by assassinating work associates. For example, the shooter in an apparent murder–suicide at the Johnson Space Center unit of NASA in 2007 had received a poor performance evaluation and feared being fired.[19] The Human

Relations in Practice insert presented earlier described one company's approach to warding off workplace violence. People involved in an unresolved domestic dispute sometimes storm into the partner's workplace to physically attack him or her. Unresolved conflict and frustration from financial, marital, or other domestic problems increase the odds of a person "going ballistic" at work.

WHAT ARE SOME TECHNIQUES FOR RESOLVING CONFLICTS?

LEARNING OBJECTIVE 3

Because of the inevitability of conflict, a successful and happy person must learn effective ways of resolving conflict. An important general consideration is to face conflict rather than letting conflict slide or smoothing over it. Ignoring or smoothing over conflict does little to resolve the real causes of conflict and seldom leads to an effective long-term solution. Here we concentrate on methods of conflict resolution that you can use on your own. Most of them emphasize a collaborative or win–win philosophy. Several of the negotiating and bargaining tactics described may be close to the competitive orientation. Self-Assessment Quiz 10-1 gives you the opportunity to think through your style of managing conflict.

Being Assertive

Several of the techniques for resolving conflict described here require assertiveness. Learning to express your feelings to make your demands known is also an important aspect of becoming an effective individual in general. Expressing your feelings helps you establish good relationships with people. If you aren't sharing your feelings and attitudes

---

SELF-ASSESSMENT QUIZ 10-1

Collaborative versus Competitive Styles of Conflict Management

Answer on a 1 to 5 scale how well you agree with each of the following statements: disagree strongly, disagree, neutral, agree, and agree strongly.

	Disagree Strongly	Disagree	Neutral	Agree	Agree Strongly
1. I like to see the other side squirm when I resolve a dispute.	5	4	3	2	1
2. Winning is everything when it comes to settling conflict.	5	4	3	2	1
3. After I have successfully negotiated a price, I like to see the seller smile.	1	2	3	4	5
4. I have a "smash-mouth" attitude toward resolving conflict.	5	4	3	2	1
5. In most conflict situations, one side is clearly right, and the other side is clearly wrong.	5	4	3	2	1
6. I think there are effective alternatives to strikes for settling union versus management disputes.	1	2	3	4	5
7. The winner should take all.	5	4	3	2	1
8. Conflict on the job is like a prize fight: The idea is to knock out the opponent.	5	4	3	2	1
9. I like the idea of tournaments in which first-round losers receive another opportunity to play.	1	2	3	4	5
10. Nice guys and gals usually finish first.	1	2	3	4	5

Scoring and Interpretation: Add the point value of your scores to obtain your total. Scores of 40 and higher suggest that you prefer a *collaborative*, or win–win, approach to resolving conflict. You tend to be concerned about finding long-term solutions to conflict that will provide benefits to both sides. Scores of 39 and lower suggest that you prefer a *competitive* approach to resolving conflict. You want to maximize gain for yourself, with little concern about the welfare of the other side.

with other people, you will never get close to them. Here we examine the nature of assertiveness and then describe several techniques for building assertiveness.

Assertive, Nonassertive, and Aggressive Behavior. As implied previously, **assertive** people state clearly what they want or how they feel in a given situation without being abusive, abrasive, or obnoxious. People who are assertive are open, honest, and "up front" because they believe that all people have an equal right to express themselves honestly. Assertive behavior can be understood more fully by comparing it to that shown by two other types of people. **Nonassertive** people let things happen to them without letting their feelings be known. They also prefer to avoid conflict. **Aggressive** people are obnoxious and overbearing. They push for what they want with almost no regard for the feelings of others.

Another representative assertive behavior is to ask for clarification rather than contradicting a person with whom you disagree. The assertive person asks for clarification when another person says something irritating, rather than hurling insults or telling the other person he or she is wrong. For example, assume someone says to you, "Your proposal is useless." Aggressively telling the person, "You have no right to make that judgment," shuts out any possible useful dialogue. You will probably learn more if you ask for clarification, such as "What is wrong with my proposal?"

Gestures as well as words can communicate whether the person is being assertive, nonassertive, or aggressive. Figure 10-2 illustrates these differences.

Becoming More Assertive and Less Shy Shyness, or not being assertive, is widespread, and about 50 percent of the U.S. population is shyer than they want to be. The personality trait of shyness has positive aspects, such as leading a person to think more deeply and become involved in ideas and things. (Where would the world be today if Bill Gates weren't shy as a youth?) But shyness can also create discomfort and lower self-esteem.[20] There are a number of everyday actions a person can take to overcome being nonassertive or shy. Even if the actions described here do not elevate your assertiveness, they will not backfire and cause you discomfort. After reading the following five techniques, you might be able to think of others that will work for you.[21]

1. Set a goal. Clearly establish in your mind how you want to behave differently. Do you want to speak out more in meetings? Be able to express dissatisfaction to coworkers? You can overcome shyness only by behaving differently; feeling differently is not enough.

2. Appear warm and friendly. Shy people often communicate to others through their body language that they are not interested in reaching out to others. To overcome this impression, smile, lean forward, uncross your arms and legs, and unfold your hands.

3. Conduct anonymous conversations. Try starting a conversation with strangers in a safe setting, such as a sporting event, the waiting room of a medical office, at an airport,

assertive

Characteristic of people who state clearly what they want or how they feel in a given situation without being abusive, abrasive, or obnoxious; open, honest, and up-front people who believe that all people have an equal right to express themselves honestly.

nonassertive

Characteristic of people who let things happen to them without letting their feelings be known.

aggressive

Characteristic of people who are obnoxious and overbearing; they push for what they want with almost no regard for the feelings of others.

FIGURE 10-2 Assertive, Nonassertive, and Aggressive Gestures

Assertive	Nonassertive	Aggressive
Well balanced	Covering mouth with hand	Pounding fists
Straight posture	Excessive head nodding	Stiff and rigid posture
Hand gestures, emphasizing key words	Tinkering with clothing or jewelry	Finger waving or pointing
	Constant shifting of weight	Shaking head as if other person isn't to be believed
	Scratching or rubbing head or other parts of the body	
Moderately loud voice	Wooden body posture	Hands on hips
	Voice too soft with frequent pauses	Voice louder than needed, fast speech

or a waiting line at the post office or supermarket. Begin the conversation with the common experience you are sharing at the time. Among them might be these:

"How many people do you estimate are in the audience?"
"How long does it usually take before you get to see the doctor?"
"What is your prediction about our plane arriving on time?"
"Where did you get that shopping bag? I've never seen one so sturdy before."

4. Greet strangers. For the next week or so, greet many of the people you pass. Smile and make a neutral comment such as "How ya doing?" or "Great day, isn't it?" Because most people are unaccustomed to being greeted by a stranger, you may get a few quizzical looks. Many other people may smile and return your greeting. A few of these greetings may turn into conversations. A few conversations may even turn into friendships. Even if the return on your investment in greetings is only a few pleasant responses, it will boost your confidence.

5. Practice being decisive. An assertive person is usually decisive, so it is important to practice being decisive. Some nonassertive people are even indecisive when asked to make a choice from a restaurant menu. They communicate their indecisiveness by asking their friend, "What are you going to have?" or asking the server, "Could you please suggest something for me?" or "What's good?" Practice quickly sizing up the alternatives in any situation and reaching a decision. This will help you be assertive and also project an image of assertiveness.

Confrontation and Problem Solving Leading to Win–Win

confrontation and problem solving

The most highly recommended way of resolving conflict; method of identifying the true source conflict and resolving it systematically.

The most highly recommended way of resolving conflict is **confrontation and problem solving**. It is a method of identifying the true source of conflict and resolving it systematically. The confrontation in this approach is gentle and tactful rather than combative and abusive. It is best to wait until your anger cools down before confronting the other person to avoid being unreasonable. Reasonableness is important because the person who takes the initiative in resolving the conflict wants to maintain a harmonious working relationship with the other party. Also, both parties should benefit from the resolution of the conflict.

Assume that Jason, the person working at the desk next to you, whistles loudly while he works. You find the whistling to be distracting and annoying; you think Jason is a noise polluter. If you don't bring the problem to Jason's attention, it will probably grow in proportion with time. Yet you are hesitant to enter into an argument about something a person might regard as a civil liberty (the right to whistle in a public place). An effective alternative is for you to approach Jason directly in this manner:

You: Jason, can I talk to you about a little problem that is bugging me?

Jason: Go ahead. I don't mind listening to a problem.

You: My problem is that when you whistle it distracts me and grates on my nerves. It may be my problem, but the whistling does bother me.

Jason: I guess I could stop whistling when you're working next to me. It's probably simply a nervous habit.

An important advantage of confrontation and problem solving is that you deal directly with a sensitive problem without jeopardizing the chances of forming a constructive working relationship in the future. One reason that the method works so effectively is that the focus is on the problem at hand and not on the individual's personality.

win–win

Belief that after conflict has been resolved both sides should gain something of value.

The intent of confrontation and problem solving is to arrive at a collaborative solution to the conflict. The collaborative style reflects a desire to fully satisfy the desires of both parties. It is based on an underlying philosophy of **win–win**, the belief that after conflict has been resolved, both sides should gain something of value. The user of win–win approaches is genuinely concerned about arriving at a settlement that meets the needs of both parties or at least that does not badly damage the welfare of the other side. When collaborative approaches to resolving conflict are used, the relationships among the parties are built on and improved.

324 CHAPTER 10

Here is an example of a win–win approach to resolving conflict. A manager granted an employee a few hours off on an occasional Friday afternoon because she was willing to be on call for emergency work on an occasional weekend. Both parties were satisfied with the outcome, and both accomplished their goals.

The opposite approach to win–win conflict resolution is *win–lose*, in which one side attempts to maximize gain at the expense of the other side. Win–lose is also referred to as a *zero-sum game*, in which one side wins nothing and the other side wins everything. Many people believe that win–lose is the best approach to resolving conflict—and that is one reason so much conflict goes unresolved in the form of physical attacks on people and bankruptcies. A person with a competitive orientation is likely to engage in power struggles in which one side wins and the other loses. "My way or the highway" is a win–lose strategy. An extreme example of a win–lose strategy would be to bad-mouth a rival so he or she gets fired.

If faced with an adversary who has a win–lose orientation, a plausible defense is to keep on pointing out the benefits of finding a solution that fits both sides. A sales representative for a company that makes steel buildings (often used for warehousing) was about to be laid off because of poor business. He proposed to his boss, "Please give me one more chance. Give me just enough salary to pay my rent and feed our newborn child. All the rest of my income will come from commissions on the sales I make." The owner conceded, and the sales rep did earn his way, so a win–lose situation emerged into a win–win.

Disarm the Opposition

When in conflict, your criticizer may be armed with valid negative criticism of you. The criticizer is figuratively clobbering you with knowledge of what you did wrong. If you deny that you have made a mistake, the criticism intensifies. A simple technique has been developed to help you deal with this type of manipulative criticism. **Disarming the opposition** is a method of conflict resolution in which you disarm the criticizer by agreeing with his or her criticism of you. The technique assumes that you have done something wrong. Disarming the opposition generally works more effectively than counterattacking a person with whom you are in conflict.

disarming the opposition

Method of conflict resolution in which you disarm the criticizer by agreeing with his or her criticism.

Another reason disarming the opposition is effective is that it implies you are apologizing for a mistake or an error you have made. An apology often gets the other person on your side, or at least softens the animosity. By offering an apology and regretting your mistake, you are likely to gain sympathy from the person who disapproves of what you have done or who you have wronged.

Agreeing with criticism made of you by a manager or team leader is effective because, by so doing, you are in a position to ask that manager's help in improving your performance. Most managers and team leaders recognize that it is their responsibility to help employees overcome problems, not merely to criticize them. Imagine that you have been chronically late in submitting reports during the past six months. It is time for a performance review and you know you will be reprimanded for your tardiness. You also hope that your boss will not downgrade all other aspects of your performance because of your tardy reports. Here is how disarming the situation would work in this situation:

Your boss:	Have a seat. It's time for your performance review, and we have a lot to talk about. I'm concerned about some things.
You:	So am I. It appears that I'm having a difficult time getting my reports in on time. I wonder if I'm being a perfectionist. Do you have any suggestions?
Your boss:	I like your attitude. I think you can improve on getting your reports in on time. Maybe you are trying to make your reports perfect before you turn them in. Try not to figure out everything to four decimal places. We need thoroughness around here, but we don't want to overdo it.

Reframing (Including Cognitive Restructuring and Asking Questions)

Another useful approach to resolving conflict is to reexamine or *reframe* the conflict situation by looking at in a different light. What follows are two practical approaches to reframing, one by searching for the positives in the situation and the other by asking questions.

Reframing through Cognitive Restructuring An indirect way of resolving interpersonal conflict is to lessen the conflicting elements in a situation by viewing them more positively. According to the technique of **cognitive restructuring** you mentally convert negative aspects into positive ones by looking for the positive elements in a situation. How you frame or choose your thoughts can determine the outcome of a conflict situation. Your thoughts influence your actions. If you search for the beneficial elements in the situation, there will be less area for dispute. Although this technique might sound like a mind game to you, it can work effectively.

Imagine that a coworker of yours, Jeff, has been asking you repeated questions about how to carry out a work procedure. You are about ready to tell Jeff, "Go bother somebody else; I'm not paid to be a trainer." Instead, you look for the positive elements in the situation. You say to yourself, "Jeff has been asking me a lot of questions. This does take time, but answering these questions is valuable experience. If I want to become a manager, I'll have to help group members with problems."

After having completed this cognitive restructuring, you can then deal with the conflict situation more positively. You might say to Jeff, "I welcome the opportunity to help you, but we need to find a mutually convenient time. In that way, I can better concentrate on my own work." To get started with cognitive restructuring, do Applying Human Relations Exercise 10-2 at the end of the chapter.

Reframing by Asking Questions. Another way to use reframing is to step back, take a deep breath, and then ask the following questions about the conflict situation arising within the work group:

- Do I fully understand the situation?
- Am I sure what my coworker is really saying?
- Is the person really angry at me or just worried and anxious?
- Have I missed something important?
- Do I have all the facts?
- What is the real issue here?
- How do I want to react in this situation?
- How would I want to be treated if the situation were reversed?

By taking such an approach, you are more likely to communicate effectively and constructively with coworkers when conflict situations arise. You carefully talk through the issues rather than becoming explosive, defensive, and argumentative. A useful scenario for reframing through questioning would be when a coworker accuses you of not carrying your fair share of the workload.[22]

Appeal to a Third Party

Now and then you may be placed in a conflict situation in which the other party either holds most of the power or simply won't budge. Perhaps you have tried techniques such as confrontation and problem solving or disarming the opposition, yet you cannot resolve your conflict. In these situations you may have to enlist the help of a third party with power—more power than you or your adversary has. Among such third parties is your common boss, union stewards, or human resource managers. Filing a lawsuit against your adversary is another application of the third-party technique, such as filing an age-discrimination charge.

In some situations, simply implying that you will bring in a third party to help resolve the conflict situation is sufficient for you to gain advantage. One woman felt she

---

cognitive restructuring

Technique of mentally converting negative aspects into positive ones by looking for the positive elements in a situation.

was repeatedly passed over for promotion because of her sex. She hinted that if she were not given fairer consideration, she would speak to the Equal Employment Opportunity Commission (EEOC). She was given a small promotion shortly thereafter. Many conflicts about sexual harassment, as well as ethnic and racial harassment, are resolved through third-party appeal.

The Grievance Procedure

The formal process of filing a complaint and resolving a dispute within an organization is the **grievance procedure**. It can also be regarded as a formal method of resolving conflict, in which a series of third parties are brought into the picture. The third-party appeal described previously skips the step-by-step approach of a formal grievance procedure. In a unionized firm, the steps in the grievance procedure are specified in the written contract between management and labor. The grievance procedure is a key part of a labor agreement because one of the union's goals is to obtain fair treatment for union members. An example of a grievance about favoritism would be, "I get the worst assignments because I'm not one of the boss's fishing buddies." An example of a grievance about discrimination would be, "I didn't get the transfer to the receptionist job because I'm fifty-five years old."

The steps in the grievance procedure may vary from one to six, depending on the labor agreement or company procedures. A summary of four typical steps in a grievance procedure is presented next and outlined in Figure 10-3. If the company does not have a labor union, a specialist from the human resources department might serve as a third party.

grievance procedure

Formal process of filing a complaint and resolving a dispute within an organization.

FIGURE 10-3 The Grievance Procedure

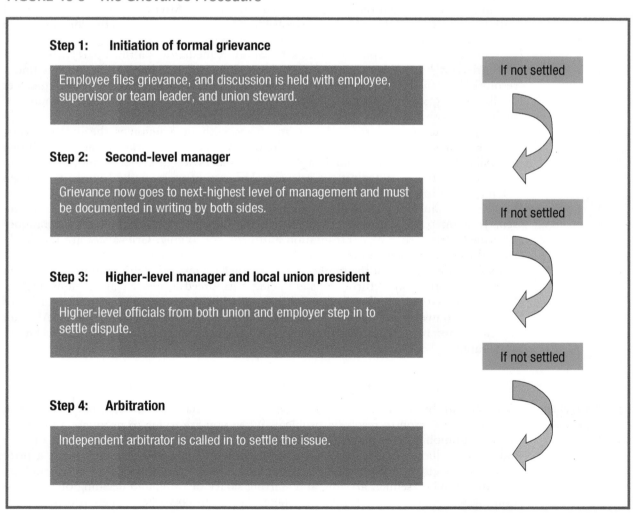

Step 1. *Initiation of the formal grievance.* Suppose that an employee feels that he or she has been treated unfairly or that his or her rights have been violated in some way. The employee then files a grievance with the supervisor (or team leader). Most grievances end at step 1 by conversation among the employee, union steward, and the supervisor. At this stage, it makes sense to use some of the techniques for resolving conflict already described. (If the workforce is not represented by a union, another type of grievance procedure might be used.)

Step 2. *Second level of management.* If the steward, supervisor or team leader, and employee cannot reach a satisfactory solution to the conflict, it goes to the next-highest level in the organization. At this point, the grievance must be documented in writing by both sides. Which people are involved at this level depends on the size of the firm. In a small firm, a high-ranking manager might be involved in step 2.

Step 3. *A higher-level manager and the local union president.* If the grievance is not resolved at step 2, higher-level officials from both the union and the employer become involved in settling the dispute. A general principle is that at each higher step in the grievance process, comparable levels of management from both company and union face each other, or a higher-level representative from the human resources department might be involved.

Step 4. *Arbitration.* If the grievance cannot be settled at lower steps, an independent arbitrator may be called in to settle the issue. Only about 1 percent of grievances go all the way to arbitration. Arbitration is often used as an alternative to a strike. The arbitrator has the authority to settle the dispute and must be a person acceptable to both sides.

In a small organization, step 2 is sometimes omitted. After the grievance is discussed with the union steward, and it is not resolved, the grievance is taken to the chief executive or business owner, and then to arbitration if necessary.[23]

Mediation is often confused with arbitration. A mediator is a third party who enters a controversy but holds no power of decision. The mediator helps the two sides find a resolution to their conflict. Relatively few labor agreements allow for mediation, yet mediation might be used to settle a strike. A mediator works like a marriage counselor by helping both sides come to agreement by themselves.

A grievance procedure used in many firms without a union is the **jury of peers**, whereby unresolved grievances are submitted to a panel of coworkers. The panel chosen is similar to a jury in a criminal case. Panel members weigh evidence and, after group discussion, vote for or against the grievant. The jury-of-peers method works well when the jury members are knowledgeable about organizational justice.

The grievance processes described are formal and legalistic. Nevertheless, to represent your interests well, it is helpful to use the informal conflict-resolution techniques described earlier, such as confrontation and problem solving. Grievances are less likely to lead to labor strikes in the current business environment, partly because labor unions in manufacturing (not in the public service sector) are less powerful than in the past. As more and more manufacturing jobs are being outsourced to lower-wage regions, including other countries, employees fear job loss. Worldwide competition has taken a lot of bargaining power away from workers and unions in the manufacturing sector. Also, an increasing number of manufacturing jobs are being automated, making workers feel more vulnerable.

Negotiation and Bargaining Tactics

Conflicts can be considered situations calling for **negotiating and bargaining**, conferring with another person to resolve a problem. When you are trying to negotiate a fair price for an automobile, you are also trying to resolve a conflict. At first the demands of both parties seem incompatible. After haggling for a while, you will probably reach a price that is satisfactory to both sides. Negotiation has many applications in the workplace, including buying, selling, arriving at a starting salary or raise, and deciding on a relocation allowance. Negotiation may also take place with coworkers when you need their

jury of peers

Grievance procedure used in many firms without a union whereby unresolved grievances are submitted to a panel of coworkers.

negotiating and bargaining

Situation of conferring with another person to resolve a problem.

assistance. For example, you might need to strike a bargain with a coworker to handle some of your responsibilities if you are faced with a temporary overload.

A sampling of negotiating tactics to help you resolve conflict is presented next. As with other techniques of resolving conflict already presented, choose those that best fit your style and the situation. Many people feel awkward at the prospects of negotiating with a stranger, yet by learning and practicing new skills most people can become better negotiators.[24]

Create a Positive Negotiating Climate.   Negotiation proceeds much more swiftly if a positive tone surrounds the session, so it is helpful to initiate a positive outlook about the negotiation meeting. A good opening line in a negotiating session is, "Thanks for fitting this meeting into your hectic schedule." Nonverbal communication such as smiling and making friendly gestures helps create a positive climate. A calm voice helps build the trust necessary for creating a positive climate.

In negotiating with coworkers for assistance, a positive climate can often be achieved by phrasing demands as a request for help. Most people will be more accommodating if you say to them, "I have a problem, and I wonder if you could help me with it." The problem might be that you need the person's time and mental energy. By giving that person a choice of offering you help, you have established a much more positive climate than by demanding assistance.[25]

Another way of creating a positive negotiating climate is to validate the other side's position by describing his or her position in your own words (a form of paraphrasing). Make a positive comment to the other person that emphasizes the value in the relationship.[26] Assume that you are renting a condo and the owner wants to raise the rent 10 percent for next year. You might state, "I recognize that your costs are rising. You are also a great a landlord. But 10 percent more rent is a little beyond my budget."

Listen First to Investigate What the Other Side Wants.   Listening skills are also part of effectiveness in negotiation. Negotiation professional Bobby Covie says, "There's a saying among negotiators that whoever talks the most during a negotiation loses." Being the first to listen helps establish trust. Listening also involves paying attention to what the other side is saying.[27] A person might begin a negotiating session claiming to want a bigger share of the division budget. Yet careful listening might indicate that he really is looking for his department to receive more respect and attention. So the issue is not financial.

As shown in the example just presented, listening helps you dig for information as to why the other side wants what it does.[28] If the other side wants a bigger budget just to have more respect, there are less expensive ways to grant respect than granting a bigger share of the budget. Perhaps the manager can give the person a classier job title, rename the department, or appoint the person to head a task force. For example, the head of marketing is renamed "chief of brands," and her department "brand development."

Allow Room for Compromise, but Be Reasonable.   The basic strategy of negotiation is to begin with a demand that allows room for compromise and concession. Anyone who has ever negotiated the price of an automobile, house, or used furniture recognizes this vital strategy. If you are a buyer, begin with a low bid. (You say, "I'll give you $60 for that painting" when you are prepared to pay $90.) If you are the seller, begin with a high demand. (You say, "You can have this painting for $130" when you are ready to sell it for as low as $100.) As negotiations proceed, the two of you will probably arrive at a mutually satisfactory price. This negotiating strategy can also be used for such purposes as obtaining a higher starting salary or purchasing excess inventory.

Common sense, and perhaps greed, propels many negotiators to allow *too much* room for compromise. They begin negotiations by asking way beyond what they expect to receive or offering far less than they expect to give. As a result of these implausible demands, the other side may become hostile, antagonistic, or walk away from the negotiations. Beginning with a plausible demand or offer is also important because it contributes to a positive negotiating climate.

Focus on Interests, Not Positions.   Rather than clinging to specific negotiating points, keep your overall interests in mind and try to satisfy them. A negotiating point might be a certain amount of money or a concession that you must have. Remember that the true object of negotiation is to satisfy the underlying interests of both sides. Among the interests you and the other side might be trying to protect are money, lifestyle, power, and the status quo. For example, instead of negotiating for a particular starting salary, your true interests might be to afford a certain lifestyle. If the company pays all your medical and dental coverage, you can get by with a lower salary. Or your cost of living might be much lower in one city than in another. Therefore, you can accept a lower starting salary in the city with a lower cost of living.

Make a Last and Final Offer.   In many circumstances, presenting a final offer will break a deadlock. You might frame your message something like this: "All I can possibly pay for your guitar is $250. You have my number. Call me when it is available at that price." Sometimes the strategy will be countered by a last and final offer from the other side: "Thanks for your interest. My absolute minimum price for this guitar is $300. Call us if that should seem okay to you." One of you will probably give in and accept the other person's last and final offer.

Role-Play to Predict What the Other Side Will Do.   An advanced negotiating technique is to prepare in advance by forecasting what the other side will demand or offer. Two marketing professors from New Zealand, J. Scott Armstrong and Kesten Green, have discovered that when people role-play conflicts, their ability to predict outcomes jumps remarkably. The researchers presented 290 participants with descriptions of six actual conflicts and asked them to choose the most likely eventual decisions. The conflicts involved labor–management, commercial, and civil disputes. Five of these conflicts were chosen for role-playing. Without the use of role-playing, the participants did not do much better than chance, with a 27 percent success ratio. Next, the researchers asked twenty-one international game theorists (specialists in predicting outcomes of events) to forecast the conflict outcomes. The game theorists were correct only 28 percent of the time. (Chance here would be one-fifth, or 20 percent.)

Next, 352 students were instructed to role-play the conflicts in the six situations. The average correct decision was 61 percent versus 27 percent for the comparable group. The authors note that in more than forty years of studying forecasting, they have never seen a technique that led to such improvement in predictive accuracy.[29]

The implication for making you a better negotiator is to role-play with a friend in advance of the negotiating session you will be facing. The role-play should help you predict what the other side and you will do so you will be better prepared. For example, if your role-play suggests that the company would be willing to give you a 15 percent bonus for incredible performance, ask for a 15 percent bonus.

Allow for Saving Face.   We have saved one of the most important negotiating and conflict resolution strategies for last. Negotiating does not mean that you should try to squash the other side. You should try to create circumstances that will enable you to continue working with that person if it is necessary. People prefer to avoid looking weak, foolish, or incompetent during negotiation or when the process is completed. If you do not give your opponent an opportunity to save face, you will probably create a long-term enemy.

Saving face could work in this way. A small-business owner winds up purchasing a network system for about twice what he originally budgeted. After the sale is completed, the sales rep says, "I know you bought a more professional networking rig than you originally intended. Yet I know you made the right decision. You will be able to boost productivity enough with the networked PCs to pay back the cost of the networking system in two years."

WHAT ARE SOME SUGGESTIONS FOR MANAGING ANGER?

Limited ability to manage anger damages the careers and personal lives of many people. The ability to manage your anger, and the anger of others, is an important human relations skill now considered to be part of emotional intelligence. A person who cannot manage anger well cannot take good advantage of his or her intellectual intelligence. As an extreme example, a genius who swears at the manager regularly will probably lose his or her job despite being so talented. Concerns about employees becoming violent have prompted many companies to offer employees training in anger management. Also, employees who become verbally abusive on the job are often sent to such training.[30] Anger-management training is likely to encompass most of the suggestions presented next. Our concern here is with several tactics for managing your own anger and that of others effectively.

Managing Your Own Anger

A starting point in dealing with your anger is to recognize that at its best, anger can be an energizing force. Instead of letting it be destructive, channel your anger into exceptional performance. If you are angry because you did not get the raise you thought you deserved, get even by performing so well that there will be no question you deserve a raise next time. Develop the habit of expressing your anger before it reaches a high intensity. Tell your coworker that you do not appreciate his or her listening to an iPod while you are having dinner together the first time the act of rudeness occurs. If you wait too long, you may wind up grabbing the iPod and slamming it to the floor.

As you are about to express anger, *slow down*. (The old technique of counting to ten is still effective.) Slowing down gives you the opportunity to express your anger in a way that does not damage your relationship with the other person. Following your first impulse, you might say to the other person, "You're a stupid fool." If you slow down, this might translate into "You need training on this task."

Closely related to slowing down is a technique taught in anger-management programs: Think about the consequences of what you do when you are worked up. Say to yourself as soon as you feel angry, "Oops, I'm in anger mode now. I had better calm down before I say something or do something that I will regret later." To gauge how effectively you are expressing your anger, ask for feedback. Ask a friend, coworker, or manager, "Am I coming on too strong when I express my negative opinion?"[31]

Managing Anger in Other People

A variation of confrontation and problem solving has developed specifically to resolve conflict with angry people: confront, contain, and connect. *Confront* in this context means that you jump right in and get agitated workers talking to prevent future blowups. The confrontation, however, is not aimed at arguing with the angry person. If the other person yells, you talk more softly. *Contain* refers to moving an angry worker out of sight and out of earshot. At the same time you remain impartial. The supervisor is advised not to choose sides or appear to be a friend.

You *connect* by asking open-ended questions such as "What would you like us to do about your concern?" to get at the real reasons behind an outburst. Using this approach, one worker revealed he was upset because a female coworker got to leave early to pick up her daughter at day care. The man also needed to leave early one day a week for personal reasons but felt awkward making the request. So instead of being assertive (explicit and direct) about his demands, he flared up.

An important feature of the confront–contain–connect technique is that it provides angry workers a place where they can vent their frustrations and report the outbursts of others. Mediator Nina Meierding says, "Workers need a safe outlet to talk through anger and not feel they will be minimized or put their job in jeopardy."[32]

Choosing a Tactic for Resolving a Conflict or Managing Anger

How does a person know which of the tactics or strategies presented in this chapter will work best for a given problem? The best answer is to consider both your personality and the situation. With respect to your personality, or personal style, pick a tactic for resolving conflict that you would feel comfortable using. One person might say, "I would like the tactic of making a last and final offer because I like to control situations." Another person might say, "I prefer confrontation because I'm an open and up-front type of person." Still another person might say, "I'll avoid disarming the opposition for now. I don't yet have enough finesse to carry out this technique."

In fitting the strategy to the situation, it is important to assess the gravity of the topic for negotiation or the conflict between people. A woman might say to herself, "My boss has committed such a blatant act of sexual harassment that I had best take this up with a higher authority immediately." Sizing up your opponent can also help you choose the best strategy. If she or he appears reasonably flexible, you might try to compromise. Or if your adversary is especially upset, give that person a chance to simmer down before trying to solve the problem.

Another perspective on conflict resolution and anger management is to ponder whether you too frequently need to resolve conflict and manage anger with coworkers (or other students). One indirect measure of being perceived as too conflict-prone, or too angry, is the extent to which you are ostracized (excluded) by other group members. Ostracism might also take place because a person is unpopular for other reasons, such as having a bland personality. Self-Assessment Quiz 10-2 gives you an opportunity to think through whether you are being ostracized from a group of which you are a member.

SELF-ASSESSMENT QUIZ 10-2

How Much Am I Being Ostracized?

Indicate how frequently each of the statements below relates to you based on a particular work group. If a recent work group does not come to mind, use a student group, athletic team, or club. 1 = Never, 2 = Once in a while, 3 = Sometimes, 4 = Fairly often, 5 = Often, 6 = Constantly, 7 = Always.

Statement	Frequency (1–7)
1. Others ignored you at work.	_____
2. Others left the area when you entered.	_____
3. Your greetings have gone unanswered at work.	_____
4. You involuntarily sat alone in a crowded lunchroom at work.	_____
5. Others avoided you at work.	_____
6. You noticed others would not look at you at work.	_____
7. Others at work shut you out of the conversation.	_____
8. Others refused to talk to you at work.	_____
9. Others at work treated you like you weren't there.	_____
10. Others at work did not invite you or ask you if you wanted anything when they went out for a coffee break.	_____
Total Score	_____

Although the authors of this scientifically developed quiz do not offer a scoring key, the higher the score, the more evident it is that you have been ostracized from the group. A score of 20 or lower would indicate almost no ostracism. Scores between 21 and 50 would indicate some ostracism. A score of 51 or higher would indicate substantial ostracism.

Source: D. Lance Ferris, Douglas D. Brown, Joseph W. Berry, and Huiwen Lian, "The Development and Validation of the Workplace Ostracism Scale," *Journal of Applied Psychology,* November 2008, p. 1366.

Concept Review and Reinforcement

Key Terms

conflict 313
personality clash 314
aggressive personalities 314
work–family conflict 315
micro-inequity 317
sexual harassment 317

assertive 323
nonassertive 323
aggressive 323
confrontation and problem
   solving 324
win–win 324

disarming the opposition 325
cognitive restructuring 326
grievance procedure 327
jury of peers 328
negotiating and bargaining 328

Summary

Conflict occurs when two sets of demands, goals, or motives are incompatible. Such differences often lead to a hostile or antagonistic relationship between people. A conflict can also be considered a dispute, feud, or controversy. Among the reasons for widespread conflict are the following:

- Competition for limited resources
- Differences of opinion on work-related issues and rights
- Personality clashes
- Aggressive personalities, including bullies
- Culturally diverse teams and factional groups
- Competing work and family demands
- Micro-inequities (semiconscious slights)
- Cross-generational conflict
- Sexual harassment

Sexual harassment is one of two types: quid pro quo (a demand for sexual favors in exchange for job benefits) and creating a hostile environment. It is important for workers to understand what actions and words constitute sexual harassment and how to deal with the problem.

The benefits of conflict include the emergence of talents and abilities, constructive innovation and change, and increased unity after the conflict is settled. Among the detrimental consequences of conflict are physical and mental health problems, wasted resources, the promotion of self-interest, and workplace violence.

Techniques for resolving conflicts with others include the following:

- Being assertive. To become more assertive, set a goal, appear warm and friendly, conduct anonymous conversations, greet strangers, and practice being decisive.
- Confrontation and problem solving leading to win–win. Get to the root of the problem and resolve it systematically. The intention of confrontation and problem solving is to arrive at a collaborative solution to the conflict. The opposite of win–win is win–lose, where each side attempts to maximize gain at the expense of the other.
- Disarm the opposition. Agree with the criticizer and enlist his or her help.
- Reframing. One approach is to use cognitive restructuring by mentally converting negative aspects into positive ones by looking for the positive elements in a situation. Also use reframing by asking questions such as, "Have I missed something important?"
- Appeal to a third party (such as a government agency).
- Use the grievance procedure (a formal organizational procedure for dispute resolution), used extensively in unionized companies.
- Use negotiation and bargaining tactics, including creating a positive negotiating climate; listening first to investigate what the other side wants; allowing room for compromise but being reasonable; focusing on interests, not positions; making a last and final offer; role-playing to predict what the other side will do; and allowing for face-saving.

Limited ability to manage anger damages the careers and personal lives of many people. The ability to manage anger is part of emotional intelligence. In managing your own anger, remember that anger can be an energizing force.

- Express your anger before it reaches a high intensity.
- As you are about to express your anger, slow down.
- Ask for feedback on how you deal with anger.
- In dealing with the anger of others, use the confront, contain (move the angry worker out of sight), and connect (ask open-ended questions to get at the real reason behind the outburst) method.

In choosing a tactic for resolving conflict, consider both your personality or style and the nature of the situation facing you. The situation includes such factors as the gravity of the conflict and the type of person you are facing. Also, think through whether if you are so conflict-prone and angry that you are being ostracized from the group.

Questions for Discussion and Review

1. Give an example from your life of how competition for limited resources can breed conflict.

2. Some conflicts go on for decades without being resolved, such as disputes between countries that last for up to a hundred years. Why is it so difficult to resolve such conflicts?

3. Imagine that after two weeks on a new job that you want, your boss begins to treat you in a bullying, intimidating manner. What would you say to that boss?

4. Many male managers who confer with a female worker in their offices leave the door open to avoid any charges of sexual harassment. Are these managers using good judgment, or are they being overly cautious?

5. Assume that a worker is being sexually harassed by the owner of the business where he or she works. How should the harassed person deal with the problem?

6. Identify several occupations in which conflict resolution skills are particularly important.

7. Visualize a person taking the road test part of obtaining a driver's license. The candidate has done a poor job of parallel parking, and the examiner looks at him or her with a frown and says, "Not very impressive." How can this candidate make best use of the tactic "disarming the opposition"?

8. How might a person use cognitive restructuring to help deal with the conflict of having received a below-average raise while expecting an above-average raise?

9. What is your explanation of the research showing that role-playing a negotiation scenario helps people make more accurate predictions about the outcome of conflicts?

10. What do you see as the potential advantages and disadvantages of having "working dates"?

The Web Corner

Labor union approach to combating sexual harassment:
www.ueunion.org Look under "Search UE."

Cognitive restructuring:
http://www.mindtools.com/stress/rt/CognitiveRestructuring.htm

Shyness:
www.shyness.com (self-quizzes about shyness, plus the opportunity to participate in research about shyness)

Internet Skill Builder

A good Web site dealing with improving your negotiating skills is www.negotiatingcoach.com. After scanning the site describe in your own words why improving negotiating skills is important and who needs to improve their negotiating skills. As the site opens, a presenter pops into view and provides an overview of the program. What is your evaluation of the presenter's communication skills? For example, how persuasive is she?

Developing Your Human Relations Skills

Human Relations Application Exercises

Applying Human Relations Exercise 10-1
Win–Win Conflict Management

The class is organized into groups of six, with each group being divided into conflict-resolution teams of three each. The members of the team would like to find a win–win solution to the issue separating each side. The team members are free to invent their own pressing issue or choose among the following:

- Management wants to control costs by not giving cost-of-living adjustments in the upcoming year. The employee group believes that a cost-of-living adjustment is absolutely necessary.

- City management has decided to take one giant step toward reducing carbon pollution by relying on giant wind turbines for some of its energy source. The people who live near the area where the windmills will be installed object strongly to the installation of these turbines, which they consider to be unsightly, noisy, and lethal for nearby birds.

- Starbucks Coffee would like to build in a new location, adjacent to a historic district in one of the oldest cities in North America. The members of the town planning board would like the tax revenue and the jobs that the Starbucks store would bring, but they still say they do not want a Starbucks store adjacent to the historic district.

After the teams have developed win–win solutions to the conflicts, the creative solutions can be shared with teammates. Explain why each of your solutions should be classified as win–win. Describe the benefits each side received from the resolution of conflict and why you classified the outcome as a benefit.

Applying Human Relations Exercise 10-2
Reframing Through Cognitive Restructuring

The following are examples of negative statements about others in the workplace. In the space provided, cognitively restructure (reframe) each comment in a positive way.

Negative: Nancy is getting on my nerves. It takes her two weeks longer than anyone else on the team to complete her input.

Positive:

Negative: Rob is so obsessed with sports he is hurting my productivity. Where does it say in the employee handbook that I have to spend thirty minutes on Monday listening to Rob's comments on his team's weekend performance? Doesn't he know that I have a job to do and that I just don't care about his team?

Positive:

Negative: My boss is driving me crazy. He's forever telling me what I did wrong and making suggestions for improvement. He makes me feel like I'm in elementary school.

Positive:

Human Relations Class Activity

Negotiating for a Bigger Raise

During good times and bad times, most people would like to receive a bigger raise than the one the company or immediate manager has decided to grant. But it is not widely known which negotiating tactic or tactics is likely to be the most effective. The purpose of this class activity is to conduct a survey of written comments about the best way to negotiate for a bigger raise than management probably had in store for you (assuming that you worked for somebody else). In addition, the class will attempt to categorize the three most frequently occurring tactics. Following the text, the categories include "be the first to listen," "allow room for compromise, but be reasonable," "make a last and final offer," and so forth.

Method of data collection: Each class member sends an e-mail to two experienced working adults in your network, perhaps including yourself. Ask the person to complete the following sentence:

The best way to negotiate for a bigger raise for yourself is to _____.

After collecting the responses, send them to a master e-mail or Web page for your class.

Method of analysis: After every class member has taken the opportunity to review the master file, each student compiles (a) what he or she considers the three most frequently used approaches to asking for a bigger raise and (b) which negotiating and bargaining tactics these approaches best fit. Here is an example for clarification: Suppose one of the most frequently used approaches is for the person wanting a bigger raise to state something to the effect of this: "Give me a bigger raise or I'll look elsewhere." This approach might be classified as "Make a last and final offer."

The analysis by individuals is then sent back to the master e-mail or Web site to prepare a final summary of the results. The class might then hold a discussion as to any takeaway lessons from this exercise.

Human Relations Case Study 10-1

The Apprehensive Sales Trainee

Maria was ecstatic about the position she just landed as a sales representative for a company that provides payroll and human resources services for small companies throughout the country. She was to be assigned a sales territory in Madison, Wisconsin, where she lived with her husband and three young children. Before working her territory, Maria had to attend ten days of training and orientation at company headquarters in Boston.

One of the key trainers in the program was the national sales manager, Todd, an energetic and successful man in his early forties. During a beverage break at the first morning of the training program, Todd approached Maria and complimented her on her "great tan," and "fabulous appearance." Maria was not particularly comfortable with the comments, but she let them pass.

Before the dinner meeting on the second night of the program, Todd came over to Maria and engaged her in a brief conversation about how she was enjoying the sales training. He then handed her a business card and said, "I imagine you might get lonely being away from home for so long, so here is my business card. Please get in touch if you would just like to hang out a little with me." Maria thought that Todd was stepping over the line of good business judgment, but she just smiled politely and said, "Thanks anyway, but I am so overwhelmed with all this great information I am receiving, I have no spare time."

The following morning, Maria received a text message from Todd on her BlackBerry that said, "Your beauty is devastating. Get back."

Maria later phoned her best friend in Madison and said, "Todd carries a lot of weight being the national sales manager. But I think his behavior toward me borders on sexual harassment. Yet five days into my job, I guess I shouldn't attempt to rat on a company executive."

Maria's friend replied, "You have got to do something. That sales manager is a predator."

Case Questions

1. To what extent is Todd engaging in sexual harassment toward Maria?
2. If Todd is guilty, what type of sexual harassment is he committing?
3. What steps should Maria take so she can stop the harassment yet still maintain a good working relationship with Todd?
4. What would be the positives and negatives of Maria filing a complaint about Todd with the company?

Human Relations Role-Playing Exercise

Maria Tries to Fend Off Todd

The case about Maria, the sales trainee, provides the background information and story line for this role-play. One person plays the role of serious-minded Maria, who wants to receive high ratings in her sales training. She does not want to create problems at the company, yet she recognizes she has the right to a harassment-free environment. Another student plays the role of Todd, who is infatuated with Maria and also believes that he is powerful and somewhat irresistible to women. Todd corners Maria during a cocktail hour prior to dinner on the third night of the sales training program. He once again starts to hit on her, and Maria wants to avoid being hit on. At least a few sets of role-players should perform in front of the class for about seven minutes.

Observers rate the role-players on two dimensions, using a 1 to 5 scale from very poor to very good. One dimension is "effective use of human relations techniques." Focus on Maria's ability to effectively deal with sexual harassment. The second dimension is "acting ability." A few observers might voluntarily provide feedback to the role players in terms of sharing their ratings and observations. The course instructor might also provide feedback.

Human Relations Case Study 10-2

Caught in a Squeeze

Heather Lopez is a product development specialist at a telecommunications company. For the past seven months she has worked as a member of a product- development team composed of people from five different departments within the company. Heather previously worked full-time in the marketing department. Her primary responsibilities were to research the market potential of an idea for a new product. The product development team is now working on a product that will integrate a company's printers and copiers.

Heather's previous position in the marketing department was a satisfactory fit for her lifestyle. Heather thought that she was able to take care of her family responsibilities and her job without sacrificing one for the other. As Heather explains, "I worked about forty-five predictable hours in my other job. My hours were essentially 8:30 a.m. to 4:30 p.m. with a little work at night and on Saturdays. But I could do the work at night and on Saturdays at home.

"Brad, my husband, and I had a smooth-working arrangement for sharing the responsibility for getting our son, Christopher, off to school and picking him up from the after-school child-care center. Brad is a devoted accountant, so he understands the importance of giving high priority to a career yet still being a good family person."

In her new position as a member of the product-development team, Heather is encountering some unanticipated demands. Three weeks ago, at 3 p.m. on a Tuesday, Tyler Watson, Heather's team leader, announced an emergency meeting to discuss a budget problem with the new product. The meeting would start at four and probably end at about six-thirty. "Don't worry, folks," said the team leader, "if it looks like we are going past six-thirty, we will order in some Chinese food."

With a look of panic on her face, Heather responded to Tyler, "I can't make the meeting. Christopher will be expecting me at about five at the child-care center. My husband is out of town, and the center closes at six sharp. So count me out of today's meeting."

Tyler said, "I said that this is an emergency meeting and that we need input from all the members. You need to organize your personal life better to be a contributing member to this team. But do what you have to do, at least this once."

Heather chose to leave the office at four-thirty so she could pick up Christopher. The next day, Tyler did not comment on her absence, but he gave her a copy of the minutes and asked for her input. The budget problem surfaced again one week later. Top-level management asked the group to reduce the cost of the new product and its initial marketing costs by 15 percent.

Tyler said to the team on a Friday morning, "We have until Monday morning to arrive at a reduced cost structure on our product development. I am dividing up the project into segments. If we meet as a team Saturday morning at eight, we should get the job done by six at night. Get a good night's rest so we can start fresh tomorrow morning. Breakfast and lunch will be on the company."

Heather could feel stress overwhelming her body, as she thought, "Christopher is playing in the finals of his soccer league tomorrow morning at ten. Brad has made dinner reservations for six, so we can make it to the *The Lion King* at 8 p.m. Should I tell Tyler he is being unreasonable? Should I quit? Should I tell Christopher and Brad that our special occasions together are less important than a Saturday business meeting?"

Case Questions

1. What type of conflicts is Heather facing?
2. What should Heather do to resolve her conflicts with respect to family and work responsibilities?
3. What should the company do to help deal with the type of conflict Heather is facing? Or should the company not consider Heather's dilemma to be their problem?

Human Relations Role-Playing Exercise

Heather Attempts to Resolve Her Work–Family Conflict

Imagine that Heather in the case just presented decides that her job is taking too big a toll on her personal life, but she still values her job and does not want to quit. She decides to discuss her problem with her team leader, Tyler. From Tyler's standpoint, a professional person must stand ready to meet unusual job demands and cannot expect an entirely predictable work schedule. One person plays the role of Heather and another the role of Tyler as they attempt to resolve this incident of work–family conflict.

Observers will look for (a) how well the conflict appears to have been resolved and (b) which techniques of conflict resolution Heather and Tyler used. Other feedback observations will also be welcome.

REFERENCES

1. Jacinthe Tremblay, "Lutte Sans Merci Entre Bud et Bud," *La Presse Affaires* (http://lapresseaffaires.cyberpresse.ca), August 18, 2007. ("Nonstop Struggle between Bud and Bud.")

2. David Enrich, "Krawcheck Is Leaving Citigroup," *Wall Street Journal*, September 23, 2008, p. C8.

3. Dominic A. Infante, *Arguing Constructively* (Prospect Heights, IL: Waveland Press, 1992); Siobhan Leftwich, "Hey, You Can't Say That! How to Cope with Verbally Abusive People," *Black Enterprise*, January 2006, p. 95.

4. "Workplace Homicides in 2007," *U.S. Bureau of Labor Statistics*, http://data.bls.gov, August 26, 2008.

5. Angela Pirisi, "Teamwork: The Downside of Diversity," *Psychology Today*, November/December 1999, p. 18.

6. Jiatao Li and Donald C. Hambrick, "Factional Groups: A New Vantage on Demographic Faultlines, Conflict, and Disintegration in Work Teams," *Academy of Management Journal*, October 2005, pp. 794–813.

7. Beth A. Livingston and Timothy A. Judge, "Emotional Responses to Work–Family Conflict: An Examination of Gender Role Orientation among Working Men and Women," *Journal of Applied Psychology*, January 2008, pp. 207–216.

8. Adapted from Sue Shellenberger, "Dinner and a PowerPoint," *Wall Street Journal*, June 28, 2007, p. D1.

9. Paul E. Spector et al. (consisting of 22 researchers), "Cross-National Differences in Relationships of Work Demands, Job Satisfaction, and Turnover Intentions with Work–Family Conflict," *Personnel Psychology*, Winter 2007, pp. 805–835.

10. Joseph G. Gryzwacz et al., "Work–Family Conflict: Experiences and Health Implications among Immigrant Latinos," *Journal of Applied Psychology*, July 2007, pp. 1119–1130.

11. The examples, but not the interpretations, are from Julie Fawe, "Why Your Boss May Start Sweating the Small Stuff," *Time*, March 20, 2006, p. 80. See also Joann S. Lublin, "How to Stop the Snubs That Demoralize You and Your Colleagues," *Wall Street Journal*, December 7, 2004, p. B1.

12. Chris Pentila, "Talking about My Generation," *Entrepreneur*, March 2009, p. 55.

13. Jennifer L. Berdhal and Karl Aquino, "Sexual Behavior at Work: Fun or Folly?" *Journal of Applied Psychology*, January 2009, p. 34.

14. Jennifer Berdahl, "The Sexual Harassment of Uppity Women," *Journal of Applied Psychology*, March 2007, pp. 425–437.

15. Chelsea R. Willness, Piers Steel, and Kibeom Lee,"A Meta-Analysis of the Antecedents and Consequences of Workplace Sexual Harassment," *Personnel Psychology*, Spring 2007, pp. 127–162.

16. Lisa Takeuchi Cullen, "Sex in the Syllabus," *Time*, April 3, 2006, pp. 80–81.

17. "Sexual Harassment Fact Sheet," www.doter.ost.dot.gov/Documents/complaint/Preventing_SexualHarassment.htm, p. 5.

18. Data synthesized in Hong Ren and Barbara Gray, "Repairing Relationship Conflict: How Violation Types and Culture Influence the Effectiveness of Restoration Rituals, *Academy of Management Review*, January 2009, p. 105.

19. Rasha Madkour, "NASA Gunman Thought He Was Going to Be Fired," The Associated Press, April 22, 2007, p. 19A.

20. Bernardo J. Carducci, *Shyness: A Bold Approach* (New York: HarperCollins, 1999).

21. Philip Zimbardo, *Shyness: What It Is, What to Do about It* (Reading, MA: Addison-Wesley, 1977), pp. 220–226; Mel Silberman with Freda Hansburg, *PeopleSmart* (San Francisco: Berrett-Koehler, 2000), pp. 75–76.

22. "Conquer Conflict with This Technique," *Manager's Edge*, September 7, 2005. As adapted from Maria Broomhower, "Dissolving Conflict through Reframing," http://www.conflict911.com.

23. Stephen P. Robbins and David A. DeCenzo, *Supervision Today!*, 4th ed. (Upper Saddle River, NJ: Pearson Prentice Hall, 2004), p. 438.

24. Marc Deiner, "Speak Up: Hate to Negotiate? That's Still No Excuse to Avoid Learning the Skill," *Entrepreneur*, September 2004, p. 79.

25. Joseph D'O'Brian, "Negotiating with Peers: Consensus, Not Power," *Supervisory Management*, January 1992, p. 4.

26. "To Agree or Disagree?" *Chicago Tribune Career Builder*, November 4, 2007, p. 1, Section 6.

27. Quoted in Brenda Goodman, "The Art of Negotiation," *Psychology Today*, January/February 2007, p. 65.

28. Deepak Malhotra and Max H. Bazerman, "Investigative Negotiation," *Harvard Business Review*, September 2007, pp. 72–78.

29. J. Scott Armstrong, "Forecasting in Conflicts: How to Predict What Your Opponents Will Do," *Knowledge@ Wharton* (www.knowledge.wharton.upenn.edu), February 13, 2002, p. 1.

30. Linda Wasmer Andrews, "When It's Time for Anger Management," *HR Magazine*, June 2005, pp. 131–135.

31. Fred Pryor, "Is Anger Really Healthy?" *Pryor Management Newsletter*, February 1996, p. 3.

32. The quote and technique are both from Kathleen Doheny, "It's a Mad, Mad Corporate World," *Working Woman*, April 2000, pp. 71–72.

Diversity

In 2009, Walgreens opened a distribution center in Windsor, Connecticut, where close to one-third of the workforce consists of people with disabilities. Employees with disabilities work alongside other team members, having the same productivity goals, and earning the same pay. Disabilities include autism and mental retardation, as well as hearing and physical impairments. An on-site training facility assists those with special needs become prepared for employment so that everyone can work productively and effectively.

"We've worked technology and creativity into every inch of this place, but the people here will amaze you," said Walgreen's senior vice president of supply chain and logistics Randy Lewis. "We originally went into this project wanting to change the work environment but soon discovered we were the ones who changed in dramatic and wonderful ways." Lewis, whose son Austin has autism, developed the idea of the outreach program for people with disabilities.

This giant 700,000 square foot facility can fit 12 football fields inside its walls, and serves hundreds of Walgreens stores throughout the Northeast. The center was planned to be 20 percent more efficient than the company's previous generation of distribution centers and has some of the most innovative logistics systems in the distribution industry.

The Windsor location and the facility in Anderson, South Carolina, that opened in 2007 are now the models for all future Walgreens distribution centers. The company's goal is to fill 10 percent of its distribution center production jobs with people with disabilities. Walgreens is more than halfway there.

For Julia Turner, a person with Down syndrome, a full-time job seemed unattainable, yet at the Southeastern

After reading and studying this chapter and doing the exercises, you should be able to

1. Recognize who fits under the diversity umbrella.
2. Describe the major values accounting for cultural differences.
3. Overcome many cross-cultural communication barriers.

distribution center in Anderson, it was possible. "I have found what I want, and I'm satisfied," Turner said as she scanned boxes at the center. Fully one-third of the workforce at the distribution center is disabled.

"For many, (working in the distribution center) is their first full-time job," said Lewis. "For a parent to finally see their (his or her) son or daughter experience what it's like to hold a job, be responsible and actually look forward, can fulfill a lifelong dream."[1]

The story about the giant drugstore company illustrates how some business firms and not-for-profit organizations value diversity in the workforce by reaching out to potential workers who may have been overlooked or discriminated against by many other employers.

Top management at business firms continues to recognize the importance of a diverse workforce as well as diverse customers. Not only is the workforce becoming more diverse, but business has also become increasingly international. Approximately 15 percent of the U.S. workforce is composed of people born in another country. Small- and medium-size firms, as well as corporate giants, are increasingly dependent on trade with other countries. An estimated 10 to 15 percent of jobs in the United States depend on imports or exports. Also, more and more work, such as call centers and manufacturing, is subcontracted to companies in other countries.

All this workplace diversity has an important implication for the career-minded individual. To succeed in today's workplace, a person must be able to relate effectively to people from different cultural groups from within and outside his or her country. Being able to relate to a culturally diverse customer base is also necessary for success. Being skilled at cross-cultural relations is also an asset in personal life because of the diversity within the society.

This chapter presents concepts and techniques you can use to sharpen your ability to work effectively with people from diverse backgrounds. To get you started thinking about your readiness to work in a culturally diverse environment, take Self-Assessment Quiz 11-1.

THE DIVERSITY UMBRELLA

LEARNING OBJECTIVE 1

Improving cross-cultural relations includes understanding the true meaning of appreciating diversity. To appreciate diversity, a person must go beyond tolerating and treating people from different racial and ethnic groups fairly. The true meaning of valuing diversity is to respect and enjoy a wide range of cultural and individual differences. Appreciating these differences is often referred to as *inclusion* to emphasize unity rather than diversity. To be diverse is to be different in some measurable way, even if what is measurable is not visible (such as religion or sexual orientation).

To be highly skilled in interpersonal relations, one must recognize and appreciate individual and demographic (group or category) differences, as well as cultural differences. People from the same demographic group often come from many different cultures. For example, the Latino demographic group is composed of many different cultures. Some people are more visibly diverse than others because of physical features or disabilities. Yet the diversity umbrella is supposed to include everybody in an organization. To value diversity is therefore to appreciate individual differences among people.

Cross-Cultural Skills and Attitudes

Directions: Listed below are skills and attitudes that various employers and cross-cultural experts think are important for relating effectively to coworkers in a culturally diverse environment. For each of the statements, check *applies to me now* or *not there yet*.

	Applies to me now	Not there yet
1. I have spent some time in another country.	_____	_____
2. At least one of my friends is deaf, blind, or uses a wheelchair.	_____	_____
3. Currency from other countries is as real as the currency from my own country.	_____	_____
4. I can read in a language other than my own.	_____	_____
5. I can speak in a language other than my own.	_____	_____
6. I can write in a language other than my own.	_____	_____
7. I can understand people speaking in a language other than my own.	_____	_____
8. I use my second language regularly.	_____	_____
9. My friends include people of races different from my own.	_____	_____
10. My friends include people of different ages.	_____	_____
11. I feel (or would feel) comfortable having a friend with a sexual orientation different from mine.	_____	_____
12. My attitude is that although another culture may be very different from mine, that culture is equally good.	_____	_____
13. I am willing to eat (or have eaten) food from other countries that is not served in my own country.	_____	_____
14. I would accept (or have already accepted) a work assignment of more than several months in another country.	_____	_____
15. I have a passport.	_____	_____
16. I know the approximate difference in value between the U.S. dollar and the euro.	_____	_____
17. I know how many hours difference there is between my time zone and at least two other overseas time zones.	_____	_____

Interpretation: If you answered *applies to me now* to 11 or more of the preceding questions, you most likely function well in a multicultural work environment. If you answered *not there yet* to 11 or more of the questions, you need to develop more cross-cultural awareness and skills to work effectively in a multicultural work environment. You will notice that being bilingual gives you at least five points on this quiz.

Sources: Several ideas for statements on this quiz are derived from Ruthann Dirks and Janet Buzzard, "What CEOs Expect of Employees Hired for International Work," *Business Education Forum,* April 1997, pp. 3–7; and Gunnar Beeth, "Multicultural Managers Wanted," *Management Review,* May 1997, pp. 17–21.

Appreciating cultural diversity in organizations was originally aimed at assisting women and minorities. The diversity umbrella continues to include more people as the workforce encompasses a greater variety of people. For example, in recent years much attention has been paid to the rights of employees included in the group GLBT (gay, lesbian, bisexual, and transsexual). Janis Walworth, co-founder of the Center for Gender Sanity, says, "The country is on a path of increasing respect for gays and lesbians as well, and transgender people are riding the coattails."[2] The rights of members of diverse religious groups are also receiving attention. At times, some of the religious groups may oppose the advances of the GLBT group.

The goal of a diverse organization is for persons of all cultural backgrounds to achieve their full potential, not restrained by group identities such as gender, nationality, or race. Another important goal is for these groups to work together harmoniously.

Figure 11-1 presents a broad sampling of the ways in which workplace associates can differ from one another. Studying this list can help you anticipate the types of differences to

FIGURE 11-1   The Diversity Umbrella

- Race
- Sex (or gender)
- Religion
- Age (young, middle-age, and old)
- Ethnicity (country of origin)
- Education
- Abilities
- Mental disabilities (including attention deficit disorder)
- Physical disabilities (including hearing status, visual status, able-bodied, wheelchair user)
- Values and motivation
- Sexual orientation (heterosexual, homosexual, bisexual, transsexual)
- Marital status (married, single, cohabitating, widow, widower)
- Family status (children, no children, two-parent family, single parent, grandparent)
- Personality traits
- Functional background (area of specialization)
- Technology interest (high-tech, low-tech, technophobe)
- Weight status (average, obese, underweight, anorexic)
- Hair status (full head of hair, bald, wild hair, tame hair, long hair, short hair)
- Tobacco status (smoker versus nonsmoker, chewer versus nonchewer)
- Styles of clothing and appearance (dress up, dress down, professional appearance, casual appearance)
- Socioeconomic status, such as some groups having low income and formal education, whereas others have high income and high formal education

understand and appreciate in a diverse workplace. The differences include cultural as well as individual factors. Individual factors are also important because people can be discriminated against for personal characteristics as well as group factors. Many people, for example, believe they are held back from promotion because of their weight-to-height ratio.

A diverse workforce is noted to have many consequences to the organization, mostly positive, but some negative. A sampling of these consequences is as follows:

- Multicultural experiences are strongly associated with creative thinking, and creative outcomes such as ideas for new products.[3] If you work with people from different cultures on the job or association with them in personal life, your creativity is likely to be enhanced.

- A diverse workforce helps generate more profits through such means as having employees onboard who look similar to and share the same customs as their customers.[4] Allstate and Wal-Mart exemplify companies whose culturally diverse workforce helps them attract more customers.

- When employees and managers working for a large retailer perceive that a positive climate (atmosphere) for diversity exists, the store is likely to prosper. A one-year study of more than 650 store units at J. C. Penney found that the largest sales growth occurred in stores wherein subordinates and managers perceived highly pro-diversity climates. In contrast, the lowest sales growth was found in stores where both managers and subordinates reported a less hospitable climate for diversity.[5]

> In this extreme war for talent, we need to create a culture of inclusion.
>
> —Lynn Weaver, vice president of human resources at Yazaki of North America

- Cultural diversity within groups can sometimes lead to so much conflict and disagreement that productivity suffers. Diversity in educational background and age can also lead to conflict. However, a study in Germany found that in teams where the need for intellectual stimulation was relatively high, team performance increased in the presence of diversity in educational experience and age.[6]
- The setting of the diverse workgroup can sometimes influence whether or not cultural diversity leads to enhanced performance. A compilation of many studies found that relations-oriented diversity led to high performance in service industry settings. (Relations-oriented includes race, ethnicity, gender, and age.) In contrast, this type of diversity had slightly negative effects in manufacturing settings.[7]

UNDERSTANDING CULTURAL DIFFERENCES

LEARNING OBJECTIVE 2

The groundwork for developing effective cross-cultural relations is to understand cultural differences. Here we discuss six aspects of understanding cultural differences: (1) cultural sensitivity including political correctness, (2) cultural intelligence, (3) respect for all workers, (4) cultural fluency, (5) dimensions of differences in cultural dimensions, and (6) avoidance of cultural bloopers. To work smoothly with people from other cultures, it is important to become competent in all six areas.

Cultural Sensitivity and Political Correctness

cultural sensitivity

An awareness of and willingness to investigate the reasons why people of another culture act as they do.

In order to relate well to someone from a foreign country, a person must be alert to possible cultural differences. When working in another country, a person must be willing to acquire knowledge about local customs and learn how to speak the native language at least passably. When working or socializing with people from different cultures, even from his or her own country, the person must be patient, adaptable, flexible, and willing to listen and learn. The characteristics just mentioned are part of **cultural sensitivity**, an awareness of and willingness to investigate the reasons why individuals of another culture act as they do.[8] A person with cultural sensitivity will recognize certain nuances in customs that will help build better relationships from cultural backgrounds other than his or her own.

Another aspect of cultural sensitivity is **political correctness**—being careful not to offend or slight anyone, and being extra civil and respectful.[9] An effective use of political correctness would be to say, "We need a ladder in our department because we have workers of different heights who need access to the top shelves." It would be politically incorrect to say, "We need ladders because we have some short workers who cannot reach the top shelves." Carried too far, political correctness can push a person in the direction of being too bland and imprecise in language. The ultra-politically person for example will almost never mention a person's race, sex, ethnicity, or health status when referring to another worker. For example, the ultra-politically person would not make a statement like, "Sadie is German, so she was a natural to be our liaison with the manufacturing group." (The cultural stereotype here is that Germans are quite interested in manufacturing technology and think precisely.)

Ultra-political correctness also involves using supposedly correct terms to describe people even if a given individual rejects the label. For example, many black people are correctly referred to as "black" rather than "African American" because they might be citizens of Africa, Haiti, England, etc. Also, the same people do not consider themselves to be African American.

Empathy is a major trait and skill that facilitates cultural sensitivity and political correctness. You have to place yourself in the other person's perspective, and ask yourself questions like, "How would I like it if somebody snarled and said an ugly word when he or she looked at my favorite food." Kim Oliver and Sylvester Baugh offer this insight into developing the type of empathy helpful in building cross-cultural relations in the workplace, "We want to try to develop an understanding for the majority about what it might be like to be the minority, and help the minority understand what it's like to be the majority."[10]

Cultural Intelligence

An advanced aspect of cultural sensitivity is to be able to fit in comfortably with people of another culture by observing the subtle cues they give about how a person should act in their presence. **Cultural intelligence (CQ)** is an outsider's ability to interpret someone's unfamiliar and ambiguous behavior the same way that person's compatriots would.[11] With high cultural intelligence, a person would be able to figure out what behavior would be true of all people and all groups, such as rapid shaking of a clenched fist to communicate anger. Also, the person with high cultural intelligence could figure out what is peculiar to this group, and those aspects of behavior that are neither universal nor peculiar to the group. These ideas are so abstract that an example will help clarify.

> *An American expatriate manager served on a design team that included two German engineers. As other team members floated their ideas, the engineers condemned them as incomplete or underdeveloped. The manager concluded that the Germans in general are rude and aggressive.*
>
> *With average cultural intelligence, the American would have realized he was mistakenly equating the merit of an idea with the merit of the person presenting it. The Germans, however, were able to make a sharp distinction between the two. A manager with more advanced cultural intelligence might have tried to figure out how much of the two Germans' behavior was typically German and how much was explained by the fact that they were engineers.*

Similar to emotional intelligence, cultural intelligence encompasses several aspects of behavior. The three sources of cultural intelligence relate to the cognitive, emotional/motivational, and the physical, shown in Figure 11-2, and explained as follows:[12]

1. **Cognitive (the Head).** The cognitive part of CQ refers to what a person knows and how he or she can acquire new knowledge. Here you acquire facts about people from another culture such as their passion for football (soccer in North America), their business practices, and their promptness in paying bills. Another aspect of this source of cultural intelligence is figuring out how you can learn more about the other culture.

2. **Emotional/Motivational (the Heart).** The emotional/motivational aspect of CQ refers to energizing one's actions and building personal confidence. You need both confidence and motivation to adapt to another culture. A man on a business trip to Africa might say to himself, "When I greet a work associate in a restaurant, can I really pull off kissing him on both cheeks. What if he thinks I'm weird?" With strong motivation, the same person might say, "I'll give it a try. I kind of greet my grandfather the same way back in the United States."

FIGURE 11-2   The Components of Cultural Intelligence

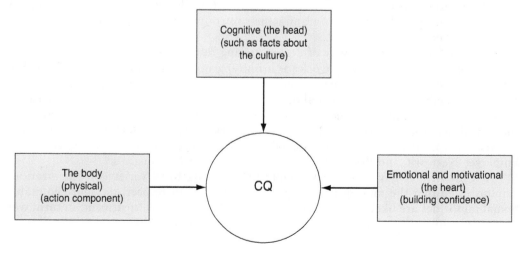

3. **The Body (Physical).** The body aspect of CQ is the action component. The body is the element for translating intentions into actions and desires. Kissing the same-sex African work associates on both cheeks is the *physical* aspect just mentioned. We often have an idea of what we should do, but implementation is not so easy. You might know, for example, that when entering an Asian person's home you should take off your shoes, yet you might not actually remove them—thereby offending your Asian work (or personal life) associate.

To practice high cultural intelligence, the mind, heart, and body have to work together. You need to figure out how to act with people from another culture, you need motivation and confidence to change, and you have to translate your knowledge and motivation into action. So when you are on a business trip to London, go ahead and hold your fork in your left hand!

Respect for All Workers and Cultures

An effective strategy for achieving cross-cultural understanding is to simply respect all others in the workplace, including their cultures. Respecting people from other cultures works equally well in personal life. An example would be not joking at the fact that an acquaintance of yours puts his head on the floor to pray.

An important component of respect is to believe that although another person's culture is different from yours, it is equally good. Respect comes from valuing differences. Respecting other people's customs can translate into specific attitudes, such as respecting one coworker for wearing a yarmulke on Friday or another for wearing African clothing to celebrate Kwanzaa. Another way of being respectful would be to listen carefully to the opinion of a senior worker who says the company should never have converted to voicemail and a voice recognition system in place of assistants answering the phone (even though you disagree).

An aspect of respecting all workers that achieves current attention is the importance of respecting the rights of majorities, particularly white males. Many of these men want to be involved in—not excluded from—bringing about cultural diversity in organizations. For example, they might want to mentor minority group members.

Company policies that encourage respect for the rights of others are likely to create a positive influence on tolerance throughout the firm. An example is that many employers have taken steps to recognize and affirm the existence of gay and lesbian workers. Among these steps are publishing formal statements of nondiscrimination, and the inclusion of issues about sexual orientation in diversity training programs. A major policy change has been to grant same-sex couples the same benefits granted to opposite-sex couples.

Another formal (official) way of demonstrating respect for all workers is to provide for the presence of **employee network** (or **affinity**) **groups.** Such a group is composed of employees throughout the company who affiliate on the basis of group characteristics, such as race, ethnicity, gender, sexual orientation, or physical ability status. The network group provides members of the same demographic or cultural group and avenue for sharing ideas with management. Employee network groups at McDonald's, for example, include the African-American Council, the Hispanic Employee Network, the Asian Employee Network, and the Gays, Lesbians and Allies at McDonald's.[13]

A study of 537 gay and lesbian employees working for a variety of organizations demonstrated that the more prevalent policies dealing with respect, the more equitably sexual minorities are likely to be treated at work. More equitable treatment, in turn, was associated with gays and lesbians being more satisfied, and less likely to leave the firm.[14]

BACK TO THE OPENING CASE

Management at Walgreens continues to be successful in building a culturally diverse workforce that includes persons with physical disabilities, as well as those with developmental (intellectual) disabilities. Management's most important approach to accomplishing this end is to show respect for all workers by treating them equally. Employees with good ideas are listened too, and both majority group members and minority group members who appear to have leadership skill have an equal shot at being part of the management training program. Should you visit a neighborhood Walgreens, you might notice that the store associates as well as the pharmacists are culturally diverse.

SKILL-BUILDING EXERCISE 11-1

Developing Cultural Sensitivity

Carefully observe products and services such as tennis shoes, notebooks, bicycles, and banking services, and attempt to find out how they are marketed and sold in other countries. For a convenient reference source, interview foreign students and foreigners outside class about these products and services. Your digging for information might uncover such nuggets as the following:

- In India, cricket champions are celebrities comparable to U.S. basketball stars who endorse soft drinks like Coca-Cola and Pepsi.

- In Hungary, peanut butter is considered a luxury food item.
- In some countries in warm climates, meat is freshly killed and hung on hooks for sale—without refrigeration or freezing.

After conducting these product and service interviews, arrive at some kind of interpretation or conclusion. Share your insights with other class members.

Source: "Teaching International Business," *Keying In,* January 1999, p. 1. National Business Education Association. Reprinted with permission.

Cultural Fluency

A high-level goal in understanding cultural differences is to achieve **cultural fluency,** the ability to conduct business in a diverse, international environment.[15] Achieving cultural fluency includes a variety of skills, such as relating well to people from different cultures and knowing a second language. Cultural fluency also includes knowledge of the international business environment, such as how the exchange rate can affect profits. Having high cultural intelligence would contribute to cultural fluency because such intelligence makes it easier to work well with people from other cultures. If you are culturally fluent, you will also find it easier to make friends (real and virtual) from other cultures.

Skill-Building Exercise 11-1 is a warm-up activity for achieving cultural sensitivity, and perhaps respect for all workers.

cultural fluency

The ability to conduct business in a diverse, international environment.

Dimensions of Differences in Cultural Values

One way to understand how national cultures differ is to examine their values or cultural dimensions. The formulation presented here is based on the worldwide research in 62 societal cultures and builds on previous analyses of cultural dimensions.[16] The cultural dimensions presented here are those most directly related to interpersonal skills. Keep in mind that these cultural dimensions are stereotypes that apply to a representative person from a particular culture, and are not meant to insult anybody. These cultural dimensions are differences between national societies and may not be representative of a given individual. As with gender stereotypes in communication, individual differences are substantial. For example, any Americans are not assertive, and many French are willing to work 70 hours per week.

1. **Performance orientation** is the degree to which a society encourages, or should encourage, and rewards group members for performance improvement and excellence. Countries high on this dimension are the United States and Singapore, whereas those low on this dimension are Russia and Greece.

2. **Assertiveness** is the degree to which individuals are (and should be) assertive, confrontational, and aggressive in their relationships with one another. Countries scoring high on this dimension are the United States and Austria, whereas those low on this dimension are Sweden and New Zealand. Assertive people enjoy competition in business, in contrast to less assertive cultural groups who prefer harmony, loyalty, and solidarity.

3. **Time orientation** is the importance nations and individuals attach to time. People with an urgent time orientation perceive time as a scarce resource and tend to be impatient. People with a casual time orientation view time as an unlimited and unending resource and tend to be patient. Americans are noted for their urgent time orientation. They frequently impose deadlines and are eager to get started doing business. Asians, Mexicans, and Middle Easterners, in contrast, are patient negotiators.

4. **Humane orientation** is the degree to which a society encourages and rewards, and should encourage and reward, individuals for being fair, altruistic, caring, and kind toward others. Egypt and Malaysia rank high on this cultural dimension, and France and Germany rank low.

5. **In-group collectivism** is the degree to which individuals express, and should express, pride, loyalty, and cohesiveness in their organizations and families. Asian societies emphasize collectivism, as do Egypt and Russia. One consequence of collectivism is taking pride in family members and the organizations that employ them.

6. **Gender egalitarianism** is the degree to which a culture minimizes, and should minimize, gender inequality. European countries emphasize gender egalitarianism, and so do the United States and Canada. South Korea is an example of a country that is low on gender egalitarianism, and is male dominated.

7. **Acceptance of power and authority** is the degree to which members of a society expect, and should expect, power to be distributed unequally. Individuals who accept power and authority expect the boss to make the major decisions. These same individuals are more formal; however, being formal toward people in positions of authority has decreased substantially throughout the world in recent years. Examples of societies that score high on acceptance of power and authority are Thailand, Brazil, France, and Japan.

8. **Work orientation** is the number of hours per week and weeks per year people expect to invest in work versus leisure, or other nonwork activities. American corporate professionals typically work about 55 hours per week, take 45-minute lunch breaks, and two weeks of vacation. Americans tend to have a stronger work orientation than Europeans but a weaker one than Asians. U.S. employees average 1,804 hours of work per year, compared with 1,407 for Norwegian workers and 1,564 for the French. Workers in seven Asian countries including South Korea, Bangladesh, and China worked 2,200 hours per year.[17]

9. **Social support seeking** is the degree to which people seek out others to help them with difficult problems through such means as listening, offering sympathy, and giving advice. Asians and Asian Americans are more reluctant to explicitly request support from close others than are European Americans. The hesitancy comes about because the Asians and Asian Americans are more concerned about negative relationship consequences, such as disrupting group

harmony or receiving criticism from the other person. Another possible reason for the hesitancy is that Asians and Asian Americans expect social support without having to ask.[18]

How might someone use information about cultural differences to improve his or her interpersonal relations on the job? A starting point would be to recognize that a person's national values might influence his or her behavior. Assume that you wanted to establish a good working relationship with a person from a high humane orientation culture. An effective starting point would be to emphasize care and concern when communicating with the individual.

Attitudes toward acceptance of power and authority can make a difference in establishing working relationships. A worker who values deference to age, gender, or title might shy away from offering suggestions to an elder or manager to avoid appearing disrespectful. This worker would need considerable encouragement to collaborate in decision making.[19] *Time-orientation* may create a conflict if you are committed to making deadlines and a team member has a laid-back attitude toward time. You might explain that although you respect his attitudes toward time, the company insists on getting the project completed on time.

Self-Assessment Quiz 11-2 will help you think about how cultural dimensions might be influencing your interpersonal relations in the workplace.

SELF-ASSESSMENT QUIZ 11-2

Charting Your Cultural Dimension Profile

Directions: For each of the nine cultural dimensions, circle the number that most accurately fits your standing on the dimension. For example, if you perceive yourself to be "highly humane," circle 6 on the fourth dimension (item 4).

1. High performance orientation   Low performance orientation

    1   2   3   4   5   6   7

2. Low assertiveness   High assertiveness

    1   2   3   4   5   6   7

3. Urgent time orientation   Casual time orientation

    1   2   3   4   5   6   7

4. High humane orientation   Low humane orientation

    1   2   3   4   5   6   7

5. In-group collectivism   In-group individualism

    1   2   3   4   5   6   7

6. High gender egalitarianism   Low gender egalitarianism

    1   2   3   4   5   6   7

7. High acceptance of power and authority   Low acceptance of power and authority

    1   2   3   4   5   6   7

8. Work orientation   Leisure orientation

    1   2   3   4   5   6   7

9. Social support seeking   Social support avoidance

    1   2   3   4   5   6   7

Scoring and Interpretation: After circling one number for each dimension, use a pen or pencil to connect the circles, thereby giving yourself a profile of cultural values. Do not be concerned if your line cuts through the names of the dimensions. Compare your profile to others in the class. Should time allow, develop a class profile by computing the class average for each of the nine points and then connecting the points.

Cultural Bloopers

An effective way of being culturally sensitive is to minimize actions that are likely to offend people from another culture based on their values. Cultural bloopers are most likely to take place when you are visiting another country. The same bloopers, however, can also be committed with people from a different culture within your own country. To avoid these bloopers, you must carefully observe persons from another culture. Studying another culture through reading is also helpful.

E-commerce and other forms of Internet communication have created new opportunities for creating cultural bloopers. The Web site developers and workers responsible for adding content must have good cross-cultural literacy, including an awareness of how the information might be misinterpreted.

- Numerical date formats can be readily misinterpreted. To an American, 4/9/13 would be interpreted as April 9, 2013 (or 1913!). However, many Europeans would interpret the same numerical expression as September 4, 2013.
- Colors on Web sites must be chosen carefully. For example, in some cultures purple is the color of royalty, whereas in Brazil purple is associated with death.
- Be careful of metaphors that may not make sense to a person for whom your language is a second language. Examples include "We've encountered an ethical meltdown" and "Our biggest competitor is over the hill."

English has become the language of business and science throughout the world, yet communicating in a customer's native tongue has its advantages. Being able to communicate your message directly in your customer's mother tongue provides a competitive advantage. Bilingualism also has career implications. Some telemarketing, banking, engineering, and financial service companies are searching for workers with bilingual skills. The two major contributing factors are the growing immigrant population in the United States, and because companies are engaged more in international business.[20]

Furthermore, according to the research firm International Data Corporation (IDC), consumers are four times more likely to purchase a product online if the Web site is in their preferred language.[21] The translator, of course, must have good knowledge of the subtleties of the language to avoid a blooper. An English-to-French translator used the verb *baiser* instead of *baisser* to describe a program of lowering prices. *Baisser* is the French verb "to lower," whereas *baiser* is the verb "to kiss." Worse, in slang *baiser* is a verb that refers to having intimate physical relationships!

Keep two key facts in mind when attempting to avoid cultural mistakes. One is that members of any cultural group show individual differences. What one member of the group might regard as an insensitive act, another might welcome. Recognize also that one or two cultural mistakes will not peg you permanently as a boor. Skill-Building Exercise 11-2 will help you minimize certain cultural bloopers.

OVERCOMING CROSS-CULTURAL COMMUNICATION BARRIERS

LEARNING OBJECTIVE 3

Cultural differences create additional communication barriers. Here are some guidelines for overcoming cross-cultural communication barriers.

1. **Be sensitive to the fact that cross-cultural communication barriers exist.** If you are aware of these potential barriers, you will be ready to deal with them. When you are dealing with a person in the workplace with a different cultural background than yours, solicit feedback in order to minimize cross-cultural barriers to communication. Being aware of these potential barriers will help you develop cultural sensitivity.

2. **Show respect for all workers.** The same behavior that promotes good cross-cultural relations in general helps overcome communication barriers. A widely used comment that implies disrespect is to say to another person from another culture, "You have a funny accent." Should you be transposed to that person's culture, you, too, might have a "funny accent."

Cultural Mistakes to Avoid with Selected Cultural Groups

EUROPE

Great Britain
- Asking personal questions. The British protect their privacy.
- Thinking that a businessperson from England is unenthusiastic when he or she says, "Not bad at all." English people understate their positive emotion.
- Gossiping about royalty.

France
- Expecting to complete work during the French two-hour lunch.
- Attempting to conduct significant business during August—*les vacances* (vacation time).
- Greeting a French person for the first time and not using a title such as "sir," or "madam," or "miss" (*monsieur, madame,* or *mademoiselle*).

Italy
- Eating too much pasta, as it is not the main course.
- Handing out business cards freely. Italians use them infrequently.

Spain
- Expecting punctuality. Your appointments will usually arrive 20 to 30 minutes late.
- Making the American sign for "okay" with your thumb and forefinger. In Spain (and many other countries) this is vulgar.

Scandinavia (Denmark, Sweden, Norway)
- Being overly rank conscious. Scandinavians pay relatively little attention to a person's rank in the hierarchy.

ASIA

All Asian employee countries
- Pressuring an Asian job applicant or to brag about his or her accomplishments. Asians feel self-conscious when boasting about individual accomplishments; they prefer to let the record speak for itself. In addition, they prefer to talk about group rather than individual accomplishment.

Japan
- Shaking hands or hugging Japanese (as well as other Asians) in public. Japanese consider these practices to be offensive.
- Not interpreting "We'll consider it" as a "no" when spoken by a Japanese businessperson. Japanese negotiators mean "no" when they say "We'll consider it."

- Not giving small gifts to Japanese when conducting business. Japanese are offended by not receiving these gifts.
- Giving your business card to a Japanese businessperson more than once. Japanese prefer to give and receive business cards only once.

China
- Using black borders on stationery and business cards, because black is associated with death.
- Giving small gifts to Chinese when conducting business. Chinese are offended by these gifts.
- Making cold calls on Chinese business executives. An appropriate introduction is required for a first-time meeting with a Chinese official.

Korea
- Saying no. Koreans feel it is important to have visitors leave with good feelings.

India
- Telling Indians you prefer not to eat with your hands. If the Indians are not using cutlery when eating, they expect you to do likewise.

Thailand
- It is considered extremely rude to point the soles of your shoes at anyone. (It's not too cool in other countries also.)

MEXICO AND LATIN AMERICA

Mexico
- Flying into a Mexican city in the morning and expecting to close a deal by lunch. Mexicans build business relationships slowly.

Brazil
- Attempting to impress Brazilians by speaking a few words of Spanish. Portuguese is the official language of Brazil.

Most Latin American countries
- Wearing elegant and expensive jewelry during a business meeting. Latin Americans think people should appear more conservative during a business meeting.

Note: A cultural mistake for Americans to avoid when conducting business in most countries outside the United States and Canada is to insist on getting down to business quickly. North Americans in small towns also like to build a relationship before getting down to business. The preceding suggestions will lead to cross-cultural skill development if practiced in the right setting. During the next 30 days, look for an opportunity to relate to a person from another culture in the way described in these suggestions. Observe the reaction of the other person for feedback on your cross-cultural effectiveness.

3. **Use straightforward language and speak slowly and clearly.** When working with people who do not speak your language fluently, speak in an easy-to-understand manner. Minimize the use of idioms and analogies specific to your language. A computer analyst from Greece left confused after a discussion about a software problem with her manager. The manager said, "Let's talk about this another time because *I can't seem to get to first base with you*." (The manager was referring to the fact that the conversation was headed nowhere because he couldn't come to

an agreement with the analyst.) The computer analyst did not ask for clarification because she did not want to appear uninformed.

4. **Observe cultural differences in etiquette.** Violating rules of etiquette without explanation can erect immediate communication barriers. A major rule of etiquette in many countries is that people address superiors by their last name unless they have worked together for a long time. Or, the superior might encourage being on a first-name basis with him or her. Be aware that an increasing number of cultures are moving toward addressing each other and customers by using the first name only. Yet, it is best to error on the side of formality.

5. **Be sensitive to differences in nonverbal communication.** Stay alert to the possibility that a person from another culture may misinterpret your nonverbal signal. Hand signals of various types, such as a thumb up or the okay sign to indicate acceptance, are the most liable to misinterpretation. Another key area of cross-cultural differences in nonverbal communication is the handshake. In some cultures, a woman is expected to extend her hand first to shake with a man. In other cultures, people, hug, embrace, or bow instead of shaking hands.[23] (With good cultural sensitivity and cultural intelligence, you can figure out what to do when meeting another person.)

   Behavioral mirroring is another example of how the effectiveness of nonverbal behavior might be influenced the other person's culture. Three experiments with bank managers required Anglos and Latinos to interact with an interviewer who was trained to mirror the behavior of the interviewee. It was found that Latino interviewees rated interviewers higher who used behavioral mirroring. Also, the Latinos experienced more anxiety when the interviewer did not mirror their behavior. [24] The intercultural explanation for these findings is that Lations, as a group, value nonverbal behavior more than do Anglos. The implication of the experiment for cross-cultural communication is to attempt to determine if you are making appropriate use of nonverbal communication techniques when interacting with a person from another culture.

6. **Do not be diverted by style, accent, grammar, or personal appearance.** Although these superficial factors are all related to business success, they are difficult to interpret when judging a person from another culture. It is therefore better to judge the merits of the statement or behavior.[25] A brilliant individual from another culture may still be learning your language and thus make basic mistakes in speaking your language. Also, he or she might not yet have developed a sensitivity to dress style in your culture.

7. **Be attentive to individual differences in appearance.** A major intercultural insult is to confuse the identity of people because they are members of the same race or ethnic group. An older economics professor reared in China and teaching in the United States had difficulty communicating with students because he was unable to learn their names. The professor's defense was "So many of these Americans look alike to me." Research suggests that people have difficulty seeing individual differences among people of another race because they code race first, such as thinking "He has the nose of an African American." However, people can learn to search for more distinguishing features, such as a dimple or eye color.[26] In this way, individual differences are recognized.

8. **Pronounce correctly the names of people you interact with from other countries.** Communication is much smoother when you correctly pronounce the name of another person. For many Americans, this is a challenging task because they are accustomed to names with one or two syllables that are easy to pronounce, such as Bob or Ann. A trouble spot for many people whose only language is English is that "H" and "J" might be silent in another language.[27] Suppose one of your work or personal associates has the first name "Hyuntak." After listening to his name for the first time, develop a phonetic spelling that will help you pronounce the name in the future. (How about "High-oon-tack"?)

Mexican Call Center Workers Learn to Deal Effectively with Americans

In a high-rise office building, one dozen young Mexicans are studying the customs of a country most of them have never visited. One by one, the students present their conclusions about the United States. "Americans think Mexicans eat mostly tacos and drink Margaritas everyday. They give big tips if they like you. Unless they are Latino-Americans, they probably speak only one language." says Maria. "People are self-centered. The average American uses a credit card even to pay for lunch in a restaurant," says Hugo.

The Mexicans, who range in age from 20 to 29, have been hired to take calls from confused or angry Americans who are having a functioning problem with their prepaid cell phone. The problem could be technical, or relating to customer service problem such as their prepaid minutes not being accurately recorded or their phone being shut down. The cell phone company works on a slim profit margin, so it cannot afford to maintain a tech support and customer service center in the United States. The company offers a Web site for providing technical support and customer service, yet many customers feel the need to interact with a live person.

To communicate with the Americans, the Mexican workers must communicate in their second language but a culture that is foreign. "We're not saying that Mexico is better or the United States is better," says their trainer, Tanya. "We just want our tech support staff to develop cultural awareness so there is better rapport when someone calls in for help."

Call centers for inexpensive cell phone service took root in Mexico when the demand for mobile phones skyrocketed in the mid-2000s, yet many people did not have good enough credit to purchase traditional cell phone service. Large prepaid cell phone providers like Tracfone wanted to provide the best tech support they could yet still remain profitable.

At first, training at the tech support centers and customer service centers was simple. The centers gave employees names that were easy for Americans to understand such as Pedro, Suzie, Maria, and Bob in cases where they had names difficult for Americans to pronounce. The new hires were instructed to watch American television shows to get an idea of American pop culture. In this way, if there was a waiting period during the help session, they could make a few minutes of small talk.

Shortly after the support center was established, problems in dealing with the Americans began to surface. Although the customers were paying the minimum price possible for cell phone service, they were often quite demanding and aggressive. One man swore at the customer service rep because he couldn't figure out how to use his phone to make a call to Ontario, Canada. Roberta, the recipient of the outrage, attempted to explain that instructions on how to telephone Canada from the United States are presented on page 8 of the manual that comes with the phone. A woman kept calling another rep a "stupid fool" because the rep couldn't understand her problem having to do with not being credited for enough minutes.

The Mexican support staff felt uncomfortable in being too firm with belligerent customers. Instead of being assertive about the company's position on a particular problem, the reps tended to be too conciliatory, often blaming the company for the problem. However, being conciliatory did not result in customers being totally satisfied. Problems were often left unresolved. As a result, the prepaid cell phone service company noticed that renewal rates were slipping. A renewal in this sense is a customer purchasing more minutes at a store or through the company Web site.

The cell phone company hired a firm that offers cultural training to help the Mexican call center workers deal more effectively with upset American customers. (Tanya was the trainer assigned to the account.) The workers were given careful instructions on how to express sympathy, using phrases such as "I am sorry that you are having this problem. I know that your phone is important to you." When a customer is explosively angry, the call center workers were coached on how to let the customer finish the outburst, and then say, "I hear that you are upset. But let us see how we can get this problem solved."

New hires as well as experienced employees were also taught to defend the company when the company is right. For example, to fix a technical problem such as the voicemail feature not working, the caller usually has to key in a long series of numbers. A frustrated customer often has difficulty with such a task. To deal with the frustration, the call center worker is taught to say something like, "Please try entering the numbers again slowly and carefully." If the customer enters the sequence of numbers incorrectly again, the worker is coached on how to be assertive, such as "This method does work. If you want to fix your phone, you have to do it carefully."

Many customer complaints that get back to the company deal with not being able to understand the English spoken by the call center workers. So the Mexican workers are coached on how to speak key English words with a general American accent. For example, instead of saying "She-ca-go" for "Chicago," the worker is taught to say "Sha-ca-go." And the workers are coached to pronounce "nine" as "nyne" instead of "neen."

Questions

1. What do you see as a major cultural difference between Mexicans and Americans that make the call center job so challenging for Mexicans?
2. Some of the call center representatives in Mexico are instructed to identify themselves as students in Kansas City, in addition to giving them American first names. What is your take on the ethics of these disguises?

Source: Case history collected from human resource specialist at the mobile phone company in question.

How Do Negative Attitudes Develop?

We learn various biases, stereotypes, and prejudices as we grow up. We can be biased in favor of or against certain kinds of foods, categories of books, styles of clothing, or types of personalities. Bias can affect decisions about what we eat, read, or wear; it can influence our choice of friends. A stereotype assumes that individuals possess certain human traits simply because they are members of a particular group. Although some traits are regarded as positive—such as blacks have rhythm, Asians are good in math—other traits are viewed as negative—certain groups are lazy, shiftless, dishonest, or violent. Although negative stereotypes are regarded as unacceptable, many people accept positive stereotypes. The problem with positive stereotypes is that they cause us to have specific expectations for individuals and groups even though we have little or no evidence for these assumptions. A positive stereotype may sabotage the process of forming a realistic and accurate perception of an individual.

During a coffee break at a midwestern university, three Asian American women employed by a student services office reminisced about their undergraduate days. They complained about how difficult math classes had been and laughed as they recalled some of their coping strategies. The student services director, an African American, walked into the room, overheard what they were saying, and interrupted their discussion to chastise them for "putting yourselves down." He said they should stop. He also said he was disappointed in them and departed.

After the director left, the three women initially were too surprised to speak. Once they started talking, they realized they were angry because his comments suggested that he assumed they all had good math skills and were not being honest when discussing their lack of math ability. The women thought the director viewed them as individuals; they were angry and hurt when they realized that he had allowed a stereotype to distort his perception of them. They were especially upset because they had not expected a person of color to believe in a stereotype—even a positive one about the math abilities of Asians—but apparently he did.

If negative stereotypes reinforce negative biases, prejudices can develop, and prejudices are always negative. Although prejudice is only an attitude, negative attitudes often lead to negative actions against an individual or a group. Taking negative action might strengthen the prejudices of a person until they become the intense hatred of bigotry, which is the basis for white supremacist groups such as the Ku Klux Klan, neo-Nazis, and the Aryan nation. Because hatred is such a strong emotion, bigots are more likely to express their hatred with *actions,* including violence. Negative behaviors are often directed against individuals from social groups based on such differences as race, ethnicity, or nationality.

What Do Stereotypes Have to Do with Uncertainty and How Do They Cause Prejudice?

Most of us only have knowledge of the groups to which we belong; often we do not know much about other groups. In the United States, schools have historically implemented curricula reflecting perspectives, contributions, and experiences of the dominant (white) group; many of our neighborhoods still tend to be segregated by race or social class. The result is that people from different racial and ethnic groups have few opportunities to learn about one another. Because of our lack of accurate information, we may believe in stereotypes as a way to convince ourselves that we know about certain groups. (See Figure 11-3.) Our stereotypes can be reinforced by images or information contained in such media as advertisements, textbooks, and films.

For an example of ignorance promoting prejudice, how many Americans know that Muslims have been in the United States from colonial times because many slaves brought to America from West Africa were Muslim? The evidence is in the names that "read like a Who's Who of traditional Muslim names"—Bullaly (Bilali), Mahomet (Muhammad), Walley (Wali), and Sambo meant "second son" to Muslim Fulbe people (Abdo, 2006, p. 66). While Americans tend to stereotype all Arabs as Muslims, the majority of Arabs immigrating to the United States in the late nineteenth century were Christians. How many Americans know that in the 1920s a small group of Muslims settled in Ross, South Dakota, and built the first mosque in the United States, or that the oldest continuously functioning mosque is in Cedar Rapids, Iowa (Abdo, 2006)?

Even if they don't know this history, how many Americans know that Muslim Americans today own over 200,000 businesses and that there are over 2,000 mosques

FIGURE 11-3 This Drawing Has Been Used for Research and in Classrooms. One Person Is Shown This Picture and Whispers a Description of the Entire Scene to Another Person, Who Then Whispers the Description to Another Person Until Each Person in the Room Has Heard It. The Last Person Is Asked to Describe the Scene to Everyone. Typically, the Person Describes a Poorly Dressed Black Man with a Weapon Preparing to Attack a Well-Dressed White Man, thus Illustrating the Power of Racial Stereotypes.

in the United States (Ansari, 2004)? How many Americans know that Muslim American adults are better educated than the average American (59% have college degrees compared to 27% of other Americans) and wealthier (a median annual income of $60,000 compared to the national median annual income of $50,000) (Barrett, 2007)? Muslims have done what America expects of immigrants. But unaware of this information, and surrounded by stereotypes and media's focus on Islamic terrorists, how many Americans harbor negative views of both the Islamic faith and Muslims? According to a 2004 survey by the Pew Forum on Religion and Public Life, nearly 50% of Americans perceived the Islamic faith as more likely to promote violence than other religions (a percentage that doubled compared to the results of a similar survey conducted two years earlier) and nearly 40% expressed a negative view of Muslims (Abdo, 2006).

When a person actually encounters individuals of a different race, ethnicity, or social class, selective perception of the behaviors of those individuals often reinforces his or her stereotypes. Stephan (1999) reported on one study where subjects were presented with equal amounts of positive and negative information about a group to which they belonged (in-group) and a group to which they did not belong (out-group). Subjects tended to recall more positive information about the in-group and more negative information about the out-group. According to Stephan, negative attitudes in our memory tend to increase over time.

Selective perception was illustrated in another study where two groups of subjects viewed consecutive videotapes: The first videotape was of a fourth-grade girl playing with friends, and the second videotape was of the same girl taking an oral test in school where she answered some difficult questions correctly but missed some easy questions. Although the second videotape was the same for both groups, the first videotape shown to one group was the girl playing in a low-income neighborhood, and first videotape shown to the other group was the girl playing in a high-income neighborhood. After watching both videotapes, subjects were asked to judge the girl's academic abilities. Those who saw her playing in the low-income neighborhood rated her academic ability lower than those who saw her playing in the more affluent neighborhood. Whether the subjects focused more on the girl's correct or incorrect answers appeared to have been influenced by the neighborhood where they believed she lived and stereotypes associated with affluence and poverty (Aronson, 2008).

Researchers have also shown that becoming more knowledgeable about others helps people overcome stereotypical perceptions. In a psychiatric hospital with an all-white staff, patients acting violently were either taken to a "time-out room" or subjected to the harsher penalty of being put in a straitjacket and sedated. In the first month of a research study, both black and white patients were admitted. Although the black patients admitted were diagnosed as being less violent than the whites, they were four times more likely to be put in a straitjacket and sedated by the staff if they became violent. The discrepancy in the white staff's use of restraints suggests that they believed in the stereotype that black people were more prone to violence. As they became better acquainted with the patients, the staff responded to violent incidents with more equal use of restraints for both black and white patients (Aronson, 2008). Stereotypes that portray a group as being prone to violence, lazy, or less intelligent can influence a person's behavior; stereotypes can also play a part in a person's self-esteem being threatened, which is another major cause of prejudice identified in research.

> "Sometimes (prejudice) is like a hair across your cheek. You can't see it, you can't find it with your fingers, but you keep brushing at it because the feel of it is irritating."
>
> — Marian Anderson
> (1897–1993)

DIVERSITY IN THE UNITED STATES

In 2005, Texas became the fourth state to have more people of color in the state's population than white people (the others are New Mexico, Hawaii, and California). Hispanic Americans constitute the largest group among people of color in all of these states except Hawaii, where Asian Americans are the largest group. In six additional states, people of color represent approximately 40% or more of the population—Arizona, Florida, Georgia, Maryland, Mississippi, and New York. And people of color are the majority of the population in the 100 largest cities in the United States (U.S. Census Bureau, 2005). White people have been the majority group in the United States since the founding of the nation, but demographers are saying that this is going to change before the end of the twenty-first century. As early as 2050, non-Hispanic whites will constitute only 53% of the U.S. population; white men will represent about 26% of the population and many of them will be retired, resulting in about half of the workforce consisting of people of color (Schaefer, 2008). For the social security system to continue to provide its promised benefits, people of color will need jobs that pay living wages. All Americans must care about diversity because in our complex, technological society we are already highly dependent on each other.

Based on data from the 2000 census, Pipher (2002) reported that one in ten people in the United States was born in another country and that one in five children in school is a child of recent immigrants. Historically, immigrants tended to settle in urban areas of a few states, primarily New York, California, and Florida, but immigrants now live in smaller cities of all states. Pipher illustrates this point by observing that in a Lincoln, Nebraska, newspaper "Our obituary column . . . is filled with Hrdvys, Andersens, Walenshenskys, and Muellers. But the births column . . . has many Ali, Nguyen, and Martinez babies" (p. 6).

Demographers track movement of people in society, yet none can predict accurately what the mix of people will be in the future. Demographers tend to be conservative in their speculations, yet the harbingers of change to come surround us. Pipher (2002) provides this example: Police in Nashville, Tennessee, have computers that explain laws and basic words for simple requests or demands in twenty languages. Rather than debate demographic predictions, it is more pertinent to consider how the current white majority responds to population changes.

How Have Members of the Majority Responded to Diverse Groups?

In any society, there is often a group hierarchy where preferred groups occupying superior positions disregard groups that are devalued by that society. As we have already seen in previous chapters, the history of the United States reveals that the white majority has never been consistently respectful of the rights of diverse groups. Terry (1993) described the relationship of dominant and subordinate groups by using an "up/down" metaphor. To determine who is up or down in a society, one must discover which groups have the most wealth, status, and power, and which have the least. In the United States, a person becomes an up by belonging to these groups: white, male, middle or upper class, Christian, heterosexual, or nondisabled. A down belongs to one or more of these groups: people of color, female, lower class, non-Christian, homosexual, bisexual, transgender, or disabled. Most individuals represent a mixture of memberships in these up or down groups.

With reference to his metaphor, Terry suggests that ups don't know much about downs, and they think they don't need to know about them because downs are not regarded as socially important. Such ignorance is one cause of prejudice as Eck (2001) noted when she described prejudice as "being down on something you're not up on" (p. 300). Ups do not compete with downs; they move in different circles. The only time ups become concerned about downs is when downs start getting "uppity" by challenging the power structure or the status quo by engaging in marches, demonstrations, or some other kind of protest about an issue. The response of ups is likely to be "What do these people want?" because they genuinely do not know. They are "dumb ups" when it comes to understanding issues affecting downs. By contrast, downs know a great deal about ups because they must; it is essential for their survival and for their success. To achieve whatever goals they have set for themselves, downs have to understand ups so that, as Terry says, they know what the ups are up to (pp. 194–196).

It is tempting to assume that if someone is a down in one category, that person will be more sensitive to downs in a category in which he or she functions as an up. Unfortunately it doesn't seem to work that way. When people are behaving as part of an up group, they tend to be "dumb ups." It's as if there are separate file folders; their experiences in one category stay in that file and don't influence other files. People living in poverty can be racist; people of color can be homophobic; gays and lesbians can be prejudiced against immigrants; immigrants can be sexist; women can be prejudiced against people with disabilities; and people with disabilities can be prejudiced against welfare recipients. Terry's "up/down" metaphor provides a useful way of thinking about the complexity involved in a society that includes diverse minority groups.

When the topic of diversity, especially racial and ethnic diversity, is addressed in the media, pundits and scholars often use negative terms rather than the positive terms that James Naisbitt used. Columnist George Will has criticized education's efforts to advocate for diversity, chastising institutions for engaging in "political correctness." Skeptical of attempts to emphasize diversity, scholars such as Arthur Schlesinger, Jr. (1991) have argued that promoting multiculturalism would lead to the "balkanization" of the United States. Others refer to ethnic conflict in the former Yugoslavia as an example of the dangers of promoting ethnic affiliations. In the wake of the destruction of New York's World Trade Center, Americans assaulted and killed Arab Americans and vandalized mosques in several cities despite appeals from religious and political leaders. Misguided responses do not bode well for our future as the nation with the most diverse population on earth.

It is imperative that Americans understand how we benefit from diversity and that we learn more about about previous and current contributions of diverse groups in our society because the real threat to our nation is not diversity but ignorance. Some Americans

> **"** It is well to remember that the entire universe, with one trifling exception, is composed of others. **"**
> —John Andrew Holmes (1789–1876)

are choosing to focus on opportunities in a diverse society rather than on problems in areas such as business, community, and education. This issue does not simply affect the United States; rather, it is global. Naisbitt and Aburdene (1990) were among the first to describe global societies becoming culturally homogenized in the 1980s. Looking ahead to the twenty-first century, they predicted a "backlash against uniformity" as people struggled to "assert the uniqueness" of their culture in the global village: "As our outer worlds grow more similar, we will increasingly treasure the traditions that spring from within" (p. 120).

ATTITUDES ABOUT DIVERSITY

Historians have long maintained that to understand the present, we must understand the past. In terms of diversity, the best way to understand historic attitudes toward societal diversity is to examine how Americans have responded to immigration, the primary source of our diversity. Although some Americans have been (and still are) guilty of anti-immigrant sentiments, many have expressed positive beliefs about immigrants assimilating into society. By reviewing past and present attitudes concerning immigration, Gordon (1964) described consistent ideological perspectives with regard to ethnic diversity: Anglo conformity, melting pot, and pluralism. Brooks (1996) and others have described a fourth perspective: separatism. Taken together, the four perspectives represent historic and contemporary American views on ethnic diversity. Curiously, despite the persistence of these ideological points of view, Anglo conformity has been and continues to be the dominant perspective on racial and ethnic diversity in the United States.

What Does It Mean to Have an Anglo Conformity Perspective?

Cole and Cole (1954) first identified **Anglo conformity** as the efforts of English colonists to institute American values, norms, and standards perpetuated ever since. Anglo conformity is an extension of English culture and European civilization. It rejects diversity in favor of homogeneity, maintaining that everyone should conform to values, norms, and standards determined by the Anglo founders of the country and modified by a continuing white majority.

Anglo conformity requires that immigrants stop speaking native languages and use only English as soon as possible. Anglo conformity requires immigrants to abandon their ethnic heritages—the customs, ceremonies, clothing, and traditions of their former culture. Even if their native lands are European, immigrants have been expected to adopt American ways and to become similar to everyone else. Barrett and Roediger (2002) explained that people of color have found Anglo conformity to be a problem because it "took place in a nation obsessed by race. For new immigrant workers the processes of 'becoming white' and 'becoming American' were connected at every turn" (p. 30). Because immigrants of color could never become white, they could never completely achieve the goal of Anglo conformity: to look and act just like the members of the white majority.

When referring to individuals assimilating into society, social scientists often use the term *Americanization,* yet it still refers to Anglo conformity. Early in our nation's history, Americanization was a process of assimilation applied even to children of indigenous people. In the late 1800s, as public schools were expected to be responsible for the Americanization of immigrant children, schools created by the Bureau of Indian Affairs (BIA) were expected to "Americanize" Native American children. Indians had long been viewed as an obstacle to U.S. expansion and occupation of new territories; Adams (1995) quoted a liberal reformer who argued that "We must either butcher them or civilize them, and what we do we must do quickly" (p. 2). The insistence on Americanizing Indian children led to the creation of BIA boarding schools. As illustrated in the photographs of Navajo student Tom Torlino (Figure 11–4), BIA boarding schools were a dramatic example of the Anglo conformity ideal.

FIGURE 11.4 Anglo Conformity Is Vividly Illustrated in These Two Pictures of a Navajo Student, Tom Torlino, Before and After Being Enrolled in a Bia Boarding School

Source: Western Americana Collections. Manuscripts Division. Department of Rare Books and Special Collections. Princeton University Library.

INSTITUTIONAL SEXISM

Institutional sexism is the consequence of established laws, customs, and practices that systematically discriminate against people or groups based on gender. Institutional sexism takes many forms, but a persistent problem is the ongoing gender discrimination in hiring. Jones and George (2003) describe a study in Philadelphia where men and women applied for restaurant jobs offering good salaries. Although their résumés were carefully constructed to make them equally qualified, men were called in for interviews twice as often as women, and five times as many men as women received job offers. Jones and George also report that women constitute 46% of the workforce in 2000, yet:

> *Only about 12 percent of corporate officers and boards of directors were women, less than 6 percent of employees with the highest status job titles are women, and only about 4 percent of women occupy positions with the highest earning levels. (p. 127)*

Even if women are successful at finding jobs, another persistent problem is the salary inequity between men and women. Historically, there is ample evidence of inequities in the salaries of men and women, but attempts have been made to address this gender gap. There is disagreement about the extent to which gender salary inequities are being resolved, but most people concur that men earn more than women, even when they work in the same jobs (see Table 11-1).

Why Are Men Earning More Than Women in the Workforce?

Four arguments address the issue of salary inequity between men and women. The first argument is the claim that significant progress has been made in closing this income gap. According to the U.S. Bureau of Labor Statistics (2008), women earned approximately

TABLE 11-1 Statewide Comparison of Gender Salaries

| Rank Earnings Gap | Median 2007 Earnings | | Female Earnings per Dollar of Male Earnings |
	Men	Women	
1 Wyoming	$45,310	$28,540	63.0
2 Louisiana	$41,980	$27,469	65.4
3 West Virginia	$40,126	$26,719	66.6
4 North Dakota	$40,028	$27,554	68.8
5 New Hampshire	$51,385	$35,722	69.5
6 Montana	$38,230	$26,598	69.6
7 Michigan	$48,512	$34,849	71.8
7 Indiana	$43,410	$31,158	71.8
9 Utah	$43,035	$31,001	72.0
10 Alabama	$40,829	$29,756	72.9
10 Mississippi	$36,819	$26,838	72.9
12 Wisconsin	$44,105	$32,265	73.2
12 Idaho	$39,413	$28,846	73.2
14 Illinois	$48,562	$35,638	73.4
14 South Dakota	$36,726	$26,965	73.4
16 Arkansas	$36,379	$26,815	73.7
17 Alaska	$51,275	$37,835	73.8
18 Ohio	$44,443	$32,853	73.9
19 Kansas	$42,041	$31,145	74.1
20 Washington	$50,269	$37,454	74.5
21 Missouri	$41,347	$30,827	74.6
22 Pennsylvania	$44,755	$33,438	74.7
22 Iowa	$41,375	$30,925	74.7
24 Kentucky	$39,920	$29,957	75.0
24 South Carolina	$40,139	$30,124	75.0
26 Maine	$41,704	$31,496	75.5
27 Connecticut	$55,394	$41,868	75.6
28 Virginia	$48,142	$36,971	76.8
28 Oregon	$42,389	$32,538	76.8
30 New Jersey	$54,846	$42,221	77.0

| | Median 2007 Earnings | | |
Rank Earnings Gap	Men	Women	Female Earnings per Dollar of Male Earnings
30 Tennessee	$39,207	$30,178	77.0
32 Minnesota	$47,602	$36,707	77.1
33 Rhode Island	$48,492	$37,475	77.3
34 Oklahoma	$37,884	$29,378	77.5
35 Nebraska	$39,070	$30,406	77.8
36 Massachusets	$53,602	$42,062	78.5
37 New Mexico	$38,366	$30,188	78.7
38 Texas	$40,344	$31,845	78.9
39 Hawaii	$44,802	$35,471	79.2
40 Georgia	$41,837	$33,351	79.7
41 Colorado	$46,230	$36,827	79.7
42 Nevada	$42,787	$34,164	79.8
43 Florida	$40,238	$32,150	79.9
44 Delaware	$47,964	$38,543	80.4
45 North Carolina	$39,447	$31,738	80.5
46 Maryland	$54,501	$44,022	80.8
47 Arizona	$41,308	$33,723	81.6
48 New York	$47,198	$38,830	82.3
49 California	$46,404	$38,903	83.8
50 Vermont	$40,834	$34,341	84.1
51 District of Columbia	$52,860	$49,364	93.4
52 Puerto Rico	$20,242	$19,812	97.9

Source: U. S. Census Bureau (www.census.gov)

60 cents for every dollar a man made from 1960 to 1980. Since then the gap narrowed, so that by 2007, American women were earning an average of 80 cents for every dollar a man earned. The answer to the salary inequity question would seem to be that men are still earning more, but that women must be getting more raises and promotions and are apparently catching up.

Careful analysis of salary data tells a different story: The primary reason for the decreasing gap is that the salaries of male workers *have not been increasing*; they have even been decreasing in some areas. The claim that women's salaries are becoming closer to men's salaries is based on the reality of salary stagnation for men. In addition, 80% of working women still earn less than $20,000 a year. It seems debatable to say that "progress" is being

> The Glass Ceiling hinders not only individuals but society as a whole. It effectively cuts our pool of potential corporate leaders by half. It deprives our economy of new leaders, new sources of creativity.
> —Lynn M. Martin (1939–)

made concerning men's and women's salaries if closing the gender gap is based on women making small wage gains while men are receiving no wage increases.

A second argument regarding gender salary inequity is based on data showing that young women entering the workforce are earning slightly more than 80 cents for every dollar a man makes. This statistic has been used to argue that the gender inequity problem is being solved and to predict that the salary gap will eventually disappear as more highly paid young women pursue their careers. Although entry-level salaries are becoming more equal, feminists argue that women who stay in the workforce lose ground to their male peers because they are not promoted as readily as men. The term **glass ceiling** was coined to refer to an upper limit, usually middle management, beyond which women are not promoted. Studies have confirmed that women are not being promoted at the same rate as men; few are promoted to top leadership roles (U.S. Bureau of Labor Statistics, 2006).

According to a recent report from the White House Project's Corporate Council, no more than 20% of women function in leadership roles in fields as diverse as business, politics, and journalism, and even fewer are leaders in the military, large law firms, and Fortune 500 companies. Using a global comparison for women's political representation, the United States ranks 69th, lagging behind such nations as Iraq and North Korea (Quindlen, 2008).

In addition, our dominant cultural expectation for women to perform housekeeping duties and raise children results in less opportunity for developing abilities, experience, contacts, and reputation. Businesses could do more to encourage women to maintain their careers while being a parent. According to Jeffery (2005), every industrialized nation except for the United States and Australia offers women paid parental leave and guarantees them a job when their leave is finished if they return to work. The reduction of the gap between men's and women's salaries for entry-level jobs is important, but the economic penalty women pay for bearing and raising children still contributes significantly to the disparity between men's and women's salaries.

A third argument about gender salary disparity is based on the fact that more American women earn college diplomas than ever before. Because more education is assumed to mean more access to careers with higher salaries, gender disparity is predicted to decrease further, and eventually to disappear. Yet statistics show that college-educated women are still paid less than men. A 2004 government study of census data reported that the average annual salary for a college-educated woman with a bachelor's degree was $35,000, but it was $36,000 for a male high school dropout. All women with college degrees (including master's and doctorate) averaged an annual salary of $42,000 compared to their male counterparts who earned an average of $77,000 (Bernstein, 2004).

A fourth argument for the gender salary inequity is that women tend to choose careers that pay lower salaries than the more highly paid professions men select. Although women account for 59% of low-paying jobs, including 70% of minimum-wage jobs, comparing the salaries of women and men within the same profession reveals that men are paid more—even in those professions where women constitute the majority of workers (U.S. Bureau of Labor Statistics, 2008; Kim, 2000).

What Are Economic Consequences of Institutional Sexism for Women?

Although people debate gender disparity in wages, Day and Newburger (2002) report that during their lifetimes women with high school diplomas can expect to be paid $450,000 less than men with high school diplomas. They also predict that women with bachelors' degrees will earn almost $900,000 less than men with similar degrees; women with professional degrees will earn $2 million less than men with professional degrees.

For middle- and upper-class women, these economic disparities make it difficult for them to pursue political power by campaigning for national or state offices. Such campaigns are expensive and require personal funds as well as aggressive fundraising. Currently, women constitute only 17% of the U.S. Congress, a percentage exceeded by fifteen African nations. In the new government of Iraq, almost a third of the members of its parliament are women (Amer & Manning, 2009; Jeffery, 2005). Another consequence of earning lower salaries over a lifetime is that women over sixty-five are twice as likely as men to be poor.

Part-time employment also illustrates the economic exploitation of women. For a variety of reasons, women constitute the majority of people working less than forty-hour weeks or working forty or more hours a week on a temporary basis. In either case, part-time workers are typically denied most or all fringe benefits provided to full-time employees, including day care, health insurance, life insurance, and employer contributions to retirement accounts.

Another economic consequence of institutional sexism concerns child support payments. When the family unit is broken, mothers are most often awarded custody of children and, as part of legal divorce settlements, fathers are almost always required to provide child support for children under the age of majority. Despite their fiscal obligation, only 40% of American fathers are observed to pay full child support during the first year following a divorce. Another 26% of divorced fathers make partial payments for only the first year (Grall, 2000). After one year, almost half of paying fathers stop making payments altogether; of those who continue, few pay the full amount, even though most can afford to make the payments (Benokraitis & Feagin, 1995; Sorenson, 1997).

For low-income mothers, lack of child support often forces them to apply for public assistance, whereas middle-class mothers often return to college to upgrade their skills so they can compete for jobs in the labor market. If divorced custodial mothers applied for loans, they would likely be rejected because child support payments are not considered a reliable source of income! Lenders are familiar with the data on child support. Despite lower salaries, lack of child support, and other economic consequences, women often work for all the same reasons as men. And they do so regardless of discrimination in salaries and promotions, and despite another frustration encountered on the job: sexual harassment.

How Is Sexual Harassment a Significant Problem for Women in the Workforce?

The behavior called *sexual harassment* is not new, but it wasn't until 1979 that Catherine MacKinnon created the term in her writings on workplace behaviors and gender discrimination (Wetzel & Brown, 2000). There were 13,867 sexual harassment complaints filed in 2008, and those making charges received $47.4 million. Sexual harassment in the workplace is not just a problem for women; men filed 15.9% of those complaints. Typically, **sexual harassment** is defined as unwelcome deliberate and repeated behavior of a sexual nature that is neither requested nor returned. Men tend to be responsible for sexual harassment, even when men are the victims. Sexual harassment is an issue of power, not sex. Most men do not engage in sexual harassment at work; it is estimated that only 5% to 10% of the American male workforce engage in harassment. Men who do harass are being pressured to change their behavior.

What Are the Most Common Behaviors That Women Regard as Sexual Harassment?

There are two common reasons that women complain about sexual harassment. The behaviors described can be regarded as illustrating a "cultural" conflict between men and women. One complaint: Men make a nuisance of themselves by persistently asking women for dates. In response, the explanation is that during childhood and adolescence, every American male is taught some version of the cliché "if at first you don't succeed, try, try again." Men taught to view persistence as a positive attribute are encouraged to be persistent in anything they do. Accused of harassment, some men have yet to understand that persistently approaching women for dates may initially be regarded as obnoxious, but eventually becomes threatening. American women tend to regard such harassment as a verbal form of stalking, and it is not surprising that many victims tend to describe harassers as disgusting, even ugly, regardless of the physical attractiveness of the harasser (Strauss & Espeland, 1992).

> " Whatever women do they must do twice as well as men to be thought half as good. "
> — Charlotte Whitton
> (1896–1975)

A second complaint has to do with men making unwelcome, sexually suggestive remarks to women, often in the form of sexual jokes sometimes told by men to each other. Now constituting almost half of the workforce, most women find this kind of humor unequivocally offensive. As our workforce continues to change, it is inevitable that some previously established norms and behaviors will also change. Men must recognize the need for reform and respond appropriately. Men must also recognize that respecting rather than resisting or criticizing reasons for reform demonstrates their respect for women.

Throughout the global economy, corporations are confronted with sexual harassment and must establish clear policies on what they consider acceptable and unacceptable behavior. The European Equal Opportunities Commission has ruled that flirting becomes harassment if it continues after the recipient has made it clear that it is offensive (Webb, 2000). How are employers at all levels supposed to monitor employee behavior in a way that is fair? The U.S. Equal Opportunities Commission has established some reasonable guidelines.

Concept Review and Reinforcement

Key Terms

cultural sensitivity 344   cultural intelligence (CQ) 345   cultural fluency 347

Summary

Today's workplace has become more culturally diverse, and business has become increasingly international. As a result, to succeed one must be able to relate effectively to people from different cultural groups from within and outside one's country. The true meaning of valuing diversity is to respect and enjoy a wide range of cultural and individual differences. The diversity umbrella continues to include more people as the workforce encompasses a greater variety of people.

A diverse workforce brings potential advantages to the organization, including higher creativity, more profits because of a demographic match with customers, and overall business prosperity. Cultural diversity within groups can lead to conflict. Results suggest that relations-oriented diversity leads to high performance in service industry settings.

The groundwork for developing effective cross-cultural relations is to understand cultural differences. Six key aspects of understanding cultural differences are (1) cultural sensitivity including political correctness, (2) cultural intelligence, (3) respect for all workers and all cultures, (4) cultural fluency— the ability to conduct business in a diverse and international environment, (5) differences in cultural dimensions, and (6) avoidance of cultural bloopers. Cultural intelligence is based on cognitive, emotional/motivational, and physical (taking action) factors.

Countries differ in their national values or cultural dimensions, leading to differences in how most people from a given country will react to situations. The dimensions studied here are (1) performance orientation, (2) assertiveness, (3) time orientation, (4) human orientation, (5) in-group collectivism, (6) gender egalitarianism, (7) acceptance of power and authority, (8) work orientation, and (9) social support seeking.

An effective way of being culturally sensitive is to minimize actions that are likely to offend people from another culture based on their values. These cultural bloopers can take place when working in another country or when dealing with foreigners in one's own country. Studying potential cultural bloopers is helpful, but recognize also that individual differences may be of significance.

Communication barriers created by cultural differences can often be overcome by the following: (1) Be sensitive to the fact that these barriers exist; (2) show respect for all workers; (3) use straightforward language and speak slowly and clearly; (4) observe cultural differences in etiquette; (5) be sensitive to differences in nonverbal communication; (6) do not be diverted by style, accent, grammar, or personal appearance; (7) be attentive to individual differences in appearance, and (8) pronounce correctly the names of people you interact with from other countries.

Cultural training is a set of learning experiences designed to help employees understand the customs, traditions, and beliefs of another culture. In today's diverse business environment and international marketplace, learning about individuals raised in different cultural backgrounds has become more important. Cultural intelligence training includes developing strategies for sizing up the environment to determine which course of action is best. Learning a foreign language is often part of cultural training, yet it can also be a separate activity.

Diversity training attempts to bring about workplace harmony by teaching people how to get along better with diverse work associates. Another goal of diversity training is to improve business performance. Most forms of diversity training center on increasing awareness of and empathy for people who are different in some noticeable way from you. Cross-cultural and cross-gender mentoring are advanced methods of improving cross-cultural relations. The minority group member or woman is assigned a mentor who helps the person advance in his or her career.

Questions for Discussion and Review

1. What is your evaluation of the fairness of Walgreens expecting workers with physical disabilities to attain the same productivity goals as those of able-bodied workers?

2. What can you do this week to sharpen your cross-cultural skills?

3. Some companies, such as Singapore Airlines, make a deliberate effort for all customer-contact personnel to be of the same ethnic group (Singapore natives). How is this practice justified in an era of cultural diversity and valuing differences?

4. Provide an example of cultural insensitivity of any kind that you have seen, read about, or could imagine.

5. What have you personally observed about Asians and Asian Americans being less likely to ask for social support when they are facing a difficult problem?

6. Many workers in the United States who were born in other countries assign themselves short names, easy-to-pronounce by Americans, such as "Joe" and "Sue." What do you see as the pros and cons of this practice of shortening a foreign name?

7. How useful is the adage "When in Rome, do as the Romans do" for someone who wants to work in another country for a while?

8. If you were a supervisor, how would you deal with a group member who had a very low acceptance of power and authority?

9. The cultural bloopers presented in Skill-Building Exercise 8-2 all dealt with errors people make in regard to people who are not American. Give an example of a cultural blooper a person from another country might make in the United States.

10. Many people speak loudly to other people who are deaf, blind, and those who speak a different language. Based on the information presented in this chapter, what mistakes are these people making?

The Web Corner

http://www.DiversityInc.com
(Extensive information including videos about cultural diversity in organizations.)

http://www.berlitz.com
(Information about language training and cultural training in countries throughout the world. Investigate in your second language to enhance the cross-cultural experience.)

Internet Skill Builder: Avoiding Cultural Insensitivity

One of the most effective ways of hampering relationships with people of another culture is to be grossly insensitive. If you can avoid these gross errors, you will be on your way toward at least acceptable relationships with people from another domestic or foreign culture. Two examples of cultural insensitivity uncovered on the Internet are: In Alberta, Canada, a sign in the window of a large chain restaurant read, "No drunken Indians allowed." Wal-Mart performed poorly in Germany because it did not recognize the cultural fact that Germans do not like to spend a lot of time shopping by walking through a giant store and waiting on line. Search the Internet for examples of cultural insensitivity. You may have to dig hard to find these nuggets of insensitivity, but the activity will help you become more culturally sensitive and aware.

Developing Your Human Relations Skills

What to Do with Shabana?

Shabana was raised in Pakistan and graduated from the University of Punjab with a major in commerce. She then moved to Chicago, Illinois, to live with her married aunt, as well as to begin a career in business in the United States. Shabana is fluent in her native Punjabi, but also has spoken and written English since the beginning of her primary education.

Having a sponsor in the United States made it possible for Shabana to enter the job market in Chicago. In addition to having a good formal education, Shabana makes a positive physical appearance that includes a warm smile, and a comfortable, relaxed manner. After a two-month long job search, Shabana found employment as a store associate in a cell-phone store of one of the major mobile phone providers. She was content with this position because she thought it would be a stepping stone to store management in the field of consumer electronics.

Shabana enjoyed interacting with the other store associates, as well as the customers. An important part of her role was explaining some of the intricacies of cell phones, as well as the contracts, to customers. She willingly worked Saturday nights and Sunday afternoons, store hours unpopular with other associates.

From time to time, Shabana was perplexed as to why some customers did not understand her. With a few of the older customers, Shabana attributed their lack of understanding to limited knowledge of technology, or hearing impairments. One customer looked straight at Shabana and said, "I do understand a word you are saying."

One day Trevor, the store manager, took Shabana aside and told her, "You are a wonderful sales associate in many ways. The other associates enjoy working with you, and you get along well with many of our customers. Yet we are getting too many complaints by e-mail and phone that many of our customers cannot understand you. It seems like some of these Chicago people just can't understand English with a Pakistani accent."

"Maybe some of our customers aren't the most sophisticated, but they are still customers. And we need every dollar we can take it to meet our sales goals. You need to become better understood by all our customers, or we can't keep you as a sales associate."

A little perplexed, Shabana replied, "I am so sorry to know that I have disappointed you and some of our valued customers. Please give me several weeks to correct this situation of my not being so well understood by all our customers."

Trevor replied, "Okay, but I am going to keep close watch on your progress."

Case Questions

1. What should Shabana do to improve her ability to be understood by more customers?
2. Is the problem of language comprehension in this case really a problem of customers not being too sharp mentally?
3. What actions do you recommend that Trevor take to help Shabana improve her ability to be understood by her customers? Or, should he just fire her?
4. To what extent do you think Trevor is practicing job discrimination by even hinting that he might fire Shabana if she is not better understood by a wider variety of customers?

Akiak Wants to Fit In

Akiak Nori was raised in Noorvik, Alaska, and then attended a career school in Juneau, Alaska, majoring in electronic technology. Approaching graduation, he sorted out dozens of job offers he had obtained, several of which did not even require an in-person interview.

Akiak accepted a position with a construction company in International Falls, Minnesota, because of the job opportunities and the long brisk winters that would be natural and comfortable for him. He was assigned to a construction team for new buildings, and was also assigned maintenance work for existing electronic systems in office buildings, factories, and mills.

Akiak's goal from the first day on the job was to perform well and fit in with his coworkers. He recognized that fitting in with a non-Eskimo group would require some patience on his part. Akiak had been counseled by several teachers that patience was not one of his strong points.

During employee orientation, two other new employees asked Akiak if his name meant kayak in Eskimo language. With a smile, Akiak replied, "No, it means brave. I guess my parents thought I would have to be brave to grow up in Noorvik, where you have to be tough to survive."

Later that morning, Akiak was asked if ice fishing and seal hunting were his two favorite sports. "Not at all," said Akiak, "We had a first-rate hockey rink in town, so I got to love hockey. And, I'm a Minnesota Viking (professional football team) fan. That's why I took a job in Minnesota." (Said with a smile.)

During lunch, Mary, another new employee, asked Akiak, "Tell me Akiak, are you an Eskimo? Or are you an Inuit? I don't want to make a mistake."

Akiak responded, "It's no mistake to call me an Eskimo. It's no mistake to call me an Inuit. Some people think that the term Eskimo is wrong, and that we should be called Inuit. It doesn't matter to me or to my friends and family. We like both terms."

"Yet, Mary, the mistake you are making is not thinking of me as just another American. Alaska is one of the 50 states. We vote. We pay and receive Social Security. And, we learn English in school, and we eat at McDonalds."

"I'm sorry," said Mary. "I was just trying to be friendly."

Ned, the supervisor of the orientation program, said to the group. "I think we have asked Akiak enough about his cultural heritage for now. Yet, I have just one favor to ask Akiak. I wish he would show us how he positions his arm, head, and body to spear a big fish."

Akiak said with a sarcastic tone, "Time out. I'm taking a break from this orientation right now. I have to go back to my igloo and chew on some frozen fish."

Case Questions

1. What does this case tell us about cultural sensitivity?
2. How might have Akiak's coworkers related better to him during the orientation?
3. How might have Akiak done a better job of relating to his new coworkers so far?
4. Does Akiak have an *attitude* (meaning negative attitude problem)?

Interpersonal Skills Role-Play

Building a Relationship with an Eskimo Electronic Technician

Several class members play the role of new workers at the company in International Falls, Minnesota, as described in the case presented above. One of the other new workers is Akiak Nori. You want to welcome him, and help him feel part of the group. At the same time, you believe that recognizing his Eskimo heritage would be part of showing respect for his culture. Yet, you do not want to be patronizing or make Akiak feel that he is unusual. Another student plays the role of Akiak who regards himself as an American, yet is also proud of his Eskimo heritage.

Conduct this role-play for about seven minutes. Observers rate the role players on two dimensions, using a 1-to-5 scale from very poor to very good. One dimension is "effective use of human relations techniques." Focus on the cross-cultural sensitivity of the workers attempting to build a relationship with Akiak. Also provide feedback about Akiak's interpersonal skills. The second dimension is "acting ability." A few observers might voluntarily provide feedback to the role players in terms of sharing their ratings and observations. The course instructor might also provide feedback.

REFERENCES

1. "Walgreens 15th Distribution Center Opens in Connecticut and Creates Jobs for People with Disabilities," *Walgreens News Room* (http://walgreens.com), April 15, 2009; "Walgreens Recruits Employees with Disabilities through New, Highly Accessible Web Site," *Medical News Today* (www.medicalnewstoday.com), July 8, 2006, pp. 1–2; Mika Brzezinski, "Program Puts the 'Able' in Disabled," msnbc.com, July 2, 2007, pp. 1–2.
2. Quoted in Diane Cadrain, "Accommodating Sex Transformations," *HR Magazine*, October 2009, p. 59.
3. Angela Ka-yee Leung, William W. Maddox, Adam D. Galinsky, and Chi-yue Chu, "Multicultural Experience Enhances Creativity," *American Psychologist*, April 2008, pp. 169–181.
4. Michael Bowker, "Corporate Diversity Driving Profits," *Hispanic Business*, September 2008, pp. 12, 14.
5. Patrick F. McKay, Derek R. Avery, and Mark A. Morris, "A Tale of Two Climates: Diversity Climate from Subordinates' and Managers' Perspectives and Their Role in Store Unit Sales Performance," *Personnel Psychology*, Winter 2009, pp. 767–791.
6. Eric Kearney, Diether Gebert, and Sven C. Voelpel, "When and How Diversity Benefits Teams: The Importance of Team Members' Need for Cognition," *Academy of Management Journal*, June 2009, pp. 581–598.
7. Apnara Joshi and Hyuyntak Roh, "The Role of Context in Work Team Diversity Research: A Meta-Analytic Review," *Academy of Management Journal*, June 2009, pp. 599–627.
8. Arvind V. Phatak, *International Dimensions of Management* (Boston: Kent, 1983), p. 167.
9. Robin J. Ely, Debra Meyerson, and Martin N. Davidson, "Rethinking Political Correctness," *Harvard Business Review*, September 2006, p. 80.
10. Quoted in "Leveraging Diversity at Work," *Hispanic Business*, November 2006, p. 70.
11. P. Christopher Earley and Elaine Mosakowski, "Cultural Intelligence," *Harvard Business Review*, October 2004, p. 140. The example is from the same source, same page.
12. P. C. Earley and E. Mosakowski, "Toward Culture Intelligence: Turning Cultural Differences into a Workplace Advantage," *Academy of Management Executive*, August 2004, pp. 154–155.
13. Ann Pomeroy, "She's Still Lovin' It," *HR Magazine* December 2006, p. 60.
14. Scott B. Button, "Organizational Efforts to Affirm Sexual Diversity: A Cross-Level Examination," *Journal of Applied Psychology*, February 2001, pp. 17–28.
15. Charlene Marmer Solomon, "Global Operations Demand That HR Rethink Diversity," *Personnel Journal*, July 1994, p. 50.
16. Mansour Javidan, Peter W. Dorfman, May Sully de Luque, and Robert J. House, "In the Eye of the Beholder: Cross Cultural Lessons in Leadership from Project GLOBE," *Academy of Management Perspectives*, February 2006, pp. 69–70. Similar were dimensions were described in Geert Hofstede, *Culture's Consequences: International Differences in Work Related Values* (Beverly Hills, CA: Sage, 1980); updated and expanded in "A Conversation with Geert Hofstede," *Organizational Dynamics*, Spring 1993, pp. 53–61; Hofstede, "Who Is the Fairest of Them All? Galit Ailon's Mirror," *Academy of Management Review*, July 2009, pp. 570–571. Dimension 8 is not included in the above research. Paul J. Taylor, Wen-Dong Li, Kan Shi, and Walter C. Borman, "The Transportability of Job Information Across Countries," *Personnel Psychology*, Spring 2008, pp. 72–76.
17. Study reported in Bradley S. Klapper, "Report: U.S. Workers Are the Most Productive," Associated Press, September 2, 2007.
18. Heejung S. Kim, David K. Sherman, and Shelley E. Taylor, "Culture and Social Support," *American Psychologist*, September 2008, pp. 518–526.
19. Lee Gardenswartz and Anita Rowe, "Cross-Cultural Awareness," *HR Magazine*, March 2001, p. 139.
20. Ellyn Ferguson, "Many Firms Seek Bilingual Workers," Gannett News Service, May 13, 2007.
21. Daren Fonda, "Selling in Tongues," *Time*, November 26, 2001, pp. B12–B13.
22. Paraphrasing of citation in Ferguson, "Many Firms Seek Bilingual Workers."
23. Carolena Lyons Lawrence, "Teaching Students How Gestures Communicate Across Cultures," *Business Education Forum*, February 2003, p. 39.
24. Jeffrey Sanchez-Burks, Caroline A. Bartel, and Sally Blount, "Performance in Intercultural Interactions at Work: Cross-Cultural Differences in Response to Behavioral Mirroring," *Journal of Applied Psychology*, January 2009, pp. 216–233.
25. Roger E. Axtell, *Gestures: The Do's and Taboos of Body Language Around the World* (New York: Wiley, 1990).
26. Siri Carpenter, "Why Do 'They All Look Alike'?" *Monitor on Psychology*, December 2000, p. 44.
27. Kathleen Begley, "Managing Across Cultures at Home," *HR Magazine*, September 2009, p. 115.
28. Mei Fong, "Chinese Charm School," *The Wall Street Journal*, January 13, 2004, p. B1.
29. P. Christopher Earley and Randall S. Peterson, "The Elusive Cultural Chameleon: Cultural Intelligence as a New Approach to Intercultural Training for the Global Manager," *Academy of Management Learning and Education*, March 2004, p. 106.
30. Kathryn Tyle, "I Say Potato, You Say *Patata*," *HR Magazine*, January 2004, p. 85.
31. Rohini Anahand and Mary-Frances Winters, "A Retrospective View of Corporate Diversity Training from 1964 to the Present," *Academy of Management Learning & Education*, September 2008, p. 356.
32. Gillian Flynn, "The Harsh Reality of Diversity Programs," *Workforce*, December 1998, p. 29.
33. Kathryn Tyler, "Cross-Cultural Connections: Mentoring Programs Can Bridge Gaps between Disparate Groups," *HR Magazine*, October 2007, pp. 77–83.

Life Plan

Time Management Resources: Calendars, Lists, and Work Space

Many a good student has fallen victim to "assignment amnesia." This occurs when otherwise smart students believe they can remember all of their assignments and appointments without writing them down and without consulting their syllabi or course outlines. Fortunately, there are measures you can take to prevent an attack of assignment amnesia: using a calendar to keep track of important deadlines and events, and maintaining a list of prioritized tasks that you need to complete.

If you use a paper calendar, you have many different types from which to choose. Once you determine the type that works best for you—a monthly, weekly, or daily calendar—make a habit of writing down your tasks, no matter how big or small. Here is an example of a typical list of a day's activities for a student like Laura:

Thursday

Make appointment to have oil changed

Pick up medicine for Mom

Turn in housing deposit for next semester

Study for history quiz on Friday

Write essay for English Composition

Turn in student club membership application

A typical monthly calendar allows you to see several weeks at once so that you can remain aware of upcoming events (Exhibit 12-1), but often there is little space on a monthly calendar to write down detailed lists such as the one above.

A weekly calendar allows you to glance at one week at a time. A benefit of a weekly calendar is that you have room to write out details of each activity; however, a drawback to a weekly calendar is it is difficult to anticipate what you must do the next week.

Daily calendars (Exhibit 12-2) usually provide the most space to write your day-to-day tasks and appointments, but this kind of calendar may be the most difficult to work with if you need to plan ahead. Since you cannot visually see the rest of the week or month, you may overlook important events or be surprised by them. Use a daily calendar if you are extremely organized and can plan ahead effectively, or use it in addition to a monthly calendar. Exhibit 12-3 shows a typical student's work and school schedule.

If you have reliable Internet access in your home, apartment, or dorm, and access to computers while on campus in computer labs, you may want to consider using a web-based, electronic calendar system and to-do list; also, consider using your phone's calendar to help you stay in track. In many cases, those phone calendars can sync to your computer, which will allow you to stay updated no matter what device you use. Electronic calendars allow you to set up events to automatically repeat themselves (e.g., calculus quiz every Thursday; Dad's birthday on March 18), rearrange priority lists without having to

EXHIBIT 12-1 Monthly Calendar

Sunday	Monday	Tuesday	Wednesday	Thursday	Friday	Saturday
					1	2
3	4	5	6	7	8	9 Picnic—noon
10	11 Work late	12	13	14	15 Pay bills	16
17	18	19	20	21 Play rehearsal 7:00	22	23
24	25 Nutrition exam 10:00	26	27	28	29	30 Birthday party 2:00

EXHIBIT 12-2 Daily Calendar

Friday March 15, 2013
7:00 Wake up, shower, get ready for school
8:00 Drive to school, arrive early and study in the library
9:00 College Algebra
10:00 English 2
11:00 Study for Biology exam
12:00 Eat lunch and review notes for College Algebra
1:00 Biology—EXAM!!
2:00 Drive to work
3:00 Work
4:00 Work
5:00 Work

rewrite them, set up reminders and alerts to prompt you about upcoming deadlines and events, and share your calendar with others so that you can coordinate team projects and family responsibilities. The added benefit of a web-based system is that you can access it anytime and anywhere you have Internet access. Google's calendar service is a popular choice among college students, and Toodledo (http://www.toodledo.com) is one option for managing all of your to-do lists and priorities. Even with these electronic systems, you

EXHIBIT 12-3   Student's College and Work Schedule

Responsibility	Contact Hours Per Week	Outside Hours Per Week	Total Hours Per Week
College Algebra	3	6–9	9–12
Composition 101	3	6–9	9–12
U.S. History	3	6–9	9–12
Reading	3	6–9	9–12
Work	25		25
TOTAL HOURS EACH WEEK: 61–73 HOURS			

can always print a copy of your calendar and to-do lists to have readily available during class or other times when you don't have Internet access. Whatever system you choose—electronic, paper-based, weekly, monthly, or daily—pick a system that works best for you and can keep you on track.

Once you've chosen a calendar system that works best for you, find your college's academic calendar on the campus website or in the catalog, and add the following deadlines to your schedule:

- Deadlines for registering and filing financial aid forms
- Date for the beginning of classes (or instruction)
- Drop/add dates for changing your schedule
- Due dates for tuition payment
- Withdrawal dates for leaving college before the semester is over
- Registration dates for the next semester
- Holidays or breaks within the semester and between semesters

The ideal calendar and to-do list are first steps to managing your time well, but there is more you can do. Creating a quiet, clutter-free space where you can study and complete assignments will also help you manage your time effectively and efficiently. If you don't have a place in your house or apartment that you can call your own, and a comfortable chair or seat at the kitchen table may be all that you can spare, make sure it is comfortable and quiet and has adequate space for books, notebooks, and other supplies. It has to be a place where you *want* to be, or it will be difficult to go there to stay on task. See Exhibit 12-4, a calendar for a typical busy student who must juggle her college work and her life.

Time Management Routines: Daily Reviews and Back Planning

With an effective calendar and to-do list in place, you can now start to establish a time management routine that helps you stay on track and maintain control over your life. For your calendar and task list to be effective, you need to establish a daily routine of reviewing and updating this information. Take a few minutes every evening to review

©Fuse / Getty Images

Schedule time to work with your classmates and talk with faculty and advisors outside of class.

EXHIBIT 12-4 Laura's Monthly Calendar

Monday	Tuesday	Wednesday	Thursday	Friday	Saturday	Sunday
6:30–7:30 Get ready for school	6:30–7:30 Get ready for school	6:30–7:30 Get ready for school	6:30–7:30 Get ready for school	6:30–7:30 Get ready for school	7:00–10:00 Clean house, shop	7:00–10:00 Study
7:30–7:45 Travel to work	7:30–7:45 Travel to work	7:30–7:45 Travel to work	7:30–7:45 Travel to work	7:30–7:45 Travel to work	10:00–11:30 Soccer	10:00–11:00 Go to church
8:00–12:30 Work	8:00–12:30 Work	8:00–12:30 Work	8:00–12:30 Work	8:00–12:30 Work	11:30–12:15 Lunch with team	11:15–12:30 Lunch with parents
12:30–1:15 Eat lunch and run errands	12:30–1:15 Go to doctor's appt.	12:30–1:15 Eat lunch with friend	12:30–1:15 Eat lunch and walk 1 mile	12:30–1:15 Eat lunch and study	12:15–2:00 Run errands	12:45–3:45 Study
1:15–4:45 Work	1:15–4:45 Work	1:15–4:45 Work	1:15–4:45 Work	1:15–4:45 Work	2:00–6:00 Go to library and do research	3:45–5:45 Do yard work
4:45–5:00 Travel	4:45–5:00 Travel	4:45–5:00 Travel	4:45–5:00 Travel	4:45–5:00 Travel	6:00–7:00 Fix and eat dinner	6:00–7:00 Eat dinner
5:00–5:45 Eat dinner and study	5:00–5:45 Eat dinner and study	5:00–5:45 Eat dinner and study	5:00–5:45 Eat dinner and study	5:00–7:00 Eat dinner with friends	7:00–9:00 Study	7:00–8:00 Walk 3 miles
6:00–9:30 Classes	6:00–9:30 Classes	6:00–9:30 Classes	6:00–9:30 Classes	7:00–9:30 See movie	9:00–10:00 Answer email and watch TV	8:00–10:00 Do laundry, get ready for next week
10:00 Go to bed	10:00 Go to bed	10:00 Go to bed	10:00 Go to bed	10:00 Go to bed	10:00 Go to bed	10:00 Go to bed

what you've accomplished and check those items off your to-do list (this will be a very satisfying experience!), add new tasks that came up that day, and then review tomorrow's calendar and to-do list so you can anticipate tomorrow's goals. Knowing what to expect for the day will make surprises less likely. Also, if you know that you have an early start tomorrow, you can make special preparations, such as preparing a lunch the night before, getting your backpack organized, making sure you know where you have to go by reviewing a map, and setting your alarm (and backups, if you tend to hit the snooze button a lot!). Stressful mornings tend to get you on the wrong track for the day, and they can typically be avoided with some thoughtful planning the night before. See Exhibit 12-5 for an example of how you can plan your day.

The second element of your time management routine that can help you manage your stress and put you in control of your schedule is a strategy called "back planning." The basic premise of back planning is to look ahead at a deadline for a task, estimate the amount of time it will take to complete the task, and establish a starting point for

EXHIBIT 12-5   Time Log Example

Time	Wednesday's Activities
7:00 A.M.	Get ready for classes; eat breakfast
7:30 A.M.	Review notes for business class
8:00 A.M.	En route to school
8:30 A.M.	Business Communications
9:00 A.M.	Class, continued
9:30 A.M.	Class, continued
10:00 A.M.	See advisor to plan next semester's classes

the task. For example, if you know that you need to write a 20-page paper for English composition, and you expect that all of the research, writing, editing, formatting, and printing will take two weeks, you can schedule time to start the project at least two weeks before its deadline. Back planning works for short-term planning, also—if you know that your morning class starts at 8:30, and it typically takes 45 minutes for you to complete your entire morning routine and find parking, then you know that you need to be walking out the door of your dorm or apartment no later than 7:45 to be on time for class. Establishing these short-term and long-term milestones will help you stay on track to meet deadlines and reduce the stress that's often associated with running behind in your schedule.

Perhaps the most important benefit of back planning is that it attacks one of the biggest threats to student success—procrastination. Procrastination is the tendency to delay starting a task until the deadline is very near. Activities such as cramming for quizzes and exams, pulling all-nighters to finish a paper or project, and missing work or other classes to finish an assignment on the due date are all evidence of procrastination. These types of last-minute, hurried efforts to meet a deadline tend to yield relatively poor academic performance and generate a tremendous amount of emotional, physical, and social stress.

BUZZ

Q

I don't normally keep a calendar or even write down what I need to do. This has served me well in high school. Why do professors make such a big deal about keeping track of my assignments?

A

You may have been able to keep track of your work in high school because you had other people helping you keep track of assignments and due dates. To stay on track to complete your work on time and remember all your appointments, here are a few tips:

- Record what you have to do each week and each day. Use either technology or pen and paper to make your list.

- Record your goals or tasks in multiple locations so that you are reminded frequently of what you need to do.

- Revise your list each day. As priorities and tasks change, make sure your list reflects these changes.

- Using a computer or cell phone, set an alarm before the task is due to remind you to complete it.

However, these desperate strategies are avoidable! With effective back planning, you can alleviate the need to stay up all night before an exam or miss other classes to finish an assignment. An example of back planning for an important assignment can be seen in Exhibit 12-6.

The single biggest obstacle you need to overcome to avoid procrastination is *starting* the project. Procrastination typically occurs when we (yes, professors sometimes procrastinate, too) are confused, intimidated, or overwhelmed by an assignment or task. Our fears get the best of us, and we choose to forget about the assignment for a while, instead of trying to get started. Once we do get started on a project, the fears tend to dissipate, and we discover that we're making more progress than we expected. The problem with procrastination is that if we wait a long time before starting the project, the fear of missing the deadline and being late begins to creep in and we lose our ability to be creative problem solvers. If you've ever tried to remember a phone number, locker combination, or some other mental note, you've probably discovered that it's more difficult to think clearly and solve problems when you're in a hurry. In the same way, it's difficult to be thoughtful and creative when you're trying to study for an exam or write a paper under time pressure.

We've spent a lot of time on procrastination, because it's such a common phenomenon in college, and we see our students suffering unnecessary consequences from it. When you are assigned homework, projects, or papers, take time to use back planning, and clearly establish your start date for the project, as well as important milestones along the way (e.g., first two chapters by September 15). Build those milestones into your calendar system, set

EXHIBIT 12-6 Back Planning Time Management

Sunday	Monday	Tuesday	Wednesday	Thursday	Friday	Saturday
		1	2	3	4	5
6	7	8 1:00 P.M. Receive paper assignment	9 6–7:30 P.M. Choose paper topic; brainstorm or freewrite on topic	10 9–10:30 P.M. Reread brainstorming list; create a draft outline	11	12
13 3–5:00 P.M. Write first draft of paper	14	15 11–12:00 noon Visit writing lab for assistance with paper	16	17	18 8:30–10:30 P.M Write second draft of paper, incorporating tutor's advice	19
20 3–4:30 P.M. Write final draft of paper	21	22	23 8–9:00 P.M. Edit paper; print out on quality paper; place in backpack	24 2:00 P.M. Turn in paper	25	26
27	28	29	30			

time aside for the work, and get started. If you can establish a solid routine of regularly reviewing your calendar and to-do list and using back planning, you'll be taking control of your time and developing skills that will serve you well in college and throughout your life.

60-SECOND PAUSE

What are two or three action items you can complete this week to establish your time management resources and routines?

MANAGE YOUR ENERGY

Just as important as managing your time is managing your energy. Think about this scenario: You have all weekend off from work and your spouse has taken the kids to visit the grandparents. Therefore, you have 48 hours of complete solitude to write a research paper that is due on Monday. Sounds ideal, doesn't it? But what if you have the flu for those two days? Does the time mean anything when you don't have the energy to do any work? What if, instead of having the flu, you've pulled two double shifts and haven't slept more than five hours in two days? Will you be able to use your free 48 hours productively, or will you need to take care of yourself?

Time, in other words, is only valuable if you have the energy to use it well. Energy includes both physical and mental sharpness and focus. Everyone experiences variations in how "sharp" they feel throughout the day. Researchers sometimes refer to this as our circadian rhythm. The key point is to understand yourself well enough to know when you are at the peak of your mental and physical alertness, and when you're not. To determine which times of the day you feel most sharp, place an "X" in the appropriate column for each time of day in Exhibit 12-7. If you work nights and sleep during most of the day, create your own chart with the times that you are awake.

In addition to the time of day, your energy levels rise and fall during the week. Do you find yourself tired on Monday mornings, but full of energy on Fridays? Or do you feel worn out by Thursday evenings, but rejuvenated on Sundays? Depending on your work, school, and personal schedules, you will find that you have regular bursts of energy at certain times of the week. To determine which days of the week you feel most energetic, write an "X" in the appropriate columns in the box in Exhibit 12-8.

EXHIBIT 12-7   Time-of-Day Energy Levels

Time of Day	High Energy	Neutral	Low Energy
6:00 A.M.			
8:00 A.M.			
10:00 A.M.			
12 noon			
2:00 P.M.			
4:00 P.M.			
6:00 P.M.			
8:00 P.M.			
10:00 P.M.			
12 midnight			

EXHIBIT 12-8   Day-of-Week Energy Levels

Weekday	High Energy	Neutral	Low Energy
Sunday			
Monday			
Tuesday			
Wednesday			
Thursday			
Friday			
Saturday			

Once you've identified the hours in the day and the days in the week when you tend to be at your best, you can build your schedule to maximize your productivity during those times, and schedule activities that don't require as much effort or concentration during times when you aren't at your peak. Activities such as writing papers, solving complex math problems, and reading articles and books for class assignments should be reserved for those "peak" times. It's during these times that you will most need your quiet, uncluttered work space, also. This will require some discipline and advanced planning, because you'll be tempted by other tasks and distractions. Take advantage of your mental and physical sharpness during these peak periods to perform activities that are the most important to your college success. Most students are at or near the peak of their mental alertness shortly after waking up in the morning. If that's also the case for you, commit yourself to productivity expert Tony Schwartz's strategy: "Another ritual I have . . . is to always do the most important task of the day first thing in the morning when I'm most rested and least distracted" (Allen, Schwartz, & McGinn, 2011, p. 85).

What should you do during those times when you aren't at your peak? First of all, recognize that it's OK to have some periods of time when you take a break from work-

ing hard. In fact, it's actually more productive to take breaks than to try to work hard all day. Again, productivity expert Tony Schwartz offers good advice: "If a person works continuously all through the day, she'll produce less than a person of equal talent who works very intensely for short periods and then recovers before working intensely again" (Allen, Schwartz, and McGinn, 2011, p. 84). The good news is that you can still get a lot accomplished, even during times when you don't feel mentally or physically sharp. During those times, you can accommodate the common "time zappers" that can rob college students of their time:

- Reviewing and sending emails
- Making phone calls
- Running errands
- Preparing meals
- Talking with roommates
- Taking a walk, swimming, or doing some other form of meditative exercise

©THINKSTOCK

Scheduling time to relax and recharge is just as important as scheduling your class work.

One way to help yourself manage your energy is by becoming aware of what activities relax you when you are stressed and what activities allow you to refill your energy reserves. In Exhibit 12-9, place an "X" in the appropriate column next to each activity. If the activity does both, place an "X" in each column. If the activity neither relaxes nor energizes, then leave both columns blank. Use this chart when planning your time. If an activity rejuvenates you and helps you recharge, you may want to schedule the activity for times when you need more energy. If an activity helps you wind down, you may want to schedule it for after you have completed major tasks.

EXHIBIT 12-9   Time and Energy Zappers and Re-energizers

Activity	Zapper	Re-energizer
Watching television		
Spending time with family/friends		
Pleasure reading		
Doing housework		
Exercising (light to moderate)		
Gardening		
Talking on the phone		
Writing		
Cooking		
Shopping		
Napping		
Participating in a hobby		
Surfing the Internet		
Organizing closets, drawers, files		
Enjoying a nice meal		

INTEGRITY MATTERS

Sometimes doing what is easiest, even if it not the right thing to do, seems like the best way to manage time effectively. For example, a student who does not have enough time to finish a paper may be tempted to download one from the Internet, use someone else's previous work, or ask someone else to write it. Such a shortcut actually shortchanges the educational process. A student who "saves time" by not doing her own work for a class risks more than not learning from the assignment; she may find herself in serious academic jeopardy when the professor confronts her with the evidence that she did not do her own work.

Your Turn

In approximately 250 words, describe what ways you have saved time by not doing something or not doing it right. Discuss how you felt about not completing the task or by not completing it to the best of your ability. Describe what you have learned about acting with integrity and managing your time.

Avoid the "Black Holes" of Television, Video Games, and Social Media

Often portrayed in science fiction movies or scientific documentaries, black holes in space absorb everything around them, including light. From the perspective of time and energy management, television, video games, and social media like Facebook have the potential to be virtual black holes in your life that can consume far too much of your time and energy. If you plan on watching TV for only 10 minutes, it's really easy to discover that you're still sitting in front of the screen two hours later, and you've accomplished nothing during that time. Video games have the capacity to be even more time consuming because of their interactive nature. Social media, like Facebook and Twitter, have emerged as another potential black hole of your time, consuming both your time and attention by feeding continual distractions to you throughout the day. As you establish your time and energy management strategies, we urge extreme caution in your use of any of these three items. They are popular activities among college students, certainly, but if they aren't consumed in careful moderation, they can absorb your time and energy, and leave you with little in return for your academic pursuits.

Multi-Tasking Should Be Used in Moderation

The process of multi-tasking—simultaneously managing several tasks or devoting your attention to more than one activity at a time—is often lauded as an admirable and even necessary skill. In fact, many people believe that you can get more done and be more productive while multi-tasking; however, the scientific evidence doesn't support this premise. In his article "Manage Your Energy, Not Your Time" (2007), Tony Schwartz explains: "Many executives view multitasking as a necessity in the face of all the demands they juggle, but it actually undermines productivity. Distractions are costly: A temporary shift in attention from one task to another—stopping to answer an e-mail or take a phone call, for instance—increases the amount of time necessary to finish the primary task by as much as 25%, a phenomenon known as 'switching time.' It's far more efficient to fully focus for 90 to 120 minutes, take a true break, and then fully focus on the next activity" (p. 67). If you have a tendency to check your emails, respond to text messages, monitor your Facebook status, and listen to your iPod while attempting to write, study, or organize your calendar, you are undermining your ability to perform well because these simultaneous tasks are sapping both your time and energy. Take the time to shut down the peripheral activities and stimuli and focus on the primary task at hand, and you'll find yourself accomplishing far more than you expected.

60-SECOND PAUSE

Now that you've considered when your physical and mental sharpness are at their peak, what are some of the changes you plan to make in your daily and weekly routine to capitalize on this insight?

MONEY MATTERS

One of the greatest challenges for students isn't meeting the academic expectations of college; it is handling the financial issues that come into play when you get there. Some students choose to go to school full-time and not work, while others juggle a job—either part-time or full-time—while going to school. No matter what their financial situation, many are adding the expense of going to college to their other obligations, or they are using grants, loans, or scholarships to cover costs.

As you know by now because you successfully enrolled in college, investing in your future takes more than courage; it also takes some cash, or at least access to funds to cover the costs. Unfortunately, as Catherine Rampell (2009) recently reported for *The New York Times*, the costs of college continue to rise and will likely increase with each passing year. So what can you do? The first step is to become financially literate. There are many resources available that can help you learn more about how to become financially fit. The next step is to create a plan for staying on a budget and for anticipating expenses in the future. The following section provides you with a brief overview of both steps.

Estimate Your College Costs

Estimating what you are going to spend in college for your education is a great first step to understanding your financial situation, and it will help you with budgeting. Since this is your first time in college, it will be helpful to see what you can expect to spend as you work on and complete your degree. Unfortunately, college tuition and fees are only part of the costs involved in earning a degree. No matter what you pay for tuition and fees, it is only a fraction of the actual costs of your education; colleges make up the difference through taxes, state and federal money, and gifts and donations.

To determine your estimated costs, you will need to get very specific about what you will need during the semesters you plan to attend. The following list is only a suggestion of possible supplies: textbooks, notebooks/binders, computer/laptop, backpack, paper (for notes and for printing), pens/pencils, calculator, computer software, jump drive, stapler, hole punch, ruler, and other specialized supplies for labs or certain classes such as photography or drawing. For specialized programs, you may have other materials that you will need to purchase. Create a list of what you know you will need, and then write down how much you think each item will cost. You will use this estimate when you create your budget.

In addition to supplies and tuition, you may also find other costs associated with going to college. For example, your transportation costs may increase as you go from home or work to campus and back. You may also discover that you need regular, reliable Internet access, which will create an additional monthly cost. Unexpected costs such as these can be an awakening to the investment of money and time that wasn't covered during new-student orientation. The following is just a suggested list of possible additional expenses that you may encounter: daycare or babysitting services, transportation (gas, car maintenance, tolls, bus pass), parking, and Internet services. You will want to talk with students who have been at your college for a few semesters or recent graduates to determine what else may be needed. These same students may also provide you with some cost-saving ideas.

Create a Budget

Creating a budget will help you manage your college costs while balancing your other financial obligations and help you stay on track. A budget doesn't have to be a headache. In fact, it is relatively easy to create a budget. The hard part is following it. First, you need to create a customized budget sheet. Exhibit 12-10 shows a sample budget form that you can start with. In the first column, you will estimate your income and your expenses. The middle column will be used to record your actual amounts of income and expenses. Record any differences in the final column by subtracting the actual amount from the estimated amount. For example, if you estimate that you earn about $1,000 a month, but this month, you earn $1,092, your difference is +$92. If you earn $997, then the difference is −$3. The budget in Exhibit 12-10 provides a sample of what you need to write down each month.

EXHIBIT 12-10 Sample Budget Form

Category	Estimated Amount Per Month	Actual Amount Per Month	Difference
Income			
Source 1 (wages/salary)			
Source 2 (scholarship, financial aid, etc.)			
Source 3 (alimony, employee tuition reimbursement, child support)			
Total Income			
Expenses			
Mortgage/rent			
Utilities			
Car payment/transportation			
Insurance			
Groceries			
Household items			
Clothing			
Gas			
Car maintenance			
Cellular phone			
Eating out			
Entertainment			
Health care (medications, doctor's visits, etc.)			
Credit cards or loans			
Total Expenses			
Net Income (Total Income minus Total Expenses)			

Once you determine the categories that fit your lifestyle, you will need to gather all the bills and paystubs that you have and add up your expenses and income. It is a good idea to review at least three months' worth of bills to get an accurate picture of your expenditures. If you have any bills that are paid less frequently than once a month, then you will need to convert them to a monthly expense. For example, if you pay $240 for car insurance every six months, your monthly expense is $40 ($240 divided by 6 months).

One key to an accurate budget that helps you track your spending is to be honest about your expenses. That means you must write down everything you spend, even the money you spend on snacks or supplies. You may find that you spend $25 a week ($100 a month) on items that are unnecessary. The more you can track unnecessary items, the better you can control your spending.

Set Goals

After you get an accurate picture of your income and expenses, you can start setting short-term and long-term financial goals. Because you are in college and probably trying to keep expenses to a minimum, you may think that creating and working toward financial goals will be a difficult undertaking until you have a job with a steady income and secure future. However, you can start setting small, short-term goals now. For example, your first short-term goal could be tracking your monthly budget and consistently spending 5% less than you earn. Another short-term goal could be to save enough money to pay for your study-abroad experience next year. Meeting these two goals will help you reach larger goals down the road.

You should also write down your long-term financial goals. One of these goals could be to start your own business. However, in order to reach that long-term goal, you will need to make a list of other, short-term goals that will help you reach your long-term goal, and start working toward them.

Don't Take Credit

Credit cards can be very tempting when you are in college, because they are so easy to use and the offers pour in just about every day. The reality of credit cards, however, is that they can cause big financial problems, ones that are sometimes difficult to pay off. Think about this: You don't want to start a new career after college that pays a good salary only to send a substantial portion of it to a credit card company.

In case you are still enticed to use a credit card, think about this sobering information. If you were to charge $1,000 on a credit card that charges 17% interest, and you make payments of $100 each month, you will be accruing more in interest than you will be paying each month. And that is only if you do not charge anything else!

Exhibit 12-11 shows that paying twice as much—$200—each month for six months only reduces the balance by $276.21—after paying $1,200. Unfortunately, some students have many more thousands of dollars of credit card debt, and with the current interest

Budgeting your money for college expenses will be crucial to your staying in college and being less stressed.

EXHIBIT 12-11 Credit Card Payments

Month	Previous Balance	Interest (17%)	Balance + Interest	Payment	Remaining Balance
Month 1	$1,000	$170	$1,170†	$200	$970
Month 2	$970	$164.90	$1,134.90	$200	$934.90
Month 3	$934.90	$158.93	$1,093.83	$200	$893.83
Month 4	$893.83	$151.95	$1,045.78	$200	$845.78
Month 5	$845.78	$143.78	$989.56	$200	$789.56
Month 6	$789.56	$134.23	$923.79	$200	$723.79

Q

You suggested that we try to avoid using credit cards, but they're so convenient. Cash transactions take longer, and then I have to hassle with the change.

A

If you like the simplicity and convenience of a credit card, here are some tips for making it better for you financially:

- Obtain a debit card from your bank.

- Make sure that the debit card doesn't allow you to overdraw your checking account, which can lead to expensive fees and penalties.

- Keep track of your purchases each day by writing them in a transaction record or by downloading them into a spreadsheet or budgeting program from your online account access.

rates, it is no wonder that students can find themselves in an endless cycle of charging and paying minimums. If it is at all possible, put the cards away until you are out of college, and then use them wisely.

Practice Good Financial Habits

A good financial plan is only good if you stick to it. The following tips can help you increase your financial literacy muscles, especially if you exercise them regularly.

- Balance your checkbook and other accounts every month. Online tools like Quicken and Moneydance can be helpful, if you're comfortable managing your finances using a computer.

- Compare your financial statements with your own recording of expenses and income. This will help you catch any unauthorized charges on your accounts or bank fees that were inappropriately posted to your account.

- Separate your bills from other mail, and create a schedule for paying them. Your paper-based or electronic calendar system is ideal for this purpose. Most bills are due on the same day each month, so you can set up a recurring reminder.

- Sign up for online payment plans if available and if it is easier to pay this way. Just be sure that you have reliable Internet access and use a consistent email addresses so you don't lose track of these transactions.

- If you have a credit card, use it for emergencies only.

- Put a small percentage of your income each month in a separate savings account for unexpected expenses. For example, for every $100 you earn, put $5 (5%) in an emergency savings account. Create a goal to increase your savings percentage.

- Check your college website every semester for updates about changes in tuition and fees.

Look at your syllabus to help determine what you need for class that will help you manage your time and money.

- What are the supply requirements listed in your syllabus for each class (e.g., textbook, notebook, graphing calculator)?

- What are the supply requirements that are needed but not listed in your syllabus for each class (e.g., printer ink, copy paper, thumb drive)?

- How much time will you need to spend a week for each class?

Protect Yourself

Budgeting and creating a plan are not quite enough to make sure that you are on firm financial foundation—you will also need to protect yourself from various scams, which can do more harm than just draining your bank account. If anyone you do not know contacts you through email or by phone to ask you to send money or provide a bank account number, delete the email or hang up the phone. Thousands of well-meaning people get scammed this way by providing access to their bank accounts, only to find out that their money is gone and their credit is ruined. If the information sounds too good to be true or doesn't seem "right," it is quite possibly a scam.

Another risk that you have to manage is identity theft. Keep your bank cards in a safe, secure place at all times, and never, ever write down your ATM PIN on a piece of paper. Also, be very cautious any time someone asks you to provide your Social Security number. Never provide it in an email, and make sure that any form requesting this number is from an official authority, like your college's financial aid office or the registrar.

Learn More

There are numerous resources available for you to explore financial matters further. There are many local, state, and federal government programs that can provide free information and counseling if you are interested in getting your finances on track. The best defense is good information about your situation and your possibilities. For starters, you can—and should—request a free credit report. A request form from the Federal Trade Commission is available at www.ftc.gov/credit. You can also find a local (and usually free) financial help center that provides workshops and counseling for people who want to know more about their financial situation. You can find these agencies online or in the phone book. Don't forget that your local library and bookstore offer many good resources on money management and financial matters. Start with a good book, such as *Personal Finance for Dummies* (Tyson, 2009), that defines common terms and provides basic information. Remember that the best way to protect your financial future—and to secure the hard work that you are doing in college to get a better job—is to empower yourself with the knowledge of what you have and what you want to do with it in the future.

60-SECOND PAUSE

What are some of your spending or financial habits that you want to avoid while in college? How can a monthly budget system help you avoid these habits?

FROM COLLEGE TO UNIVERSITY

How to Handle the New Pressures on Your Time

A good time management strategy that works for you will serve you well when you transfer to a university. Yes, there will be more work and more expected of you when you get closer to completing a bachelor's degree, but there may also be less direction from professors. They will assume you have solid time management skills. The more you practice now, the better you will be able to handle even more restrictions on your time. Additionally, there will be more for you to do as you work toward completing a four-year degree. You may find yourself participating in a career-related club, interning to get experience for your resume, talking to professors about graduating, and putting together applications for jobs.

Try out a few strategies and find what works, but also talk to students who have already transferred to find out what new expectations you will encounter.

©iSTOCKPHOTO

Improving Time Management on the Job

If you decide to go directly from college to work, or back to work, your time and stress management skills can be the difference between a dreaded job and a life-fulfilling career. Time management will be even more important on the job because your actions will affect more people. Just like a move from college to university, the more you practice good time management skills, the more likely you will be able to complete assignments on time. Beware, though, that on the job, the stakes will be much higher than they were in college. Using a calendar and writing down daily tasks will help you keep on top of your to-do list. There may be times when you won't be able to manage your time as effectively as you wish, but if you can be honest and speak up quickly, you may be able to save others time as well.

©iSTOCKPHOTO

YOUR PHYSICAL HEALTH MATTERS A LOT IN COLLEGE

Think about this scenario: You have just bought a brand-new car and you are about to drive it off the lot. Before you do, the salesperson provides you with an owner's manual and begins to tell you how often you will need to fill the tank, replace the oil, check the brakes, and rotate the tires. You tell the salesperson you don't need to know any of that stuff, and you drive the car off the lot. Besides, you know that the car needs to be filled up whenever the light on the dashboard comes on. What else is there to know?

For those who own and drive cars, you can imagine what will happen next. One day, maybe in a few months or a few years, you will find the car stops working regularly or stops working at all. In some cases, the repairs are minimal; in other cases, major repairs must be made to get the car into shape. The costs could be astronomical, so much so that you find yourself without a car and without hope for getting another one any time soon.

Now, consider that the car is your body. You know when you are hungry and when you are tired, when you feel happy and when you are stressed, but do you know how to take care of yourself? Maybe you do know that exercising will improve your health and help you manage your stress, but you won't make the time to include fitness as a part of your weekly routine. Just as a car may drive well for a while without regularly scheduled maintenance, there will come a day that the neglect will keep it from running properly or at all.

Learning to take care of your physical and mental health is crucial to getting where you want to go. To continue the car analogy, you won't be arriving at your destination if the vehicle is not in proper working order. One of the benefits of higher education, as stated earlier, is that you learn to make better choices, and that includes making better choices about your health. You can do that by understanding what you can control and how to get information to stay physically and mentally healthy.

Nutrition Gives You Fuel

One key to living a healthy life is making it a priority to eat nutritious food. Getting the recommended daily allowances of fruits, vegetables, whole grains, proteins, and fats is a commonsense approach to healthy eating, but as a society, we are choosing less healthy foods that are quick and easy—and loaded with calories, fat, salt, and sugar. Some of the reasons for poor nutritional choices include lack of time, too little information, and limited access to healthy alternatives. Increased stress is another reason that students make poor food choices; they may choose comfort food over nutritious alternatives.

Making good food choices is the foundation for overall good health.

To make healthier choices, arm yourself with information. As with any aspect of your health, the more you know, the better choices you can make. Learn what healthy foods are and seek them out. Read about and pay attention to serving sizes; too much of even a healthy food can add unneeded calories and contribute to weight gain. Read and learn to interpret food labels and ingredient lists that provide information about what is in the food and how much of it represents recommended daily values. The U.S. Food and Drug Administration (2011) provides detailed information on its Web page "How to Understand and Use the Nutrition Facts Label," which can be accessed at http://www.fda.gov/food/labelingnutrition/consumer information/ucm078889.htm. It provides helpful information about what percentages of fat, sodium, and sugars you should limit.

Another way of getting nutritional information is to talk with a physician or a nutritionist to get a better idea of what kinds of food will be best for you to consume. Regular doctor visits will determine if you have any potential health risks, such as high blood pressure or diabetes, which will make your food decisions even more crucial to good health. Keeping chronic illnesses in check with monitoring and medication will not only help you feel better, but it will also keep you healthy for the long term.

Eating healthy means eating regularly. Most experts recommend eating smaller meals more frequently, rather than heavy meals five to seven hours apart. At the very least, start the day with a healthy breakfast, even if you don't have enough time to sit down and eat a full meal (Zellman, 2011). You will feel more alert and energized throughout the early morning. However, what you eat for breakfast is just as important as eating something. Powdered doughnuts and a sugary, caffeinated soda will not provide you with the nutrients you need to be at your best. A piece of fruit and a cup of yogurt, for example, would be a better choice if you have to eat on the run. In addition to smaller, frequent, nutritious meals, drinking plenty of water throughout the day has numerous health benefits, including regulating body temperature and assisting digestion, but you should also consider drinking juices to get more nutrients (Zellman, 2011).

Avoiding fad diets is another strategy for staying healthy. Although they may promise increased energy and weight loss, the results may be short lived and potentially harmful. A better approach to eating healthy is to stick to the recommended guidelines from the Food and Drug Administration or a health expert. Be aware, too, of the potential for eating disorders, such as anorexia and bulimia. Anorexia, a condition in which people strictly control how much food they eat, and bulimia, a condition in which people cycle between overeating (binge-eating) in a short amount of time and then purging (through vomiting or abusing laxatives), are two eating disorders that can cause serious physical and psychological harm. Students who suffer from anorexia or bulimia, or believe they do, should see a health professional as soon as possible. The website nationaleatingdisorders.org provides definitions of eating disorders as well as a helpline for those who need to talk to an expert.

Why should you be concerned about what you eat and how much you eat? One benefit of eating healthy is that it improves your body's functions. You may find that eating better improves your ability to sleep or reduces the fatigue you feel by the end of the day. Eating well also improves your mental abilities. Studies have shown that eating certain foods, such as fish, can improve your test-taking abilities. Finally, eating healthy and avoiding overeating helps keep stress under control, which in turn keeps stress-related illnesses at a minimum. See Exhibit 12-12 for tips.

EXHIBIT 12-12   Tips for Healthy Eating in College

Find and read reliable information about health issues.

Eat consciously and take time to appreciate the nourishment you are receiving from healthy foods.

Plan your meals and snacks ahead of time so that you are not susceptible to last-minute, poor choices.

Take bottled water in your backpack, and drink it throughout the day.

Take healthy snacks with you to eat between classes to avoid making unhealthy choices at the vending machines or at the student union.

Pay attention to serving sizes, and eat what you need to stay healthy, not the amount that you want to eat.

Make wise choices at vending machines by avoiding food that is high in fat, caffeine, sugar, and salt content.

Make any changes gradually; think long-term health, not short-term results.

Exercise Gives You Energy and Relieves Stress

We all know that making good choices about nutrition and exercise is part of a healthy lifestyle, but busy students often find it difficult to squeeze in time to work out. Take into consideration that as a student, you will spend many hours sitting down studying or working on the computer. Even if you have had a regular exercise routine, you may find that you have to make studying a higher priority.

Because you may have less time for exercise, it will be even more important that you find time to include some exercise in your busy schedule because of the numerous health benefits. At the very least, getting regular exercise will help you relieve stress.

Regular exercise can lower blood pressure, increase your metabolism, improve muscle tone, and lessen your chances of suffering diseases that are directly related to a sedentary lifestyle. It can also improve your mood and your self-confidence. Experts vary on how much exercise is ideal, but most agree 30 minutes of sustained activity three or four times a week will provide you with health benefits.

If you have trouble getting started or staying in an exercise routine, consider setting fitness goals that are reasonable and achievable. Reward yourself whenever you meet your goals, and don't get discouraged if you fall short now and then. Exercising regularly should be a lifestyle, not a short-term activity, so think of your progress as part of a long-term plan to live better. As with any exercise program, see a doctor before you begin and start gradually if you are not usually physically active.

TECHNOLOGY TIPS

Using Technology to Get Ahead

The Internet provides many quality resources for maintaining your health and wellness. Seek sound face-to-face medical advice from your physician if you have a serious health issue.

Recommended Sites

- http://www.choosemyplate.gov: This website provides important nutritional information and allows you to analyze your diet and make a personalized plan for eating healthy.

- http://www.mayoclinic.com/health/stress-management/MY00435: The Mayo Clinic provides resources for minimizing the negative effects of stress.

- http://www.webmd.com/fitness-exercise/guide/default.htm: WebMD offers exercising information for everyone, including the beginner.

EXHIBIT 12-13   Tips for Exercising in College

Take a physical education class at your college.

Use the exercise facilities and equipment on your campus.

Take advantage of walking trails or paved walkways on your campus.

Park farther away from the buildings and get extra steps in.

Join a gym and go regularly.

Ask a friend to exercise with you.

Incorporate short sessions of exercise into your studying routine by taking walking or stretching breaks in between reading or writing papers.

Learn how to play a new sport, or investigate a new form of exercise.

Some students feel like it's not worth the time to work out if they can't be in the gym for an hour or more. Once their schedules get busy, especially during midterms and finals, those one- and two-hour time slots quickly disappear. The truth is that even if you only have 20 minutes, you can engage in a worthwhile physical activity that can improve your health and relieve stress. You can also do interval training, or "alternating bursts of intense activity with intervals of lighter activity," such as incorporating short bursts of running into your walking (Mayo Clinic, 2011). Varying the activities, length, and intensity of your workout will keep boredom at bay and help you keep it up. See Exhibit 12-13 for tips for exercising while balancing your college work.

Sleep Recharges Your Batteries

Getting an adequate amount of sleep each night is as important to maintaining good health as what you eat and how often you exercise, but most people in the United States, especially college students, do not get enough sleep to maintain their health. Experts say that adults should get seven to nine hours of sleep a night to function normally throughout the day, but millions regularly get six hours or less. While you are in college, you may believe that six hours a night sounds like a luxury as you juggle your multiple responsibilities. For sure, there will be times that, because of circumstances, you will not be able to get enough sleep, but those times should be few and far between. Maintaining a regular schedule of going to bed and getting up will help you get the amount of sleep you need. Despite the myth of what college life is like, pulling all-nighters to study for tests and complete assignments is strongly discouraged, because it will make you less likely to perform well the next day.

For some students, the idea of keeping a regular sleeping and waking schedule seems impossible because of other factors that limit their ability to sleep. The reasons for many students' sleep deprivation are varied, but may include health problems, such as breathing obstructions and stress. If you believe your lack of sleep is the result of a medical problem, consider seeing a health care professional. For stress-related sleep problems, practicing the stress-relieving strategies discussed earlier in this chapter will help alleviate the symptoms; however, if you find that relaxation techniques do not improve your ability to sleep well, then consider seeing a general practitioner or mental health professional for issues regarding stress.

What you put into your body can affect your sleeping habits. Eating high-fat and high-sugar foods near bedtime can slow you down, even if they seem to speed you up at first. Good sleep can also elude you if you consume alcohol and caffeine—even in small amounts—close to the time that you go to bed. Drugs, including medications for common illnesses, can deprive you of sleep or make you feel sluggish after you take them. Avoid consuming food, drink, or medications that overstimulate or make you drowsy

Q

I have heard about the "Freshman 15," and I have noticed I have put on some weight since I have been in college. What can I do to avoid gaining more weight and maybe even lose some?

A

Gaining weight in college doesn't have to happen if you plan ahead and make your health a top priority. Here are some tips for avoiding packing on the pounds:

- Talk to your physician or a health provider at your college before doing anything.
- Plan your meals before you are hungry. Find out what healthy choices are available to you, and commit to eating them most of the time.
- Pack healthy snacks and avoid vending machine junk food.
- Park farther away and walk more. Find ways to incorporate exercise throughout the day.
- Check out the college health center or physical activity opportunities.

right before bedtime. Never abuse prescription or over-the-counter medications or illegal drugs to stay awake.

In addition to what you put into your body, what you do to it will affect your ability to get a good night's rest. Exercising too close to bedtime will make it harder to fall asleep. However, too little physical exertion during the day can also contribute to difficulty falling and staying asleep. Experts suggest exercising early in the day—an activity as easy as walking for 30 minutes will suffice—in order to sleep more productively at night. Regular exercise will also help you alleviate the negative effects of stress. If you find, though, that you cannot "shut off" your mind because thoughts overwhelm you, consider writing down your worries—anything you may stay up thinking about after the light is off—in a journal, which will help you unwind and put away your day's thoughts.

Because sleep deprivation can contribute to irritability, depression, and physical health problems, it is important to make getting enough sleep a priority throughout the semester. If you have difficulty sticking to a regular sleep schedule, treat it like any other goal and write down what you want to do. Make it easier to achieve your goal by keeping your bed and bedroom free of clutter and by avoiding using your bed as a place to do homework or watch television. In other words, creating a sanctuary in your bedroom, a place where you can truly relax, may alleviate stress and anxiety that contribute to sleeplessness. Finally, avoid taking naps during the day, even on weekends, because they can throw off your sleep schedule. If you have an irregular schedule because of working different hours each day of the week, find a system that is relatively regular and that works for you. You may have to be creative about how you get enough sleep each evening or day.

The bottom line is that sleep deprivation can be dangerous and deadly. How little sleep you get should not be a medal of honor that demonstrates how much you work or how dedicated you are to meeting your goals. Getting enough sleep is a necessary part of living well, enjoying what you do accomplish, and being enjoyable to be around when you are awake.

Drugs and Alcohol Can Quickly Derail Your Health and Life

There are some habits that we know are potentially hazardous to our health, yet some people still do them. Smoking and using tobacco products, taking drugs, and consuming too much alcohol are known risks, but college students sometimes pick up these poor health habits because of peer pressure, a desire to fit in, and a need to find a way to relax or escape.

According to the American Heart Association (2008), about a quarter of Americans smoke, and people with the least education (9–11 years in school) are more likely to smoke than people with more education (more than 16 years in school). Smoking or chewing tobacco carries with it increased risks of heart disease, stroke, high blood pressure, cancer, and emphysema. The more educated you become about the health risks that are associated with smoking and using smokeless tobacco, the more it will be obvious that using tobacco products can cause serious health consequences. There are a variety of methods for quitting; it is worth investigating what your college and community offers if you are a smoker or a user of smokeless tobacco. Your college may provide information, support groups, or physician referrals for students who want to quit.

Alcohol and drugs are two other health issues that affect college students—sometimes even before they get to college. Having parents, partners, or friends who have abused drugs or alcohol is one way students can be affected. They may feel that they have to take care of others who drink too much or take drugs, which can take a toll on their time and emotional well-being. Students may also suffer from abusing drugs and alcohol while in college—and the effects can be far reaching. According to Facts on Tap (2008), a website that offers drug and alcohol education and prevention information, 159,000 first-year college students will drop out of college because of issues related to drug and alcohol abuse.

Being drunk or high can have grave consequences, the least of which is that you will do something you later regret. You increase your risk of having an unwanted sexual experience and causing physical harm to yourself and others. Death from overdosing on drugs and alcohol can happen, even for those who are first-time users. Whether they are consumed for recreational purposes or because of other more serious health reasons, abusing drugs and alcohol should not be a part of your college career because you will find it more difficult to reach your educational and personal goals. See Exhibit 12-14 for guidance on avoiding drugs and alcohol.

In addition to abusing alcohol and illegal substances, using medications for purposes other than for what they were prescribed can have grave consequences, including death. Excessive use of medications that contain amphetamines and narcotics may seem like a good idea at first if you have trouble staying awake or going to sleep, but using them for a longer period than they have been prescribed can lead to dependency.

Yes, We Do Need to Talk about Sex

A discussion of health issues would not be complete without talking about sexual health. Most colleges and universities strive to educate their students, especially those who are recently out of high school, about sexual responsibility, sexual assault, and common sexually transmitted diseases (STDs). Many experts and college officials have been alarmed at the recent statistics that show 73% of students report having unprotected sex while they are in college. More disturbing is that 68% of those having unprotected sex do not consider themselves at risk (Gately, 2003). This last statistic points to a major reason that

EXHIBIT 12-14   Tips for Avoiding Drugs and Alcohol in College

Educate yourself about the effects of abusing drugs and alcohol.

Cultivate relationships with people who have healthy habits.

Avoid situations in which you know drugs and alcohol will be present.

Take walking breaks instead of smoking breaks.

Find other ways to relax that are healthy, free, and legal.

Talk with a counselor or health care professional if you feel you are about to make a poor decision regarding the use of drugs and alcohol.

Appeal to your vanity, if all else fails: Drugs, alcohol, and tobacco make you look and smell bad.

students, despite sex education in high school or elsewhere, continue to engage in risky sexual behavior. Because most STDs lack immediate visible or physiological symptoms, students who are at risk for contracting a sexually transmitted disease rarely ask to be screened for signs of infection.

Risky behavior, which includes having sex with multiple partners and having unprotected sex, opens the door to possible infections and illnesses such as chlamydia, gonorrhea, genital herpes, HIV, and AIDS (see Exhibit 12-15). Some diseases can be transmitted in ways other than sexual intercourse. Hepatitis B and C are both diseases that can be contracted through shared razors, toothbrushes, body piercings, and tattooing.

If you are sexually active, it is important to be screened regularly for STDs even if you do not have symptoms. Your long-term health and the health of those you come in contact with are at risk if you do not. As with any health issue, educate yourself with the facts about risk factors and symptoms. Then, monitor your behavior, practice safe sex, and see a doctor regularly to maintain good health.

Sexual assaults in the college environment are a troubling phenomenon that you shouldn't ignore. Some of the most common incidents of sexual assault are related to excessive consumption of alcohol and date rapes, which involve two people who actually know each other. The Rape, Abuse, and Incest National Network (RAINN) provides numerous resources that students can use to educate themselves about the risks, consequences, and preventive actions. Some important tips for reducing your chances of being involved in such a tragedy, and for helping others avoid risky situations, include the following:

- Be aware of your surroundings at all times. This means take out earphones and avoid talking on your phone when walking, and pay attention to where you are hanging out and who is there.
- Walk tall. Act confident and self-assured when you are moving from one place to another. RAINN calls it "walk[ing] with a purpose."
- Listen to your "little voice." If you feel uncomfortable in a situation or environment, remove yourself. You often know best when something is not right.

One particular type of unhealthy relationship that occurs most frequently among traditional college students is date or acquaintance rape. Simply defined, date rape is a forced sexual act in which one party does not actively consent; often, the two people

EXHIBIT 12-15 Common Sexually Transmitted Diseases

STD	Symptoms	Treatment
HIV and AIDS	May have no symptoms; extreme fatigue, rapid weight loss	No cure, but prescribed medication can keep the virus from replicating
Chlamydia	May have no symptoms; abnormal discharge, burning during urination	Antibiotics
Genital herpes	May have no symptoms; itching, burning, bumps in the genital area	No cure, but prescribed medication can help treat outbreaks
Gonorrhea	Pain or burning during urination; yellowish or bloody discharge; men may have no symptoms	Antibiotics
Hepatitis B	Headache, muscle ache, fatigue, low-grade fever, skin and whites of eyes with yellowish tint	No cure, but prescribed medication can help guard against liver damage

involved are not complete strangers—hence the terms "date rape" and "acquaintance rape." Both men and women can be victims of date rape, although women are more often victims. Alcohol or a date rape drug such as Rohypnol may be involved in the incident. Many experts warn college-age women and men about the risk factors for date rape and encourage them to get to know who they are going out with, to not get intoxicated, to make sure their food or drinks are not handled by others, and to communicate loud and clear if they find themselves in an uncomfortable situation.

Depression and Suicide Are Sad but Real Occurrences in College

The pressures to succeed and juggle multiple priorities can lead to negative stress and feelings of being overwhelmed. Many times, feeling a little stressed during the semester is normal, but there are times that students can feel as though they are in over their heads, with no hope of getting out. It is no wonder that one of the most common mental health issues on any college campus is depression.

Problems with depression often start before students enroll in college: "Students arrive already having started various medications for depression, anxiety and attention deficit disorders" (Schoenherr, 2004). Signs of depression include loss of pleasure in activities, feelings of hopelessness, inability to get out of bed, increased use of alcohol or drugs, changes in appetite or weight gain or loss, changes in sleep patterns (sleeping too little or too much), extreme sensitivity, excessive crying, lack of energy or interest in participating in activities, and lack of interest in taking care of oneself.

Suicide is another mental health issue that is associated with depression. With the startling statistic that 25% of college students have contemplated suicide, it is no wonder that college health and counseling centers strive to educate students about the signs of severe depression and potential suicide attempts. Thoughts of ending your life should always be taken seriously, and you should seek help immediately. Call a college counselor, an advisor, a hospital emergency room, or 911 if you are thinking about committing suicide. If one of your friends or roommates exhibits any behaviors or says anything that implies suicidal thoughts, do everything you can to put them in contact with professionals on campus or at the local hospital who can help.

60-SECOND PAUSE

Give yourself a grade of A, B, C, D, or F on each of the health-related practices mentioned in this chapter: nutrition, exercise, sleep, and healthy choices relating to drugs, alcohol, and sex. What are the primary risk factors you face, based on your current activities and habits?

HEALTHY LIVING IS A CHOICE YOU MAKE FOR LIFE

There is more to life than just eating well and exercising. Healthy living is a practice that involves all parts of your well being: physical, mental, and spiritual.

A Balanced Life Is a Healthy Life

Living a balanced life means paying attention to and improving all areas of your life—from relationships to cardiovascular health to your inner peace. If one area is overdeveloped, then the other areas will suffer from the lack of balance. There will be times that you will need to put in more hours at work and school, throwing the balance off slightly, but be careful that you make some time for the other areas that have been neglected.

A great way to stay balanced is to strive to create relationships with people on campus. Having healthy relationships with professors, advisors, and classmates will not only enable you to stay connected with your college work, but it will also provide you a personal support network in case you feel as though you need help with the stresses of being in college.

Balancing your life to eliminate stress also entails evaluating your values and priorities whenever you begin to feel stressed. You can then identify areas in your life that are getting out of balance and put those areas higher up on your list of priorities. For example, if you value exercise and are stressed because you realize that you have been spending most of your time at work or at school, you can make working out a higher priority, creating better balance in your life.

Relationships Impact Your Health

Maintaining healthy relationships is as much a part of your good health as eating nutritious foods and exercising, but there are some issues that are signs of unhealthy, even dangerous, relationships.

Incorporating regular exercise into your routine will help you alleviate some of the negative effects of stress.

One type of unhealthy relationship issue is abuse: physical, mental, verbal, and sexual. Being in a relationship with someone who is abusive is not healthy. Although the previous statement sounds like common sense, take time to think about it. No one deserves to be hit, controlled, or humiliated, ever.

Although we know that someone who makes us feel bad physically or emotionally can prevent us from being our best, studies find that abused men and women find it difficult to get out of abusive relationships. One reason people stay with abusive partners is that the abusers are—at first—charming, attentive, and loving. Usually, abusers begin to show subtle signs that something is not right; they may be extremely jealous, verbally insulting, and focused on your every move. Victims may also be dependent financially or emotionally on their abusers, which makes eliminating their influence difficult.

Maintaining a healthy relationship takes time and energy, but there are many ways to make sure your relationships are positive experiences. For example, get to know people well before spending time alone with them. Learn to communicate your wants and needs effectively. Say "no" loud and clear when you do not want something to happen. Watch for signs of abusive and controlling people; sometimes, people show you signs of their true selves in smaller, subtler ways early in a relationship. If a situation makes you uncomfortable, get out of it immediately. Last but not least, do not abuse alcohol and drugs, which can impair your ability to judge situations. If you feel as though you have no options in removing yourself from an abusive relationship, seek professional help.

For most of your relationships, communication will be key to balance and satisfaction. Whether it is your family, friends, roommates, or significant others, you will want to be an advocate for your own feelings and needs and to express them in a respectful manner. Learning to listen actively and critically will also help you strengthen relationships. Good, solid relationships are built on honesty, communication, and a healthy respect for others' physical and emotional well-being.

Getting Help When You Need It

An important part of making good choices and staying healthy is to get regular checkups and to see a health professional whenever you experience pain, difficulty, or even uncertainty about a health issue. Your college may provide access to a health clinic or health fairs. Free screenings, health seminars, and dispensing of over-the-counter medications are possible services that your college clinic may offer. Take advantage of these types of services, such as blood pressure checks or information about handling diabetes, because they may provide you with life-improving or life-saving information. If your college provides only limited access to health services, then you will need to find other ways to monitor your health. Regular checkups are part of taking care of yourself, both in the short term and the long term.

60-SECOND PAUSE

How do you rate the health of your relationships? Is there a relationship that you can improve? What tips from above will you use to strengthen that relationship?

FROM COLLEGE TO UNIVERSITY

How Your Stress Will Change and How to Handle the New Pressures

There are many possible stressors awaiting you when you make that move from your community college to university. For example, your professors will be asking more from you academically. To meet the challenges that await you, be honest about them. In addition, recognize the fact that you will be graduating in just a few semesters and that you should plan for life after school. With some work—and the good habits you form at your community college—you can overcome stress with the same success.

Regardless of the new challenges, once you transfer, you will be making connections with people whom you hope will help you get a job after college. Along with your family, these relationships can provide you with a system for handling the demands of a four-year university. Practice stress-reducing activities regularly; you will then be more relaxed and more confident in your abilities.

©SHUTTERSTOCK

FROM COLLEGE TO CAREER

Making Healthy Lifestyle Changes Is a Good Long-Term Strategy

The purpose of making better choices should be a long-term strategy to create a better life for you and your family. After graduation, you may have to change the time or place that you work out. Maintaining healthy relationships with those who have positive influences on your life is one way to keep stress levels at a minimum and to create a safety net of friends and family when you may need them. Avoiding drugs, alcohol, and other poor health choices will be crucial to performing your best on the job.

Because of the importance of good health, some employers have made healthy choices a top priority. Talk with the human resources department about what your company offers its employees to support healthy habits. They may offer free screening, free or reduced-cost vaccinations, time off for doctors' appointments, health insurance, discounted gym memberships, and planned physical activities.

©iSTOCKPHOTO

Concept Review and Reinforcement

Questions for Discussion and Review

1. What activities and responsibilities will you have to manage while you are in college? How will managing your time help you stay on top of these tasks?

2. Name and describe two time management strategies. List the advantages and disadvantages of each.

3. What are the different reasons for procrastinating? What strategies are available to eliminate procrastination?

4. What money issues do you need to consider as a college student? Which will you work on while you are a student? Why?

5. What are the different ways students can incorporate exercise into their busy schedules?

6. What are the major health issues that college students face?

7. What can students do if they find themselves in an unhealthy relationship?

8. What are some of the effects for a student who makes poor health choices during a semester?

Apply & Analyze

Critical Thinking

1. What will be your greatest challenges to managing your time effectively? What have you learned so far, either from this chapter or from being in college, about what will be expected of you in terms of managing your time?

2. What do you see as your greatest time management strengths? What are your time management weaknesses? What will you do to build upon your strengths while also addressing your weaknesses?

3. Working within a group or with another classmate, describe the types of activities that can zap students' time and energy; then create solutions for managing them. Present your ideas to the class.

4. What stress-relieving techniques are most helpful to you and why? How will you be sure to find time to relieve stress while you are in college? What possible effects will not managing your stress have on you?

5. When you have a conflict with a person, what can you do to make sure the relationship remains healthy and open?

6. What health issues would you like to work on this semester? How do you intend to make time for working on them? What changes in your lifestyle and time management do you intend to make and why?

Evaluate

Case Scenarios

1. Janice has been doing very well in her classes. She has been able to manage her time wisely and adjust her schedule anytime something unexpected has come up. However, Janice has had a hectic week. Her boss expects her to stay late for the week to finish a special project; she has an important exam on Thursday evening; her daughter has been sick with a stomach virus; and her husband has been out of town for the last two weeks. Her goal is to take care of each problem without jeopardizing her job, her grade, or her daughter's welfare, but she cannot always balance all of these at all times. She decides to ask her professor if she can take her exam the following week after her boss's special project is finished, and she asks a good friend to take care of her daughter so that she can work late until she finishes the project. For Janice, at this point, her top priority is her job.

Use the following scale to rate the decision that has been made (1 = Poor Decision, 5 = Excellent Decision). Be prepared to explain your answer.

Poor Decision ← **1** — **2** — **3** — **4** — **5** → Excellent Decision

2. Glenn is a constant procrastinator. He feeds on the adrenaline that runs through his veins when he waits until the last minute to complete an assignment. The last time he did this, for a computer programming class, he ended up failing the assignment because he ran out of time and was exhausted for three days because he had stayed up for 36 hours straight. Glenn really wants to break his bad habits, so he creates a study group in which they work on assignments together to get them finished. For example, in his accounting class, each group member completes one of the homework questions and the group then compiles the answers to turn in individually. He also borrowed a friend's paper from a history class and is using it as the foundation for his so that he doesn't have to spend so much time starting his paper from scratch.

Use the following scale to rate the decision that has been made (1 = Poor Decision, 5 = Excellent Decision). Be prepared to explain your answer.

Poor Decision ← **1** — **2** — **3** — **4** — **5** → Excellent Decision

3. Korto has started a new job while she is in college so that she can pay for minor living expenses now that she has moved into an apartment by herself. Because her financial aid has been delayed, she cannot pay for both her apartment and her tuition and books at the beginning of the semester. Her college has offered to provide a monthly payment plan, but she has to complete her payments in three months, which she is not sure is enough time if her financial aid does not arrive before then. Thus, she has decided to use her credit card to pay for college expenses because she knows she can at least afford the monthly minimum until her financial aid comes in.

Use the following scale to rate the decision that has been made (1 = Poor Decision, 5 = Excellent Decision). Be prepared to explain your answer.

Poor Decision ← **1** — **2** — **3** — **4** — **5** → Excellent Decision

4. Vin-Singh has been having trouble sleeping since he started college. He shares an apartment with another student who likes to stay up late and play loud music. Vin-Singh eats well and avoids caffeinated drinks, but he does not exercise regularly and often feels anxious when he tries to sleep. He has a research paper due in one week and a final exam that is worth 50% of his overall grade that he must take in three days. Because he has not been able to sleep well, he has been feeling overwhelmed by what he has left to do before the semester is over. A friend suggested that he get some power energy drinks and caplets to get him through the last week and promised him that once he finishes his final assignment, he will be back to feeling better. Vin-Singh gets the energy boosters and starts taking them.

Use the following scale to rate the decision that has been made (1 = Poor Decision, 5 = Excellent Decision). Be prepared to explain your answer.

Poor Decision ◄——— 1 ——————— 2 ——————— 3 ——————— 4 ——————— 5 ——► Excellent Decision

5. Wanda has not exercised since she was in high school, and now, 20 years later, she sees the importance of improving her health. In fact, she wonders if the 30 pounds she has gained since high school are keeping her from feeling her best as she juggles the demands of college. She is about to start her last year in college, one that will be stressful for her as she takes classes that will help her pass a nursing licensing exam and get a good job. She also wants to lose the weight and start an aggressive exercise program. Wanda has decided to start lifting weights three times a week, running four times a week, and restricting her calories to 1,200 a day.

Use the following scale to rate the decision that has been made (1 = Poor Decision, 5 = Excellent Decision). Be prepared to explain your answer.

Poor Decision ◄——— 1 ——————— 2 ——————— 3 ——————— 4 ——————— 5 ——► Excellent Decision

6. Ever since D.J. started college, he has focused on his studies and has cut out all activities that do not help him achieve his educational goals. He has told his friends that he won't be able to hang out with them; he has cut back on his hours at work; he has stopped playing basketball and running; he has even stopped attending religious services so that he can have time to take as many class hours as possible each semester. He wants to graduate with a degree as fast as he can and start working, and his grades are good. Although he has been feeling depressed and tired most days, he knows that these feelings are short-term and that he will return to his routine after he completes his degree. He has 10 months left before he reaches his goal of graduating.

Use the following scale to rate the decision that has been made (1 = Poor Decision, 5 = Excellent Decision). Be prepared to explain your answer.

Poor Decision ◄——— 1 ——————— 2 ——————— 3 ——————— 4 ——————— 5 ——► Excellent Decision

Create

Research It Further

1. Search the Internet to find three videos of unique ways to manage time. Share those videos with your classmates, and ask them to rank the strategies from most effective to least effective.

2. Create a survey that asks your classmates how they manage their time in college. Once you collect your data, determine which time management strategies are the most used and suggest why you think they are popular. Report your results to the class.

3. What resources are available on your campus to help students manage their money effectively? Investigate resources in the library as well as any offices or departments that provide workshops or financial counseling for students. Compile a one-page list of these resources for your classmates.

4. Studies have shown that community college students have higher rates of depression and suicide than students at four-year universities. Do you think this is true? After interviewing your classmates or surveying a number of students, record the various reasons that this may be true; then create a list of local resources that could help such students at your institution.

5. Search the Internet for national statistics regarding violence against college students. Determine what groups are more likely to experience physical and sexual abuse. Inform your class of your findings.

6. What does your college offer in terms of health care for its students? Create a list of services and events, along with contact numbers for community services that students may need. Present your list to your classmates.

Take This With You

Based on the goals we set at the beginning of this chapter, here's how you can take this learning with you toward college success:

- Get a calendar (electronic or printed) and start using it on a daily basis.
- Start practicing a work and activity routine based on your personal energy patterns.
- Establish a monthly budget, set goals, and start tracking your progress.
- Continue learning about financial matters so that you can make smart decisions about your money.

- Identify which stressors you presently experience and which you can reasonably anticipate this semester.
- Create a plan to reduce stress in your life.
- Start working on health issues that are important to you.
- Develop a personal approach to maintain balance in your overall health.

REFERENCES

Allen, D., Schwartz, T., & McGinn, D. (2011). Being more productive. *Harvard Business Review, 89*(5), 82–88.

American Heart Association. (2009). Cigarette smoking statistics. Retrieved from www.americanheart.org/presenter.jhtml?identifier=4559

Dodd, P., & Sundheim, D. (2005). *The 25 best time management tools and techniques: How to get more done without driving yourself crazy.* Chelsea, MI: Peak Performance Press.

Facts on Tap. (2009). Alcohol and student life. Retrieved from www.factsontap.org/factsontap/alcohol_and_student_life/index.htm

Gately, G. (2003, August 23). College students ignoring risks of unprotected sex. *Health Day News.* Retrieved from www.hon.ch/News/HSN/514968.html

Hindle, T. (1998). *Manage your time.* New York, NY: DK.

Leland, K., & Bailey, K. (2008). *Time management in an instant: 60 ways to make the most of your day.* Franklin Lakes, NJ: Career Press.

Mayo Clinic. Interval training: Can it boost your calorie-burning power? Retrieved from http://www.mayoclinic.com/health/interval-training/SM00110

Nelson, D. B., & Low, G. R. (2003). *Emotional intelligence: Achieving academic and career excellence.* Upper Saddle River, NJ: Pearson.

RAINN. (2011). Reducing your risk of sexual assault. Retrieved from http://www.rainn.org/get-information/sexual-assault-prevention

Rampell, C. (2009, October 20). The skyrocketing costs of attending college. *The New York Times.* Retrieved from http://economix.blogs.nytimes.com/2009/10/20/the-skyrocketing-costs-of-attending-college

Schoenherr, N. (2004). Depression, suicide are the major health issues facing college students, says student health director. *News & Information, Washington University–St. Louis.* Retrieved from news-info.wustl.edu/tips/page/normal/4198.html

Schwartz, T. (2007). Manage your energy, not your time. *Harvard Business Review, 85*(10), 63–70.

Sibler, L. (1998). *Time management for the creative person: Right-brain strategies for stopping procrastination, getting control of the clock and calendar, and freeing up your time and your life.* New York: Three Rivers Press.

Tyson, D. (2009). *Personal finance for dummies* (6th ed.). New York, NY: Wiley.

U.S. Food and Drug Administration. (2011). How to understand and use the nutrition facts label. Retrieved from http://www.fda.gov/food/labelingnutrition/consumerinformation/ucm078889.html

Zellman, K. M. (2011). 10 ways to lose weight without dieting: Simple changes to your lifestyle can help you lose weight and keep it off. *WebMD.* Retrieved from http://www.webmd.com/diet/features/10-ways-to-lose-weight-without-dieting

INDEX

A

Achievements, recognizing, 50
Active listening, 171–73, 180
Adverse environmental conditions, 286–87
Affective component, of attitude, 207
Affinity groups, 346
Age discrimination, 117
Aggressive personalities, 314–15, 323
AIDS, 391
Airport security, nonverbal
    communication and, 160–61
Alcohol use, 389–90
Americanization, 358
American Standard Code for Information
    Interchange (ASCII), 123
Anger, 312–39
Anger management, 330–32
Anglo-conformity perspective, 358
Appearance, 82
Appearance, nonverbal communication
    and, 159–60
Appointments, 87
Arbitration, 328
Aryan nation, 354
Ash, Mary Kay, 191
Assertiveness, 322–24, 348
Attendance, 296
Attention deficit disorder, environmentally
    induced, 288
Attitudes, 186–231
Attitudes, about diversity, 358
Attitudes, as communication roadblocks, 163
Attitudes, changing, 209–10
Attitudes, components of, 207–13
Attitudes, empowered, 166
Attitudes, formation of, 208
Attitudes, in workplace, 89, 114–15
Attitudes, negative, 353–54
Attitudes, personal productivity and, 295–98
Attitudes, positive, 209
Authority, acceptance of, 348

B

Back planning, 372–76
Balance, attaining, 296–97
Bargaining tactics, 328–30
Barriers to communication, 155
Behavioral component, of attitude, 207
Behavioral interview question, 75
Behavior detection officer, 160
Belbin, R. Meredith, 46
Bias, 353, 354
Big picture, 52
Blind area, in Johari Window, 13
Blogs, company, 174–75
Blogs, ethics and, 261
Body piercings, in workplace, 84–85
Brain, hemispheres, 23

Branden, Nathaniel, 191
Brooks, Arthur C., 217
Budgets, creating, 380–81
Bullies, 314–15
Bureau of Indian Affairs (BIA), 358
Burnout, 283–84
Business cards, 108
Business ethics, 256–57
Business etiquette, 85
Business networking, 86–87
Business process improvement, 298

C

Calendars, 370–72, 373
Career, choosing, 103–5
Career choices, learning styles and, 24–25
Career goal setting, 251
Career objective, 105, 116
Career success, self-esteem and, 191
Carlson, Richard, 218
Carnegie, Dale, 209
Carpal tunnel syndrome, 287
Casual workdays, 83
Challenge stressors, 282
Channels, formal communication, 174–77
Character trait, 255
Childhood experiences, self-esteem and, 189–90
Cholesterol, stress and, 285
Chronological layout, of résumé, 118
Cigarette smoking, 390
Citizenship, 53
Cleanliness, valuing, 296
Code of Ethics and Business Contact, 269
Cognitive behavioral approach to stress
    management, 289
Cognitive component, of attitude, 207
Cognitive dissonance, 208
Cognitive restructuring, 326, 335
Cold-warm dimension, 155, 156
Collaboration, 17–18, 49
Collaborative management style, 322
Collaborative workplace, 37
Collectivism, 317
Collectivism, in-group, 348
College, depression and suicide in, 392
College, nutrition in, 385–86
College, physical health in, 385–92
College costs, 380
College students, goals and values of, 242–44
Combat communication overload, 168
Communication, 152–85
Communication, barriers to, 155
Communication, building bridges to, 165–68
Communication, cultural and language
    barriers to, 164–65
Communication, defensive, 167
Communication, gender barriers to, 169–70
Communication, nonverbal, 156–61
Communication, one-way, 162

Communication, poor skills, 164
Communication, roadblocks to, 161–65
Communication barriers, cross-cultural, 350–54
Communication overload, 163
Company blogs, 174–75
Company-specific research, 68
Competence, feelings of, 195
Competition, for limited resources, 313–14
Competitive management style, 322
Compromise, 329
Computer ethics, 262
Confidential information, 261
Conflict, 312–39
Conflict, cross-generational, 317
Conflict, micro-inequity as source of, 317
Conflict, positive and negative
    consequences of, 320–22
Conflict, work-family, 315–17, 338
Conflict of interest, 261
Conflict resolution, 322–30, 331–32
Confrontation, 331
Confrontation and problem solving, 324–25
Confrontations, minimizing, 49
Consensus, 52
Consumer protection, 384
Conti, Regina, 245
Cooperation, 49, 212
Corporate ethics programs, 268–71
Corporate resources, 261–62
Cost of living, 106
Courtesy, 85, 212
Cover letters, 124–25, 136, 137, 138–39, 140,
    141, 142
Cover letters, tailoring, 125
Covie, Bobby, 329
Creativity, employee, 20
Credit cards, 382–83
Credit history, in job search, 66
Criticism, 5, 50
Cross-cultural communication barriers,
    overcoming, 350–54
Cross-generational conflict, 317
Cultural barriers, to communication, 164–65
Cultural bloopers, 350
Cultural differences, self-evaluation and, 14
Cultural differences, understanding, 344–50
Cultural fluency, 347
Cultural intelligence (CQ), 345–46
Culturally diverse teams, 315
Cultural mistakes, avoiding, 351
Cultural sensitivity, 344
Cultural sensitivity, developing, 347
Cultural values, differences in, 347–49

D

Daily reviews, 372–76
Deadlines, focus on, 52
Decision making, ethical, 265–67, 268
Decoding, 154

Defensive communication, 167
Defining moment, 262–64
Deliberate practice, 296
Denial, 167
Depression, 392
Devaney, Earl E., 260
Developmental opportunity, 11
Diet, healthy, 290
Dietary guidelines, 290
Dining, 87–89
Dining etiquette, 88–89, 99
Disarming the opposition, 325
Discrimination, 75–76
Distance, communication and, 157
Distortion, of information, 163
Distractions, minimizing, 172–73
Diversity, 340–69
Diversity, attitudes about, 358
Diversity, in United States, 356–58
Diversity, majority response to, 357–58
Diversity, workplace, 19–20
Dominate communication, 155
Downsizing, 288
Dress, influences of in professional
      environment, 82–83
Dress code, 82
Drug use, 389–90
Dunn and Dunn Learning Styles Assessment, 23

E

Electronic communication, in collaborative
      workplace, 38–39
Electronic formatted résumés, 123
Electronic image, 107
Electronic job search portfolio, 107
Electronic work, control of, 300
Embarrassments, bouncing back from, 202–3
Emotional contagion, 206
Emotional intelligence, 203–7, 225
Emotional intelligence, human relations and, 205
Emotional labor, 287–88
Empathy, 171, 228
Employee Assistance Programs (EAP), 307
Employee network, 346
Employee rights, 75–76
Employees, creativity and innovativeness of, 20
Employee violence, ending, 316
Employment applications, 109
Encoding, 154
Energy, increasing, 297–98
Energy, managing, 376–79
Environmental audit, 271
Environmental conditions, adverse, 286–87
Environmental consciousness, 271
Equal Employment Opportunity Commission
      (EEOC), 327
Ethical decision making, 265–67, 268
Ethical problems, prevalence of, 257–64
Ethical screening, 265
Ethics, 254–79
Ethics, business, 256–57
Ethics, computer, 262
Etiquette, 85, 89–90
Etiquette, dining, 88–89, 99
Executive presence, 81
Exercise, as stress reliever, 387–88
Ex-offenders, tips for, 125
Expectations, setting high, 200–201
Experience, 197
Expertise, 245
Extreme job, 285
Extreme job hunting, 62, 63
Extrinsic motivation, 245
Eye contact, 159

F

Facial expressions, 159
Factional groups, 315
Feedback, 10–11, 12, 13, 172, 191
Feedback, checking for communication
      through, 166–67
Feelings, 218
Figure of speech, 172
Financial habits, practicing good, 383
Flat maximum, 168
Flight-or-fight response, 281
Flow, 201
Fluency, cultural, 347
Follett, Mary Parker, 16
Fonts, in résumés, 123
Forgiveness, 265
Formal communication channels, 174–77
Frame of reference, 166
Frank, Robert H., 192
Fredeig, Randi, 168
Functional layout, of résumé, 118

G

Galatea effect, 200–201
Gender barriers, to communication, 169–70
Gender egalitarianism, 348
Gender salaries, statewide comparison of, 360–61
Glass ceiling, 362
GLBT (gay, lesbian, bisexual, and transsexual), 342
Globalization, 19–20
Goals, 232
Goals, attributes of, 235
Goals, habits versus, 235
Goals, influences of, 232
Goals, long-term, 233
Goals, motivation and, 234–37
Goals, of college students, 242–44
Goals, short-term, 233
Goals, SMART, 234
Goals, types of, 235–37
Goal setting, 232–53
Goal setting, career, 251
Goal setting, in money matters, 382
Golden Rule, 215
Google Talk, interviewing with, 74
Gossip, 168
Green, 271
Grievance procedure, 327–28
Group interviews, 75
Groupthink, 42
Groupware, 39
Guilt, 316

H

Habits, 235
Habits, financial, 383
Hall, Douglas T., 197
Hand gestures, 158–59
Handshakes, 85–86
Happiness, 213–18, 226
Happiness, keys to, 214–18
Harassment, 318–19
Hawthorne effect, 15
Hawthorne studies, 14, 15
Healthy living, 392–94
Hedonic adaptation, 215
Helping, 212
Hidden area, in Johari Window, 13
Hindrance stressors, 282
Hollenbeck, George P., 197
Home office, productive work from, 300–301
Honesty, 265

Human behavior, 6
Human behavior, ethical, 264–73
Human behavior, general information about, 10
Human behavior, influences on, 21–23
Human behavior, questionable workplace, 259
Humane orientation, 348
Human relations, 2–28
Human relations, benefits of studying, 4–7
Human relations, emotional intelligence and, 205
Human relations, history of, 17
Human relations, workplace challenges and, 17–21
Human relations journal, 31
Human relations movement, 14–17
Human relations skills, developing, 31–34
Hygiene rules, 84

I

Illegal interview questions, 76
Inclusion, 341
Independence, 265
Industrial humanism, 16
Industrial Revolution, scientific management and, 14
Industry research, 106
Informational interview, 113
Information heading, 121
In-group collectivism, 348
Inner critic, rebutting, 194
Innovativeness, employee, 20
Institutional sexism, 359–64
Institutional sexism, economic
      consequences of, 362–63
Integrity, 265, 267, 378
Intelligence, cultural, 345–46
Intelligence, emotion, 203–7
Intelligence, emotional, 225
Interactive values-goals model, 234
Internet search skills, 301
Interpersonal communication, relationship
      building and, 155–56
Interpersonal relationships, 5, 367–68
Interpersonal skills, 368
Interruptions, 173
Interview methods, 74–75
Interview portfolio, 69–70
Interview questions, 74–75, 76–77
Interview questions, illegal, 76
Interview questions, practicing, 70
Interviews, 67–75
Interviews, closing, 77–78
Interviews, informational, 113
Interviews, one-on-one, 74
Interviews, phone and technology-based, 73–74
Intimacy, circles of, 158
Intimate distance, 157
Intranets, 176–77
Intrinsic motivation, 245
Introductions, in workplace, 86–87
Intuition, 267

J

Jacobi Voice, 159
Jewelry, in workplace, 84–85
Job boards, 65
Job dissatisfaction, 9
Job insecurity, stress and, 288
Job leads, sources of, 110–11
Job loss, stress and, 288
Job-oriented interpersonal skills, 353
Job performance, influences on, 21–23
Job performance, stress and, 282–83
Job problems, coping with, 6
Job satisfaction, positive attitudes and, 210–11
Job search, 103

Job search, conducting, 60–67
Job search, targeted, 106
Job search portfolio, 107–9
Job search portfolio, electronic, 107
Job-specific skills, 119
Johari Window, 12–13
Judge, Timothy A., 201
Jury of peers, 328
Justice, 265

K

Knowledge base, developing, 198
Ku Klux Klan, 354

L

Labor, emotional, 287–88
Labor-waste elimination systems, 19
Language, clarity of, 351–52
Language barriers, to communication, 164–65
Layout, of résumé, 118
Leadership, upward ethical, 272–73
Learning preference comfort zone, 24
Learning styles, career choices and, 24–25
Letters if recommendation, 109
Lifelong learning (LiLA), 21
Life plan, 370–401
Limited resources, competition for, 313–14
Listening, active, 171–73, 180
Listening skills, enhancing, 170–73
Living space, high self-esteem, 196
Long-term goals, 233
Lovell, Pamela, 50

M

Management style, collaborative, 322
Management style, competitive, 322
Managers, 22
Margolis, Joshua D., 203
Marketing strategy, developing, 63
Mayer, John D., 203
Mayo, Elton, 16
McGregor, Douglas, 16–17
McNatt, D. Brian, 201
Mediation, 328
Medical exams, 79
Meditation, 291
Mental health, self-esteem and, 191
Micro-inequity, 317
Mirroring, 168
Mission statement, 295
Mixed signals, 162–63
Moods, 218
Moral intensity, 257
Motivation, 213, 232–53, 244
Motivation, extrinsic, 245
Motivation, goals and, 234–37
Motivation, intrinsic, 245
Multiculturalism, 343
Multitasking, 299, 379
Myers-Briggs Type Indicator (MBTI), 23

N

n Ach factor, 242
Negative affectivity, 285
Negative attitudes, development of, 353–54
Negative self-talk, 200
Negotiation, 328–30
Neo-Nazis, 354
Networking, 94–95, 111–12, 113
Networking, business, 86–87
Networking, in job search, 63–64

Network list, 113
Noises, 155
Nonassertive people, 323
Nonverbal communication, 156–61
Nonverbal communication, airport
    security and, 160–61
Nonverbal communication, differences in, 352
Nutrition, 385–86

O

Objectives, 233
Offshoring, 164
One-on-one interview, 74
One-way communication, 162
Online approaches, to job hunting, 64
Open area, in Johari Window, 13
Opposition, disarming, 325
Optimism, 239
Optimists, explanatory style of, 201
Orderliness, valuing, 296
Organizational behavior, 4
Organizational citizenship behavior (OCB), 211–13
Organizational effectiveness, 4
Organizational success, 191–92

P

Panel interviews, 75
Paperwork, control of, 300
Paraphrasing, 172
Parker, Glenn, 51
Peak performance, 201–2
Peer evaluations, 11
PEPS Learning Styles Inventory, 23
Perceived control, 284
Perfectionism, 303–4
Performance evaluation, 11
Performance orientation, 347
Personal appearance, 159–60
Personal commercial, 68–69
Personal communication style, 173
Personal distance, 157
Personality, 46–47
Personality, aggressive, 314–15, 323
Personality, job factors contributing to
    stress and, 284–88
Personality clashes, 314
Personality types, 24
Personal life, work and, 8–9
Personal problems, coping with, 6
Personal productivity, high expectations for, 18–19
Personal productivity, improving, 293–304
Personal productivity, work habits and, 298–301
Personal profile, 105, 116
Personal references and recommendations, 109
Personal relationships, health and, 393
Personal strengths, awareness of, 193
Personal support, 212
Perspectives, 163
Phone interviews, 73–74
Physical exercise, stress and, 289–90
Physical fitness, 217
Physical health, in college, 385–92
Physiological reactions, to stress, 282
Piracy, 259
Political correctness, 344
Portfolio, job search, 107–9
Positive attitudes, importance of, 209
Positive attitudes, job satisfaction and, 210–11
Positive self-talk, 72, 199–200
Positive visual imagery, 200
Posture, 157–58
Power, acceptance of, 348
Power words, 120

Practice, pre-interview, 70–72
Pre-employment tests, 79
Prejudice, causing, 354–56
Prejudices, 353
Preparation, for job search, 107
Present moment, principle of, 218
Pride, 265
Privacy, protecting, 113–14
Private self, 10
Problem solving, confrontation and, 324–25
Procrastination, 293–95, 374–75
Productivity, 265
Productivity, personal, 293–304
Profanity, 90
Professional code of conduct, 272
Pronunciation, 352
Psychological functioning, principles of, 218
Public distance, 157
Public self, 10
Punctuality, 296

Q

Questions, interview, 74–75

R

Rape, Abuse, and Incest National Network
    (RAINN), 391
Rapport building, 169
Rationality, 264
Rawady, Donna, 63
Recognition, 33
Recommendations, letters of, 109
References, personal, 109
Reframing, 326
Relationship building, interpersonal
    communication and, 155–56
Relationship management, 204
Relationships, with work associates, 268
Research, industry, 106
Resilience, 241
Resolution, conflict, 322–30
Respect, 85
Respect, for cultures, 346, 350
Responsibility, 51
Rest, importance of, 290
Results-only work environment (ROWE), 300
Résumé package, building, 115–25
Résumés, 116, 127, 128, 129, 130, 131,
    132, 133, 134–35
Résumés, electronic formatted, 123
Résumés, layout of, 118
Résumés, sharing, 122–24
Résumés, tailoring, 125
Role ambiguity, 286
Role overload, 285
Roles, self-oriented, 47
Roles, team member, 42–47

S

Salary negotiation, 78–79, 98, 335–36
Saving face, 330
Scientific management, 14–15
Self, 9
Self-assessment quizzes, feedback from, 11
Self-awareness, 203
Self-confidence, 202
Self-confidence, developing, 197–203
Self-confidence, importance of, 197
Self-disclosure, 13
Self-discovery, 103
Self-efficacy, 202

Self-efficacy, importance of, 197
Self-efficacy, low, 284–85
Self-esteem, 186–231
Self-esteem, childhood experiences and, 189–90
Self-esteem, enhancing, 192–96
Self-esteem, high, 190–92
Self-esteem, of group members, 196
Self-esteem calendar, 196
Self-evaluation, traps in, 13–14
Self-image, positive, 193
Self-management, 203, 204
self-nurturing, 194–95
Self-oriented roles, 47
Self-talk, negative, 200
Self-talk, positive, 72, 199–200
Self-understanding, 9–14
Seligman, Martin, 190, 216
Semantics, 162
Sender, credibility to, 162–63
Setbacks, bouncing back from, 202–3
Setting, nonverbal communication and, 157
Sex, 390–92
Sexism, institutional, 359–64
Sexual harassment, 261, 317–20, 333, 363–64
Sexually transmitted diseases (STD), 390–91
Short-term goals, 233
Silo mentality, 18
Situational constraint, 288
Skill acquisition, upward mobility *versus,* 21
Skills, job-oriented interpersonal, 353
Skills, job-specific, 119
Skills, soft, 119
Skills, transferable, 119
Skype, interviewing with, 74
Slavery, 354
Sleep, necessity of, 388–89
Sleep deprivation, 389
Small talk, 168
SMART goals, 234
SMART method, 233, 234, 238–39, 251
Social awareness, 204
Social distance, 157
Social loafing, 42
Social media, as time consumer, 379
Social networking, 175–76
Social support, 348–49
Soft skills, 119
Software, illegal copying of, 259, 260
Special events, dress for, 83
Stereotypes, 353, 354–56
Stoltz, Paul G., 203
Stress, 280–311
Stress, burnout and, 283–84
Stress, job insecurity and loss and, 288
Stress, job performance and, 282–83

Stress, personality and job factors contributing to, 284–88
Stress, physiological reactions to, 282
Stress, symptoms and consequences of, 281–84
Stress busters, 292
Stress management, 281–93
Stress management, methods for, 288–93
Stressor, 281
Stressor, challenge, 282
Stressor, hindrance, 282
Stressor, modifying, 289
Stress reduction, visualization for, 291
Stress relief, exercise as, 387–88
Structured interview question, 75
Subordinate communication, 155
Suggested activity, 241
Suicide, 392
Support network, 291
Sustainable environment, contributing to, 270
Synergy, 40

T

Targeted job search, 106
Tattoos, in workplace, 84–85
Team building, 36–59
Team play, interpersonal aspects of, 47–51
Team play, task aspects of, 51–54
Teams, 37–40
Teams, advantages and disadvantages of, 40–42
Teams, culturally diverse, 315
Teamwork, 17–18
Technical expertise, 51
Technology-based interviews, 73–74
Telecommuting, 20–21
Television, as time consumer, 379
Theory X, 16–17
Theory Y, 16–17
Thinking, 218
Third party, appeal to, 326–27
Time log, 374
Time log, maintaining, 302
Time management resources, 370–72
Time management routines, 372–76
Time orientation, 348, 349
Time wasters, overcoming, 301–2
Time zappers, 377, 378
Timing, communication roadblock and, 164
Traits, character, 255
Transferable skills, 119
Trigger words, 104
Trust, team members and, 48–49
Trust, virtual team and, 40
Type A behavior, 285

U

Unethical boss, confronting, 273
Unionization, threat of, 16
United States, diversity in, 356–58
Unknown area, in Johari Window, 13
Unstructured interview question, 75
Upward ethical leadership, 272–73
Upward mobility, skill acquisition *versus,* 21
Utilitarian predisposition, 258

V

Values, 217, 247, 254–79
Values, cultural, 347–49
Values, of college students, 242–44
VARK questionnaire, 25, 28
Video games, as time consumer, 379
Violence, employee, 316
Virtual office, 20
Virtual office, productive work from, 300–301
Virtual teams, 38–40
Virtual workplace, 20–21
Virtuousness, developing, 264–65
Visual imagery, positive, 200
Visualization, for stress reduction, 291
Voice quality, 159

W

Wage inequity, 359–62
Wainwright, Tony, 172
Walworth, Janis, 342
WebEx, interviewing with, 74
Webinars, 177
Whistleblowing, 273
WIFO (worst in, first out) principle, 294, 305
Win-win, 324, 335
Workaholism, 296–97
Work-family conflict, 315–17, 338
Work habits, personal productivity and, 298–301
Work life, personal life and, 8–9
Work orientation, 348
Workplace, attitude in, 89
Workplace, challenges in, 17–21
Workplace, diversity in, 19–20
Workplace, questionable behavior in, 259
Workplace, tips for, 80
Workplace, virtual, 20–21
Workplace, wage inequity in, 359–62
Work wardrobe, 83

Z

Zero-sum game, 325